America's 100 Best Places to Retire

Edited by Richard L. Fox

VACATION PUBLICATIONS

HOUSTON

America's 100 Best Places to Retire

Edited by: Richard L. Fox

Art Direction and Cover Design: Fred W. Salzmann

Assistant Editor: Elizabeth Armstrong

Back cover photo by Dean Chavis

Published by Vacation Publications, Inc.
1502 Augusta Drive, Suite 415
Houston, TX 77057

Library of Congress Catalog Card Number: 00-104481
ISBN 0964421674

Printed in the United States of America

The Contributors

Mary Lu Abbott
Jean Allen
Mary-Ann Bendel
Brenda Blagg
Betsy and John Braden
Ron Butler
Jay Clarke
Julie Cooper
Karen Feldman
Richard L. Fox
Dixie Franklin
Diane Freeman
Fred Gebhart
Diana C. Gleasner
Carol Godwin
Janet Groene
Linda Herbst
Tracey B. Holyfield
Dave G. Houser
John A. Johnson
Bern Keating
Bob Lane
Adele Malott
Stephen H. Morgan
Honey Naylor
Mary Lou Nolan
Stanton H. Patty
Peggy Payne
Ruth Rejnis
Carolyn Rice
George L. Rosenblatt
Genevieve Rowles
William Schemmel
Marcia Schnedler
Alan Silverman
Lan Sluder
Constance Snow
Molly Arost Staub
Nina J. Stewart
Dana Tims
John Villani
Judy Wade
Claire Walter
Loralee Wenger
David Wilkening

Table of Contents

Low-Cost Edens 💔   Undiscovered Havens ☀

By State

America's 100 Best Places to Retire

The Top 10

Best Art Towns
Ashland, OR
Brevard, NC
Jackson Hole, WY
Key West, FL
Palm Desert, CA
Rockport, TX
Ruidoso, NM
Santa Fe, NM
Sarasota, FL
Scottsdale, AZ

Best Budget Towns
Eufaula, AL
Fayetteville, AR
Hattiesburg, MS
Hot Springs, AR
Mountain Home, AR
Natchitoches, LA
Ocala, FL
Oxford, MS
San Antonio, TX
Vicksburg, MS

Best Lake Towns
Coeur d'Alene, ID
Eagle River, WI
Eufaula, AL
Gainesville, GA
Lake Conroe, TX
Lake Havasu City, AZ
Marble Falls, TX
Mount Dora, FL
Paris, TN
Petoskey, MI

Best Undiscovered Towns
Cashiers, NC
Celebration, FL
Grants Pass, OR
Sequim, WA
Eagle River, WI
Thomasville, GA
Paris, TN
Mountain Home, AR
Natchitoches, LA
New Bern, NC

Best Beach Towns
Carlsbad, CA
Cape Cod, MA
Cape May, NJ
Charleston Barrier Islands, SC
Golden Isles, GA
Longboat Key, FL
Myrtle Beach, SC
Naples, FL
Ormond Beach, FL
Whidbey Island, WA

Best Low-Crime Towns
Camden, ME
Door County, WI
Georgetown, TX
Green Valley, AZ
Longboat Key, FL
Mountain Home, AR
Pinehurst, NC
Punta Gorda, FL
San Juan Capistrano, CA
Venice, FL

America's 100 Best Places to Retire

Best College Towns
Asheville, NC
Athens, GA
Chapel Hill, NC
Charlottesville, VA
Clemson, SC
Eugene, OR
Fayetteville, AR
Gainesville, FL
Oxford, MS
Williamsburg, VA

Best Small Towns
Beaufort, SC
Brevard, NC
Camden, ME
Edenton, NC
Fairhope, AL
Mount Dora, FL
Oxford, MS
Port Townsend, WA
Punta Gorda, FL
Waynesville, NC

Best Four-Season Towns
Bend, OR
Boise, ID
Camden, ME
Charlottesville, VA
Door County, WI
Fort Collins, CO
Greenville, NC
Maryville, TN
Santa Fe, NM
Wilmington, NC

Best Mountain Towns
Asheville, NC
Bend, OR
Brevard, NC
Cashiers, NC
Fort Collins, CO
Jackson Hole, WY
Prescott, AZ
Ruidoso, NM
Santa Fe, NM
Waynesville, NC

San Juan
Islands

Sequim ● ● Whidbey
Island
Port
Townsend ●

Coeur d' Alene ●

Lincoln
City ●
Eugene ●
● Bend

Grants Pass ●

Boise ●

● Ashland

Jackson
● Hole

Reno ●

Fort Collins ●

St. George ●

Las Vegas ●

Santa Fe ●

San Juan
Capistrano ●
Palm Desert ●
Prescott ●
Lake Havasu ●
Wickenburg ●
● Carlsbad
Scottsdale ●

Ruidoso ●

Tucson ●

Green Valley ●
●
Sierra Vista ●

Georgetown ●
Marble Falls ● ●
Kerrville ●
San Antonio ●

Rockport ●

America's
100
Best
Places
to
Retire

Camden

Eagle River

Petoskey

Door County

Cape Cod

Cape May

Charlottesville

Williamsburg

Chapel Hill
Edenton

Brevard
Asheville
Greenville

Branson
Mountain Home
Paris
Waynesville
Pinehurst
New Bern

Maryville
Hendersonville
Wilmington

Fayetteville
Cashiers
Greenville
Clemson

Oxford
Gainesville
Myrtle Beach

Hot Springs
Athens
Aiken
Charleston
Barrier Islands
Beaufort
Hilton Head

Vicksburg
Eufaula
Golden Isles

Natchitoches
Thomasville

Hattiesburg
St. Augustine

Lake Conroe
Pensacola
Gainesville
Ormond Beach

Fairhope
Seaside
Ocala
DeLand
Mount Dora
Celebration

Dade City
Winter Haven

Bradenton
Vero Beach

Longboat Key
Jupiter

Sarasota
Boca Raton

Siesta Key
Fort Lauderdale

Venice

Punta Gorda
Naples

North Fort Myers

Key West

Introduction

After our retirement, my wife and I set out on what some would consider to be a dream assignment for *Where to Retire* magazine: to visit the best retirement towns in America and find out — firsthand — what makes them so popular.

From the Atlantic to the Pacific, from the Rio Grande Valley to the Great Lakes, we sampled more than 400 communities favored by retirees. In the most promising of these towns, we gathered data on health care, taxes, crime, climate and so on. But we also took the time to try to get a feel for the place and its people, and we accomplished this by talking to everyone from newspaper editors to chamber of commerce directors and real estate agents. Our most important discussions in any town were with retirees themselves, and we always interviewed at least three couples who had relocated from out of state.

What really sets this book apart is the insight brought to its pages by these retirees, folks from all walks of life who have moved in search of a better quality of life. Al Donaubauer said of Kerrville, TX, "Next to San Diego, it's the best climate in the country." Kate Minnock claimed of life on St. Simons Island, GA, "When we're here on the island, we don't think about personal security." Priscilla Aronin observed about Eugene, OR, "Here, you only need a few minutes and you can be in the mountains, at the coast or canoeing on lakes and rivers."

These illuminating comments, and thousands more, led us to the unexpected but not altogether surprising conclusion that most retirees want roughly the same things: a favorable climate (not synonymous with 365 sunny days annually); access to shopping, fun, games and entertainment (but not necessarily in their own back yards); community (large or small, as long as their neighbors are friendly and compatible); security (not only from criminals, but from excessive taxation, bureaucratic bungling and inadequate zoning); competent health care (and they don't mind driving a reasonable distance for it); and means of escape (a commercial airport and interstate highway within an hour's driving time). Given these qualities, anything else is just icing on the cake.

Eventually, all of the best communities we visited came to be featured in *Where to Retire* magazine. "America's 100 Best Places to Retire" is a compilation of these articles, each updated to reflect the most current data available.

You'll find among the profiled cities some "Low-Cost Edens (💲)," some "Undiscovered Havens (☀)," and some of the most popular vacation resorts in America — Branson, MO; Las Vegas, NV; and Myrtle Beach, SC, to name a few. The fact is, almost all good retirement towns are great places to visit.

No matter what you expect out of your retirement home, if you get through this book and haven't felt a strong bonding with one or more places profiled, you might as well close the book and plan to stay where you are. The place you're looking for probably doesn't exist.

On the other hand, if you're about to become one of the 400,000 Americans who move across state lines to retire every year, we hope we've helped you narrow the search. Happy hunting and happy retirement. — *Richard L. Fox*

Aiken, South Carolina

South Carolina town has charm, culture and an equestrian heritage

By William Schemmel

Aiken, situated in the gently rolling and densely wooded Sand Hill country of western South Carolina, always has proved irresistible to newcomers, although today's residents need not have fortunes or horses in order to be socially accepted. Still, at least a pastoral interest in the ponies doesn't hurt.

Almost as quick as train tracks were laid down, locomotives brought wealthy 19th-century plantation owners from steamy Charleston and the Low Country to the new town of Aiken. Many of them grew fond of the area's quiet beauty and temperate climate and built second homes.

Even before the Civil War, Aiken's reputation as a health resort well-suited to the genteel sports of horse racing, steeplechasing and fox hunting spread to the cities of the North. After the war, wealthy Northerners established what became known as the Winter Colony, building magnificent 50- to 100-room "cottages" with plenty of acreage to raise and run horses.

Aiken was introduced to polo in 1882, only six years after the sport crossed the Atlantic from Europe. Thoroughbreds, harness horses and steeplechasers took immediately to the balmy year-round climate. Nowadays, there's hardly a major race in America without an Aiken-reared blue blood at the starting gate.

The city's love for horses reaches a crescendo in late March and April when the Aiken Triple attracts equestrian sports lovers from all over the world to flat races, steeplechasing and harness racing on three successive weekends. From September to November and February to July, the public is invited to the Aiken Polo Club's Sunday afternoon matches. In this easy-living town, several small streets are left unpaved in deference to horses, and pedestrian "walk" buttons are placed high on poles in easy reach of riders on horseback.

Alan and Marjorie (Marge) Wood moved to Aiken in 1993. They don't ride horses, "but like everybody else in town,

we go to the racing events in the spring," says Marge.

Alan was global marketing manager for the Delaware Port Authority in Philadelphia when he retired, and Marge had a career with the U.S. Department of State, her last assignment with the economic development department of the U.S. Embassy in Malaysia. The Woods vow they'll never move again.

"We love it here," says Marge, a vivacious redhead in her mid-50s. "There's tremendous diversity among the people who live in Aiken, and there's always something to do. We have our own symphony and ballet, a good amateur theater and outdoor concerts in the summer. For a small city, we have an amazing number of good restaurants and many opportunities to get outdoors."

Several of the town's resources are legacies of the Winter Colony. Banksia, the Aiken County Historical Museum, was originally a 32-room Winter Colony mansion. Now it's the city's fascinating "municipal attic," with numerous exhibits that trace the area's colorful past.

The Thoroughbred Hall of Fame and Museum at Hopeland Gardens was a gift from Mrs. C. Oliver Iselin, a member of the Winter Colony. When she died in the late 1960s, she willed her estate to the city. Photos and trophies earned by 39 home-grown champions are proudly displayed in the hall of fame. Each has won major races like the Kentucky Derby, Preakness Stakes or Belmont Stakes.

The rest of the estate became a 14-acre public garden with canopies of magnolias, live oaks and cedars, seasonal flowers, fountains, classical statuary and a touch-and-sense trail for the visually impaired. On summer Monday evenings, Aikenites enjoy free concerts in Hopeland's amphitheater.

Also left from the Winter Colony is Hitchcock Woods, a 2,000-acre preserve originally part of the estate of Thomas Hitchcock, a wealthy New York sports-

man who brought steeplechasing to Aiken in the 1890s. Trails winding through the woods attract legions of horseback riders, walkers, joggers and bikers. Hitchcock Woods is the setting for fall and winter fox hunts and Thanksgiving Day's Blessing of the Hounds.

"Shopping is excellent," adds Marge Wood, "and when we want a change of pace or something we can't find here, we're close to Augusta and Columbia, and Atlanta is a short drive. The North Carolina, Tennessee and Georgia mountains and the beaches at Charleston and Hilton Head Island are also a short drive."

The Woods began thinking about retirement while living in India in 1980. "We wanted a place with a four-season climate," Marge says. "I'm originally from Vermont and Alan was born in England and lived in the tropics for 30 years. Neither of us is fond of severely cold weather, but we didn't want to live in Florida where it's warm all the time. We really enjoy Aiken's four seasons. And the people here are so friendly and generous."

The Woods looked at retirement sites in Louisiana, Florida and Georgia and visited Aiken several times before making their decision. They bought property in Kalmia Landing, an adult community, in 1985 and built their house in 1988. They moved permanently in January 1993.

"I wish we'd done it a lot sooner," says Alan, 72. "We like just about everything, except maybe the fire ants. The cost of living here wasn't a major factor in our decision, but housing and other things are less expensive than most of the other places we've lived."

Patio homes in Kalmia Landing offer 1,600 to 2,200 square feet of living space and sell for $90,000 to $135,000. Condos in the community are $55,000 to $65,000. Clubhouse facilities include a library, dance floor, kitchen, exercise room, pool and tennis courts.

Marge feels secure at Kalmia Landing and considers proximity to medical services a big plus. "Two years ago, Alan had a stroke and I was able to get him to the Aiken Regional Medical Center in two minutes," she says.

"While he was recuperating, it was great for me to be so close."

Rodney and Geneva Grandy, both in their early 60s, considered Hilton Head Island and Kiawah Island in South Carolina and Raleigh-Durham in North Caro-

Aiken, SC

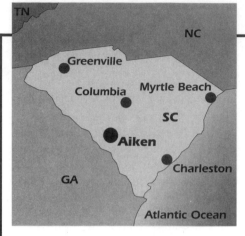

Population: 24,929 in Aiken, 134,000 in Aiken County.

Location: Extreme western South Carolina, 17 miles east of Augusta, GA, and 60 miles southwest of Columbia, SC. Lightly rolling country, 527 feet above sea level.

Climate:

	High	Low
January	51	35
July	90	74

Aiken has four distinct seasons, with warm summers and mild winters.

Average relative humidity: 60%

Rain: 47.5 inches.

Cost of living: 94.5, based on national average of 100.

Average housing cost: $147,000

Sales tax: 5%

Sales tax exemptions: Prescriptions, dental prosthetics and hearing aids.

State income tax: Graduated in six steps from 2.5% to 7%, depending on income.

Income tax exemptions: Social Security benefits. Retirees under age 65 who are drawing income from qualified retirement plans may deduct up to $3,000 of that income. At age 65, residents may deduct up to $15,000 in income.

Intangibles tax: None.

Estate tax: None, except the state's "pick-up" portion of the federal tax, applicable to taxable estates above $675,000.

Property tax: $184.20 per $1,000 of assessed value in unincorporated county; city residents pay an additional $21 per $1,000. Residential property up to five acres is assessed at 4% of actual appraised value, over five acres assessed at 6%. The average tax on a $147,000 house on less than five acres is $1,083 in the county,

$1,206 in the city. Tangible personal property, including vehicles and boats, is subject to a personal property tax that varies by county district; it is assessed at 10.5% of appraised value.

Homestead exemption: $20,000 off market value for homeowners age 65 and older.

Security: 62.2 crimes per 1,000 residents, higher than the national average of 46.2 crimes per 1,000 residents.

Religion: More than 100 churches and synagogues represent some 20 denominations.

Education: The University of South Carolina-Aiken offers full four-year programs in a wide range of studies and continuing-education and evening classes. The Academy for Lifelong Learning, affiliated with USC-Aiken, has exercise classes, forum and lecture meetings, field trips, study groups and cultural programs for those 55 and older. Aiken Technical College has two-year programs in many practical areas. The main campus of the University of South Carolina is 60 miles away at Columbia. Tuition at all South Carolina public colleges is free for those 55 and older.

Transportation: No public bus system. Regularly scheduled commercial air service is available at Bush Field in Augusta, GA (35 miles), and Columbia Metropolitan Airport, SC (40 miles).

Health: Aiken Regional Medical Center is a 225-bed acute-care complex with 24-hour emergency service, neurosurgery, urology/lithotripsy, cardiac care, Carolina Cancer Center, Women's Lifecare Center, Aiken Medical Imaging Center, plastic/reconstructive surgery, nuclear medicine and orthopedics/sports medicine. About 110 physicians practice in Aiken County. Public health centers, assisted living, nursing homes and hospice programs are available.

Housing options: Housing ranges from apartment, condo and manufactured-home communities to Winter Colony mansions with extensive grounds and stables that sell for $1 million or more. **Cedar Creek**, (800) 937-5362, is a

1,150-acre golf community. Its neighborhoods include Summit Hills, with 1,800- to 3,500-square-foot homes priced from $160,000. Carriage houses in Carriage Run, with 1,500-2,000 square feet, are priced from $150,000. The 18-hole Golf Club at Cedar Creek, lighted tennis courts and a 25-meter competition swimming pool are among features. **Kalmia Landing**, (800) 722-7356, has about 70 1,500- to 1,700-square-foot patio homes from the high $90,000s to $135,000. Two- and three-bedroom condos are $55,000-$65,000. A bridge connects the adults-only community to Aiken Regional Medical Center, and all homes have special lights to direct emergency vehicles. **Woodside Plantation**, (803) 643-4653, is a golf-course community, with 300 to 400 homes priced from the high $90,000s to about $600,000. Homes include club villas and attached houses. There's full-time gated and staffed security. Amenities also include a swimming pool, tennis courts and a clubhouse. **Houndslake**, (803) 648-6805, has villas, patio homes and attached houses in three areas. Most are 2,500 to 3,500 square feet and sell for $130,000 to $300,000. The few available lakeside lots sell for about $75,000; other lots are $59,000-$69,000. Among amenities are three nine-hole golf courses, tennis, swimming pool and clubhouse. **Summit Place**, (803) 642-8444, is an assisted-living community with studio apartments and one- and two-room suites for individual and shared living. The single-story brick building on four wooded acres has a community dining room, library, beauty shop and activity rooms.

Visitor lodging: Holiday Inn Express, two locations, $55-$85, double occupancy, (800) 465-4329. The historic Willcox Inn, $99-$150, double occupancy, including continental breakfast, (803) 649-1377.

Information: Greater Aiken Chamber of Commerce, 121 Richland Ave. E., Aiken, SC 29802, (800) 542-4536, (803) 641-1111 or www.chamber.aiken.net.

lina before relocating from New Canaan, CT, in June 1991. Geneva had lived in Aiken in the late 1970s, when things were different.

"It's changed a lot, for the better, in the last 15 years," she says. "The downtown area has made a big turnaround. It wasn't very attractive when I lived here the first time, but they've landscaped the streets and there are many new businesses, restaurants and shops. I seldom go to Augusta for shopping — we have everything we need right here."

A lower cost of living was among other attractions. "Having lived in the Northeast, I knew living in the South would be a lot less expensive," Rodney says. "But cost was only one consideration. I had a successful 37-year career with Exxon, with excellent retirement benefits and good investments. So we were really looking for a place where life would be easier."

And the Grandys believe they have found that easier life. "After six years here, I have a hard time finding anything I don't like," Rodney says. "Occasionally I have to sit in traffic a whole minute or two, I don't buy as many suits as I used to, and I can't remember the last time it snowed."

For Rodney and Geneva, the easier life they found in Aiken is an active one. "It's a can-do city — people are active; they don't just sit around," says Rodney.

Three times a week, Geneva attends exercise classes at University of South Carolina-Aiken's Academy for Lifelong Learning, a program for persons 55 and older that also includes field trips, study groups, discussion groups and cultural programs. The academy also is affiliated with the Elderhostel Institute Network, which offers programs worldwide.

The Grandys are active in several civic clubs and public health and social service agencies. They play golf, climb mountains and ski in neighboring North Carolina.

The Grandys live in a lakeside home in Woodside Plantation. One of Aiken's most prestigious residential developments, Woodside has its own golf course, tennis courts and swimming pool. Homes range from the high $90,000s to about $600,000.

Golf is a popular pastime all around Aiken. In 1997 *Golf Magazine* hailed Aiken's new Cedar Creek community as the No. 4 semiretirement golfing community in the country, which took Cedar Creek residents and management

by pleasant surprise.

"It's incredible. You can't buy that kind of advertising," says Cedar Creek vice president Ray Jackson. "People here want to live their retirement in a different way than they did their working life. They're not hanging it up, they're just changing address, getting to a warmer climate where they can be active 365 days a year."

Cedar Creek is attracting newcomers whose idea of retirement is full-time action on the golf course. The community is a mix of retirees, semiretirees and families with small children and pets.

Plans call for 850 homes to be built over a 10-year development plan. Homes range in size from 1,500- to 1,600-square-foot carriage houses, selling from $149,000, to custom-built houses with 2,000 to 6,000 square feet, selling from $180,000 to $550,000.

Architect Arthur Hills laid out the 7,206-yard, 18-hole golf course first. Housing sites were arranged around the course, which has gently changing elevations, creeks and streams, tree-lined Bermuda fairways and a few sand bunkers to keep the game interesting. The Cedar Creek Club House, designed like an English country manor house, has a full-service dining room, pro shop and outside porches.

Residents also enjoy lighted tennis courts, a 25-meter competition swimming pool with a 5,000-square-foot sun deck, and a 3.5-mile nature trail. Cedar Creek's 1,150 acres of pristine woods are a bird and wildlife sanctuary.

Lois and Larry Potter fell in love with Aiken when they were scouting the Carolinas four years ago. Larry was retiring as an IBM engineer in Manassas, VA, and Lois was a former teacher and director of a voluntary action center. The couple already had ruled out Florida and other states when they discovered Aiken.

"We visited Aiken four times, and each time it looked better," says Lois, 65. "We're still very happy here. By coincidence, not long after we moved here, our daughter, son-in-law and grandson moved to Columbia, SC, and my mother just moved to the new Cumberland Village senior living community from Florida."

Cumberland Village, an upscale senior living community on 35 wooded acres, welcomed its first residents in 1996. Housing options include furnished studio, one- and two-bedroom apartment rentals and

privately owned 1,350- to 1,600-square-foot patio homes with full services and access to an indoor swimming pool and other amenities. The Personal Care Center is designed for residents who require assistance with daily activities.

The Potters live in Gem Lakes, an older neighborhood 10 minutes from downtown. Ranch and colonial-style homes with about 2,000 square feet sell for around $160,000. Residents range from retirees and semiretirees to young couples with children. Although Gem Lakes is not a planned community, the neighborhood has a recreation center, tennis courts, private lakes for swimming and a playground for kids.

Larry, 68, says property taxes on the couple's $160,000 house are "miniscule" compared to what they paid in Virginia. With deductions that seniors get at age 65, their annual taxes are only about $1,000. "Even without the deduction, taxes here are much lower than they were in Virginia," Larry says.

They've found plenty to keep them occupied. "We keep very busy," Lois says. "We're in the hand-bell choir at our Presbyterian church. We do volunteer work and take part in activities at the Academy for Lifelong Learning. We're also doing archaeological work with the University of South Carolina in Columbia."

For couples like the Potters, Grandys and Woods who enjoy the outdoors, recreation is abundant. Lake Thurmond, a massive U.S. Army Corps of Engineers reservoir on the nearby Savannah River, and Lake Murray, near Columbia, lure fishermen, boaters, swimmers, water-skiers and campers. Aiken State Park, 16 miles east of the city, has four lakes, nature trails and campsites.

The Blue Ridge Mountains of the Carolinas, Georgia and Tennessee are less than three hours north of the city. Due east, the same drive time will get you to such popular Atlantic Ocean resort areas as Hilton Head Island, Myrtle Beach and Kiawah Island. Big-city shopping, sports, entertainment and dining are less than an hour away in Columbia, South Carolina's capital, and two and a half hours west in Atlanta.

"The people here, our rich history, low taxes, excellent medical care, cultural and recreational activities are among the many positive things that make Aiken such a great place to retire," says Ray Jackson.●

Asheville, North Carolina

This small, vibrant city in the North Carolina mountains attracts active retirees from all over the country

By Mary Lu Abbott

While George W. Vanderbilt came to Asheville for its beautiful setting and built a 250-room chateau in the late 1800s, retirees today are finding they, too, can have the good life in the mountains of western North Carolina — and in smaller abodes.

On a high plateau surrounded by the gentle, often-misty Blue Ridge Mountains, Asheville has been a natural crossroads for centuries, creating a richly diverse community in the new millennium. Coming from such distant, and disparate, locales as New England and California, retirees today find a spirit that's simpatico with a variety of individual interests.

Settling here in 1994 from Connecticut, Jack and Sheila Ingersoll wanted a place they could truly call home after having moved many times.

"I wanted to put down roots, to know people in the town and to greet them as you walk around. I thought Asheville gave us that opportunity," says Sheila, 66. "It's somewhat a spiritual community. I thought the people had a caring spirit, and now I know they do."

Jack, 70, says, "I wanted to give back some of the good I had received over the years, and I thought there would be the opportunity here — and there has been."

An executive with IBM, Jack continued working as a consultant for several years after they moved to Asheville, then retired in 1998 and delved into a program called Leadership Asheville Seniors, which explores the history of the area, introduces participants to community leaders and matches work skills with volunteer needs.

From Marin County north of San Francisco, Louaine Elke focused on lifestyle rather than a region or particular towns for retirement. "I wanted a co-housing community, a concept started in Denmark," says Louaine, 67. While residents have their own private living unit, they also share some meals together in a community house and donate time keeping up the common grounds and tending to community business, she says.

Louaine, a college instructor with degrees in fine arts and architecture, had investigated some co-housing communities in California after her husband died in 1994 but found them all too expensive. At the invitation of a former student, she came to Asheville in 1996 to see its architecture and crafts and discovered a co-housing unit was being developed in town. "I went to a meeting (of those planning the community) and I liked the people. I felt it would go. Sometimes people sit around and talk about doing this but it never goes. In a week, I made a deposit," she says.

Beyond the lifestyle concept, "I liked Asheville — the size, the old buildings, the university campus, the arts community," she says. She returned three times to watch progress of the community, located adjacent to a creek and wooded area, and moved here in 1998.

Rick and Linda Ricordati retired here from Rhode Island in 1997, after having lived most of their lives in the Chicago area. They discovered Asheville about 20 years ago when vacationing along the Blue Ridge Parkway and Skyline Drive, a scenic route that connects the Shenandoah Mountains in the north and the Great Smoky Mountains southwest of Asheville.

"Any time we traveled, we would look at a place and say, 'Could we live here?'" says Linda, 58. "The decision about Asheville was a process of elimination. I did not want a lot of heat and humidity. That ruled out Florida and Arizona — I don't care how dry it (Arizona) is, 110 degrees is 110."

Rick adds that they checked out San Diego but felt traffic was too congested, and it was too far from their children in the Midwest. "We looked at the coasts of North and South Carolina. The winters are mild, but the summers are brutal," he says.

"There are ocean people and mountain people, and we are mountain people," says Linda.

On a master checklist of desirable qualities in a retirement destination, Asheville scores high — a small but sophisticated city with excellent health care, a reasonable cost of living and the added bonus of a university with a cutting-edge program for active seniors. Well-located, it's on Interstate 40 and the slow-paced Blue Ridge Parkway, approximately 200 miles from Atlanta, GA; 120 miles from Charlotte, NC; 110 miles from Knoxville, TN; and 60 miles from Greenville, SC.

Once they decided on the Asheville area, the Ricordatis visited several times and talked to many residents before buying property in a new development of free-standing homes. They like the diversity of Asheville. "It isn't filled with all the same types of people — all the same age or who all play golf," says Rick, 58, who retired from marketing. The cultural, educational and medical hub of a region that encompasses more than 200,000 residents, Asheville has a makeup that mixes retirees with college students, young families and professionals of all ages. Health care, manufacturing and tourism are major industries.

"We like the manageability of living here," says Linda. "It's easy to do things — to go to the grocery store or the cleaners. And if there's a little traffic, you don't mind it because the scenery is so beautiful."

"In general, the whole city is friendly and laid-back," Rick says. "It's unusual to bump into anyone who's not pleasant."

Since moving here in 1994, the Ingersolls have seen the city gain momentum. "It has gotten better. It's growing — but not too much — and downtown is really coming to life," Sheila says.

"We had dinner downtown the other night," says Jack, " and people were still walking around at 9 or 10. It's drawing a variety of ages."

Asheville entered its first boom in the early part of the 1900s, as Vanderbilt's elegant Biltmore Estate focused attention on the area. Its clean, cool mountain air soon made it a favorite resort among presidents and celebrities. Luxury accommodations opened, among them the still-grand 1913 Grove Park Inn, a massive hotel built in the style of a rustic lodge with walls of granite boulders. The down-town area blossomed with new buildings in art deco and modern designs, and farmland became housing developments with mountain views. When the Great Depression hit, Asheville and surrounding Buncombe County reeled under a massive debt and struggled for nearly five decades to pay off all its obligations rather than default on the loans. Only in the 1970s did the city really begin to recover, but there was an unexpected benefit to its long-term decline: Since the city had no extra funds for urban renewal projects popular in the '50s and '60s, its classic buildings

Asheville, NC

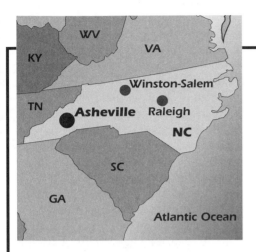

Population: About 68,000 residents in the city, 195,000 in Buncombe County. Asheville is the county seat and regional cultural, medical and educational hub.

Location: In the Blue Ridge Mountains of western North Carolina, about 200 miles northeast of Atlanta, GA, and 120 northwest of Charlotte, NC. It's on the Blue Ridge Parkway about 50 miles from Great Smoky Mountains National Park. Elevation varies, with the average being 2,200 feet.

Climate:

	High	Low
January	47	25
July	83	63

Average relative humidity: 58%

Rain: 48 inches.

Snow: 15 inches.

Cost of living: 103.8, based on national average of 100.

Average housing cost: $89,782 for a two-bedroom home, $142,656 for a three-bedroom home. Monthly apartment rents average $535 for one bedroom, $625 for two bedrooms.

Sales tax: 6%

Sales tax exemptions: Prescriptions and services. Motor vehicles are taxed at 3 percent.

State income tax: Graduated in three steps from 6% to 7.75%, depending on income.

Income tax exemptions: Social Security benefits. Each taxpayer also can exempt up to $4,000 in local, state or federal government retirement benefits and up to $2,000 in private retirement benefits, but the total of these exemptions cannot exceed $4,000 per person.

Intangibles tax: None.

Estate tax: None, except the state's "pick-up" portion of the federal tax, applicable to taxable estates above $675,000.

Property tax: City residents pay a combined city-county tax rate of $1.15 per $100 of assessed value, and county residents pay a rate of $.63 per $100 of assessed value, with all homes assessed at 100 percent of market value. Annual taxes on a $142,000 home are about $1,633 in the city, $895 in the county.

Homestead exemption: Those age 65 and older can exempt $20,000 off the valuation if their income is less than $15,000 annually.

Personal property tax: Same rate as home taxes noted above apply to vehicles, boats, motor homes, mobile homes and other specified belongings.

Security: 76.3 crimes per 1,000 residents, lower than the national average of 46.2 crimes per 1,000 residents.

Religion: The city has about 300 places of worship, representing Protestant, Roman Catholic, Greek Orthodox and Jewish faiths.

Education: The city has several colleges and universities, augmented by campuses in surrounding communities. The University of North Carolina at Asheville has degree programs and is home to the North Carolina Center for Creative Retirement, which has numerous programs for retirees, including the College for Seniors with four terms of noncredit classes annually.

Transportation: Asheville Regional Airport provides commuter and jet service, and the Asheville Transit Authority runs buses in the city.

Health: A regional medical center, Asheville has five hospitals and more than 500 doctors, providing a range of health care including heart and cancer centers, trauma services and emergency air transport by helicopter.

Housing options: Some retirees choose to buy older homes in city neighborhoods, while others relocate to new developments in suburban areas or adjacent communities in Buncombe County. Some developments cater to active adults but many are composed of all ages. Among choices: In the eastern part of the city, **ViewPointe**, (800) 601-8622, is a gated community of maintenance-free cluster homes for active adults, with a clubhouse for activities; homes are in the $160,000s-$190,000s. To the north in Weaverville, about 20 minutes to downtown Asheville, **Reems Creek Golf Club**, (828) 645-3110, attracts all ages, offering townhomes from $175,000 and homes from the $260,000s. To the south at the community of Arden, about 10 minutes from Asheville, **High Vista Falls**, (828) 890-1234, is a gated community for all ages with golf course, clubhouse and patio homes from the $277,000s and townhomes from the low $300,000s.

Visitor lodging: A popular vacation hub, Asheville has a wide choice of lodging, from budget to luxury and including bed-and-breakfast inns. The grand dame is Grove Park Inn, (800) 267-8413, a legendary mountainside resort with a rustic elegance; rates start at $130. Contact the Asheville Bed & Breakfast Association, (877) 262-6867, for information on most of the B&Bs.

Information: Asheville Area Chamber of Commerce, P.O. Box 1010, Asheville, NC 28802, (800) 257-1300 or www.ashevillechamber.org. North Carolina Center for Creative Retirement, (828) 251-6140 or www.unca.edu/ncccr.

didn't succumb to the wrecking ball.

Recognizing their architectural treasures from the early 20th century, residents and developers began restoring the art deco, Queen Anne, Revival and Romanesque structures and recycling them for new uses. Today more than $50 million is pledged for downtown redevelopment. Among the restorations downtown, Pack Place now houses three museums, a theater and cultural center. Galleries and shops showcase outstanding arts and crafts created in the region, augmenting the extensive collection of mountain crafts at the Folk Art Center outside town on the Blue Ridge Parkway.

Asheville's extensive cultural venues are a drawing card for many retirees who are eager to escape the hassles of living in metropolitan areas but still want some of the big-city amenities. "It's easy and inexpensive to go to performances here," says Louaine, noting that the area has community theater, university drama presentations and current productions by touring groups. It takes her as little as 10 minutes to get to performances, which usually cost less than $20 — "I figured it cost about $100 to go into San Francisco for an evening performance," she says.

Although the cost of living in Asheville runs slightly above average, it's less than metropolitan areas, and all those interviewed cited lower costs as a factor in choosing Asheville.

Each chose a different option for housing. The Ingersolls bought an older home, which they renovated. "It's 10 minutes from downtown but feels like it's in the country," says Sheila. The Ricordatis wanted a new development where they felt that making friends would be easier than in a neighborhood of longtime Asheville residents. "We pretty much built our house by phone and fax," Rick says, noting that they shuttled to and from Rhode Island during construction. They were pleased with the work, though. "The real surprise (of their move) was that we could build a house without being here, and it come out 98 percent the way we wanted," he says with a laugh.

Louaine's co-housing community has 24 units in close clusters of three or four attached homes that range from one to three stories and from one to five bedrooms. Each has a private back yard but the front yards are common. All parking is close to the street with walkways to the houses, an architectural design intended to encourage residents to meet and greet their neighbors as they go to and from their homes.

"We have a very interesting group (of residents), ranging from a 4-month-old baby to 70s," says Louaine. "This is part of the appeal to me — I didn't want all seniors." It's a friendly group that looks after each other, she says, and takes time to chat when crossing paths outside.

"In Denmark, co-housing residents eat dinner at the community house daily. Here we do it twice a week and sometimes the men do brunch on Sunday," she says. The community house has a restaurant-size kitchen, and residents sign up for work on the cooking team. A community garden provides vegetables and herbs for the shared meals, and residents also can have their own gardens. Louaine, who is an avid gardener, has an arbor where she grows Asian pears and kiwis, among other fruits.

A guiding force for many seniors who move to the Asheville area is the North Carolina Center for Creative Retirement, established in 1988 as part of the University of North Carolina at Asheville. With "creative" an operative part of its title, the center reached out to the growing number of seniors who want to stay active in retirement and designed programs that have become national models. Its mainstay is the College for Seniors, which offers four terms annually with classes in such far-ranging topics as Understanding the Balkans, King David vs. King James, Getting Started With Computers and U.S. Leadership in Today's Global Economy. UNCA faculty, community residents and retirees who are experts in varying fields teach the noncredit classes, which draw about 1,500 seniors annually.

The Ingersolls, Ricordatis and Elke are involved in classes at the College for Seniors, which they also found to be a good way to meet people, make new friends and learn more about the community. Jack serves on the boards of the College for Seniors and Leadership for Asheville Seniors, another program of the center. Rick serves as the university's representative to United Way, and both he and his wife volunteer to assist with the center's Creative Retirement Exploration Weekend. Held over the Memorial Day weekend, the event an-

nually draws about 150 seniors who attend workshops to discuss the economic, social and psychological factors of relocating to this region when they retire. Participants hear firsthand experiences from seniors who have come here from all parts of the country and have time to see Asheville and surrounding communities.

With mountains at their doorsteps, Asheville residents enjoy a variety of outdoor sports, including hiking, rafting, biking and fishing. The area has a mild four-season climate with a colorful spring and fall.

The retirees interviewed consider the health care here excellent, and Louaine notes that besides traditional medicine, the city has choices of alternative medicine. Although the crime rate is above average, many retirees agree that it didn't affect their decision to move to Asheville. "It's still a place where a lot of people don't lock their doors," says Rick.

All voice a common concern about increased air pollution, which usually occurs in summer. There has been a slight upward trend in air pollution recently, with the increased population driving more motor vehicles and pollutants drifting into the area from the west, according to representatives of the Western North Carolina Air Pollution Control Agency, which monitors air quality. They say that while in the summer of '99 Asheville had some days when the ozone level rose to moderate levels, the city had only two days when air quality was rated unhealthy for sensitive groups (those susceptible to asthma and other respiratory problems) and no days rated generally unhealthy.

Rick says most people who've relocated here like it so much they sound "like a voice for the chamber of commerce — we've become that way." As for seniors considering places to retire, Rick adds, "I think Asheville should be on your list. It was right for us but it may not be for everyone." He says a golfer would find plenty of courses to play but a "water person" or boating enthusiast might not be as happy here.

Jack says that after living so many different places, "This is home — where I want to be." Sheila adds, "No matter where I lived I enjoyed it, but I never made an attachment and I wondered if I would ever find a place I could. It's happened here." ●

Ashland, Oregon

A lively town in pretty southern Oregon sets the stage for Shakespeare

By Stanton H. Patty

Sometimes it seems as if all of Ashland's 19,220 residents are hooked on Shakespeare. That includes retirees who have settled here in southern Oregon to partake of Ashland's award-winning Oregon Shakespeare Festival.

"We've seen plays all over the world, but none better than right here in Ashland," says Gerald Garland, a retired educator. But the play hasn't always been the thing in Ashland-upon-Interstate 5.

Back in 1935, Angus Bowmer, an instructor at Southern Oregon Normal School (now Southern Oregon University), dreamed of producing a Shakespeare festival on the grounds of an abandoned theater once used for events on the Chautauqua circuit. Chautauqua was the 19th-century movement that aimed to bring culture and entertainment to rural areas around the country. Celebrities such as bandmaster John Philip Sousa and orator William Jennings Bryan drew crowds here.

Ashland's city fathers agreed to give Bowmer $400 for expenses — with the provision that a boxing match be presented on the same program. The thrifty city officials reasoned that pugilism would cover the Shakespeare show's certain losses.

The fights lost money, but that first festival's two Shakespeare plays — "Twelfth Night" and "The Merchant of Venice" — turned a profit. Ever since, the annual Oregon Shakespeare Festival has been a hit.

And ever since, this pretty, little town snuggled against the Siskiyou and Cascade mountain ranges has been blending scenic beauty and the lyrics of the Bard. More than 358,000 visitors were counted here last year. The economic impact of the nine-month-long Oregon Shakespeare Festival alone was estimated at $90,203,600 last season.

Many of Ashland's retirees say they "discovered" Ashland during frequent trips here to attend the Shakespeare series. Others allow that they didn't have a burning interest in Shakespeare's works until getting involved in volunteer assignments at the festival.

John and Norma Yovich, both retired teachers, moved to Ashland 17 years ago after giving retirement a try in the U.S. Virgin Islands. The Yoviches had friends who were conducting a study of the best places to live for retirees. The friends decided on Medford, 17 miles north of Ashland by way of Interstate 5. The Yoviches traveled to Medford for a visit.

"But then we looked at Ashland and just fell in love with the town," recalls Norma. Ashland, she says, offered "just the right mix" — location, small-town living, an array of cultural assets, excellent medical care, a gentle climate for gardening, interesting neighbors and scenic mountain views.

"The (Shakespeare) festival was not the most compelling reason for moving here," says John (Jack) Yovich. "What I really liked was the idea of having a college in town." The Yoviches, both 76, are regulars at Ashland's Southern Oregon University for concerts, lectures and Elderhostel sessions.

But now they also are Shakespeare enthusiasts. "I'm hooked," says Norma Yovich, who, along with dozens of other retirees, volunteers for tasks ranging from costume repairs to ticket-taking at the festival's three theaters.

What happened in Ashland is that the Tony Award-winning Oregon Shakespeare Festival made the town a major-league destination. Along with Shakespeare came other theaters, a symphony orchestra, a range of lodging accommodations (including 62 bed-and-breakfast inns, at last count),

outstanding restaurants, art galleries and antique shops. These are all attractions sought by retirees who are determined to continue creative, vigorous lives after their working years.

For them (with apologies to the Bard of Stratford-upon-Avon), it's Ashland as they like it. An Ashland Chamber of Commerce publication states it this way: "Ashlanders don't talk much about 'quality time' because it's all quality time."

Richard and Mary Mastain didn't even consider another retirement spot before moving here from Sacramento, CA, in 1989. "I can't think of any negatives," Mary says of Ashland.

Richard, 73, was director of California's Commission on Teacher Credentialing for 16 years. Before that he was employed at Yale University, and before Yale he served in the Peace Corps in Nigeria. Mary, now 71, and their four children went along on the African adventure. Mary, a longtime reading specialist in a Sacramento-area school district, taught in a Nigerian school for a year.

It was the Oregon Shakespeare Festival that introduced Ashland to the Mastains. "We had been to Ashland two or three times for the festival and just liked the town very much," says Mary.

During one visit, the couple expressed interest in buying a 100-year-old house on Granite Street in downtown Ashland but had to wait four years before the owner was ready to sell. Their 2,800-square-foot home is across from Lithia Park, Ashland's 100-acre gem of a park where early-day locals and visitors used to imbibe a so-called healing elixir called Lithia Water.

Ashland's enterprising merchants had hopes back then that their town would become a renowned European-style spa, but interest waned. Fortunately for Ashland, Shakespeare

Ashland, OR

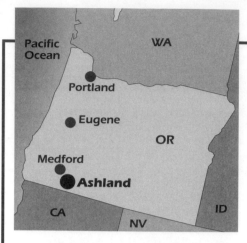

Population: 19,220 in Ashland, 172,800 in Jackson County.

Location: On Interstate 5 between San Francisco (365 miles to the south) and Portland, OR (290 miles to the north). Ashland, at an elevation of 2,000 feet, is at the southern end of the Rogue Valley, 15 miles north of Oregon's border with California.

Climate:

	High	Low
January	48	32
July	85	52

Average relative humidity: 83% in winter, 52% in summer.

Rain: 19 inches.

Cost of living: Above average (specific index not available).

Median housing cost: $176,161 in the city, $220,205 in rural areas.

Sales tax: None as such, but Ashland does have a 5% "food tax" that applies to restaurant meals, takeout foods and deli purchases within grocery stores. There is no tax on other groceries.

State income tax: Graduated in three steps from 5% to 9%, depending on income.

Income tax exemptions: Social Security benefits are exempt. You may be able to subtract some or all of your federal pension income, based on the number of months of federal service before and after Oct. 1, 1991.

Intangibles tax: None.

Estate tax: None, except the state's "pick-up" portion of the federal tax, applicable to taxable estates above $675,000.

Property taxes: For the 1999-2000 tax year: $14.26 per $1,000 of assessed value for city property owners, and ranging from $9.27 to $12.64 for rural property owners, depending on taxes assessed by school and fire districts. Homes are assessed at 85% of market value. The tax on a $176,000 home in the city would be about $2,133. The tax on a $220,000 home in a rural area would be about $1,733 to $2,364. Property-tax relief is available for low-income seniors.

Homestead exemption: None.

Security: 45.8 crimes per 1,000 residents, lower than the national average of 46.2 crimes per 1,000 residents.

Religion: 36 churches or religious affiliations, including synagogues and a Buddhist congregation.

Education: The Ashland School District has seven schools with enrollment estimated at 3,400. There also are several private schools. Southern Oregon University, founded in 1869, is part of the Oregon University System. Its main campus is in Ashland, with a branch campus in neighboring Medford. There are more than 5,000 undergraduate and graduate students. Rogue Community College, with its main campus in nearby Grants Pass, OR, offers a full range of community college programs.

Transportation: The regional airport is Rogue Valley International-Medford Airport, 20 miles north of Ashland. The airport is served by United Airlines and Horizon Air, a sister company of Alaska Airlines. Bus service is available from Greyhound-Trailways and, locally, from Rogue Valley Transportation District, which offers low-cost public transportation throughout Ashland. For rail service, the nearest Amtrak station is in Klamath Falls, OR, 70 miles east of Ashland.

Health: Ashland Community Hospital is an acute, primary-care facility fully accredited by the Joint Commission on Accreditation of Healthcare Organizations. The 49-bed hospital provides 24-hour emergency services, inpatient medical and surgical services, outpatient services, an intensive-care unit, an alternative family-oriented birthing center, a hospice unit and other facilities. Other medical facilities in the region include Providence Medford Medical Center (168 beds) in Medford, and Rogue Valley Medical Center (305 beds), also in Medford.

Housing options: Many Ashland-area retirees buy single-family homes, but the city also has high-quality retirement facilities. Among these is **Mountain Meadows**, (800) 337-1301, an award-winning retirement center occupying a 41.5-acre campus about one mile northeast of downtown Ashland. Options include single-family homes (with two or three bedrooms) priced from $260,000 to $325,000, depending on square footage, and condominiums (with one, two or three bedrooms), from $130,000 to $290,000. Attached houses (with two or three bedrooms) range from $245,000 to $270,000. Mountain Meadows also has an assisted-living center with 75 apartments and 32 special-care units. Prices begin at $1,700 a month. Madeline Hill, a former administrator of the state of Oregon's Senior Services Division, founded Mountain Meadows 10 years ago "when I saw what was not available for my older friends." Mountain Meadows was honored by the National Council on Seniors Housing as being the best small active-adult community in America. Another Ashland retirement center with facilities for independent or assisted living is **Mountain View**, (541) 482-3292, in downtown Ashland. Mountain View has 111 apartments, including 25 apartments for assisted-living guests. Monthly rates for independent-living tenants range from $995 to $1,360 for a studio apartment, and from $2,200 to $2,305 for two-bedroom apartments. Assisted-living services are an additional $800 to $1,100. There is a waiting list that ranges from one to three months. Mountain View is part of a chain, Holiday Retirement Corp., with 25,000 units in the United States, Canada and England. Medford also offers retirement centers, including **Rogue Valley Manor**, (800) 848-7868, with accommodations for about 750 residents.

Visitor lodging: Ashland's lodging establishments — including more than 60 bed-and-breakfast inns and country inns — offer a total of about 1,200 beds. Among motel options: Windsor Inn, $65-$85, (800) 334-2330, and Bard's Inn Best Western, $72-$95, (800) 528-1234. Among B&B options: Chanticleer Inn, $75-$170, (800) 898-1950, and Bayberry Inn, $65-$100, (800) 795-1252.

Information: Ashland Chamber of Commerce, P.O. Box 1360, Ashland, OR 97520, (541) 482-3486, or fax (541) 482-2350. Internet: www.ashlandchamber.com. Oregon Shakespeare Festival, P.O. Box 158, Ashland, OR 97520. For tickets, call (541) 482-4331. For administration offices, call (541) 482-2111. Internet: www.orshakes.org.

soon replaced the bitter bubbly from Lithia Springs as the mainstay of Ashland's economy.

Richard and Mary Mastain have a full schedule. Mary is a volunteer at the local chamber of commerce, serves on Ashland's library board and guides walks through Lithia Park. Richard plays tennis regularly with partners that he describes as "terrific people from all walks of life." A recent tennis turnout of retirees included an oral surgeon, a Navy physician, two airline pilots, a businessman and a still-performing Shakespearean actor.

The Mastains celebrated their 50th-wedding anniversary in Lithia Park. They needed a major space for the party because more than 150 guests from throughout the United States attended. "We're having a wonderful time here," says Mary Mastain.

Cherie and Gerald Garland began their retirement years in Ashland in 1990 by buying a two-story house on 45 acres of land — and adding three goats, two cats, a dog and 100 head of beef cattle. They since have traded the house and the menagerie for a condominium at Ashland's Mountain Meadows retirement community, which won the National Council on Seniors Housing award as the best small active-adult community in America.

"There comes a time," says Cherie of the switch to condo living.

Gerry, 71, was a high-school English teacher for 24 years in Oklahoma and California. Later the couple owned an educational-supplies business with stores in California and Arizona. It was the Shakespeare festival that brought them to Ashland.

"We started coming to the festival about 25 years ago," says Cherie, 67. "We'd usually see eight plays or so, then go home and jump back into the business."

But one day, while returning through stop-and-go freeway traffic to their home in Pomona, CA, there was what Gerry calls "a gray blanket of fog" hanging over the Los Angeles Basin. It was time to leave, he said.

Destination: Ashland — and the 45 acres of pasture with the big house. "We had just sort of fallen in love with the town," Gerry remembers.

Then came the day when they decided to move into Mountain Meadows. Their Ashland house sold after only five days on the market, and all the animals found good homes. The cats stayed with the property, and the dog went to live with friends. The goats moved two houses away. The cattle belonged to someone else, who had been leasing the Garlands' property for grazing. And so the Garlands settled happily into a brand-new 1,500-square-foot Mountain Meadows condominium.

"There has not been one moment of regret," says Cherie. "It was a big decision, but we were able to make it while we were of sound mind and in good health. That's the important thing."

Both sing in church choirs. Cherie also is active in the local garden club, and Gerry plays tennis several times a week. Travel also is on their schedule, and they have journeyed from Bali to Africa.

"Nothing to it," says Cherie. "We just go out the front door and lock it."

Geography — Ashland's mainline location between San Francisco and Portland, OR — was an important decision-making factor for many retired couples here. "We wanted to be in driving distance of our children in California," says Mary Mastain.

Ashland is 15 miles north of the California border — 365 miles north of San Francisco, 290 miles south of Portland. About the only drawback for Ashlanders, says Jack Yovich, is what he terms "somewhat limited air transportation." The nearest airport — Rogue Valley International-Medford Airport — is 20 miles north of Ashland. It currently is served by only two carriers, United Airlines and Horizon Air, an Alaska Airlines sister company.

"It's not a serious thing, but does makes airline travel a bit more complicated for us," Jack says.

"And yet," says Jeanne Thomas, a 22-year resident of Ashland, "things have really improved over the years here for air travel. We are getting more special fares and better service than before," says Jeanne, a receptionist at the Ashland Chamber of Commerce.

Another key factor in attracting retirees to Ashland is excellent medical care. There are first-rate hospitals both in Ashland and in neighboring Medford. And Ashland's full menu of cultural offerings is encouraging big-city physicians to move here to rear their families.

"There's so much culture here that it's sort of mind-boggling," says Mary Mastain.

And Shakespeare isn't Ashland's only attraction. Residents of all ages in this Oregon playground are outdoor-minded. They exercise along a network of walking and bicycle trails inside the city, and they golf on eight courses scattered through the Ashland-Medford region.

Close by — and, incidentally, owned by the city of Ashland — is the Mount Ashland ski area. Mount Ashland, 7,533 feet high, receives more than 300 inches of snow each Thanksgiving-through-April ski season. Cross-country skiers find more than 80 miles of trails, and downhillers have a choice of 23 runs.

Emigrant Lake, six miles to the east, is popular with water-skiers, swimmers and boaters. Crater Lake National Park (Oregon's only national park) is a drive of about two and a half hours from Ashland. And then there is Oregon's Rogue River, with world-class rafting, kayaking, jet-boating and sport fishing. Guides and outfitters are available for adventure outings.

For generous helpings of history and music, there is Jacksonville, five miles west of neighboring Medford. Jacksonville, born of a gold rush in the 1850s, is home to the Britt Festivals, a summertime musical series running the scale from jazz to the classics.

But it is the Oregon Shakespeare Festival that continues to hold the spotlight here. The 65-year-old festival is billed as the nation's oldest and largest professional regional theater company. The extravaganza begins in February and ends in October and features nearly a dozen plays.

If all the world's a stage, as the Bard said, Ashlanders will tell you that center stage is right here in southern Oregon. Verily!●

Athens, Georgia

Historic university sets the pace in Georgia city

By William Schemmel

In Athens, GA, unlike many other cities today, the action centers on downtown, where the scene is reminiscent of *Saturday Evening Post* covers.

Students and townspeople crowd the sidewalks, drifting in and out of shops that sell books, bagels, clothes, CDs, hardware and a myriad of other goods.

They settle into restaurants serving everything from tofu burgers and "California inventive" cuisine to Southern-style home cooking, barbecue, Indian, Mexican, Cajun, Chinese, Japanese and German dishes.

The lively downtown "looks like the downtowns many people remember when they were younger," says Joan Zitzelman, spokeswoman for the Athens Convention and Visitors Bureau.

A major contributor to the action is the University of Georgia, temporary home to about 30,000 students. From downtown, the landmark Arch serves as a commemorative gateway to the historic campus.

UGA is the nation's oldest chartered state university, founded in 1785, but buildings and classes didn't come until 1801, with the birth of the town of Athens. City fathers named the community for the Greek capital, seeking to establish it as another "classic city" known as a center of culture and learning.

Indeed, the new Athens did become a major educational center, with UGA fostering great pride and a fervent following among Georgia residents and its graduates.

Today UGA's abundance of cultural, educational and recreational activities draws not only young students but also seniors seeking an active retirement lifestyle. Here they find theater, lectures, films, the Georgia Museum of Art, the State Botanical Garden, a continuing-education center with extensive enrichment classes and the popular Georgia Bulldogs athletic programs.

Many graduates come back to Athens when they retire.

Helen Rode, 63, grew up in Athens and attended the university. She and her husband, Ed, 66, lived in the Chicago area for most of his 40-year ministry with the United Methodist Church.

When he retired, they considered a few other areas, "but we wanted the cultural activities and other amenities of a university town, and I remembered what a wonderful place Athens was," she says. "We were delighted to find that it still has a wonderful small-town feeling, even though it's much larger than it was then."

The city now has a population of about 90,000, including students. Large oak and elm trees shade historic homes and churches, including many antebellum mansions with tall white columns. At the university, the Greek Revival-style chapel, the president's residence and several other buildings on the original campus date back to the early or mid-1800s.

Ed says another factor in choosing Athens was its below-average cost of living, which he calls "much lower than in Illinois."

"We have a modest income and we needed an affordable home. Plus, we wanted to get out of the cold Chicago winters. It stays hotter here than it does in Illinois, but it rarely snows, and the falls are beautiful," Ed says.

They purchased a 30-year-old home in a subdivision of medium-sized houses. "It's a lovely home that was really well cared for," he says. "I've always had a dream of having a home in a community I enjoyed being in. It's very satisfying."

Helen adds, "It's such a beautiful town, with so much going on all the time. It's hard to be bored. But we can get to Atlanta in about an hour or so, and we're also within a short drive of the Georgia mountains and a few hours from the Georgia and South Carolina beaches."

Okel and Gennis Dawson moved to the Athens area after their home of 32 years in Homestead, FL, was destroyed by Hurricane Andrew in 1992.

"We'd been thinking about moving away from South Florida for a good while," says Gennis, 70. "When the hurricane took everything, we didn't see any reason to stay.

"Our son had become the dean of environmental design at the University of Georgia, and he encouraged us to move to the Athens area. We're very happy with the decision.

"Everything, especially property taxes, is much cheaper here, and property values are much better," she says.

The Dawsons live in the Great Oaks subdivision in Oconee County, a rapidly growing bedroom community about 10 minutes south of downtown Athens. Houses in Great Oaks are valued at $120,000 to $175,000.

"We have a two-story house on two-and-a-half acres of land. That enables us to have a garden," says Gennis, adding that it helps cut down on their grocery bills.

The Dawsons found a warm welcome in their new home.

"I didn't know my next-door neighbor in Homestead," Gennis says, "but when we went to a church of 150 members here, 120 shook our hands. People are so friendly."

The Dawsons often go into Athens for dining, football games and other activities. They say they feel safer from crime here than they did in South Florida.

"We're happy where we are," says Okel, 76, a machinist who retired from International Paper Co.

Other residents are equally enthusiastic about the area's assets.

"First-class health care is abundant," says Buddy Allen, president of

Heyward Allen Motor Co. Athens is a medical center for northeast Georgia, offering two acute-care facilities, Athens Regional Medical Center and St. Mary's Hospital. Both have advanced surgical technology and treatment programs.

Jack Wilson, who moved from Atlanta a year ago, finds the city a comfortable place for singles.

"There are plenty of inexpensive apartments and rental houses," he says. "You can get a decent place for much less than you'd pay in Atlanta or other big cities. There's always something to do here. You can eat very well and very inexpensively. Athens has crime problems like every other place, but I generally feel safe here."

The average housing cost in Athens is $120,000. Property taxes are reasonable, aided by a $10,000 homestead exemption.

The city takes up most of Clarke County, which is the state's smallest county in land area and one of its most densely populated. Although much of the available land in Clarke County has been developed, a few new subdivisions are still being built.

Athens, GA

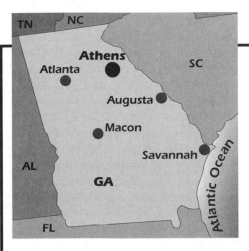

Population: 120,000, including 30,000 University of Georgia students.
Location: In Georgia's southern Piedmont Plateau region, 65 miles northeast of Atlanta.

Climate:

	High	Low
January	48	31
July	92	69

Average relative humidity: 60%
Rain: 52 inches.
At an elevation of 750 feet, Athens has a moderate four-season climate with cool winters, colorful falls and hot, humid summers. Snow is infrequent and light when it occurs.
Cost of living: Below average (specific index not available).
Average housing cost: $120,000
Sales tax: 7%
Sales tax exemptions: Prescriptions, hearing aids, eyeglasses.
State income tax: Graduated from 1% to 5% on first $7,000 (singles) or $10,000 (couples filing jointly), then 6% on greater amounts.
Income tax exemptions: Social Security benefits; up to $13,000 in retirement income is exempt.
Intangibles tax: None.
Estate tax: None, except the state's "pick-up" portion of the federal tax, applicable to taxable estates above

$675,000.
Property tax: $32.70 per $1,000 of assessed value, with homes assessed at 40% of fair market value. With homestead exemption listed below, yearly tax on a $120,000 house is $1,242.
Homestead exemption: $10,000 off assessed value for full-time residents.
Security: 80.6 crimes per 1,000 residents, higher than the national average of 46.2 crimes per 1,000 residents.
Religion: More than 200 churches and synagogues serve all denominations.
Education: The main campus of the University of Georgia offers undergraduate and graduate programs, day and evening classes, community classes without credit and a wide range of continuing-education courses in languages, cultural studies and other subjects. College classes are free for all Georgia residents age 65 and older; continuing-education classes have fees. The Athens Area Technical Institute offers day and evening vocational and technical courses.
Transportation: Athens Transit System provides bus service throughout the area, and the university operates a bus system for use by students, faculty and staff. There are daily commuter flights to Charlotte, NC, a hub for air connections nationwide; regularly scheduled limousine service goes to the Atlanta airport.
Health: Athens is a regional health care center. St. Mary's Hospital (private) and Athens Regional Medical Center (public) together have about 500 beds and offer 24-hour emergency care and all other major services. More than 170 physicians practice in all medical specialties. The Navy Corps

Supply School has medical and dental facilities available to military retirees.
Housing options: Five Points is a quiet neighborhood near downtown and the university, with frame and brick homes built in the '30s-'50s; prices range from about $80,000 to $200,000 and up for older homes. In Clarke County, the **Village at Jennings Mill** has large contemporary homes from $109,000 on an 18-hole private golf course. **Kingston Greens**, a golfing community in Madison County, about 20 minutes north of downtown Athens, has new three-bedroom homes on large wooded lots from the low $100,000s. South of Athens in Oconee County, **Stonebridge** has three- and four-bedroom homes for $175,000-$230,000, and **Laurel Shoals** homes start in the upper $100,000s. The Athens area has numerous rental apartments, condos and houses.
Visitor lodging: Holiday Inn, adjacent to downtown and UGA campus, doubles $79-$107, (706) 549-4433; Courtyard by Marriott, near downtown and campus, $79 double, (706) 369-7000; Holiday Inn, near campus and downtown, $79 double, (706) 546-8122. Rivendell Bed and Breakfast, between Athens and Watkinsville, contemporary country home in a quiet wooded setting about 15 minutes from downtown, $70-$85, (706) 769-4522. Rates at most Athens area lodgings are higher on football weekends.
Information: Athens Convention and Visitors Bureau, P.O. Box 948, Athens, GA 30603, (706) 546-1805. Athens Area Chamber of Commerce, 220 College Ave., No. 7, Athens, GA 30601, (706) 549-6800 or www.aacoc.org.

Large wooded lots in Hampton Park start at $23,900, and three-bedroom homes with tennis and pool privileges start at $127,000.

Those who enjoy in-town living in an older neighborhood prefer the Five Points area. Close to downtown and the university campus, most of the frame and brick homes were developed between the 1930s and early 1950s. The neighborhood shopping area has grocery stores, a deli, antique shops, bookstores and a good mix of locally owned restaurants and shops. Smaller homes that need work sell for about $60,000, while brick homes in good condition are in the low $120,000s. Some newer homes are selling for $200,000 or more.

Much of the area's new growth is taking place in once-rural counties like Oconee to the south and Madison to the north. New developments such as Harrowford Estates, Skipstone, Laurel Shoals, Great Oaks and Twelve Oaks in Oconee County and Kingston Greens in Madison County are priced from $120,000 and up. Some large custom-built homes are valued at $1 million-plus.

Although many residents consider their neighborhoods and downtown Athens to be safe, the Athens crime rate is higher than the national average, with 80.6 crimes per 1,000 residents at press time, compared to a national figure of 46.2 crimes per 1,000 residents.

Local police say the figures don't tell the complete story. Sgt. Greg Paul, who works in crime analysis for the Athens/Clarke County Police Department, says the higher crime rate can be attributed in part to a much larger city population than 120,000 at given times. For instance, college events such as football games draw tens of thousands of extra people, and the work force includes commuters from adjacent counties, but these people aren't counted in the population upon which the crime rate is based.

As for specific crime problems, he notes, "Many of the reported crimes are student-related thefts from dorm rooms and parked cars and other petty crimes. Many are drug-related and crimes involving domestic violence."

The overall crime has declined, in part due to an increased number of police, bike and foot patrols and community awareness and action programs.

In addition to its thriving downtown and neighborhood shopping areas, Athens has numerous other shopping districts and one major regional mall. Georgia Square has four anchor department stores — Macy's, Penney's, Sears and Belk — as well as specialty shops, services and cinemas.

Residents offer little criticism of the city, though newcomers must adjust to the huge influx of football fans, who help fill the 82,000-seat stadium.

Ed Rode notes that traffic can be heavy and "there are plenty of 'Chicago drivers' down here," referring to the aggressive nature of some on the road.

The Rodes can think of only one thing they miss from their previous home. "You can't get Illinois corn in Georgia. Fresh corn out of the field just can't be replaced, but then you can't get good Georgia peaches, watermelons and peanuts in Illinois," he says.

The city hosted some segments of the Summer Olympic Games in 1996, furthering its bond with ancient Greece. The university's football stadium was the setting for the semifinals and finals of women's and men's soccer, and its 10,000-seat basketball coliseum was the scene of Olympic volleyball competition.

In the months before the games began, the city was the training site for national Olympic teams from several different countries, including Australia and Sweden.

"We know we have a wonderful community, and we enjoyed showing it off to people from so many states and foreign countries," says Zitzelman of the Athens Convention and Visitors Bureau.●

Beaufort, South Carolina

Newcomers settle into island life in coastal South Carolina

By Lan Sluder

An irresistible combination of dependably warm weather, laidback island living, historical charm and welcoming attitude to newcomers has turned the once-sleepy community of Beaufort into one of the fastest-growing retirement areas in South Carolina.

The town of Beaufort, about midway between Charleston and Savannah, is the seat of Beaufort County, which in recent years has led the state in population growth. The county has doubled in population since 1980, and the Greater Beaufort area has almost 15,000 residents, a gain of 56 percent from 1990.

Beaufort is in the heart of what's called the Lowcountry. The Lowcountry is more a state of mind than a specific geographic locale, but roughly it runs along the coast from around Georgetown, SC, to somewhere south of Savannah, GA. It includes the South Carolina Sea Islands of which Beaufort is a part.

Even if you've never been within miles of Beaufort, you've probably seen the town. Beaufort (pronounced as in "beautiful," say local boosters) was Forrest Gump's hometown in the blockbuster film of the same name. Beaufort and its collection of atmospheric Southern mansions have been featured in many other movies, including "The Prince of Tides" with Barbra Streisand and Nick Nolte and "The Big Chill" starring William Hurt and Glenn Close.

Because Beaufort was a Union headquarters and hospital zone in the Civil War, it was spared the destruction of many other Southern towns. Beaufort's 304-acre historic district has 150 antebellum and pre-Revolutionary homes. The oldest, the Thomas Hepworth House, dates to 1717.

While suburban areas around Beaufort have their share of franchise sprawl, Beaufort's historic district is an almost picture-perfect Southern coastal town. The graceful old homes on Bay Street, one of the town's main thoroughfares, have views of the Beaufort Bay (a part of the Beaufort River) framed by ancient live oaks and palmetto palms.

But it's not history or Hollywood that draws most retirees to Beaufort. It's that magic five-letter word — water, says Ron Kay, 57, who moved here with wife Carrol from Miami in 1989 to open a bed-and-breakfast inn, TwoSuns Inn B&B.

"People don't necessarily want to live on the water, just be near it," says Ron, who notes that almost one-half of the guests at his six-room inn are considering Beaufort for retirement or relocation.

Peggy Masterson, 62, who with husband Greg, 70, moved to the Beaufort area in 1991 from Barrington, IL, agrees. "Our interest was very much being in a community at the ocean. We are both beach people, and I swim daily in the ocean," she says. Peggy and Greg live at Fripp Island, a gated community on the water about 17 miles east of downtown Beaufort.

The city of Beaufort itself is on an island, Port Royal Island, and most of the surrounding communities are on the scores of islands that together make up the South Carolina Sea Islands. However, these are not islands edged with sandy beaches, but barrier islands whose shores are mostly salt marsh. The nearest ocean beach is at Hunting Island, about 16 miles from downtown Beaufort.

As you drive east from Beaufort on Highway 21 toward the Atlantic, you are struck by the beauty of the marshes, which are washed twice a day by tides with a tidal variation (the difference between low and high tides) of up to 11 feet. Vistas of the dominant cordgrass, which grows to five or six feet in the marsh, may remind you of enormous fields of wheat.

Here, east and south of the town of Beaufort on a cluster of islands, some so close together that you may not realize that only short bridges separate one from another, are a growing number of planned communities. Prized waterfront building lots with deep-water access go for $200,000 or more.

Beaufort's coastal setting, however, is a curse as well as an attraction. Hurricanes are a fact of life, although most recent transplants have never experienced a killer storm. In 1893, a fearsome hurricane — by all accounts the strongest storm to hit the region in recorded memory — killed more than 2,000 people as a tidal wave rushed over low-lying areas. Another hurricane in 1940 did serious damage. Beaufortonians note with irony that a scale developed to measure the force of wind is called the Beaufort scale after the early 19th-century British admiral who invented it.

Twice in 1996 area residents faced mandatory evacuations because of hurricane threats. These storms, however, veered off and didn't do much damage. Still, the sea and usually fine weather are the main reasons people move to Beaufort, says Jean Lebro, executive vice president of the Greater Beaufort Chamber of Commerce.

That holds true both for those moving to escape cold Northern or Midwestern winters and for those from Florida and other hot-weather areas who like the fact that Beaufort has a four-season climate. While summers can be hot and humid — and in Beaufort summers begin in March and end around Christmas Eve, some say — sea breezes exert a moderating influence. Homes in Beaufort traditionally all faced south to catch the prevailing breezes.

Maybe it's the weather or something in the water, but the Beaufort lifestyle is definitely laid-back. "There's a peace and serenity here that you don't find in some other towns," says Peggy Masterson.

Another couple, Norm and Suzanne Green, who moved to Dataw Island from Chester Township, NJ, in 1994, also like the Beaufort style. "We liked the gentle lifestyle — it has a nice rural feel to it," says Norm, 69. Dataw is a gated planned community of about 500 homes on an 870-acre island developed by ALCOA about six miles east of Beaufort. Villas and homes sell for $140,000 to $650,000.

"It offers the type of atmosphere we were used to," says Nancy Hicks, 70, who with husband Scott, 71, moved from Peterborough, NH, to Dataw in 1996. This area has "the feel of a small town, yet it's close enough to Charleston for big-city amenities," she says.

Residents note that Hilton Head is only about 35 miles from Beaufort, but the pace of life is entirely different. Hilton Head has a population of about 30,000, of whom about one-third are retirees, but the island gets more than 1.8 million visitors a year. Tourists come to play its

Beaufort, SC

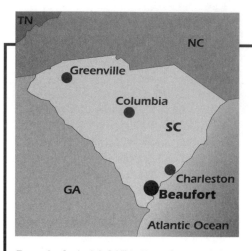

Population: 14,967 in Beaufort, 118,337 in Beaufort County.

Location: The city of Beaufort is in northern Beaufort County on the southeastern coast of South Carolina. By car it is about one hour north of Savannah, GA, and one and a half hours south of Charleston, SC. Hilton Head is about 45 minutes away.

Climate:

	High	Low
January	59	38
July	89	71

Beaufort has a mild, four-season climate, although summers are very warm. Hurricane season is June-November. Average water temperature in the Atlantic Ocean is 52 in January and 84 in July.

Average relative humidity: 53%

Rain: 49 inches on average, with the most rain May through August. Light snow occurs very rarely.

Cost of living: About average (specific index not available).

Average housing cost: $105,000

Sales tax: 6%

Sales tax exemptions: Prescriptions, dental prosthetics and hearing aids. There is a maximum of $300 sales tax on motor vehicles. Those 85 and older are exempt from 1% of sales tax.

State income tax: Graduated in six steps from 2.5% to 7%, depending on income.

Income tax exemptions: Social Security benefits. Retirees under age 65 who are drawing income from qualified retirement plans may deduct up to $3,000 of that income. At age 65, residents may deduct up to $15,000 in income.

Intangibles tax: None.

Estate tax: None, except the state's pick-up portion of the federal tax, applicable to taxable estates above $675,000.

Property tax: In the city of Beaufort, $219.50 per $1,000 of assessed value, with homes assessed at 4% of appraised value. Annual tax on a $150,000 home in the city would be about $1,317. Tax rates in districts outside Beaufort range from $169.90 to $235.60. Tangible personal property, including vehicles and boats, is subject to a personal property tax that varies by county district; it is assessed at 10.5% of appraised value.

Homestead exemption: $20,000 off market value for residents age 65 or older.

Security: 115.8 crimes per 1,000 residents, above the national average of 46.2 crimes per 1,000 residents.

Religion: More than 25 churches and synagogues.

Education: The University of South Carolina has a campus in Beaufort offering four-year and continuing-education programs. Members of the USC-Beaufort's Creative Retirement Center — now totaling about 600 — can take an unlimited number of special CRC courses for a flat fee of $100. Webster University and Park College, based elsewhere, offer degree programs locally. Technical College of the Lowcountry offers courses in computers and other subjects.

Transportation: Major airlines serve the airports in Savannah (45 miles) and Charleston (70 miles).

Health: Beaufort Memorial Hospital is a fully accredited 170-bed hospital with more than 80 board-certified doctors on staff. Larger hospitals and more specialists are available in Charleston and Savannah.

Housing options: The Beaufort area offers a wide choice of housing options, from antebellum homes in the historic district (a large renovated antebellum home may be $600,000 or more) to waterfront or golf-course living in a planned community. Among the planned communities in the area are **Callawassie Island**, (800) 221-8431, with homesites from $45,000 to $400,000 and homes from $270,000 to $600,000; **Dataw Island**, (800) 848-3838, with homesites from $50,000 and homes ranging from $230,000 to $650,000; and **Fripp Island**, (843) 838-2411, with homesites from around $30,000 to $250,000, and villas and homes from under $100,000 to $650,000. The houses at **Newpoint**, (800) 831-4536, are inspired by the traditional coastal architecture of historic homes in Savannah and Charleston and feature old-fashioned porches and picket fences. The neighborhood is on Lady's Island, across the river from Beaufort. Home prices range from the low $200,000s to more than $500,000. West of Beaufort on the Broad River, **Habersham**, (803) 846-1000, offers interior lots from the $30,000s and marsh-front lots from the $90,000s, and homes from the mid-$100,000s to more than $400,000. Homes in other neighborhoods around Beaufort County start at under $100,000. Two-bedroom rental apartments range from around $400 to $800 a month.

Visitor lodging: Beaufort has nine inns and several chain motels. Beaufort Inn has 13 luxurious rooms, $125-$225, and an award-winning restaurant, (843) 521-9000. The more casual six-room TwoSuns Inn B&B occupies a 1917 building overlooking Beaufort Bay, $130-$155, (800) 532-4244. Best Western Sea Island Inn is an attractive motel in downtown Beaufort, $79-$119, (843) 522-2090. Hunting Island State Park has rental cabins for $73-$116 and a 200-site campground near the beach, (843) 838-2011.

Information: Greater Beaufort Chamber of Commerce, P.O. Box 910, 1106 Carteret St., Beaufort, SC 29901, (800) 638-3525 or (843) 524-3163 or www.beaufortsc.org.

30 golf courses and 300 tennis courts and to shop its many factory outlet stores.

It's nice to be able to go to Hilton Head for outlet shopping, says Peggy Masterson, or to Savannah (less than an hour away) or Charleston (about an hour and a half by car) for major purchases and entertainment. Still, she notes, it's good to come back to the quieter atmosphere of Fripp Island and Beaufort.

But transportation is a concern for some residents. The nearest interstate, I-95, is about 25 miles away. Both Savannah and Charleston have airports, but flying from them often requires a change of planes in Atlanta or Charlotte.

For those who look for it, however, there's plenty to do in the area. There are thriving little theater groups and music societies. Beaufort's art galleries, many specializing in Lowcountry art, are known throughout the region.

Good food is important to Beaufortonians, and while Beaufort doesn't have the selection of ethnic eateries to be found in larger cities, the best of Beaufort restaurants rival those in Charleston or Savannah. Locals gather at Plums or Bananas, two popular downtown lunch spots, dine expansively at Beaufort Inn or get together for a Lowcountry boil. Lowcountry boil, also known as Frogmore stew after the Frogmore section of Beaufort County, is a combination of shrimp, sausage, corn on the cob, red potatoes, onions, seafood seasonings and sometimes crabs, all boiled together in a large pot.

The Beaufort area offers almost unlimited outdoor recreational opportunities. In addition to nearby Hilton Head's golf options, there are 11 public and private courses around Beaufort, including nationally noted ones at Fripp, Dataw, Callawassie, Spring and Cat islands, among others.

Boating is big in Beaufort, and many planned communities have their own marinas. Hunting Island, near Fripp, is one of South Carolina's most popular state parks. The 5,000-acre park has four miles of beach, a lighthouse and a subtropical maritime forest of great beauty. The ACE Basin, a large coastal wilderness area defined by the Ashepoo, Combahee and Edisto rivers, is just north of Beaufort.

Alligators thrive at Hunting Island and elsewhere around the Sea Islands. As dangerous as gators can be — they occasionally devour dogs and can outrun humans for short distances — the peskiest creatures on the islands also are among the smallest. No-see-ums, biting gnats so tiny they can get through screen doors and windows, are bugaboos of many retirees. Mosquitos can be fierce in remote marsh areas and at Hunting Island State Park but are not much of a problem in areas where there is regular mosquito control sprayings, residents say. Cockroaches (locals call them palmetto bugs) are big and not at all rare.

Many Beaufort residents point to the Creative Retirement Center at the University of South Carolina at Beaufort as an important source of local activities and educational opportunities. Through the campus in Beaufort, and at satellite locations serving Hilton Head and the Del Webb Sun City development near Bluffton, the CRC offers more than 50 courses for members in everything from gardening to Greek history. CRC members can take as many courses as they wish for a flat fee of $100, says Peggy Masterson, who edits the CRC newsletter, Second Wind.

The Beaufort area also occupies a special place in African-American history. Penn Normal School on St. Helena Island east of Beaufort was established by Quaker missionaries as the first school for freed slaves. In the early 1960s, Dr. Martin Luther King Jr. used Penn Center, as it is now known, as a training and meeting facility for civil rights workers. Today its mission is to preserve Gullah heritage, the culture developed by former slaves on the Sea Islands. Sea Island Creole, also called Gullah, combines elements of English and West African languages and still is spoken by some people in the area.

Critics say that Beaufort's special lifestyle could eventually be threatened by the area's growing popularity.

The chamber of commerce's Jean Lebro says her office gets about 40,000 requests for information a year, many from people considering relocation to Beaufort. But she admits that there is some local resistance to more growth. Those who moved to Beaufort some time ago note that traffic congestion has increased, especially on some of the two-lane roads.

If water, weather and lifestyle are Beaufort's big selling points, it is an intangible quality that clinches the sale for many transplants. Put simply, Beaufort is one of the most welcoming and friendliest places anywhere.

Old towns, especially old port towns in the South, often have a veneer of hospitality, but scratch that and you find that newcomers — those whose roots go back less than three or four generations — are never quite fully welcomed into the heart and soul of the community.

But for a variety of historical and cultural reasons, Beaufort isn't like that. The Civil War broke the back of an aristocratic plantation economy that once made Beaufort one of the richest areas of America, famed for its Sea Island cotton and rice. Many of Beaufort's old guard moved away, replaced by contingents of Northerners who stayed on after the war ended or moved here later. This infusion of new blood has continued, off and on to the present day, because of Beaufort's growing lure for retirees and other transplants.

In 1891, a U.S. Navy station was established on Parris Island (it's now a Marine Corps boot camp and training base). Along with Parris Island, a naval hospital and Marine air station have pumped millions of dollars into the local economy, but they also have added a cosmopolitan layer to the area. Today the Beaufort area is home to a sizable group of retired military, including a number of senior officers such as Gen. Norman Schwarzkopf, the Gulf War commander, who has a place here.

All of these factors mean that Beaufort, while its roots run deep, is neither provincial nor closed to outsiders. Says innkeeper Ron Kay, "Beaufort is one of the most hospitable small towns on the entire East Coast. Period."

"It was so easy to make friends here," says Suzanne Green. "Everyone is in the same boat, looking for new friendships."

Even the head of the Greater Beaufort Chamber of Commerce, Jean Lebro, is a relative newcomer. A self-proclaimed "damn Yankee from Boston," Jean moved to Beaufort four years ago. "Beaufort really welcomed me," she says.

Still, there's a limit to Beaufort's hospitality. "Never say, 'this is how we did it up North,'" Jean advises potential newcomers.●

Bend, Oregon

Pine forests and rugged mountains make Central Oregon hard to resist

By Fred Gebhart

Most days, Mirror Pond in downtown Bend looks like the perfect picture postcard. Its waters reflect the snowcapped Cascade Range along with towering ponderosa pines, blazing yellow roses and a sapphire sky. River otters blithely scamper across bike paths, and bald eagles cruise nearby rivers looking for a meal. On winter days, you wonder how rainbows happen over one shoulder while falling snow obscures the silhouette of the Cascades on the other side.

Bend sits on the sunny eastern side of the Cascade Range in Central Oregon, and it's easy to see why early explorers like Kit Carson escaped harsh mountain winters and blistering desert summers by lingering along the Deschutes River as it rushed through the high desert near Bend.

For financial planner Max Jacobs and his wife Sandra, these attributes were exactly what they were seeking in retirement. One of Max's five business partners in Laguna Beach, CA, had grown up in Bend and suggested that the couple give the small Oregon town (population 33,700) a look when it came time to retire. And as it turned out, the area's jumble of jagged lava flows, waterfalls, buttes, acres of forests, alpine lakes and crystal-clear rivers suited Max and Sandra perfectly.

"We checked into the River House, a hotel that straddles the Deschutes River, in 1992, and walked outside to Drake Park," Max remembers. "We were just enchanted when we saw Mirror Pond. We knew we wanted to leave the Los Angeles area when I retired in 1994, and this looked like the place."

Californians Dick and Joan Gilles had the same reaction. Both liked the San Francisco area where they were living but wanted a smaller home with what Dick called "a little bit of land" around it when he retired from his longtime job as product engineering director for an aerospace company.

"The trail that led us to Bend was a long one," Dick explains. "We started looking up and down the West in 1990. One of Joan's friends had a sister in Bend who suggested we look here for the golf and the fishing. Once we saw Bend in 1994, we kept coming back three or four times a year until we found the right property."

Bend offers everything from manufactured housing in long-established parks to custom-built mansions overlooking forests that will never be developed. Dick, now 67, and Joan, 66, looked at, and passed over, traditional subdivisions, gated communities and one of the most successful resort developments in the Pacific Northwest, Sunriver.

The basic equation, Dick explains, was a combination of housing budget, space and facilities, especially golf. The plan was to sell their 2,400-square-foot house in San Ramon, CA, and pay cash for something smaller. It had to be far enough from the neighbors that they didn't hear toilets flushing and TVs blaring. And Dick wanted to store their 32-foot trailer on site.

"There are a lot of communities that are terrific," he found, "but many restrict you to parking your RV in a parking area instead of on the property. I want our trailer where I can work on it at my leisure, not theirs."

They had considered Florida for retirement, but heat and humidity sent them back to the West. They also looked in coastal Oregon, Palm Springs and Las Vegas before Joan's friend brought Bend's charms to their attention.

"We had plenty of choices from Sunriver to Redmond," Dick says. "There are a lot of opportunities for less money than we ended up paying. But when you talk value for the money, we're still convinced it was a bargain."

The bargain was $220,000 for a 9-year-old, 1,800-square-foot house on 2.7 acres in Boones Borough, a rural development eight miles north of Bend. The one-square-mile subdivision has 225 lots surrounded on three sides by untamed juniper forests controlled by the Bureau of Land Management. The nearby Deschutes and Crooked rivers and Tumalo Creek lure fly-fishers from around the world eager to test their catch-and-release skills against wily trout and salmon. And there are more than two dozen golf courses within a 30-minute drive.

That's not to say that Bend is a garden of Eden. Gardening, in fact, can be a challenge because of the short growing season. Although the sun shines close to 300 days most years, the gardening season is barely three months long. Central Oregon was settled by cattle ranchers, not farmers, and while there's no shortage of water for home gardens, frost can come to the high desert anytime from Labor Day to Memorial Day.

"I've lost two crops of tomatoes this year," Dick sighs. "I planted too early. I'm probably not going to get any tomatoes at all, but the peppers survived."

Max, 64, and Sandra, 61, don't mind the short growing season, but they aren't avid gardeners. They came to Bend for the natural beauty, the small-town feel and the outdoor activities.

"It never gets really hot in summer, although it can get cold for a few days in winter," says Max. "That's hard for somebody from Southern California, but compared to Idaho or Montana, Bend is a piece of cake. And if you're a golfer, which we aren't, this is paradise. The courses are all affordable and most of them are open to the public."

The Jacobses bought their property

as an investment, sight unseen. They fell in love with the area and saw growth potential in Boones Borough.

Back in Southern California, they instructed a real estate agent to buy a lot in their $24,000 price range.

When they finally saw their property nine months later, 2.5 acres bordering BLM forest with more than 80

Bend, OR

Population: 33,700 in Bend, 101,200 in Deschutes County, with 15.5 percent of city residents age 65 or older.

Location: In the high desert of Central Oregon, just east of the Cascade Mountains, Bend is the economic and recreational hub of the eastern two-thirds of the state. Bend sits astride Highway 97, 180 miles north of Medford, 162 miles south of Portland and 121 miles east of Eugene. Elevation is 3,628 feet.

Climate:

	High	Low
January	39	18
July	85	46

Average relative humidity: 45%

Rain: 12 inches. **Snow:** 34 inches. Bend averages 280 days of sun annually.

Cost of living: 109.1, based on national average of 100.

Median housing cost: $139,551 in Bend, $205,991 for a single-family home on rural acreage. The value of rural property is determined largely by the availability of water.

Sales tax: None.

State income tax: Graduated in three steps from 5% to 9%, depending on income.

Income tax exemptions: Social Security benefits are exempt. You may be able to subtract some or all of your federal pension income, based on the number of months of federal service before and after Oct. 1, 1991.

Intangibles tax: None.

Estate tax: None, except the state's pickup portion of the federal tax on taxable estates in excess of $675,000.

Property tax: The tax rate in Bend is $14.92 per $1,000 of assessed valuation. Tax rates in Deschutes County range from $8.77 (desert areas) to $19.11 (Redmond) per $1,000 of assessed valuation. Since the passing of Measure 50 in 1997, homes are assessed at 90% of the 1995 market value; for subsequent years, the growth in assessed value is limited to 3% a year. The yearly tax on a home currently assessed at $140,000 in Bend is approximately $2,089.

Homestead exemption: None.

Security: 82.4 reported crimes per 1,000 residents, higher than the national average of 46.2 crimes per 1,000 residents.

Religion: There are more than 100 places of worship in Bend, nearly all Christian and conservative.

Education: Central Oregon Community College, which has 1,600 students, offers noncredit classes and workshops at centers in Bend, Sunriver, Redmond and other nearby towns. Seniors age 62 and older receive discounted tuition for some classes.

Transportation: The nearest air access is Redmond Municipal Airport, 16 miles north, served by Horizon Airlines and United Express with service to Portland and Seattle. Avis, Budget, Hertz and National have car-rental outlets at the airport. Bend Municipal Airport (5.5 miles northeast) and Sunriver Resort Airport (17 miles south) have general aviation services, charters and car rentals. Amtrak provides passenger service via Chemult, 60 miles south of Bend.

Health: St. Charles Medical Center has a trauma center with its own air ambulance service, Air Life. The 181-bed facility offers the latest in medical technology with more than 200 local physicians on staff. Specialties include radiation oncology, neurology, neurosurgery, open-heart surgery, radiology, urology, pathology, emergency medicine, rehabilitative medicine, family practice, cardiology, dermatology, orthopedics, psychiatry and men's and women's health services.

Housing options: Many retirees buy homes in existing neighborhoods in Bend, with average home prices around $140,000. Prices are somewhat less in nearby Redmond, and higher in **Sunriver**, (541) 593-1000, a 3,300-acre mountain resort 15 miles south of Bend. A quarter of the resort's 3,200 homes and 600 condominiums are occupied full time, primarily by retirees drawn to 54 holes of golf, 35 miles of paved bike paths, a 5,500-foot private airstrip and nearly two dozen restaurants. Prices range from $90,000 for a studio to well over $1 million for a 10,000-square-foot mansion; the median price is $242,000. At **Broken Top**, (800) 382-7600, homes start at $290,000, or residents can custom-build homes on lots starting at $65,000. The gated community is on the west side of Bend and offers a 27,000-square-foot clubhouse and 18-hole golf course. **The Falls at Eagle Crest**, (888) 70-FALLS, opened in 1998, north of Bend in Redmond. The 208-home neighborhood for those 55 and older offers homes for $149,900-$224,900. **Bend Villa Court**, (541) 389-0046, has 123 apartment units for independent or assisted living. Monthly fees range from $1,380 for a studio to $1,735 for two bedrooms. All units are unfurnished, but fees include three daily meals (plus a fully equipped kitchenette), housekeeping and laundry, local transportation and utilities. **The Summit Assisted Living**, (541) 317-3544, has 65 units, studios to two-bedrooms, ranging from $1,500 to $2,350 per month with all meals, light-duty nursing, housekeeping and activities included.

Visitor lodging: There are more than 2,400 hotel and motel rooms in Bend, with another 2,000 rooms in nearby towns and recreational areas, including Best Western Inn and Suites, $59-$79, (541) 382-1515; Hampton Inn, $89, (541) 388-4114; and The Riverhouse, $69-$129, (541) 389-3111.

Information: Bend Area Chamber of Commerce/Visitor and Convention Bureau, 63085 N. Highway 97, Bend, OR 97701, (541) 382-3221, (800) 905-6323 or www.bendchamber.org.

full-grown junipers of their own, it was a gem. Max retired on schedule in 1994·and the couple moved to a rented house in Redmond, about 20 minutes north of Bend. The interim move got them out of crowded Southern California and gave them the time to look for the perfect house in Bend.

Eventually, though, they decided to build on the lovely lot they had bought as an investment. "We just couldn't find an existing home that really met our needs," says Max, who with Sandra decided on plans for a two-story, 2,400-square-foot country farmhouse with porches on all four sides and passive solar heating. The solar design tempers both the occasional 90-plus summer days and winter nights that drop into the teens.

Snow rarely stays on the ground more than a few days, Max says, though he warns prospective buyers to check weather with potential neighbors. The area is a checkerboard of microclimates that change dramatically with elevation, exposure and rivers.

Sunriver, for example, 15 miles south of Bend, turns its three golf courses and 30-plus miles of bike trails to cross-country skiing every winter. Mount Bachelor, another 15 miles south, is one of the top downhill ski destinations in the West.

Sunriver is an important part of the Bend community. Several of the area's finest restaurants are in Sunriver, supported by the 1,500 or so permanent residents as well as the 3 million tourists who visit Bend every year. The Sunriver Music Festival brings some of the biggest names in classical and jazz to Central Oregon every August.

The music festival meshes with Bend's own Cascade Festival of Music as well as the free Munch & Music series that fills Drake Park with up-and-coming pop, blues and world beat groups on midsummer Thursday evenings. Central Oregon Community College provides live theater, an activity that will boom in 2000 when a new county performing arts center opens in Redmond with the area's first space for touring theater and performance companies.

There is, of course, a downside to Bend. The nearest international airport is Portland, a 3.5-hour drive or an expensive commuter flight from Redmond. "There just isn't enough business to push the airlines to drop their prices," Max gripes, "although that's changing as the population grows. We have double the number of daily flights that we had two years ago."

Traffic is another complaint. Highway 97, the main north-south artery, has regular traffic jams in Bend. But a bypass due in 2000 will leave local roads to local traffic and ease the congestion. And while downtown Bend is alive with boutiques and art galleries, the closest upscale department stores are in Portland. Local shopping malls tend toward Kmart, Home Depot and Sears.

Jobs are another sore point. Bend is traditionally a ranching and lumber region, with little skilled and professional employment. Population growth and the resulting housing boom is creating construction jobs, but retirees should count on living on their retirement income or make plans to create their own jobs. Sandra Jacobs found part-time work in a local accountant's office, but such opportunities are rare.

Taxes are on the high side — what taxes there are, that is. There's no state sales tax, for instance. "We get hit pretty hard on property taxes and personal income taxes," Max says. "But I just saved 8 percent on a Ford Ranger over what I would have paid in California. That kind of savings goes a long way toward easing the pain of income taxes."

Indeed, Bend's charms far outnumber its few drawbacks, Max says. "It's a vibrant place, a gorgeous place — art galleries, festivals, restaurants, scenery, hiking, out-of-this-world photography," says Max. "We love it."●

Boca Raton, Florida

Arts and culture and cool sophistication characterize this Florida resort community

By Jay Clarke

Retirement is a time to slow down and take it easy, right? Florida would seem to be just the spot, but Boca Raton may not be the place to rest on your laurels. There's an industrious quality to life in retirement here.

"I am tremendously busy," says Aaron Lintz, 68, who moved to Boca Raton in 1990 from Washington, DC. "I play golf six days a week, and I'm a volunteer with the Service Corps of Retired Executives and with RSVP (Retired Senior Volunteer Program)."

Aaron, a salesman during his working years, also keeps a finger on the pulse of his telemarketing business. His wife, Elaine, plays golf three times a week, enjoys bridge and does volunteer work.

Bruce Benefield reports a similar experience. "For the first two years after I retired, I was busy adding on to this house," says Bruce, 69, who also moved from the Washington, DC, area to Boca Raton six years ago. "Then I got involved in the homeowner association and became president."

Still at it, Bruce, a retired Air Force colonel and vice president of TRW, is on the alumni board of directors of his alma mater, the University of Miami, and does some volunteer tax counseling. His wife, Barbara, 66, is active in the local garden club and tends the beautiful garden that surrounds their waterfront home. She's also into aerobics and started a local chapter of her sorority, Kappa Kappa Gamma.

"I have to be busy," says Stan Perlstein, 71, who moved to Boca Raton from the Philadelphia area just a year ago. An interior designer, Stan says that for the first two weeks of his retirement, he "stood at the refrigerator all the time" and gained unwanted weight. So now he's working in design again. "I have to get out of the house."

So does his wife, Gladys, 56, who taught kindergarten and once worked at Bloomingdale's. "Maybe I'll go work in a department store again," she muses.

For all three couples, retirement is not an abdication of life but an opportunity to grow in different ways.

"What this (retirement) has done for me is that it's given me the opportunity to do things other people did, and I love it," says Aaron, whose career in sales kept him out of town and away from home for long periods. "I never played golf before we moved here.

"In some ways, we're living life like we did up North," he says of the lifestyle he and his wife have chosen. "We lead separate lives during the day, but we go out to eat a lot and we spend weekends together."

"It took us a while to get acclimated to retirement," Elaine admits, but neither now misses their former home. The first time they went back to Washington, DC, after moving to Boca Raton, Elaine says, "We stayed a month. Next time it was three weeks, then two weeks. Then it was 10 days, and now my husband says that's too long."

"We broke away from the North completely," confirms Aaron. "This is our home; this is the way we want to live."

The Benefields, too, have settled comfortably into their home in a residential neighborhood where there's a mix of ages. "When we moved in, there were no children on our block," says Barbara. "Now there are seven. We like that."

Barbara even has adjusted to the climate. "What I like about Florida is that it rarely rains all day," she says, noting that downpours occur but soon end. In Washington, she says, day-long drizzles are more common.

Bruce also had little trouble adapting to Florida. "I even bought a convertible — always wanted one," he says. And, like a lot of other Floridi-

ans, the Benefields have a boat. Since they live on a canal, their 23-footer is docked just a few steps from their back door — providing a quick escape to the water if the mood strikes.

Stan and Gladys Perlstein, who live near the Benefields, also have a boat. Stan bought the 42-footer when he lived in a Philadelphia suburb before he retired, but he didn't get to use it as often as he would have liked. Now he believes he'll be able to put it to more frequent use.

But Stan actually is somewhat surprised to find himself living here. "I really hated Florida," he admits. "Dad lived on Collins Avenue (in Miami Beach), and when I came to visit, all I saw were old people. There were nurses in the lobby. I didn't want to live like that when I retired."

Stan thought about moving to Mexico but now is glad he settled on Boca Raton. One reason may be that Boca is unlike most other communities that attract retirees. It does not make any special pitch for retirees, doesn't have subdivisions just for retirees and, frankly, doesn't want to become known primarily as a retirement haven.

Says Mike Arts, president of the Boca Raton Chamber of Commerce, "Our median age has been going down — from 44 to about 41 — since I came here 11 years ago."

Particularly noticeable, he says, is the increasing number of second homes. "Boca's population increases 12 percent in the winter season."

Though they may not live in communities especially designed for them, retirees find that Boca Raton has much to offer. "You won't find much ticky-tack here," the editor of the *Boca Raton News* said in a 1992 profile of the city. "We don't have an underclass. We don't have smokestacks or even industry that's unsightly. It's what we don't have that makes this place what it is," said Wayne Ezell, the editor in 1992.

That still holds true. Boca always has attracted clean industries. Giant IBM built personal computers here and had a massive presence for years. It has since moved most of its PC manufacturing out of state, but newer companies keep moving in.

Culture plays an important role in Boca Raton, whose location in south Palm Beach County puts its residents within easy reach of the arts in Fort Lauderdale and West Palm Beach.

Boca Raton has its own cultural scene, as well. Partly because it is an upscale community, Boca is home to many art galleries. It also boasts an art museum, pops orchestra, theater and concerts at Florida Atlantic University and many other venues for music and drama. The new International Museum of Cartoon Art expects to draw close to a million visitors in its first year.

Boca, too, has an undeniable panache. Comedians like Jay Leno and Billy Crystal work "Boca" into their gags, usually coupled with "money." The city's upscale reputation is so widespread that the often-heard phrase, "It's *so* Boca," is instantly understood even outside Florida. Being Boca means being upscale in an unmistakable but not flashy way.

Nowadays, what's *so* Boca in Boca is Mizner Park. It's Florida upscale, a palm-

Boca Raton, FL

Population: 70,000 within city limits, 195,000 in the metropolitan area.

Location: On the Atlantic Coast of Florida between Fort Lauderdale and West Palm Beach.

Climate:

	High	Low
January	76	63
July	90	78

Average relative humidity: 75%

Rain: 60 inches

May-October is the rainy season, October-April the dry season.

Cost of living: 102.7 in Palm Beach County, based on state average of 100.

Average housing cost: Single-family homes average $215,000, with the range running from $70,000 into the millions of dollars. Average condo co-op cost is $118,198.

Sales tax: 6%

Sales tax exemptions: Groceries, medicines, professional services.

State income tax: None.

Intangibles tax: Assessed on stocks, bonds and other specified assets, with some investments exempt. Tax rate is $1 per $1,000 of value for assets under $100,000 for individuals or $200,000 for couples, and $1.50 per $1,000 of value for greater amounts. First $20,000 for

individuals ($40,000 for couples) is exempt.

Estate tax: None, except the state's "pick-up" portion of the federal tax, applicable to taxable estates above $675,000.

Property tax: $23 per $1,000 of assessed value, with homes assessed at 100% of market value. Annual taxes on a $215,000 home are about $4,370, with the homestead exemption noted below.

Homestead exemption: $25,000 off assessed value of permanent, primary residence.

Security: 55.5 crimes per 1,000 residents, higher than the national average of 46.2.

Religion: There are more than 50 houses of worship in Boca Raton.

Education: There are five institutions of higher learning in Boca Raton, including a state community college, Palm Beach Community College, and a state university, Florida Atlantic.

Transportation: Boca Raton is conveniently located about halfway between Palm Beach International Airport (25 miles north) and Fort Lauderdale International Airport (20 miles south). Miami International Airport (47 miles south), with direct flights to many foreign destinations, is about an hour away. Boca Raton Airport is home to about 225 corporate and individually owned aircraft and has a station on the Tri-Rail commuter train line, which runs between West Palm Beach and Miami. Ten to 15 trains run in either direction daily. Amtrak's two northbound and two southbound trains daily stop at nearby Delray Beach and Deerfield Beach. Palm Beach County bus service is provided by PalmTran; fare is $2 for adults with discounts for seniors and disabled passengers. Door-to-door service is available to

seniors and disabled adults under a Dial-a-Ride program.

Health: The not-for-profit Boca Raton Community Hospital, with 394 beds and 24-hour emergency service, is the largest in south Palm Beach County. West Boca Medical Center, a private facility, has 185 beds and 24-hour emergency care. Several other hospitals are in the area, including Delray Community Hospital in Delray Beach, North Broward Medical Center in Pompano Beach and North Ridge Medical Center in Fort Lauderdale. A number of specialized health-care centers also are found in Boca Raton, including the Mae Volen Senior Center.

Housing options: The older coastal communities tend to be more expensive, with condominium units starting at $500,000, while new developments in unincorporated areas west of the city offer many amenities in lower price ranges, with condos and estate homes starting at $200,000.

Visitor lodging: Rates are seasonal — lowest in summer, highest in winter. The Boca Raton Resort and Club, built by Addison Mizner, is the most prestigious hotel in the region, charging about $165 in summer, $315 in winter, (561) 395-3000. Among chain hotel choices are Best Western University Inn, about $59 low season, $120 high season, (561) 395-5225; Holiday Inn West Boca, about $74 low season, $99 high season, (561) 482-7070; and Shore Edge, $250 per week for a low-season efficiency, $700 per week for a high-season efficiency, (561) 395-4491.

Information: Greater Boca Raton Chamber of Commerce, 1800 N. Dixie Highway, Boca Raton, FL 33432-1892, (561) 395-4433 or www.bocaratonchamber.com.

lined mall of more than 50 specialty shops, cafes and art galleries. A Jacobson's department store and the museum of cartoon art are important anchors in the tony mall, whose design and ambiance would have pleased 1920s society architect Addison Mizner.

It was Mizner who created Boca Raton 71 years ago. The man who had designed many of the grand mansions and clubs of Palm Beach wanted to create a town all his own 22 miles south of that bejeweled resort. It was his grandest vision.

Mizner sketched out polo fields, grand plazas, playhouses, a golden-domed city hall and lavish homes for the wealthy. He planned to build a castle on an island in a lake for himself and a cathedral for his mother. He even designed modest bungalows for workers.

"All of the charms of the Riviera, Biarritz, Menton, Nice, Sorrento, the Lido and Egypt are to be found in Boca Raton," a Mizner brochure boasted immodestly.

Alas, only part of his plan became reality. Mizner did build the hotel, now known as the Boca Raton Resort and Club. One of the top hotels in Florida, the landmark pink hostelry counts among its assets a half mile of private beach, two 18-hole golf courses and 34 clay tennis courts.

Mizner also built a grand avenue, El Camino Real, that was 20 car lanes wide and had a canal in its median. The road still exists, although the canal was filled in long ago. He built 29 modest homes for workers and an administration building, all in the Spanish Mediterranean style he created for Palm Beach, and they, too, still are in use.

But Florida's real estate bubble burst in the 1920s and the rest of Mizner's dream never was realized. The hotel, though, provided an image that set the stage for Boca Raton's resurgence after World War II.

Living costs in upscale communities can be a problem, but the Lintzes say their overall costs in Florida are less than they were in the Washington, DC, area. Dining out costs less, Aaron reports, and there's no state income tax. Clothing also costs less — and is far more casual. Aaron hasn't bought a suit since moving to Boca Raton.

The Benefields and the Perlsteins also agree that lifestyles are more informal in Florida than in their preretirement communities. Suits and other dressy outfits stay mostly in the closet, they say. But some costs creep higher. Entertainment options in Boca Raton are good but on the expensive side, says Aaron Lintz. "We pay $65 for the theater."

Home insurance, too, has been on the rise since Hurricane Andrew caused billions of dollars in damage to South Florida in 1992. In fact, the Benefields find quite a few costs to be higher in Boca Raton than in Washington. They say their real estate taxes have doubled. "And homeowner's insurance is also at least twice as high," says Bruce. "Fuel is higher here, too," Stan Perlstein notes.

So with many choices available to today's retirees, what made this trio decide to move to Boca Raton? All cite location and easy access to airports, cultural facilities, shopping and climate.

"Boca Raton is not as densely populated," says Aaron. "People here are pretty friendly," Bruce observes. And, adds Stan, "Everyone knows Boca."

Indeed, everyone knows Boca. After all, Boca Raton still reflects much of the spirit and ambiance Mizner planned for it. Even though newer homes and buildings no longer mimic Mizner's designs, his grand style still overlays the city — one of the reasons it has become such a stylish retirement haven.●

Boise, Idaho

In booming Idaho valley, emphasis is on the outdoors

By Genevieve Rowles

Jerry and Carol Larson beat the "California gold" rush to Boise, retiring to the Idaho capital before it was discovered as a clean, green haven by West Coast residents.

Since their arrival here several years ago, the Larsons have watched as the population and price of housing have escalated, creating mixed feelings for Boise residents.

"Boise's growing too fast, but you can't keep a good secret," Jerry says.

While he's candid about the city's growth pains, he's still sold on its many attractions. "I wouldn't discourage anyone from retiring here," he adds.

Jerry, 63, and Carol, 59, relocated to Boise from Anchorage, where he was deputy state soil conservationist. Previous career postings took the Larsons to five Western states. At retirement, they considered settling in Whitefish, MT, Reno, NV, and Boise; they had relatives in all three places. They found Reno housing expensive and Whitefish winters too severe, so they decided on Boise.

The Larsons enjoy the outdoors and were drawn by Boise's recreational opportunities, including nearby mountains for camping and fishing.

Set in a gentle river valley in the southwestern corner of the state, Boise's head is pillowed by rolling hills rising gradually to the mountains edging the vast River of No Return Wilderness Area to the north. At Boise's feet, extending south and west, sprawl some of the West's most fertile truck gardens, orchards and vineyards.

The sparkling Boise River runs through the center of town like a necklace showing off the city's jewels against green velvet. Several years ago, Boise scored an urban redevelopment coup by transforming the lands bordering the river into a 25-mile greenbelt laced with walking and biking paths and studded with wetlands, pedestrian bridges, museums and gardens.

Tubing and rafting the shallow river are favorite summer weekend activities for residents. The Happy Hoofers, a seniors walking group, make good use of the shady paths in nice weather, and cross-country skiers enjoy the greenbelt's level terrain when snow falls.

Boise State University's attractive campus faces downtown and the domed State Capitol from across the river. A short walk from the greenbelt, the rejuvenated downtown boasts a new convention center, shops, eateries, hotels and open squares with fountains.

The Larsons enjoy sampling downtown Boise's numerous restaurants, but their main interests are golfing and fishing. They take advantage of the area's 10 golf courses and its wonderland of mountains, lakes and rivers teeming with fish. They also attend Boise State University basketball and football games.

"Have golf clubs and RV, will travel" could well be their motto. If they are not golfing, they are off in their 25-foot fifth-wheel RV, camping in Idaho's scenic state parks and forests, visiting relatives or "snowbirding."

"I wouldn't want to live in it full time," Jerry says, but they do take off in their RV for two winter months. They travel to warmer climes — Arizona and Texas are favorites — and use a "golf card" for a reduced-rate entree to 2,500 courses nationwide.

While Boise winters are cold, its elevation of slightly less than 3,000 feet keeps it from having as severe weather as in the mountainous regions of the state. The average annual snowfall is 21 inches, comparatively low considering how far north it is.

Much of Boise's previous growth was tied to the processing of Idaho's famous potatoes and other agricultural products. In the past few years, though, the population explosion has resulted from Boise's proximity to outdoor recreational opportunities and success in attract-

ing diversified industry.

The city has become a regional medical center, with two state-of-the-art health facilities. St. Alphonsus Regional Medical Center provides the latest in cancer treatment, and St. Luke's Regional Medical Center offers comprehensive cardiac care and a transport van equipped to meet intensive-care needs. Boise also has Veterans Affairs and rehabilitation hospitals.

The metropolitan population has grown to about 387,800, with the fastest expansion coming in southwestern Boise and the suburb of Meridian, whose 2000 population has doubled since 1990.

The Boise area's median home price has shown a healthy increase over the past few years. The home that the Larsons bought in 1989 for $64,000 is now worth $125,000.

For Californians such as Ralph and Arlene Way, the comparatively lower housing costs in Boise are a major attraction. One reason they left the San Francisco Bay area, where they had lived for 26 years, was the high cost of housing there. The Ways first considered Arlene's native Nebraska but were dissuaded by the rough winters. Then Boise won their hearts.

"We fell in love (with Boise) the first time we drove into the Boise Valley," says Ralph, 68, of the day when he and Arlene came to visit their daughter and her family, who had recently moved to Boise.

After a half dozen visits over a year's time, they returned to stay. Now they wouldn't live anywhere else.

Ralph purchased the couple's ranch-style house without Arlene, 65, having seen it.

"I even furnished it before she came. We've been married 45 years, so she's pretty used to me," he adds with a smile.

Their home is on a 1-acre lot, giving Ralph room to indulge in a favorite hobby, raising a big vegetable garden. Good soil and a fairly long growing season make gardening popular in the area.

Ralph, a native Californian, retired at age 62 following a jack-of-all-trades career. He stays active in building construction with occasional projects to augment his pension and the investments he made before retiring.

Ralph's carpentry skills helped open the door to new friendships when they moved to the area. They joined the Christ Lutheran Church in Meridian and Ralph volunteered to oversee a church building project.

Volunteering opportunities make Boise attractive to those who want to become active in the community. The Retired Senior Volunteer Program

(RSVP) coordinates opportunities in 130 local agencies, including hospitals and nursing homes. RSVP volunteers work with at-risk children, tutor in the schools, help staff museums and nature centers, drive other seniors to doctor appointments and contribute their time and talents in a variety of other ways.

"People seem to be very friendly here," Ralph says. While Californians often receive a cool reception because so many are moving into the Boise area, "that wasn't true for us," he adds.

The Ways consider Boise less congested and polluted than the San Francisco area where they formerly lived. The Larsons, who've been in Boise longer however, have seen problems grow with the heavy influx of newcomers. Jerry Larson cites three downsides he

has seen to the growth: traffic congestion due to the city's lack of north-south arteries, inadequate public transportation and worsening air pollution. Like Denver and Salt Lake City, Boise sits in a "bowl" that prevents polluted air from rising in certain winter conditions.

The Larsons also have a gripe with the Air National Guard. Jerry knew of the proximity of Gowan Field when they bought their home, but says, "I wasn't aware of the Guard's tremendous activity. If anyone else made that much noise, they'd put them in jail." The F-4 jets are his pet peeve noisemakers.

Yet, Jerry adds, the problems don't make him want to move. "We have too many things here that we enjoy."●

Boise, ID

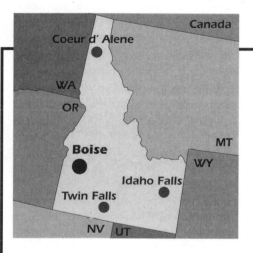

Population: 168,258 in city, 387,800 in metropolitan area.

Location: In southwest Idaho where the Boise National Forest gives way to the Snake River Plain, on Interstate 84.

Climate:

	High	Low
January	37	23
July	91	59

Average relative humidity: 43%

Rain: 11.7 inches.

Snow: 21.4 inches.

Boise has a four-season climate with cold winters, with temperatures dipping to zero. Summer days can be hot, but humidity is low and nights are cool. Though earthquakes can occur, severe quakes are not a concern; while there are thunderstorms, it is not tornado country. Elevation is 2,838 feet.

Cost of living: 96.7, based on national average of 100.

Median housing cost: $123,500

Sales tax: 5%

Sales tax exemptions: Prescription drugs, prosthetic devices, professional services.

State income tax: Graduated from 2% to 8.2%, depending on income. Every taxpayer required to file must pay a $10 permanent building fund tax.

Income tax exemptions: Social Security benefits are exempt, and some deductions apply for those age 65 and older receiving federal pensions.

Intangibles tax: None.

Estate tax: None, except the state's "pickup" portion of the federal tax, applicable to taxable estates above $675,000.

Property tax: Tax rates vary within the city and suburban areas. Rates vary from 1% to 2.7% of market value, with homes assessed at 100% of market value (average rate is 1.7%). Average annual tax on a $123,500 home would be about $1,250, with the exemption noted below.

Homestead exemption: State law exempts 50% or $50,000 (whichever is less) of assessed value of the primary residence, exclusive of land value.

Security: 53.3 crimes per 1,000 residents, higher than the national average of 46.2 crimes per 1,000 residents.

Religion: Worship centers represent many denominations and include a synagogue. The Church of Jesus Christ of Latter Day Saints (Mormon) and Roman

Catholic are predominant.

Education: Boise State University offers adult education courses. The Boise city schools offer enrichment classes.

Transportation: Boise Urban Stages provides public transportation. Both major and regional air carriers serve the city, and Amtrak's Pioneer stops in Boise.

Health: Boise's two regional medical centers, VA hospital, two psychiatric hospitals and rehabilitation hospital have more than 1,200 beds. The St. Alphonsus and St. Luke's regional medical centers cover most critical-care needs. There are 750 licensed physicians serving the area.

Housing options: Most housing options are single-family existing homes or development homes in the $80,000-$300,000 range. There are some condominiums. The **Columbia Village** development, (208) 342-4600, offers townhomes and single-family homes priced from $80,000 to $250,000. **Meadow Creek**, (208) 853-8028, has homes with resort amenities from $140,000.

Visitor lodging: J. J. Shaw House Bed & Breakfast Inn, $79-$119, (877) 344-8899; Idaho Heritage Inn, $65-$105, (208) 342-8066.

Information: Boise Area Convention and Visitors Bureau, 168 N. Ninth St., Boise, ID 83702, (800) 635-5240. Boise Area Chamber of Commerce, P.O. Box 2368, Boise, ID 83701, (208) 344-5515 or www.boise.org.

Bradenton, Florida

Newcomers find it easy to get involved in this town on Florida's west coast

By Karen Feldman

Spanish conquistador Hernando DeSoto, who landed in Bradenton in 1539, searched the region in vain for gold. But modern-day visitors can mine all manner of riches with just a bit of digging.

At first, the casual observer might see little happening in this laid-back city of 48,000. But on closer inspection, they'd discover a community on the move, endowed with sprawling beaches along the Gulf of Mexico and a multitude of golf courses, plus easy access to Sarasota to the south and sprawling Tampa-St. Petersburg to the north.

"Sometimes newcomers can't fully appreciate the city initially," says Marie Deitrich, vice president of the Manatee County Chamber of Commerce. "But we have everything here: We still care about each other as neighbors.... We've got beautiful beaches and still have a community feel. You go to a baseball game and see people you know. People here are more savvy than some give them credit for."

Marie, who has lived in the area for 30 years, thinks Bradenton "has come into its own. Everything is happening at the same time: There's downtown waterfront development, a new city center, and Lakewood Ranch (a new housing development) has been a humongous boon to the area."

The city is connected to the rest of the world by Sarasota-Bradenton International Airport, from which 10 carriers transport 1.6 million travelers a year. And less than an hour away lies the even larger Tampa International Airport, from which two dozen airline companies serve 11.5 million passengers annually.

It was this mix of accessibility and sense of community that prompted Paul and Janet Trudeau to leave Burlington, CT, their home of 34 years, in October 1996. They'd considered and ruled out other locales, including southern California as well as the Carolinas, where winters would still be too chilly for their taste.

"I like to go in the water any time of year," says Paul, a retired insurance company executive. "We both love the ocean."

While staying at a relative's home in nearby New Port Richey, he says they "drove around Florida until we found Bradenton. We wanted proximity to the Gulf. We wanted a community with arts and theater, a college town."

Bradenton already has those things and continues to grow in scope and population, drawing most of its residents from the northeastern and midwestern states. More than 50 percent of the population is 45 and older. As a result, there are many recreational, medical and housing options that cater to this older population.

With all the cultural opportunities of Sarasota within easy reach, the Trudeaus found an apartment close to the Gulf at a price that suited them. And it didn't take long for them to find friends. "We joined a church right away. We met people in the apartment complex. And we attended dances," says Paul, 60.

They also volunteered their services to a variety of organizations and met still more people that way. Paul joined the Elks. They linked up with Volunteer Service of Manatee, through which they got involved with the chamber of commerce, a landscaping project at a school, helping out at Bradenton Ballet performances and serving as museum tour guides. "There aren't too many days when we are at home just sitting around," says Janet, 59.

Retired elementary school teachers Ben and Georgette Thomas had a similar experience. After living in South Windsor, CT, for 28 years, the couple moved to Bradenton in June 1991. They'd considered Asheville, NC, and Florida's Gulf coast from St. Petersburg south.

They wanted warm weather — which eliminated Asheville from consideration — as well as a place where they'd have access to culture and be able to be a part of it, too. "Within a reasonable distance, we wanted a symphony orchestra, a theater large enough to bring in the Broadway touring companies, an opera guild, community theater. It began to narrow the scope," says Georgette, 67, who refers to Bradenton as "a big small town."

"Prior to our teaching (Georgette is a graduate of the Juilliard School of Music), we both performed opera and musical comedy," says Ben, 72, "and we were looking for a place where we could perform. We found that Bradenton is probably the best place in Florida. Within three-quarters of an hour, I'm in Sarasota or Tampa. There are any number of theaters in the area."

It didn't take the Thomases long to get involved in their new community. They joined RSVP — Retired Senior Volunteer Program — and helped create Seniors Offsetting Schools (SOS), through which retirees work with schoolchildren. Both perform in community theater. Not long ago, Georgette played Miss Daisy in a community theater production of "Driving Miss Daisy."

A diabetic, Georgette knows regular exercise is vital, so she walks daily — along the beach when she can. Ben likes to take his boat out to fish in the tranquil bays of the region.

They purchased a 1,650-square-foot home in Highland Lakes, a development with 126 homes, a small clubhouse and a pool, about seven miles from the beach. Over the time they've had it, the house has appreciated about 40 percent, according to Georgette. "We live here instead of Sarasota because our home would have cost $10,000 more than here," Ben says.

Those looking for property will find a wide range of housing options and price ranges, says Lynn Parker, the relocation director and branch manager for Wagner Realty in Bradenton. Four golf communities — all with easy access to Interstate 75 — offer maintenance-free villas, patio homes and single-family homes, with prices starting at $140,000 for a villa, $170,000 for a patio home and about $200,000 for a single-family home.

Along the bays and on the county's two barrier islands, Anna Maria Island and Longboat Key (half of which lies in Sarasota County to the south), the choices are condos or single-family homes, she says. A modest home

Bradenton, FL

Population: 48,029 in Bradenton, 247,028 in Manatee County.

Location: On the west coast of Florida just north of Sarasota, 45 miles south of the Tampa-St. Petersburg area. Easily accessible via Interstate 75 and Interstate 275 as well as Sarasota/Bradenton International Airport and Tampa International Airport.

Climate:

	High	Low
January	72	50
July	91	72

Average relative humidity: 52%

Rain: About 52 inches annually

Cost of living: 104.5, based on national average of 100.

Median housing cost: $126,900 for a new single-family home ($117,500 for condominiums).

Sales tax: 7%

Sales tax exemptions: Food and medicine.

State income tax: None.

Intangibles tax: Assessed on stocks, bonds and other specified assets, with some investments exempt. Tax rate is $1 per $1,000 of value for assets under $100,000 for individuals or $200,000 for couples, $1.50 per $1,000 of value for greater amounts. First $20,000 of assets ($40,000 for couples) is exempt.

Estate tax: None, except the state's "pick-up" portion of the federal tax, applicable to taxable estates above $675,000.

Property tax: $19.87 per $1,000 in Bradenton, with homes assessed at 100% of market value. The annual tax on a $126,900 home, with exemption noted below, is $2,025.

Homestead exemption: $25,000 off the assessed value of a permanent, primary residence.

Security: 54.8 crimes per 1,000 residents, above the national average of 46.2 crimes per 1,000 residents.

Religion: There are 165 Protestant and seven Catholic churches, four synagogues and 62 other houses of worship in Manatee County.

Education: Manatee Community College operates a branch in Bradenton. In Sarasota, there are several colleges, including the University of South Florida, Eckerd College, the Ringling School of Art and Design, New College and the University of Sarasota. In Tampa, there are campuses of the University of South Florida, Eckerd College, Tampa College, the University of Tampa and the University of Sarasota. These colleges offer a variety of degrees ranging from associates to doctorates. Noncredit courses for adults also are available.

Transportation: Sarasota-Bradenton International Airport provides service to many U.S. cities with a combination of major air carriers and commuter carriers. Tampa International Airport, 45 minutes north, offers hundreds of flights daily to destinations throughout the world. Amtrak provides train service to much of the United States from Tampa. Manatee Area Transit provides local bus service.

Health: There are two primary health-care hospitals: Manatee Memorial with 512 beds and Columbia Blake Medical Center with 383 beds. Charter Hospital of Bradenton is a psychiatric hospital. There are 36 licensed nursing and congregate-care facilities. The county has 534 physicians and 130 dentists.

Housing options: There are many options available in the Bradenton area, including single-family and condominium complexes. **Lakewood Ranch,** (800) 30-RANCH, a 4,000-acre working ranch and farm, now has a housing community under development, with an 18-hole golf course, tennis club and housing by several builders, ranging from modest condos to estate homes in the $500,000 range. Other golf communities include **Rosedale, Palm Aire, University Park** and **Tara,** offering maintenance-free villas and patio homes starting at about $140,000 and single-family residences at about $200,000. Along the Gulf of Mexico, modest dwellings can be had for about $150,000. Boating communities, with access to the Intracoastal Waterway and Tampa Bay, offer condos in the $90,000-to-$100,000 range and single-family residences ranging from $175,000 to $500,000. In inland neighborhoods that aren't on the water, a two-bedroom home with a pool averages $125,000, while a condominium can be had for $75,000 to $80,000.

Visitor lodging: Hotels and motor inns abound in this popular tourist destination. A sampling includes the Comfort Inn-Bradenton, $53-$99, (941) 747-7500; Holiday Inn-Riverfront, $124-$149, (941) 747-3727; and the Park Inn Club and Breakfast, $84-$114, (941) 795-4633. For those seeking a waterfront spot, there's Tradewinds Resort, $79-$145, (941) 779-0010 on Bradenton Beach. There are beach-front accommodations on Longboat Key at the Colony Beach and Tennis Resort, $195-$1,195, (941) 383-6464; the Longboat Key Hilton Beach Resort, $99-$239, (941) 383-2451; and the Resort at Longboat Key Club, $170-$345, (941) 383-8821. Rates are per night, double occupancy.

Information: Manatee County Chamber of Commerce, 222 10th St. W., P.O. Box 321, Bradenton, FL 34206, (941) 748-3411 or www.manateechamber.com.

on the Gulf might be had for about $150,000. More affordable for many people are neighborhoods where homeowners can dock their boats in canals behind their homes and still have access to the Intracoastal Waterway and the Gulf of Mexico.

Among the newest and most popular developments in the area is the 4,000-acre Lakewood Ranch. "It still is an active ranch and farm," Lynn Parker says, "but they've broken off part and created a new community that has homes geared to young upscale families and active retirees." Builders offer a range of housing, from small condos to regal estate homes.

It was precisely because of the myriad choices that the Trudeaus opted to rent for a while so they could thoroughly investigate various neighborhoods before deciding where to buy a place. Their experience as renters has been a positive one in a 200-apartment complex about four miles from the Gulf of Mexico. They find their neighbors and other city residents to be "warm-hearted, friendly people," Paul says.

"People whom we have just met briefly have invited us into their homes," he says. "One day a lady on a bicycle — she must have been 85 years old — led us to a friend's home just to show us something of the neighborhood."

Though both couples have wide circles of friends, there are a few parts of their Northern lives they miss, such as family and old friends. "And Connecticut in the fall. I really miss that season," Georgette says.

On the other hand, Ben says, "I was happy to get rid of the snow blower, lawn mower, the responsibilities of a larger home. My life has changed so much. I can't consider going back. I'd be bored to death in Connecticut."

Boredom isn't something from which either the Trudeaus or the Thomases suffer. "If you are bored in retirement, it's because you are boring," Georgette says.

The city offers a wealth of volunteer opportunities, fraternal groups and more than 230 houses of worship. Keep Manatee Beautiful, a group that encompasses volunteers, businesses and government agencies, provides year-round opportunities to help beautify beaches, roads and public places. The Art League of Manatee County displays the works of local artists, offers classes, demonstrations and workshops, and teams up with other groups to sponsor cultural events. The league works with the Goodtime Jazz Club, for example, to sponsor Jazz on the Riverfront, a weekend of live jazz during the winter tourist season.

While its larger neighbors to the north and south get most of the publicity, Bradenton boasts much of interest, especially of a historical nature, a rarity in a state where development often paves over the past.

The city proudly claims its connection to DeSoto, who began his four-year, 4,000-mile trek through the southeastern portion of the country in his futile search for El Dorado, the lost city of gold. Modern-day visitors can get a taste of DeSoto's 16th-century world at the DeSoto National Memorial along the Manatee River where, from December through March, park employees dress in period costumes and portray the way the early settlers lived, including cooking and musket-firing demonstrations. Each spring, the city hosts a month-long Florida Heritage Festival to commemorate DeSoto's landing.

The Manatee Village Historical Park focuses on the region's 19th-century life, with a collection of historical buildings, including a Cracker farmhouse, one-room schoolhouse, church and smokehouse. Staff members here also wear period dress.

Downtown at the South Florida Museum lives the city's mascot, Snooty the manatee, in a 60,000-gallon aquarium. At age 46-plus, the 750-pound vegetarian is the oldest living manatee in captivity, having taken up residence at the museum at the age of 10 months. He and his companion Mo afford a rare close-up view of these gentle sea mammals that seek out Florida's warm waters during the winter months. The museum also displays various aspects of the region's history, maintains an old-time medical wing and runs star and laser shows at the Bishop Planetarium.

During the winter, the Royal Lipizzaner Stallions of Austria take up residence at Colonel Hermann's Ranch in Manatee County. And come March, residents and visitors alike flock to McKechnie Field to watch the Pittsburgh Pirates play spring-training games.

For culture, Sarasota has few equals of its size. It is home to the Asolo Theatre Company, The Players, Sarasota Opera, Sarasota Ballet of Florida, the Florida West Coast Symphony and a number of vocal and chamber ensembles. It draws big-name entertainment to the Florida State University Center for the Performing Arts and Van Wezel Hall.

There are still more cultural opportunities in Tampa and St. Petersburg. A sampling includes the Salvador Dali Museum, The Florida Aquarium, the Florida International Museum, the Museum of Fine Arts, the Tampa Bay Performing Arts Center and Busch Gardens. Tampa's Ybor City has a rich Cuban heritage and has become a popular nightspot. In St. Petersburg, the Pier is a multilevel complex filled with restaurants, shops and clubs.

Many retirees are drawn to Florida by the weather and the opportunity to be outdoors. In Bradenton, options include golfing at any of 30 courses, tennis and racquetball, fishing and, of course, the beaches on Anna Maria Island and Longboat Key.

The mix works well for many, as the Trudeaus and Thomases can attest. Neither couple has plans to move out of the area anytime soon. For others considering relocation, Georgette Thomas suggests, "Make an itemized list of what you need to keep yourself mentally and physically healthy in your retirement, and certainly explore Bradenton, because there is such a variety of things to do." ●

Branson, Missouri

Missouri Ozarks are alive with the sound of music

By Mary Lou Nolan

Puffs of mist cling to Table Rock Lake, holding up the start of the Tri-Lakes Triathlon. So 50 swimmers wait, waist-deep in water, shivering under their orange rubber caps.

Nearby are dozens of volunteers, many of them retirees, in orange vests, orange caps or orange buttons, just as alert as the athletes, but smiling, not shivering. It's a crisp September morning, a bright sun is burning off the last of the mist, and an event they have worked on for months is about to begin. Swimming, biking and running courses are laid out, checkpoints are staffed, stop watches are set.

As a whistle splits the air, the athletes — and the volunteers — plunge into action. You can't tell who will enjoy it more.

Volunteers are integral to the quality of life in Branson, MO, a country-music-mad boom town in the Ozark Mountains. They staff the Branson/Lakes Area Visitor Center, stamp books at Taneyhills Community Library and raise money for the expanding Skaggs Memorial Hospital. New businesses struggling for a foothold in the self-proclaimed "America's Live Entertainment Capital " get help from SCORE, the Service Corps of Retired Executives.

"I think this town would collapse without volunteers," says Norma Root, the library's only paid employee.

Retirees underpin the volunteer community here, mixing good works with golf and fishing, bridge matches, dinner clubs and church socials. Their lives are full — too full for some of their spouses — and the strains of country music only add to their enjoyment.

"I'm about ready to leave him and get a man who stays home," jokes Effie Evans, who retired here with her husband Ken.

But the music boom also has strained local resources. Lower-income housing is in short supply, and some residents worry about trees being cut and lake water being dirtied as a result of the expansion. On the other hand, traffic, once a legendary nightmare, has undergone tremendous improvement.

The boom also has brought a new sense of urgency to some volunteer pursuits. A spinoff group of 19 local churches, for example, assists people with little money who come to Branson in search of jobs. The Christian Action Ministry, with about 70 volunteers, helps with food, rent and utility payments. It operates a pantry and is considering opening a shelter, with community support, says Charles G. Mitchener, a retiree who spearheads the program.

The ministry is just one of the volunteer activities that Mitchener threw himself into when he and Ellie, his wife, moved to Branson from Carmel, IN, near Indianapolis, nine years ago. The couple considered spots in North Carolina and the Cumberland Plateau area in Tennessee before buying a four-acre lot north of Branson and building a home. Then Mitchener, who retired as chief financial officer for a Midwestern farm cooperative, got busy.

"I decided when I retired that I would like to put some of those skills back into a community," says Mitchener, 67.

He's also active with the Red Cross, SCORE and Lives Under Construction, a ranch for troubled teenage boys southwest of Branson. And Mitchener was on hand at Table Rock State Park that crisp Saturday morning in September, working as a volunteer. He and Ellie checked in athletes as they crossed under the balloon-festooned goal posts that marked the finish line.

Retirees in orange Tri-Lakes Triathlon Volunteer buttons chatted like golf buddies before the race got under way. Bob Glenn, a retired state patrolman, and his wife, Jerrie, moved here from Ames, IA, 10 years ago. Glenn started working on the triathlon in January. His condo neighbor, Bill Silva, a retired

Speed Queen employee from Ripon, WI, helped get members of the Amateur Radio Club in Kimberling City involved as volunteers.

Much of what appeals to retirees about the Branson area was apparent at Table Rock State Park that day.

The land itself is a big draw. Steep wooded hills of the Ozark Mountains fall away to sprawling Table Rock Lake, one of three that define the Branson/Lakes Area in western Taney and southern Stone counties. Table Rock, with 750 miles of shoreline, is known for water sports and bass fishing; Taneycomo, which winds northeast like a river channel for 22 miles, is known for trout; Bull Shoals, east of Branson, flows through the least populated, least developed land.

The climate is mild, especially compared to the Upper Midwest, from where many residents have moved. But the four seasons are distinct, usually with some snow in the winter and hot, humid days in the summer.

Climate and green, open spaces were a big draw for the Glenns. "I like the four seasons," Jerrie Glenn says, adding that the foot of snow blanketing the hills in February "is beautiful — I love this."

There also is a neighborliness nurtured by Branson's small-town atmosphere. Its relatively low cost of living and crime rate, low taxes and conservative values have attracted many retirees over the years. Perhaps that's why complaints about growth, and especially traffic and the lengthening tourism season, are so common.

"You lose all patience when you have to deal with it every day," Ellie Mitchener says.

"I've learned to be quite a wild driver now, with all the tourists," she says, smiling. "You learn to take the back roads, and to go out in front of the tourists, who are wondering which way to go."

Branson has only 5,039 residents, while the Lakes Area has about 33,000. But more than 5.7 million people visited in 1999 as more big-name entertainers opened music shows here.

Four new dinner theaters opened in 1995, bringing the total number of indoor entertainment centers to 42, with a total seating capacity in excess of 60,000. Branson's main strip, 76 Country Boulevard, also is home to some 7,000 motel rooms, more than 140 restaurants and huge amounts of neon.

Some of the long-time music shows, with locally known entertainers and hillbilly humor, have suffered as bigger, fancier shows have opened. But the big-name entertainers now draw fans to Branson from across the country. Among country musicians performing here are Mel Tillis, Willie Nelson, Jim Stafford, Cristy Lane, Ray Stevens and Charlie Pride. Andy Williams broadened the scene a bit when he opened the $8 million Moon River Theater in '92, and Wayne Newton has his own theater.

Tourism, long the area's leading industry, got a significant — some say overwhelming — boost in December '91, when "Sixty Minutes" aired a segment on Branson's boom. The chamber of commerce tripled the number of phone lines, added staff and began moving toward a year-round season.

" 'Sixty Minutes' launched us, in giving us an identity internationally," says Dawn Erickson, the chamber's communications director. "We have not had what you would call a quiet time since then."

"I'm a country-western music lover from way back," Jerrie Glenn says, although the effect of the intense publicity concerns the Glenns. Both worry that the influx of tourists will lessen the quality of life in Branson, but the Glenns still feel at home here. A recent three-week trip to the South-

Branson, MO

Population: 5,039 in town, 33,000 in area.

Location: Busy commercial, entertainment center in Ozarks of southwestern Missouri. Hilly, wooded terrain in two counties with three major lakes.

Climate:[1]

	High	Low
January	41	22
July	93	68

Average relative humidity: 58%

Rain: 41 inches.

Snow: 15 inches.

Has four distinct, though not harsh, seasons. Snowfall normally light. Spring and fall are mild, summers warm and humid.

Cost of living: Below average (specific index not available).

Median housing cost: $107,276 for single-family house in Taney County; prices higher in many areas popular with retirees. A lake-front house runs from $125,000 to $3,400,000.

Sales taxes: 7.225%.

Sales tax exemptions: Prescription drugs, some medical supplies, professional services.

State income tax: Graduated in 10 brackets from 1.5% to 6%, depending on income.

Income tax exemptions: $6,000 government pension income exempt for married couples filing jointly with taxable income of less than $32,000.

Intangibles tax: None.

Estate tax: None, except the state's "pick-up" portion of the federal tax, applicable to taxable estates above $675,000.

Property tax: Rate is $4.49 per $100 of assessed value in Branson, including schools, fire, ambulance, health and city taxes. Homes are assessed at 19% of market value. Property tax on a $107,276 home is about $915.

Homestead exemption: There is a property tax credit for homeowners age 65 and older filing jointly with a household income of $17,000 or less.

Security: 32.5 crimes per 1,000 residents, lower than the national average of 46.2 crimes per 1,000 residents.

Religion: 36 Christian churches in Branson.

Education: Classes available at The College of the Ozarks, a private, four-year liberal arts college.

Transportation: None. Car necessary. Springfield Regional Airport is 45 miles north.

Health: Skaggs Community Hospital, a non-profit care center with 107 beds and a staff of more than 400 has completed a $7 million expansion to double the size of its emergency room, add a helicopter pad and expand outpatient services at Springfield.

Housing options: Most retirees live in single-family homes outside the city. Besides resale homes, there are new homes in the $85,000-$500,000 range available within a five-mile radius. Custom-built homes on the south side of Table Rock Lake are popular with retirees. The **Branson North** development has $100,000-plus homes on spacious lots in a quiet, wooded area. Kimberling City, also on Table Rock Lake, attracts upper-income retirees; Forsyth and Hollister attract moderate-income retirees. Condominiums are available, both in Branson and on the lakes, and two complexes, **Oak Manor and Branson Manor**, offer subsidized housing for the elderly in Branson.

Visitor lodging: More than 20,000 motel/resort rooms available, with rates of $20 to $250-plus a night. New Super 8 Motel, (417) 334-8880, by Branson's main strip, $60 on summer weekdays. Deer Run Motel near Silver Dollar City, (417) 338-2223, $55. Big Cedar Lodge, (417) 335-2777, a 72-year-old resort overlooking Table Rock Lake, $119 and up.

Information: Branson/Lakes Area Chamber of Commerce, P.O. Box 1897, Branson, MO 65615, (417) 334-4136 or www.bransonmo.com.

[1]Climate data based on information for nearby Springfield.

west only confirmed that.

"We talked to our friends and saw some nice places, but they didn't sway us," Bob Glenn says. "We like it every bit as much here as any place we've seen."

"Sixty Minutes" also lured people looking for work, some of whom just packed up and moved to Branson, says Al Moon, a real estate agent and retired banker. Jobs were available, but they often were seasonal with wages of $5 and $6 an hour. And lower-income rental housing is in very short supply in Branson, where land values have climbed.

Efforts are under way to add rental housing and to build the labor force. One potential answer is to recruit retiring military people who are looking for income to supplement pensions, Moon says.

Major traffic relief is in the works. Branson voters approved $10 million in taxes in 1991 for city road improvements, and a $100-million-plus project that will build an Ozark Mountain Highroad around Branson is in progress.

The music boom also may be affecting the type of retirees drawn here. For years they tended to be well-to-do people who vacationed in the Lakes Area because of its natural beauty, Moon says. A couple bought land, often with a lake view, built a spacious home and took in an occasional music show.

As the music industry grows, and more visitors and bus tours pass through, Moon thinks more retirees will be moderate-income music fans.

Retirees now looking in the area are typically from the Midwest and are searching for homes in the $65,000-$100,000 bracket, Moon says. Older homes in Branson run $60,000-$65,000; moderate-priced housing typifies the nearby communities of Forsyth, Hollister and Rockaway Beach. Kimberling City, with homes in the $100,000-plus range, is at the high end.

The area seems especially popular with Californians, some of whom are Midwestern natives who want to put the West Coast lifestyle behind them.

"This is just a better place to live, a better life for them," Moon says.

That's what Ladd Chase found here. Over a bridge hand at the Branson Community Center, Chase describes how he left the furniture business behind in Long Beach, CA, when he moved into a Branson condo six years ago.

"I like the lakes, I like the fishing, I like the country music shows. I wouldn't live anywhere else," says Chase, 75. "Traffic doesn't bother me — I know the back roads."

Not everyone agrees. Just ask people at the next bridge table.

Ethelmae Henss and her husband helped develop Branson North, an older suburban development of spacious homes on wooded lots. But after more than 30 years in the area, she's concerned about the rapid pace of growth. "It happened too fast," she says, echoing many older residents.

As the Branson area grows, residential development is pushing outward, says Rex L. Asselin, a real estate broker and a chamber of commerce director. He speaks from experience.

In 1992 Asselin sold the 4,400-square-foot home he and his wife built in 1968 to the company that built Wayne Newton's new theater. The house was bulldozed, and a 3,000-seat theater, restaurant and two motels were built on the 32-acre plot in a once-rural area on Branson's outskirts.

Asselin himself moved 12 miles north of Branson, where he built a 5,500-square-foot house with indoor pool on a large tract of land.

"Branson's not a quiet place," he says. "But you can live within a 15-minute drive of Branson and have a quiet country living."

That describes Dean and Peg Courtney, who recently added a deck to their three-bedroom mobile home on a secluded lot south of Hollister. The couple vacationed in the area for about 10 years, then moved down after Dean Courtney retired as postmaster in Caney, KS.

Courtney, who is a member of the Lions Club, says his church "adopted" the couple after their first visit. "We haven't sat still since we got here," he says.

He also works at Silver Dollar City, a theme park where turn-of-the-century crafts and amusement rides are featured. During the busy season last year, he worked in cash control in the office.

"It's just like a bank," Courtney says. "It's office work without the responsibility of the postmaster."

Courtney says his wages help pay for "extras," and he enjoys the fellowship. During winter months the couple often travels to a warmer location, like the Texas coast.

"I feel like a person who retires and then goes back to work looks at it differently," says Courtney, 59. "If you are using it as supplemental income, you have a different attitude. You don't have to do it."

Ken and Effie Evans were drawn here more than 20 years ago from Oak Park, IL, when Ken was about to retire from Swift & Co. in Chicago. He was a native of northern Missouri and the couple had traveled in the area. Then their daughter took a teaching job south of Kansas City, about four hours away.

" 'I know when Daddy retires he's going to come back to Missouri,' " Evans recalls his daughter saying. "Well, I don't remember telling her that, but she could feel how much we enjoyed it."

The Evanses bought a lot in the Branson North subdivision in 1970, built a spacious one-story home and moved in 1974.

"Coming from Missouri, loving the hills and the Ozarks, this was it," Evans says.

The growing traffic and congestion is irritating. And Ken has never liked the humid summer days. But the Evanses keep a busy schedule. As sight chairman for the Lions Club, Ken helps arrange glasses and surgery for needy people. And both are active in the Presbyterian church.

Still happy here?

"Wouldn't be anywhere else," Ken says.

"Yes, I've been very happy here," Effie agrees. "You have your church, and we have a dinner club we belong to. And we have lots of friends here."

But Effie advises potential visitors to find out the best routes for traffic in advance.

"Anyone who wants to come should send for a map," she says.●

Brevard, North Carolina

Small-town friendliness adds to beauty of North Carolina town

By Diana C. Gleasner

With a main street worthy of a Norman Rockwell painting, Brevard sits tucked neatly in a valley surrounded by the heavily forested mountains in western North Carolina.

People gather for summer concerts in the park, and going to the bank is as much a time to visit with neighbors as to do business.

The 2,230-foot altitude contributes to a moderate four-season climate with mild winters and cool summers, and crime is not a serious concern.

Yet for many residents, these attractions aren't the main appeal of Brevard.

"It's the friendliness of the people and the pace of life we like best," says Bob Reaume, 63, who moved with his wife, Joyce, 61, from Connecticut four years ago.

Joyce adds, "At the slightest problem, neighbors come to help."

George and Eva Stephenson, 63 and 51 respectively, moved from Florida and like the small-town atmosphere and feeling of safety in Brevard, which has only about 7,100 residents.

"It's a dry county (no liquor sales) and that has a tranquil effect on adults and children alike, since the children don't have to suffer through the hangovers of their parents," says Eva. She thinks the area's lower drug usage helps keep crime down, too.

Jack and Barbara Cronin, formerly of Princeton, MA, didn't want to retire to an adult-only community. They appreciate the mix of ages in Brevard, and the laid-back attitude and relaxed lifestyle, says Jack, 64. Barbara, 61, likes the opportunity to take an active role in a "real community."

Making friends in Brevard was easy, says Jack. "We went to church and before we got home people were waiting at our door to welcome us."

All three couples assimilated quickly by taking a course at Brevard College called "Inside Transylvania," which introduces newcomers to the facilities of the community and Transylvania County.

"We met the local politicians, medical professionals and academics," says Joyce Reaume. Other speakers acquainted new residents with the Brevard Music Center, police department, volunteer agencies and the nearby Pisgah National Forest.

Brevard College, a two-year liberal arts school, offers a range of courses. Joyce, who currently is taking macrobiotic cooking and landscaping, sometimes teaches a course in sign language. One of the Reaumes' five children is hearing-impaired, and Joyce had been a full-time teacher of the deaf before coming to Brevard.

Bob Reaume took beginning piano and cartooning, and both he and Joyce enjoyed a course called "Great Decisions," an analysis of the U.S. role in international affairs. The Cronins, who are in a swimming program at the college, took conversational French and a course in Chinese cooking.

The three couples have further woven themselves into the community by contributing their time and talents. Jack Cronin teaches adult students as part of the Transylvania Literacy Council and serves as the council's chairman and president. Barbara also works with literacy students, is a full-time church organist and takes calls on the 911 mental health hot line.

The Reaumes tutor in the School of Forestry, in the public schools and in the literacy program. George Stephenson is active in Kiwanis and both he and his wife plan to get involved in the literacy program or in the public schools.

The town's rich cultural scene centers on Brevard College, the Blue Ridge Community College campus in Brevard and the Brevard Music Center. During its annual six-week Summer Music Festival, the center sponsors more than 50 events including Broadway musicals, operas, chamber music, symphony and pops concerts featuring internationally renowned guest artists. The center has a nationally recognized summer music camp for promising young artists.

Aficionados of authentic mountain music may drop in at Silvermont Mansion any Thursday evening for a live performance. These inspired (and free) concerts set the toes tapping as the dulcimer, fiddle, banjo, bass fiddle, guitar and harmonica celebrate the musical heritage of the region's original Scotch-Irish settlers.

Brevard Little Theater presents popular plays, while the Arts Council sponsors a weeklong annual Festival of the Arts in mid-July. It features musicians, tours, food, special events and the arts and crafts of local artists.

Retirees enjoy the natural beauty of the Blue Ridge Mountains. The county's 200 waterfalls have given it a nickname, Land of Waterfalls. At 411 feet, Whitewater Falls is the highest cascade east of the Rockies, while beautiful Looking Glass Falls is probably the best known. Sliding Rock, a 150-foot natural water slide, is a popular local attraction. Shining Rock Wilderness area and more than 200 miles of clear streams and rivers add to this idyllic scene. The area has more summer camps than any county in the country.

Pisgah National Forest just north of Brevard covers more than a third of Transylvania County. It has 470 miles of hiking trails plus opportunities for rock climbing, cross-country skiing and tubing. At Cradle of Forestry, where scientific forestry was first taught in America almost 100 years ago, the U.S. Forest Service operates an interactive hands-on museum. The forest shelters a black bear sanctuary and has one of the largest trout hatcheries in the East. Visitors to the fish hatchery can see the origins of the trout that later stock local streams.

Golf enthusiasts find year-round challenges on public and private courses in the area. Sapphire Lakes, a private 18-hole championship course, has been listed among the top 50 of *Golfweek* magazine's "Best of the Best." Etowah Valley Championship Club in Henderson County is open to the public. Glen Cannon, although private, allows guests from out of the area. Among other private courses are Sherwood Forest, Lake Toxaway Country Club's Holley Forest, Horsepasture Club and Connestee Falls.

Other area recreational opportunities include tennis, swimming, fishing, hunting, square dancing, camping, canoeing, kayaking and horseback riding.

Nearby attractions lure visitors who come to experience the Blue Ridge Parkway, considered one of America's most scenic drives, and Great Smoky Mountains National Park. Asheville, a 40-minute drive north, offers additional shopping and amenities. At Asheville, the 250-room Biltmore Estate, largest private residence ever built in the New World, has guided tours through the home and gardens. Thomas Wolfe's boarding house, the setting for his novel "Look Homeward, Angel," has been restored

Brevard, NC

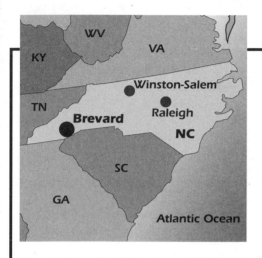

Population: 7,112 in town, 28,481 in Transylvania County.

Location: In the scenic Blue Ridge Mountains of southwestern North Carolina, 30 miles south of Asheville. Brevard, the county seat, is adjacent to Pisgah National Forest. The French Broad River flows through the area, creating mountain streams and waterfalls. Elevation is 2,230 feet.

Climate:

	High	Low
January	50	25
July	85	61

Average relative humidity: 55%
Rain: 66 inches.
Snow: 6.2 inches.
Moderate four-season climate with mild winters and cool summers. Average number of days with snow coverage is five.
Cost of living: Below average (specific index not available).
Average housing cost: $150,000
Sales tax: 6%
Sales tax exemptions: Prescription drugs, eyeglasses, some medical supplies.
State income tax: Graduated in three steps from 6% to 7.75%, depending on income.
Income tax exemptions: Social Security benefits. Each taxpayer also can exempt up to $4,000 in local, state or federal government retirement benefits and up to $2,000 in private retirement benefits, but the total of these exemptions cannot exceed $4,000 per person.
Intangibles tax: None.
Estate tax: None, except the state's "pick-up" portion of the federal tax, applicable to taxable estates above $675,000.
Property tax: City tax rate is $5.20 per $1,000 valuation and county rate is $6.41 per $1,000 valuation, with homes assessed at 100 percent of appraised value. City residents pay both city and county taxes. Tax on a $150,000 home within the city is about $1,806 yearly, including $65 solid-waste assessment. Tax on a $150,000 home in the county is about $1,026, including the solid-waste assessment.
Homestead exemption: Homeowners age 65 and older, or disabled, living in the home and earning $11,000 or less per year qualify for an exemption of $15,000.
Security: 54.5 crimes per 1,000 residents, higher than the national average of 46.2 crimes per 1,000 residents.
Religion: More than a dozen denominations are represented.
Education: Brevard College, a two-year liberal arts college, offers an extensive continuing-education program, and Blue Ridge Community College's Brevard campus offers a wide variety of courses. Transylvania County Library's 65,000 volumes include large-print books. Bookmobile covers rural area.
Transportation: No public transportation. Car necessary. Asheville Regional Airport is 25 miles away.
Health: Transylvania Community Hospital has 94 beds and provides in-patient medical, surgical, obstetrical, coronary and intensive care, outpatient services, in-home services, drug and alcoholism treatment. Emergency services are staffed 24 hours. Highland Hospital Resource Center offers psychiatric services. Three-level care at Brian Center, a 140-bed facility, includes skilled, intermediate and nursing home care.
Housing options: College Walk, (800) 280-9600, a retirement community adjacent to Brevard College, offers apartments from $950-$2,150 per month; cluster homes and 20 assisted-living units cost $135,000-$145,000. **Deerlake Village**, (828) 884-7007, has cottages, homes, condominiums, homesites and some lakefront properties; homesites cost $35,000-$120,000, detached homes $140,000-$240,000. **Glen Cannon Properties**, (828) 966-4242, has wooded residential homesites from $25,000 and condos starting at $150,000; Glen Cannon Country Club, to which residents may belong, has a golf course, tennis courts, pool and clubhouse.
Visitor lodging: Inn at Brevard, $95-$165, (828) 884-2105, has 12 guest rooms in a historic bed-and-breakfast setting. Womble Inn, $62-$72, (828) 884-4770, a B&B, has seven guest rooms furnished in antiques, all with private bath. Located 17 miles west of Brevard, Greystone Inn, (828) 966-4700 or, outside the state, (800) 824-5766, offers resort accommodations in a historic mansion on Lake Toxaway; prices are $285-$550 per couple, including meals.
Information: Brevard Chamber of Commerce, P.O. Box 589, 35 W. Main St., Brevard, NC 28712, (828) 883-3700, (800) 648-4523 or www.brevard.org.

to its 1906 image.

The gentle mountains have become a haven for retirees who enjoy a four-season climate without lengthy cold winters or long hot summers. Besides attracting retirees from the Northeast, the area draws people from Florida seeking to escape its steamy summers.

Eva Stephenson, a native Floridian, fell in love with the mountains on a vacation. When she and her husband moved here, she was thrilled with the first big snow. She says she doesn't miss Florida's hot weather — "it zaps your energy."

Jack Cronin is quick to say he doesn't miss what he calls the "Taxachusetts" government he left behind in Massachusetts, and his wife adds that she doesn't miss the heating bills from their New England house.

A favorable economic climate in Brevard, while not the primary motivation for most retirees to relocate here, is a definite attraction. According to the North Carolina Department of Budget and Management, Brevard's cost of living is below the national average.

In looking ahead to retirement, Bob Reaume, a former engineer, developed a detailed financial plan and for years focused on building a nest egg to meet their goals. Each month Bob calculates the couple's net worth and makes appropriate adjustments. So far the Reaumes are on target with money to meet their needs.

"If we want something, we buy it," he says. "Joyce is a frugal shopper and I don't have great needs. Every once in a while I buy a new tool for my wood shop."

The Reaumes find the cost of living, especially housing and taxes, lower than in Connecticut, although the difference is not dramatic.

The Stephensons are delighted that insurance is much less expensive than where they lived in Haines City, FL, but they now have to pay a state income tax, which Florida did not have.

The Cronins find small-town living much more economical than life in a big city. While Jack jokes that retirement is a time when "my wife is blessed with twice as much husband and half as much money," these parents of five admit they have more discretionary income than ever before. "Not that it's that much, but we have fewer people helping us spend it," Jack says.

Medical services are especially important, as Jack puts it, "to those of us who are getting less young." Transylvania Community Hospital provides medical, surgical, coronary and intensive care, diversified in-home care and 24-hour emergency services. He describes the local hospital as "terrific, reflective of this caring community."

Bob Reaume, whose cardiac problems began in his 40s, checked area medical resources thoroughly before retiring to Brevard. The Reaumes' peace of mind is helped by having a hospital "right up the road" and emergency helicopter service that transports patients to an Asheville cardiology group in just 11 minutes. A recent trip to the Mayo Clinic for a second opinion confirmed Bob's conviction that he is getting excellent local care.

Joyce Reaume says they looked into continuing-care facilities before making a decision to move to Brevard.

"We didn't want to burden our children, and we also didn't want to have to pick up and move to a whole new area of the country," she says.

Brian Center, a 140-bed facility, offers various levels of care as do local communities with assisted-living units.

If Brevard has flaws, retirees have to think long and hard to come up with them. Bob Reaume is surprised at the amount of rain, lightning and thunder. Jack Cronin notes that the laid-back style of living does not apply to mountain drivers, and he misses the fresh fish and seafood he and his wife enjoyed in New England.

While the Cronins take great pleasure in the nationally acclaimed Brevard Music Festival, Barbara mentions the increase in summer traffic and congestion generated by the festival's popularity. George Stephenson misses Florida's warm winter weather.

All three couples suggest that prospective retirees spend time in the area before making a decision to move here. When the Reaumes arrived in Brevard, they thought they would just love living way up on a mountain, but renting such a home for a year brought them back down to earth.

"With 24 curves you couldn't see around, we wore out brakes and tires like you wouldn't believe," says Bob.

The Reaumes now are settled in a self-designed home two miles from downtown in a woodsy area called Deerlake Village. They describe it as a community within a community, with a current population of 80 families that includes seniors as well as young couples with new babies.

Eva Stephenson, however, yearns for a house higher on the slopes, declaring, "All that's missing from my paradise is a wide-open view of the mountains." Husband George concurs, adding, "We found beautiful views with a lousy house, and beautiful houses without views, so we had to compromise on the view somewhat."

Jack Cronin says, "I only regret we didn't find Brevard earlier."●

Camden, Maine

Despite high cost, Maine coastal town's natural beauty makes it perfect for some retirees

By John A. Johnson

When Al and Ina Doban decided to retire seven years ago, they had the financial means to move anywhere in the country.

They chose Camden, a small town on the coast of Maine.

It was a move that startled their friends and neighbors in Hagerstown, MD. After all, Maine is not generally recognized as a premier retirement area.

"Our friends were surprised we chose Camden, but they had never been here," says Ina, 59. "Al and I vacationed here in 1987 and it was the first vacation I had ever been on that I didn't want to go home."

Al, 64, agrees: "Our one-week vacation in Maine turned into a four-week stay. When it was time to retire, Camden seemed the perfect place for us to go."

Nestled at the base of the Camden Hills, which rise almost 1,400 feet above one of the state's most picturesque harbors, Camden is considered special not only by retirees and vacationers but also by Maine natives.

Camden was settled in 1769 by James Richards, his wife, Betsy, and their cook. The family came to cut timber and fell in love with the natural beauty of the mountains and the sea.

That beauty attracted other families, and Camden was incorporated in 1791 as the 72nd town in Maine. There were 331 residents at the time.

Over the years the town became a center for boat building, gristmills and tourism. A summer colony soon sprang up and today the population of 5,060 swells to almost 15,000 during June, July and August.

Generally, people who retire to Camden are financially comfortable. The cost of living is higher than in many parts of the country, especially when it comes to buying a house and paying real estate taxes.

"The same house you pay $400,000 for in Camden probably would cost $150,000 back in Maryland," Al says.

"But that didn't deter us. Ina and I sat down to look over potential retirement spots in Florida, North Carolina, Arizona and California and we compared everything to Camden."

Ina explains it simply: "We asked ourselves if we wanted to save $1,000 a year and live in North Carolina or a few thousand a year living in Florida. The answer was always no. We wanted to live in Camden. It's worth the extra costs."

The Dobans aren't alone in their feelings. Many Camden residents are retirees. In fact, more than 30 percent are age 55 or older. They have come from all across the United States, but primarily from the Northeast — Massachusetts, New York and New Jersey. Most have spent vacations in the Camden area or have lived in Maine at one time or another.

Sandy and Mary Lou MacKimm, for example, lived in Waterville, ME, for five years during the early 1960s. "We moved all around the country for Sandy's work, but we loved Maine the most," says Mary Lou, 63. "We have a summer camp in another part of the state, so it was natural for us to consider Maine for our retirement home."

The only other spot the MacKimms considered was in North Carolina. "We have five children and two grandchildren. We knew they would visit us in Maine, but we weren't sure about (their coming to) North Carolina," Sandy, 64, says.

The MacKimms retired here from Barrington, IL, choosing Camden in part because they felt it would be easy to make friends.

"Sandy was an executive with a chemical company, and there are many retirees here with similar educations and company responsibilities," Mary Lou says. "We felt comfortable right from the start."

Town manager Roger A. Moody says, "Our retirees seem to like the fact that Camden is a real town, that it wasn't created just for those of retirement age. We have all age groups and occupations here, and there's a vitality to the town that retirees seem to enjoy. In addition, our neighborhoods are mixed and the retirees don't feel isolated."

The town has two subsidized housing developments for older people but no other retirement communities.

A popular yachting center, Camden is home to many of the passenger schooners offering weekly summer trips along the Maine coast. It's also a popular stop for private yachters as they tour Penobscot Bay.

Many of Camden's activities center on its harbor, home port for several yacht races throughout the summer, including the annual race from Camden to Castine. During these events, as the boats head home toward the Camden Yacht Club, they raise their spinnakers and create an exciting parade of color that tourists and residents alike eagerly flock to each year.

Along Camden's typical New England Main Street, fine clothing boutiques, gift and book stores, handcraft shops and galleries keep visitors browsing for hours. A variety of restaurants can be found throughout the town, and accommodations range from fine inns to cozy bed-and-breakfasts.

In addition to the waterfront, activity in Camden centers on the public library, located at the top of Main Street. Next door is the Camden Amphitheatre, which is the town green and the arena for summer and fall arts and craft shows and various entertainment.

Across from the green is the town park, bounded by a beautiful waterfall and one of the oldest boatbuilding shops in the United States. With its grand view of the harbor, the park is a lovely spot for boat watching and picnicking. Prominently placed in the town park is a Robert Willis sculpture of Edna St. Vincent Millay, the Pulitzer Prize-winning poet and Camden's most famous native.

Mementos of Millay still abound in Camden — from the stately Cushing-Hathaway Mansion that she owned on Chestnut Street to the plaque on Mount Battie commemorating her most famous work, "Renascence."

Just north of the town along coastal U.S. 1, Camden Hills State Park spreads across 5,000 acres at the foot of Mount Battie. A paved road ascends from the campground to Mount Battie's 900-foot summit, which offers a wonderful panorama of Penobscot Bay, nearby towns and the rolling inland countryside.

Camden claims to be the only town on the East Coast where you can ski from the top of a mountain (at the Camden Bowl) and see the Atlantic Ocean as you descend. The area has golf courses and health clubs.

Outdoor activities are important, the town manager says, because retirees who move to Camden tend to be younger and more active.

Vaughan and Vera Lee, 64 and 63 respectively, retired to Camden from Stratford, CT. They enjoy hiking, swimming, boating, golfing, canoeing and cross-country skiing, all of which are found in the Camden area.

"Camden affords us almost a total lifestyle," Vera says. "Because of our proximity to the lake and the town, which is only five to seven minutes away, we feel we have the best of all worlds."

Sandy MacKimm says Camden offers plenty of opportunities to stay busy. Retirees spend a lot of time doing volunteer work with such groups as Habitat for Humanity, the Rotary Club, the garden club, the book club, the yacht club, or just visiting sick townspeople. The Longstreet Society, engaged in historic preservation, is a favorite organization for many retiree volunteers.

"I've had to learn to say 'no' to some requests," says Vera. "When you come to Camden, you aren't allowed not to become involved."

Full medical care is available at the Penobscot Bay Medical Center and Camden Health Care Center.

Recently when Sandy was ill, he found care came from more than the doctors and nurses at Penobscot Bay Medical Center.

"I found an outpouring of love that was just great," he says. "Our friends and neighbors cooked for us, stopped

Camden, ME

Population: 5,060
Location: Midcoast Maine, about one hour north of Portland and one hour south of Bar Harbor. Surrounded by Camden Hills and Penobscot Bay.

Climate: High Low
January   32   14
July   75   55

Average relative humidity:[1] 59%
Rain: 46 inches.
Snow: 35-40 inches.
Coastal conditions are tempered by the Atlantic Ocean, resulting in cooler summers and warmer winters than in other regions of the state.
Cost of living: Above average (specific index not available).
Average housing cost: $165,000
Sales tax: 6%
Sales tax exemptions: Food at gro-

cery stores, except snack foods, professional services, prescription drugs, eyeglasses.
State income tax: Graduated in four steps from 2% to 8.5%, based on taxable income.
Income tax exemptions: Social Security income.
Intangibles tax: None.
Estate tax: None, except the state's "pick-up" portion of the federal tax, applicable to taxable estates above $675,000.
Property tax: Rate is 15.37 per $1,000 of assessed value, with homes assessed at 100% of full market value. Tax on a $165,000 home is $2,536.
Homestead exemption: There is a property tax rebate for homeowners with a total household income of $25,800 or less, based on amount of property taxes paid. There also are exemptions for veterans.
Security: 9 crimes per 1,000 residents, lower than the national average of 46.2 crimes per 1,000 residents.
Religion: 18 churches, one synagogue in Camden-Rockport area.
Education: Husson College, a four-year accredited business school, offers courses at the local high school. A branch of the University of Maine-Augusta is located 12 miles south of Camden in Thomaston.

Transportation: None; car needed. Nearest commercial airport is in Bangor, about one hour away.
Health: Penobscot Bay Medical Center has 109 beds, 79 physicians and is a full-service regional hospital.
Housing options: Most housing is neighborhood single-family homes. The **Lily Pond Drive** and **Chestnut Street** areas are popular with retirees; housing prices are $175,000-$650,000. The Assisted Living Unit of the **Camden Health Care Center**, (207) 236-8381, offers six apartments. There are two subsidized elderly housing projects, **Highland Park** with 44 units and the **Megunticook House** with 34 units; both have income limits.
Visitor lodging: The Lord Camden Inn, (207) 236-4325, a historic property on Main Street, starting at $118 off-season, $148 in season. The Lodge at Camden Hills, (800) 832-7058 or (207) 236-8478, rooms and suites (some with fireplaces, kitchens and Jacuzzis) in a wooded setting, starting at $89 off-season, $129 in season.
Information: Rockport-Camden-Lincolnville Chamber of Commerce, P.O. Box 919, Camden, ME 04843, (207) 236-4404 or www.camdenme.org.

[1]Relative humidity based on readings for Portland.

by to see me in the hospital and were willing to do anything we needed. There are some very caring people in this area."

Although residents accept Camden's cold weather and higher costs as prices to pay for living here, these factors are unattractive to some retirees. While winters are milder on the coast than elsewhere in Maine, they're still cold — January highs hover at the freezing mark and the lows dip into the teens. Snowfall averages 35-40 inches a winter, but the warming effect of the water prevents heavy accumulation.

Most retirees live year-round in Camden because they enjoy activities in all seasons. Spring — or lack of it in Maine — is the exception.

"We like to go away each spring to Europe, especially Portugal," says Mary Lou. "It's the only time that Maine is not beautiful. There is no real spring."

But that doesn't dampen her enthusiasm for Camden.

"I would recommend Camden to anyone willing to live in a colder climate and able to put up with a few inconveniences, such as the lack of a big department store," Mary Lou says.

Retirees say the only major drawbacks to living in Camden are the traffic in the summer and the lack of parking in town.

Unless retirees have friends here, getting to know people can take some reaching out, the couples note.

"We had an advantage because Vaughan's family had been vacationing here each summer for several years," Vera says. "We fit right into the social scene."

Both the MacKimms and the Dobans met people through organizations they joined and through volunteer work.

For those interested in retiring to Maine, the cost of living is a factor. While some costs are kept down because of the mix of retirees and a working class, most consider Camden to be expensive.

With the average cost of a home at $165,000, according to the town assessor, and a tax rate of $15.37 per $1,000 of assessed value, the average property tax bill is more than $2,500 a year. There are some veterans' exemptions available, however.

"I don't dare think about what it's costing me to live here," says Al. "But we planned well for our retirement (the Dobans both worked at Mack Truck). We worked with a financial planner and had a 30-year plan."

The MacKimms and Lees also planned for retirement for many years and were well prepared. Still, with interest rates falling and costs rising, they have had to be more aware of finances than they thought would be necessary.

None of the couples has changed their lifestyles, however, although traveling has become more of a luxury.

"We used to do a trip a year," says Vaughan. "We've cut that out. Of course, I've bought a boat and that has something to do with it."

While each has different reasons, they all love Camden, agreeing that the pros outweigh the cons.

Vera Lee sums it up best: "Vaughan and I have traveled worldwide, and there's no place else that has the ambiance that Camden has for us."●

Cape Cod, Massachusetts

When summer crowds depart, residents settle in for the quiet life

By Stephen H. Morgan

Summer is high season on Cape Cod, southern New England's favorite beach vacation spot. Traffic picks up on the bridges over the Cape Cod Canal from Friday afternoon through Monday morning, clogging the Cape's main arteries and making it tough to get around — unless you know the back roads. Beaches are crowded, their parking lots full. And tee times, restaurant tables, ferry tickets — well, everybody seems to want the same things at the same time.

All that changes after Labor Day, when the summer people head home to work and school. "It's quieter, less traffic, less hassle, and you can make left turns easily," says Edward Kleban, 64, a retired certified public accountant from White Plains, NY.

What's left are weekending couples, late-season vacationers whose children are too young for school and, of course, the small-town community life of Barnstable County's 211,922 year-round residents, about 22 percent of whom are age 65 or older.

"The Cape is swarming with retirees," says Carol Kleban, 61, a retired marketing-research executive who is current president of the Nauset Newcomers Club. The club keeps its nearly 800 members hopping from Labor Day to Memorial Day but shuts down in summer because everybody is too busy. "We struggle with an inundation of guests in season," Carol explains.

At the September monthly meeting, members sign up for interest groups, which include everything from canoeing, bicycling and horseback riding to bridge, dine-around groups (both at restaurants and in members' homes), square dancing and needlework. People get a chance to make friends through common interests and to connect with local organizations that need volunteers.

"When we moved here in May '94, we literally knew no one," says Carol, despite having vacationed here on and off for 15 years. Neighbors told them about the club, and they've since gotten involved in local cultural and civic groups. "Now it's unbelievable."

Most retirees settle in the Upper Cape — the part closest to the canal — or the Middle Cape, says Michael J. Frucci, executive director of the Cape Cod Chamber of Commerce in Hyannis. Some are snowbirds who head south in winter, and about 85 percent come from Massachusetts, Connecticut, New Jersey and New York.

"Most everybody comes first as a visitor," says Frucci. "Then they buy a vacation home, which becomes a permanent home."

One couple who bucked that trend is Peter and Carolyn McDermott of Glendale, CA. "On the Cape, they call you a 'wash ashore' if you weren't born here," says Carolyn, 54, a Los Angeles native who never saw snow until she was 21. "I was a 'drag ashore.' . . . I never thought I would ever move to a cold climate."

The McDermotts had scouted other retirement locations before buying a home in Harwich, a small Outer Cape town of beaches and cranberry bogs. Sun City, AZ, was "too organized a retirement place," says Peter, 64. "We wanted to be involved in a community and see children . . . and mix with all kinds of people." They also spurned the gated community they visited in Las Vegas and the heat of Phoenix and Palm Springs.

A hospital administrator for Los Angeles County who had grown up in the New York-New Jersey area, Peter often traveled back East for hospital seminars. Carolyn, who worked for the county health services department, came along on one trip in 1992, and they tacked on a Cape visit with Peter's cousin in Orleans.

On a lark, they asked a real estate agent to show them around. They ended up offering a "ridiculously low"

$200,000 for a cedar-shingled Williamsburg colonial — with an asking price 50 percent higher — that had been sitting vacant on an acre of land in a tiny development near Round Cove Pond. The real estate market was sliding, and to their surprise the offer was accepted. "We didn't believe we could buy this much house," Peter said.

Two years later Peter moved into the Harwich home to oversee renovations, and two years after that they sold their $400,000 Glendale home and Carolyn retired. Now they're involved in a dizzying array of activities.

Through the Nauset Newcomers Club, they go saltwater canoeing in Pleasant Bay, Carolyn is learning how to garden the Cape's sandy soil and Peter is learning how to get on the Internet. Together they are uniformed volunteers with the Coast Guard Auxiliary, advising boaters on marine safety and courtesy, and Carolyn is the volunteer coordinator for the Harwich Cranberry Festival, the town's biggest annual event.

Peter loves the seasonal Cape climate, something he missed in California. For Carolyn, after a rainy first summer, "the jury's out" regarding weather, but not on her West Coast worries about "snobbish" New Englanders. "Here I know my neighbors," she says, "which I never did in L.A."

Cape Cod's climate is cool compared to the Sunbelt, but it is probably the mildest climate in New England because of the moderating waters surrounding it.

The climate was the main attraction for Doris Childs, a social-studies teacher from Manlius in upstate New York's snow belt. She retired two years ago, not long after her husband, William, died. "I wanted to live somewhere the climate was mild and where it was close to the ocean," she says.

She considered coastal Maine, where she has friends, and the New Jersey shore, where she had once lived. But she liked the Cape's ambiance better and settled on a $200,000 three-bedroom contemporary home with a cathedral ceiling in Brewster. "It's like living in the country without being in the country," she says.

Doris is only two blocks from the beach on Cape Cod Bay, whose waters are warmer and tides more dramatic than the Atlantic Ocean or Nantucket Sound beaches. "The tide goes out a mile and you can walk way out," she says. "Then the water comes in and you can swim."

The 65-mile-long Cape, a peninsula that varies from one to 20 miles wide, basically is a sandbar left by the last glaciers. It was made into an island by the completion of the Cape Cod Canal in 1914.

Wind, tide and overuse take their toll annually on the Cape's natural resources. In the 1960s, a 27,000-acre swath

Cape Cod, MA

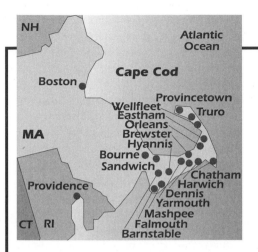

Population: 211,922 in Barnstable County; 22% are 65 and older. Town of Barnstable (which includes Hyannis) 43,699, Falmouth 30,560, Yarmouth 23,546, Sandwich 20,577, Bourne 17,236, Dennis 13,254, Harwich 12,043, Brewster 9,473, Mashpee 13,159, Chatham 6,800, Orleans 6,827, Eastham 5,171, Provincetown 4,675, Wellfleet 3,057, Truro 1,845.

Location: In southeastern Massachusetts, Cape Cod is an arm-shaped peninsula separated from the mainland by a canal and extending into the Atlantic Ocean.

Climate:

	High	Low
January	40	25
July	78	63

Average relative humidity: High.

Rain: 45 inches at Chatham.

Snow: Usually minimal, occasionally heavy.

Cost of living: Higher than average (specific index not available).

Median housing cost: In most towns $154,000-$178,000 for a single-family home. Higher in Orleans ($219,000), Chatham and Truro ($212,000). Lower in Mashpee ($142,000), Provincetown ($148,000) and Yarmouth ($149,000).

Sales tax: 5%

Sales tax exemptions: Groceries, clothing priced less than $175, prescription drugs, some medical supplies.

State income tax: 5.95% on earned income and interest earned from a Massachusetts bank (12% on dividends, capital gains and interest not earned from a Massachusetts bank).

Income tax exemptions: $700 per person age 65 or older in addition to a personal exemption. Social Security benefits and federal and state contributory pensions are exempt.

Intangibles tax: None.

Estate tax: None, except the state's "pickup" portion of the federal tax, applicable to taxable estates worth $675,000 or more.

Property tax: Per $1,000 of valuation, with property assessed at 100% of market value: Barnstable $12.80, Bourne $14.46, Brewster $11.92, Chatham $10.08, Dennis $8.64, Eastham $11.71, Falmouth $11.46, Harwich $11.70, Mashpee $14.92, Orleans $8.46, Provincetown $9.90, Sandwich $16.03, Truro $7.65, Wellfleet $9.43, Yarmouth $13.06.

Homestead exemption: $500 off the property tax for persons over age 70 under certain conditions.

Security: Reported crimes per 1,000 residents is 41.5 in Barnstable, 48.2 in Bourne, 40.2 in Dennis, 39.7 in Falmouth, 27 in Harwich, 29.4 in Mashpee, 73.2 in Provincetown, 18.6 in Sandwich and 33 in Yarmouth, compared to the national average of 46.2 crimes per 1,000 residents.

Religion: Well over 100 churches throughout the Cape cover a variety of denominations; Hyannis has a synagogue.

Education: Adult education classes are available at Cape Cod Community College in Barnstable, at high schools and regional vocational technical schools and, through Elderhostel, at institutions such as the Marine Biological Laboratory in Woods Hole and the Cape Cod Museum of Natural History in Brewster.

Transportation: Cape Cod Regional Transit Authority provides bus service along three routes on the Upper and Middle Cape, plus Hyannis-Provincetown. Its B-Bus minibuses make door-to-door trips throughout the Cape with pickups by reservation one day ahead. Plymouth & Brockton Street Railway buses go to downtown Boston and Logan Airport. There's air service and (summers only) Amtrak service from Hyannis to Boston and New York. Ferries to Nantucket and Martha's Vineyard depart from Woods Hole and Hyannis.

Health: Cape Cod Hospital, a 258-bed acute-care hospital in Hyannis, and 110-bed Falmouth Hospital have merged; they are affiliated with 22 medical-service providers around the Cape. The 60-bed Rehabilitation Hospital of the Cape and Islands is in East Sandwich.

Housing options: Single-family homes, condos (starting about $70,000), rental homes and apartments. Retirement communities include **Thirwood Place**, (508) 398-8006, $124,000-$148,000 or on a rental basis; **Heatherwood at Kings Way**, (508) 362-4400, $165,000-$295,000; **Mayflower Place**, (508) 790-0200, all in Yarmouth. **Wise Properties**, (508) 945-5291 in Chatham and Harwich, $118,000-$294,000. **New Seabury**, (508) 477-9400, is a second-home community in Mashpee with prices of $140,000-$2 million. Golf communities include **Ballymeade** in Falmouth, **Willowbend** in Mashpee and **The Ridge Club** in Sandwich with average new-home prices of $300,000-$500,000.

Visitor lodging: Hotels, motels, housekeeping units, bed-and-breakfast inns and weekly rentals of cottages and condos are among options. Call the chamber of commerce for listings.

Information: Cape Cod Chamber of Commerce, P.O. Box 16, Hyannis, MA 02601, (508) 790-4980 or www.capecodchamber.org. The Cape Cod Canal Region and most towns also have their own chambers of commerce.

from Orleans to Provincetown — including wetlands, forest and some 30 miles of beaches — was set aside as the Cape Cod National Seashore. Other protected areas include the Audubon Society's Wellfleet Bay Wildlife Sanctuary, the Ashumet Holly Reservation and Wildlife Sanctuary in Mashpee and the Monomoy National Wildlife Refuge in Chatham.

All these areas are accessible for hiking, bird-watching and other outdoor activities. There's also Nickerson State Park in Brewster and miles of paved bicycle paths of the Falmouth Shining Sea Bikeway and the South Dennis-to-Eastham Cape Cod Rail Trail, about 80 beaches, more than 20 golf courses (public and private), and no end of places to go fishing or put a boat in the water.

Many retirees cite the Cape's cultural attractions as favorites, such as the summertime Monomoy Theatre in Chatham and Cape Cod Melody Tent in Hyannis, as well as the year-round Cape Cod Symphony Orchestra, the Academy Playhouse in Orleans, museums in Provincetown, Brewster, Sandwich and other places, and an endless variety of adult-education classes and library events.

Some like to visit Boston, one and a half to two hours away by car, with its art and science museums, theater and musical events, sightseeing, restaurants and night life. Providence, RI, also is a cultural mecca. There are major shopping malls in Falmouth, Hyannis, Mashpee and South Dennis.

Maude and Raymond Dugan were Cape Cod regulars by the time they moved to Chatham year-round in June 1984. With their five children, they had vacationed in Brewster, an easy drive from their home in Ramsey, NJ. They bought a large lot in South Chatham in 1973 and built a three-bedroom Cape ranch house as a year-round home rather than an uninsulated cottage, even though it originally was used as a vacation home.

"We always knew we wanted to retire to Cape Cod, but not necessarily to this house," says Maude, 72, who worked as a registered nurse in northern New Jersey high schools, then in hospices.

When Ray, now 75, retired from New Jersey Bell's management in 1983, they hired a local builder to enclose the side porch and convert it to a dining and reading room with beautiful built-in bookcases while they took the "trip of a lifetime" through the South Pacific.

The cozy cedar-shingled home — on a private way where few cars pass — is only a 10-minute walk from Ridgevale Beach, one of the small so-called private beaches that serve local renters and year-rounders while tourists head to Harding's, the town beach nearby. The neighborhood association maintains two footbridges that give access to the beach, arching the tidal streams that ebb and swell in grassy wetlands where geese and herons feed.

For Maude, Chatham offers a great library ("I read a lot") and convenience to community theaters, chamber music and Cape Cod Symphony concerts, plus opportunities to volunteer at hospices, join the choral group and take community college classes. Ray golfs in spring and fall ("it's too crowded in summer"), and in winter drives north to Vermont, New Hampshire and Maine to ski with old friends from New Jersey.

The Dugans find Cape prices comparable to New Jersey, where they still visit friends and family — but their property taxes are about $5,000 lower. And they don't feel put off by Chatham's wealthy image. "It's quiet money," explains Maude. "The guy you see at the hardware store with no toes on his sneakers is probably the one who is president of some large corporation."

Residents say each of the 15 Cape Cod towns has its own character. Chatham, surrounded by water on three sides at the Cape's "elbow," is notable for its shop-lined, walkable center; Harwich has several centers. Brewster is a bedroom town; Orleans a commercial hub. Outer Cape towns have a quiet, beachy feel until you reach busy, urban Provincetown at the tip.

Back toward the canal, parts of Dennis are quietly suburban, while Yarmouth has a bit of highway honky-tonk. Hyannis is an urban center and one of seven villages that comprise sprawling Barnstable. Falmouth is a leafy retreat, despite its big ferry terminal and famous oceanographic institute at Woods Hole.

The Cape's biggest town, Barnstable, has less than 45,000 people. Most towns are governed by a board of selectmen, and some hold the traditional New England town meeting each year.

Sunbelt-style retirement communities aren't yet a big part of the Cape's senior scene, but they are growing in popularity, particularly as a second move.

Among options is The Melrose in Harwichport, which Betty Budell, 78, describes as "like living in a fine resort hotel" because of the 29-unit development's attractive common rooms, 24-hour concierge service and good security. She and her husband, Bill, 84, call it "an ideal setup."

Prices at The Melrose go up to $294,000 for a 1,500-square-foot, two-bedroom unit; at Heatherwood they're up to $275,000, plus hefty monthly fees for meals and use of facilities. New Seabury resort in Mashpee, while defining itself as a second-home community rather than a retirement community, is another attractive option, with condos starting at $140,000 and single-family waterfront homes with prices into the stratosphere.

In comparison, a modest home on the Upper or Middle Cape might go for $90,000 to $100,000, says chamber of commerce director Frucci. That's for a two-bedroom house with living room, dining room and kitchen, a full basement and one-car garage, on a 1,500- to 2,000-square-foot lot.

Few retirees complain about prices, except that gasoline costs more in the summer tourist season. Most say their property taxes went down dramatically, even when making an even trade in terms of housing prices. Peter McDermott found haircuts half the price of cuts in California, but the Klebans say food and dry-cleaning costs are higher than in New York state.

None expresses concerns about personal safety. "We still have our California attitude," says Peter McDermott, who locks his car and put a security system in their house. "But crime is no big deal here. You get the occasional theft, but it's nothing like in a metropolitan area."

Doris Childs says her neighbors check the furnace when she's away and look out for each other in other ways. "I feel very safe here," she says.

It's a quiet lifestyle that tends to draw you in with the beauty and comfort of the surroundings.

"You tend to fall in love with the Cape," says Doris.●

Cape May, New Jersey

History and nature combine in a unique Jersey shore town

By Carolyn Rice

When Jane and Jim Bonner retired to Cape May in 1993 from Philadelphia, they weren't sure what they were going to do with their time

"Between raising eight children and our careers, we hadn't developed any hobbies," says Jane, 66. "Still, we had no intention of taking on new jobs." But that changed in a hurry in Cape May, where a spirit of loyalty and volunteerism is infectious.

Cape May could be called the "big toe" of New Jersey. The peninsula sits at the state's southeastern point where the Delaware Bay meets the Atlantic Ocean. Like most shore towns, Cape May boasts beaches, ocean breezes, great seafood restaurants and a bulging summer population.

Cape May, however, adds a lot more to the usual coastal mix. It has the largest concentration of 19th-century houses in the United States and a year-round schedule of events and activities.

It was Cape May's spirit and vision that kept it from becoming just another shore town. When a huge spring storm destroyed the town's boardwalk and much of its beach in 1962, the town used federal disaster funds to restore and preserve its historic buildings — instead of tearing them down for modern motels, as many developers wanted to do. When the wrecker's ball loomed again in 1970 over the Emlen Physick Estate, a masterpiece of Victorian architecture, the townspeople rallied once more, founding the Mid-Atlantic Center for the Arts (MAC).

MAC volunteers raised $90,000 to buy the decaying property, patched the roof, installed windows and mowed the lawn. Since then, the entire downtown district of Cape May has been declared a national landmark, the Physick Estate has become a fascinating museum of Victorian-era culture, and volunteers and part-time employees conduct a year-round series of walking and trolley tours for thousands of annual visitors, using the proceeds to finance MAC operations.

When senior staff at MAC learned that Jane Bonner had been the executive director of the senior volunteer program in Delaware County, PA, they offered her a part-time job as volunteer coordinator. Jim, 72, a former sales agent for an air freight company, was recruited to be the part-time manager of the city's recycling program.

Beyond their part-time jobs, the Bonners have converted part of their sprawling 1912 "cottage by the sea" into a guest house and host a local cable TV program called "Gray Matters." On the show, they give information about activities and services available to seniors and interview politicians and area senior citizens who have unusual hobbies or skills.

"Cape May turns out to be a great place for retirees who want to volunteer or work part-time. MAC prefers to hire retirees to be guides because they provide continuity and enthusiasm," notes Jane.

Retirees with an interest in history find it easy to become involved in MAC, which pays volunteers and prospective employees to take its extensive training program. This includes a complete history of Cape May and the Physick Estate, a grounding in the day-to-day life of Victorians, and lectures on architecture and art of the 19th century. Anyone who takes a paid position must pass a comprehensive test.

Volunteers (some 200 of them) may do anything from gardening, driving a trolley, or opening up their homes to various tours. "The inside of Cape May's Victorian homes can be just as fascinating as the outside. We're so lucky that so many people volunteer to show their homes to strangers," says Jane.

Opening one's home to the world can only be done in a place that feels safe, and Cape May does. Chief Robert Boyd of the Cape May Police Department says burglary and other property crimes are rare. "Our most common crime is bicycle theft," he says, adding that the police force doubles in size during the summers to add the security necessary to control seasonal crowds.

One thing that draws visitors to the Cape is its extensive collection of historic accommodations. The community has more than 50 bed-and-breakfast inns, many of them owned and managed by people who have retired from other careers.

When Terry and Lorraine Schmidt sought to retire from their banking and administrative careers in Trenton, they knew they wanted to live near the ocean. "But we didn't want to live in a town that closes the day after Labor Day," says Lorraine.

Still in their 40s when they left their jobs in the state's gritty capital for small-town Cape May in 1987, the Schmidts wanted to go into business for themselves. As a former executive with the New Jersey Casino Control Commission, Terry understood something about taking a gamble, but he also knew to develop a business plan.

"Our decision to open an inn in Cape May was more a business one than an emotional one, but we're very happy we made it," notes Terry.

The Schmidts' retirement business is the Humphrey Hughes House, a home originally built for a Philadelphia physician in 1903. "Once we chose Cape May, we contacted a Realtor to find out what was available. We bought the Humphrey Hughes House for $700,000. It's worth at least twice as much today," explains Terry.

The inn has been successful enough to now have a full-time manager. The Schmidts have purchased a private residence a few blocks away, giving them some much-needed privacy. While the inn is open year-round, during the winter it only accommodates guests on weekends. "As we get older, we intend to work less and less," Lorraine says.

She is enthusiastic about Cape May as a retirement hometown for anyone who loves history or just wants to live in a friendly, walk-everywhere kind of place. "I don't see any negatives," she says, noting that property values are increasing.

Peg Roth, a real estate agent and third vice president of the Chamber of Commerce of Greater Cape May, echoes that sentiment. "We see a steady stream of retirees coming into Cape May. Most come from Maryland, Philadelphia and northern New Jersey," she says.

A popular area for retirees is Village Green near the Coast Guard base. A two-bedroom quad unit costs as little as $85,000. Single-family homes in the heart of town start around $179,000 and can cost much more if the home has historic significance or coveted ocean views. (There are very few ocean-front properties.) "Many people purchase second homes in Cape May and eventually retire to them," says Peg Roth.

That's the approach Edward and Jane Zane took. Having fallen in love with Cape May in the 1950s (even though other shore resorts were much more fashionable at the time), the Zanes bought a duplex in 1976 for weekend use. They lived in Turnersville, NJ, near Philadelphia. Edward, 69, was a line installer for New Jersey Bell and Jane, now 75, worked for a bank in Philadelphia.

"Where else is there a seaside resort town with tree-lined streets for walking?" asks Jane. "We don't like the gated, more wealthy communities where every house has a huge fence or gigantic hedge to block the

Cape May, NJ

Population: 4,300 in the city, 105,000 in Cape May County.

Location: In southeastern New Jersey. Cape May is a thumb-shaped peninsula separated from the mainland by a canal. It divides Delaware Bay and the Atlantic Ocean.

Climate:

	High	Low
January	40	24
July	85	68

Average relative humidity: 73%

Rain: 46 inches. **Snow:** 16 inches (snow cover rarely lasts more than a day).

Cost of living: Above average (specific index not available).

Median housing cost: $150,000. Housing costs are higher in town than in the surrounding area. Average monthly rent is $600.

Sales tax: 6%

Sales tax exemptions: Groceries, clothing, and prescription and non-prescription drugs.

State income tax: For married couples filing jointly, graduated in six steps from 1.5% to 7% of taxable income.

Income tax exemptions: Social Security benefits are exempt.

Intangibles tax: None.

Estate tax: None, except the state's "pick-up" portion of the federal tax, applicable to taxable estates above $675,000.

Property tax: $1.64 per $100 of assessed value, with homes assessed at 100% of market value. Annual tax on a $150,000 home is about $2,460.

Homestead tax exemption: First $25,000 of assessed value of a primary, permanent residence for households with gross incomes of less than $100,000.

Security: 66.6 crimes per 1,000 residents, higher than the national average of 46.2 crimes per 1,000 residents.

Religion: There are 11 churches in Cape May City, and the nearest synagogue is in Wildwood. Cape May County has 116 houses of worship.

Education: Adult education classes are available at Atlantic Community College, Cape May Institute, Rutgers University Extension programs and Cape May County Technical School.

Transportation: New Jersey Transit provides bus service to Atlantic City, Philadelphia and New York City. The nearest airports are Atlantic City International and Philadelphia International. The County Department of Aging provides free transportation for seniors to medical facilities (including Veteran's Hospital in Wilmington, DE) and essential shopping.

Health: Burdette Tomlin Memorial Hospital, 10 miles north, has 258 beds. Major medical facilities are available in Philadelphia and Wilmington, both a 90-minute drive. Atlantic and Cape May counties have 139 physicians per capita.

Housing options: Village Green, a 10-year-old area with ranch-style homes, has quad units for $85,000-$100,000 and duplex units for $125,000-$135,000. Houses in the historic district start at $179,000 and go into the millions if they have been renovated as inns.

Visitor lodging: The Virginia Hotel is a full-service, luxury hotel in the historic district, $130-$345 depending on season, including continental breakfast, (609) 884-5700. The Humphrey Hughes House is an elegant B&B inn, $90-$235 depending on season and type of room, (609) 884-4428.

Information: Chamber of Commerce of Greater Cape May, P.O. Box 556, Cape May, NJ 08204, (609) 884-5508 or www.capemaychamber.com. Cape May County Chamber of Commerce, P.O. Box 74, Cape May Court House, NJ 08210, (609) 465-7181 or www.cmcc ofc.com.

views of passers-by. In Cape May, people are proud of their houses and gardens and want them to be seen." The Zanes' garden is a case in point, having won the Cape May Garden Club's monthly award.

Knowing that they would move to Cape May when Edward retired from his job at age 65, the Zanes bought an older single-family house near the beach in 1991, tore it down and rebuilt it before moving in four years ago. They also sold their first duplex and purchased another one, which they rent to year-round residents.

"There's always something to do here," says Edward, who served as treasurer for the local historical society and as a volunteer for Cold Spring Village, a re-creation of a 19th-century farming village just a few miles from town.

While history buffs and antique collectors find Cape May almost divine, they aren't the only folks who enjoy the good life in New Jersey's far south. Nature lovers and anyone who likes being active outdoors will take to Cape May.

For starters, the climate generally is welcoming. The ocean takes the edge off both winter and summer, and temperatures drop below freezing only 15 days a year. Snow melts before it becomes a nuisance. While some may find 46 inches of annual rainfall and an average humidity of 73 percent a little too wet, the gardens love it.

The Cape also is a good place to view wildlife. It is rated as one of the 10 best bird-watching destinations in the world by the Audubon Society. In prehistory, migrating birds selected the narrow peninsula as their resting and feeding ground on annual flights between the Arctic and South America. Butterflies, too, make the Cape a way station — as do several species of whales and dolphins.

"Cape May is ideal for many migrating species because it is halfway between their northern and southern habitats," explains Dr. Paul Kerlinger, director of the Cape May Bird Obser-vatory. Commonly observed species include red-throated loons, snowy egrets, ospreys, peregrine falcons and many types of sandpipers and terns. Many retirees get caught up in birding once they settle on the Cape and take part in the observatory's annual census.

Biking and walking also are popular. People who might not have enjoyed bicycling back home find that the area's lightly traveled roads and flat terrain make it quite pleasurable. Walkers have their choice of venues, and the walker-friendly historic district is particularly popular with retirees.

The shopping district is a pedestrian mall, and sidewalks are in good repair on block after block of brightly painted, garishly trimmed Victorian houses. After the infamous 1962 storm that blew away the boardwalk, it was replaced with a concrete promenade. "It's easier to walk on than a boardwalk," says Jane Zane.

Boardwalk aficionados will find miles of it in Cape May Point State Park, bridging marshes and meandering through mangroves to various birding lookouts. When the grandchildren come to visit, retirees take them to the Wildwood boardwalk eight miles north of Cape May. This is where they'll find beach amusements and the widest expanse of white sand in the state. While Cape May's beach has been slowly eroding, Wildwood's beach is growing.

Although Cape May residents may not have a huge beach to brag about (it's a more-than-adequate strip of sand), most are glad to be living on solid ground. Unlike most shore towns in New Jersey, Cape May is not on a barrier island.

With the convergence of two large bodies of water, fishing and boating enthusiasts will find plenty of opportunities to pursue their interests. Cape May has the second-largest commercial fishing port on the East Coast — a tribute to the wealth of these waters.

Golf, too, is a popular sport with 10 courses in the surrounding area, including the 18-hole Cape May National Golf Club. Tennis courts are abundant; seniors particularly like the town courts next to the Emlen Physick Estate.

Like most shore towns, Cape May has its share of eateries featuring fried fish, hot dogs, saltwater taffy and hamburgers. The town also boasts top-rated restaurants, most of which are open all year, but a few close January through March.

There's also a three-season roster of cultural, educational and just plain fun events and festivals. Spring kicks off with tulip, kite and music festivals. The Cape May Music Festival features a six-week schedule of classical, jazz and blues artists. In the summer, there are antique shows, a seafood festival, a wine-and-food festival, and theater — including the Cape May State Equity Theater, the Speak-eezy musical revue, and the Cape May Kids Playhouse.

Activities peak during a 10-day period in October known as Victorian Week, which features historic house tours, Victorian fashion shows and sing-alongs. The Christmas season also is jammed with activities. Things get quiet during the winter, and many retirees choose that time to vacation in warmer climates.

The Cape May Institute offers a year-round roster of Elderhostel programs. It also conducts photography, writing and preservation workshops at various times of year, and a summer series of philosophy lectures.

For more extensive entertainment opportunities, Cape May residents like the area's proximity to Philadelphia (80 miles) and Atlantic City (49 miles). Public transportation is available to both at reduced rates for senior citizens.

Convenient location, mild climate, lots to do, and a friendly atmosphere all make Cape May rate highly as a retirement locale. As Jane Zane puts it, "A day doesn't go by when we don't say how blessed we are to live here."●

Carlsbad, California

Sea breezes and Mediterranean charm sweeten life in this Southern California coastal town

By Richard L. Fox

It's springtime in this coastal Southern California village, and massive fields of ranunculuses and other hard-to-pronounce flowers erupt in blazing colors of red, orange, pink and yellow, drawing thousands of visitors from across the Southwest. It's summertime, and hordes of youngsters and their parents and grandparents stream into one of the world's largest family-oriented theme parks. It's autumn, and golfers, fishermen, sunbathers and festival-goers flock to this sun-splashed oceanside resort seeking refuge, recreation and relaxation.

Into this magical potpourri of sun, sand, surf and surprises, New Jersey retirees Jack and Gwen Nelson came seeking the perfect place to spend their retirement years. "We were looking for a community with sidewalks, a nearby college and a good library," says Jack. "We found that and a whole lot more in Carlsbad."

Carlsbad evokes images of a charming Mediterranean town, with balmy sea breezes, sun-splashed sidewalk cafes and delightful antique shops and boutiques. Its attributes also include a predictably temperate climate, scenic vistas, excellent shopping and diverse residential neighborhoods, and San Diego is within easy range for more shopping options, cultural and sporting events, dining and entertainment.

For centuries the area was the home of Luiseno Indians, who camped by and fished in coastal lagoons that dot the landscape. In the mid-18th century, Spanish explorers staked claim to this remote territory for their king. In 1798, Franciscan missionaries established the largest of 21 missions in California, Mission San Luis Rey, a few miles north.

With the discovery in the 1880s of mineral waters believed to have healing properties, Carlsbad borrowed its name from the popular Karlsbad Spa in Bohemia and began establishing a reputation as a tourist destination. A giant step was taken in the opening of these coastal lands between Los Angeles and San Diego when the Arizona Eastern Railway built the Carlsbad Depot (now the Tourist Information Center) in 1887.

The introduction of irrigation waters in 1914 brought an economic boom to the area through increased cultivation of vegetables, fruits and flowers. Now more than 200,000 people visit Carlsbad's famous Flower Fields, a mile-long garden of multicolored blossoms that has attracted spring visitors for more than 60 years. The area's newest attraction, Legoland, opened last March to enthusiastic crowds and was expected to bring 1.8 million youngsters and chaperones to the Danish toy manufacturer's only U.S. theme park in its first year of operation.

For many retirees, California's reputation for expensive real estate and high costs of living has precluded relocation. But some, including the Nelsons, have done comparison shopping and found the state more affordable than they thought.

"We had decided to write off California for retirement because of everything we read about high costs of housing, taxes and general living expenses," says Jack. "Then we read an article that caused us to compare property, sales and income taxes in New Jersey and California. We found that New Jersey was much higher than California."

Pleasantly surprised, the Nelsons looked at 10 towns in Southern California, from Santa Rosa to San Diego, and also considered Boulder, Fort Collins and Colorado Springs, CO; Las Cruces and Albuquerque, NM; Seattle, WA; and Philadelphia, PA. Just as the Nelsons thoroughly researched places to retire, they looked hard at available housing before selecting their retirement home.

"We looked at 80 houses, and this was the best built," says Jack, a 66-year-old former Rutgers University professor. "The contractor built it for his mother."

They bought a 2,300-square-foot ranch-style home with stucco and wood siding in May 1998 for about $300,000 "in old Carlsbad, less than a mile from downtown and 1.5 miles from the ocean," says Jack. It's an ideal location for two favorite hobbies, walking on the beach every morning and sampling new restaurants. "We test a lot of restaurants," Gwen adds.

Carlsbad's wide array of housing styles complements the diverse lifestyle choices of its residents. Oceanside condominiums and expansive estates are available for those who enjoy a close relationship with surf and sand. Victorian cottages and beautifully restored historic homes in walking distance of downtown are favored by those seeking convenient access to small-town living. New, upscale suburban developments, notably Aviara and La Costa east of Interstate 5, offer a choice of golf course, lagoon and ocean views from high-end homes running $300,000 to $1,000,000-plus. Carlsbad by the Sea, a luxurious, oceanfront continuing-care retirement community in California mission-style architecture, provides on-site health care, a diverse recreational program, transportation and an innovative program of services fostering good health and well-being.

Manley and Linda Sarnowsky chose a home in the upscale planned community of Aviara, just off Interstate 5 and only minutes from the ocean and downtown, when they moved from St. Louis, MO, in April 1998. Manley, a 58-year-old retired Ralston-Purina executive, and Linda, 57, had visited potential retirement sites in North Carolina, New Mexico and other areas of California before settling on Carlsbad. "We stayed here three full weeks and bought on our first visit," Linda recalls. "We knew we wanted to be near the coast, and we wanted new housing. Once we found the right house we knew this was the place. Carlsbad Village is so attractive, and we just fell in love with the area."

"We had always thought about (retiring in) California, but we thought it would be too expensive," says Manley. "We set a limit on what we would pay for a house, and it turned out to be what we paid almost to the dollar."

"The cost of living is higher than St. Louis," Linda adds, "but that's the only negative here. There are trade-offs. You may have to pass up some things you would like in order to live in a beautiful place."

Asked how they made new friends after moving to Carlsbad, Manley says, "It was easy for me. We joined El Camino Country Club, and I went to the golf course. I play just about every day." Manley says he misses the golf courses back in St. Louis, but they were more crowded. "I have three courses (here) I can get on quite easily," he says.

Linda doesn't golf, but she does "a lot of walking and reading." She joined the Newcomers Club, American Association of University Women, Aviara Women's Club and an investment club. "We've also been inundated with houseguests since we moved out here. I sometimes feel like I'm running a B&B — but I love it," she adds.

Another transplanted couple, Morris and Gladys Hayes, were pleased to find their living expenses in California less than what they were in their preretirement days in Altoona, WI. Morris and Gladys had lived in Altoona for 30 years when they decided their annual one-week stay in a time-share unit at Carlsbad Inn was just

Carlsbad, CA

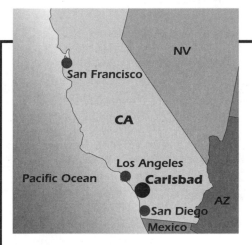

Population: 73,700

Location: On the California coast, 31 miles north of San Diego.

Climate:

	High	Low
January	65	47
July	78	68

Average relative humidity: 69%

Rain: 7.15 inches.

Cost of living: Above average (specific index not available).

Average housing cost: $303,000

Sales tax: 7.75%

Sales tax exemptions: Food products, prescription medicines and services.

State income tax: Graduated from 1% to 9.3%, depending on income and filing status.

Income tax exemptions: Social Security payments are exempt.

Estate tax: None, except the state's "pickup" portion of the federal tax, applicable to taxable estates above $675,000.

Property tax: 1.02013% to 1.05949% of appraised value. With the exemption noted below, the annual tax on a home valued at $303,000 would be $3,020 to $3,136.

Homestead exemption: $7,000 on owner-occupied property.

Security: 32.1 crimes per 1,000 residents, lower than the national average of 46.2 crimes per 1,000 residents.

Religion: There are 26 churches and synagogues.

Education: California State University at San Marcos, 10 miles east, offers undergraduate and graduate degree programs. Two nearby community colleges, MiraCosta in Oceanside and Palomar in San Marcos, offer vocational and general education courses.

Transportation: Coaster is a commuter rail service to San Diego. San Diego International Airport is 30 miles south.

Health: Tri-City Medical Center, just north in Oceanside, is a 450-bed general and acute-care facility. Just south of Carlsbad, Scripps Memorial Hospital-Encinitas has 139 beds. There are 48 physicians and surgeons in Carlsbad, and more than 400 in the area.

Housing options: Homes on or near the ocean, within walking distance of downtown, in historic neighborhoods and in new, upscale suburban developments are available in escalating price ranges. Plan to spend $125-$200 per square foot for new housing. Older homes can be purchased for around $100 per square foot. **Carlsbad by the Sea** is an award-winning continuing-care retirement community housed in an attractive California mission-style complex near the Pacific Ocean. Programs focus on health and well-being, and amenities include a fitness center, lap pool, hydro-therapy pool and spa services such as facials, massages and herbal wraps. Floor plans range from 800 to 1,800 square feet. Entrance fees are $149,000 to $475,000 and monthly service fees are $1,555 to $3,300. For information, call (800) 255-1556 or visit www.carlsbadbythesea.com.

Visitor lodging: Twenty hotels, motels and bed-and-breakfast inns in the community offer a wide range of accommodations and prices. Carlsbad Inn Beach Resort, $169-$238, (800) 235-3939. Pelican Cove Inn, a bed-and-breakfast inn, $90-$180, (760) 434-5995. La Costa Resort and Spa, $315-$500, (800) 854-5000. Four Seasons Resort, Aviara, starting at $355, (800) 332-3442. Rates are per night, double occupancy.

Information: Carlsbad Chamber of Commerce, 5620 Paseo del Norte, Suite 128, Carlsbad, CA 92008, (760) 931-8400 or www.carlsbad. org. Carlsbad Convention and Visitors Bureau), 400 Carlsbad Village Drive, P.O. Box 1246, Carlsbad, CA 92018, (760) 434-6093 or www.carlsbadca.org.

not enough.

"We liked coming here so much that we decided to think about retiring here," says Gladys, 78, a former high school music teacher. "We wintered here in 1996-97 and started looking at real estate. We looked at five properties and bought within 24 hours — four blocks from the ocean."

They found that their property taxes were half what they paid back in Altoona, "and utility bills are about a seventh of what we paid in Wisconsin," Morris says. He estimates their home in a 70-unit condominium development has appreciated modestly since they purchased it in February 1997 — "about $3,000," he says.

Morris, 80, a former music professor at the University of Wisconsin-Eau Claire, says they were captivated by the "quaintness" of Carlsbad Village.

"They built the shopping area about four miles from the village," he says, "and the city fathers have made a point, religiously, to keep fast-food chains and things like that out of the village. Crime is low, and the transportation system is excellent."

Carlsbad is getting its share of relocating in-state retirees as well. Bill and Pat Northridge had lived in La Crescenta, north of Los Angeles, more than 40 years when they decided to seek relief from the increasingly frenetic pace of their hometown. "It took awhile to shake the L.A. County hurries," Pat says, "but the laid-back attitude of the people here in San Diego County has finally rubbed off.

"When our real estate agent found this area in Aviara we did not hesitate to buy," she adds. "One mile to the ocean, which is always in view, yet we're in a forest of protected vegetation and trees all through the hills running up from the Pacific."

Bill and Pat enjoy Aviara's scenic trails, which boast ocean views and wind through exotic vegetation and past a cool, clear lagoon. Bill attends San Diego Padres baseball games, and they both engage in "a bit of competition (among neighbors) to have a beautiful community and keep it that way," says Pat.

Carlsbad's population has grown from about 300 at the turn of the century to about 75,000. There are nine retail shopping centers in the area, including Carlsbad Company Stores, an eclectic mix of upscale retailers, designers, manufacturers' outlets, art galleries, restaurants and financial institutions. With the opening of Legoland, and a large luxury resort, golf course and upscale shopping facilities on the drawing board, some residents worry that the small-town, resident-friendly atmosphere of Carlsbad is being threatened.

But at this point, there's only one thing Linda Sarnowsky doesn't like about Carlsbad: "It's a little far from downtown San Diego," she says. "It takes 30 to 40 minutes to get downtown."

Those who want to avoid busy Interstate 5 to San Diego can take a more leisurely scenic drive down coastal Highway 101. Better yet, residents can board the popular Coaster at one of two Carlsbad stations and enjoy a comfortable commuter train ride downtown.

Normally quiet and uncrowded, Carlsbad draws a crowd of 90,000 shoppers during the Carlsbad Village Faire, the largest one-day street fair in California, in May and November, and a popular farmers market fills downtown streets with eager buyers during the peak growing season. Among major sporting events attracting large numbers of visitors to Carlsbad annually are the San Diego Marathon, with more than 5,000 competitors; the Carlsbad 5000, a premier racing spectacular with more than 10,000 runners participating; and the Mercedes PGA golf championship and Toshiba Tennis Classic held on the grounds of La Costa Resort and Spa.

Seniors can take courses at MiraCosta College, next door in Oceanside, and Palomar College, 15 minutes away in San Marcos. Both are community colleges. The Cal State University campus in San Marcos provides a range of undergraduate and graduate courses.

Jack and Gwen Nelson are glad they made the move from New Jersey. When they aren't walking on the beach or "testing restaurants," Jack is busy revising his latest college textbook and Gwen is either reading, knitting or cooking.

"We may eventually move out of Carlsbad, but not for a long time," Jack says. "We may need an assisted-living home some day, but it will be in this area."

If you're planning a move to Carlsbad, "you better hurry up," advises Linda Sarnowsky. "It's not getting any cheaper. Try to get in on the front end of a new development."●

Cashiers, North Carolina

This western North Carolina village has the ambiance of a mountain resort

By Mary Lu Abbott

In search of "downtown" Cashiers, I pulled into the corner gas station/food mart at U.S. Highway 64 and State Highway 107 and interrupted a conversation of local patrons to ask, "Where's the main part of town?"

They looked at each other, chuckled and nodded to the young clerk to provide an answer. "Well, I guess this is it, ma'am," she said.

Indeed, city folks sometimes have a hard time recognizing Cashiers. In the blink of an eye you've passed through town and again are deep in the mountains and forests of western North Carolina.

Called the "crossroads" by residents, the intersection of highways 64 and 107 forms the heart of Cashiers, an unincorporated community that attracts many retirees. To one side of the intersection the small Village Green acts as a gathering spot and playground, and beyond it is a cluster of enticing shops and businesses with a mountain resort ambiance. Down from the Village Green on Highway 107 north, a few gift stores and crafts galleries, antique shops, professional offices and a hardware store and mercantile occupy small wood and stone buildings nearly hidden among tall fir trees.

Gloria Joseph, a former resident of West Bloomfield, MI, a Detroit suburb, is happy that Cashiers is small. "I don't want it to be built up. The purpose in coming here is to get away from all development," she says, although she acknowledges that at first she was reluctant to settle in this mountain community about 65 miles southwest of Asheville.

"Friends told us about Cashiers, and when we went to Florida for a wedding, we stopped here on the way back. My husband fell in love with it and bought a lot then," says Gloria, 58, who worked for a steel company before she retired. "I didn't want to leave Michigan. We had built our home there and had a lot of blood, sweat and tears in it."

Gloria changed her mind over the next five years, though, as she and Jeff, 64, a Chrysler employee, came back to vacation in the area. They built a home in the Sapphire Valley Resort area east of Cashiers and moved permanently in 1990.

Situated at 3,486 feet, the town is surrounded by mountains 4,000 to 5,000 feet high. Narrow two-lane roads twist and turn through canyons, climb through forests and skirt the edge of ridges with precipitous drop-offs. On some mountain curves, the narrow road makes it difficult for one large vehicle to pass another, and the speed limit in many stretches is only 20 to 30 mph. Those who know the area navigate the snaking roads faster than newcomers and visitors. Road signs suggest that slower drivers pull over to let others pass.

"At first, I was terrified by the roads with no guardrails, but now I drive with one hand — the other's on the armrest — and people have to pull off for me," Gloria says with a laugh.

For hundreds of years people have found their way over these mountains and into Cashiers Valley, first American Indians coming to hunt, then permanent settlers in the early 1800s. By the mid-1800s, it was gaining a reputation as a summer resort where well-to-do Southern families came to escape the heat and humidity of coastal areas. Mountain lodges and second homes sprang up, and an active social scene developed among the "summer people." The early activities of hunting, fishing and horseback riding soon expanded to include golfing, hiking, swimming and tennis.

Now Cashiers is more popular than ever as a resort, its permanent population of about 1,250 residents mushrooming to 8,000 or more with the summer people, many of whom have second homes they've built or bought in developments around Cashiers. While Cashiers draws vacationers from a variety of areas, the migration of Southerners has remained strong. Residents of metropolitan Atlanta frequently escape here for the weekends, but perhaps the largest contingent comes from Florida. Residents of South Florida in particular pack up and head to the cool mountains for the entire summer to escape their sultry season.

Lester and Mary Freeman of Miami, FL, built a vacation home outside Cashiers in 1988 and moved permanently in 1991. Like the Josephs and many others who summer here, when it came time to retire, the Freemans decided there was no better place than Cashiers.

"We didn't have to think about it," says Mary, 67. "We loved the atmosphere when we visited here during the summer months. We liked the scenic beauty, and we had friends with summer homes here."

When John and Rosalyn Perdue prepared to retire and leave Mobile, AL, their home of 36 years, they knew they wanted to relocate to these mountains but weren't sure exactly where to settle.

"We looked all over western North Carolina. We wanted a cooler climate with a change of seasons. When we saw Cashiers, we knew this was the place," says John, 74.

Like other retirees, the Perdues were drawn by the scenic beauty of the area, with its gentle, often misty mountains, many waterfalls and clear streams.

"It's centrally located between a lot of larger towns for shopping, cultural and entertainment needs," John adds. The hub of the region is Asheville, about an hour away. Greenville, SC, is about 70 miles to the southeast, and Charlotte, NC, and Atlanta each are about two hours away.

Retirees are settling in several towns in the area, in particular Highlands, 10 miles southwest on Highway 64, and Franklin, about 30 miles farther west on Highway 64. Highlands sits highest, at an altitude of about 4,100 feet, while Cashiers is lower by about 600 feet, and Franklin, the largest town, spreads over the foothills at about 2,100 feet.

"Franklin gets hot in the summer," says Rosalyn, 71. "We wanted someplace cooler. We looked at Highlands but were discouraged by the (high) prices. We were on our way back to Greenville (where their daughter lives) and decided to go through Cashiers. We were impressed at how it had cleaned

Cashiers, NC

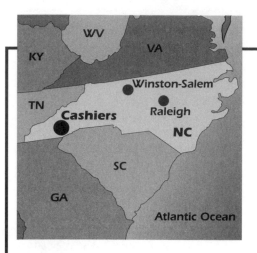

Population: About 1,250 year-round residents in Cashiers, about 8,000 in summer. Jackson County has about 29,000 residents.
Location: In the Blue Ridge Mountains of western North Carolina, about 65 miles southwest of Asheville. Elevation is 3,486 feet.

Climate:

	High	Low
January	46	26
July	82	59

Average relative humidity: 56%
Rain: 91 inches.
Snow: 12 inches.
Cost of living: Below average in Jackson County (specific index not available), but homes tend to be higher-priced in the Cashiers area.
Average housing cost: About $150,000, though many homes are in the $200,000 range and some go above $1 million.
Sales tax: 6%
Sales tax exemptions: Prescriptions, services and automobiles.
State income tax: Graduated in three steps from 6% to 7.75%, depending on income.
Income tax exemptions: Social Security benefits. Each taxpayer also can exempt up to $4,000 in local, state or federal government retirement benefits and up to $2,000 in private retirement benefits, but the total of these exemptions cannot exceed $4,000 per person.

Intangibles tax: None.
Estate tax: None, except the state's "pick-up" portion of the federal tax, applicable to taxable estates above $675,000.
Property tax: Residents of Cashiers pay the Jackson County tax rate of $5.30 per $1,000 of assessed value. Homes are assessed at 100 percent of market value, but appraisals are done only every eight years. Taxes currently are based on 2000 appraisals. Annual taxes on a $150,000 home are $795.
Homestead exemption: Those age 65 and older can exempt $20,000 off the valuation if their yearly income is less than $15,000.
Personal property tax: Same rate as real property (homes) on the depreciated value of boats, mobile homes, motor homes and campers and other specified belongings.
Security: 30 crimes per 1,000 residents in Jackson County, lower than the national average of 46.2 crimes per 1,000 residents.
Religion: The community has several Protestant, Roman Catholic and non-denominational places of worship, but no synagogue.
Education: Southwestern Community College in Sylva and a branch in Franklin offer classes. The University of North Carolina at Asheville, about 65 miles away, has an extensive program and activities for seniors.
Transportation: There's no local bus service. Nearest airports are at Asheville and Atlanta, about two hours away.
Health: The community has a medical clinic affiliated with the Highlands-Cashiers Hospital, about six miles from Cashiers on U.S. Highway 64. The 24-bed hospital offers extensive services, including cardiac care, and is linked with regional medical facilities to provide specialized care locally. For ad-

vanced surgical procedures, residents go to Asheville or Atlanta.
Housing options: There are many residential communities in the Cashiers-Glenville-Sapphire area, offering lots and new and resale homes, townhouses and villas in the mountains and on lakes and golf courses. Most construction is wood and stone. Among popular options for retirees are **Holly Forest**, with homes priced from $110,000-$450,000, and **Emerald Cove**, $175,000-$225,000 (contact Fairfield-Sapphire Valley Resort, (828) 743-3441, for information on these two communities); the new **Trillium Links and Village**, (888) 464-3800, custom homes $175,000-$400,000, homesites $42,000-$120,000; **Country Club of Sapphire Valley**, $175,000-$950,000; and **Cullowhee Forest**, $250,000-$650,000. The chamber of commerce provides a directory listing several real estate agencies in the area.
Visitor lodging: Options range from log cabins to elegant homes, bed-and-breakfast inns, resorts and lodges. Oakmont Lodge, (828) 743-2298, offers log cabins with fireplaces starting at $59 November to June and $72 the rest of the year. Cottage Inn, (828) 743-3033, has accommodations for $80-$100, depending on season. The Millstone Inn Bed & Breakfast, (888) 645-5786, open March through December, has 11 rooms starting at $146. Sapphire Valley Resort, (800) 533-8268, about three miles outside Cashiers, has golf, tennis, hiking, fishing, canoeing and a variety of accommodations from hotel rooms to four-bedroom homes; hotel rates are $90-$250 a night.
Information: Cashiers Area Chamber of Commerce, P.O. Box 238, Cashiers, NC 28717, (828) 743-5941 or www.cashiers-nc.com.

up. It used to have a lot of junkyards and old cars along the highway.

"We stopped to see a realtor and five months later bought a lot. We wanted to buy something to renovate. We said we would never build another house (after building one in Mobile) but we couldn't find anything we wanted, so we did build," says Rosalyn.

When they moved in 1991, theirs was the third house in an area a couple of miles from Cashiers on Highway 64 toward Highlands. "We were the first full-timers in the area and we thought we were going to be alone out here for a while. Now there are 18 homes and four of us are full-timers," Rosalyn says. She retired from a position as a school library media specialist, and John concluded a career as a structural engineer.

Cashiers residents say their community and Highlands are more resort-oriented than Franklin. Gloria thinks Cashiers has more pizazz because of its specialty shops, which purvey fine art, mountain crafts, gourmet foods, decorative arts, gardening gifts and antiques.

"We're similar to Highlands, but they're more commercialized, more developed. They're incorporated and we're not. There are advantages and disadvantages to incorporation," says Jeff. Without a local governing authority, development can be helter-skelter, but "a few wealthy families bought a lot of the land around here and make sure that what goes in is desirable," says Jeff. "There are a lot of very active people who are guiding growth control. It's in good shape."

Cashiers relies on Jackson County and local volunteers to provide needed services. Emergencies are handled by a volunteer fire department, a rescue squad with a full-time ambulance crew supplemented by volunteers, and the Jackson County Sheriff's Department. Cashiers residents take pride in their new branch of the Jackson County Public Library, which also has a meeting room for concerts and other programs. A community center hosts activities for seniors. The local Cashiers Medical Center is affiliated with the Highlands-Cashiers Hospital, located between the two communities.

"The hospital was a deciding factor in our move," says Rosalyn. "We're five miles and about eight minutes from the hospital. It took longer than that to get to a hospital in Mobile. This is a good hospital — it's hooked up (for electronic consultations) with other medical facilities in the region, and some staff from Emory University Hospital (in Atlanta) come for visits or are on call. Some Emory doctors have homes up here."

For all three couples, a major factor in relocating here was its lower cost of living. "We can live here 40 to 50 percent cheaper than we can in Miami," says Lester, 70, who owned a telecommunications company. "Taxes and insurance are much less. We used to do a lot of dining out — on-the-town sort of thing. We have far fewer opportunities to spend money." And that includes "even the places to buy clothes — there's no Bloomingdale's," adds his wife, Mary.

For Jeff and Gloria, the savings were dramatic. "Michigan taxes were $10,000-$12,000 annually. Here they are $1,000-$1,200," Jeff says. "Transportation expense is far less. When we were in the city we spent about 25 percent of our lives in a car. We went from two cars to one when we moved here. We live right across the street from the golf course and I have a golf cart."

High among the attractions cited by residents are the outdoor activities, including hiking, walking, golfing, fishing and rafting. The area is "good for your health because it's hard not to be involved in physical activities," says Jeff.

The beauty of the changing seasons also beckons people outdoors. Red maples and pink azaleas herald spring, followed by the rosy hues of rhododendrons, white and pink mountain laurels and fragrant magnolia blossoms covering the mountains into the summer. Fall paints the peaks and knolls a myriad range of reds, oranges and golds.

Winter brings chilly days and several snowfalls, but extreme cold and heavy snow are rare. Retirees have mixed reactions to the winters, depending on where they have lived previously. Those who came from the North, such as the Josephs, consider the winters quite mild. Some people from the South love the opportunity to see snow, and others consider January and February good times to flee like "snowbirds."

"We love the snow," says Rosalyn, who rarely encountered it in Mobile. "We don't mind being snowed in with a fireplace. We have four-wheel-drive vehicles. You really need them up here," she says, while noting that highways are plowed for snow and remain open in winter.

The Freemans don't like the "rainy, dismal days" that sometimes come in winter, so they escape back to Miami frequently. "When you live in South Florida, the sun shines every day. I am very much affected by gloomy weather," says Mary. Lester adds that they experience "horizon deprivation" when they are surrounded too long by mountains rather than skies. The Freemans suggest that anyone considering retiring to Cashiers full-time rent for a year and try it out through a winter.

The Josephs advise retirees resettling here to compare the price of buying furniture in North Carolina to the cost of moving furnishings. Since so much furniture is manufactured in the state, it's often less expensive here.

The retirees find more to praise than to fault in Cashiers. Those who moved from metropolitan areas like its low crime and the lack of congestion. Being a resort area has fostered the growth of good cafes, delis and gourmet restaurants, though some close for a while during winter. The couples say it's easy to meet people and step into the active social scene through churches and community volunteer programs.

For Rosalyn and John Perdue, living in Cashiers is like one long vacation. "Our friends wondered how we found the place and how we could drive on the (narrow, twisting) roads without being bothered, but we're not," says Rosalyn. "We have exactly what we want," adds John.●

Celebration, Florida

Retirement dreams come true in this Florida town created by Disney

By David Wilkening

The idea of retiring to Walt Disney World may seem like a childhood fantasy, but when Disney founded a town adjacent to its Orlando theme park in 1994, it was a dream that became reality. The first residents moved into their homes in Celebration four years ago, and while the development is not age-restricted, many of its residents are young-at-heart retirees. In accordance with general Disney philosophy, residents here are supposed to live happily ever after. For many, that's not a difficult assignment.

New residents Rod Owens and his wife, Peg, found that it really is a small world after all, as the Disney ditty goes. They had planned a retirement relocation, and their search for a new community took them about 17,000 miles in a small motor home. But eventually they found their new home only 30 miles from the old one.

"After my husband retired, we started traveling. But we were always looking for someplace else to live," recalls Peg Owens. The couple had what seemed an almost perfect retirement location on a lake in Central Florida near the garden-rich tourist attraction of Cypress Gardens. But while living on a lake sounds like a fine lifestyle, "it was quiet but boring," says Peg.

The couple wanted to live in the South in a community with good sidewalks. "My husband jogs every day, and we knew we wanted somewhere with the mobility of being able to walk on sidewalks," she says. They were considering various places they visited, but their search came to an end on the day they read about a new community planned by Walt Disney World in Florida.

Celebration, less than an hour from their home, was so popular before it even opened that a drawing was held to determine the buyers of the first

500 homesites available. There were 5,000 entries, and Rod, a retired dentist, and Peg were among the lucky ones.

Their good fortune allowed them to become two of Celebration's first residents when they moved into their home in the summer of 1996. What they found when they arrived was a small-town atmosphere and a downtown that featured retail shops, restaurants, a town hall, a post office, grocery store, offices and cinema. Not only did they have sidewalks on which to jog, they also had access to a lake ringed with a wide promenade that is a focal point of the town.

One of Disney's theme parks, EPCOT (Experimental Prototype Community of Tomorrow) originally was to have been a place where people lived and worked. Walt Disney died long before that ever took place, but he probably would have approved of the magic of Celebration, a community with Southeastern ambiance and pre-1940s-style architecture. When complete, it will have 12,000 to 15,000 residents in homes overlooking plenty of green space. The 4,900-acre site just south of busy U.S. Highway 192 near Interstate 4 is surrounded by a 4,700-acre protected greenbelt.

Disney wanted its community to be perfect, just like its theme park, and it is said that the creators of Celebration spent a decade studying successful towns of the past and present to create a close-knit community — but one that also is technologically advanced to meet the needs of the 21st century. Famous architects of Disney's new town included Robert Stern, Aldo Rossi, Michael Graves and Philip Johnson.

The technology is evident in various ways, such as Florida Hospital Celebration Health, a 1,432-bed health-care facility offering compre-

hensive care and a 60,000-square-foot fitness and wellness center. Another example is the community's own Intranet, which links homes, schools, health-care facilities, office and retail areas, providing such online services as e-mail, chat rooms and bulletin board announcements.

But there are homey small-town touches such as homes with front porches designed to promote social interaction. Even the par-72 Celebration Golf Course has been designed to have the feel of a city park. Popular with retirees such as the Owenses are the many miles of nature trails and bicycle paths.

Also popular among retirees is an over-50 group of volunteers. But what the Owenses and others find particularly enticing about Celebration is its wide mix of age groups that all seem to share a sense of community.

"You get a great feeling of community here that I don't think you find at mobile home parks or retirement areas," says Peg Owens. Virtually everyone she knows at Celebration is involved in some type of charity or civic organization. Her husband, Rod, 57, helps out with Give Kids the World. Peg, 51, started a garden club when Celebration first opened and has watched it grow from 15 to almost 60 members.

If there is a negative side to Celebration, the Owenses feel it is nearby busy U.S. Highway 192. "We do hate the traffic there," Peg says. As best they can, the Owenses and other residents avoid getting out at rush hour and other peak traffic times.

The Owenses praise the wide choice of housing available, ranging from apartments to garden, village, cottage and estate homes. Prices start at $189,000 for a garden home and reach $550,000 to $1 million at the estate level. The Owenses chose a 2,400-square-foot home that has a small lot but provides them with plenty of privacy because of the layout.

Houses are designed in six styles: Classical, Victorian, Colonial Revival, Coastal, Mediterranean and French. There are six home types: estate, village, cottage, garden, townhouse and bungalow. These types allow for a variety of lifestyles that range from a traditional large home on a golf course that might be 90 feet wide by 130 feet deep to compact cottage homes like those found in the downtown areas of some of Florida's cities and towns. Bungalow homes, the smallest at 39 feet wide by 79 feet long, are reminiscent of Coral Gables, FL, or Pasadena, CA, in the early 1900s. Thirty-seven of 47 bunga-

low sites were snapped up the first day they became available last September.

The community is not gated, but the Owenses say that's no detriment. Perhaps partly because there always are people out participating in various activities in the community, there is little concern about crime.

"All ages are here. We love seeing and hearing the children. There are wide sidewalks everywhere. Children are skating by. Families are walking by. You feel perfectly safe," says another resident, Melie Sue Ablang. She and her husband, Ernie, a physician, also were among the lucky lottery winners who first moved here. Like the Owenses, the Ablangs read about

Celebration in a magazine.

At the time, they were living in Chesapeake City, MD. "Ernie had always loved Disney, so we flew down and took a look," Melie Sue says. They made up their minds almost immediately. Sight unseen, evaluating it from a picture, they bought a village home with a garage apartment.

"Back home in Chesapeake City, we told our kids we were packing up and retiring to Disney World. Their mouths were open. Their eyes were wide. They said, 'You're doing what?' But they quickly got over the shock," recalls Melie Sue.

The Ablangs helped start the Celebrators, an over-50 retirement club that now has about 60 members and

Celebration, FL

Population: About 2,700, eventually reaching 12,000 to 15,000 when the development is completed.

Location: In the northwest corner of Osceola County, 10 miles southwest of downtown Orlando and just south of Walt Disney World, about 20 minutes from Orlando International Airport.

Climate:

	High	Low
January	72	49
July	92	73

Average relative humidity: 55%

Rain: 48 inches annually.

Cost of living: 100.5, based on national average of 100.

Median housing cost: The average home in Celebration costs $377,000, according to a local real estate company.

Sales tax: 7%

Sales tax exemptions: Food and medicine.

State income tax: None.

Intangibles tax: Assessed on stocks,

bonds and other specified assets, with some investments exempt. Tax rate is $1 per $1,000 of value for assets of less than $100,000 for individuals or $200,000 for couples, $1.50 per $1,000 of value for larger amounts. First $20,000 of assets ($40,000 per couple) is exempt.

Estate tax: None, though there's a "pick-up" portion of the federal tax, applicable to taxable estates above $675,000.

Property tax: $16.4615 per $1,000 of assessed value. Real property is assessed at 100% of value. The annual tax on a $377,000 home, with exemption noted below, is about $5,794.

Homestead exemption: $25,000 off the assessed value of a permanent, primary residence.

Security: 72.24 crimes per 1,000 residents in Osceola County, higher than national average of 46.2 crimes per 1,000 residents. Specific figures for Celebration not available.

Religion: All major religions are represented in Osceola County. Community Presbyterian Church is located in Celebration.

Education: Four-year colleges in the area include the University of Central Florida and Rollins College. There also are several junior colleges, including Seminole Community College, Valencia Community College and others. Noncredit classes for adults are avail-

able at various outlets, including The Knowledge Shop.

Transportation: Orlando International Airport is a major airport providing direct service both nationally and internationally. But the area's major bus transportation system, Lynx, does not serve Celebration.

Health: Florida Hospital Celebration Health, a 1,432-bed facility that offers acute care, is located in Celebration. There are several other major hospitals in the Orlando area.

Housing options: New residents can choose from apartments to estates. Prices start at $189,000 for garden homes, $250,000 for townhomes and cottages, $349,000 for village homes and $550,000 for estates, according to Re/Max Properties Southwest. Monthly rentals can be had for $2,500-$2,800 for furnished townhomes, $2,000-$3,000 for unfurnished homes and townhomes, and $650-$950 for garage apartments.

Visitor lodging: The 115-room Celebration Hotel is built in 1920s-style wood-frame design, with rooms from $165 to $380, (888) 499-3800 or (407) 566-6000. Near the theme parks are other options in all price ranges.

Information: Celebration Realty, 700 Celebration Ave., Celebration, FL 34747, (407) 566-HOME or www.celebrationfl.com.

meets monthly to hear guest speakers. Melie Sue is active in the garden club and does work with the Celebration Foundation, an independent, nonprofit organization established to promote and conduct activities in the town's community buildings. She and Ernie also are active in the local Presbyterian church.

Like the Owenses, Melie Sue and Ernie don't want to live in a community peopled entirely by retirees. They relish the variety of age groups they encounter daily. And, "there's always something going on," says Melie Sue. Community-sponsored events range from St. Patrick's Day treasure hunts, periodic car shows, pumpkin-carving events at Halloween, founders day weekends, basketball tournaments and even artificial snow at Christmas.

Along with the Ablangs and the Owenses, Pat and Joe Storey also were among the first settlers here. And the Storeys have equal praise for Celebration, though they are moving — very reluctantly and by necessity, says Joe, a retired Navy pilot. He had already retired and they were living in another part of Orlando when Celebration first came to their attention.

"Our next-door neighbor was an architect and construction project manager for Celebration," recalls Joe. "He kept us advised what was going on down here.

"We figured that if someone who was on the inside of this project was enthusiastic enough to plan to move here, we would just follow along and see what was going on."

The Storeys visited the preview center and watched a presentation. "We liked what we saw," but that early in development, "it was a leap of faith," says Joe. However, Pat thought so highly of the plans for Celebration that she told her husband, "We should move there even if we have to live in a closet."

Needless to say, they didn't have to live in a closet, and they relied on Disney's longstanding reputation for high quality in making their decision to buy. "We knew about their track record, and judging by that, we thought it would be a beautiful place. And it is. It's a great, great place," Joe says.

Then why are they moving? "We're moving to a CCRC (continuing-care retirement community) because of our health. To get to places you have to visit, such as getting your car repaired, you have to drive down a very busy highway (U.S. Highway 192) for at least five minutes. My wife hates it. As long as you don't leave Celebration, that's no problem. But outside the gates, access gets less convenient as you get older," Joe says.

The Storeys particularly liked the sense of community in Celebration, and they found it easy to make friends.

They say they will miss those friends when they move, but they had no trouble selling their home. "Homes only last about two weeks on the market," Pat says. And some homes have appreciated $100,000 or more since Celebration opened just a few short years ago, she adds.

That level of appreciation is lamented by friends of the Owenses who considered Celebration but instead retired in Tampa. Now the Owenses say their frequently visiting friends wish they had moved to Celebration. But it's too late — they can no longer afford the prices.

The Ablangs also are thinking of moving again, although they say they love their home. But they'll be staying in Celebration, perhaps moving to a larger home so Ernie can have more space for his hobby, woodworking. Both Ernie and Melie Sue do miss their children, "but they visit a lot because business conferences bring them to the Orlando area. We get to see them often," Melie Sue says.

And that brings up one of the best things about Celebration — its proximity to Walt Disney World. With the theme park just a short drive away, residents who have children and grandchildren say they've never been more popular. "We even have a back road that takes us straight to Disney World without getting on the busy highways," says Melie Sue Ablang.●

Chapel Hill, North Carolina

A top university attracts retirees to this 200-year-old North Carolina town

By Richard L. Fox

Two worlds mingle in Chapel Hill. Presidents from John F. Kennedy to Bill Clinton have chosen this town as a stage for worldly pronouncements. Yet on a warm summer evening, the muted chirps and croaks of crickets and bullfrogs can be heard rising from shallow marshes along Jordan Lake.

Such scenes illustrate the dual essence of Chapel Hill. The small, 200-year-old city, set amid the forests and lakes of central North Carolina, grew up around the University of North Carolina, the nation's first state university. The school's contributions to research, medicine and higher education have helped make Chapel Hill one-third of the acclaimed "research triangle," which also includes Raleigh, site of North Carolina State University, and Durham, home of Duke University.

The university's sprawling 729-acre, oak-covered campus is bordered on three sides by residential neighborhoods of large, historic homes and fraternity houses. The fourth side is edged by Franklin Street, the main thoroughfare and heart of downtown Chapel Hill.

"It's a beautiful place, full of friendly, honest, hard-working people," says Frances Stein, 61. In 1990 she and her husband, Richard, moved to Chapel Hill from Sanibel Island, FL, where they were happily retired.

"We were attending the 40th reunion of my class at Yale University when old friends invited us to visit them in Chapel Hill," Richard, 72, recalls. "The university community always has lots going on. There are cultural and educational opportunities, seminars and meetings. And when you spread the faculty throughout the community, there are opportunities to meet lots of interesting people."

Finding educational outlets is not hard in this quintessential college town. Popular courses are offered on the UNC campus through the Carolina College for Seniors. Weekend courses are presented in a series titled "Adventures in Ideas," and both credit and non-credit courses are available at the William and Ida Friday Continuing Education Center. A local publication, *Think Again*, lists continuing-education opportunities and lectures that are open to the public.

The university has fostered a rich cultural environment, boasting museums, theaters and arts generally found in much larger cities. The Ackland Art Museum hosts traveling exhibitions and houses a 14,000-piece permanent collection that includes works by Degas, Delacroix and Rodin. The North Carolina Symphony conducts part of its season on the UNC campus, performing in Memorial Hall and occasionally giving outdoor concerts on the steps of South Building. The Carolina Playmakers Repertory Company, a renowned professional theater company based at UNC, has produced well-known actors, playwrights, composers and musicians, among them actor Andy Griffith, author Thomas Wolfe, band leader Kay Kyser and composer Richard Adler.

Morehead Planetarium, the first on a university campus, opened in 1949 and served as an early celestial navigation training facility for NASA astronauts. Today there are daily presentations at its Star Theater, plus free science and art exhibits.

Cultural fare is not limited to the college campus. The ArtsCenter, in adjoining Carrboro, offers year-round musical events including jazz, folk, and popular and country music. A favorite outdoor retreat in Chapel Hill is the North Carolina Botanical Garden. With 600 acres of gardens, trails and preserved lands, it is the largest collection of native plants and herbs in the Southeast.

For a local history lesson, the Chapel Hill Preservation Society recommends a self-guided walking tour of downtown. The society's map of Franklin Street and adjacent blocks highlights homes and buildings that date from the early 1800s to the early 1900s, most of them built for UNC professors. The architecturally interesting Kennette House was built in 1897 by a chemistry professor. The Horace Williams House, an 1840s farmhouse later occupied by faculty members, now serves as headquarters for the Preservation Society.

Thanks in large part to Chapel Hill's commitment to preserving its past, it's not hard to imagine Franklin Street as former university chancellor R.B. House once described it in the UNC alumni magazine: "I have experienced an immense exhilaration of spirit every day since I first saw Chapel Hill in September 1912, rode through the red dust of Franklin Street bordered by a forest, walked on the gravel of the campus paths, got grit in my shoe and got Chapel Hill in my soul."

Franklin Street still is a main gathering place for residents and students, which gives it a villagelike ambiance. A post office, churches, drugstores, restaurants, bookstores, clothiers and banks front its tree-shaded sidewalks.

All it takes is a look beyond Franklin Street to see how the community is growing. Chapel Hill's borders, once confined to Franklin Street and the university, now meet with those of neighboring communities like Carrboro to the west. Where open, empty road once stretched northeast to Durham, malls, restaurants, fast-food establishments and gas stations now vie for business.

Yet despite the growth, much of the land surrounding Chapel Hill remains heavily forested, with only lakes, farms, meadows and upscale housing developments punctuating the landscape.

The Steins moved to a small rural development about 15 minutes south of Chapel Hill. Their new home sits on a two-acre lot at the edge of a woodland. "We use part of the meadow as garden space," says Richard. "We have deer, raccoons, rabbits, hedgehogs and plenty of possums in the area."

It was another neighborhood that drew Bob and Ruth Tiemann to the Chapel Hill area. The couple lived in New Jersey and several Midwest states before moving in 1987 to Fearrington Village, a 20-year-old planned community 10 miles outside Chapel Hill. They considered Williamsburg, VA; Pinehurst, NC; and Keowee, SC, before settling here.

"The university, cultural activities, excellent medical facilities and four-season climate sold us on this area," says Bob. "But the main attraction for us is Fearrington Village and its people. We sing in choral groups, belong to various clubs for crafts and investments, and joined a golfing group that plans and plays in tournaments on various area courses from March through November."

Housing options in Chapel Hill vary from planned communities, mostly outside the town limits, to more central historic neighborhoods. New homes in Fearrington Village start at around $230,000, and resales start at about $150,000. Prices for large, custom-designed, single-family homes begin at around $250,000.

Closer to town is Southern Village, situated on 300 acres of woodlands just a mile south of the university and hospital. New homes in this self-described "new, old neighborhood"

Chapel Hill, NC

Population: 44,015, including more than 23,000 university students.

Location: In the gently rolling hills of central North Carolina, about two hours from the Blue Ridge Mountains and the Atlantic Coast.

Climate:

	High	Low
January	48	25
July	88	65

Average relative humidity: 54%

Rain: 46 inches. **Snow:** 7.5 inches. A mild four-season climate with pretty springs, hot and humid summers, and colorful fall foliage that peaks in October. Snows are rare in winter and melt away after a few days. Elevation is 487 feet.

Cost of living: 112.5, based on national average of 100.

Average housing cost: $231,000

Sales tax: 6%

Sales tax exemptions: Prescription drugs and services. Automobiles are exempt from sales tax but incur a 3% highway use tax at the time of purchase.

State income tax: Graduated in three steps from 6% to 7.75%, depending on income.

Income tax exemptions: Social Security benefits. Each taxpayer also can exempt up to $4,000 in local, state or federal government retirement benefits and up to $2,000 in private retirement benefits, but the total of these exemptions cannot exceed $4,000 per person.

Intangibles tax: None.

Estate tax: None, except the state's "pick-up" portion of the federal tax, applicable to taxable estates above $675,000.

Property tax: $17 per $1,000 of assessed value, with homes assessed at 100% of market value. Yearly tax on a home valued at $231,000 is $3,927 without exemption.

Homestead exemption: Homeowners age 65 or older, or disabled, living in the house and earning $11,000 or less per year qualify for an exemption of $15,000.

Personal property tax: Same rate as real property on depreciated value of cars, boats, mobile homes and airplanes.

Security: 62.7 crimes per 1,000 population, higher than the national average of 46.2 crimes per 1,000 residents.

Religion: There are two Catholic, one Jewish and 76 Protestant places of worship.

Education: The University of North Carolina at Chapel Hill offers undergraduate, graduate and continuing-education courses.

Transportation: Chapel Hill Transit Authority provides local bus service. Raleigh-Durham International Airport, a 20-minute drive from downtown, is serviced by major airlines with more than 100 passenger flights daily.

Health: The UNC Hospitals complex includes a medical school, 665-bed hospital, Family Practice Center, North Carolina Clinical Cancer Center and children's, women's and neuroscience hospitals.

Housing options: Fearrington Village, (919) 542-4000, has resales starting at $150,000 and new homes from about $230,000. **Southern Village** offers sales through Coldwell Banker, (919) 933-4422, with new homes from the $150,000s to $400,000s. **Carol Woods,** (800) 518-9333, and **Carolina Meadows,** (800) 458-6756, are accredited continuing-care retirement communities; both often have waiting lists.

Visitor lodging: Carolina Inn, from $159 double occupancy, (919) 933-2001. Hampton Inn, from $84 double occupancy, (800) 426-7866 or (919) 968-3000.

Information: Chapel Hill-Carrboro Chamber of Commerce, 104 S. Estes Drive, P.O. Box 2897, Chapel Hill, NC 27514, (919) 967-7075 or www.herald-sun.com/cchamber. Chapel Hill/Orange County Visitors Bureau, 501 W. Franklin St., Suite 104, Chapel Hill, NC 27516, (919) 968-2060 or www.chocvb.org.

range from the $150,000s to the $400,000s. Five miles from downtown is the 1,600-acre Governors Club, a master-planned community that features a Jack Nicklaus-designed golf course and luxurious homes on wooded hillsides.

For those who want to live in town, there are rare chances to purchase a home in one of the historic neighborhoods. Many of these old homes have been bought and restored by relocated retirees.

From Chapel Hill's central location, residents can be in the Blue Ridge Mountains or at the sandy beaches of the Atlantic Ocean within little more than a two-hour drive. Interstate highways 85 and 40, both minutes from downtown, put the state's major cities within easy round-trip driving distance, and Atlanta and Washington, DC, are a comfortable same-day drive away. Raleigh-Durham International Airport is 20 minutes away via the interstate.

Chapel Hill's ideal location and pleasant climate are what attracted Bill and Barbara Anderson. After 20 snowy winters in Huntington, NY, the Andersons retired to Chapel Hill in 1980.

They visited Chapel Hill 10 times over five years before making the decision to move. Bill says they stayed for "the climate plus Carolina athletics and the Chapel Hill Country Club." They divide much of their time between playing golf and serving on various committees.

While winters generally are mild enough to pursue golfing and other outdoor activities and snow is rare and short-lived, summers can be humid and hot. To cope with the heat, residents sometimes escape for the day to the nearby mountains, where a few thousand feet of altitude nets cooler temperatures.

Chapel Hill's health-care facilities became an unexpectedly important factor for Bob Tiemann. He had major medical problems after retiring to the area but rates the treatment he received here as superior. "The university hospital and doctors have been outstanding," says Bob.

The UNC medical complex includes one of the country's premier medical schools. Providing some of the most advanced medical care in the Southeast, UNC hospitals are leaders in transplants and transplant therapies, burn care and gene therapy.

When asked about drawbacks, the Steins note that their taxes are higher than in Florida. The elimination in 1995 of North Carolina's intangibles tax on investments has eased the tax load for many residents.

The Steins also warn that the much-heralded Tar Heel athletic programs have a downside: Up to 60,000 fans from the far corners of the state converge on Chapel Hill for football and basketball games, causing heavy traffic congestion and excessive auto emissions.

Chapel Hill has come a long way since the time when an unpaved Franklin Street was the only source of retail and commercial services in town. Yet the university remains the center of attention, and Franklin Street retains its picture-window view of earlier times. As Thomas Wolfe, UNC alumnus and author of "You Can't Go Home Again," once said, "You can always come home again to Chapel Hill and feel like you've never been away."●

Charleston Barrier Islands, South Carolina

South Carolina coast combines resort living with Colonial charm

By William Schemmel

In Charleston, church bells chime the hours as they've done since 1670, when the city was chartered in the name of England's King Charles II. Stately mansions, Colonial cottages, churches and public buildings — many older than the American Revolution — stand shoulder to shoulder on broad streets and winding lanes. The rhythmic clip-clop of horse-drawn carriages and the sing-song voices of tour guides and sweetgrass basket vendors fill the air.

Adjacent to this aristocratic South Carolina city of Old World charm lies a string of barrier islands where seniors are finding New World amenities they want for a retirement location. From the Isle of Palms on the north end to Seabrook Island on the south, this area fronting the Atlantic Ocean is known for its mild climate and natural beauty — long beaches with sand dunes and sea oats, lush vegetation including pines and palmettos, and protected harbors and coves perfect for boating.

Retirees settle into quiet, secluded communities on the islands — away from big-city hassles, yet close enough to Charleston to take advantage of its cultural scene, shopping and medical facilities.

Officials at the Center for Carolina Living predict that in coming years the Charleston metropolitan area will draw a larger share of the 10,000 people age 50 and older who move to South Carolina every year.

Patrick Mason, executive director of the center, formerly the South Carolina Retirement Communities Association, sees relocation patterns changing in the state. "Traditionally, Myrtle Beach, Aiken and Hilton Head have been the most popular destinations for retirees in South Carolina," he says. But with in-creased tourism to the Charleston area, more seniors are enticed to consider it for retirement.

"Many of them come on vacation, and they enjoy the lifestyle here so much, they want to retire here," says Amy Blyth of the Charleston Area Convention and Visitors Bureau. "Others have served in the military here, and when they retire this is their first choice. The Charleston area's many military bases provide them with inexpensive shopping, medical care and recreation."

Most of the area's retirees come from Northeastern and Midwestern states such New York, New Jersey, Pennsylvania, Massachusetts, Connecticut, Illinois, Ohio and Michigan.

Charles and Carolyn Betz moved to Seabrook Island from New Canaan, CT, in 1993.

"We wanted a warmer climate and a coastal view," says Charles, 56, a former IBM executive. Although they had been vacationing on the island for a number of years, they scouted the coastline before making up their minds about a retirement site.

"We took a three-week trip through North Carolina, South Carolina and Georgia, up and down the coast, spending three to four days in each place, to 'kick the tires,'" says Charles.

They looked at Hilton Head Island, Charleston, Wild Dunes (a beach-golf resort community) on the Isle of Palms and Savannah, but ended up where they started — at Seabrook. A small island with limited access, Seabrook has about 500 permanent residents. There are no hotels on the island, but many condominiums are available to rent for vacation.

"We decided on Seabrook Island because it's not commercial," he says. "It has magnificent scenery and some won-derful people. The security is superb, the amenities are outstanding, and there's a strong town government."

The Betzes built a home on a site with a marsh in front, a creek in back and boat access to the ocean 500 yards away.

Also among newcomers to Seabrook in 1993 were Charles and Gloria Mangee from Kalamazoo, MI. For more than 10 years, during company meetings and vacations they had looked at possible retirement sites, including Palm Springs, CA; Phoenix and Scottsdale, AZ; and the east and west coasts of Florida.

"We went to Kiawah first for a meeting. We loved that — the geography," says Charles, 63, a former vice president with Upjohn Pharmaceuticals. Then they discovered Seabrook, vacationed there for two years and bought a lot.

Gloria, 65, adds, "We liked the size of the island, the natural beauty and serenity. Also the security and proximity to Charleston."

The Mangees built an oceanfront house, which Charles describes as a blend of contemporary and classical Sea Island architectural traditions. Annual property taxes are about a quarter of what he'd pay on a similar house in Michigan, he says.

Stuart and Sheila Christie settled on Seabrook Island in 1993 after looking up and down the East Coast. "We had a home in Florida — Boca Raton — but it was too crowded and had no seasons," says Stuart, 69.

"We wanted moderate weather, change of seasons, near a city with some cultural activities, good transportation and medical facilities. It (Seabrook) has friendly people and good restaurants. It's a family-oriented island," Stuart says.

Seabrook is a private island held by the property owners, whose association maintains the streets, provides the 11-member, 24-hour security force, garbage pickup and other services. The association's architectural code assures that homes and other structures are consistent with the island's environment; development is kept low profile. The Seabrook club has two 18-hole golf courses, designed by Robert Trent Jones Sr. and Willard Byrd, a 13-court tennis center, equestrian center and other recreational amenities.

The island is a chartered municipality, with a mayor and town council; Charles Mangee serves on the council.

Charleston Barrier Islands, SC

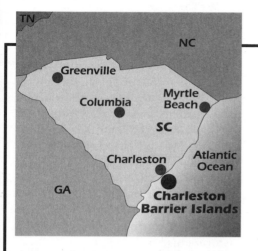

Population: 88,133 in city of Charleston, 316,482 in Charleston County, including Seabrook Island, Kiawah Island, Johns Island, Isle of Palms, North Charleston and Mount Pleasant. Seabrook Island's population is 1,064.

Location: Near the middle of South Carolina's Atlantic coast, halfway between Miami and New York City.

Climate:

	High	Low
January	60	37
July	89	71

Average relative humidity: 56%
Rain: 52 inches.
Snow: Infrequent.
Hot, humid summers, modified by ocean breezes. About 40 percent of annual rainfall occurs in summer. Winters are mild, but temperatures can go below freezing. Area is subject to hurricanes; the last one to hit was Hugo in 1989, which inflicted heavy damage. Elevation nine feet.

Cost of living: 103, based on national average of 100.

Average housing cost: Overall $151,241 for 1,800-square-foot three-bedroom home. Island prices range from the low $100s on James Island to $400,000-$600,000 on Kiawah Island and slightly less on Seabrook Island. Average rent for a two-bedroom apartment is $677 a month.

Sales tax: 6%

Sales tax exemptions: Prescription drugs, eyeglasses, some medical supplies and most services.

State income tax: Graduated in six steps from 2.5% to 7%, depending on income.

Income tax exemptions: Social Security benefits. Retirees under age 65 who are drawing income from qualified retirement plans may deduct up to $3,000 of that income. At age 65, residents may deduct up to $15,000 in income.

Intangibles tax: None.

Estate tax: None, except the state's "pick-up" portion of the federal tax, applicable to taxable estates above $675,000.

Property taxes: All homes are assessed at 4% of market value. The tax rates are: Kiawah Island and Seabrook Island, $260 per $1,000 of assessed value; city of Charleston, $317.30 per $1,000; Mount Pleasant, $278 per $1,000. Yearly taxes: on a $300,000 home on Seabrook, about $3,120; on a $151,241 home in Charleston, about $1,958; on a $135,000 home in Mount Pleasant, about $1,500. All calculations are without the age 65-and-older homestead exemption noted below.

Homestead exemption: $20,000 off market value for residents age 65 or older; none for those under 65 unless disabled.

Security: Officials say there's little crime on the islands, which have limited access, private security forces and communities with gates. The crime rate in Charleston is 104.1 crimes per 1,000 residents, higher than the national average of 46.2. Mount Pleasant's crime rate is 46.7 per 1,000 residents.

Religion: Hundreds of churches and synagogues in the area represent every faith.

Education: Charleston Southern University and College of Charleston offer day and evening continuing-education courses. Trident Technical College specializes in business, engineering, industrial and health fields. Johnson & Wales University offers degrees in culinary arts and hospitality management.

Transportation: No public transportation on the islands but there is public bus service in the city of Charleston and some close-in Charleston County suburban areas.

Health: A full range of health care is provided by 172-bed Charleston Memorial Hospital, 597-bed Medical University of South Carolina, 300-bed Trident Regional Medical Center, 362-bed Bon Secours St. Francis Xavier Hospital, 462-bed Roper Hospital, 235-bed R.H. Johnson U.S. Veterans Administration Medical Center and other major private and public facilities.

Housing options: On Seabrook Island and Kiawah Island, single-family houses start at about $250,000; for information, contact **Seabrook Island Resort**, (800) 845-2475, and **Kiawah Resort Associates**, (800) 654-2924. James Island has homes starting in the $90s. Mount Pleasant, a small city 15 minutes from downtown Charleston, offers homes at a median price of $135,000; older homes are as low as $90,000, and golf communities such as **Charleston National** and **Dunes West** have homes for $145,000 and up.

Visitor lodgings: Wide range of historic bed-and-breakfast inns, deluxe hotels, moderately priced chain motels and furnished villas and condos on the resort islands. Days Inn, (800) 325-2525, historic district, $129-$139 for a double; Holiday Inn Riverview, (800) HOLIDAY, $99-$199; Kiawah Island Resort, (800) 654-2924, from $195; Seabrook Island Resort, (843) 768-1000, from $175; and Wild Dunes Resort, (800) 845-8880, from $165 (seven-day stay required).

Information: Charleston Metro Chamber, P.O. Box 975, Charleston, SC 29402-0975, (843) 577-2510 or www.charlestonchamber.net. Center for Carolina Living, 4201 Blossom St., Columbia, SC 29205, (803) 782-7466 or for its Relocation Resource Line, (800) 849-6683.

The county maintains a full-time fire station on the island, as well as emergency medical services and a mobile library.

"Grocery stores and other shops are close by, but the downside to living here is that we are on an island, 22 miles from Charleston. But after a while, you get used to the drive. The city has so much to offer in the way of cultural activities and other opportunities. The *New York Times* recently did a story on the city's great restaurants. Once a month we have a bus that takes residents to the symphony," says Charles Mangee.

Charleston hosts the world-renowned Spoleto Festival USA, which brings the world's finest singers, dancers, classical, jazz and choral musicians to the "Holy City," as it is nicknamed, each May. Throughout the year, residents enjoy an excellent symphony orchestra, resident theater and dance companies, art exhibitions and performances by touring shows.

"Most of the residents on Seabrook are retirees," Charles adds, "and some of them are working on master's degrees at the College of Charleston. Others, including myself, use their fax modems to do consulting work. You can do everything you ever imagined, except you're in a quiet, secure, beautiful environment."

Most retirees — like the Mangees — custom-build their homes, but many "spec" houses also are available. Single-family homes on Seabrook and neighboring Kiawah Island start at about $250,000. Condos begin in the $190,000s and go up to $300,000-$400,000, depending on size and location near beaches and golf courses.

Kiawah — a mile from Seabrook — also has a chartered town government, but unlike its much smaller neighbor, the island is jointly owned by residents, developers and the Kiawah Island Resort. It's considerably larger and has more commercial development than Seabrook. Although some retirees call Kiawah home, the average age of its approximately 700 year-round residents is about 50.

"We welcome retirees, but we don't target any specific age group," says Jim Stuckey, a realty executive with the Kiawah Resort Associates, which owns all the undeveloped land on the 10,000-acre island. Kiawah Island Resort includes a hotel and about 1,500 privately owned condos, cottages and villas, many available for short-term rental by tourists.

According to Stuckey, the island's least expensive homes, away from the ocean, with three bedrooms and two baths, sell for $245,000. Most homes cost $400,000-$600,000 on Kiawah, slightly less on Seabrook. Kiawah, a gated community, has its own security force and a county fire department. Residents and visitors enjoy five 18-hole championship golf courses, tennis courts, swimming pools, restaurants and shopping.

On the less expensive side, many retirees choose James Island, across the Ashley River southwest of downtown Charleston. Homes in Cross Creek, Harbor Woods and other new developments sell from the low $90,000s to low $100,000s. Also on James Island, the Bishop Gadsden Retirement Community, supported by the Episcopal Diocese of South Carolina, has completed a $30 million expansion to its facilities with 44 one-and two-bedroom cottages with dens and suites and 148 apartments with up to 1,650 square feet. A three-story community center has a modern dining room, swimming pool and fitness center. Monthly rates of $1,200-$1,800 include one daily meal, assistance with medications, social activities, group transportation and other amenities. Bishop Gadsden has a 90-percent refundable entrance fee of $90,000-$200,000, with other refund plans available.

Mount Pleasant, a city of about 32,000 across the Cooper River Bridge 15 minutes northeast of downtown Charleston, is preferred by growing numbers of middle-income retirees. Chuck Aydlette with Coldwell Banker/O'Shaughnessey Realty says the median price of a three-bedroom, two-bath home in the city is $135,000.

"Most of these homes were built in the past five years," Aydlette says. "Some very nice older homes, in excellent condition, are available in the $90s. Many of the neighborhoods have their own community swimming pools, tennis courts and other amenities."

Also in Mount Pleasant, homes in Charleston National, a golf community, start at $145,000. At Dunes West, a golf community developed by Georgia-Pacific Corp., one- and two-story homes on one-acre lots start at about $150,000.

Besides beaches, golf, tennis and water sports, the area has numerous attractions. The city is brimming with historic homes, many open for tours either year-round or during the spring, when gardens are blanketed in azalea and dogwood blossoms. The King Street antiquing district offers one of the largest selections in the South. Patriots Point, just across the Cooper River Bridge from Charleston, is the country's largest maritime museum. Its star attraction is the WWII Yorktown aircraft carrier, open to the public as a historic museum.

Seafood restaurants line both sides of Shem Creek, home of Charleston's shrimping fleet. Sullivan's Island and Isle of Palms are two of the area's best public beaches. All beaches in South Carolina are public domain, but resort communities such as Seabrook and Kiawah have limited access.

Most retirees have few complaints about the area. Summers can get hot, but ocean breezes usually make the islands slightly cooler than the city. Although the cost of living for Charleston is slightly above average, some of the retirees interviewed noted little change in their costs from previous places.

Crime on the islands reportedly is rare. Andrew Fine of Seabrook Island Resort, which markets the properties, says, "There's only one road onto the island and only one road off. We have full-time gated security, and unless you're a homeowner or a guest in one of the rental properties, you can't use our beaches, golf course or other facilities. So crime just doesn't happen."

The retirees interviewed cherish the beauty and serenity of the environment.

"You get a sense of life's true value living on nature's edge," says Charles Mangee. "You get to see how it all works — the tides, the effect of the moon's gravity on us. You understand how fragile life is by living in a very fragile area." ●

Charlottesville, Virginia

Retirees follow Jefferson's lead to Virginia

By Bob Lane

In 1809, after finishing his second presidential term, Thomas Jefferson knew exactly where to retire: Monticello, his mountaintop home outside Charlottesville, where Virginia's rolling green countryside meets the misty Blue Ridge Mountains. Jefferson considered this area to be "the Eden of the United States."

With equal certitude, Carlos and Jean Burns think they made the right decision to retire at Lake Monticello, a 1,500-home subdivision a few miles from its namesake. They came south from Wilton, CT.

"I still marvel at the almost perfect balance of retirement factors in this community," says Jean. "We have good neighbors, low taxes, reasonable living costs, safety and great medical facilities. This place is Brigadoon."

Her enthusiasm can be understood by glancing out their living room window at the peaceful setting. A pontoon boat rocks idly at water's edge. Around a 350-acre lake are homes situated among loblolly pines, tennis courts, a golf course, community pool and a wide, sandy beach.

While they live in a community filled with 20th-century amenities, the area surrounding them is steeped in early American history. Michie Tavern, circa 1770, was built on land granted to Patrick Henry's father and is one of the oldest homesteads in the state. Charlottesville itself has more than 200 historic buildings, including a courthouse originally built in 1762 and rebuilt in 1803. In the early days, the courthouse served as the "common temple," where townspeople came for worship and political gatherings. And, near Jefferson's estate is Ash Lawn, the home of President James Monroe.

Jean and Carlos describe their lives and their community in superlatives. "We are perfectly happy here," Jean says. "It is a gorgeous community.

When we moved here, our property taxes were $600 versus $4,000 back in Wilton for a similar house. Up North, I had a burglar alarm by my bed; down here we have guarded gates and two police cars roving our streets 24 hours a day. And we have 60 neighbors who comprise a really gung-ho fire and rescue squad."

Carlos tested the rescue squad the hard way when he suffered a heart attack four years ago. His neighbor, a cardio-technician on the rescue squad, quickly came to his aid until the ambulance arrived. "It always seemed like half the people on the golf course carried beepers, and I now keenly appreciate that fact," says Carlos, a golfer.

Jean says it's a caring community: "Someone is listening for you all the time."

Jean and Carlos stay busy in retirement. Jean was elected to the board of directors of Lake Monticello's homeowners association, and Carlos started his own business, a self-serve ministorage warehouse, in 1992. A former executive with General Foods, he enjoys the challenge of steering a company on his own. "No one has total say in the corporate world," says Carlos. "This little business will test my judgment."

Jack and Mary Matthewman selected a different option when they were home-shopping in the area. They already had retired once, back in 1975, to a contemporary single-family home on the second tee of a golf course in Grantham, NH.

Jack's last job before retirement was as a sales executive for Texaco in Boston, commuting from Wellesley. They liked the Northeast, so a move to Grantham kept the couple close to the kids and provided the skiing and golfing they enjoy. They also liked New Hampshire because it had no income tax or sales tax, Jack says.

But after 15 years, the ice and snow got to them. At first, the solution was an annual winter sojourn to Naples, FL, for a month or so. On their trips, Jack and Mary stopped several times at Charlottesville, which struck them as a "nice little place." It's about 70 miles northwest of Richmond and only about 20 miles from the scenic Blue Ridge Parkway and Skyline Drive in the Blue Ridge Mountains.

When they decided to move to a warmer clime, they added Charlottesville to the list of communities recommended by their friends: Aiken and Kiawah, SC, and Pinehurst and Advance, NC.

Over several years, Mary researched a move south in travel and retirement magazines and books. When the time came to move, both agreed that Charlottesville had the best mix of culture and weather.

"Charlottesville reminded me of Wellesley," Mary says. "It is an attractive, wooded college town, with concerts, lectures, football games — all the things that make a town vibrant."

The city is home to the acclaimed University of Virginia, which swells the town's population of about 41,000 by another 16,000 when classes are in session. The school, an integral part of the community, was founded and designed by Jefferson. Its classic architecture is considered outstanding.

Many cultural events — plays, concerts, exhibits — are offered on campus. The historic downtown area has been turned into a pedestrian mall of shops and restaurants and is the site of live summer concerts. Ash Lawn is the setting for comic operas in the summer.

Throughout the area, springtime brings a burst of color and celebrations, including the Dogwood Festival and Historic Garden Week, when many private estates are open to the public.

Besides the cultural opportunities, the Charlottesville area offers a variety of recreation in all seasons. There are 33 golf courses, 45 local tennis courts and 13 public lakes. Nearby Wintergreen resort has skiing, and the Shenandoah National Park, with 174 trails, is a favorite getaway for hikers. Civil War buffs can visit 84 sites in the area.

Both the mountains and the Atlantic Ocean protect the area from extreme temperatures, winter and summer.

The Matthewmans, lifelong New Englanders, found that Charlottesville had as hot a climate as they wanted. "We have never lived in air-conditioning before this," Mary says.

They toured the area with a real estate agent and bought a townhouse in Branchlands, a retirement community centrally located near shopping and entertainment.

In retirement, Jack and Mary already had tried life in a single-family house. The second time around, they wanted someone else to handle the painting, gutters, landscaping and other such chores that the $90-per-month Branchlands dues buy for them. And they wanted to be close to shopping and recreation.

Standing at the rear bay window of their four-bedroom, three-bath town-home, Mary gestures to the north at Fashion Square, the premiere shopping mall in Charlottesville. Its 65 stores are anchored by Sears and Penney's, and the mall opens at 8 a.m. for walkers.

"Just over the rooftops three blocks away is a magnificent senior center," Mary points out. This 14,000-square-

Charlottesville, VA

Population: 41,000 in Charlottesville, plus 18,000 students at the University of Virginia during the school year. Three-county metropolitan area has 131,000 residents.

Location: The city sits just east of the Blue Ridge Mountains, about 120 miles southwest of Washington, DC.

Climate:

	High	Low
January	45	27
July	87	67

Average relative humidity: 52%
Rain: 46 inches.
Snow: 24 inches.
Summer days aren't as humid as many places on the East Coast, and surrounding mountains make winters warmer than locations west of the mountains.

Cost of living: Average (specific index not available).
Median housing cost: $134,000
Sales tax: 4.5 percent (raised only once since 1968).
Sales tax exemptions: Prescription drugs, eyeglasses, some medical supplies, professional services.
State income tax: Graduated in four steps from 2 percent to 5.75 percent, depending on income.

Income tax exemptions: Social Security benefits. There is an $800 personal exemption for residents age 65 or older. There is a $6,000 deduction per person from adjusted gross income for residents age 62-64, and a $12,000 deduction per person for residents 65 or older.
Intangibles tax: None.
Estate tax: None, except the state's "pick-up" portion of the federal tax, applicable to taxable estates above $675,000.
Property tax: Rates are $11.10 per $1,000 in Charlottesville and $7.20 per $1,000 in Albemarle County, based on 100% of fair market value. In the city, the tax on a $134,000 home is $1,487, and in the county, $965.
Homestead exemption: Homeowners age 65 or older with a gross income of less than $22,000 and assets of less than $75,000 (excluding home value) receive an exemption of a portion of property tax due.
Security: 70.6 crimes per 1,000 residents, higher than the national average of 46.2 crimes per 1,000 residents.
Religion: More than 50 churches represent 16 denominations.
Education: Adult courses at Charlottesville-Albemarle Technical Education Center, Piedmont Virginia Community College and the University of Virginia's School of Continuing Education.
Transportation: City-county bus lines into many neighborhoods. Richmond International Airport is 75 miles away.
Health: City is a major regional health-care center. A teaching hospital at the University of Virginia's Medical School has 550 beds and 19 operating rooms. The renovated Martha Jefferson Hospital has 221 beds, and Piedmont Health Care Center has 230 beds for long-term care.
Housing options: Lots at **Lake Monticello,** (804) 589-8263, start at $10,000 inland, about $40,000 on the golf course and $100,000 on the waterfront. Three-bedroom homes start at $80,000 on an inland lot. At **Glenmore,** (804) 977-8865, lots from $140,000 to more than $200,000 surround a golf course. Two- to four-bedroom cottages start from $380,000. **Forest Lakes,** (804) 973-7222, is a close-in, midpriced, single-family subdivision ($117,000 and up) with recreational amenities. At **Branchlands,** (804) 973-9044, villas close to the Senior Center sell for $92,000-$131,000. Life-care facilities: **Westminster Canterbury,** (804) 980-9164, is a not-for-profit facility with fees. **Our Lady of Peace,** (804) 973-1155, has no entrance fees. **The Colonnades,** (804) 971-1892, is associated with the University of Virginia and managed by Marriott Corp.
Visitor lodging: 20 hotels and motels, including the Hampton Inn, $77, (804) 978-7888. An alternative is Charlottesville Bed and Breakfast Reservation Service, (804) 979-7264.
Information: Charlottesville Regional Chamber of Commerce, P.O. Box 1564, Charlottesville, VA 22902, (804) 295-3141 or www.cvillechamber.org. Also, the Senior Center, (804) 974-7756. For a local real estate publication that includes mortgage rates, contact Real Estate Weekly, (804) 977-8206.

foot facility, built in 1991 from private funds, has three cavernous meeting rooms, a craft shop and door-to-door handicapped-accessible bus service. For annual dues of $35, almost 3,000 residents participate in dances, lectures, travel tours, fashion shows, potluck suppers, crafts, clubs, card games and Bible studies.

Ned and Fran Morris also moved twice in retirement. They sought still another lifestyle option: "lifetime security," a contractual package that has a real estate component but long-term health care as well.

They retired to Charlottesville from New York. At the time their son was working on his doctorate at the University of Virginia, so they had visited Charlottesville frequently. Their first retirement house was an 1845 estate on three acres outside Charlottesville. Ned, a former advertising executive, and Fran, a self-described "household engineer," enjoyed fixing up and adding to the little farm. But they always thought the best solution for their retirement years eventually would be a life-care community.

They were elated when, in the mid-1980s, a not-for-profit organization known as Westminster Canterbury of the Blue Ridge (WCBR) started a facility overlooking Charlottesville. Even more fortunate, WCBR admired Ned's marketing background and put him on its board of directors. Ned and Fran decided this was the retirement community they wanted. Entering the development early allowed them to put custom touches in their duplex, like a brick fireplace, a sun room and 9-foot ceilings to give 6-foot-4 Ned some breathing room.

Ned says that while retirees considering life-care communities often suffer "sticker shock" from entrance fees, they need to understand what they're getting for their money.

For example, the smallest one-bedroom cottage at WCBR requires a minimum entrance fee (with three refund options) of $182,686 for two persons, plus a monthly maintenance fee of $2,335.

But, Ned notes, that money buys more than just real estate. "You are buying a contract with an institution to take care of you and your spouse the rest of your life, no matter what happens to you," he says.

Contracts differ among communities that provide health care. What Ned likes most about his contract is that there are no extra fees if either he or his wife ever needs the services of the nursing care facility on the grounds.

"The best thing you can do at age 60 is to sit back and figure out how to take care of yourself and your spouse in the years to come," says Ned. "We figure the kindest thing we could do for our kids was to sign up in a life-care community, even if they don't inherit a red cent."

Obviously, the Burnses, Matthewmans and Morrises planned their retirement from three different viewpoints — but all three couples share a conviction that the Charlottesville area is right for them.

As it was for Jefferson, writing to a friend in 1787. His words are engraved on a wall at the area visitor center: "All my wishes end, where I hope my days will end, at Monticello."●

Clemson, South Carolina

College spirit enriches this lakeside town in the rolling South Carolina hills

By Mary Lu Abbott

Two centuries ago, as calendars turned into the 1800s, Americans were discovering a verdant corner of South Carolina, building second homes there and retiring to enjoy the scenery and climate. As the new century unfolds, the scenario plays anew for modern-day retirees in the foothills of the mountains that bond the Carolinas and Georgia.

Known as the "upcountry," or upstate, the region about halfway between the metropolitan areas of Atlanta and Charlotte retains its natural beauty, the rolling hills and towering trees enhanced by a string of lakes. Glimpses of the distant Blue Ridge Mountains provide visible evidence for their name. Historically agricultural, the region also is attracting light industry and high-tech companies, some of their buildings set along country roads where signs still alert drivers to the possibility of deer darting from the woods.

Nestled in the hills of historic Pickens, Oconee and Anderson counties are a number of small towns, the most notable being Clemson about 11 miles from the traffic on Interstate 85. On the shores of Lake Hartwell and partially hidden among canopies of trees, Clemson exudes a serene aura, blending history and tradition with the energy and vibrancy of the renowned university for which it's named.

David and Julia Wise had plane tickets to Arizona to check out retirement sites there when a friend suggested they consider the Clemson area. "We came and liked it so much we bought a house in two days," says Julia. "We like the weather and the four seasons — spring and fall are glorious. We're close to the mountains, and it's a half-day drive to the ocean."

David was a veterinarian with the Air Force, so the Wises moved frequently, and they sampled a couple of other retirement sites before settling here. After spending a summer in Beaufort, SC, on the coast, they decided it was "too hot and buggy," and after a year in Cascade, CO, they thought it was too isolated. When they came to this region, they first bought in Seneca, about five miles from Clemson, and for several years David served the university as veterinarian. In 1994, they moved to the Clemson Downs retirement community, where they have a spacious apartment and enjoy community activities that include classical concerts in a new entertainment facility.

Chuck and Betty Cruickshank, who lived in upstate New York outside Rochester, discovered Clemson when they came through the area to visit their sons at the University of Georgia at Athens. "The Finger Lakes area (of New York) looks like this. It reminded us of home — without the snow," says Betty, 68. They also considered retiring to nearby Asheville, NC, and to Florida.

Though the town's population is only about 12,000, that represents a major growth since 1960 when residents numbered about 1,500. Each fall, the population more than doubles as about 17,000 undergraduate and graduate students start classes at the university.

Beyond simply sharing names, the town and university are closely intertwined and form an integral part of South Carolina history that's dear to the hearts of thousands of Southerners. Clemson was home to the eminent orator and statesman John C. Calhoun, 1782-1850, who was in national politics for 40 years, serving about 20 years in Congress (most of them as a senator), as secretary of war for James Monroe, as vice president for John Quincy Adams and Andrew Jackson and as secretary of state for John Tyler. Many may recall from U.S. history classes that Calhoun, Daniel Webster and Henry Clay were eloquent, powerful speakers of their time and that Calhoun became a staunch states' rights advocate.

Born at Abbeville to the south, Calhoun bought a small two-story cottage here in 1825 when he was vice president and expanded it for his family, establishing a plantation known as Fort Hill. The community became known as Calhoun and was part of the Pendleton District, which was attracting wealthy, well-educated plantation owners and other well-to-do families who wanted to escape the sultry summers in the "lowcountry," as the swampy coastal area is called. They came "upcountry" to build homes in the mountains where summers were more moderate and there were cool streams and abundant waterfalls.

Calhoun's daughter, Anna Maria, married Thomas Green Clemson, an advocate of science education and its application in agriculture. Clemson bought the plantation from Calhoun, and like other Southerners after the Civil War pondered the economic future of the region. Upon his death in 1888 without any heirs, he bequeathed the plantation and the rest of his estate to South Carolina to start an agricultural and mechanical college. Thus Clemson was founded in 1889, graduated its first class in 1893 and over the years diversified its curriculum and became a major university. A national historic landmark open to visitors, the Calhoun home sits on a tree-covered hilltop surrounded by college buildings. Most of the campus and some of the town that grew around it, now named Clemson, were part of the plantation.

"The combination of small town and university gives it a unique quality," says Walter Cook of the attributes that he and his wife, Grace, like about Clemson. "Students bring a vitality and energy to the community."

In their 60s, the Cooks were pleasantly surprised at the numerous events in which they could participate and the educational stimulation from the university. They moved here in 1991 from western Pennsylvania after he retired from Quaker State Corp., and for three years he worked in corporate development for the university.

The Wises, who are in their early 70s, like the Clemson area for its "large number of people with the same cultural and educational level and social interests as ours," says David. Julia enjoys the diversity of the town, from its many university offerings to its proximity to Atlanta.

The Cruickshanks also take advantage of the cultural programs, entertainment and sports provided by the

Clemson, SC

Population: About 12,100 residents in town, about 17,000 enrolled in Clemson University.

Location: In the foothills of the Blue Ridge Mountains in the northwestern corner of the state, about 30 miles southwest of the booming Greenville area and about 125 miles from Atlanta to the southwest and Charlotte to the northeast. Altitude is 850 feet.

Climate:

	High	Low
January	50	30
July	88	68

Average relative humidity: 54%
Rain: 51 inches.
Snow: 6 inches.
Cost of living: Average (specific index not available).
Average housing cost: $124,160 in the Clemson-Pendleton area, including some lake property.
Sales tax: 6%
Sales tax exemptions: Prescription drugs.
State income tax: Graduated in six steps from 2.5% to 7%, depending on income.
Income tax exemptions: Social Security benefits. Retirees under age 65 who are drawing income from qualified retirement plans may deduct up to $3,000 of that income. At age 65, residents may deduct up to $15,000 in income.
Intangibles tax: None.

Estate tax: None, except the state's portion of the federal tax, applicable to taxable estates above $675,000.
Property tax: Clemson homeowners pay a tax rate of $286.20 ($82 city, $204.20 county) per $1,000 in valuation, with homes assessed at 4% of market value. Owners receive sales tax credits from the city (currently .001543 of the market value) and county (currently .001496 of market value) and property tax relief from the state for up to $399.20 for homes valued above $100,000. Gross yearly tax on a $124,160 home would be about $1,421; with credits noted, the tax drops to about $645.
Homestead exemption: In addition to the credits noted above, at age 65 owners receive an exemption of $20,000 off the market value of their homes and further credits based on the homestead exemption.
Personal property tax: Same city and county tax rates and sales tax credits apply to vehicles and boats, which are assessed at 10.5% of market value.
Security: 31.2 crimes per 1,000 residents, below the national average of 46.2 crimes per 1,000 residents.
Religion: There are about two dozen places of worship in the immediate area. Jewish synagogues are located in nearby Anderson and Greenville.
Education: Seniors can audit classes free at Clemson, which also offers some noncredit, continuing-education programs.
Transportation: Clemson Area Transit runs free bus service around the campus and town. There's Amtrak service, and Greenville-Spartanburg Airport has commercial jet flights.
Health: The 160-bed Oconee Memorial Hospital, located in neighboring Seneca, has 110 doctors and provides

emergency services, including cardiac care. More extensive medical services are available in Anderson, about 20 miles away, and in Greenville, the regional hub, about 30 miles away.
Housing options: There are older neighborhoods and newer subdivisions in Clemson and adjacent Pendleton, and there are gated communities, some with golf courses, around the adjacent lakes, particularly Keowee. Among options popular with retirees: **Heritage Oaks**, a landscaped subdivision with green spaces in Pendleton, is about 3 years old and has homes from the $99,000s to the $140,000s. **Magnolia Point** in Pendleton includes lawn maintenance for its single-family homes, which run $98,000-$102,000. In Clemson, **Country Walk** is a master-planned community with a pool, clubhouse and putting green among amenities; homes start at $200,000. **Clemson Downs**, (864) 654-1155, is a retirement community with private homes and apartments, assisted-living apartments and a nursing care center. Around the lakes, **Keowee Key**, (800) 537-5253, is one of the region's premier resort communities with a golf course, country club and water sports; condominiums and townhomes start around $65,000 and homes from about $125,000. Among the real estate agencies that can help locate homes is Carolina Real Estate, (864) 654-6202.
Visitor lodging: The Clemson-Pendleton area has B&B lodging, motels and rental properties on the lakes. Among choices are the Hampton Inn, (800) HAMPTON, which has double rooms from $69.
Information: Clemson Area Chamber of Commerce, P.O. Box 1622, Clemson, SC 29633, (800) 542-0746, www.clemsonchamber.org.

university. "The new Brooks Center for the Performing Arts is a beautiful theater with perfect acoustics, and there's a Clemson Little Theater," says Betty. Besides numerous university productions and performances, there are concerts and programs by emerging and established artists from elsewhere. Betty says ticket prices usually are lower here than in larger cities nearby.

Come fall, Clemson's colors show not only in beautiful foliage but also in university sports as the orange carpet is rolled out for the football team to come thundering into Clemson Memorial Stadium to the roar of 80,000-plus fans. The site is more commonly known as Death Valley Stadium, so named back in the 1940s by an opposing coach whose team suffered frequently at the hands of the Clemson Tigers. The nickname was enhanced in the 1960s when an alumnus placed a rock from Death Valley, CA, on the players' route into the stadium. Facing a tough foe, the Clemson coach suggested the players rub the Death Valley rock for good luck as they passed it. After the win that day, the ceremonial touching of the rock by each player has become an opening tradition for every game.

With many championships to their credit and repeated trips to bowl games, the Tigers draw large crowds to their stadium, which officially seats about 80,000. Rising 177 feet on one side and 159 feet on the other side, the stadium exerts a commanding presence in this small community where trees are taller than nearly all the buildings. The stadium also hosts major concerts.

With years of experience, the town seems to know how to handle an influx of 80,000 or more fans for games and other events. Several highways provide access, and main routes become one-way into town before major events and one-way out afterward. Those in the know come early or stay late and enjoy tailgate parties. The town also has many restaurants and more accommodations than many other towns its size.

Betty says the football fans, many of them repeat visitors and alumni, generally know where they're going and where to park, but traffic problems sometimes arise when first-time visitors come for concerts in the stadium. School spirit and support run high throughout the community. Orange tiger paw prints color streets, and merchants in the downtown shops adjacent to the campus offer Clemson memorabilia and items in the school's dominant colors, orange and white.

A part of the Calhoun plantation, the South Carolina Botanical Garden by the campus showcases the area's colorful and fragrant seasons, from camellias in winter to azaleas and daffodils in spring, with wildflowers, rhododendron and honeysuckle leading into summer's annuals and perennials and chrysanthemums and bright foliage in fall.

The Cruickshanks volunteer at the botanical gardens and established a namesake garden of hostas, which they tend regularly. They play golf and hike in the mountains. The Wises enjoy gardening, walking and bird-watching and have assisted in rehabilitation of injured wild animals. Julia helped found the "Keep Oconee Beautiful" Association, which now numbers more than 500 members and assists in keeping the county clean.

The Cooks both do several types of volunteer work at the university, particularly at the Brooks Center for the Performing Arts, and they play golf and tennis. The university has a golf course, and several others are located in the surrounding counties.

Some retirees relocate here for the lake recreation and outdoor sports. Sailing, windsurfing, water-skiing, fishing, canoeing and boating are popular on Lake Hartwell, which borders the town, and adjacent lakes Keowee and Jocassee, both taking names from the Cherokee Indian heritage of the area. Many gated communities are built along the lake shores; the best-known development is Keowee Key with its country club, golf course, marina, hiking trails and condominiums, townhomes and homes for sale and rent. For those who want action, the nearby Chattooga River rushes through the mountains, offering white-water trips through rugged back country.

All three couples say it's easy to make friends in the community, which is accustomed to welcoming new students each year. "I know someone's life history after standing with them for five minutes in the checkout line," says Julia, who was born in England and adjusted to making new friends often as the Wises moved in the Air Force.

The couples find little to fault in the area, though Grace dislikes the summer humidity, which can be high at times. She and her husband were surprised by a personal property tax on cars and found their state income tax higher here than in Pennsylvania. The Wises were surprised to see abandoned vehicles and appliances outside some homes in the country, a reminder of rural poverty.

For those who might consider the area for retirement, David says, "I would encourage them, but they need to understand that this is not a big city."

"Come well ahead of time and look it over; talk to people who live here. Be curious and satisfy yourselves that it's a fit," says Walter.

Chuck, who's 71, suggests not moving too far out from town. "The action is here in Clemson. We could have bought a place at Keowee Key but we wanted to be close-in to take advantage of what the university offers," he says.●

Coeur d'Alene, Idaho

The Idaho Panhandle offers a playground of rivers, mountains and lakes

By Richard L. Fox

Lewis and Clark put it on the map. French-speaking explorers and fur traders named it. Now tourism, retirees and refugees from urban concerns are shaping Coeur d'Alene, the hub of Idaho's panhandle.

In the course of their expedition to find a Northwest Passage in the early 1800s, Meriwether Lewis and William Clark were met by the Nez Perce Indians 100 miles south of present-day Coeur d'Alene. Dispatches to President Thomas Jefferson recounted their explorations and brought new details about this great Western territory to map makers, opening the region for exploration and eventual settlement.

The name Coeur d'Alene, roughly translated as "heart like an awl," refers to the keenly sharp negotiating skills of the Schee-Chu-Umsh Indians, whose village occupied the area when French traders arrived several decades after Lewis and Clark.

Today, the Coeur d'Alene Indians are based about 30 miles to the south, where they have achieved economic success with a popular bingo and gaming casino. The rugged wilderness and mystique of which Lewis and Clark wrote still permeate this region.

"When I first came here, the town reminded me of my hometown of Newport Beach, CA, when I was a child," says Shirlee Wandrocke. "The town, the lake, the mountains just overwhelmed me (along with) the warm, congenial, lovely people. I just have a spiritual feeling living here."

Shirlee, 59, made what might be termed a reconnaissance move to the area in 1983, leaving husband Dick, 63, in Newport Beach to manage the family business. She commuted back and forth until 1990, when Dick turned the business over to their son and joined Shirlee in Coeur d'Alene. Their first home sat on a hillside over-

looking the Spokane River where it joins Lake Coeur d'Alene, but they recently moved to a new home that sits on one acre of land right in town.

The Wandrockes looked at potential retirement sites in Washington, Oregon and Jackson Hole, WY, before deciding on Coeur d'Alene. "It measured up to all of our requirements. We had to live within an hour's drive of a large city (Spokane) for concerts and symphonies. We also wanted to be near an airport because of our children living in Southern California. We had to be in sight of water . . . and it had to have a decent hospital, because I was bringing my mother with me," Shirlee says.

The desire to live "in sight of water" is shared by natives and newcomers to the area. Rustic cabins, lake villas, condominiums and 10-acre estates all share spectacular views of the lake and surrounding mountains.

With a population greater than 32,000, Coeur d'Alene is the seat of Kootenai County in the northwest Idaho Panhandle. It sits on the north shore of Lake Coeur d'Alene near forests and mountains that beckon climbers, hikers, bikers, skiers and snowmobilers. Some might expect this town to be merely a launch pad for recreational opportunities in the hinterlands.

"Not so," says Dick Compton, 63, who spent 33 years traveling around the country and the world for IBM before retiring to Coeur d'Alene in 1993 with his wife, Janette, a native of the town.

Janette, 64, likes the small-town atmosphere. "It doesn't matter who you are or where you've been — you are accepted," she says.

"Cultural opportunities are good, health-care facilities are good — and getting better — and crime is a minimum issue. There are no gangs and (there is) good law enforcement," says

Dick, who finds that civic leaders are more accessible in Coeur d'Alene. "You can know the people who are prominent and influential in the city and become involved much easier than in a large city like Seattle. It's the right size," he says.

Shortly after retiring here, Dick became involved in local politics and was elected chairman of the Kootenai County Board of Commissioners. He also serves on the board of Jobs Plus, which recruits small businesses to the area.

Coeur d'Alene has experienced a growth spurt in the last few years, creating mixed feelings among residents. "Whether you like it depends on whether you are buying or selling," says Dick. "Prices of real estate have gone up considerably. We're having a tough time absorbing the growth that's going on — the social and economic changes."

He feels that the local economy is good. "When we grew up around here there wasn't a lot of employment... there's more now — more opportunities for young people to go to work in meaningful jobs," he says.

Residential sales statistics chart Coeur d'Alene's growth. In 1990, permits were issued for construction of 526 new residences. In 1999, 1,294 permits were issued. The average home sale price was $77,419 in 1990, rising to $129,669 in 1999.

Jim and Margie Porter moved to the area from Diamond Bar, CA, in 1990. "Our home has probably tripled in value since we bought it," says Jim. "Five acres used to run $20,000. Now it runs from $60,000 to $80,000."

The influx of new residents has increased local traffic, as Dick Wandrocke notes. "When Shirlee moved here (in 1983) there were two stoplights. When I moved here (in 1990) I could go anywhere in town from my home in five minutes. Now it takes 20 to 25 minutes. I still haven't adjusted to that, and I'm frequently late for meetings," he says.

Shirlee takes it in stride. "You could not drag me back to California — just too many people," she says. The traffic is horrendous. I go insane when I drive down there."

With more than 300 businesses, shops and restaurants, downtown Coeur d'Alene is clean, open and tourist-oriented. The trendy, fashionable shops of Coeur d'Alene Resort Plaza spill into the downtown shopping district. Other shopping venues include Silver Lake Mall and, in neighboring Post Falls, a factory outlet mall with 60 stores.

Small, picturesque communities that range in size from 225 to 10,000 residents cozy up to the borders of Coeur d'Alene. Jim and Margie Porter chose Hayden Lake (population about 7,000), eight miles to the north.

"We found a perfect place in Hayden Lake," says Jim, 67. "A great house... five acres of timber. It's just heaven."

"We built a barn and bought a horse for Jim and a pony for our grandchildren," adds Margie, 63. "We have an acre of grass. When you're out on the patio you feel like you're in the national forest."

Jim's 10 bypasses and a pacemaker were not enough to move the couple from their home in Hayden Lake, though Jim did travel to famed Scripps Institute in California for his most critical surgical needs. He still splits his own firewood, storing up enough for winter. "When I can't chop wood, take care of that acre of lawn (and) my horse, and put the hay up for the winter, we'll probably have to move," he says.

"But we won't move out of the area," Margie declares.

Lake Coeur d'Alene is the nucleus that binds together the town, a large resort and many recreational areas. Just one of some 60 lakes in a 60-mile radius, this 26-square-mile, huckleberry-hued playground is an outdoor paradise.

Homesites and boat docks line the lake's forested 135-mile shoreline. Standing out on the horizon is the Coeur d'Alene Resort, an expansive complex with a multistoried hotel, marina, boat rentals, private beach, cross-country and downhill skiing and more. The fairways of the resort's championship golf course frame the water's edge, and cruise boats ferry sightseers for a close-up view of the nearly five-million-pound, one-of-a-kind floating green on the 14th hole.

The steamboats that moved mining

Coeur d'Alene, ID

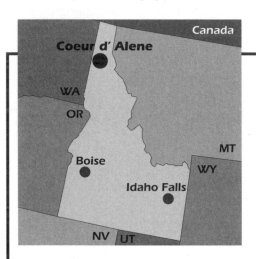

Population: 32,200 in Coeur d'Alene, 104,200 in Kootenai County.
Location: At the edge of scenic Lake Coeur d'Alene in northern Idaho's panhandle. Elevation is 2,187 feet.
Climate:

	High	Low
January	35	22
July	86	52

Average relative humidity: 46%
Rain: 27 inches. **Snow:** 80 inches.
Cost of living: Slightly above average (specific index not available).
Average housing cost: $129,669, according to the Kootenai County Assessor's Office.
Sales tax: 5%
Sales tax exemptions: Prescription drugs and most services are exempt.
State income tax: Graduated from 2% to 8.2%, depending on income.
Income tax exemptions: Social Security benefits are exempt, and some deductions apply for those age 65 and older and receiving pensions.
Intangibles tax: None
Estate tax: None, except the state's "pick-up" portion of the federal tax, applicable to taxable estates above $675,000.
Property tax: At the average rate of $14 per $1,000, the annual tax on a $129,669 home would be about $1,115, with homestead exemption noted below.
Homestead exemption: State law exempts 50% or $50,000 (whichever is less) of assessed value of the primary residence, exclusive of land value.
Personal property tax: None
Security: 80.4 crimes per 1,000 residents, higher than the national average of 46.2 crimes per 1,000 residents.
Religion: 26 Catholic and Protestant denominations are represented.
Education: Lewis-Clark State College's Coeur d'Alene Center offers the final two years of a baccalaureate degree program in a number of disciplines. The University of Idaho Coeur d'Alene Center allows students to complete undergraduate and graduate degrees.
Transportation: Spokane International Airport, 35 miles west, is served by seven major carriers.
Health: Kootenai Medical Center has 187 beds and 24-hour emergency care. The North Idaho Immediate Care Center and North Idaho Cancer Center, both in Coeur d'Alene, offer additional healthcare facilities. Six major medical centers and hospitals are less than an hour away in Spokane, offering advanced medical and surgical procedures.
Housing options: Arrow Point Resort offers two-bedroom, two-bath condos on the lake starting at $180,000. **Coeur d'Alene Place**, with parks and a trail system, has new homes priced from $100,000 to the low $200,000s. Lake-view homesites are expensive, starting at $160,000 in one area minutes from town.
Visitor lodging: The Coeur d'Alene Resort, $79-$229 in winter, $99-$429 in summer, (800) 688-5253. Comfort Inn, $59-$62 in winter, $71-$95 in summer, (800) 424-6423.
Information: Coeur d'Alene Area Chamber of Commerce, P.O. Box 850, Coeur d'Alene, Idaho 83816, (208) 664-3194 or www.coeurdalene.org.

and lumbering supplies in the early 1900s are gone. Now boats take off with parasailers in tow, and sailboats and cabin cruisers barely leave a wake as they lazily ply the calm waters. Heron and osprey circle high above the vessels in summertime, and in January and February avid bird-watchers scan the skies for bald eagles, which fish the lake for kokanee salmon as they migrate to warmer climes.

The Coeur d'Alene, Spokane and St. Joe rivers, flowing in and out of the lake, abound with salmon, trout and bass. In some places, white-water rapids provide a thrill a minute for rafters, canoeists and kayakers.

Mountain peaks are visible to the north, south and east of Coeur d'Alene. National forests and state parks make up more than 50 percent of the Idaho Panhandle.

"Camping is absolutely wonderful up here," says Shirlee Wandrocke. "You can go anywhere and find camp-grounds — primitive or with all of the facilities."

There also are opportunities for bik-ing, hiking and climbing, and it's not uncommon to spot a moose, elk, deer or mountain lion in the higher eleva-tions during summer months.

When temperatures dip (the aver-age January low is 22 degrees), boats are put in dry docks, and snowmo-biles, skis, snowshoes and ice skates are brought out of storage. Those who enjoy ice fishing break out their ice picks and cold-weather gear to try their luck on area lakes.

Four alpine ski resorts at eleva-tions of 6,000 to 7,000 feet offer trails for downhill skiers, while literally hundreds of miles of cross-country and snowmobile trails crisscross the mountains.

Jim and Margie Foster love the cold and snow. "We don't go south like the snowbirds," Margie says. "We stay here with our two snowmobiles and play." But she cautions those think-ing about moving here to consider the weather. "Everyone can't handle the winters. Some friends tried it for four years, gave up and moved to Arizona," says Margie.

"The good news is there's four sea-sons. The bad news is there's four seasons," jokes Dick Compton. "We get some snow and we get some win-ter. If you're concerned about being able to cope with that, you may want to look south." ●

Dade City, Florida

Forget beaches – this Florida town has hills, oak trees and antique shops

By Carol Godwin

In a state known for its palm trees and beaches, Dade City boasts neither.

"Florida isn't all beach," observes Louis Sclafani. "People normally think Florida is flat, but the Pasco County countryside has rolling hills, citrus groves and ranches."

"It's not the Florida most people envision," adds Richard Barraclough. "No (or few) palm trees — they're an hour drive south to the other Florida. Dade City is a very friendly small-town America."

Janet Chouinard surprises most people when she says, "I live on a hill" — something she didn't expect to find in Florida.

To Josephine Bellows, Dade City "reminds us of a quiet town on Long Island. The traffic is not heavy and there are no crowds of vacationers. I-4 (slicing the state east and west near Tampa) is like the Long Island Expressway."

The Sclafanis, the Barracloughs, the Bellowses and Janet Chouinard, all former residents of the Northeast, have found Dade City an ideal place to retire. And for good reason — Dade City is a quaint, award-winning small town nestled in Central Florida's undulating hills northeast of Tampa. A recognized Main Street community, the city's people-oriented Streetscape Plan of canopied oaks, fine eateries and shops are a welcome change of pace from increasingly crowded, busy cities.

"Dade City is clean and picturesque, with nice little lunch places and a Main Street full of antique shops and boutiques my wife loves," says Louis Sclafani.

The late Florida Gov. Lawton Chiles dubbed Dade City "Florida's Outstanding Rural Community of the Year - 1994." Of the 99 cities and towns profiled by authors Richard and Betty Fox in "Where to Retire in Florida," Dade City is one of only five places that each author ranked a five-star retirement place. High on the list of good impressions is the warmth, friendliness and helpfulness of the townspeople.

Long known for its graceful oak trees that shade neighborly byways, the town of about 6,000 residents was recognized as a Tree City USA by the National Arbor Day Foundation, a non-profit educational organization dedicated to tree planting and environmental stewardship.

Incorporated in 1889, Dade City originally was settled as an agricultural community in Florida's rich citrus region. Succulent fruit still comes from the environs, including the little community of St. Joseph, known as the Kumquat Capital of the World. Several back-to-back winters of hard freezes forced some citrus farms to other options that now include hothouses of decorative foliage and hillsides of fresh Christmas trees popular with the locals and families who drive from Tampa to cut their own.

Dade City's small 2.8-square-mile city limits harbor a treasure trove of historical sites, with 63 structures listed on the historical registers of the Dade City Historical Advisory Board and the Pasco County Preservation Committee. The Pioneer Florida Museum clusters six historic buildings on 21 acres, giving an authentic glimpse of early Florida.

Proof that everything old is new again, the newly renovated, circa-1912 Seaboard Coastline Railroad Depot is back in service, thanks to Amtrak making Dade City the first new addition to its train schedule in seven years and the only stop in Pasco County.

One of Florida's first Rails-to-Trails Programs created a 47-mile linear park on a former railroad right-of-way stretching from Citrus Springs to Dade City. Today, the Withlacoochee State Trail is a wonderful place for walking, hiking, jogging, skating, bike riding or horseback riding. The park's new welcome center occupies the old Trilby railroad yard.

Proud of his roots, tennis professional Jim Courier is a favorite son who let the French Open crowd know exactly where Dade City is on the map. Baseball's Mud Cat Grant, country singers the Bellamy Brothers and opera star Janette Thompson also are proud to claim Dade City as their mutual hometown.

More and more retirees are discovering the area, settling in Dade City or outlying communities. In Pasco County, 32 percent of all residents are age 65 or older.

Phyllis Smith, executive director of the Greater Dade City Chamber of Commerce, says, "As Tampa continues to grow north, many larger developments are moving into Pasco County. People come to look, discover our charming Main Street and quiet neighborhoods and can't believe this place is here."

As natives, Phyllis and her husband, Eugene, an agent with Dade City Realty, have been enthusiastic about the community for years.

In mid-1995, Louis and Barbara Sclafani retired to the Dade City area after 32 years in New Windsor, NY, on the Hudson River 10 miles from the U.S. Military Academy at West Point. "We were (football) season ticket holders," says Louis, 58, who drove for 30 years and more than 1 million accident-free miles for United Parcel Service. Barbara, 57, retired from Cigna after 22 years in medical insurance.

"Now we're both enjoying free golf for life where we live at Tampa Bay Golf and Tennis Club. We always wanted to retire in Florida and considered Sun City until we came here," Louis says.

Richard and Joan Barraclough came to Florida seven years ago from the Wilmington, DE, area. With three grown children on the East Coast, they set Florida, Georgia and North and South Carolina as retirement options. Their first move was to a manufactured-home community in Ruskin, south of Tampa Bay Golf and Tennis Club.

"We discovered this area while living in Ruskin," says Richard, 62, a classroom teacher for 33 years when he retired. "A sign on the highway said 'free golf for life' and I was hooked. I got involved in arranging golf games before the pro came. We had golf in Ruskin but the community was not like this one."

Joan, 61, a housewife and former bookkeeper, likes to dabble in ceramics, crafts and water aerobics and to browse Dade City's appealing Main Street shops.

Located eight miles from downtown Dade City in the small community of San Antonio, Tampa Bay Golf and Tennis Club is a new, planned adult community with a number of amenities. Along with a championship 18-hole golf course and the development's limited-time offer of free golf for life with the purchase of a home, a second clubhouse is being built with a fitness center and full restaurant. Site-built block and stucco homes range in price from $90,000 to $250,000.

"We discovered Dade City totally by chance and are happy to be here," says Josephine Bellows. "We were coming down to look at an apartment

Dade City, FL

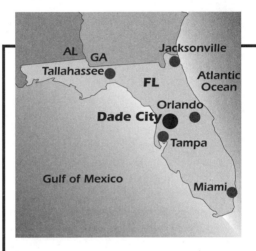

Population: 6,000 in town, 115,468 within 20 miles.

Location: Rural community in west-central Florida, about 45 minutes north of Tampa Bay area.

Climate:

	High	Low
January	75	51
July	92	71

Average relative humidity: 60%
Rain: 58.8 inches.
Winters are mild; summers are long and hot, often with high humidity. Heavy thunderstorms are common, and hurricanes are a threat. No major hurricane has hit the Tampa Bay area for 40 years, though Hurricane Elena caused damage in 1985 as it sat offshore. Elevation is 78 feet.

Cost of living: Below average (specific index not available).

Median housing cost: $87,000. Median rent is $435 a month in Pasco County.

Sales tax: 6%

Sales tax exemptions: Groceries, medicines, professional services.

State income tax: None.

Intangibles tax: Assessed on stocks, bonds and other specified assets, with some investments exempt. Tax rate is $1 per $1,000 of value for assets under $100,000 for individuals or $200,000 for couples, and $1.50 per $1,000 of value for greater amounts; first $20,000 for individuals and $40,000 for couples is exempt.

Estate tax: None, except the state's "pick-up" portion of the federal tax, applicable to taxable estates above $675,000.

Property tax: In Dade City, $26.40 per $1,000 of assessed value, with homes assessed at 100% of market value. Yearly tax on an $87,000 home is about $1,636, with the exemption noted below.

Homestead exemption: $25,000 off assessed value of primary, permanent residence.

Security: 134.7 crimes per 1,000 residents, higher than the national average of 46.2 crimes per 1,000 residents. The Pasco County crime rate is 47.1 crimes per 1,000 people.

Religion: The Greater Dade City area has a total of 64 places of worship, representing numerous denominations.

Education: Nearby St. Leo College offers a four-year liberal arts degree and continuing-education programs; Pasco-Hernando Community College has two-year degrees transferable to the state university system and many continuing-education courses.

Transportation: Local bus service is run by Pasco County Star. Amtrak serves Dade City, its only stop in the county. Tampa International Airport is 45 minutes away, and Interstate 75 is minutes outside town.

Health: Both Columbia Dade City Hospital and East Pasco Medical Center at nearby Zephyrhills are 120-bed acute-care facilities, providing 24-hour emergency services.

Housing options: Single-family homes and apartments are available in town and adjacent communities in the county. **Tampa Bay Golf and Tennis Club**, (352) 588-2100, at nearby San Antonio has an 18-hole championship golf course and other amenities; homes are $90,000-$250,000. **South Fork Mobile Home Community**, (352) 523-0022, offers swimming pool, clubhouse and other amenities; lots are leased, and manufactured homes cost $37,000-$65,000. **Edwinola**, (352) 567-6500, is a large, modern congregate-living facility with resort amenities.

Visitor lodging: Azalea House Bed and Breakfast, (352) 523-1773, is a restored 1890 home on the historic register, one block from Main Street antique shops. All guest rooms have king beds and private bath; rates are $69-$79 a night, including complementary breakfast and afternoon wine. Saddlebrook Golf and Tennis Resort, (800) 729-8383, 20 minutes away in Wesley Chapel, has double rooms starting at $132 a night.

Information: Greater Dade City Chamber of Commerce, 14112 Eighth St., Dade City, FL 33525, (352) 567-3769 or www.dadecitychamber.org.

in Lake Wales (south of Orlando) and got off I-75 because the drive was boring. We took Highway 301 to Highway 98, saw the big sign for South Fork Mobile Home Community, went in and fell in love with it." Josephine, formerly with the New York Department of Environmental Conservation, and her husband, Albert, both 62, lived all their married life in Patchogue, in Suffolk County, NY, before moving to Dade City.

"I always wanted to retire at 62 so I could be home with Albert, who was disabled on the job with the post office. We'd thought about retiring in Pennsylvania to be close to our son, but the weather there was not what we wanted. It's much easier and much nicer to be where it's warm," Josephine says.

Janet Chouinard came from Chicopee, MA, to central Florida several times to look for possible retirement locations when her husband became ill three years ago. With a sister in Zephyrhills, 20 minutes from Dade City, and friends living at Blue Jay Mobile Home Community in Dade City, she stopped next door to check out South Fork. Janet liked its quiet yet friendly atmosphere so much that she bought a place there the same day and moved in three days later. South Fork's neighborly warmth reached out to her when her husband died in late '94.

"I was down and didn't do much for a while," says Janet, 63, mother of six and grandmother of 14 grandchildren scattered throughout Massachusetts, North Dakota and Idaho. Janet, a computer technician for 16 years with Digital Equipment Corp. in Westville, MA, now stays busy with the St. Rita Catholic Church Women's Club and South Fork activities, including crafts, line dancing, swimming, bingo, exercise and potluck dinners. "And," she adds, "I'm crocheting 14 afghans for my little ones."

South Fork, an adult mobile-home community offering swimming pool, shuffleboard and clubhouse with ac-

tivities, is about five miles from downtown Dade City and two miles from a shopping center. Manufactured homes here cost from $37,000 to about $65,000; residents lease the lots for their homes. The park currently has about 150 spots occupied but can accommodate approximately 200 homes.

"Most homes in Dade City are under $100,000," says Eugene Smith of Dade City Realty. "A good portion are in the median range of $60,000 to $75,000."

The low cost of living was a big factor in the Bellowses relocating in the area. "My retirement is at a minimum and New York apartments are simply too high. If my husband passes away, I do not receive his pension. The cost of living is much better in Florida," says Josephine. "Albert planned our retirement by saving through IRAs, 401(k)s, watching the financial news and reading books on the subject. He did the best with the money we had."

The Sclafanis saved through retirement plans at work and agree that the cost of living in the area is much less than in New York. "We got a lot for our money here," Louis says.

For the Barracloughs, Richard says, "Cost weighed a lot. The mobile home we first lived in was reasonable and we were able to pay cash for it from the sale of our previous home, but we leased the land. Now we own our home and the land it sits on. We planned for retirement by working with a financial planner and going over different things to do, but we're not real good at budgeting. It's been six and a half years now, and so far so good."

Investing in Individual Retirement Accounts at work helped Janet Chouinard save. Thanks to the sale of a large home in Massachusetts, she was able to pay cash for her South Fork home and make the upgrades she desired, such as ceramic sinks and mirrored wall and chandelier in the dining room.

All moves have some surprises. For the Bellowses, the Dade City area's excellent medical facilities and health-care systems proved unexpectedly welcome. Since their relocation, Albert underwent another back operation and recently suffered a heart attack. He highly praises the care he received at both Columbia Dade City Hospital and East Pasco Medical Center.

"The care was a great surprise," adds Josephine. "Albert is progressing slowly and when he's back on his feet we'll do a lot more in the community."

Dade City's annual calendar of events keeps people on the go to everything from quilt and antique shows to bluegrass festivals, Seminole War battle reenactments and sporting events.

Decembers are wrapped up with gala goings-on that include the Magical Night Christmas Parade, Country Christmas Stroll down Main Street with shopping galore and tasty treats, entertainment and carriage rides, Christmas Open House at Pioneer Florida Museum, Church Street Christmas and a Bluegrass New Year's Eve Party.

"We may have to turn on the air conditioning to enjoy a Yuletide fire while we decorate the Christmas tree," says Phyllis Smith, "but it's better than shoveling snow." The North's icy chill and the job, says Louis Sclafani, are the things they — and other retirees — miss least. Friends and family are missed the most.

"But it only takes the kids two and a half hours to fly down from New York," adds Josephine Bellows. "They could spend that much time in traffic."

Janet Chouinard hopes some of her six children will eventually follow her to Florida.

All pleased with their choice for retirement, only Louis Sclafani would have done something differently: "If I'd only known how well everything was going to work out, I'd have retired sooner." ●

DeLand, Florida

University scene enriches life in central Florida town

By Janet Groene

Bypassed by interstates and eclipsed by its more famous neighbors, Walt Disney World and Daytona Beach, little DeLand seldom gets attention amid all the attractions of central Florida. But seniors are discovering that this quiet community of 20,000 residents has many makings of a nice retirement town.

From its stately domed courthouse to oak-lined streets and elegant Greek Revival, Victorian and Tudor university buildings, DeLand evokes a sense of permanence. Its mixture of architecture is more reminiscent of classic Small Town U.S.A. than nouveau Florida, where concrete-block construction dominates.

In DeLand and the surrounding area, retirees find a blend of cultural and recreational opportunities. As the home of Stetson University, a private school with 2,045 students, it offers a wide range of cultural pursuits for a town its size. And, it's a recreation crossroads, ideally located near Ocala National Forest, 45 minutes west of the Atlantic beaches and in the middle of central Florida's pleasantly hilly lake district.

Retirees from urban areas of the North have found this small town has more of what they're looking for in retirement than many other places.

Vic Laumark, 63, and his wife, Muriel, 54, considered New Hampshire, the western Carolinas and northern Florida for retirement after living in a New York City suburb and overseas while he was with Exxon.

But after three visits to DeLand in a three-month period, they chose the town for its good fishing, hunting and social opportunities, they say.

Norman and Kay Laws, in their mid-60s, looked for five years at spots in Hawaii, California, Arizona, Texas and central Florida before retiring to DeLand when he left Chicago State

University, where he was a professor.

Al Reeves, 63, and his wife, Jean, 60, also considered other Florida sites and Chapel Hill, NC, before moving to DeLand from Rochester, NY, where he was with Kodak.

"We've found a real home here. We're really happy," says Jean as she and Al exchange greetings and banter with neighbors in Whisperwood. On a sunny Sunday, the manufactured-home community crackles with activities and conversations among residents.

The couples say the small, college-town atmosphere and the music, drama and lecture programs of Stetson University, one of the South's oldest and best liberal arts schools, were a major draw.

While DeLand's cultural offerings aren't as extensive as in the metropolitan areas where they formerly lived, retirees say there are trade-offs. They have to drive only a few miles to attend world-class speeches, symphonies, operas or touring theater productions under university auspices. Plus, parking is hardly a problem at these events.

Recent appearances have been made here by such luminaries as Archbishop Desmond Tutu, ex-President Jimmy Carter, author Derek Humphrey, Russian poet Yevgeny Yevtushenko, and jazz great Taj Mahal. An even wider choice of events, including national sports, is within a 30-minute or one-hour drive to Daytona or Orlando.

Beyond its cultural events, Stetson plays an integral part in the community. Its students mingle with senior citizens in funky coffeehouses and avant-garde theaters, giving the community an eclectic blend that is lacking in some Florida cities.

The town was founded in 1876 by Henry A. DeLand, a manufacturer from New York, who planted oak trees

50 feet apart to border the streets. Development started along the St. Johns River, a major waterway that brought settlers to the state long before roads were built, but the town grew away from the river when U.S. 17, now a quiet byway, became a major route between Miami and New York.

DeLand persuaded John B. Stetson, the hat-maker, to establish a school in the town. Founded as DeLand Academy in 1883, it later became Stetson University and is the home of the oldest higher education school building in the state. The original Henry DeLand home now is restored as a museum, open to the public.

The towering oaks that once lined the stately streets and earned the town the nickname "Athens of Florida" have been decimated by storms and street projects, but new live oak trees have been planted along Woodland Boulevard, locally known as "The Boulevard."

Outdoors enthusiasts enjoy such nearby attractions as a wildlife refuge with a smorgasbord of bird life; DeLeon Springs State Park, thought to be the original Fountain of Youth; and Blue Springs State Park, one of the state's most fabled manatee refuges.

The area's sprawling St. Johns River system is a fishing and boating bonanza, yielding lunker bass on its lakes and drawing swimmers and divers to its sweetwater springs and wildlife enthusiasts to jungle-lined shores.

Aboard rental houseboats, awed visitors from all over the world roam the river, looking at colorful birds, curious raccoons, sunning turtles, manatees munching fragrant water hyacinth, alligators, and even a colony of wild monkeys along the banks.

One of the nation's biggest, freshest and folksiest farmer's markets is held each Wednesday at the county fairgrounds west of downtown. And the historic downtown area itself is becoming a magnet for antique shoppers and nostalgia buffs.

Lower costs of living, better climate, less pollution and lighter traffic are factors that attract retirees to this area.

"The cost of living, including no state income tax, was a large influence," says Vic Laumark of the move to DeLand. "We figure we can live here for $3,500 less annually than in New Jersey."

The three couples interviewed

waltzed happily into local life through the Newcomers Club, church and the many volunteer opportunities they found. New residents must leave the newcomers group after three years, so all three couples have "graduated" — with regrets — but are busier than ever.

The Reeveses enjoy chess, bicycling, crafts and bowling. Both are involved as volunteers in a Florida state program for first-time juvenile offenders in which they hear juvenile cases and recommend courses of action to the judge.

Muriel Laumark's enthusiasm as a newcomer led her to a new career, welcoming other new arrivals for the Florida Greeting Service.

The Lawses, who live on a canal just 10 minutes by water from the St. Johns River, are active in the yacht club and other water-oriented activities as well as church, garden club and service clubs.

In sharing tips for other retirees planning a relocation move, both the Laumarks and the Reeveses point to things they would do differently.

DeLand, FL

Population: 20,000 in DeLand, 425,000 In Volusia County.
Location: In central Florida's hilly lake district, about 20 miles from Daytona and about 40 miles from Orlando.
Climate:[1]

	High	Low
January	72	49
July	92	73

Average relative humidity: 55%
Rain: 48 inches.
Winters are warm and dry; summers are hot and muggy.
Cost of living: 95.6 for Volusia County, based on state average of 100.
Median housing cost: $72,750 ($73,894 for single-family home, $80,870 for a condo and $38,012 for a manufactured home on owned property). Prices for new three-bedroom, two-bath homes start at $85,000.
Sales tax: 6%.
Sales tax exemptions: Medical services, prescription drugs, most groceries.
State income tax: None.
Intangibles tax: Assessed on stocks, bonds and other specified assets. Tax rate is $1 per $1,000 of value for

assets under $100,000 for individuals or $200,000 for couples, and $1.50 per $1,000 of value for greater amounts; first $20,000 for individuals and $40,000 for couples is exempt. Some investments are exempt.
Estate tax: None, except the state's "pick-up" portion of the federal tax, applicable to taxable estates above $675,000.
Property tax: $30.82 per $1,000 of assessed value, with homes assessed at 100% of market value. Tax on a $72,750 home is about $1,472, with homestead exemption noted below.
Homestead exemption: $25,000 off assessed value for primary, permanent residence.
Security: 138.7 crimes per 1,000 residents, higher than the national average of 46.2 crimes per 1,000 residents.
Religion: 56 Protestant churches, one Catholic church and one synagogue.
Education: Stetson University, a private liberal arts college in DeLand, offers non-degree classes and Elderhostel programs geared to those age 60 and older. DeLand also has a branch of Daytona Beach Community College.
Transportation: There's no local bus or air service. DeLand is served by Greyhound, Amtrak and several taxi and van services to the Daytona Beach and Orlando airports, 20 and 40 miles respectively.
Health: The 156-bed West Volusia Memorial Hospital is the area's major health facility. New 97-bed Fish Hospital is south of town in Orange City.

Many local patients go to Orlando or Daytona Beach for specialized services. There are 150 medical doctors.
Housing options: There's a wide range of single-family homes, condos and manufactured-home communities, some catering to adults only. **Trails West** and **Brandywine** are planned urban developments of single-family homes and townhomes; **Bent Oaks** and **Longleaf Plantation** have upscale homes, and **Whisperwood** offers manufactured homes starting at $39,000 on rented lots. Independent living in continuing-care communities is available at the **Alliance Community**, (904) 734-3481; **Florida Lutheran Retirement Center**, (904) 736-5800; and **John Knox Village**, (904) 775-0788. Retirement apartment complexes include **Hugh Ash Manor**, (904) 736-2500; **College Arms Towers**, (904) 734-2299; and **Woodland Towers**, (904) 738-2700.
Visitor lodging: DeLand has many small, private motels, campgrounds and fish camps. Other options include the DeLand Country Inn, $49-$59, (904) 736-4244; Holiday Inn, $69, (904) 738-5200; and Quality Inn, $49-$64, (904) 736-3440. Book early; rooms fill quickly during special events at Stetson or at the Daytona International Speedway.
Information: DeLand Area Chamber of Commerce, 336 N. Woodland Blvd., DeLand, FL 32720, (904) 734-4331 or www.delandchamber.org.

[1]Climate data for nearby Orlando, from National Climatic Data Center.

When moving, number your boxes and keep an inventory of everything you pack, the Laumarks caution. They also advise insuring your goods for replacement value. In their move, some of their boxes were lost, and they couldn't prove the boxes even existed, let alone the value of the contents.

Jean Reeves' chief regret was that they got rid of too many items from their home in Rochester.

"We had a big house sale and sold almost everything we owned, so we had to purchase many of the items here at higher prices," she says.

The Lawses credit "a lot of planning" with their smooth transition.

DeLand's wide choice of local housing is reflected by the three lifestyles chosen by the couples: manufactured-home subdivision, waterfront property and acreage in the country.

The Reeveses didn't want the expense and upkeep of a standard house so they looked for a manufactured home in an adult community — one that also would accept their 80-pound dog. After a search, they found what they wanted in a development in which manufactured homes start at $38,900 and sites rent for $169 monthly. The monthly fee covers lawn mowing, recreation facilities and other amenities. By contract, their rental fee cannot rise more than 6 percent a year.

The two other couples have homes built on site, one on three country acres and the other on a canal leading to the St. Johns River.

Like many others in the area, all three couples consider themselves De-Landites but actually live in neighborhoods outside the city limits, which cover only a small area. Because of the large number of county government and university buildings in DeLand, 34 percent of the city's property is tax-exempt. As a result, the town has one of the highest property tax rates in the county. Adjoining and nearby neighborhoods zealously guard against annexation, although thousands of their residents come into DeLand for shopping, church, medical treatment, meetings, entertainment and recreation.

While Florida does not have a state income tax, it does have a tax on intangible assets, which applies to stocks, mutual funds and some bonds, though there are some exclusions. The tax is a bookkeeping nuisance since taxpayers must compute the value of all applicable holdings as of Jan. 1 each year. Taxes are based on the asset's value that date, regardless of the value when the tax is paid, which can be as late as the following June 30.

Although one couple interviewed reports that this tax costs them $1,400-$1,500 yearly, they say that's much lower than the taxes they paid where

they previously lived. With its exemptions, the Florida intangibles tax has little effect on many taxpayers. It falls heaviest on those who have large stock portfolios.

The state sales tax rate is 6 percent. Volusia County, unlike some neighboring counties, hasn't voted in a local optional 1 percent additional sales tax, but there is a constant clamor for more money in government coffers because of school overcrowding and a growing crime problem.

Both the Laumarks and the Reeveses express concern about crime. The Reeveses were distressed at a rash of burglaries nearby — "seven and eight homes in one night" — that prompted their community to organize a neighborhood watch program.

The Lawses note that power outages are frequent in their area, and say they must reset clocks three or four times a month.

Al and Jean Reeves miss having a major shopping center nearby.

The medical care is not as extensive as found in metropolitan areas, the Lawses add, but they find it adequate. For more specialized care, residents usually go to Daytona Beach or Orlando, both nearby.

Would any of them move away? No — but Al and Jean Reeves would like to have a summer home in North Carolina. Florida's summer weather is more humid than they expected.●

Door County, Wisconsin

Outdoor beauty, quaint villages distinguish the Wisconsin shore

By Dixie Franklin

A narrow strip of land with rolling hills and hardwood forests protrudes from northeastern Wisconsin like a "pinkie" finger into the waters and bays of Lake Michigan, its shoreline of limestone bluffs and pebbled coves defining Door County.

Most of its dozen or so quaint villages hug the 250-mile shoreline, offering hundreds of summer studios, galleries and crafts shops. Spreading inland are apple and cherry orchards, fields of wildflowers, tree-lined roads marked by low stone fences and scenic countryside dotted with weathered barns, white farmhouses and friendly inns.

In the summer, slightly more than 27,000 permanent residents mix with three times as many visitors and seasonal inhabitants to enjoy a climate tempered by breezes off the water, which is never more than 10 minutes away.

The same beauty that attracts tourists to Door County also beckons retirees. Some are "snowbirds," retirees who arrive in May and remain to enjoy the balmy weather through the colorful fall, then flee south for winter. But others choose to stay year-round.

Those who stay on the Door all year are the lucky ones, says Fran Burton, 59, who retired with her husband, Paul, 62, to the village of Ephraim. In the off-season, Door is more serene and tranquil as residents return to a slower pace after the summer crowds leave.

"The real people of the Door are here in winter," she says.

Many seniors like Fran and Paul retire here gradually after vacationing in the area for years. Fran had been coming here longer than most people, first visiting from St. Louis with her parents in 1939.

Fran and her husband spent summers on the Door and 11 years ago built Stonehill Crafts gift shop in Ephraim with the goal of moving here when Paul, a professor at the University of Kansas in Lawrence, retired.

Leo and Jill Mortensen, ages 67 and 63 respectively, moved to Sturgeon Bay from a suburb of Milwaukee six years ago. However, Leo, a banker, continued to work by phone and fax, spending two weeks a month away until he retired here permanently last year.

With a population of slightly more than 9,600, Sturgeon Bay is the peninsula's largest city, boasting the area's only hospital, the seat of county government, the county newspaper and the most year-round shopping opportunities. Many retirees prefer to settle in smaller villages to the north, such as Egg Harbor, Fish Creek, Ephraim, Sister Bay, Ellison Bay and others scattered along the only two highways, routes 42 and 57.

Leo says they searched the Midwest for six or eight years looking for a place to retire.

"We had been vacationing and sailing here in the past and were looking for good sailing for retirement," Leo says.

Local history began from the water, with fishing, then shipment of lumber harvested on the peninsula. With completion of the Sturgeon Bay ship canal in 1891 came shipbuilding and the beginning of the tourism industry. Farms and orchards followed lumbering, which cleared much of the land. Today, the area is a major producer of cherries.

Early settlers left a rich ethnic heritage in architecture, foods, churches and customs. An Icelandic community adds a colorful flavor to Washington Island. Sister Bay boasts of Scandinavian ties, and Ephraim's Moravian heritage still influences the community to remain free of alcohol sales.

The ethnic heritage is shared at traditional Scandinavian "fish boils" such as found at Pelletier's Restau-

rant in Fish Creek. Whitefish filets fresh from the lake are boiled with potatoes and onions in a huge black cauldron over an open fire. When flames leap up into a steaming "boil-over," the meal is ready to serve. The dessert is hot cherry pie, made with fruit from Door orchards.

Another Door County tradition is dining on Swedish specialties at Al Johnson's Swedish Restaurant at Sister Bay. First-timers are surprised to see goats grazing along its sod roof.

The first retirees were primarily tourists who had developed close ties to the peninsula as vacationers. They came from the Chicago area, Minneapolis and St. Paul, St. Louis and the Quad Cities of Davenport and Bettendorf, IA, and Rock Island and Moline, IL. Gradually the geographical mix has expanded to include much of the Midwest.

A main attraction of Door Peninsula remains the water.

"We can be on the waters of Sturgeon Bay in minutes," says Leo. "Five miles east and we are on Lake Michigan, and five miles west, we are on the bay of Green Bay. The Door offers the best of waters."

The Mortensens feel they have most everything they enjoyed in a metropolitan area: good city government, good roads, cable TV, snow removal, garbage pickup and other services.

"Outside my window, I see cedar waxwings at the feeder. On the bay are sea gulls, and we're on the fall and spring migrating pattern of all kinds of birds and waterfowl. When the six grandchildren come, they can enjoy our canoe, a 10-foot dinghy, fishing boat or powerboat. Overall, this is exactly what we wanted," Leo says.

Single-family cottages and homes dominate the real estate market. Dennis Starr of Starr Realty in Sturgeon Bay says most retirees seek property with a view, frequently choosing a place with no neighbors nearby.

"We have a clean, safe environment, so people are not afraid to live out (of town) a bit," Starr says. "Most do not live in condos but prefer their own properties, not only shorefront properties but places with a country view."

Retirees say property taxes are on the high side but community services are good and dependable.

Retirees seem undaunted by limited health services, with only one facility in the county, the 89-bed Door County Memorial Hospital at Sturgeon Bay, which has primary and emergency care. About 45 doctors practice in the county. For life-support services, county residents look to a dual network of first-responders and paramedics; the average response time is five minutes. The paramedics service was the first such rural program established in Wisconsin. Three nursing homes serve senior needs.

"If additional health needs are indicated, we refer patients to one of the three hospitals in Green Bay," says Door County Memorial Administrator Jerry Worrick. "We find that we can transport patients by ground as fast as we could send them by helicopter." Green Bay is about 45 miles southwest of Sturgeon Bay.

Fran says community involvement is a necessity for those retiring in a tourism-oriented area.

"Village government goes on year-round. In our village of only 240 residents, we can't sit back and wait for someone else to do things," she says.

Retirees spearhead library and hospital projects, cultural activities and other community functions.

Fran spends part of her summer days at the shop, while Paul keeps busy with civic projects, including the village government and the Ephraim Foundation, which is dedi-

Door County, WI

Population: 27,125

Location: This popular vacation area is an 85-mile-long wooded peninsula jutting into Lake Michigan northeast of Green Bay. Sturgeon Bay and shipping channel slices the peninsula. The largest town is Sturgeon Bay, the county seat with about 9,600 population.

Climate:

	High	Low
January	23	9
July	80	60

Average relative humidity: 74%

Rain: 27.44 inches.

Snow: 39.8 inches.

Area has four-season climate with colorful springs and falls. Temperatures are moderated by the surrounding waters of Lake Michigan and Green Bay. Elevation is about 590 feet.

Cost of living: Average or slightly below (specific index not available).

Average housing cost: Single-family inland, $73,748; single-family waterfront, $257,728; condominium, $134,215.

Sales tax: 5.5%

Sales tax exemptions: Groceries, prescription drugs, professional services, hearing aids, eyeglasses, prosthetic devices.

State income tax: Three-tier structure with tax rates of 4.9%, 6.55% and 6.93%, depending on income.

Income tax exemptions: No more than 50% of Social Security benefits are included in Wisconsin taxable income. There is a credit of up to $25 for those 65 and older.

Intangibles tax: None.

Estate tax: None, except the state's "pickup" portion of the federal tax, applicable to taxable estates above $675,000.

Property tax: Rates vary by town; property assessment rates also vary, although most properties are assessed at 85%-100%. A house in Sturgeon Bay with a 76.62% assessment ratio and $133.19 lottery credit has a net tax rate of $16.84 per $1,000. Tax on a $73,748 home in the Sturgeon Bay area would be about $1,250 annually, without any exemptions.

Homestead exemption: For homeowners with a gross income up to $19,154, the state allows a homestead credit of $10 to $1,160 based on income and property taxes paid.

Security: 20.2 crimes per 1,000 residents, lower than the national average of 46.2 crimes per 1,000 residents.

Religion: 50 churches representing 18 denominations. Majority are Lutheran or Catholic. No synagogues closer than Green Bay, about 45 miles south of Sturgeon Bay.

Education: Northeast Wisconsin Technical College has campuses at Sturgeon Bay and Green Bay, with some non-credit courses at $3 each. University of Wisconsin Extension offers four Elderhostels a year, averaging $300 each, and a Learning in Retirement program with $50 membership fee. The Clearing, an adult school of the arts, literature and ecological studies, has classes in Ellison Bay.

Transportation: No public transportation; car necessary. Airport at Green Bay is closest with commercial service.

Health: Door County Memorial Hospital, an 89-bed 24-hour emergency facility served by 45 physicians, with primary and specialized care, in- and outpatient surgery, neurology and diagnostic imaging center affiliated with Green Bay hospital. EMT and paramedic service has five-minute response time county-wide. Closest acute care is in Green Bay.

Housing options: Most retirees buy single-family homes in Sturgeon Bay, smaller communities to the north and in the countryside. **Hillcrest** in Sturgeon Bay, has two- and three-bedroom condo units for $85,000-$120,000. Condos in Fish Creek run $165,000-$263,500.

Visitor lodging: Best Western Maritime Inn in Sturgeon Bay, $88 for a double in summer, $53.50 in winter, (920) 743-7231; Landmark Resort in Egg Harbor, rates start at around $148 for a one-bedroom condo in summer, $75 in winter, (920) 868-3205.

Information: Door County Chamber of Commerce, P.O. Box 406, Sturgeon Bay, WI 54235, (920) 743-4456 or www.door countyvacations.com.

cated to preserving historical buildings and documenting the past.

The Burtons point with pride to the Door Community Auditorium, an 8-year-old, 750-seat cathedrallike structure attached to Gibraltar High School in Fish Creek. It attracts nationally known artists in theater, music and dance, as well as local talent. Paul serves as president of the board of directors overseeing the auditorium.

The Door Peninsula with its four seasons tempered by surrounding water has become a haven for retirees who still enjoy a strong work ethic. Mike and Marilyn Hagerman, both 57, said they "changed gears" when he was offered early retirement from his position with IBM in Waukesha, WI, a suburb of Milwaukee.

The Hagermans built the log bed-and-breakfast Wooden Heart Inn in a forest near Sister Bay. It includes their home, three guest rooms and gift shop, where they sell their homemade bird feeders and perches.

"We wanted to do something different while we were still young enough," Marilyn says. They had been vacationing in the Door for 20 years and were drawn to retirement by "so many interesting people and crafts-oriented classes that we wanted to be part of it."

The Clearing, an adult vacation school of the arts, literature and ecological studies, offers courses in a forest setting north of Ellison Bay. From mid-May to mid-October, there are more than 40 weeklong courses, ranging from crafts to the arts, from

philosophy to French.

The Clearing also is a popular gathering place for year-round residents in winter. Then, classes meet only once a week and are so much in demand that sign-up is by a lottery system, Fran says.

Fran and Paul enjoy the Door's strong performing arts scene. She serves on the board of the Peninsula Music Festival in Ephraim, which presents 10 well-attended classical concerts in the late summer.

The Peninsula Arts Theatre and American Folklore Theatre have professional stage productions and a summer season under the stars at the Peninsula State Park theater in Fish Creek. Fall performances move into the Fish Creek Town Hall. Peninsula Players Theatre in Fish Creek is America's oldest professional resident theater, with more than 60 years of productions in a scenic setting of forests and gardens.

For recreation, retirees choose from eight golf courses, boating, fishing, bicycle paths and stables. Winter offerings include more than 100 miles of snowmobile trails plus cross-country ski trails.

The peninsula boasts five state parks, including the sprawling Peninsula State Park in Fish Creek with an 18-hole golf course, hiking, biking, cross-country ski trails and more. The park's 1868 Eagle Bluff Lighthouse is one of 12 lighthouses ringing the peninsula, giving Door County more than any other county in the nation.

The area has four distinctive sea-

sons, each with its own appeal. In spring colorful blossoms spread across the cherry and apple orchards. In summer, the beat picks up with the bustling tourist scene. Autumn brings a blaze of color across hardwood forests and apples ripening in the orchards. Winter introduces another world, the "quiet time" of the Door, with light snows and crisp, clean air. Winters can be bitterly cold, particularly in December and January; year-round residents often take extended vacations during some winter months.

The remote nature of the Door is part of its appeal yet presents problems.

"There are hundreds of gift shops, but where do you get necessities?" Fran asks.

Stores and services are limited, even more so in the winter. Residents go to Green Bay for their major shopping.

When fall comes, most lodgings, gift shops and restaurants close; winter sports still bring tourists but not enough to justify keeping shops open. However, two discount stores remain open all winter.

"If you want to eat out in winter, choices are limited," Fran says.

While life slows down in the winter, retirees say they're not bored by the quieter period. The Hagermans find more time for their crafts, and the Mortensens cross-country ski when the bay freezes.

Fran says new retirees are more surprised at the obligation to get involved with government and village affairs than the cold and "small inconveniences" of winter.●

Eagle River, Wisconsin

Wisconsin lake area sparkles with fresh air, clear water

By Dixie Franklin

The north-central Wisconsin town of Eagle River is a life-size diorama, with low storefronts bordered by flowers in summer and roofs silhouetted against winter snow by strings of tiny holiday lights. In this dioramic setting moves a parade of tourists and local residents — including a growing number of retirees.

The natural beauty of four seasons, a clean environment and a perfect combination of woods and waters help attract retirees to the town of 1,645 people. A laid-back lifestyle and the spontaneous friendliness of its people add to its charm. Folks like to boast that the air here is fresher, the lakes clearer, forests greener and snows whiter than anyplace else.

"I came from a place where you could see the air," says Bob Johnson, a retiree who didn't stay retired long. Formerly a merchant and clothing manufacturers' representative, he now is executive director of the Eagle River Information Bureau.

After retiring to Arizona and living in a community where he had to purchase bottled drinking water, he and wife Carol returned to northern Wisconsin. "The other day while fishing, I could see my lure in 17 feet of water," he marvels.

Summers bring idyllic 85-degree temperatures, and autumns mean glorious displays of reds, oranges and bronzes painted across the forests. Winter snow comes in mid-November and lingers until March, with mid-January temperatures in the high teens and 20s. Most year-round retirees are defensive about their winters and are reluctant to admit to "cabin fever."

"From a calendar standpoint, our winters are long, but I have an unbelievable number of personal projects that keep me busy," says Adrian Willis, a retired marketing manager who lived in Battle Creek, MI, before mov-

ing to Eagle River. "And there is a side benefit to our winters. Once it gets cold, it stays cold, as opposed to ups and downs in temperature."

Johnson agrees. "In winter, it's cold, but it's white, clean and crisp. There is no isolation. Our infrastructure is good, and roads are plowed immediately after a snow."

The town and its surrounding lakes and forests make it a popular year-round tourism destination. The town of Eagle River sits in a bend of the river of the same name. The river links 28 navigable freshwater lakes known as the Eagle River Chain of Lakes, one of the world's largest such inland chains. Summer population increases to 6,500 in the immediate area. For residents living along the chain of lakes, the easiest way to town may be by water. There's a marina just a block from the heart of town.

Many storefronts along the seven-block business district are reminiscent of the 1920s and 1930s, with a railroad depot converted to an information center, a corner bank-turned-gift shop, an old-fashioned soda fountain and a cinema that shows first-run movies through the summer months.

There are souvenir and craft shops, boutiques, galleries, antiques, a candy store, markets and restaurants. At the Colonial House ice cream parlor and restaurant, visitors still can drop coins in the nickelodeon while waiting for their sodas. B.J.'s Butcher Block makes its own sausages, and Bonson's Bakery bakes the famous Wisconsin Kringles, fruit-filled pastries with just enough dough to hold the filling together.

First as summer tourists, then as year-round residents, retirees are discovering the pleasures of an area that they boast is "above the tension zone," free of city hassles. The area is especially attractive to outdoor enthusiasts who are as happy here in winter as summer because of the snow sports.

And artists wax creative in a North Woods setting where it is not unusual to see whitetail deer, otter, beaver and occasionally a bear during an afternoon drive.

Eagles still nest in the forests of tall, craggy pines along the Eagle River, which flows from Watersmeet Lake on the Wisconsin River to connect the Eagle Chain. Before 1870, the only Europeans to pass this way were occasional fur traders.

In the 1870s, lumberjacks came to harvest virgin white pine. They built a large sawmill in the river's bend, and the town grew around it. Lumbering and the forests still fill a vital role in the economy, both in the harvest of timber and creation of a natural environment of forests and lakes for tourism. The Nicolet National Forest to the east and Northern Highlands State Forest to the west guarantee many outdoor opportunities.

Vilas County, of which Eagle River is the county seat of government, boasts 549 named lakes and 773 smaller unnamed lakes among its rolling, forested hills. Seventy-three rivers and streams carve their way through forests predominantly of pine, maple and birch. Lakes and rivers are enjoyed by fishermen, boaters, waterfowl hunters — and just plain romantics who relish a sunrise or sunset across a placid lake.

Fish catches include the legendary fighting muskies, walleye, northern pike, bass, trout and many species of pan fish. Most any summer weekend will find lakes teeming with fishing boats, sailboats, pontoons, canoes, kayaks and jet skis.

Retiree Herman Smith, formerly a recreation and resource agent for the University of Wisconsin Extension Service, says he saves his fishing for midweek when waters are less crowded, leaving weekends for the tourists.

With such a wealth of recreational

opportunities, it's no surprise that real estate on the water is most popular, especially along the Eagle River Chain of Lakes. Residential properties range from summer cabins to impressive year-round homes worth $275,000 and more.

Bruce Bryer of Tri-County Realty, a local agency, says the average cost of homes near Eagle River has increased as much as 20 percent in the last two years. Newcomers should plan to spend up to $200,000 for a 1,200-square-foot cottage on the water, Bryer says.

A municipal water and sewer system serves the city and adjacent area, although some homeowners depend on private wells and septic systems. There are three banks, a public library, pharmacies, insurance agencies and a fire department staffed by 28 volunteers. A county newspaper is published weekly.

Homes in town offer many advantages, but shoreline property is the first choice of many retirees. Adrian Willis lives on the river, which provides entertainment year-round — even in winter, when the current prevents it from freezing over entirely.

Adrian and his wife, Gen, moved to Eagle River when their two sons purchased a marina on the Chain of Lakes. They spend pleasant spring days watching minks build dens in the banks of the river. Later in the season the minks parade their young across the lawn.

James Slagle first came to Eagle River as a tag-along on his father's fishing trips. The retired school principal lived in Minnesota and elsewhere in Wisconsin before moving to Eagle River.

"From childhood on, I've always enjoyed the woods," he remembers. Four years ago, James and his wife, Sandra, purchased an "insulated shell of a house on Lower Nine Mile Lake east of Eagle River, and I did much of the remodeling myself." Summer evenings often find the Slagles paddling their canoe on the lake.

Herman and Betty Smith are not newcomers; they have lived in the same big house on the edge of town for the last 40 years. Herman says it is time to move to a smaller house, but they're not moving far. They're looking at a house down the street.

Eagle River, WI

Population: 1,645 in Eagle River, 21,277 in Vilas County.

Location: Eagle River is in the lake country of north-central Wisconsin, 140 miles northwest of Green Bay. Elevation is 1,642 feet.

Climate:

	High	Low
January	25	10
July	85	60

Average relative humidity: 50%
Rain: 28 inches.
Snow: 60 inches.
Idyllic summers, long winters (from late November to May).

Cost of living: Average (specific index not available).

Average housing cost: $90,000 for a 1,200-square-foot house away from the water, $200,000 on the water. Water frontage costs $900 per foot on the Eagle River Chain of Lakes, $500 on other boatable lakes. New construction averages $80 per square foot.

Sales tax: 5.5%

Sales tax exemptions: Groceries, prescription drugs, professional services, hearing aids, eyeglasses, prosthetic devices.

State income tax: Three-tier structure with tax rates of 4.9%, 6.55% and 6.93%, depending on income.

Income tax exemptions: No more than 50% of Social Security benefits are included in Wisconsin taxable income. There is a credit of up to $25 for those 65 and older.

Intangibles tax: None.

Estate tax: None, except the state's "pick-up" portion of the federal tax, applicable to taxable estates above $675,000.

Property tax: About $35 per $1,000 of assessed value, which is set at 90.28% of market value. Yearly taxes on a $150,000 home would be about $4,725.

Homestead exemption: For homeowners with a gross income up to $19,154, the state allows a homestead credit of $10 to $1,160 based on income and property taxes paid.

Security: 62.6 crimes per 1,000 residents, higher than the national average of 46.2 crimes per 1,000 residents.

Religion: 12 Protestant churches, one Catholic church.

Education: Nicolet College and Technical Institute at Rhinelander, a two-year school, offers classes at Eagle River. Average tuition for students age 62 and older is $3 per course.

Transportation: There's no public transportation, but the Kalmar Senior Center arranges some city transportation. Regional transportation is available via commercial commuter service at Eagle River Regional Airport and by commercial commuter service at Rhinelander-Oneida County Airport, 25 miles south.

Health: The 41-bed Eagle River Memorial Hospital handles general health care with 14 medical doctors. The town has 10 dentists, and an additional 19 doctors from Rhinelander and Woodruff offer satellite services.

Housing options: Homeowners choose among lakeside and river properties, forested acreages and city-size lots. Many homes are summer cottages that have been winterized; others represent new construction. Some lake areas have property and homeowner associations.

Visitor lodging: Rustic cabins and modern resorts are located throughout the area. In addition: American Days Inn-Eagle River, $74, (715) 479-5151; Chanticleer Inn, $69, (715) 479-4486.

Information: Vilas County Chamber of Commerce, 330 Court St., Eagle River, WI 54521, (715) 479-3649 or www.villageprofile.com/wisconsin/eagleriver.

There are no planned housing facilities for retirees, and as the area has become more popular for year-round living, housing availability has become more limited. Some retirees are solving the problem by building new homes or purchasing older summer cottages and remodeling them for year-round use.

Even though he has faced a heart attack and bypass surgery, Herman Smith doesn't worry about the availability of medical service. The 41-bed Eagle River Memorial Hospital maintains an active medical staff of 14, with specialists in surgery, urology, cardiology, internal medicine, orthopedics and occupational therapy. It maintains 24-hour ambulance service, with trained emergency medical technicians. An air ambulance also is available to transport patients to other regional hospitals or to medical facilities in Milwaukee.

The hospital is affiliated with the 99-bed Howard Young Medical Center at Woodruff, 25 miles west, which has a staff of 45 physicians plus consultants. The medical center was named for a New York art dealer who owned a summer home in nearby Minocqua. Upon his death, he be- queathed $20 million to the hospital.

The Eagle River Hospital can arrange for Meals on Wheels for homebound residents who require special diets prescribed by a physician. Other senior meals are served at the local Kalmar Senior Center.

There's no public transportation in Eagle River, but Kalmar Senior Center schedules free senior van service for medical appointments and shopping. For other chores, residents say there often seems to be a neighbor going in the right direction.

"There is so much to do, I don't feel like I'm retired yet," says James Slagle, who is among the many who add vitality to the community by volunteering through the hospital, churches, clubs and Senior Eagle River Volunteer Enterprise (SERVE).

Through church activities, the Slagles have made many new friends. They also participate in the Youth Futures Committee, a group of students and mature citizens who are developing ideas and activities as an alternative to alcohol and drugs for area youth. James also serves on the hospital board.

Some retirees take advantage of continuing-education programs offered through Nicolet College and Technical Institute at Rhinelander. The college brings classes to Eagle River, and discounts are available to students age 62 and over.

For entertainment, retirees tend to look first to outdoor recreation. Eagle River has one 18-hole golf course and one nine-hole course (there are 16 golf courses within a 20-mile radius) as well as tennis courts, parks, beaches and picnic areas. After summers spent fishing (the license is $5 for persons age 65 and older), boating and hiking, residents look forward to winter ice fishing, snowmobiling and cross-country skiing over miles of forest trails.

Shows at a community theater liven up the winters. At Hazelhurst, 30 miles southwest, the Northern Lights Playhouse presents professional theater throughout the year. There also are numerous festivals, including the October Cranberry Fest.

For dining out, opportunities range from fast foods to nice supper clubs. A number of restaurants offer access from land and water.

Herman Smith sums it up for many retirees who live in Eagle River. "For us, there is no other place," he says.●

Edenton, North Carolina

North Carolina bay-front town takes pride in its Colonial past

By William Schemmel

Many retirees search coast to coast before finding a community that fits all their criteria. But for Murphy Moss and his wife, Mary Ann Coffey, the decision to move was easy. Edenton, on the Atlantic coast of North Carolina, was the hands-down choice.

"We didn't really think about retirement sites. We just wanted to move to Edenton," says the 65-year-old Moss, formerly the managing partner of New Orleans' largest law firm. "We were looking for a place that had distinct, but not extreme, climate changes and was reasonably close to population centers. We definitely didn't want to be in a city."

His wife adds: "We wanted to settle in a real town — not a suburb or resort. Edenton just made us feel so welcome. We bought our house on Good Friday, and that same day one of our new neighbors came over and invited us to Easter Sunday dinner. We knew right then we'd made the right choice."

Incorporated in 1722, Edenton looks like a page from a Colonial American picture book. The town of 5,300 was built around an English-style village green on a small bay of Albemarle Sound, on the northern coast of the state. Scores of homes, churches and public buildings predate the American Revolution.

Cupola House, a national historic landmark completed in 1725, is considered by historians to be the finest wooden structure south of Connecticut. Also on the national register, Georgian-style Chowan County Courthouse has meted out justice since 1767. The county jail, though no longer a functioning detention center, was first built in 1788 and rebuilt in 1828.

Beautifully maintained Federal, Colonial and Victorian homes preside over spacious lawns and year-round gardens. Many of these historic showplaces were built by Colonial-era merchants and sea captains who prospered from commerce flowing through Edenton's port.

Soon after the famous "tea party" in Boston, the ladies of Edenton signed a proclamation declaring they would drink no more tea and wear no more English clothing until the British Parliament abolished its excessive taxes.

In the early 1800s, a canal built through the Great Dismal Swamp drained the life from the town's port; Norfolk eventually became the favored anchorage. But, happily for residents and newcomers, Edenton has been able to preserve its historic heritage while adopting the most attractive features of modern American life.

A community theater, art galleries and seasonal festivals enhance the town's cultural life. Retirees can become involved in a variety of civic and social clubs, churches, charitable organizations and historical preservation societies. Those who enjoy active sports can play golf and tennis, walk and hike, and fish in Albemarle Sound. North Carolina's nearby Outer Banks area also offers a wealth of sand-and-sea recreation.

Large shopping centers on the tourist-oriented Outer Banks complement retail stores and markets in downtown Edenton. The town has one full-service hospital and one long-term nursing home. Major medical centers, including several on U.S. military installations, are 60 miles north at Norfolk, VA. Others are about two and a half hours west in Raleigh and Durham, NC. Edenton residents also travel to these metropolitan neighbors for dining and entertainment options.

Along with its historic homes, Edenton's housing mix includes new single-family homes, condos and apartments. Many of them have attractive locations on the bay. Housing costs range between $80,000 and $1 million. Property is taxed at a rate of $10.45 per $1,000 of assessed valuation.

Among the things Mary Ann Coffey likes most about Edenton is its just-right size.

"It's a real community with most everything you'd find in a city, brought down to a manageable scale," she says. "We have shopping, good public services, an active cultural community with the Little Theater and art galleries. But we don't have big-city traffic and safety problems."

Her advice to potential newcomers: "Be prepared to contribute and participate. This is a very interconnected town, and if you want total privacy, go elsewhere. They (local residents) are open to ideas but don't want to be told how you did it better where you came from. A popular bumper sticker says, 'We Don't Care How You Did It Up North!' "

Moss and his wife live in a Victorian-style house originally built in 1900 and modernized in 1975. For "something to do," they made their own renovations, which have appreciated the value of the home.

Along with renovating their home, Moss and his wife find plenty of things to keep them busy. She is secretary-treasurer of the Little Theater, vice president of the Society for the Prevention of Cruelty to Animals, and a columnist for the weekly newspaper. Her husband takes an active role with the Edenton Historical Commission, zoning adjustment board and the Chowan County Arts Council.

John and Patty Thomas moved from Indianapolis following an extensive search that included four visits to Edenton. John, 69, was an executive with Eli Lilly & Co., a pharmaceutical company. His wife was associate dean of students at Pennsylvania's

Waynesburg State College. They moved to Edenton at the same time her brother moved from Scarsdale, NY.

"My sister-in-law and I were quite methodical with our site-selection process," says Patty, 65. "We decided we'd all retire to the same community, so we made lists of things we wanted and didn't want. We were looking for a place on the water, but we didn't want to be in a kind of senior citizens' compound. We liked Edenton from the first day we saw it. We went down our list, and it had almost everything we were looking for. In two days, we both bought houses."

Edenton's major selling points were its visual beauty, friendly people and lack of congested traffic. Personal safety was another factor. "We walk all over town," she says, "and never worry about our safety.

"My brother and his family moved into their house six months before we did," she says. "They were impressed by Edenton's cost of living, which is very low compared to Scarsdale. They also found it's very easy to make friends here. Just after they moved in, they gave a dinner party and invited the whole block. You can meet people just walking to the post office and stores."

Like other retirees, the Thomases emphasize that Edenton is ideal for those seeking a quiet, peaceful lifestyle. "But," says Patty, "if you're looking for urban anonymity, you won't find it here."

John Thomas says with a chuckle: "You pass somebody on the street, and they say, 'Did you have a nice time?' And you weren't even aware that they knew you had gone anywhere."

He and his wife are involved in a wide range of civic and cultural activities. Patty tutors at the Adult Literacy Center, and John helped start the Edenton Foundation, an educational and youth-oriented community improvement group.

Would they consider moving from Edenton? "Emphatically no! We really love it," they answer.

Bob and Elizabeth Will took a long look before moving to Edenton from Chagrin Falls, OH.

"We first saw Edenton in 1960," says Bob, 63, a former design construction engineer. "We came back several times in the early 1980s and liked the fact that it was a real, working community. Although it's a small town, we have the best of two worlds. We're close to Norfolk and Raleigh.

"We bought our house in 1983 and rented it until we moved here perma-

Edenton, NC

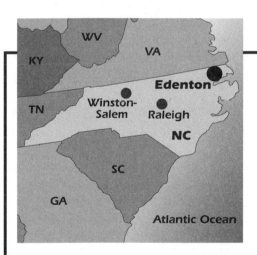

Population: 5,300 in Edenton, 14,325 in Chowan County.

Location: On Edenton Bay of Albemarle Sound on North Carolina's Atlantic coast. Picturesque town known for its many pre-Revolutionary landmarks and well-kept private homes.

Climate:

	High	Low
January	52	34
July	88	72

Average relative humidity: 57%
Rain: 48 inches
Mild winters, hot summers.

Cost of living: Below average (specific index not available).

Average housing cost: $125,000
Sales tax: 6%

Sales tax exemptions: Prescription drugs, eyeglasses, some medical supplies.

State income tax: Graduated in three steps from 6% to 7.75%, depending on income.

Income tax exemptions: Social Security benefits. Each taxpayer also can exempt up to $4,000 in local, state or federal government retirement benefits and up to $2,000 in private retirement benefits, but the total of these exemptions cannot exceed $4,000 per person.

Intangibles tax: None.

Estate tax: None, except the state's "pick-up" portion of the federal tax, applicable to taxable estates above $675,000.

Property tax: $10.45 per $1,000 valuation, with homes assessed at 100% of market value. Yearly tax on a $125,000 home is $1,306.

Homestead exemption: Homeowners age 65 and older, or disabled, living in the home and earning $11,000 or less per year qualify for an exemption of $15,000.

Security: 72.3 crimes per 1,000 residents, higher than the national average of 46.2 crimes per 1,000 residents.

Religion: 36 places of worship, representing most denominations.

Education: Classes for seniors available through the College of Albemarle (a community college in nearby Elizabeth City, with a branch in Edenton) and Elizabeth City State College.

Transportation: No public bus system, but almost everything is within walking distance. Nearest airport is at Norfolk, VA, 60 miles away.

Health: 127-bed, full-service hospital and a long-term nursing home. Major medical complexes are in Norfolk.

Housing options: A mix of historic homes (some dating to the mid-1700s) and newer single-family houses, with few rental apartments or condos. **Riverton** has new homes for $85,000-$130,000. **Village Creek** in town has homes for $175,000. **Chowan County Senior Citizens Center** is housed in an old school renovated into efficiency apartments starting at $300 a month.

Visitor lodging: Trestle House Inn B&B, $80-$95, (252) 482-2282. Governor Eden Inn, $85, (252) 482-2072. Outer Banks area has wider range of lodging.

Information: Edenton-Chowan County Chamber of Commerce, P.O. Box 245, Edenton, NC 27932, (252) 482-3400. Historic Edenton, P.O. Box 474, Edenton, NC 27932, (252) 482-263. Check out a Web site at www.edenton.com.

nently in 1987," he says. "It turned out to be a good move, because we were able to get a four-year tax depreciation advantage."

They also bought a piece of history. Built in 1743, their house is believed to be one of Edenton's oldest residences. It was renovated in 1927 but still has many original features, including the mantels and floors. The Wills originally paid $98,000 for it and spent $50,000 on renovations. They are confident they could sell it at a profit.

But, "my wife would never let that happen," Bob laughs. The Wills don't plan to move. They don't miss northern Ohio's snowy winters, and they are adjusting to long, hot summers on the North Carolina coast.

"We pay a penalty on our homeowner insurance because we're in a hurricane zone," Bob says. "But we've never had a hurricane come into the area. Barrier islands protect us from tidal flooding."

They find ample opportunities to stay busy, productive and useful. The Wills, Murphy Moss and Mary Ann Coffey and two other retired couples started an audience-participation singing program with Christmas caroling on the courthouse square. It was well-received, and the group hopes it will become one of old Edenton's newest traditions.

"I was pleasantly surprised by the number of things to do in Edenton," says Elizabeth Will, 64. "We live two blocks from downtown, and it's amazing how many things I can do without ever getting in the car. I've been so busy that I haven't been able to get my housework done."

But like other retirees, Bob Will advises potential newcomers to look hard before leaping into Edenton.

"If you're not accustomed to a conservative Southern town, you need to give it a try — perhaps spend a few days — before you make a decision to buy a house here," Bob says.●

Eufaula, Alabama

Alabama town prides itself on Southern heritage and good fishing

By William Schemmel

For nearly 170 years, the picture-book little town of Eufaula has preened in its antebellum glory, sitting on a 200-foot-high bluff overlooking southeast Alabama's Chattahoochee River.

Until recently, it's been a secret place shared mainly by bass fishermen and lovers of Southern architecture and easygoing Old South ways.

Thanks to the Retiree Attraction Committee of the Eufaula/Barbour County Chamber of Commerce, the secret's out, and the town of 17,000 is catching the eye of increasing numbers of active retirees.

Jim Hallman, a former IRS regional director, retired here from northwest Alabama and likes the area so much he served five years as co-chairman of the committee to attract more retirees.

He says the reasons for Eufaula's popularity are easy to see: the beauty of both the area and the town itself, the outdoor recreational opportunities and the small-town environment.

Hallman points to Lake Eufaula, a 45,000-acre reservoir created by a dam on the Chattahoochee.

"It's one of the best bass fishing places in the whole United States," he boasts. "The woods and fields around here are excellent country for hunting deer, dove and wild turkey.

The rolling farmland is a prime peanut-growing area.

Of the town, Hallman says, "Eufaula's historic district has over 700 buildings on the National Register of Historic Places. Our lifestyle is peaceful and relaxed. And, taxes are unbelievably low."

Hallman pays about $525 per year in property taxes on his seven-bedroom Victorian house.

"It was built in 1879, in the heart of the historic district. I call it my Tara," he says.

Alabama has a state income tax of 5 percent on a taxable income in excess of $6,000 and 2 percent to 4 percent on lesser amounts. But most retirement benefits — including military, government and private pensions — are exempt.

There's no state inheritance or estate tax beyond what part the state claims if you are subject to federal taxes, applicable on estates of $675,000 or more.

State and local sales taxes tend toward the high side, at 7 percent in Eufaula and 6 percent in unincorporated Barbour County. Prescription drugs and medical services are exempt.

Hallman said the county's retiree recruitment program has drawn several hundred new residents to Barbour County.

"Many are former Florida retirees who found the cost of living there too high. We're also getting a lot of military people and early retirees," he says.

Eufaula's moderate year-round climate and nearness to big-city amenities are important pluses.

"Weather is the No.1 attraction for many Northerners," says Malinda Ross, who came from Indiana eight years ago and fell in love with Eufaula. "I would never go back to all that ice and snow and winter confinement. It rarely gets cold enough here for anything heavier than sweatsuits and sweaters."

According to the U.S. Weather Service, the area has a mean temperature of 71 degrees, with a moderate 43 degrees in January. Yearly rainfall of about 52 inches can make summer days uncomfortably humid, though.

The Rosses had so many winter visitors that they converted their 1850s Italianate mansion into St. Mary's Bed & Breakfast, Eufaula's first historic inn.

Many retirees pitch in during the Spring Pilgrimage, in early April each year. Thousands of visitors come to tour the historic homes against a colorful backdrop of azaleas and dogwoods and to browse through arts and crafts displays by local and regional artists. Many of the Greek Revival, Victorian, Georgian and Italianate showplaces in the Seth Lore and Irwinton Historic District are open to the public only during the pilgrimage. Shorter Mansion, a Corinthian-columned Greek Revival home, welcomes visitors year round.

When they're not taking care of guests, the Rosses find plenty to keep them busy. Robert Ross, a native Alabamian, is an avid fisherman and hunter. Like other Eufaula newcomers, the Rosses frequently make the two-and-a-half-hour drive to Atlanta for shopping, dinner, night life, professional sports, theater and other activities.

Florida and Alabama Gulf Coast beaches are about a three-hour drive. Greyhound racing and Montgomery's renowned Alabama Shakespeare Theater are an hour's drive away, as are cultural activities, shopping and dining at Dothan, AL, and Columbus, GA, which have airports.

In Eufaula, shoppers have a choice of family-run retail shops in the typical small-town downtown and chain stores in three shopping centers. Local talent comes to the forefront in theater, choral groups and other artistic outlets. The Eufaula Arts Council brings singers, orchestras and theater companies from around Alabama and surrounding states.

Most restaurants feature fresh fish and seafood, Southern home cooking, steaks and barbecue. There's a growing selection of fast food, and mixed drinks, beer, wine and package spirits are available.

House-hunters have a choice of historic mansions, such as Hallman's, and contemporary brick and frame houses. There also are more than 20 mobile-home parks and 15 apartment complexes on both sides of the river.

Recreation is abundant along the Chattahoochee. In Alabama, the 85-mile-long waterway formed by the dam is known as Lake Eufaula, but Georgians call it Lake George, in honor of Walter F. George, their revered U.S. senator from 1922 to 1957. Most mornings, rain or shine, fishermen line the red clay banks under the bridge connecting the two states.

Lakepoint Resort State Park outside of Eufaula lures fishermen and family vacationers with a marina, lakeside lodge, furnished cottages, campgrounds and an 18-hole golf course.

At Tom Mann's Fish World, bass, catfish and other Chattahoochee natives are on view in a 38,000-gallon aquarium and 10 1,400-gallon tanks. A granite tombstone with a sculpted likeness honors "Big, Bad Leroy Brown," a legendary largemouth bass that lived in the aquarium. He had become a mascot, so the fishermen mourned his passing. Proprietor Tom Mann never tires of telling the tale of how Leroy was laid to rest in a tackle box — then kidnapped, but rescued and returned for a proper burial. The tombstone assures that his legend lives.

The Eufaula National Wildlife Refuge, on the Chattahoochee north of town, is a peaceful place to see ducks, geese, egrets, herons and other migratory waterfowl in completely natural surroundings. From a nature trail and observation tower, you also may sight families of deer, beaver, bobcats, foxes and raccoons.

George T. Bagby State Park, on the Georgia shore, is a comfortable roosting place for migratory humans. Its rustic-contemporary amenities include a 30-room lodge and dining room, swimming pool and river beaches, marinas, campsites and furnished cottages with kitchens for cooking the day's catch.

At Providence Canyon State Park, near Lumpkin, GA, an easy hike takes you through a dozen earthen chasms, as deep as 200 feet. Also at Lumpkin is Westville, a living history village of the 1850s with two dozen authentic buildings and craftsmen demonstrating basket-weaving, candle-making, blacksmithing and other pioneering skills.

In health care, Eufaula has the 78-bed Lakeview Community Hospital, owned by National Healthcare. It has a staff of 15 doctors, including two surgeons, a cardiologist, two OB/GYNs, a pediatrician and a surgeon/family practitioner. Medical specialists are nearby at Dothan and Columbus, and both Atlanta and Birmingham have world-renowned medical centers.

Hallman thinks Eufaula's health

Eufaula, AL

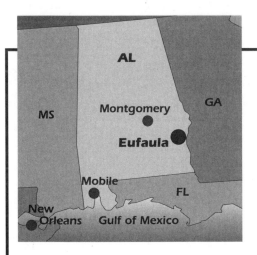

Population: 17,000
Location: Historic town dating back to the 1830s on the Chattahoochee River by the Alabama-Georgia state line. It's about 160 miles south of Atlanta and about 80 miles from Montgomery.

Climate:

	High	Low
January	57	32
July	91	68

Average relative humidity: Not available.
Rain: 51.5 inches.
Moderate climate, with chilly but not severe winters, warm summers.
Cost of living: Below average (specific index not available).
Average housing cost: $93,000

Sales tax: 7%
Sales tax exemptions: Prescription drugs, medical services.
State income tax: Graduated in three steps from 2% to 5%, depending on income and filing status.
Income tax exemptions: Social Security benefits and most private and government retirement pensions are exempt.
Intangibles tax: None.
Estate tax: None, except the state's "pick-up" portion of the federal tax, applicable to taxable estates above $675,000.
Property tax: Rate is $44 per $1,000 of assessed value, and homes are assessed at 10% of appraised value. Tax is $409 on a $93,000 home, before exemptions.
Homestead exemption: Up to $4,000 of assessed value exempted for state tax and up to $2,000 of assessed value exempted for county tax. Age 65 and older exempt from paying state portion; disability and low-income exemptions also available.
Security: 51.3 crimes per 1,000 residents, higher than the national average of 46.2 crimes per 1,000 residents.
Religion: 25 Protestant and Catholic churches.
Education: Seniors can take classes at Wallace Community College.
Transportation: No public transportation system. The nearest airport is in Columbus, GA, about 50 miles away. Atlanta International Airport is three hours away.
Health: 30 physicians in Eufaula; Lakeview Community Hospital has 78 beds.
Housing options: The historic district has older homes for $60,000-$130,000. Lake Eufaula waterfront homes cost $120,000-$200,000, and waterfront townhomes start at $80,000. Manufactured homes outside the city limits start at $40,000.
Visitor lodging: Kendall Manor B&B, $114-$124, (334) 687-8847; Lakepoint Resort State Park, $59 in lodge, $158 in two-bedroom cottage, (800) 544-5253; George T. Bagby State Park, $55-$60 in lodge, $85-$90 in cottages, (912) 768-2571.
Information: Eufaula/Barbour County Chamber of Commerce, P.O. Box 697, Eufaula, AL 36072, (334) 687-6664 or www.eufaulaalabama.com.

care will get even better with the influx of new residents.

"Services always follow demand, and our hospital is working steadily to upgrade its staff and facilities," Hallman says.

Many retirees lend their career skills to volunteer programs. Bob Smith, former co-chairman of the Retiree Attraction Committee with Hallman, "discovered" Eufaula after taking early retirement as a broadcaster for the U.S. Information Agency's Voice of America.

"At age 56 I decided I'd had enough," Smith says. "We looked around for a place to settle, and kept coming through Eufaula. Finally I told my wife, 'Let's stop by the water.'

"We bought a fishing camp with a boathouse and a couple of old mobile homes and just fished for a couple of years. Then the little radio station here burned down, and I helped the owner put it back in operation. I now do a news-at-noon show, with plenty of local and Alabama news, sports and meeting schedules. I'm also a ham radio operator," Smith says.

Hallman says the community welcomes the skills of retirees, but "you have to be assertive. Eufaula still has some of the trappings of a closed community. If you wait to be invited to participate, you can get mighty lonesome.

"I'm involved with many activities that I always wanted to do but never had time for while I was working. I think that goes for most of us who've chosen Eufaula for our retirement," Hallman says.●

Eugene, Oregon

Oregon valley proves it's a paradise for building a new life

By Dana Tims

Eugene Skinner knew a good deal when he saw one. So when he trekked into Oregon's southern Willamette Valley in the spring of 1846, he realized immediately that his cross-country search for a new home was at an end.

"The land is as rich and verdant as any I have ever laid eyes on," an ecstatic Skinner wrote in a letter to his sister. "I have found paradise."

For all his hard work clearing and settling the area, Skinner, the first European to set foot in the valley, was honored by having it named after him.

In the intervening 150 years, thousands of people have found that Skinner's vision of paradise made him as much a prophet as it did a pioneer. Retirees are continuing to discover that paradise today, flocking to Eugene in numbers that prompt some local residents to wonder how much longer Eugene will be a small city.

Few doubt, however, that Eugene, with its population of 133,460, will continue to grow and accommodate the needs of those drawn to a variety of lifestyles. Options include everything from rugged mountaineering in the breathtaking Cascade Range to countless arts and theater experiences within reach of any home in the city.

When Keith and Sharon Munson were toying with the thought of early retirement, their only goal was to leave Alaska, where Keith had worked for 20 years as an oil exploration engineer with Houston-based Schlumberger Co., and Sharon had taught third grade. They wanted to remain on the West Coast, but not in a climate where cold feet can turn into frostbite.

"If I had stayed up there, I never would have quit working," says Keith. "I didn't want to be retired in a place that had nine months of winter."

Seattle attracted the couple's attention first but was ruled out because of its size and traffic congestion. Portland, 110 miles north of Eugene, got the next look but was scratched off the list because of its sprawling freeways.

The Munsons, both 54, already were familiar with Eugene, having driven through it frequently on their way to the famed Oregon Shakespeare Festival productions in the tourist hamlet of Ashland. On a hunch and a whim, they decided to give Skinner's paradise a try, and they haven't looked back.

"It's just mind-boggling how much there is to do here," says Sharon, who is taking writing and film classes at nearby Lane Community College. She also has met new friends by joining three book groups and taking weekly mountain hikes and canoe trips. "We're building a new life here very comfortably," she says.

The Munsons were delighted from the start when they realized that in Eugene they could buy a larger home at less cost than their Anchorage residence. The influx of retirees into the area, in fact, has produced a market rewarding both to buyers and sellers. And an end to the good deals does not appear to be in sight.

"My feeling is that anybody who invests in real estate in the next several years in the Eugene area is going to see quite a bit of appreciation on their investment," says real estate agent Jerry Ramey. "It stands to be an excellent prospect for some years to come."

The Munsons' next surprise came the first time they shopped at the local grocery and produce markets.

"In Alaska, everything had to be trucked or shipped up and you seldom got the kind of fresh fruits and vegetables that we love so much," Sharon says. "In Eugene, we were delighted to find fresh berries, vegetables, all kinds of fruits and apples,

for months on end."

Year-round golf was another plus for Keith and Sharon, as it is with other retirees who frequent the nine public golf courses located within 45 minutes of downtown Eugene. Many of the emerald-green fairways are lined with towering Douglas firs, the same kind of wooden giants that carpet the rolling foothills of the Cascades and coat the craggy mountains. The rugged spine of the Cascades divides the moist western part of the state from the dry, arid high-desert plateau of the east.

For many, the ability to enjoy four distinct seasons adds to Eugene's charm and livability. Snowfall on the sprawling valley floor, 400 feet above sea level, is rare. Yet only 65 miles east, several ski areas are open from November through April for both downhill and cross-country skiing.

Summer daytime temperatures rarely exceed 90 degrees, and humidity levels stay low enough to keep the climate breezy and comfortable. Frequent rain showers produce damp springs and quips that "Oregonians don't tan, they rust." But locals are quick to note that showers are necessary to produce the rainbow of colors that pop up each May in Eugene's dazzling public and residential gardens.

"We don't have Southern California's weather all the time," Keith observes. "But we don't have their traffic jams and smog, either."

Elliot and Priscilla Aronin say they have found their own kind of paradise in Eugene since retiring from East Brunswick, NJ, where Elliot managed the fleet division of a large transportation company and Priscilla worked as an elementary school librarian.

The couple first visited Eugene 20 years ago to see their son, who was attending the University of Oregon, the state's largest university and home of a long line of track and field stars, including Alberto Salazar. For the Aronins, who are both 66, it was love at first sight.

"In New Jersey, you had to have at least a whole weekend if you wanted to get away somewhere," Priscilla says. "Here, you only need a few minutes and you can be in the mountains, at the coast or canoeing on lakes and rivers. It's quite a nice change."

Contrary to popular myth, it's not just Californians who are retiring to Oregon, the Aronins have learned. They have met people from all over the country who have found retirement refuge in Eugene.

"We've discovered a lot of wonderful people here," Priscilla says. "Getting to know people has been really easy."

Elliot has found time to pursue his first love, cross-country skiing, by volunteering to help teach and coordinate winter outings for two different programs. One is run by Campbell Senior Center, which is open to anyone age 55 or older. The other is operated by the Eugene Parks and Recreation Department.

The area's nationally award-winning network of bicycle paths has allowed Elliot and Priscilla to virtually give up their automobile on many days. Both enjoy pedaling leisurely past soaring osprey and great blue herons on tree-shaded paths that

Eugene, OR

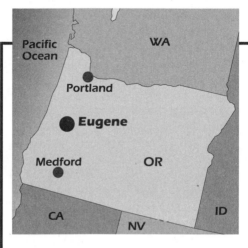

Population: 133,460 in Eugene, 313,100 in Lane County.
Location: Situated at southern end of Willamette Valley in west-central Oregon, 110 miles south of Portland.
Climate:

	High	Low
January	45	35
July	79	53

Average relative humidity: 60%
Rain: 49 inches.
Eugene has generally mild weather, with a wet season from November through April. Annual snowfall is not measurable, and marine air from the Pacific Ocean 60 miles to the west keeps summer temperatures in check. Elevation is 419 feet.
Cost of living: 107.4, based on national average of 100.
Median housing cost: $157,500
Sales tax: None.
State income tax: Graduated in three steps from 5% to 9%, depending on income.
Income tax exemptions: Social Security benefits are exempt. You may be able to subtract some or all of your federal pension income, based on the number of months of federal service before and after Oct. 1, 1991.

Intangibles tax: None.
Estate tax: None, except the state's "pick-up" portion of the federal tax, applicable to taxable estates above $675,000.
Property taxes: $15.36 per $1,000 of assessed value. Homes are assessed at 100 percent of market value. Yearly tax on a $157,500 home is $2,411.
Homestead exemption: None.
Security: 90.1 crimes per 1,000 residents, higher than the national average of 46.2 crimes per 1,000 residents.
Religion: All major religious denominations are represented.
Education: The University of Oregon, the state's largest university, and Lane Community College both offer continuing-education classes. The university's Learning in Retirement program, open to students age 62 and older, costs $100 for unlimited use. Students age 62 and older at the community college receive a 50 percent tuition discount, bringing tuition to $15 per credit hour.
Transportation: The entire area is served by Lane Transit District buses. Seniors pay 35 cents per ride, compared to a regular fare of 75 cents, and can obtain monthly passes costing half the regular charge of $22. Eugene Airport is served by United Airlines.
Health: Sacred Heart Medical Center, with 433 beds and 500 affiliated physicians, is one of the largest general-care facilities in Oregon. It offers every type of medical treatment except transplant services and severe burn treatment. Its Cancer Care Center, Oregon Heart Center and Oregon Rehabilitation Center make it among the foremost facilities in the nation. Another 62 physicians are affiliated with the Eugene Clinic, which spe-

cializes in out-patient treatment programs. The city has medical practitioners in fields ranging from chiropractic to therapeutic massage.
Housing options: Many retirees buy single-family homes in existing neighborhoods in the city. Several retirement communities also are available. **Willamette Oaks Retirement Living Community,** (541) 343-2688, is a managed living facility on the banks of the Willamette River three miles from downtown Eugene. Units range from $885 per month for a 350-square-foot studio apartment to $2,000 for a two-bedroom, two-bath unit. Services include light housekeeping and daily dinners. **Washington Abbey,** (541) 342-6077, offers the option of renting ($880-$2,160 per month) or buying an apartment. **Churchill Estates,** (541) 485-8320, features independent and assisted-living facilities tucked into a quiet southwest Eugene neighborhood. Cost is $795-$1,210 per month depending on size of unit.
Visitor lodging: Eugene has a wide variety of overnight accommodations, from upscale downtown hotels to numerous new bed-and-breakfast inns. Among the options: Valley River Inn, $180-$230, (541) 341-3460; Best Western New Oregon Motel, $78, (541) 683-3669; Oval Door Bed and Breakfast, $75-$125, (541) 683-3160.
Information: Convention and Visitors Association of Lane County, 115 W. Eighth Ave., No. 190, Eugene, OR 97440, (800) 547-5445. Eugene Chamber of Commerce, 1401 Willamette St., Eugene, OR 97440, (541) 484-1314 or www.eugene-commerce.com.

meander along the green banks of the Willamette River.

One of their favorite stops along the bike paths is pristine Alton Baker Park, where several hundred acres of inviting grasslands and open areas draw weekend picnickers. Music and crafts events often are held here. Linked by bicycle and foot bridges crossing the Willamette River to a downtown pedestrian mall, the park provides the perfect resting point on an afternoon tour.

Priscilla has pursued her learning goals by taking adult education courses in bird-watching and Russian culture at Lane Community College. The college, nestled into scenic hills just south of Eugene, offers a tuition discount of 50 percent for students age 62 or older. For a flat fee of $100, classes also are available through the University of Oregon's Learning in Retirement program. Subject matter ranges from breakthroughs in the study of DNA to the origins of early American jazz.

Priscilla also has found a bounty of arts offerings through plays and concerts at the university's intimate Robinson Theater and at the Hult Center for the Performing Arts, located in an imposing cement structure near the downtown pedestrian mall.

When the Hult Center opened in 1982, organizers jokingly referred to it as "San Cemente" because of its gray, stodgy exterior appearance. "But the outside is only part of it," according to Luke Bandle, a former marketing director for the center. "We put all of the goodies on the inside."

Indeed, the building, with the elegant, basket-weave design of its Silva Concert Hall, has attracted top names in theater, opera and classical and pop music. Eugene pulled off an artistic coup of sorts in 1991 when the New York Philharmonic, with renowned conductor Zubin Mehta on the podium, made the Hult Center its only West Coast stop.

"It's a tremendous bonus," says Priscilla Aronin. "The Hult Center is considered one of the top halls of its kind in the nation."

The center serves as the home for a number of local performing arts groups, including the Eugene Opera, the Eugene Ballet and the Eugene Festival of Musical Theatre.

It also is home to the Oregon Bach Festival, whose two-week run in late June and early July has drawn some of the world's foremost classical musicians for the past 30 years. Retirees are offered a $3 discount on tickets. In addition, they can enroll in the festival's Elderhostel program, which allows 50 participants to enjoy two weeks of behind-the-scenes entree to concerts, lectures and workshops.

The Campbell Senior Center, Eugene's largest senior facility, offers classes and programs in a wide variety of fields, including foreign languages, crafts, outdoor recreation and general science. Weekly workshops teach participants about such varied topics as health care and living wills.

One-day field trips are available on a regular basis, and overnight ventures include hiking in Mount St. Helens National Volcanic Monument in southwestern Washington. Whitewater rafting on the turbulent Rogue River in southern Oregon is another favorite, while other participants prefer cross-country skiing in the nearby high Cascades.

Kaufman Senior Center, another popular meeting spot for retirees, provides classes and social outings for more than 1,400 people monthly. It is open to anyone 55 years and older and is located in a quiet suburban neighborhood within easy walking distance of downtown.

More than 200 local retirees have made friends and found needed assistance through the Community Time Share project, which is run by longtime Eugene resident Frank Hales. The project enables retirees to earn one "share" for every hour of work they log doing tasks for others. The tasks range from shopping or running errands to providing relief for home-care assistance volunteers. Participants can cash in their "shares" whenever they find themselves in need of household chores they can't handle themselves.

"The idea is similar to the old-fashioned barn raisings of the past," says Hales. "You have the security of knowing your help for someone else will be returned when you need it."

Residents who need more help than neighbors can provide take comfort in premier health-care facilities at Sacred Heart Medical Center and the Eugene Clinic. The hospital's Senior Health Service, open to those 55 years of age and older, has more than 5,000 members. For a flat fee of $13 per couple, they can take classes covering all aspects of health care. They also are eligible for programs that provide in-home monitors and daily safety checks.

The hospital also offers 24-hour trauma and emergency services, as well as nationally recognized cancer, coronary and rehabilitation centers.

For shopping, Eugene residents head to the downtown pedestrian mall, which opened in 1970. It drew criticism in recent years as one small business after another closed, stung by the economic recession. But several new construction projects, along with renewed interest from businesses wanting to locate there, has re-energized the area. As a result, new restaurants and new specialty shops featuring fabrics, antiques, household goods and clothing have opened.

Only two blocks from the mall is the popular Fifth Street Historic District, featuring the European atmosphere of the Fifth Street Public Market. Its 57 small shops and restaurants fill a graceful, three-story brick building that in days gone by served as a hub for the city's early industrial core. Historic signs across the street direct visitors to where the city's first saw and cotton mills were built more than 100 years ago.

Although it was a desire for warmer weather that originally drew Keith and Sharon Munson to Eugene from Alaska, the couple is convinced they have long since gotten their money's worth.

"We couldn't have asked for more than we've found here," Sharon says. "It's just been ideal."

Eugene Skinner couldn't have said it any better.●

Fairhope, Alabama

Eastern shore of Alabama's Mobile Bay charms world travelers

By William Schemmel

When the whole world is under consideration, how does an American who lived 40 years in Europe end up retiring in a quiet coastal town in Alabama?

For newlyweds Gene and Christiane d'Olive, the decision wasn't difficult.

"While we were visiting Sanibel Island (in Florida), I told Christiane I would bring her over and show her where I spent much of my childhood," remembers Gene, the 73-year-old former director of ITT Europe.

The side trip ended a worldwide search for a retirement locale. The d'Olives discovered that Point Clear, near Fairhope on the eastern shore of Mobile Bay, met their priorities for "a quiet, warm small town with heart and soul," says Christiane, 51.

A resort and residential community of 2,360, Point Clear is home of Marriott's Grand Hotel, an award-winning resort on Mobile Bay with some of the finest golf, tennis and boating facilities in the Southeast.

Nearby Fairhope, with 10,481 year-round residents, is an arts colony with several good restaurants, galleries and upscale shops. The Eastern Shore Art Association/Whiting Art Center exhibits regional and national oils and watercolors, weaving, sculpture and pottery and also offers concerts, film and lecture series.

The Fairhope Municipal Pier is part of a beautiful bay-front park with duck ponds and seasonal landscaping by the town's horticulturist.

Fairhope's residential neighborhoods are characterized by large single-family homes, many with cedar shake roofs, gardens, patios and swimming pools. They are on large lots shaded by live oak trees and lush stands of camellias, azaleas and other flowering plants.

Neighboring Daphne, population 15,300, is another charming old shore town now being discovered by retirees.

Numerous attractions draw people to this area. Gulf Shores, a 30-mile-long island with glistening white sand beaches on the Gulf of Mexico, has hotels, restaurants, amusements and other resort amenities. Also on the Gulf, 14-mile-long Dauphin Island has parks, marinas, wildlife sanctuaries and about 1,000 year-round residents.

Big-city attractions are within reach. Mobile, Alabama's second-largest city, is 25 miles across Mobile Bay. Pensacola and the rest of the Florida Gulf Coast are to the east.

Fairhope, Point Clear, Daphne, Dauphin Island and Gulf Shores are all in Baldwin County. Baldwin is the state's fastest growing county and like most of Alabama has low property taxes, a low crime rate and an overall cost of living below the national average. All were factors in the d'Olives' decision to retire here.

Plus, there was a family connection. "My father's ancestors settled in the Mobile area a long way back, and my mother's parents came down here from Chicago for summer holidays," says Gene. "I visited them as a small child. Then I left and lived in Europe for 40 years."

Gene retired first in Annecy, France. He remarried after his first wife died, and he and Christiane started looking at new retirement sites four years ago. They considered "the whole world," says Gene.

Christiane, formerly an inspector for the French Ministry of Education, initially wanted to live somewhere in the Pacific. They investigated Hawaii and California but also considered the west coast of Florida.

The d'Olives moved into a custom-built home that Gene describes as "a very large cottage." The house is in a large, secured subdivision with a country club, golf, tennis and other recreational amenities.

They have been pleasantly surprised by the friendliness of their new neighbors.

"In France, people are so much colder than they are here. They don't come to visit you," says Christiane. "Here, they come and they're very hospitable. It's a quiet, charming area, with nice homes and vegetation, wildlife and birds. It's like living in a big park."

Gene does miss the European restaurants and cuisine. "Food is important. The restaurants here mostly have local seafood. I got used to the European atmosphere, customs and society," he says.

Ironically, his French wife is more forgiving. In France, she says, "most people live in high-rises and lead very sterile lives. Here the buildings are quaint and all different styles."

But they both had to adjust to the hot humid weather of south Alabama.

"The first year, we tried living with the windows open as we did in Europe," Gene recalls. "But it was too hot, and everything was ruined by mildew. So now we live indoors (with air conditioning) during the summer like everybody else."

Like the d'Olives, Ric and Kay Lahti also considered exotic retirement locales but chose the Eastern Shore area instead. Ric, a retired Air Force colonel, and Kay, a newspaper and magazine journalist, moved to Daphne.

"We considered Hawaii for our retirement home," says Ric, 53, "but we thought about things we'd enjoy at age 65, and this area seemed to offer the best opportunities."

While he was stationed at Maxwell Air Force Base at Montgomery, AL, the Lahtis spent several short holidays at Marriott's Grand Hotel.

"We liked everything about the area," says Kay, 50, "especially the climate, the location and the easy lifestyle."

The Lahtis lived in a rented condo for six months before buying a home in Lake Forest, a development of single-family homes in Daphne that has attracted many retirees. Amenities include a 27-hole golf course, swimming pools and a marina with boat access to Mobile Bay.

"On our last assignment, we lived in a large, old historic home," says Kay. "It was fine, but when we were planning our retirement home, we decided we didn't want something like that again."

Like the d'Olives, the Lahtis have enjoyed making new friends.

"The people here are terrific, warm and outgoing," says Kay. "Right after we moved in, the Lake Forest community gave us a coffee and 30 or

more women attended."

The Lahtis have become active in their new community. She's president of the Lake Forest Garden Club and joined the Women's Club and the Eastern Shore Welcome Wagon. He's joined the local chapter of the Retired Air Force Officers Association.

With the proximity of so many natural attractions, they can indulge in their favorite activities — swimming, fishing, golfing, sailing, gardening and relaxing on the Gulf Coast beaches.

World-famous Bellingrath Gardens, Mobile's antebellum homes and annual Mardi Gras and springtime Azalea Trail Festival are nearby options. So are greyhound racing in Mobile

and Pensacola and casino gambling on the neighboring Mississippi Gulf Coast.

"I'd like to live here forever," says Kay. "We don't miss anything about our former homes except our friends, but they come to see us and we visit them."

The area's heat and humidity are the only major drawbacks, they say. They advise other prospective newcomers to spend at least six months in the area — ideally in midsummer when the heat and humidity are their most oppressive — before making a decision on retirement here.

Charlie and Judy Wilson also chose Lake Forest when they made their

Fairhope, AL

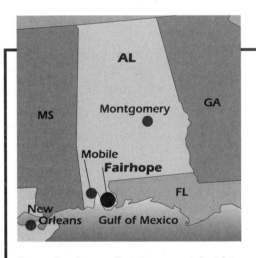

Population: Fairhope, 10,481; Daphne, 15,300; Point Clear, 2,360; Gulf Shores, 4,200; Baldwin County, 136,006.

Location: On the eastern shore of Alabama's Mobile Bay, 50 miles from Mobile, 40 miles from Gulf of Mexico beaches and the Florida Gulf Coast.

Climate:

	High	Low
January	62	42
July	91	72

Average relative humidity: 73%

Rain: 67 inches.

Subtropical climate with mild winters, balmy springs and delightful autumns. Summers are long, hot and muggy with frequent thunderstorms. There are occasional hurricane threats, usually in September and October.

Cost of living: Below average (specific index not available).

Average housing cost: $190,000

Sales tax: 6%

Sales tax exemptions: Prescription

drugs, medical services.

State income tax: Graduated in three steps from 2% to 5%, depending on income and filing status.

Income tax exemptions: Social Security benefits and most private and government retirement pensions are exempt.

Intangibles tax: None.

Estate tax: None, except the state's "pick-up" portion of the federal tax, applicable to taxable estates above $675,000.

Property tax: In Fairhope, $42.50 per $1,000 of assessed value, with homes assessed at 10% of market value. Taxes on a $190,000 home are $807 a year, before exemptions.

Homestead exemption: Up to $4,000 of assessed value exempted for state tax and up to $2,000 exempted for county tax. Age 65 and older exempt from paying state portion; disability and low-income exemptions also available.

Security: 42.5 crimes per 1,000 residents, lower than the national average of 46.2 crimes per 1,000 residents.

Religion: Over 80 Protestant, Catholic, Greek Orthodox and Jewish houses of worship.

Education: Faulkner State Community College and the University of South Alabama both have campuses in Fairhope. Non-credit courses are offered by the Eastern Shore Institute for Life Long Learning.

Transportation: No public transpor-

tation system. A car is a necessity. The state-operated Mobile Bay Car Ferry connects Dauphin Island and Gulf Shores. Mobile Regional Airport is 30 miles away.

Health: Thomas Hospital (150 beds) in Fairhope has 24-hour emergency and other specialized services. Helicopters can transfer patients to hospitals in Mobile and Pensacola.

Housing options: Many new residents live in country club-style residential communities with single-family homes, golf, tennis, marinas, security and other features. Beach condos are for sale and rent. Among popular developments are **Lake Forest** in Daphne, (334) 626-0788; **Quail Creek** in Fairhope, (334) 928-4411; and **Rock Creek** between Daphne and Fairhope, (334) 928-2223.

Visitor lodging: Marriott's Grand Hotel, doubles from $89 in winter and $159 in summer, (334) 928-9201. (Ask about honeymoon, golf and tennis packages.) Gulf State Park, an Alabama resort park at Gulf Shores, from $49 in winter and $113 in summer, (800) 544-GULF. (Accommodations include hotel rooms, furnished cabins and campgrounds, and there are many recreational options.)

Information: Eastern Shore Chamber of Commerce, P.O. Drawer 310, Daphne, AL 36526, (334) 621-8222 or www.eschamber.com.

retirement move.

"We had a Realtor who knew exactly what features we wanted," says Judy. "She didn't waste our time trying to sell us something we didn't want."

Charlie, 60, was an IBM manager in the Chicago area. Judy, 52, was director of administration for the chamber of commerce in Boca Raton, FL, where the couple lived for almost eight years.

"We considered Rochester, MN; Tucson; and south Alabama, all places where we'd lived at one time or another," explains Judy. She and Charlie visited Daphne twice within six months before they decided to move there.

"We finally decided to retire here because it has a high quality of life for the dollar," says Charlie. "The taxes are low. The state of Alabama doesn't tax pensions. We've got a golf course in our back yard, and the Gulf of Mexico is 40 miles away."

To fund their retirement, the Wilsons put money into a tax-deferred 401(k) plan, stocks and other investments.

"We didn't want to reduce our standard of living, so we concentrated on our finances," says Charlie. "I plan to live at least another 30 years, and I want to live as comfortably as possible. I think it's a big mistake for retirees to start thinking about dying the day they quit working full-time."

They have economized in some ways. "We travel a lot less than we used to when we were both working," Judy says. "But with all the opportunities for outdoor recreation around here, we don't have to take many vacations."

Transfers during Charlie's career made the Wilsons savvy movers, so they knew how to adjust to a new town when they retired.

"With IBM, we moved six or seven times," says Charlie. "We developed skills that come into play with each new move. One way to get acquainted with the community is to join the Newcomers Club and other civic organizations."

They both miss some foods — "especially the bagels," says Judy — and other amenities of former homes, including accessibility to shopping, entertainment and cultural events. But there are local specialties that Judy appreciates.

"The local produce is so good — Baldwin County is famous for its potatoes — and the seafood is abundant and inexpensive," she says.

Charlie wishes there were fewer local political squabbles, but high on the Wilsons' not-missed list are pollution, crime, population density and cold weather.

Do they anticipate moving again anytime soon?

"No," they answer with big smiles.●

Fayetteville, Arkansas

Arkansas Ozarks town mixes education, business, crafts

By Brenda Blagg

Fayetteville's visual mix of historic structures with high-rise buildings, the clear link between business and education and the easy intermingling of blue-jeaned crafters and bankers in suits and ties say something about the character of this place.

Clearly one of Arkansas' most eclectic cities, Fayetteville is a thriving city with small-town quaintness, including an active town square.

Fayetteville's square is a defining element of this northwest Arkansas city, where local leaders rejected the urban renewal of the 1970s to restore the downtown area. As in so many cities around the country, Fayetteville's downtown had suffered as retail businesses moved to shopping malls. Many buildings on the square stood empty, some falling into disrepair.

Today, the Old Post Office Gathering Place anchors the square. Developers preserved the historic exterior, which dated to 1911, and transformed the interior into one of the city's best eateries. Competing banks cooperated to establish public gardens and, with the city government, provide for their perpetual care. The two banks and a third one that opened in 1987 hold down three sides of the square, which has become the financial hub of a fast-growing region.

Several days each week, beginning in spring and extending into autumn, farmers bring their fruits and vegetables to sell at the local Farmers Market. They join area crafters who bring every kind of art and craft to peddle from trucks and vans backed up to the square.

Catty-corner to all that activity stands the University of Arkansas' Continuing Education Center, which with its physical link to Fayetteville's Hilton Hotel attracts a wide range of conferences year-round, including a growing Elderhostel program for those age 60 and older.

Participation in one of more than a dozen Elderhostels held each year offers seniors a weeklong introduction to Fayetteville and has prompted several attendees to retire to the region. Cost is roughly $300 for hotel, meals and a program that includes a sampling of local culture.

Across the horizon from the Fayetteville square, and towering over the University of Arkansas System's main campus, is Old Main, a building that has become the symbol of higher education in Arkansas. University teams routinely reward enthusiastic sports fans with runs at national titles. The UA's flagship campus, like all institutions of higher learning in Arkansas, offers tuition-free classes to qualifying seniors.

The most popular route between the city center and the university is along Fayetteville's famed Dickson Street, which is undergoing a metamorphosis as shops and restaurants cater to theater patrons attracted by a new performing arts center. The city's Walton Arts Center, named for benefactors Sam and Helen Walton, has three theaters and other facilities and programs, including several targeted to seniors.

Fayetteville has room for all kinds of people with all kinds of interests. That's part of what Marion Wyckoff, 65, likes best about the city and what her husband Robert, 69, calls its "latter-day hippy population."

The friendliness of the people is Fayetteville's strong point, she says, defining the city as a progressive town with a "fairly liberal outlook" where people are "accepting, non-judgmental and cosmopolitan."

She passes along advice given her by another retiree before the Wyckoffs got to Fayetteville: One of the best ways to make friends is to join the local League of Women Voters.

Marion followed the advice. Within nine months, she was president of the local chapter, a role that put her in contact with then-Gov. Bill Clinton. His election to the presidency provided Fayetteville with yet another tool for recruiting tourists.

Bill and Hillary Rodham Clinton, both former faculty members in the UA School of Law, were married here and had their first home in Fayetteville. He launched his political career from Fayetteville, losing a first run for the U.S. Congress, then winning a statewide race for attorney general.

The Wyckoffs retired to Fayetteville from Minneapolis. The city had been on the route between their home and her mother's place in south Arkansas, but they had never stayed overnight until about two years before they retired.

By their second stopover, they were house hunting and never really considered retiring anywhere else — although they looked at nearby Eureka Springs, a resort community even more eclectic than Fayetteville. But the Wyckoffs liked the idea of moving to a university town.

They first bought a rental property in Fayetteville and fixed it up before finding their permanent residence.

"I'm supremely happy," says Marion. "I've never regretted the move. Neither has Bob."

In fact, she adds, "We'll stay here forever. Bob says they'll have to haul him out feet first."

At age 60, Bob left a high-stress job in social work as director of family services in Minneapolis. The family came to Fayetteville while the Wyckoffs' youngest son was still in high school, which factored into their choice.

"I'm the financial manager," says Marion. "I knew it would be cheaper to live here." Tax rates are comparatively low. Some utilities, notably water, are higher, she says, and the absence of a city transit system forced them to buy a second car. But overall, costs are less — 15 percent below Minneapolis, from which the Wyck-offs came, according to data from AC-CRA, a research group.

Even if the costs of living here hadn't been lower, says Marion, "We would have come anyway. That was sort of an added bonus."

Public transportation and more choices among restaurants are what she misses most about Minneapolis. But she was glad to leave the harsh winters behind. "That is one of the most glorious things here," she says. "I love the change of seasons here. I just wish you wouldn't say too much about it."

A location high in the Ozark Mountains gives Fayetteville four distinct seasons. Snowfall averages five to six inches, just enough to satisfy any longing for wintry scenes. Although wind chills occasionally drop below zero, even winter weather usually accommodates the year-round golfer.

In spring, dogwood and redbud trees flower on the hillsides. As summer comes, lush green leaves protect the many hardwoods that will, in autumn, paint the Ozarks with color.

Dr. Malcolm and Hulda Knowles, both 80, came to Fayetteville as many newcomers do, pulled here by a relative who wanted them near. Malcolm, who still teaches as an adjunct professor at the University of Arkansas, is professor emeritus of adult and community college education at North Carolina State University. A pioneer in the field, he has written 19 books, several of which continue to be used as textbooks nationally.

He went to North Carolina State in 1964 from Boston University, then

Fayetteville, AR

Population: 52,662 in Fayetteville, 136,728 in Washington County.

Location: In the Ozark Mountains of northwest Arkansas, Fayetteville is 25 miles from the Arkansas-Missouri boundary and 14 miles from the Arkansas-Oklahoma boundary. Fayetteville (elevation 1,400 feet) is the county seat.

Climate:

	High	Low
January	45	23
July	89	68

Average relative humidity: 55%

Rain: 44 inches.

Snow: 6 inches.

Cost of living: 89.8, based on national average of 100.

Average housing cost: $118,500 for a single-family home.

Sales tax: 6.5%

Sales tax exemptions: Prescription drugs, medical services, prosthetic devices.

State income tax: Graduated in six steps from 1% to 7%, depending on income.

Income tax exemptions: Social Security benefits and $6,000 of employer-sponsored public and private pensions exempt.

Intangibles tax: None.

Estate tax: None, except the state's "pick-up" portion of the federal tax, applicable to taxable estates above $675,000.

Property tax: $47.30 (city $4.80, county $6.30, school district $36.20) per $1,000 valuation, with property assessed at 20% of market value. Tax on a $118,500 home in the city is about $1,121 a year.

Homestead exemption: Residents age 62 and older with income of less than $15,000 may qualify for a homestead property tax refund up to $250.

Security: 47.7 crimes per 1,000 residents, slightly higher than the national average of 46.2 crimes per 1,000 residents.

Religion: There are 73 Protestant churches, two Catholic churches and a synagogue.

Education: Fayetteville is home to the flagship campus of the University of Arkansas System. An Elderhostel affiliate through the UA Division of Continuing Education hosts seniors from other states and countries and offers participation for local seniors. Vocational programs are available through Fayetteville High School West Campus and Northwest Technical Institute in neighboring Springdale.

Transportation: There is limited local bus transportation on university transit routes and complimentary tourist transportation. There are commuter flights into Fayetteville's Drake Field.

Health: Fayetteville has five hospitals with 714 beds, three nursing homes with 439 beds and 32 clinics. There are 254 medical doctors.

Housing options: There's a wide selection of homes and apartments. Housing developments include **Oak Manor**, older homes ranging from $90,000-$150,000; **Boardwalk**, with community pool, clubhouse and tennis courts, $150,000-$200,000; and **Paradise View Estates**, large homes backed up to a private golf course, $150,000-$250,000. Two retirement facilities are available. **Hillcrest Towers** offers federally subsidized apartments for seniors in a downtown high-rise. **Butterfield Trail Village** is a life-care retirement community on the city's north side near a major shopping mall. Entrance fees range from $52,000 for a studio apartment to $187,600 for a two-bedroom cottage.

Visitor lodging: Fayetteville Hilton, $93-$152 double, (501) 442-5555. Clarion Inn, $69-$79, (501) 521-1166. Many other motels and seven bed-and-breakfast inns are available. Book well in advance of autumn weekends because of UA football, area arts-and-crafts fairs and fall foliage. UA basketball similarly fills accommodations in winter months.

Information: Fayetteville Chamber of Commerce, P.O. Box 4216, Fayetteville, AR 72702, (501) 521-1710 or (800) 766-4626 or www.fayettevillear.com.

retired into a consulting business that he still operates, although at a slower pace. He and Hulda, his Swedish-born wife of 58 years, moved into a life-care retirement community in Raleigh, NC, expecting to stay. Their son, a University of Arkansas professor, badgered them to move to Fayetteville. "We were propagandized to come here to be part of an extended family," Malcolm says.

The Knowleses had visited the city once and found it strikingly similar to Raleigh. Both are university towns and, since they are at the same latitude, have almost identical weather. The cost of living, says Malcolm, was about the same, although the big economic issue for them was whether to forfeit the $115,000 entrance fee they had invested in a two-bedroom apartment in Raleigh.

"We decided it was worth the difference," he says, noting that Butterfield Trail Village in Fayetteville, the life-care community to which they moved, is much like the one they left and has a similar entrance fee. Royalties from his books have held up well, says Malcolm, acknowledging that his income combined with pensions allowed them to make the switch from one life-care facility to another.

The Knowleses knew no one in Fayetteville except their son and his family, but they found that friendships come easily here. Their closest alliances are with the people they lunch with, he says, noting that he and Hulda choose to have the noon meal in Butterfield Trail's cafeteria.

Hulda suffered a stroke in 1985 and is less mobile. Malcolm gives Fayetteville's medical facilities high marks but says Raleigh, 19 miles from Duke University, had a wider variety of health care. The University of Arkansas' Medical Sciences campus is in Little Rock, roughly 200 miles away from Fayetteville. But the city has an expanding medical community with a variety of specialists and outpatient facilities concentrated in its North Hills Medical Park.

Malcolm finds his Butterfield Trail neighbors to be "fairly intellectual," a product of Fayetteville being a university town. Someone who is "strictly a playboy type" might not be as comfortable here, he says.

William and Marian Rankin also are among retirees who are comfortable and happy in Fayetteville, although they preferred a residential neighborhood to a retirement center. William, 72, and Marian, 70, moved to Fayetteville from Des Moines, IA.

If the decision had been Marian's, the Rankins would never have left Des Moines, where they were nearer to children and grandchildren. But William wanted out of the cold and into a less-expensive lifestyle.

Although William decided they should move, the choice of location was Marian's.

Now she is satisfied that "we did the right thing" and is a strong advocate for their adopted home, where she is active in Welcome Wagon and her church.

Her only complaint is that there is little public dancing for their age group. Otherwise, says Marian, "We love it. It's a pretty little town."

The Rankins started their search about two years before the move and knew they were headed to either Missouri or Arkansas, where William expected to find good fishing and hiking. The Rankins also were looking for warm weather but didn't like Arizona or Florida.

"We came down and Marian fell in love with it," William says.

The next trip, they found their future home. The city met all their criteria, William says, noting that major draws included nearby Beaver Lake and the many mountain trails they could hike. Their favorites are along the bluff-lined Buffalo National River and at Devil's Den State Park just a few miles from Fayetteville.

William especially likes not having to drive long distances to pursue their hobbies and being able to do a lot "with little or no money." Another appeal was the range of medical services here. William had heart bypass surgery several years ago and wanted to be sure the necessary care was available.

"If I'd known it was this delightful, I would have moved years before. The people are absolutely lovable. I've never seen any nicer people," says William, who traveled frequently during a career arranging international sales for U.S. factories.

He also likes the casual lifestyle. "Down here, it's just a little more relaxed. I only put a necktie on to go to church."

The Rankins' move to Fayetteville, like all the others in their life together, was "blind." They knew no one but easily made friends. They were prepared for more problems than they experienced during the move.

"We realized there was a culture change. We were afraid we would run into the Civil War complex," he says. But none of those fears materialized.

His only trouble is that grooming an oversized yard cuts into his fishing time. What does he miss about Iowa? "Not one single bloody thing," he says.●

Fort Collins, Colorado

Colorado city intent on preserving beauty, quality of life as it grows

By Claire Walter

Massachusetts-born John and Camille Trolla lived in Southern California for more than 40 years. When it came time to retire, they moved within sight of the Rocky Mountains.

The Trollas picked Fort Collins, CO, because, as John, a former school teacher puts it, "You see blue sky with clouds, smell clean air, watch the leaves changing."

John, 68, retired two years before their California house sold. As soon as it did, Milly, 66, left Disneyland after 24 years in personnel and purchasing, and in two weeks they had relocated to a new life in Fort Collins.

Jack O'Neill of Huntington, NY, spent four days in Fort Collins while visiting a brother in Denver.

"I was impressed by the cleanliness and beauty," the former high school guidance counselor recalls. "I was also impressed by the young people. Then I saw a house I liked." He phoned his wife, Ellen, and said, "I'm going to make a bid on a house, OK?" She agreed.

That deal didn't fly, but Jack told the real estate agent he wanted something in that neighborhood. The O'Neills bought a home sight unseen, didn't even attend the closing, and the agent found tenants for the house until the O'Neills were able to move.

"Everything was handled by mail," Ellen marvels. "In New York, you don't do anything without lawyers."

The couple, now both 60, say people are amazed that they would buy a home without seeing it first. They recall one woman's reaction when they related the story while asking her for directions to their new home when they first arrived.

"You let him buy a house you had never seen!" the woman exclaimed to Ellen.

"I never saw it either," Jack piped up.

But the house turned out to suit them perfectly, even fulfilling a longtime dream. "I always wanted to live on a cul-de-sac,"
says Jack — and now he does.

Set where the prairie crumples into rolling foothills, Fort Collins offers a palpable sense of space and freedom, yet has such urban amenities as good shopping, a lively cultural scene, fine health care and decent public transportation. Founded as a military post on the Cache La Poudre River, Fort Collins made the transition to a civilian settlement in the 1870s, when Colorado A&M (now Colorado State University) was founded. CSU, Colorado's second-largest college, has more than 20,000 students, who bring to the city a youthful energy that appeals to retirees.

The downtown area, known as Old Town, is a national historic district and remains the vibrant heart of the city, with a classic main street. Although Fort Collins has two major indoor malls and many neighborhood shopping areas, Old Town draws residents and visitors alike to its interesting shops, cafes, restaurants and street festivals.

The city's major thoroughfares are spaced a mile apart, forming a neatly planned grid. Most retail and commercial development is clustered around big intersections and along the boulevards. Neighborhoods often are complemented by parks providing green space.

The community has made a concerted effort to preserve and enhance the beautiful setting. Height limitations on buildings assure that the foothills, not skyscrapers, will dominate the view. Utility lines are buried, and there's been an aggressive tree-planting program.

Broad, tree-lined boulevards are easy to drive, but Fort Collins is not totally car-dependent. Nearly 60 miles of bike routes and a 14-mile protected path for cycling, jogging and walking get heavy year-round use, and a downtown river walk is in the works. Additionally, the city's Transfort bus system is gaining riders at 30 percent a year.

Despite being close to the Rockies,
the weather is relatively mild. Hot summer days are moderated by cool nights, and cold winter nights usually turn into warm, sunny days. With low humidity, even extreme temperatures rarely are uncomfortable. At Fort Collins' 4,979-foot elevation, snow melts quickly and is usually off streets and sidewalks in hours. (Even the indoor climate is good: Restaurants with 30 or more seats must have a no-smoking section, and many are totally smoke-free.)

This booming city of 109,000 — up an average of about 2.5 percent annually since the mid-'80s — is working to balance a healthy economy with planned growth, rather than the kind of mindless development that has driven people from other places.

Ward Luthi is a land-use and transportation planner by profession and founder of Walking the World, a hiking program for people age 50 and older. His Citizen Planners is a grass-roots group studying environmental and development issues.

"We're seeing an exodus from California, and one place they're coming is Colorado," Luthi says. "It tells you there's something here that people want, and there's something out there they don't want anymore. Remember, those people went to California not too long ago because California had what we have now."

Fort Collins' healthy climate, both physically and fiscally, has fueled robust growth, but natives and newcomers alike are concerned with retaining quality of life. Few want to squelch growth, but most residents want to manage it.

"I left Hawaii because we ruined paradise," says 72-year-old John Peacock, retired president of a commuter airline there. He got involved with Challenge Fort Collins, a citizens' group studying and planning Fort Collins' future.

Like other cities in the state, Fort Collins is seeking ways to get residents out of their cars and into some form of public transportation. Peacock envisions the Front Range Railroad, a high-speed train linking Fort Collins with Denver International Airport and other Front Range cities along the eastern edge of the Rockies. He foresees managed growth along the rail corridor rather than at random.

A consensus is growing that, in order to preserve the prized sense of community in the area, there should be buffer zones, or green areas, established between towns. Such zones would keep towns from growing into each other and becoming a congested megalopolis. Residents are still discussing what constitutes buffer zones, though, with one camp wanting them to remain as farmland and another finding golf courses, parks or individual houses on 35-acre tracts acceptable.

While big skies and open spaces provide an expansive umbrella for the whole city, its lifestyle and weather continue to captivate residents. Norman and Eleanor Christiansen, both 71, lived all over the country while he was a newspaper publisher. In the early '70s, they spent five years in Boulder, another

Fort Collins, CO

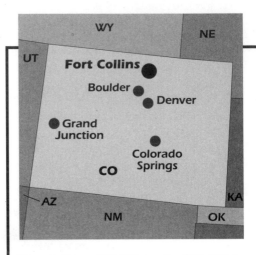

Population: 109,000 in city, 200,000 in Larimer County.

Location: In northeastern Colorado, 60 miles from Denver. The city, at an altitude of 4,979 feet, perches on rolling plains against the backdrop of the Rocky Mountains.

Climate:	High	Low
January	40	13
July	86	56

Average relative humidity: 37%
Rain: 15 inches.
Snow: 51 inches.
The city has a sunny, four-season climate, averaging 296 days of sunshine a year, 116 of them clear and 180 partly sunny. There's measurable snowfall (1/10 inch or more) on an average of 25 days a year, with 3 inches or more falling on five of those days.
Cost of living: 103.4, based on national average of 100.
Average housing cost: $144,000
Sales tax: 6%
Sales tax exemptions: Professional services, prescription drugs, some medical supplies.
State income tax: 5% of gross income.
Income tax exemptions: Social Security benefits and first $20,000 in pensions exempt for those age 55 and older.

Intangibles tax: None.
Estate tax: None, except the state's "pick-up" portion of the federal tax, applicable to taxable estates above $675,000.
Property taxes: The property tax rate in Fort Collins is $82.82 to $91.80 per $1,000 of assessed value, with homes assessed at 12.86% of market value. The tax on a $144,000 home is about $1,534 to $1,700 a year.
Homestead exemption: There is a state tax deferral program for taxpayers age 65 or older.
Security: 45.2 crimes per 1,000 residents, lower than the national average of 46.2 crimes per 1,000 residents.
Religion: The city has 73 churches and two synagogues.
Education: Colorado State University has continuing-education non-credit classes days and evenings; tuition is half-price for students age 60 and older. Front Range Community College's Larimer campus offers more than 90 low-cost adult-education classes through its continuing-education program. Fort Collins Parks and Recreation also has classes, and Poudre Valley Hospital's Aspen Club for people age 55 and above offers many free services and classes on health, wellness and other issues.
Transportation: Transfort, the city bus system, operates daily except Sunday on nine routes; the fare for those age 60 and older is 35 cents, and transfers are free. Care-A-Van provides free on-request or regularly scheduled door-to-door rides for registered clients age 60 and older and for citizens with disabilities. (A modest fare system is under study.) There's frequent bus service to Denver and Cheyenne, WY,

and Airport Express operates hourly buses to the new Denver International Airport (about an hour-and-a-half drive from Fort Collins). There are commuter flights between Denver and Fort Collins-Loveland Airport.
Health: Poudre Valley Hospital, with 250 beds, has in- and outpatient services, including regional heart and neurosciences centers. Specialty and teaching hospitals are located in Denver. There are assisted-living facilities and nursing homes in Fort Collins. In addition, Meals on Wheels provides hot meals to the home-bound, Elderhaus offers day care for the elderly and Senior Chuckwagon delivers lunches for those 60 and older.
Housing options: More than 65 percent of the homes in Fort Collins have been built since 1970, many in new subdivisions. Most are single-family homes, but patio homes, condominiums and a few full-service, high-rise apartment buildings also are available. Among the new subdivisions, **Paragon Point** has homes for $175,000-$400,000, **Stone Ridge** offers homes for $199,000-$325,000, and **South Ridge** has patio homes for $148,000-$186,000. Two older subdivisions include **Indian Hills**, $150,000-$200,000, and **Nelson Farm**, $150,000-$250,000.
Visitor lodging: The city has 20 hotels and motels, including the Fort Collins Marriott, (970) 226-5200, $89-$99 for a double room, and Plaza Inn, (970) 493-7800, $65.
Information: Fort Collins Area Chamber of Commerce, 225 S. Meldrum St., P.O. Drawer D, Fort Collins, Colorado 80522, (970) 482-3746 or www.fc chamber.org.

Colorado university town.

"We chose Colorado because of its climate and beauty," Eleanor says. "We love the mountains, the outdoors, nature. Fort Collins has everything — cleanliness, beauty, bike paths, culture. And it's the right size — between a big city and a tiny town."

Norman says their moves have allowed them to analyze many different places to live. He adds, "There are no negatives here. It's nice to go to the theater one evening and the next day put on your fishing clothes and go fishing."

Carl and Grace Hittle have lived all over the world, but they settled in Fort Collins. Carl, an eastern Colorado native, received his doctorate in agronomy from what is now CSU, where he met Grace, daughter of a professor. His career took them to Central America, Sri Lanka, Nepal and India. The couple, both 72, selected Fort Collins because it is a college town with good medical care and access to the mountains.

Carl is part of a group that hikes once a week in summer and snowshoes in winter, usually in Rocky Mountain National Park, the Indian Peaks Wilderness or Roosevelt National Forest for the day.

The Trollas also hike, but they've discovered greater joy in paleontology. They prospect a ridge above a local cement plant (they've befriended the company's geologist), and sometimes they head for Wyoming's rich fossil beds. They identify and clean the specimens and mount them on wooden plaques that John shapes and Milly finishes.

The Christiansens prefer sightseeing, with a lunch stop in a picturesque town. "We take trips all around the mountains," Norman says. "In the East and Midwest, people are so confined in winter. In Florida where we once lived, people don't go out in summer."

The Fort Collins climate, with lots of sunny days, fosters year-round outdoor activities. While winter brings snow and cold temperatures, heavy snowfall and long stretches of freezing temperatures are uncommon.

For the O'Neills, who retain a distinct Eastern, urban outlook (Ellen grew up in Boston, Jack in New York), having

the Rockies as a visual backdrop and occasional destination suffices. When their daughter, a New York City police officer who patrols Times Square, visited, she said the neighborhood was so quiet that she couldn't sleep. "Is everyone dead around here?" she asked the first morning.

Fort Collins may seem too quiet to an NYPD Blue, but retirees find lots to do. The Christiansens participate in Bible study, and Norman swims at a local pool. The Hittles found the Newcomers Club an excellent way to make new friends. Their "Retired Couples Out to Lunch" group grew so large that it had to be split into two eating parties.

Carl also joined Poudre Golden K, a Kiwanis group for men age 55 and older. "I never had time for that before," he says.

RSVP — the Retired Seniors Volunteer Program — provides another avenue to be involved in the community and meet people.

Ellen O'Neill, a former nurse, took a temporary job one Christmas as a cooking demonstrator at a local store and found it "so much fun" that she stayed on three days a week. With a low 4.8 percent unemployment rate, Fort Collins has part-time jobs for retirees who want them. Jack is an officer (and self-appointed social director) of his community homeowners' association and was accepted in the Fort Collins Civilian Police Academy. His interest in police procedure stems from his youngest daughter's career.

Most housing subdivisions in Fort Collins have no clubhouse, outdoor pool or golf course, but these facilities are available in the community. Of the six golf courses, three are municipal, two are private and one is a country club. EPIC — the Edora Pool and Ice Center — opened in 1987 and has a year-round ice rink and swimming facilities. A 40,000-square-foot senior center recently opened with a swimming pool, fitness center, library, wood and metal shops, and other facilities.

Boyd Lake, Carter Lake and Horsetooth Reservoir offer beaches and boating, and both cross-country and downhill skiing are nearby. Sports fans attend CSU varsity games or go to Denver for Broncos, Nuggets and Rockies games. Free summer concerts, a fine

local symphony and shows at Lincoln Center, an exceptional performing-arts facility with two stages, provide Fort Collins' cultural underpinnings.

Single-family homes still dominate the housing scene, but patio homes are increasing in favor, especially among retirees. Paragon Point, South Ridge and Stone Ridge are three new subdivisions in the southeastern part of town. Stone Ridge has only single-family detached homes to retain the look of a traditional neighborhood.

"Many retirees like a semblance of what they left," says Linda Hopkins, of The Group, Fort Collins' largest real-estate agency. She says most area retirees prefer homes where no one lives above or below them.

"They want enough maintenance provided so they can travel and know the chores are covered but without a burdensome homeowners' organization running everything. The developer puts in the front yard and mows and maintains it, but residents have a courtyard to do with as they wish. A lot of people are willing to give up mowing, but they still like a petunia and a tomato plant. They give up the chores and keep the fun," Hopkins says.

Among other housing options, Park Lane Towers, a high-rise near Old Town, offers security and full building services. "When a unit comes on the market, it's snapped up right away," says Helen Gray, relocation director at The Group. The Preserve, a large apartment complex near the university, is popular with seniors. Collinwood is a new, exceptionally attractive assisted-living facility. Many of the 74 units are suites, and all are furnished with residents' own possessions. Meals, housekeeping, laundry and 24-hour nursing service are provided.

"People retire here because of the climate and the size of the community," says Gray, "The university is also a big drawing card, not necessarily for educational purposes but for the diversity and activities it brings to town. Every college town has a vitality. People often say, 'Fort Collins reminds me of such-and-such,' and the place they name is usually a college town.

"When people come to Fort Collins, it feels like a nice place to be. It's comfortable and safe," says Gray.●

Fort Lauderdale, Florida

Climate and shorts-sandals lifestyle make Florida beach resort a hit with retirees

By Jean Allen

Ask retirees what they like best about living in Fort Lauderdale, FL, and they'll talk about the beaches and golf courses, the shorts-and-sandals lifestyle — and the main reason they moved here in the first place: climate.

"When we go back to Philadelphia, it's gray, it's cold. I just feel old," says Lois Ginsberg, 57, who with husband, Sam, 58, moved to Fort Lauderdale from Bala Cynwyd, PA, in the Philadelphia area. Before retiring after careers in real estate, they had vacationed here for five years in the high-rise apartment on the beach where they now live.

"You don't realize how wonderful it is until you move," says Sam.

Climate also is what finally convinced Bill and Margaret Bauman to move here instead of to Bill's original choice, Myrtle Beach, SC. The Baumans — she was a teacher, he was with IBM — moved from White Plains, NY.

"Bill loves golf, but in Myrtle Beach I felt confined," says Margaret, 61. "It was too cold at times to go to the beach."

Now they live in a beach-front apartment, and there is no shortage of golf for Bill, 63. Greater Fort Lauderdale has 19 private golf courses and 22 public links.

"There is so much to do, so many good things in recent years. The Center for the Performing Arts is fabulous," notes Margaret, a volunteer usher at the center.

If the subtropical climate with year-round sun, easy living and no heating bills is what brings retirees here, they soon find that Fort Lauderdale offers more than the restaurants, hotels, racetracks, outdoor recreation, festivals and cruises expected in a good beach resort. It also has a fast-growing cultural scene — performing arts venues, libraries, museums, operas, ballet and symphonies — and nearby professional teams

in every major sport. And if they need it, there is excellent medical care and a vast range of services and perks for senior citizens.

Living in Fort Lauderdale is not the same as visiting: It's better, retirees say. "If you come down for three weeks or three months, you don't get the feeling until you move here for good," says Sam Ginsberg.

On any typical South Florida day, Sam and Lois might be out antique-hunting, playing tennis or just hanging out. Sam, who wishes they had moved to Florida sooner than they did, says, "I'm so busy doing nothing, I'm three months behind."

Bill Bauman will be playing his daily round of golf while Margaret walks on the beach outside their apartment, swims in the surf or plays bridge. She says that to meet people when they moved here, "I just read the papers and joined everything I could find — a bridge club, a choral group and so on."

Jack and Debby Smookler probably can be found on the golf course at their club, a 20-minute drive from their condominium apartment on the beach. Jack, 73, took up golf only after they moved here from Newton Center, MA, near Boston. Debby, 67, is a longtime golfer. The pair had bought a home here for vacations and never considered another retirement site.

Fran and Peg Lorenzen will be playing duplicate bridge, their favorite pastime, at a recreation center. One reason they live here, Fran says, is the many chances to play duplicate.

"I've been playing since I was 21," Fran says. "I've moved around a lot through the United States and Canada in various careers — as an accountant, business manager and consultant. Wherever I go, duplicate bridge players are always welcomed, so I never had trouble meeting people."

Fran is 87 and Peg is 77, but they

haven't slowed down. One regular stop on their card-playing rounds is at Holiday Park in Fort Lauderdale, a city recreation department social center across the street from where the park's tennis pro taught his daughter Chris to play tennis. Jimmy Evert is still the pro at the tennis complex.

Fort Lauderdale, with a population of 150,000, is the center of a metropolitan area known as Greater Fort Lauderdale, including Pompano Beach, Hollywood and Broward County's 21 other municipalities.

It stretches from the Atlantic Ocean to the Everglades and is so laced by canals and rivers that it's called the Venice of America. Thousands of pleasure boats are docked at waterfront homes and in marinas. Water-skiers zoom on lakes, and a pretty canopy of subtropical trees and shrubs dresses up the scenery.

Fishermen and boaters can saltwater fish on charter boats or ocean piers, drop lines off bridges for freshwater catches or ride airboats through the 'Glades. They can call a water taxi for a ride to a restaurant or to see a show at the riverfront Center for the Performing Arts. They can cruise the Intracoastal Waterway and New River on a paddlewheeler, ride a sightseeing trolley around town or take a ride in the Goodyear blimp. They can sightsee or catch a ball game by riding Tri-Rail, a light-rail train, to Palm Beach to the north or Miami to the south.

Spectator sportsmen could hardly ask for more variety: Major-league football (Dolphins), baseball (Marlins) and basketball (The Heat) are in play, and NHL hockey arrives this fall when the Florida Panthers take the ice. Thoroughbreds run at Gulfstream Park and Calder Race Track, pacers and trotters at Pompano Beach Harness Track and greyhounds in Hollywood. There is parimutuel Jai Alai at the Dania Fronton, golf and tennis tournaments attract top pros, and national meets are held at the International Swimming Hall of Fame.

Beach walkers along Fort Lauderdale's 25 miles of public beaches find mostly families there; the spring break collegians who once swarmed here are long gone, moved to Daytona Beach and other spots. The city likes it that way.

Other leisure options include playing golf, joining a mall-walking group, visiting the Museum of Discovery and Science or Butterfly World, or watching big cruise ships come and go at Port Everglades, a major leisure seaport.

Shopping is outstanding. Greater Fort Lauderdale attracts shoppers who arrive by the busload daily to hunt bargains at two notable shopping spots: The Swap Shop, a sprawling flea market with free circus performances and country music concerts, and Sawgrass Mills, with 255 outlet and discount stores, said to be the world's largest discount mall. Retail malls are found in every area, and East Las Olas Boulevard with its many boutiques is the city's version of California's Rodeo Drive.

Festivals and special events range from jazz concerts along the downtown River Walk, sidewalk art shows, food fests and health fairs to the Florida Derby at Gulfstream and the Christmas Boat Parade when decorated yachts parade along the Intracoastal Waterway.

But even paradise has problems, and Fort Lauderdale has some minuses. It's a large city and carries with it the

Fort Lauderdale, FL

Population: 149,377 in city, 1.5 million in county.
Location: On Florida's lower east coast, 25 miles north of Miami. Greater Fort Lauderdale (Broward County) stretches from the Atlantic Ocean to the Everglades. City is laced with waterways and has miles of pretty Atlantic beaches.
Climate:

	High	Low
January	73	52
July	89	74

Average relative humidity: 62%
Rain: 60 inches.
Subtropical with warm rainy summers, mild dry winters; elevation 12 feet.
Cost of living: 103.3 for Broward County, based on state average of 100.
Median housing value: $108,000
Sales tax: 6%
Sales tax exemptions: Groceries, medical services, prescription drugs.
State income tax: None.
Intangibles tax: Assessed on stocks, bonds and other specified assets. Tax rate is $1 per $1,000 of value for assets under $100,000 for individuals or $200,000 for couples, and $1.50 per $1,000 value for greater amounts; first $20,000 for individuals and $40,000 for couples is exempt. Some investments are exempt.
Estate tax: None, except the state's "pick-up" portion of the federal tax, applicable to taxable estates above $675,000.
Property tax: Rates are $25.85 per $1,000 of assessed value. Homes are assessed at 100% of market value. Tax on a $108,000 house with homestead exemption noted below is $2,145.
Homestead exemption: $25,000 off assessed value for primary, permanent residences.
Security: 115.7 crimes per 1,000 residents, higher than the national average of 46.2 crimes per 1,000 residents.
Religion: 230 churches and 16 synagogues.
Education: Adult credit and enrichment courses available at several local campuses. Tuition waivers are offered to persons age 62 and older at state-assisted institutions.
Transportation: Broward County Transit bus system has limited routes; TriRail, a light-rail system, operates from West Palm Beach through Greater Fort Lauderdale to Miami. Fort Lauderdale-Hollywood International Airport is served by most major airlines; Greyhound buses and Amtrak trains serve the area.
Health: Greater Fort Lauderdale has 27 hospitals, four psychiatric care centers, 33 nursing homes and 200 adult congregate living facilities (ACLFs) with on-site medical care. City has a Veterans Affairs clinic; full-service VA hospital is in Coral Gables, 35 miles away.
Housing options: Areawide, 57% of residents live in multiple-family housing; 39% live in single-family homes, and 4% live in mobile homes. Condo prices range from $50,000 to $1 million plus. Resales include waterfront condos from $100,000, non-waterway from $55,000. New home enclaves to the west include villas, townhouses and houses. **King's Point**, in Tamarac, has garden apartments and lakefront condos from the $60,000s, villas with garages from the $120,000s. For information on retirement housing, contact Senior Placement Services of South Florida, (800) 866-8677.
Visitor lodging: Hundreds of accommodations in a range of prices, many offering senior discounts. Lowest off-season rates available after Easter to mid-December. Comfort Suites, (800) 228-5150, $79-$179 for a couple depending on season, is one of several all-suite properties with cooking facilities. Several small owner-operated beachfront motels have weekly rates and some kitchenettes, including Sea Chateau, from $45 per night off-season, from $65 in season, (954) 566-8331.
Information: Greater Fort Lauderdale Chamber of Commerce, P.O. Box 14516, 512 N.E. Third Ave., Fort Lauderdale, FL 33301, (954) 462-6000 or www.ftlchamber.com. Greater Fort Lauderdale Board of Realtors, 701 Promenade Drive, Pembroke Pines, FL, 33026, (954) 431-5300.

problems common to metropolitan areas. Because of the great influx of new residents in South Florida, traffic is heavy and the crime rate is high.

As in other metropolitan areas, though, a high crime rate doesn't mean that crime is a problem in all neighborhoods. The retirees interviewed did not indicate that crime was a primary concern. The Ginsbergs consider crime to be less of a problem in Fort Lauderdale than in their previous home in Pennsylvania, though the Baumans and Smooklers say crime is worse than in their previous homes in New York and Massachusetts.

Fran Lorenzen thinks that crime isn't as much of a problem as the lax enforcement of traffic laws. "Every time we drive down Federal Highway (U.S. 1), without exception, we see cars running red lights," he says.

The weather has its drawbacks. Summers are hot and humid, but Sam Ginsberg likes it that way. He calls summer "the best-kept secret in Fort Lauderdale. No waiting in restaurants — it's wonderful."

But Margaret Bauman voices the opinion of many when she says Florida summers are "just too hot." Thousands of residents escape Florida in summer for cooler climes. She and Bill go to White Plains, NY, where they still have an apartment.

Residents also face the threat of hurricanes each season and the economic impact of being in a hurricane area. Although the center of 1992's killer Hurricane Andrew missed Greater Fort Lauderdale, the area sustained property damage. As a result, home insurance rates rose, policies were canceled and coverage is harder to find. Before Andrew, the last hurricane in the Fort Lauderdale area struck in 1964.

While retirees who move from the North are happy to find much lower utility bills in the winter, what is saved on heating often is spent on air conditioning, particularly during the hottest months. According to Florida Power and Light, an average electric bill for a 1,400 square-foot, all-electric house is $72 for the month of January and $155 for July.

Most retirees find that clothing costs are lower, mainly because people don't wear much. "All you really need are three tennis outfits and a bathing suit," says Sam Ginsberg with only slight exaggeration.

Taxes are lower here than in the North, retirees say. Currently the property tax rate in the city is $25.85 per $1,000 of assessed value.

Overall, Fort Lauderdale satisfies retirees. What seniors want, they probably can find in the city. Older residents have economic and political clout here because of their numbers. One in three area residents is age 50 or older, and one in five is 65 or beyond.

New York is the biggest provider of Fort Lauderdale's retirees, and when New York City was near bankruptcy and delayed payment of city pensions a few years ago, local merchants complained as loudly as the many New York retirees living here. Any security force at gated communities and apartment complexes here is likely to include one or more retired New York City police officers.

Residents of mostly retiree condo complexes can and do swing area elections. Many complexes organize parties, picnics, concerts, craft classes, sightseeing and theater expeditions and have their own minibus transportation to shopping and appointments.

Besides the reduced-price early-bird dinners and other discounts, seniors can find hundreds of available classes and lectures at local colleges, universities and public schools. Agencies cater to senior citizens with health screenings, lectures and assistance. Other agencies help seniors find paid or volunteer jobs.

Greater Fort Lauderdale has 200 adult congregate living facilities (ACLFs), state-licensed and certified facilities for seniors who are mobile but need or want on-site medical availability, some or all meals furnished and other services.

"There are all sorts of retirement centers," says Debbie Romero, who operates a free placement service that matches seniors with appropriate places that suit their tastes and pocketbooks.

"There's everything from converted beach motels to private homes and very deluxe apartment complexes, with from five beds to 504, and prices from about $500 to over $2,000 a month," she says. Prices depend on the level of luxury, number of meals and other services desired, and whether the retiree is independent (taking care of all his own needs) or assisted (needing help with dressing and care). Rental apartments are available fully furnished or with just appliances and carpets.

Average age of residents entering retirement homes is 75, Romero says. Younger retirees tend to buy houses or condominium apartments, often in complexes with mostly older adults.

Jack Smookler, a neighbor of the Ginsbergs, says he was surprised at how much Fort Lauderdale offers for senior citizens, "although we don't take advantage of much of it." Jack and Debby say they currently are too active to need or want special services for seniors.

The Lorenzens, like many Fort Lauderdale area retirees, met and married here after losing their mates. Both lived in the same beach-front condominium building.

"He sold his apartment and moved into mine," says Peg, who moved to Fort Lauderdale from the Boston area. Both had lived here part-time since the 1970s. Fran, who moved from Ontario, is one among thousands of Canadians who retire or winter in the Fort Lauderdale area.

Sam and Lois Ginsberg, on the other hand, were high school sweethearts. "I feel, living here, we are two people in high school without the homework," says Lois. "I want to live the last years of my life in an environment like this." ●

Gainesville, Florida

Renowned medical facilities and Florida's largest university attract retirees

By David Wilkening

Some people move to Gainesville for the climate, the culture and the easygoing Florida lifestyle. But there are a lot of other reasons — including a top-rated university and excellent medical care — that help account for the fact that almost one in every 10 residents of the city is 65 or older.

Joe Werner moved to Gainesville because he got tired of traveling to town by ambulance. Joe retired in 1991 after a career as an attorney in St. Petersburg and, seeking a peaceful country life, he bought a five-acre farm in rural Dixie County, home to only 10,000 residents. But when a touchy pancreas required emergency care, Joe was rushed three times to the renowned Shands Hospital 50 miles away in Gainesville.

"After about the third trip of 50 miles, when the ambulance was bumping over rutted back roads and the medics were trying six or seven times to get an IV into my arm, I said to myself, 'I'm going to move'," recalls Joe.

Joe sold his farm and found another home for the 75-pound stray dog who had moved in with him there. Then he bought a condominium in Gainesville near the million-square-foot Oaks Mall and paid just under $50,000 for it.

The area's geographic location is midway between Atlanta and Miami and about 120 miles north of its better-known cousin, tourist-famous Orlando. A city of 100,000 people in the heart of north-central Florida, Gainesville basks in Gulf breezes that make summer days generally warm, with dry and mild winters. The most prominent city in Alachua County (population about 213,000), Gainesville has an average year-round temperature of 69 degrees.

The mild climate was an important consideration for Lucille Schlichting, who moved to Gainesville in 1989 from Long Island, NY, five years after her late husband, Bill, had a stroke that paralyzed his right side.

"We decided that we were tired of the cold weather and the rising tax rates," recalls Lucille, who recently celebrated her 70th birthday. The Schlichtings followed their daughter and son-in-law, who had moved to Gainesville from Long Island to start an auto upholstery business. The younger couple had determined they could better afford a start-up business in Florida over higher-taxed and generally more expensive New York.

A talented commercial artist before his stroke, Bill Schlichting died in 1992. "But he was comfortable in his last years here because the climate was easier on him and he had a chance to watch his grandchild grow into a beautiful and talented artist herself," says Lucille.

Just as Orlando is heavily influenced by tourism, the face of Gainesville is shaped largely by Florida's oldest and largest university, the University of Florida. Walter Gardner, 80, says that the university was one of the three major reasons he and his wife, Jacky, moved here after first leaving their native Minneapolis, MN, to retire in Virginia.

"Gainesville has the finest medical facility in the Southeast. And there are no snowbirds," smiles Walter, who along with Jacky, 75, is active in various university-related clubs and associations.

The Gardners first came to Gainesville to visit friends. They said their initial reaction was that it was a friendly town with a good climate that is influenced culturally by the presence of the university.

The sprawling school of almost 40,000 students serves as a major focal point. The college's sports teams are nationally known, particularly the NCAA champion football team. The university's cultural facilities include an impressive 1,800-seat Center for the Performing

Arts, a venue for everything from popular music to opera, jazz and country music concerts. The university also lures a variety of speakers and a host of cultural events throughout the year.

Even in the summer, when school attendance dwindles, there is no shortage of cultural activities. There's the small but distinguished Hippodrome State Theater, where plays are acted out on a round stage in a former U.S. Post Office building constructed in 1909. Plays also are produced by the Gainesville Community Playhouse, the Santa Fe Players, Across-Town Repertory Theater and Florida Players Theater.

Other performing arts groups also have flourished, including the Gainesville Civic Chorus, Gainesville Ballet Theater, Danscompany, Dance Alive!, Gainesville Symphony Orchestra and Gainesville Friends of Jazz. Art lovers often find their way to the new Samuel P. Harn Museum of Art, which houses five permanent exhibits.

It's not unusual for retirees to continue their education by enrolling in the University of Florida. Santa Fe Community College also offers a variety of noncredit courses.

Gainesville's strong lure for nature lovers is as obvious as the presence of the university. Almost two-thirds of Alachua County's 969 square miles is a wilderness of forests, punctuated with scenic lakes and wetlands.

The 62-acre Kanapaha Botanical Gardens has paved pathways for wheelchairs that lead to a herb- and plant-strewn rock garden. The largest bluff oak tree in Florida is found here. For the more adventurous, the Devil's Millhopper is a giant sinkhole with a half-mile nature trail and a 232-step wooden stairway to take visitors to the bottom.

Parks abound in the area. There are 40 nature parks within 50 miles of Gainesville for picnicking, hiking, swimming, camping, boating and fishing. The Gainesville Parks and Recreation Department maintains 30 parks and plans a year-round schedule of recreational activities and competitive sports for all ages. Area anglers have easy access to six freshwater lakes, all with boat ramps, and two provide accommodations and camp-sites with covered boat slips.

Golfers can choose among seven courses, five of which are public or semiprivate. Lighted golf at night is as inexpensive as $9.50 a round between March and November at the Villages of West End Golf Club, a predominantly par-three course. For those who want to make their way around on bicycles, Gainesville has 60 miles of roadways with on-street bicycle lanes that have won the city a ranking among the top 10 in the United States by Bicycling Magazine.

The median housing price is an affordable $95,820, according to the

Gainesville, FL

appraised value. The tax on a $95,820 home would be about $1,916 a year, with the homestead exemption.

Homestead exemption: $25,000 off assessed value for permanent, primary residences.

Security: 106.4 crimes per 1,000 residents, higher than the national average of 46.2 crimes per resident.

Religion: There are approximately 300 places of worship for all faiths in the Alachua County area.

Education: Gainesville is home of Florida's oldest and largest university, the University of Florida. Santa Fe Community College offers a variety of noncredit enrichment courses. The area's Community Education Program offers classes in subjects as diverse as arts, computers, natural history and sports. Alachua County Library District has 10 locations and bookmobile service, and books can be mailed to homebound patrons. The library also sponsors dozens of free programs throughout the year.

Transportation: The Regional Transit System provides local bus service as well as minibus transportation for the handicapped. The Gainesville Regional Airport offers 32 nonstop flights each day, linking the area with hub cities such as Atlanta, Charlotte, Miami and Orlando via five major carriers. Amtrak provides rail passenger service. Interstate bus transportation is offered by Greyhound-Trailways. There is good highway access; Interstate 75 skirts Gainesville on the west, making it the main link with major metropolitan centers such as Atlanta and the Tampa-St. Petersburg area. U.S. Highway 301, U.S. Highway 441 and State Highway 26 join Gainesville with other communities in Alachua County and northern Florida.

Health: Shands Hospital and the Uni-versity of Florida Health Systems (UFHS) is the area's best-known medical complex, encompassing four acute-care hospitals with a total of 800 beds, two specialty hospitals and two licensed home-health agencies. North Florida Regional Medical Center is a 278-bed acute-care facility. Gainesville Veterans Affairs Medical Center is a 480-bed medical, surgical and psychiatric facility.

Housing options: Haile Plantation is a master-planned community composed of walking and bicycle trails, tennis courts, playgrounds, swimming pools and an 18-hole golf course. Homes are priced from the mid-$100,000s. **The Village** is an apartment complex on 80 wooded acres complete with a pond and walking trails, in a setting less than 15 minutes from shopping malls, restaurants and other amenities. There are various amenities such as a pool, hot tub, library, greenhouse and gardening areas. Efficiencies start at $1,160 a month, single occupancy. For high-rise living, the 12-story **Lakeshore Towers** near the university and Shands is an adult-oriented rental community offering both furnished and unfurnished apartments with balconies and a view. Security includes a door attendant on duty after hours. Air conditioning and heating are included in rental fees, which start at $1,050 a month for an efficiency unit of 400 square feet. The standard lease agreement is for one year, but the rental community works with newcomers who are unsure of their housing plans.

Visitor lodging: University Inn, $50, is near the University of Florida and Shands Hospital, and shuttle service is available, (352) 376-2222.

Information: Gainesville Area Chamber of Commerce, P.O. Box 1187, Gainesville, FL 32602-1187, (352) 334-7100 or www.gainesvillechamber.com.

Population: About 100,315 in Gainesville, 212,997 in Alachua County.

Location: In north-central Florida midway between Atlanta and Miami, about 120 miles north of Orlando. Jacksonville is 78 miles northeast.

Climate:

	High	Low
January	66	43
July	91	71

Rain: 52 inches.
Alachua County has a 255-day growing season and an average temperature of 69 degrees.

Cost of living: Below average.

Median housing cost: $95,820

Sales tax: 6%

Sales tax exemptions: Groceries, prescription medicines and professional services.

State income tax: None.

Intangibles tax: Assessed on stocks, bonds and other specified assets with some investments exempt. Tax rate is $1 per $1,000 of value for assets under $100,000 for individuals or $200,000 for couples, and $1.50 per $1,000 of value for greater amounts. The first $20,000 for individuals and $40,000 for couples is exempt.

Estate tax: None, except the state's "pick-up" portion of the federal tax, applicable to taxable estates above $675,000.

Property tax: In Gainesville, $27.06 per $1,000, with homes assessed at 100% of

Gainesville Chamber of Commerce, and it is possible to find a new 1,800-square-foot single-family home on an 8,000-square-foot lot for not much more than $100,000. Such a home typically would have three bedrooms, two full baths, a living and dining area, a family room with a fireplace, and a two-car attached garage. There also are many luxury apartment complexes, condominiums and retirement communities.

One popular retirement area is Bailey Village, a residential assisted-living community where a monthly fee covers three meals a day, daily housekeeping, weekly linen and laundry service, supervised medication and an extensive activity program. Programs are tailored to the needs of residents, either on a long- or short-term care schedule.

Lucille Schlichting has lived in the Cedarwood Apartments complex since she came to Gainesville seven years ago. Her unit is in a heavily treed complex with tennis courts and a swimming pool that she enjoys virtually every day. Her large two-bedroom apartment often serves as a temporary hotel for the many guests and relatives who pass through town.

Because Shands Hospital is a leading referral center for the state and the entire Southeast, people from all over — some with rare, diagnostically baffling diseases — are drawn to Gainesville. Because so many guests at the nearby Radisson Hotel are hospital visitors, the hotel boasts in brochures that it "treats patients, too" and offers free hospital transportation. Shands Hospital's 576-bed tertiary-care facility on the campus of the university includes cardiovascular medicine, neurological services, cancer services and transportation.

Shands at Alachua General Hospital, also in Gainesville, is a full-service center with 423 beds and 200 physicians on staff. The facility offers cardiac care, cancer care, neuroscience, neonatology, women's health and emergency care. Of particular note to seniors, the hospital sponsors Senior Advantage, a health-benefits program for people age 55 and older.

Other area hospitals include North Florida Regional, a facility with a maternity unit rated one of the top 10 in the country by Child Magazine. Veterans Affairs Hospital is a 480-bed federally funded medical center that provides medical, surgical and psychiatric patients with primary, secondary and tertiary care. And the Gainesville area supports six nursing homes offering a variety of care and a dozen retirement communities providing independent and assisted living.

Special services for retirees are offered by the Center for Aging Resources, a unit of the Mid-Florida Area Agency on Aging, (800) 262-2243. It was set up in 1986 to help seniors and their families negotiate the maze of programs and benefits that serve the elderly. Resource specialists at the agency use a computerized network to access a wealth of practical information about local, state and national resources — everything from local transportation services to pharmaceutical resources.

In part because of the hospitals, there are an unusual number of local opportunities for volunteers to perform various types of social work. Under the umbrella of the Retired Senior Volunteer Program, several hundred retirees work in museums, libraries, hospitals and nursing homes.

Among the volunteers are Joan and George Nehiley. George, 77, regularly visits local hospitals to help patients confined to wheelchairs. Joan, 73, spends part of each Thursday helping to distribute meals at a local food bank.

Before they retired, George was a guidance counselor for Dade County schools, and Joan was a secretary-treasurer. After they found themselves victims of crime several times in Miami, they moved to Gainesville about 12 years ago. They already were familiar with the area, where George attended the university before embarking on his own educational career.

The Nehileys like the warm climate and felt welcome in their new community. "There are a lot of active senior programs, and it's just a very friendly town," says Joan.

In common with much of Florida, Gainesville's growth as a city came only after the turn of the century. As early as 1529, Spanish explorers trekked through what now is Alachua County. Later they built missions and used the area's fertile land for the production of food and cattle to feed themselves and the Seminole Indian population.

The British occupied Florida from 1763 to 1783, when Spain regained control. In 1817, the Spanish king granted nearly 300,000 acres of northern Florida land to a powerful Cuban merchant. The land grant was voided two years later when Florida became a U.S. territory.

Alachua, believed to have been named after a Seminole word for a large sinkhole in a wetlands area, became the territory's ninth county. Gainesville, which was established in 1854 at the end of the Second Seminole War, was named in honor of a military hero, Gen. Edmund Gaines. The new city grew from a core of only 250 original settlers, and until the late 1800s, Alachua County was little more than a citrus capital. However, a series of freezes in the late part of the century pushed that industry farther south.

Today, visitors to the area often come to see Florida's second-oldest town, Micanopy, founded in 1821. The small city just 13 miles from Gainesville is popular for its antiques, art and curio shops.

Gainesville itself has a distinct personality in that it is home both to retirees who have their careers behind them and young college students who have yet to decide what to do with their lives. This is not always an easy truce, as Joe Werner points out.

"This town is not exactly built around retirees," Joe says when pushed to find fault with the area. He is reminded of that fact when driving too slow to suit young motorists behind him or when he pauses a little too long at a traffic signal. Students sometimes are quick to lean on the horn, he says.

Still, that seems to most retirees a small price to pay for living here. The Nehileys, who live in a subdivision that offers a mix of younger residents and retirees, put it in perspective. "Young people help keep you young," suggests Joan.●

Gainesville, Georgia

Georgia setting wins a gold medal from retirees

By William Schemmel

The secret was safe for a while, but many residents of Gainesville say the word spread during the summer of 1996: This small north Georgia city is a nice place to live.

That's when the summer Olympic Games were held in Atlanta, and communities on Lake Sidney Lanier had front-row seats. A section of the lake three miles north of downtown Gainesville was selected as the venue for canoeing and rowing competitions.

City officials say that some Olympic visitors have returnd permanently since they experienced the beauty of the lake and the mountains surrounding Gainesville.

Lake Lanier — a 38,000-acre U.S. Army Corps of Engineers reservoir with a 607-mile wooded shoreline — is one of the most popular inland waterways in the nation, and it is a major reason retirees are moving to Gainesville.

With a population of 19,672, Gainesville is the largest city on the lake. Almost 22,000 acres of this mammoth inland sea, created by a dam on the Chattahoochee River, are in Hall County, which has nearly 125,000 residents.

Gainesville also is the gateway to northeast Georgia's Appalachian Mountain vacation lands. National forests, mountains as high as 4,800 feet, waterfalls, lakes, scenic rivers, craft towns and tourist centers are a short drive north of the city.

For visitors who elect to stay here permanently, Gainesville boasts an attractive selection of residential communities, moderate property taxes, excellent medical care and plenty of indoor and outdoor recreation. Proximity to metropolitan Atlanta — only 52 miles south on an interstate highway — is another major plus.

Pat and Bud Schick visited Gainesville and Hall County many times over a five-year period before making their move from LaCrosse, WI.

"When I retired (from the Wisconsin Highway Department) at age 55, we got a trailer and spent 10 to 12 weeks at a time on the road," says Bud, 62. "We seriously considered the Asheville, NC, area and several Tennessee Valley Authority lakes. But we kept coming back here.

"We decided on it for several different reasons," he says. "It's sheltered from storms by the Appalachians and has a pleasant four-season climate. We get some cold weather and even a little snow — but nothing like we had in Wisconsin. And the fall foliage in the mountains is as beautiful as you'll find anywhere.

"We like being close to the mountains and, of course, to Lake Lanier. We enjoy fishing, swimming, boating, golf, tennis — all of which the lake has plenty of."

Pat adds: "It's the people that really decided us. They're so friendly — I was surprised at being so readily accepted. We can enjoy the advantages of a small town, and we're only an hour from the shopping, dining, entertainment and other advantages of Atlanta."

The Schicks enjoy the best of Gainesville's two worlds. They're only a few minutes from town, but their three-story brick home in the Cherokee Forest subdivision is only a few yards from the lake.

Developed originally in 1988, Cherokee Forest is typical of the area's many lake-front residential communities. About a third of the 140 homes, on large, wooded, gently rolling lots, are owned by retirees or preretirees who enjoy the lake, a pool and tennis courts on the property.

Lake-front lots sell for $75,000-$250,000. Away from the lake, lots with mountain views are $27,000 and up. Homes in Cherokee Forest are valued at $250,000-$400,000.

Another option is Chestatee North, a patio-home community on Lake Lanier. About half of its residents are retirees, and the 45 homes here average about $175,000. Amenities include pools and tennis courts.

Royal Lakes is another subdivision popular with retirees. The 500-acre community is not on Lake Lanier, but it has two small lakes on the property and a golf course. Lots sell for $30,000-$80,000, with homes from $190,000-$400,000.

Bob and Gloria Molloy moved to the Chattahoochee Country Club area of Gainesville from Lufkin, TX. They lived in an apartment while their home was under construction.

The Molloys' home is 500 feet off the road and backs up to Lake Lanier. "The good Lord willing, we'll die in that house," Gloria laughs.

"I miss my wonderful friends in Texas, but I have made some wonderful friends here, so I would not go back," Gloria says. "It's a great town if you want to pitch in and take part in the life of the community. Organizations and clubs welcome your participation, but you have to reach out."

Both Gloria and Bob are involved in church activities, and Gloria also donates time to the Newcomers Club and does some bell-ringing for the Salvation Army.

One of the few drawbacks to the area, she says, is a lack of good restaurants, although they are readily available in Atlanta. The Molloys like to travel, so they also appreciate the proximity to Hartsfield International Airport in Atlanta.

"The people here are very friendly," says Gloria, 66. "But it's more than that. The two colleges (Brenau University and Gainesville College) and the military academy (Riverside Academy) give the town a special mix of people."

Brenau University, a small, private college, and Gainesville College, a two-year unit of the state university system, both offer day and evening continuing-education courses. BUL-LI (Brenau University Learning and Leisure Institute) is extremely popular with retirees.

Many retirees also appreciate the cultural opportunities available through the colleges. "The colleges offer a lot of entertainment and music," says Janet Hutts, 68, who moved to Gainesville from Rhode Island with husband Wilsie, 71.

"I like living close to the water and the mountains, " says Wilsie. "And I like Gainesville because it's still small — you can go anywhere in town in 20 minutes."

They originally considered several other retirement areas in Georgia, South Carolina and Texas, but Gainesville's climate, medical services and proximity to Atlanta and their children and

Gainesville, GA

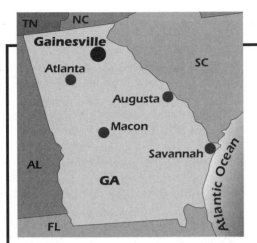

Population: 19,672 in Gainesville, 123,571 in Hall County.

Location: In the foothills of northeast Georgia's Appalachian Mountains, 52 miles north of Atlanta.

Climate:

	High	Low
January	50	31
July	87	67

Average relative humidity: 60%

Rain: 53 inches.

Snow: 3 inches.

Elevation of 1,279 feet fosters a moderate four-season climate. Hot summer days cool off in the evening. Severe cold spells, with some light snow, are brief. Fall foliage is spectacular.

Cost of living: Below average (specific index not available).

Average housing cost: $105,150

Sales tax: 7%

Sales tax exemptions: Prescription drugs, hearing aids, eyeglasses.

State income tax: Graduated from 1% to 5% on first $7,000 (singles) or $10,000 (couples filing jointly), then 6% on greater amounts.

Income tax exemptions: Social Security benefits; up to $13,000 in retirement income is exempt for those age 62 and older.

Intangibles tax: None.

Estate tax: None, except the state's "pick-up" portion of the federal tax, applicable to taxable estates above

$675,000.

Property tax: In Gainesville, $9.75 per $1,000 of assessed value, based on 100% of fair market value plus $7.64 per $1,000 based on 40% of market value. With $2,000 homestead exemption noted below, annual taxes on a $105,000 home are $1,319. In unincorporated Hall County, the rate is $22.75 per $1,000 assessed valuation, based on 40% of fair market value. With homestead exemption, taxes on a $105,000 home are about $937.

Homestead exemption: $2,000 off assessed value for full-time residents. Taxpayers who are 62 or older and have an income of less than $12,000 can request a school tax exemption.

Security: 99.8 crimes per 1,000 residents, higher than the national average of 46.2 crimes per 1,000 residents.

Religion: About 100 Protestant churches, one Catholic church. Nearest Jewish congregations are in Atlanta and Athens (30 miles).

Education: Brenau University, a small, private school, offers evening and weekend programs. Gainesville College, a two-year unit of the University System of Georgia, offers day and evening continuing-education courses. Lanier Technical Institute also offers continuing-education courses in many practical fields. The main campus of the University of Georgia is 30 miles away at Athens.

Transportation: Hall Area Transit public bus system. Atlanta's international airport is 60 minutes south.

Health: Northeast Georgia Medical Center, a 294-bed facility, serves a 20-county area of northeast Georgia, offering emergency care and extensive specialized and critical-care services.

Lanier Park Regional Hospital is a fully accredited 124-bed acute care medical and surgical hospital with 24-hour emergency care, also. Lanier Park's "Seniority" program offers a package of health-related services for those age 55 and above, available for a one-time $20 membership fee. About 200 medical doctors and 70 dentists practice in Gainesville and Hall County. The county has seven nursing homes with about 600 beds.

Housing options: Subdivision communities on Lake Lanier are the most popular retirement locations. Cherokee Forest, Brittany Pointe, Chestatee North, Royal Lakes and other developments offer large, wooded lots on gently rolling terrain. Some have lake frontage ($75,000 and up); some interior lots have mountain views (high $20,000s and up). Some older resale homes are available in Gainesville, which also has a limited number of rental apartments and condos. Two-bedroom units rent for $500-$800 a month.

Visitor lodging: The Dunlap House Bed & Breakfast, a 1910 home in the Green Street Historic District downtown, $85-$155 including breakfast, (770) 536-0200. Holiday Inn, in downtown Gainesville with pool, restaurant and lounge, $59-$72, (770) 536-4451. Lake Lanier Islands Hilton Resort, with pool, tennis, restaurant, lounge, water sports and golf, $149, (770) 945-8787. Campsites at Lake Lanier Islands, with water and electricity hookups, hot showers and picnic areas, are $20-$30 a night, (770) 932-7270.

Information: Greater Hall Chamber of Commerce, P.O. Box 374, Gainesville, GA 30503, (770) 532-6206, www.ghcc.com or www.gainesville.org.

grandchildren won them over.

An industrious city with many well-kept residential neighborhoods, the center of Gainesville is the downtown courthouse square. Most of the art deco-style government buildings were constructed after a disastrous tornado in April 1936. Some of the city's most important cultural activities take place on Green Street, a tree-shaded avenue of stately Victorian homes a few blocks from the square.

The Georgia Mountains Museum is a repository of information about the culture and history of the mountains. Permanent exhibits include books, arts and handicrafts by North Georgians. The Mark Trail Memorabilia Exhibit honors north Georgia native Ed Dodd, who created the nationally syndicated comic strip character.

The neighboring Quinlan Art Center has a year-round schedule of art exhibits, films, lectures, classes, workshops and music performances. The city's arts umbrella includes the Gainesville Symphony Orchestra, Gainesville Chorale, Gainesville Music Club, Pro Musica, Children's Theater, the Northeast Georgia Writer's Club and Gainesville Ballet. The Gainesville Theatre Alliance, a joint program of Brenau University and Gainesville College, offers half a dozen yearly stage productions.

Excellent and readily available medical service is cited by numerous retirees. The Northeast Georgia Medical Center is a 308-bed complex that serves a 20-county area of northeast Georgia. Services include cardiac catheterization, intensive care and coronary care units, an outpatient surgery center, cancer care, dialysis, endoscopy, enterostomal therapy, nutritional counseling, cardiology lab and a gynecologic and urologic care unit.

The city and county parks departments operate more than two dozen recreation areas, with tennis courts, swimming pools, softball fields, boat ramps, picnic pavilions and other amenities. Eight golf courses are open to the public.

Two 18-hole courses are in the Lake Lanier Islands recreation area. Operated by a state recreational authority, it was developed on the hilltops that bobbed above the waters of the lake when it was formed in 1958. In addition to the two championship golf courses, Lanier Islands' numerous recreational amenities include two resort hotels (Stouffer's Pine Isle and the Lake Lanier Hilton Resort), a sand swimming beach with boat rentals and water slides, festivals and summer concerts, camping and cottages, and some of the finest fishing in North America.

Many Gainesville retirees dock their boats at Lanier's spacious marinas. The U.S. Army Corps of Engineers has developed several multipurpose recreation areas around the lake.

Gainesville claims to be the "broiler chicken capital of the world," and many retirees originally came here as executives in the poultry industry. Other Gainesville retirees have backgrounds in diversified manufacturing and service industries. Some pre-retirees commute to jobs in metropolitan Atlanta.

"It has the values we were brought up with, and the culture of a small Southern town," says Gloria Molloy. "I hope we will never have to move."●

Georgetown, Texas

This award-winning Texas Hill Country town carefully preserves its history

By Nina J. Stewart

Given its modern sophistication, it's sometimes hard to believe that the fastest-growing city in the fastest-growing county in Texas once was a rough-and-tumble staging town for vast cattle drives up the old Chisholm Trail. Located on the banks of the San Gabriel River on the edge of the Central Texas Hill Country, Georgetown is a progressive town of 26,400 with a rich pioneer history.

Georgetown residents came together in 1998 to celebrate their town history with a sesquicentennial blowout, which featured gala parties, parades, a mock longhorn cattle drive and other historical remembrances. Founded as an agricultural community in 1848, early Georgetown settlers — mostly Czechs, Germans, Mexicans and Swedes — realized prosperity after the railroad arrived 30 years later.

Residents then forsook their simple log or frame houses for more elaborate and stylish Victorian homes and shops. This surge of building and planning can be seen in the beautiful old town district, which was awarded a Great American Main Street Award in 1997 for its charming renovation and preservation of 180 historic buildings and houses.

Georgetown is so proud of its old town and Victorian structures that its Heritage Society keeps a trained staff of docents available to give tours and lectures designed to bring the town's pioneer history to life. The olden-days flavor is enhanced by antique street lamps that grace brick walks and tree-shaded streets.

No county seat in Texas is complete without a town square, and Georgetown does not disappoint. Bed-and-breakfast inns, city administration offices, quaint restaurants and lovely shops all grace the town square, which is crowned at its center by Williamson County's domed courthouse, erected in 1910. Visitors are reminded of Texas' participation in the Civil War by a statue on the courthouse lawn that pays tribute to its Confederate forces.

History buffs and budding anthropologists can find plenty more in the area to intrigue them. "Leann," one of the earliest-known immigrants to Texas and estimated to have lived between 8,000 to 7,000 B.C., was discovered by archaeologists in a burial ground near Georgetown. The area once was home to roving bands of Tonkawa Indian tribes in centuries past, and the discovery of pottery and arrowheads is not uncommon.

One tourist draw is the Inner Space Caverns, only a half-mile from downtown. Discovered in the late 1960s, the living caverns were formed nearly 80,000 years ago, and its depths are reached by cable car. Visitors take in the stunning stalactites and stalagmites as well as remains of prehistoric mastodons, wolves and other Ice Age animals captured for eternity in the caverns.

Housing in Georgetown is plentiful and varied, with a median housing cost of $137,000. One of the new housing developments designed in a "neotraditional" manner is Georgetown Village, an ungated community. An attractive feature of the development is the notion that housing should reflect the more appealing look of a traditional village, with smaller streets, a town center and pleasant living and work spaces. Housing prices start at $136,000 and run to $500,000.

But certainly one of the most powerful reasons retirees flock to the area is Del Webb's beautiful Sun City Georgetown. Harold and Jean Steadman bought a lot in the desirable community in 1995 and built their dream home the following year. "We would not have moved to Georgetown without Sun City, although we have come to enjoy the town," says Harold, 74.

The former Houston-area Southwestern Bell sales manager and his wife, a retired teacher, lived in Buchanan Dam, TX, for 10 years before moving to Sun City. Jean, 72, says she found making friends easy even though she and Harold didn't have friends or relatives already living in the area. "There are so many activities at Sun City, you can't help but meet people," she says.

Both find satisfaction in community involvement. Harold is president of the drama club at Sun City and is a director of the convention and visitor's bureau and the Palace Theatre. Jean volunteers with Friends Who Care, an organization that provides mentoring for schoolchildren. She also tapes books for the blind in Austin at the Texas State Library, and both are active in their church. "We started a new Methodist church with 15 initial members in March of 1997," says Harold. "Now we have about 225 members."

But not everyone prefers planned retirement communities. Ann McVey, 79, found Georgetown another way — through "trial and error." Just before her husband died, he urged her to move from Odessa in search of a retirement lifestyle that suited her. So, in 1993, with a pioneering spirit that would have made her ancestors proud, she left her home of 47 years and moved to Georgetown.

"I stayed at the Ramada Inn and looked at property in Georgetown's Berry Creek Country Club. I immediately fell in love with it and picked out a lot," says the former State Farm insurance employee. She built a 2,200-square-foot home to her liking in the prestigious development, choosing a screened porch, tile roof and stucco exterior. "My children liked it so much that they wanted to move with me," Ann says.

Making friends was made easy with the help of her neighbor, a friend of 30 years who also happened to be her State Farm underwriter. While Ann misses her friends in Odessa, she doesn't miss the West Texas sandstorms and hail in the spring. She keeps busy by volunteering with the Georgetown hospital auxiliary and works in the public affairs office.

Another local retiree, Bob Jones, 51 and a retired major in the U.S. Marine Corps, already knew of Georgetown's charm, since he had spent his boyhood school days here and had visited friends and family periodically during his military career. Georgetown's excellent school system was another draw when he and his wife, Jerri, a lieutenant colonel in the Marine Corps, considered retirement locales. They have two sons still in school.

While still on active duty and living in Okinawa, Japan, the Joneses selected a building site six miles from

Georgetown, TX

Population: 26,400 in Georgetown, more than 235,000 in Williamson County. Georgetown is the county seat of Williamson County.

Location: On the eastern edge of Central Texas' Hill Country, 26 miles north of Austin off Interstate 35, 40 miles south of Temple, and equidistant from Houston and Dallas-Fort Worth. Altitude in Williamson County ranges from 454 to 1,265 feet.

Climate:

	High	Low
January	59	39
July	95	74

Average relative humidity: 56%

Annual rainfall: 34.2 inches.

Snow: Trace.

Cost of living: Below average (specific index not available).

Median housing cost: $137,000

Sales tax: 7.25% (state sales tax is 6.25% and the city sales tax is 1%).

Sales tax exemptions: Food and produce, pharmaceuticals, some agricultural services.

State income tax: None.

Intangibles tax: None.

Estate tax: None, except the state's "pickup" portion of the federal tax, applicable to taxable estates above $675,000.

Property tax: $2.31 per $100 valuation, with homes assessed at 100% of market value, less homestead and age exemptions. Georgetown Independent School District levies $1.625 per $100, Williamson County levies $.348 per $100, and the city levies $.34 per $100. The tax on a $124,000 home is about $2,818, with the $15,000 homestead exemption noted below.

Homestead exemptions: $15,000 off the assessed value of permanent, primary residences. Taxpayers over age 65 get an additional $10,000 off the assessed value.

Security: 24.2 crimes per 1,000 residents, lower than the national average of 46.2 crimes per 1,000 residents.

Religion: More than 40 churches serve 16 denominations.

Education: Southwestern University, a four-year liberal arts college in Georgetown, has 1,200 students. In nearby Austin, opportunities include the University of Texas (48,000 students), St. Edward's University (3,200 students) and Austin Community College (25,000 students), among other options.

Transportation: North/south Interstate 35 runs west of downtown Georgetown. Austin's new international airport, Bergstrom, is about a 45-minute drive. Georgetown has a municipal general utility airport for business and executive jet activity.

Health: Georgetown Hospital is a 98-bed general, acute-care facility with surgical, diagnostic and emergency services. Scott and White Clinic at Sun City Georgetown has internists and family practitioners. Georgetown also is home to a range of therapy and rehabilitation clinics as well as a cardiovascular center. Residents can select from 134 doctors and 21 dentists.

Housing options: Options range from single-family residences and apartments to manufactured homes, estates on acreage, farms and planned communities. Many retirees choose to buy property and build a home in developments or subdivisions near town. **Sun City Georgetown** (888) 932-2266, a Del Webb retirement community, offers housing ranging from cottages to luxury homes from $95,000 to more than $300,000. Ask about a Vacation Getaway program that allows visitors to sample lifestyles at the development for a small fee. **Berry Creek Country Club,** (512) 930-9995, offers five neighborhoods and existing housing with a median price of $175,000, from garden homes to estates as well as acreage home sites. The country club has two championship 18-hole golf courses, swimming, tennis and racquetball courts. **Georgetown Village,** (512) 930-2322, is an ungated community with homes starting at around $136,000 in "neotraditional" style.

Visitor lodging: Visitors can choose between five motels (Comfort, La Quinta, Rodeway, Days Inn and San Gabriel Motel) or eight bed-and-breakfast inns. Average motel room costs are $79 per night, double occupancy. A historic Victorian landmark, Inn on the Square, is a bed-and-breakfast inn featuring antiques and stained glass. Rooms range from $85 to $125 per night, (888) 718-2221 or (512) 868-2203. There also are four RV parks.

Information: Georgetown Chamber of Commerce, P.O. Box 346, 100 Stadium Drive, Georgetown, TX 78627-0346, (512) 930-3535 or www.georgetownchamber.org. Georgetown Convention and Visitors Bureau, P.O. Box 409, Georgetown, TX 78627, (512) 930-3545 or www.georgetown.org.

Georgetown in 1995 and built a one-story, four-bedroom, 3,100-square-foot brick home on two acres. The development is not a planned community, but homesites are restricted to a minimum of one-acre lots on paved streets.

The Georgetown area's semirural setting has become a popular draw in Central Texas, especially among retirees who ache to spread out on their own land. "There were only about 30 homes in our neighborhood when we built. Now there are over 100 homes," Bob says.

Jerri, 46, is a dedicated golfer and president of the Women's Golf Association. Bob's hobbies are closer to home, where he gardens and enjoys coin collecting. Both volunteer with the chamber of commerce, their church and the school system. Jerri recommends that retirees moving to Georgetown "get involved early on within the community in order to meet people."

Jerri likes the fact that Fort Hood, with its commissary and medical services, is only 40 miles north in Killeen, making Georgetown even more attractive to military retirees like the Joneses. Also popular with local retirees is the opportunity to participate in college courses. Options are many in nearby Austin, home of the University of Texas, first in the nation in National Merit scholars. But one of the jewels in Georgetown's crown is Southwestern University, Texas' oldest educational institution.

Formed in 1873 when the Texas Conference of Methodist Churches decided to consolidate schools, Southwestern has a reputation for being one of the most prestigious private universities in the South, bringing cultural and economic benefits to the city. It also has a pretty campus with lovely limestone architecture welcoming all who enter. Plus, retirees in Sun City can take advantage of the Senior University in the development, where visiting college professors in the area provide lectures on a wide range of topics.

And there's outdoor recreation as varied as the imagination. Lake lovers enjoy the five miles of Lake Georgetown, only a few minutes by car from town. The park and lake offer residents and visitors alike wilderness hiking trails, fishing, swimming, boating, camping and picnicking. The U.S. Army Corps of Engineers maintains the lake and ensures its health and beauty.

In addition to the lake, the city offers two country clubs, three swimming pools, four golf courses, 38 tennis courts, a racquet club and 14 parks totalling 200 acres. Ann McVey no longer golfs, but that doesn't stop her from walking the golfing paths of Berry Creek Country Club every day.

Sports fans also have plenty to cheer about. Austin's Ice Bats, a minor league hockey team, and sports teams at the University of Texas provide the excitement. And local baseball fans soon will realize a dream: Hall-of-famer Nolan Ryan won approval to bring a minor league team to nearby Round Rock, and voters recently approved the construction of a new stadium.

Situated between rich, black farmland and rolling Central Texas hillsides, the Georgetown area also is considered desirable for its beauty and its temperate climate. The hills are rich with limestone cliffs, granite outcrops, wildlife, springs and gorgeous wildflowers. Winter freezes are few and far between, and summers are hot but not uncomfortably humid. Rapidly changing weather can include the threat of tornadoes, but the twisters normally are less powerful than those farther northwest in the Texas-Oklahoma "tornado alley" corridor.

The city's allure and natural beauty have attracted many new residents and businesses, making Georgetown part of the second-fastest-growing metro area in the United States. Georgetown's Convention and Visitors Bureau is proud of the city's rapid growth, but not everyone is completely pleased. Jerri Jones feels road construction has not kept up with the influx of residents, which causes traffic complaints.

Others simply like the charm of Georgetown and don't want it to change. "Some people would like to put a fence around Georgetown and keep everybody out, but that's not the way the world works," says Harold Steadman. "Besides," says Jean Steadman, "we are beginning to get some nice restaurants here because of the population growth, and I'm not opposed to that."

And despite the growth, Georgetown seems to be winning the battle to maintain its quaint atmosphere. Bob Jones marvels that Georgetown "still has that small-town feel, yet the closeness to metropolitan amenities." And that, he says, is reason enough to make him glad he moved to Georgetown.●

Golden Isles, Georgia

Georgia's coast has history, nature and a 'kinder, gentler' lifestyle

By William Schemmel

On the Golden Isles, a string of barrier islands on Georgia's Atlantic Coast, there's a sense of history and security that's hard to find in today's world. For many retirees who move here, the islands offer a convenient escape to a different time and place.

"There's a wonderful magic about this part of the world. It has recaptured the feeling, the ambiance, the security of the 1950s," says Kate Minnock, who has found retirement contentment on Georgia's St. Simons Island. It's the most populous of the Golden Isles, which include Jekyll Island and Sea Island.

While some retirees are attracted by the less-developed nature of the islands, others prefer being closer to mainland amenities, choosing homes in nearby Brunswick and elsewhere in Glynn County. The area is midway along the coast between Savannah, GA, and Jacksonville, FL.

About the size of Manhattan, 14,000-acre St. Simons is connected to Brunswick, the county seat, by a toll causeway (35 cents per car). Resort hotels, condos and private homes are thinly spread along the hard-packed sand beaches. The 17,250 islanders, and thousands of yearly visitors, can play golf and tennis, shop in major supermarkets, art galleries and gift shops and dine and enjoy nighttime entertainment in a variety of restaurants and clubs.

However, most of the island remains an undeveloped realm of forests and salt marshes teeming with birds and wildlife. At the island's southern end, St. Simons Lighthouse has been a landmark since 1872.

Like all the Golden Isles, St. Simons is rich in history. In the late 1730s, the English who founded the Georgia colony built Fort Frederica at the island's northern end as a defense against Spanish invasion from Florida. The fort — whose ruins are now a national monument — never was tested, but when the Spaniards did invade in 1742, their defeat at the Battle of Bloody Marsh left England firmly in control of the Georgia coast.

Bloody Marsh is the back yard to Kate and Tom Minnock's five-bedroom, two-story Cape Cod house in the central part of the island. They moved to St. Simons after first retiring to Hawaii from California, where he was an educator and she was a marketing executive.

If they had it to do over, "I would skip Hawaii and come straight to St. Simons Island," says Tom, 60. "When we first thought about retirement, Hawaii was our first choice. We spent the first few months doing nothing, got bored and went back to work."

After five years in Hawaii the Minnocks decided to move back to the mainland. "We looked at places all along the Georgia and South Carolina coasts, but we always kept coming back to St. Simons," he says.

Boredom is not a problem on St. Simons. Both Minnocks find plenty of ways to stay busy. Tom was coordinator for cultural, arts and athletic activities in conjunction with the 1996 Summer Olympic Games in Atlanta and nearby Savannah. Kate, 51, is administrator at a shelter for abused children in Brunswick. The Minnocks enjoy walking the island's beaches, fishing, crabbing, biking and golfing.

"The Newcomers Club is very active with new retirees," says Tom. "We also take trips with Friendship Force International, which is a people-to-people organization that enables you to stay in the homes of people in places like Russia, Ireland and Australia. There are also civic clubs, historical and arts groups."

Weather, security and cost of living were other attractions for the Minnocks.

"I like the weather," says Tom. "It's a little cooler here than Hawaii and Florida, and hurricanes are rare. I think the last one that did any damage was about 30 years ago."

The Minnocks feel safe on St. Simons, even though the county as a whole has a crime rate that is higher than the national average. Glynn County had 62.9 crimes for every 1,000 residents at press time. The national average is 46.2 crimes per 1,000 residents.

"Especially when we're here on the island, we don't think about it (personal security)," Kate says. "When I'm in Brunswick I might lock my car doors. But if you examine crime records, you find that the majority of serious crime occurs in low-income neighborhoods in Brunswick where people are poor, overcrowded and feel they have no future."

Residents and police also cite Interstate 95, along the west side of Brunswick, as a contributor to crime problems. The main north-south route between Florida and New York is considered a corridor for drug trafficking.

The cost of living was another factor in the Minnocks' move.

"Most everything, including real estate, taxes and food, is much more reasonable here than in California or Hawaii," says Tom.

Gail Kellis, president of the Brunswick/Golden Isles Board of Realtors and an agent with Golden Isles Realty, says that St. Simons' relaxed atmosphere, mild climate, stately live oak trees draped with Spanish moss and other assets attract increasing numbers of retirees.

The island offers them a wide range of housing options, from country club communities around golf courses to single-family homes on the beach and one- and two-level condos. But the days of inexpensive beach houses are gone, she says.

"It's getting to the point that you really have to look hard to find anything on St. Simons for under $100,000," she says.

Although St. Simons is undergoing rapid changes, the Minnocks say they're not concerned about overdevelopment. "Every once in awhile, a genius will come in who wants to change this into a mecca when it already is one," says Kate.

"When you're at ground level, it seems like we're being overdeveloped, but when you go up in a plane, as we did recently, you can see that maybe only 10 percent is being developed," she says. "The Sea Island Co., which owns The Cloister resort, owns so much of St. Simons. They allow only a small part to be developed at a time, and it's always very carefully planned."

Golden Isles, GA

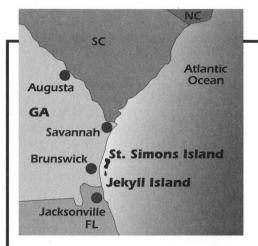

Population: 67,779 in Glynn County, 14,651 in Brunswick, 17,250 on St. Simons Island, 700 on Jekyll Island, 700 on Sea Island.

Location: Georgia's Atlantic Coast, 75 miles south of Savannah, GA, and 65 miles north of Jacksonville, FL. St. Simons, Sea Island and Jekyll Island are connected to the mainland by toll causeways from Brunswick.

Climate:	High	Low
January	61	42
July	90	74

Average relative humidity: 60%
Rain: 55 inches.
A subtropical climate boasts short, mild winters and hot, humid summers with frequent thunderstorms. The last hurricane causing serious damage was Hurricane Dora in 1964. Elevation: Brunswick, 10 feet; the islands, 0-30 feet.

Cost of living: Below average (specific index not available).

Median housing cost: $100,000 in mainland Glynn County and Brunswick; $237,500 on the islands.

Sales tax: 6%

Sales tax exemptions: Prescription drugs, hearing aids, eyeglasses.

State income tax: Graduated from 1% to 5% on first $7,000 (singles) or $10,000 (couples filing jointly), then 6% on greater amounts.

Income tax exemptions: Social Security benefits; up to $13,000 in retirement income is exempt.

Intangibles tax: None.

Estate tax: None, except the state's "pick-up" portion of the federal tax, applicable to taxable estates above $675,000.

Property tax: In Brunswick, $39.39 per $1,000 valuation, with property assessed at 40% of market value. Tax on a $100,000 home, with $6,000 homestead exemption noted below, is $1,339. In the islands and other unincorporated areas, $25.14 per $1,000 valuation with property assessed at 40% of market value. Tax on a $237,500 home, with homestead exemption, is $2,237.

Homestead exemption: $6,000 off assessed value for full-time residents. Other age- and income-related exemptions available.

Security: 62.9 crimes per 1,000 residents in Glynn County, higher than the national average of 46.2 crimes per 1,000 residents.

Religion: More than 100 churches and synagogues represent a wide spectrum of denominations.

Education: Coastal Georgia Community College, a two-year unit of the state university system, offers day and evening classes in the arts and sciences, languages and vocational/technical fields.

Transportation: No public bus system; a car is necessary. There's frequent commuter air service to Atlanta from Brunswick; nearest major airports are at Savannah, GA, and Jacksonville, FL.

Health: Southeast Georgia Regional Medical Center in Brunswick is a comprehensive 345-bed complex with complete diagnostic facilities and a 24-hour emergency department, coronary intensive care, mental health unit, breast imaging center and radiation oncology center. The county has 134 physicians and four nursing homes.

Housing options: On St. Simons Island, choices include country club communities such as **The Island Club** and **Sea Palms Resort,** with single-family homes on the golf course for $150,000-$500,000 and above. Condos in the **Village** area, near the lighthouse and marina, are $150,000-$250,000. There are inland condos available on St. Simons Island from $65,000 and up. Ranch and stucco homes in **East Beach** start at about $165,000. On Jekyll Island, development is restricted and no new homes are planned. The island has 586 residences, most of them ranch-style dwellings built in the '50s-'70s. Prices range upward from $140,000, with three-bedroom oceanfront homes starting at about $280,000. On Sea Island, condos in **River Club** start at about $250,000; virtually all homes on Sea Island are custom-built. In Brunswick and mainland Glynn County, options range from secured-gate country club developments such as **Oak Grove** ($150,000-$550,000) to **Marshes by Mackay** and **Windward Acres** ($90,000-$250,000) and **Deerfield** ($50,000s-$70,000s). **Bell Point** ($59,000-$265,000) is popular with the 1,400 personnel at the Federal Law Enforcement Training Center.

Visitor lodgings: Jekyll Island Club Hotel, a restored Victorian-style hotel in the historic district, has standard doubles for $139-$269, (912) 635-2600. Villas-by-the-Sea, a hotel condominium on the Jekyll Island beach, has one- to three-bedroom suites with kitchens for $139-$239, (800) 342-6872 in Georgia and (800) 841-6262 elsewhere. The King & Prince Hotel, a deluxe resort on the St. Simons beach, has doubles for $160-$189, depending on season, (800) 342-0212. Days Inns of America, away from the beach on St. Simons' main commercial thoroughfare, is $85, (800) 325-2525. To rent a house ($500-$2,000 per week), call Parker-Kaufman Realty, (912) 635-2512 on Jekyll Island or (912) 638-3368 on St. Simons.

Information: Brunswick & Golden Isles Visitors Bureau, 4 Glynn Ave., Brunswick, GA 31520, (912) 265-0620, or Brunswick and Glynn County Development Authority, P.O. Box 1079, Brunswick, GA 31521, (912) 265-6629 or www.brunswick-georgia.com.

A small bridge divides St. Simons from Sea Island. Owned by the Sea Island Co., the tiny island is home of The Cloister, one of the most distinguished resort hotels in the country. Spanish-style villas and other huge estates along the Sea Island beach are valued in the millions of dollars.

Neighboring Jekyll Island, reached by its own causeway from Brunswick ($2 per car toll), also has an illustrious history. From 1885 to 1942, the island was the private retreat of many of America's wealthiest families. Vanderbilts, Rockefellers, Morgans, Pulitzers, Goodyears, Cranes and Astors built elegant "cottages" where they spent their winters socializing and making big deals.

In 1947, the state of Georgia purchased the island, including the plutocrats' cottages, for the modest sum of $650,000. It's now a state park administered by the Jekyll Island Authority.

Ten miles of sand beaches are uncrowded even on the busiest holidays. Jekyll Island homeowners and visitors also enjoy 63 holes of golf, miniature golf, a driving range, picnic shelters, a fitness center, an outdoor summer theater festival, nature trails, indoor and outdoor tennis, marinas, water slides, an indoor Olympic-size swimming pool and other amusements.

The millionaires' cottages are a main attraction. Several are restored and open to the public in the attractively landscaped Jekyll Island Club Historic District. The Jekyll Island Club, the turreted Victorian landmark where the aristocrats dined and socialized, now is a full-service resort managed by Radisson Hotels.

The 700 full-time residents on Jekyll Island live in 586 mostly ranch-style homes built from the mid-1950s to the mid-1970s. Since state law stipulates that no more than 35 percent of the island's high ground can be developed, no new residential areas are foreseen.

Residents have full ownership of their homes and may make any changes they desire. However, the state retains ownership of the land, which is leased to homeowners under long-term agreements. Leases are about $300 to $350 a year.

Jack and Pat Overholt purchased their three-bedroom ranch-style home near the ocean in 1977. After renting out the house for 10 years, they moved into it in 1987.

"When we bought it, it was a typical Jekyll Island rancher, with about 2,000 square feet," says Jack, 66, a former executive with Sara Lee Bakeries in Chicago. "We've since put on a significant addition. Before you can make additions, you have to submit your plans to the Jekyll Island Authority for approval. They're fairly flexible and are mainly concerned that you don't infringe on your neighbors."

The Overholts' home now is valued at about $200,000 on land leased until 2049. Frank Cerrato, a broker with Parker-Kaufman Realty, says large homes that front the ocean sell for $280,000 to $395,000, while some homes away from the beach can be found for about $140,000.

Potential retirees who might want to test the island's waters, literally and figuratively, can rent a place for $300 to $2,000 a week. They may find the cost of living and the island's subtropical climate attractive inducements to move here. Both were major points in the Overholts' decision.

"After living in the Chicago area, you look for a milder climate," says Pat, 61, a former elementary school teacher. "We had looked in Florida, but we preferred a little more change of seasons. Very rarely does it get so cold here that you can't go out and be active, even in the middle of winter."

Jack enjoys having a variety of activities. "I think the thing I like best is the lack of restrictions on our lifestyle," he says. "We're outdoor people, and neither of us wanted to retire and go into limbo."

Pat works with the Elderhostel program, which offers educational programs to senior citizens about the history, culture and environment of the Golden Isles. Jack is involved with Jekyll Island Museum Associates, which provides volunteers as workers and docents in the historic area.

The Overholts like to fish and play golf and tennis, activities available in abundance. "But we wouldn't want to be stuck here all the time," says Jack. "Jekyll gets pretty quiet when the summer vacationers go home. We travel a lot, visiting relatives and seeing other parts of the country and places overseas."

Among the things she misses, Pat says, is "the accessibility to a large city. But I don't miss the congestion and hard winters."

Jekyll's shopping, dining and nightlife are limited. A strip shopping center has a small grocery store, drugstore, bank and a few other shops that cater mainly to the island's visitors. Most dining and entertainment are in the 10 hotels.

The Overholts gladly endure the minor inconveniences for the peace and security of Jekyll Island. "We have very little crime here," says Jack. "I can't remember the last time there was a robbery. Since the island is owned by the state, the Georgia State Patrol is our police force. They take very good care of us."

For serious shopping and a choice of restaurants, the Overholts must make the half-hour trip into Brunswick, where malls have chain supermarkets and other major stores. Convenience to shopping and medical services prompts many retirees to buy homes in Brunswick.

"About 20 percent of the people in Brunswick are retirees," says Winifred Capps with Capps-Century 21 Realty. "Many of them have come from Florida and the Northern states. Housing in Brunswick is less expensive than the islands, and many of the older houses are brick, which many people prefer to frame or stucco."

Oak Grove, one of the most exclusive communities, has 24-hour gated security and an 18-hole golf course. Homes sell for $150,000-$550,000. Homes in older developments facing the picturesque tidal marshes start at $90,000. Restored Victorian houses in the Old Town District near downtown Brunswick sell for about $150,000, while fixer-ups cost $50,000 or less.

The area's major medical center and only commercial airport are in Brunswick. Only commuter air service to Atlanta is available; many residents drive 65 to 75 miles to larger airports in Savannah and Jacksonville.

While the Minnocks and the Overholts like to travel, they also like to come home to Georgia's Golden Isles.

"There is a great deal of love, understanding and trust among the people who live here," says Tom Minnock. "I have never met a more gracious, warm, loving group of people."●

Grants Pass, Oregon

Oregon's Rogue River Valley invites casual living

By Dana Tims

Zane Grey, the popular 19th- and 20th-century writer, sold millions of books chronicling the trials and travails of the Old West. But when he wanted to relax, Grey didn't head for any dude ranch in Durango. Instead, he made a beeline for the bounding Rogue River and its meandering tumble through the bucolic southern Oregon town of Grants Pass.

"Deep and dark green, swift and clear, and pure as the snows from which it springs, the river has its source in the mountains under Crater Lake," Grey wrote of his favorite vacation spot while holed up in a one-room cabin on the Rogue in 1920.

"It is a river at its birth, gliding away through the Oregon forest with hurrying momentum, as if eager to begin the long leap down through the Siskiyous. Twisting through Grants Pass, it chafes and fights its way rushing over the rocks until, finally, it enters the canyoned wilderness of the Coast Range."

Grey, a first-rate American writer, is also regarded as one of the first tourists to extol the virtues of the Rogue Valley as it slices through Grants Pass toward the Pacific Ocean.

In his wake, thousands have followed, making Grants Pass one of the Pacific Northwest's premier settling points for retirees looking to combine breathtaking scenery and a mellow lifestyle with the affordability that residents say can't be beat.

"Grants Pass is basically a retirement mecca," says Norm Eckl, a local real estate agent. He notes that more than 50 percent of the town's 20,565 residents are retirees, many of them drawn to the area from other parts of the country including California, Nevada, Idaho and points east.

"There's virtually everything a retiree could want here, including a climate that has been called a little banana belt," he says.

The climate — with summer temperatures in the mid-80s and winters that may include an occasional dusting of snow but few hard freezes — proved an irresistible drawing card for Paul and Pat Van Auken. They left the congestion of San Jose, CA, for a slower and more affordable lifestyle in Grants Pass.

"One reason we came to Grants Pass is that we felt we could live better for the same amount of money," says Paul, 64, who retired after a 36-year career as a design draftsman for General Electric. "But we also love the slow pace of life. We couldn't be happier here."

Pat worked for years as an office manager. In fact, she stayed in San Jose nearly 18 months after Paul officially retired to Grants Pass.

"For a while there, I had the absolute best of both worlds a man could hope for," quips Paul, who kept himself busy gardening and reading volumes of social and military history. "I was retired up in Oregon, while my wife continued to work and bring home the paycheck in California."

The couple initially had viewed Nevada as prime retirement territory. They were so serious about it, in fact, that they purchased a parcel of property in Spring Creek, NV. The climate, however, soon forced them to look elsewhere. "The growing season was about three days long," says Pat, knowing that Paul's gardening would founder in ground that was frozen much of the year. "The winters were just too severe."

Then they remembered Grants Pass, where they spent a night on a trip north. They had liked the town, cradled 960 feet above sea level in the lush, rolling foothills of the Siskiyou Mountains 50 miles north of the California-Oregon border.

"We both came from small towns, and Grants Pass just looked like a nice place to stay," Paul recalls. "But what really got me interested was a brochure listing real estate prices in the area. Compared to where we were living in California, the real estate was really quite reasonable."

The closer they looked, the better they liked what they saw — abundant urban and rural hiking trails; no fewer than 18 public parks located within a 20-minute drive of downtown; community service organizations looking for volunteers (Paul delivers dinners to seniors weekly as part of the area's Meals on Wheels program); a local historic district with 29 residences dating to the late 1800s; proximity to national forests and national monuments, including the Oregon Caves subterranean labyrinth and Crater Lake National Park; lots of local shopping, bolstered by the 119-store, 750,000-square-foot Rogue Valley Mall in Medford, 25 miles southeast; and easy access to the world-famous Oregon Shakespeare Festival in Ashland, 35 minutes southeast. Grants Pass, Medford and Ashland all are on Interstate 5.

"We found that it had everything we could ever want, plus a more informal lifestyle that was just really appealing," says Paul. "Here, we can go out to dinner in the evening wearing sweatshirts and casual slacks and it's no problem at all. That really sealed it for us."

They sold their 1,530-square-foot home in San Jose and bought a 2.3-acre plot in Grants Pass with an equal sized, three-bedroom, two-bath house that cost $110,000 less than its California counterpart. "It's actually a little bigger than what we were looking for," Paul says. "And it has everything we want."

Avid golfers, Pat and Paul joined the golf league at nearby Colonial Valley Golf Course, just a 10-minute hike up a quiet road lined by willowy birches and firs. Like the other nine year-round courses located within easy driving distance from their home, it features everything from ponds populated by Oregon ducks and Canada geese to fairways guarded by stately spruce trees and the occasional giant redwood.

Pat, 62, made numerous friends by joining a dance group that regularly visits local nursing homes. She also serves as secretary for the Colonial Valley Property Owners' Association. On evenings when the Van Aukens are strictly looking for enjoyable entertainment, they hit the road for a quick sojourn south to Ashland, where for between $10 and $25, they can take in a play at the Shakespeare Festival.

A primary drawing card for many retirees in Grants Pass, county seat of timber-laden Josephine County, is the climate. Moderate summer tempera-

tures, cooled by breezes from the Pacific Ocean 60 miles to the west, rarely exceed 90 degrees. Indian summers are common, making the surrounding Rogue Valley one of the only areas in Oregon capable of producing deep red wines such as cabernet sauvignon that are more commonly associated with California's Napa and Sonoma valleys.

Autumn triggers brilliant oranges and reds among the maples and birches blanketing the hills overlooking the town, while just enough snow dusts Grants Pass in the winter to give schoolchildren a day or two of

sledding fun. Only in December does the average overnight low temperature dip below freezing.

The moderate climate was just what Gene and Helen Clark were looking for after spending 14 years in Anchorage, AK. Although Gene, who retired as vice president of administration for Enstar Natural Gas Co., occasionally finds himself longing for cooler summers and the world-class fishing available in his former home state, he snaps back to reality when thoughts of Alaska's subarctic cold come to mind.

"Don't get me wrong," says Gene, 65.

Grants Pass, OR

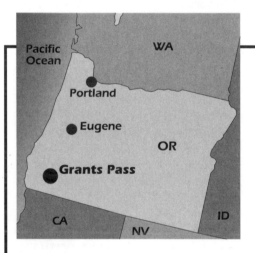

Population: 20,565
Location: In the heart of the Rogue River Valley in southwestern Oregon, 245 miles south of Portland, 56 miles north of the Oregon-California border and about 60 miles inland from the Pacific Ocean.

Climate:

	High	Low
January	49	34
July	88	52

Average relative humidity: 61%
Rain: 32 inches.
Snow: 2.3 inches.
Four-season climate is generally mild, with a wet season from December through March and occasional freezes. Cooling marine air tempers periodic summer heat waves. Autumns are warm and pleasant. Elevation is 960 feet.
Cost of living: Slightly above average (specific index not available).
Average housing cost: $129,000 in Grants Pass.
Sales tax: None.
State income tax: Graduated in three steps from 5% to 9%, depending on income.

Income tax exemptions: Social Security benefits are exempt. You may be able to subtract some or all of your federal pension income, based on the number of months of federal service before and after Oct. 1, 1991.
Intangibles tax: None.
Estate tax: None, except the state's "pick-up" portion of the federal tax, applicable to taxable estates above $675,000.
Property tax: Rate is $14.42 per $1,000 of assessed value, with homes assessed at 100% of market value. The yearly tax on a $129,000 home is about $1,860.
Homestead exemption: None.
Security: 93.5 crimes per 1,000 residents, higher than the national average of 46.2 per 1,000 residents.
Religion: All major religious denominations and many smaller ones are represented in more than 100 churches and synagogues in Josephine County.
Education: Rogue Community College offers continuing-education classes. Fees are $15-$35 per course.
Transportation: Rogue Transportation operates a private bus service on weekdays for $1 per ride. The company also runs taxi and airport shuttle services. The Medford/Jackson County Airport, a 30-minute drive, has flights daily to major points in the region.
Health: Three Rivers Community Hospital and Health Center offers a full range of acute care on two campuses; it was formed by the recent merger of Josephine Memorial Hospital and Southern Oregon Medical Center. The 144-bed hospital has 80 affiliated

physicians, community health-education classes at little or no cost and the Home Health Agency, which provides 24-hour Medicare-certified nursing and rehabilitative services. The town has numerous smaller clinics, some retirement centers and a number of homes for the disabled elderly.
Housing options: Many retirees buy single-family homes in existing neighborhoods in the town or outlying areas. For example, Colonial Valley, just northeast of downtown Grants Pass, has homes starting at $150,000. There are several retirement communities. Among them: **Oak Lane Retirement Community**, (541) 476-7727, a managed-care facility near downtown, offers assisted-living and independent units, with studio apartments starting at $1,010 per month for two; services include 24-hour security, beauty and barber shops, housekeeping and food service. **Rogue Valley Retirement Center**, (541) 479-6400, an independent-care facility within walking distance of downtown, has studio, one-bedroom and two-bedroom apartments starting at $1,250 a month for two.
Visitor lodging: Among the many options: Sweet Breeze Inn, $65 for two, (541) 471-0598, and the Redwood Motel, $80, (541) 476-0878.
Information: Grants Pass/Josephine County Chamber of Commerce, P.O. Box 970, Grants Pass, OR 97528, (541) 476-7717 or www.grantspasschamber.org. Grants Pass Visitors and Convention Bureau, P.O. Box 1787, Grants Pass, OR 97528, (541) 476-5510.

"I love Alaska, but 20-below does get a little nippy."

Helen, who has joined several local women's organizations and a bowling league, first thought of Denver or Spokane, WA, when the couple began planning their retirement. But the urban sprawl and biting winters of those places turned their attention to Grants Pass, where Helen had stopped for a night once while driving between Alaska and California. Gene also knew about the Rogue Valley since he attended high school in Oregon and later logged a year in Eugene, 135 miles to the north.

Gambling everything on Grants Pass turned out to be the smartest thing the Clarks ever did, they say.

"We knew we were going to be on a fixed income, so it was important that we could live comfortably and still make ends meet," says Helen, 60, who worked as a bookkeeper for an Anchorage bank before retirement. "And we've found that living here has more than allowed us to do that."

Lovers of privacy, they searched the area's ample supply of available housing before finding 2.5 acres of land located four miles west of town. Oak and pine trees dot the property, which features a spacious shop area where Gene can pursue his love of tuning old engines and maintaining the chain saws he uses to tame vegetation near the house.

They also have stayed active in community life. Gene, with years of experience as a certified public accountant, serves as a volunteer counselor at the Small Business Development Center downtown. Operated by nearby Rogue Community College, the center provides information and tips for fledgling businesses. The college also offers a large number of courses in continuing adult education.

Both Gene and Helen say that Grants Pass has grown a little more crowded since they moved there seven years ago. Property values also have crept up during that time. The median price for a three-bedroom, two-bath home with plenty of yard and garden space is about $129,000 in Grants Pass itself and about $140,000 in surrounding Josephine County.

As far as the Clarks are concerned, things couldn't be better. "Our kids are through school, we have no house or car payments and we're living life just the way we want to," Gene says. "For me, it was kind of a lifetime goal to end up back in Oregon."

While Gene calls Grants Pass "the greatest place in the world," he does caution about winter fog. "The whole month of December was foggy one year, and I felt like I was in a Frankenstein movie," he says.

A number of community programs and activities are available for retirees in Grants Pass, which according to local legend was named in honor of Ulysses S. Grant's military victory at Vicksburg during the Civil War. More than 350 clubs and organizations, including the American Association of Retired Persons, give newcomers numerous opportunities to meet people.

The Rogue Craftsmen, a non-profit organization founded in 1964 for the sole purpose of furnishing retired hobbyists with an outlet for their creative abilities, is a popular meeting spot. A board of directors and a manager run the shop, while volunteers staff the front counter daily. For some of the store's nearly 200 members, it is a means of livelihood. Others use it as an avenue for selling an array of crafts, including ceramics, jewelry, toys, paintings, clothing, stained glass, floral arrangements and much more.

Lovers of the arts in Grants Pass find they do not have to travel to Ashland or even the world-renowned Britt Musical Festival in nearby historic Jacksonville for cultural pleasures. Instead, they can spend pleasant summer evenings beneath the stars enjoying musical presentations at Rogue Community College's outdoor theater. The main attraction is the Rogue Music Theater, an independent, non-profit corporation that every season employs professional actors, directors, choreographers and technical staff to enhance their productions.

For Dick and Elly Dunn, the best thing about Grants Pass is its affordability.

The Dunns lived in Belmont, CA, 20 miles south of San Francisco, until they retired. Both worked for a major electronics company, with Dick, 65, managing quality assurance and Elly, 62, as a supervisor in production control. Both were familiar with Grants Pass, since the company operated a manufacturing facility in the area. When it came time to retire, they knew they wanted to leave the congestion and smog of the Bay Area behind in favor of something quieter and more friendly.

What they got in the process was nothing less than a steal. The Dunns sold their modest three-bedroom, one-bath Belmont townhouse for a whopping $370,000. In exchange, they landed a 2,500-square-foot home situated near the frolicking Rogue River on eight acres of rural land nestled among oaks, pines, fir and madrone. Their buying price of only $180,000 enabled them to stuff a sizable chunk of cash into the bank and virtually end any future money worries.

"We retired on a pension before we were eligible for Social Security, so we couldn't afford to live in California due to the cost of living," Dick says. "In addition to being able to buy our home up here with cash, eliminating any house payments, we also found that taxes were considerably less. So we are living on our pensions, saving money, and our living standard has changed. Not a bad deal, I'd say."

The Dunns also have found Grants Pass an ideal launching point for ventures in their motor home. The ocean is an hour's drive, much of it on a quiet highway weaving through towering redwoods more than 700 years old. Crater Lake National Park, with its newly restored historic lodge and famed Wizard Island, is less than 70 miles to the northeast. To the north is Wildlife Safari, a 600-acre drive-through park where animals from Africa, Asia and North America roam free.

Closer to home, Dick has found a niche serving on the Grants Pass Community Service Advisory Board. He's a participant in the Retired Senior Volunteer Program, providing tax advice to seniors. He also puts his business skills to use by tutoring students at Rogue Community College.

"Other than that, we've been able to sleep late, eat when we wish and do essentially what we want to do," Dick says. "It's just marvelous having no dictates on our time any more." ●

Green Valley, Arizona

Retiree-friendly community is an oasis in the southern Arizona desert

By Judy Wade

The 5,000 acres that comprise Green Valley lend a sense of history and tradition to a community only three decades old. The land was part of the original San Ignacio de las Canoa land grant conveyed to members of the Spanish monarchy more than 400 years ago. Today the names Canoa and San Ignacio figure prominently in the names of Green Valley streets and developments.

This unincorporated town 25 miles south of Tucson is a community of age-restricted retirement developments mixed with a few family subdivisions. Located in the Santa Cruz River Valley at an elevation of 2,900 feet, Green Valley is consistently seven degrees cooler than Tucson and 10 degrees cooler than Phoenix, two and a half hours to the north.

Green Valley is long and narrow, radiating out from both sides of Interstate 19, with main thoroughfares fed by quiet residential streets. To the east, the Santa Rita Mountains provide magnificent views as well as pine-forested venues for picnicking and hiking. On the horizon to the west is the Duval Copper Mine, a working mine that appears as a distant berm kept watered and treed so as not to create dust or become an eyesore.

The Santa Cruz River, mostly dry but subject to occasional flooding, parallels the freeway. The general impression is of a neat and tidy community that fits comfortably into the desert's austere beauty.

The weather was a deciding factor when Dave and Jan Evans moved from Rockford, IL, six years ago. Winters were cooler than they expected. "I have an orange and a grapefruit tree, and I have to cover them about a dozen times in the winter," says Dave, 68.

Green Valley's first small houses were built in the 1960s by a company that expected retirees to buy them as second homes. By 1973, Fairfield Homes, a large developer, had become the dominant builder and was offering two-bedroom villas at first intended as winter homes. But it didn't take long for residents to realize that Green Valley was delightful all year, and arriving newcomers wanted larger, full-time homes.

Today Fairfield, the area's largest builder, offers townhouses and single-family homes beginning under $80,000. But large estate homes with more than 2,500 square feet on mountain-view lots can exceed $500,000. Buyers can choose from a number of neighborhoods.

"The last few years, Fairfield has responded to an ever-younger retiree who may want a home office, a hobby room or a large guest room for kids and grandkids, which means larger homes overall," says sales associate Inez Peters. She adds that this trend extends to Fairfield's recreation centers, where lap pools and meeting rooms are in demand and the fastest-growing groups are computer clubs.

Helen and Gene Honderich, both 77, chose a Fairfield home when they moved from Grosse Pointe, MI, in 1989. Their townhouse overlooks the 16th fairway of the San Ignacio Golf Course, with a 270-degree view of the Santa Rita Mountains beyond. They say the view more than makes up for leaving a home on the Detroit River with access to Lake Erie.

"We discovered Green Valley while visiting Tucson and were impressed with its newness, good traffic flow and absence of slums," says Gene. They also were pleased to find property taxes considerably less than in Michigan.

Green Valley also has a variety of resale housing options. Red tile roofs create a Mediterranean atmosphere in some areas, and flat-roof territorial styles establish a Southwest feel in others. Most have desert landscaping, with few traditional grass lawns.

This diversity is one of the town's big attractions, says Joe Steinmetz, associate broker with Long Realty. "We have a lot of older little townhomes and villas in the $30,000-to-$40,000 price range that are especially popular with retirees, as well as $400,000 homes," he says.

Pueblo Estates, a manufactured home community that is age-restricted, has resales from about $53,500 to $98,500, including the lot, according to Steinmetz. La Posada, a continuing-care retirement community, is set in a shady mature pecan grove. It offers garden homes, apartments and assisted living and always has a waiting list.

When the Evanses moved from Illinois, they purchased one of the town's oldest homes, built in 1964. An add-on room provides art studio space for Jan, 67, where she works in mixed-media acrylic. Although their home is air-conditioned, they say they rarely use it, preferring an evaporative cooler that works efficiently in the dry climate. The large yard backs up to a wash, where the Evanses occasionally see coyotes. Finches, doves, flickers, cactus wrens and Gila woodpeckers are frequent visitors to the desert plantings in their yard.

Nature plays a large part in Green Valley's personality. On either side of a main street called Camino del Sol, lush fairways connect velvety golf course greens. Almost a third of Green Valley residents are golfers. Two of the town's seven courses are private, with the remaining five open to public play.

Green Valley sits on a productive aquifer, a subterranean zone that stores accessible water and keeps these desert greens grassy. It is projected to meet the town's water needs for decades to come, relieving dependency on ground sources and allowing Green Valley to live up to its name.

Green Valley Recreation Inc., a non-profit organization, is the equivalent of a municipal department of parks and recreation. It operates four major recreational complexes and six neighborhood centers with swimming pools, meeting rooms, a theater and auditorium, and other sports, recreation and leisure facilities. Membership is based on the deed restrictions of each residential property. The Evanses, avid tennis players, note that their court fees went from more than $150 per month to zero when they moved to Green Valley.

Everyone in Green Valley is careful to emphasize that it is a town rather than a city. "A city and all its ills is something that many of our residents are trying to escape," says Inez Peters. "This is a small town with neighborhoods and a feeling of community."

Green Valley's small-town personality appealed to Dave and Dee Haynes, 64 and 62 respectively. They left Cupertino, CA, because of its traffic, crowds and high cost of living. "We bought our first place here in 1980 and vacationed here until I retired, then moved permanently," says Dave. In 1988 they purchased a single-family home in an area of Green Valley that is not age restricted.

With a median age in Green Valley of 70.8 years, and 80 percent of the population over the age of 55 and retired, it's no surprise that senior sensibilities run high. Fairfield builds only age-restricted communities, with one buyer in a couple required to be at least 45 to 55, depending on the community. A few local builders offer family subdivisions, but it is the retirement market that prevails.

Four shopping centers have major supermarkets and department stores as well as large discount stores and major drug chains. Small boutique apparel shops and specialty stores are part of the retail mix. Residents say they do as much shopping as possible in Green Valley to take advantage of the town's 5 percent sales tax. In nearby Tucson, the sales tax is 7 percent.

But residents seek health care in

Green Valley, AZ

Population: 25,000 in Green Valley, 728,425 in Pima County.
Location: In the Santa Cruz River Valley midway between Tucson, AZ, and Nogales, Mexico. Elevation 2,900 feet.

Climate:

	High	Low
January	65	37
July	98	71

Average relative humidity: 25%
Rain: 16 inches.
Snow: Rare.
Clean desert air and low humidity are big drawing cards. From July through September, humid air from Mexico rushes north to cause afternoon thunderstorms with lightning displays, helping to keep the area cool.
Cost of living: Below average (specific index not available). Tucson, 25 miles north, has a cost-of-living index of 96.8, under the national average of 100.
Average housing cost: $109,000

Sales tax: 5%
Sales tax exemptions: Prescription drugs, groceries.
State income tax: Graduated in five steps from 2.9% to 5.17%, depending on income.
Income tax exemptions: Social Security and up to $2,500 of federal, state and local government pensions are exempt.
Intangibles tax: None.
Estate tax: None, except the state's "pick-up" portion of the federal tax, applicable to taxable estates above $675,000.
Property tax: $90.10 per $1,000 of assessed value, with homes assessed at 10% of market value. Taxes on a $109,000 home are approximately $982 a year.
Homestead exemption: None.
Security: 15.7 crimes per 1,000 residents, lower than the national average of 46.2 crimes per 1,000 residents.
Religion: 21 churches represent more than a dozen denominations.
Education: College courses are offered at local off-campus facilities by the University of Arizona and Pima Community College. In Tucson, the University of Arizona offers a wide range of degree courses, some of which are available to seniors at no cost on a space-available basis.

Transportation: There's no town transportation. Citizen's Auto Stage provides bus service between Nogales, Tucson and Phoenix, stopping in Green Valley. Tucson International Airport is 23 miles north, with shuttle service to and from Green Valley.
Health: Green Valley has four medical clinics, six dental offices, two nursing homes and four ambulances with trained emergency medical technicians. Full-service hospital care is available in Tucson.
Housing options: There's a wide selection of new and resale homes ranging from $24,000 to $500,000. Two apartment rental complexes have one-bedroom rentals from $300 per month on an annual basis, $900 per month for a furnished unit during the peak winter season.
Visitor lodging: Best Western, $59-$119, double occupancy, (800) 344-1441. Tubac Golf Resort (20 miles south of Green Valley), $75-$125 summer, $140-$195 winter, (520) 398-2211. Fairfield Homes offers accommodations at the Fairfield Green Valley Lodge for $45-$85, (800) 528-4930.
Information: Green Valley Chamber of Commerce, P.O. Box 566, Green Valley, AZ 85622, (800) 858-5872, (520) 625-7575. Also see www.arizona guide.com.

Tucson because Green Valley is not yet large enough to support its own hospital. Gene Honderich appreciates the fact that area doctors and hospitals are accustomed to treating a large geriatric population.

Fine dining and cultural opportunities also are best sought in Tucson, where a renowned symphony orchestra, ballet season and theatrical events are part of an active cultural scene. Green Valley has the usual fast-food chains as well as a couple of cowboy steakhouses and good Mexican restaurants, and there's a bowling alley and a branch of the Tucson Public Library. There's no movie theater yet, but a local arts council regularly schedules exhibits and sponsors musical and dance performances.

Fifteen miles south of Green Valley, the little city of Tubac is a hub of artistic activity with more than 80 galleries and studios, shops and restaurants. It offers a series of exhibitions and performing arts presentations September through May.

The variety of churches appealed to the Honderichs, who were attracted to Valley Presbyterian because of its aesthetics. "It is architecturally de-signed with a beautiful view of the mountains, and it has an excellent musical program. We both belong to the choir," says Gene, who also is active in barbershop quartet singing.

A landmark just a few miles north of town is the stunning mission San Xavier del Bac. It appears on the horizon to the west of Interstate 19 as a magnificent monument to the tenacity of early Catholic fathers. "The White Dove of the Desert" is considered one of the finest examples of Spanish mission architecture in the country. It is open for tours and daily mass.

Other things to do in the area include exploring the cool, shadowy depths of Madera Canyon, about 15 miles east of Green Valley. Just 40 miles south, the Mexican border city of Nogales offers unique shopping opportunities. An hour's drive south, Patagonia Lake has recently opened for fishing and boating.

One of the most-visited attractions is the Arizona-Sonora Desert Museum, a 45-minute drive from Green Valley. Native plants and animals in their natural habitat give visitors an opportunity to get close to desert big-horn sheep, coyotes, javelinas and more.

The Pima County Sheriff's Department is the primary law enforcement agency for the area, keeping the crime rate far below the national average. Many residents belong to Friends in Deed, the largest and oldest of several service organizations. It provides no-cost blood pressure checks and assistance with Medicare, and its members visit the homebound and arrange for wheelchairs, crutches and walkers.

Most residents move to Green Valley from other areas of Arizona, but a large wall map in the chamber of commerce office shows that other states are well-represented — 1,918 from California, 1,700 from Illinois, 1,124 from Colorado, 1,056 from Minnesota and 984 from New York.

If there is a drawback to life in Green Valley, Dave Haynes attributes it to snowbirds who come only for the winter, doubling the population. Traffic is a little heavier and grocery lines are a little longer, at least temporarily.

But Dave acknowledges that there's another way to look at it: In the winter, there's double the number of friendly neighbors in Green Valley.●

Greenville, North Carolina

North Carolina city combines small-town warmth, sophistication

By Peggy Payne

Once fueled by the tobacco industry, the city of Greenville in eastern North Carolina today banks on education and medicine for its future.

Set in a gentle landscape of bays, wide rivers and large brackish sounds, the city of 56,000 combines an engaging small-town warmth with the sophistication of a university community and major medical center.

It offers the "best of both worlds" in several other ways. The climate is mild enough for year-round golf, yet there are four distinct seasons. Ocean beaches are close enough for an easy day excursion, but housing costs are comparable with those of an inland town rather than resort area.

"It has the attributes of a large city without the crowds," says Tom Parrish, who, with his wife, Marge, retired to Greenville after 21 years in Chicago.

The Parrishes, both 70, can reel off a list of reasons they chose to come to Greenville. Climate, says Marge, boating, the cultural activities of the university and good medical facilities. It's the warmth of the people that they like best, though, yet they "didn't know a soul" when they arrived.

"The biggest surprise," says Tom, a former FBI agent, "was the absence of cliquishness, which the press would have you believe is rampant in the South."

The town has a gentle nature, a feel of "softness," says Marge, a former high school English teacher.

Janice Whitaker, 63, agrees. She and her husband, Joe, 69, had lived in Geneva, Switzerland, and Wilmington, DE, in the years prior to his retirement from a position in international industrial and labor relations.

"This town just opens its arms," Janice says of Greenville, where they have lived now for 10 years.

The first Colonial settlers came to this area by boat, on the Tar River running at the edge of the Town Common in downtown Greenville. The Tar, khaki-colored and wide as an interstate road with trees leaning low over the water, served as the area's first highway.

Early settlers grew tobacco on the riverbanks. As recently as the 1950s, Pitt County, where Greenville is located, was selling more flue-cured tobacco than any other county in the United States.

You can still feel the agricultural heritage as you drive past Gold Leaf Warehouse on the street that leads to the 35,000-seat football stadium close to the center of town. Or if you're downtown and step into Globe Hardware, with its antique pine floors and 1926 cash register, you'll see the spring yard flags, some bearing the image of a big gold tobacco leaf and others with a bird or a flower or a college sports mascot.

In recent years, Greenville has made a graceful transition from a town that ran on tobacco to a small city that has attracted a diverse range of industry but revolving mainly around East Carolina University.

The university campus faces East Fifth Street, a narrow avenue of tall shade trees. Its brick buildings, many tile-roofed with archways and Palladian windows, have an old, comfortable feel. With nearly 18,000 students and more than 100 undergraduate programs, ECU is the third largest university in North Carolina. It offers a wide range of studies, from medical degrees to continuing-education classes for those who simply enjoy learning but don't want to earn credits.

The arts calendar is one of the university's greatest gifts to Greenville, with more than 1,500 cultural events presented each year under the auspices of local arts councils and the university. The ECU School of Art is the only such program in North Carolina accredited by the National Association of Schools of Art and Design.

The Wellington B. Gray Gallery provides exhibition space for work by faculty and students, as well as for traveling exhibitions. Faculty and alumni from ECU's schools of art and music have performed at Lincoln Center's Alice Tully Hall and the Kennedy Center, and the work of ECU artists has been displayed at the Smithsonian and Pushkin Galleries.

John Shearin, chairman of the ECU Department of Theatre Arts, says, "Our audience is active, sophisticated and expects high quality in concept and performance. We deliver the goods."

Driving into the city from the west, the first part of Greenville that you see is an outlying branch of the campus: the University Medical Center of Eastern North Carolina-Pitt County. About 25 years ago, Dr. Leo Jenkins, then head of the university, waged a now-legendary political battle in the halls of the North Carolina Legislature to get the money to build a medical school at ECU and to make Greenville a regional medical center.

Today, the school has grown into a massive complex spread across a spacious campus, with a heart center, a center for family practice, a high-rise tower for outpatient care, and the Leo W. Jenkins Cancer Center.

The outstanding medical care was one reason that the Whitakers chose to come to Greenville, Joe says.

With extremely sophisticated treatment locally available, "people don't have to go to Raleigh or Chapel Hill....it's such a blessing," says Greenville's former mayor Nancy M. Jenkins, a longtime Greenville booster and the widow of Leo Jenkins, the campus founder whom she married in his retirement years.

"I'm unabashedly Greenville's cheerleader," says Nancy, who has served as a member of the city council and of the local school board. She has traveled over much of the world but "wouldn't want to live anywhere but Greenville."

In the 32 years she has been in the city, it has moved from provincialism to urban sophistication, she says. "Now, instead of being suspect of strangers, we're interested in them,

we welcome them," she says.

She's particularly proud of a festival that celebrates the area's ethnic diversity. Held on the downtown mall in late October, the International Festival uses food, music, dance and crafts to celebrate the more than 40 nationalities represented in the county.

Don Edwards, who runs the University Book Exchange, a downtown business, sees the sociology of the town in a slightly whimsical way.

"Sometimes I think of (some of the) other eastern North Carolina towns like a banana republic, a small class of people who have the wealth. In Greenville, we were never that rich. Instead, we have a broad-based middle class with a lot of professionals. We have tremendous industry and all the doctors and college professors," he says.

The town is diverse, he says, and the "economics positive."

Housing costs are among the at-

Greenville, NC

Population: 56,788 in Greenville, 126,263 in Pitt County.
Location: In eastern North Carolina on the wooded coastal plain, fronting the Tar River; it's an hour and a half to ocean beaches and less than two hours to Raleigh.
Climate:

	High	Low
January	49	28
July	92	73

Average relative humidity: 54%
Rain: 46.32 inches.
A mild climate, with four distinct seasons. July through September can be hot and sometimes muggy. Snow is rare. Passing hurricanes may cause heavy rain, but the town has not been hit by a hurricane since the 1950s. Elevation is 55 feet.
Cost of living: 97.7, based on national average of 100.
Average housing cost: $125,000
Sales tax: 6%
Sales tax exemptions: Prescription drugs, eyeglasses, some medical supplies.
State income tax: Graduated in three steps from 6% to 7.75%, depending on income.
Income tax exemptions: Social Security

benefits. Each taxpayer also can exempt up to $4,000 in local, state or federal government retirement benefits and up to $2,000 in private retirement benefits, but the total of these exemptions cannot exceed $4,000 per person.
Intangibles tax: None.
Estate tax: None, except the state's "pick-up" portion of the federal tax, applicable to taxable estates above $675,000.
Property tax: The combined city-county tax rate in Greenville is $12.30 per $1,000 of assessed value, with property assessed at 100% of market value. The yearly tax on a $125,000 home is $1,538.
Homestead exemption: People age 65 or older, or disabled, with an income of no more than $11,000 receive a $15,000 reduction in the property tax valuation of their permanent residence.
Security: 113.7 crimes per 1,000 residents, higher than the national average of 46.2 crimes per 1,000 residents.
Religion: 76 congregations in the Greenville area, including two Catholic churches, one synagogue and churches of more than a dozen other denominations. Baptists and Free Will Baptists make up the largest group.
Education: East Carolina University, the third largest school in the University of North Carolina system, offers baccalaureate, graduate and continuing-education courses. Pitt Community College provides vocational and technical training, as well as a continuing-education program.
Transportation: There is local bus ser-

vice. Pitt-Greenville Airport provides commuter service to Raleigh and Charlotte.
Health: The 731-bed University Medical Center of Eastern North Carolina-Pitt County is the primary teaching facility of East Carolina University School of Medicine. It is one of the leading medical centers in the state, with one of the four Level One Trauma Centers in North Carolina. The hospital has an active medical staff of more than 400.
Housing options: There's a wide choice in the type and price of housing. Recent listings include: an older country home for $54,000, a three-story five-bedroom older brick home for $87,500 and two-bedroom condos with cathedral ceilings for $58,900. **Cypress Glen**, a continuing-care retirement community on the Tar River, has apartments renting for $1,214-$2,235 per month, and homes for $82,000-$123,000. Other options include **River Crest**, with a boat ramp and some houses fronting the Tar River, in the $135,000-$200,000 range; and **Cypress Landing** on Chocowinity Bay, 20 minutes from Greenville, has a marina, yacht club and 18-hole golf course, with lots starting in the mid-$30,000 range and homes starting at $170,000.
Visitor lodging: Greenville Hilton, $99-$104 double, (800) 445-8667; Ramada Plaza Hotel Greenville, $84 double, (800) 228-2828.
Information: Greenville-Pitt County Convention and Visitors Bureau, P.O. Box 8027, 525 S. Evans St., Greenville, NC 27835, (800) 537-5564 or www.visitgreenvillenc.com.

tractions for many retirees. Carl Esslinger, 58, cited excellent, affordable housing as one reason that he and his wife, Anne, moved to the city from Danville, IL. The couple's best friends from their 48 years in Danville had moved to Greenville and invited them for a visit. They quickly decided to move south, too.

Both the Whitakers and Parrishes also cited good value in housing, with Greenville prices being about half those in Chicago, Tom Parrish estimates. Latest figures show the average housing cost is about $125,000.

The Parrishes found the general cost of living much lower than in Chicago. Tom estimates that they paid for their move on the basis of a year's savings on auto insurance alone.

Retirees to the area mention a variety of other benefits they have found in Greenville: good city government, the politeness and promptness of people, the excellent retirement facility Cypress Glen, the many Colonial historic sites in the region, the ease of meeting people and making friends, an outstanding library system and the beauty of the city and area.

Residents do have some complaints, including humidity, the distance to ski slopes and the flatness of the area. The Esslingers note that crime seems to be more of a problem than in their previous home in Danville. Latest FBI figures indicate a higher-than-average crime rate in the city. The FBI Uniform Crime Index for Greenville shows 113.7 crimes per 1,000 residents; the national average is 46.2 crimes per 1,000 people.

Greenville Chief of Police Charles Hinman says that when he took the job in 1991, he went on the "rubber chicken circuit," making speeches urging better reporting of crime. In the next two years, he says, more crimes were reported, "larcenies and other incidents," than had been in the past. At the same time, the department "was grossly understaffed." More officers have been hired, and Hinman says the crime rate has been steadily dropping.

While forests and mountains distinguish western North Carolina, water dominates the eastern third of the state. The Tar River runs through the center of Greenville, to enter the wider Pamlico only 20 minutes away in the waterfront town of Washington. The Pamlico River, crisscrossed by ferries, widens until it is part of the huge Pamlico Sound that lies behind the barrier shore of the North Carolina Outer Banks. Just to the north is Albemarle Sound. By car, the ocean is about an hour and a half away.

"I love the natural environment and the small coastal towns nearby," Carl Esslinger says. "I'm a history buff, and eastern North Carolina is a treasure store of history."

Just downriver is North Carolina's first town, a 1690s settlement that became the town of Bath in 1705. Now a deeply shaded riverbank community about a mile long, Bath in the early 18th century was the haunt of the pirate known as "Blackbeard." Today, the oldest church in the state and a few 18th-century Bath homes blend perfectly into the rest of this small, quiet village.

Also to the south of Greenville is a town with a splashier display of Colonial history. In New Bern, Royal Gov. William Tryon built his 18th-century palace. The reconstructed Georgian buildings, set in formal gardens, are open to the public. New Bern, which on its riverfront resembles a small Charleston, has more than 150 landmarks on the National Register of Historic Places. Washington and Beaufort also are historic towns.

Within a few hours' drive are the sandy windblown strip where the Wright brothers made their first flight, the island where Sir Walter Raleigh planted the first colony in America, Revolutionary and Civil War sites and early archaeological discoveries.

"I can't imagine what anyone would offer me," Joe Whitaker says, "to cause me to move."●

Greenville, South Carolina

A downtown renaissance adds to the appeal of this growing South Carolina city

By Mary Lu Abbott

In the rolling hills of northwestern South Carolina known as the upcountry, Greenville catches the eyes of many soon-to-be-retirees searching for a new place to live. It's neither too far south nor too far north and sits close to scenic lakes and mountains. Azaleas, dogwood and rhododendron announce the arrival of spring and summer, and brilliant red, orange and gold leaves signal football season. Peach orchards and pine trees scent the air. A vibrant city with a newly enlivened downtown, Greenville anchors a burgeoning six-county metropolitan area with nearly 1 million residents, though the city itself has only about 59,000 residents.

After living in Michigan and upstate New York, Lowell and Vione Hull wanted to settle somewhere in the middle South with a milder climate that wasn't too hot but had definite seasons. They considered Lexington, KY; Hendersonville and Asheville, NC; and Knoxville, TN. After visiting the Greenville area four times over two years, they decided it was the right place for them.

"We liked what we saw," says Vione, 67, of this area. It offered "a combination of climate, university atmosphere, good cost of living and low taxes," adds Lowell, 69.

A number of colleges, including nationally known schools, are located in and around Greenville. Furman University, a liberal arts college, has a tree-shaded campus next to a lake on the edge of town. Bob Jones University, a Christian-based liberal arts college in town, is noted for an outstanding collection of religious art, and well-known Clemson University is about 30 miles southwest. All three have programs for seniors and cultural events that attract residents throughout the area. A statewide favorite football team, the Clemson Tigers play to crowds of 80,000 or more on fall weekends.

For most of their working years, Bob and Marjorie Halladay lived overseas while Bob completed assignments as an engineering design manager in the Middle East and Europe. They met in Kuwait, where Marjorie, who's from Scotland, was teaching. After living in London for more than six years, he took a job in Greenville in the late 1980s. They began thinking of retirement in the early '90s and checked out places from Virginia to Louisiana, including golfing communities in Florida. But eventually they decided to stay in Greenville.

"A lot of people are transferred here and then make a conscious decision to stay when they retire," says Marjorie.

While the Halladays liked the climate and location, they viewed the town from different perspectives at first. Bob, 68, liked the size of Greenville — "not too big nor too small" — but Marjorie, 60, at first found its smallness depressing after leaving London.

"When we first came here, I couldn't find gourmet items in the grocery stores and I went to Atlanta to buy clothes, but that has changed. You now can find anything you want here," says Marjorie.

Both the Hulls and the Halladays have witnessed tremendous changes in the community since they moved to the area in 1988-1990, before the Greenville-Spartanburg area entered a boom era that has continued into the new millennium. In the mid-1990s, automaker BMW located its North American manufacturing plant at neighboring Greer, on the Greenville-Spartanburg county line. Michelin, the tiremaker and publisher of maps and guidebooks, has its North American headquarters in Greenville and has expanded production at plants throughout the upcountry. Besides bringing in employees themselves, these companies have fostered the growth of other light industry in the area.

"Greenville is not the same community we moved to," says Marjorie. "It has grown dramatically."

The figures testify to the change. Greenville County's population has jumped from approximately 320,000 in 1990 to 353,000 in 1999. Adjacent Spartanburg County has grown from about 226,000 to 247,000 from 1990 to 1999. Growth in the six-county area has been nearly 100,000 in the last decade.

Shopping and housing developments have covered the hills outward from Greenville, Spartanburg and Greer, a town in the middle, so the communities tend to run together. The Hulls have an address in Greer but say their neighborhood is actually nearer Greenville than Greer.

Both couples applaud some changes effected by the growth and bemoan other impacts. "We didn't have the Peace Center for the Performing Arts (when they first moved here). Now we have all the cultural activities you could want — Broadway shows, Bette Midler, little theater," says Marjorie. Located downtown in a renovated factory area along the Reedy River, the Peace Center includes a concert hall, theater and outdoor amphitheater. It's augmented with the Bi-Lo Center, a sports and entertainment arena. Both Clemson and Spartanburg also have major entertainment venues, and Greenville has a regional orchestra and a community theater.

A rejuvenated downtown bustles with activity day and night, with numerous buildings already renovated and others being restored to serve as offices, stores and restaurants. Main Street entices residents and visitors to browse along tree-shaded walkways, and joggers and bikers follow trails that connect from the Peace

Center gardens to the adjacent Reedy River Falls Park and nearby Cleveland Park. On Main Street, the historic 1920s-era Poinsett Hotel is undergoing a $20 million renovation. Among nearby historic properties, the

Greenville, SC

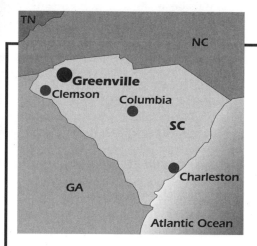

Population: 59,125 in the city, about 353,000 in the county and 918,000 in the six-county metropolitan area.

Location: In northwestern South Carolina on Interstate 85, about 140 miles northeast of Atlanta and 99 miles southwest of Charlotte, NC. From the rolling hills and wooded areas, the Blue Ridge Mountains can be seen to the north, and there are several lakes nearby. Elevation ranges from 800 to 1,100 feet.

Climate:

	High	Low
January	50	30
July	88	68

Average relative humidity: 54%

Rain: 51 inches.

Snow: 6 inches.

Cost of living: Average (specific index not available).

Average housing cost: $140,928 in the greater Greenville area.

Sales tax: 5%

Sales tax exemptions: Prescription drugs.

State income tax: Graduated in six steps from 2.5% to 7%, depending on income.

Income tax exemptions: Social Security benefits. Retirees under age 65 who are drawing income from qualified retirement plans may deduct up to $3,000 of that income. At age 65, residents may deduct up to $15,000 in income.

Intangibles tax: None.

Estate tax: None, except the state's "pick-up" portion of the federal tax, applicable to taxable estates above $675,000.

Property tax: For owner-occupied homes in the city, the combined city-county tax rate is $313.40 per $1,000 valuation, with homes assessed at 4% of market value on a statewide basis. The state allows a property tax relief on school taxes based on market value of the home, with the maximum credit of $364.40 for homes valued at $100,000 and above. Gross yearly tax on a $140,928 home would be about $1,766.67. With the noted credit, the tax drops to $1,402.27. For residents who live in the county, the tax rate varies from $220 to $318 per $1,000 in valuation.

Homestead exemption: In addition to the credits noted above, at age 65 owners receive an exemption of $20,000 off the market value of their homes and further credits based on the homestead exemption.

Personal property tax: The same city and county tax rates apply to vehicles, boats and other specified personal property, which is assessed at 10.5% of market value.

Security: 99.7 crimes per 1,000 residents, higher than the national average of 46.2 crimes per 1,000 residents.

Religion: All types of places of worship are represented in the area, and several colleges have religious affiliations. Several area churches are historically significant, some dating to the early 1800s.

Education: Greenville and nearby communities have more than a dozen colleges and universities. Furman University, Bob Jones University, Greenville Technical College and the University Center in Greenville have programs for older adults. Nearby are Clemson University in Clemson and Converse College, Wofford College and the University of South Carolina-Spartanburg, all in Spartanburg.

Transportation: The Greenville-Spartanburg International Airport has jet service, and Amtrak trains run through Greenville. There is local bus service with eight routes but no runs in the evenings or on Sundays.

Health: The city has state-of-the-art medical care through two major hospital systems and additional health facilities. The Greenville Hospital System, a teaching and research network that is the largest in the state, provides advanced medical care with more than 1,100 beds in varying locations. The St. Francis Health Care System has two major hospitals, including one specializing in women's care.

Housing options: Greenville itself has both historic and new neighborhoods, and there are numerous housing communities in the county and around nearby lakes with mountain views. The historic **Hampton Pinckney** district has tree-shaded streets with Victorian homes that start at about $150,000. **Windstone** and **1200 Pelham** are new developments with homes of varying sizes starting in the low $200,000s. Among several golfing communities, **Green Valley Country Club** has townhomes starting in the $200,000s. On nearby Lake Keowee, **Keowee Key**, (800) 537-5253, is one of the region's top resort communities with a golf course and country club. It has condos from around $65,000 and homes from about $125,000. **Rolling Green Village**, (864) 987-9800, is a lakeside continuing-care community with homes and apartments offering independent and assisted living, a nursing center and a special-care unit for residents with Alzheimer's disease. Homes start in the high $90,000s. The area also has rental apartment retirement communities offering meals, activities and other services.

Visitor lodging: Accommodations include hotels, motels and bed-and-breakfast inns. Options include several Hampton Inns, (800) HAMPTON, from about $60-$70 a night.

Information: Greater Greenville Convention and Visitors Bureau, P.O. Box 10527, Greenville, SC 29603, (800) 351-7180. Greater Greenville Chamber of Commerce, P.O. Box 10048, Greenville, SC 29603, (864) 242-1050 or www.greatergreenville.com.

Carpenter Brothers Drugstore, with a soda fountain, dates to 1883.

"We have 66 restaurants on Main Street now," says Marjorie, who volunteers at the visitor center of the Greater Greenville Convention and Visitors Bureau in City Hall downtown. "We have music on Main Street Wednesday through Saturday nights, and you can eat alfresco and stroll. We're drawing all ages downtown, from Generation X to retirees." The outdoor concerts run from April through August.

While it evokes a feeling that is both modern and young, the city actually dates to the 1770s, when a trading post was established here. Settlers took advantage of the Reedy River and its falls, built mills and developed a textile industry that flourished. Over the past several decades, as automotive, engineering and high-tech businesses began to dominate the economy, the river and its environs degenerated. As part of the downtown renaissance, the river area was cleaned up, scenic overlooks and nature trails were created and gardens were added. The historic Falls Cottage, built in 1838 as a shoemaker's home and shop, now serves as a cozy restaurant. Nearby, a once-rundown warehouse area has been turned into the West End Market, a trendy complex of plazas, an antiques and crafts village, restaurants and fresh-foods market.

One of the city's cultural gems, the Greenville County Museum of Art on the edge of downtown, displays works by the acclaimed American painter Andrew Wyeth, who calls this the "very best collection of my watercolors in any public museum in this country." The museum also has excellent works featuring Southern lifestyles.

While the couples interviewed tick off all the attributes that make the area appealing, they're also realistic in advising retirees what to expect as the area continues to boom. "Greenville has gotten a lot more congested. We have some traffic problems. The infrastructure hasn't kept pace with the growth," says Lowell Hull. "We're not against growth — we just wish there was more planning for it."

Lowell believes local politicians are strongly pro-business and pro-civic development. He notes that even though some projects have been rejected by voters in tax referendums, politicians have forged private-public partnerships to accomplish the goal. For instance, the Bi-Lo Center, a major entertainment venue for the region, was rejected by voters, then built with mostly private funding and a small amount of public funds that did not require a county tax hike. It has been well-received and its events well-supported.

Marjorie and Bob Halladay also have noticed increased traffic congestion in the area, but Marjorie says most residents learn back routes to get places faster. "You can't live here without a car — I guess you could, but it would really be difficult. There's limited local transportation," says Marjorie.

Lowell advises newcomers to shop carefully for housing because zoning laws allow a mixture of businesses and homes in some areas. Marjorie also notes that Greenville is in the heart of the Bible Belt and that a religious fervor surfaces at times. While both the Hulls and the Halladays have made friends through their neighborhoods, newcomers club, golf clubs and volunteering, Vione felt "some resentment to outsiders," mainly by older women who've always lived in the area.

"Greenvillians are very friendly if you get involved, but they will leave you alone if you are detached," says Marjorie. She became active with a garden club, serves as president of a women's club and volunteers at a hospital. Both she and Bob volunteer as ambassadors for the city at the airport. Lowell Hull volunteers with a group that helps the elderly prepare their taxes, and Vione teaches line dancing at the senior center.

"For the retiree who wants to be involved and active, there's every club you could want here. A lot of retirees take part-time jobs, too. A lot of women usher at the Peace Center," says Marjorie.

Marjorie notes that the Greenville area is attracting many younger retirees, some in their 50s who are buying property and plan to settle here later. Many come from Northern states. In addition to settling in the city or neighborhoods in adjacent counties, some buy homes or condos on nearby scenic Lake Keowee.

While the Halladays like their neighborhood, they've long harbored the desire for a different house, preferably a one-story patio home, but they haven't found one to suit their wishes. "It has to have a certain view, face in a certain direction, ideally on a small lake or a golf course," says Bob. Both couples advise other retirees considering the area to come and stay for a while before settling permanently. "Don't move in cold turkey," says Marjorie.

Because of the fast growth, Lowell and Vione have thought of moving, but they haven't found a community they like better than Greenville. "We still haven't found anything better (than) the climate, activities, cost of living, the vibrancy of the college community here," Vione says. As for the Halladays, they've lived in Greenville longer than anywhere else in their married life.

"We recognize Greenville as home," says Marjorie.●

Hattiesburg, Mississippi

Newcomers quickly feel at home in Mississippi university town

By Richard L. Fox

In the early 1990s, Tom and Jane Moseley were looking for a town where they could spend their retirement years — "just a nice place where we could be integrated into the community," Tom recalls.

They left their home near Atlanta in 1992 and settled into Hattiesburg, a city of about 50,000 residents in southern Mississippi. Now Tom, 60, a retired IBM engineer, and his wife, Jane, 58, a homemaker, are so well integrated into their new community that Tom is the featured commentator on a retiree-attraction videotape produced by the Hattiesburg Area Development Partnership.

"The first and foremost attraction for us was its friendly people," says Tom. "This is a thriving town . . . the leaders have a great 'can-do' attitude."

This also is a town that rolls out the red carpet for retirees. In January 1995 the Mississippi Department of Economic and Community Development named Hattiesburg the first "certified retirement city" of its Hometown Mississippi Retirement program. The statewide mission promotes Mississippi as a retirement haven and helps city leaders market their communities to relocating retirees. Cities must meet a long list of criteria in order to be certified, including good health-care facilities, available housing, educational and cultural opportunities and a retiree-attraction committee.

An integral part of Hattiesburg's retiree-attraction effort is the Retirement Connection. A division of the Area Development Partnership, this organization is staffed by senior volunteers — called "connectors" — who contact prospective new residents and share information about Hattiesburg as well as their own experiences.

Charles and Helen Short received a phone call from a Hattiesburg connector shortly after visiting the town. "The information and assistance we received

from that group was vital in our decision to move to Hattiesburg," says Helen, 67. The Shorts moved in June 1995 after 35 years in Rochester, NY.

"When we moved down here, we were the 100th retired couple," recalls Charles, 69. "So we got a little publicity from that." They also got a reception, a key to the city from the mayor and a basket of goodies.

"A few months later we sat down and wrote a letter saying, 'Thank you, Hattiesburg,' for all of the things Hattiesburg had done to make us feel so warmly received. We got quite a bit of press from that and made even more new friends as a result. We had about 20 calls from people saying, 'We're so glad you're here,'" says Charles.

Bill and Nancy Litwiller, 68 and 65, moved to Hattiesburg from Hampstead, NC, where they had lived for 10 years after a long career in overseas government service. They found the Retirement Connection to be a tremendous help to their relocation. "We had friends we didn't even know — before we arrived here," says Nancy, who along with her husband now is active in the group herself.

Recently Hattiesburg has been cited in a number of national publications for its "livability," low cost of living and retiree-oriented programs. The U.S. Conference of Mayors awarded the city the Livability Award for communities of less than 100,000 residents.

If there's one thing upon which everyone in Hattiesburg agrees, it is that 12,000-student University of Southern Mississippi and 2,200-student William Carey College are largely responsible for the town's growing reputation as a great place to live.

Prominently situated on a pretty, oak-shaded campus just west of downtown, USM is credited for bringing a youthful exuberance and vitality to Hattiesburg, along with social, cultural and educational opportunities generally found in

much larger cities. William Carey College is a private, Baptist-affiliated, four-year liberal arts college.

For many retirees, the university's Institute for Learning in Retirement (ILR) is the ultimate example of the community's outreach to its retired population. Established under the auspices of the university and Mississippi Hometown Retirement, the organization is run by retirees for retirees and offers dozens of courses year-round, with retirees often serving as instructors.

Seminars and a luncheon lecture series bring large numbers of people to its off-campus location. Members attend ILR classes for about $15 each and, if 65 and older, can obtain a $30 "listener's license" to audit regular university classes on a noncredit basis. Other perquisites include discounts on all continuing-education courses at USM and honorary University Club membership.

The Litwillers have taught and taken courses at the institute and number it high among their reasons for retiring to Hattiesburg. Helen Short, who was a microbiologist at the University of Rochester in New York, lectures at ILR, and she and Charles, a former marketing executive, regularly attend classes there.

Helen credits what she calls the "centrality" of Hattiesburg for its special qualities. "It has a small-town environment and yet all of the amenities," she says. "At Christmastime, people come from 100 miles away to do their shopping and participate in festivities."

Heavily traveled Hardy Street is Hattiesburg's primary east-west artery. It is named for founder Capt. William H. Hardy, who first recognized the area's potential when surveying a new railroad route; the city itself is named for his wife, Hattie. Hardy Street connects a busy, attractive downtown to the university, hospitals, restaurants and shopping malls that extend to the west.

Hattiesburg boasts a number of restored late 19th- and early 20th-century homes, churches and commercial buildings listed on the National Register of Historic Places. A 1985 historic conservation ordinance encourages the restoration of homes and buildings in six separate historic districts. The largest is 23-block Hattiesburg Historic Neighborhood District, which features Victorian, Queen Anne and Greek Revival-style homes. During a Victorian Christmas celebration each December, the district becomes a holiday wonderland.

A striking new 53,000-square-foot public library near downtown features a circular 167-foot mural in its atrium. Painted on sandblasted stainless steel by local artist William Baggett, the mural depicts life in Mississippi before a 16th-century visit by explorer Hernando de Soto, and scenes extend all the way to contemporary times. Other library highlights include a 100,000-volume collection, computer lab, books by mail and a growing collection of large-print books. At Lunch With Books sessions held at the library, university professors and writers host lunchtime discussions on such topics as rare book col-

Hattiesburg, MS

Population: 49,667 in Hattiesburg (not including 19,000 college and university students).

Location: In southeastern Mississippi, 115 miles northeast of New Orleans.

Climate:

	High	Low
January	59	39
July	91	70

Average relative humidity: 74%

Rain: 60 inches.

Cost of living: 94.3, based on national average of 100.

Average housing cost: $106,700. The average rent for a 950-square-foot apartment is $425 per month.

Sales tax: 7%

Sales tax exemptions: Prescription drugs.

State income tax: Graduated in three steps of 2%, 3% and 4% of taxable income.

Income tax exemptions: Qualified retirement income is exempt, including Social Security benefits, public and private pensions, IRAs and annuities. There is an additional $1,500 personal exemption for residents age 65 and older.

Intangibles tax: None.

Estate tax: None, except the state's "pick-up" portion of the federal tax, applicable to taxable estates above $675,000.

Property tax: In Hattiesburg, $163.48 per $1,000 of assessed value, with homes assessed at 15% of appraised value. The rate in unincorporated areas of the county is $111.98 per $1,000. For those age 65 or older, homes are assessed at 10% of appraised value. With exemptions noted below, annual property tax on a home in Hattiesburg appraised at $100,000 is about $2,212 for homeowners under age 65 and about $654 for homeowners age 65 or older.

Homestead exemption: There is a $240 tax credit for all homeowners. For those age 65 and older, the first $60,000 of appraised value is exempt from taxation.

Personal property tax: For automobiles, there is a tax of $165.38 per $1,000 based on 30% of the depreciated value, less a tax credit of 5% of the assessed value. Tax due on a car valued at $15,000 would be about $519.

Security: 80.7 crimes per 1,000 residents, higher than the national average of 46.2 crimes per 1,000 residents.

Religion: There are more than 150 places of worship, including churches and synagogues.

Education: The University of Southern Mississippi offers undergraduate and graduate degree programs. William Carey College is a four-year private liberal arts school. USM's Institute for Learning in Retirement is a self-run, self-directed association of retirees offering a variety of courses.

Transportation: Amtrak offers direct service from Hattiesburg east as far as Atlanta and west as far as Los Angeles. Hattiesburg-Laurel Regional Airport has connecting flights to Memphis. Jackson International Airport is 90 miles away, and New Orleans International is 105 miles away.

Health: Forrest General Hospital is a 537-bed, full-service regional medical center serving 17 counties. Wesley Medical Center has 201 beds. More than 300 medical professionals in Hattiesburg practice 32 specialties.

Housing options: Prices for condominiums and townhomes in older developments start around $60,000. Currently, a limited number of condominiums and townhouses are available, but more are planned. **French Cove** has garden patio homes priced from $104,900 to $124,900. **Timber Ridge** has three-quarter-acre lots from $10,500 and homes with underground utilities from $110,000. There are several manufactured-home parks in the city and rural areas with new homes for $50,000-$75,000. Homes in historic districts go on the market for about $120,000-$250,000. Master-planned developments include **Canebrake**, (601) 264-0403, a lakeside golf-course community with homes for $200,000-$1 million; **Timberton**, (601) 264-1900, a popular golf community just minutes from downtown with homes for $140,000-$300,000; and **Lake Serene**, (601) 545-3300, which has homes on large, wooded lakeside lots with resale prices of $150,000-$300,000.

Visitor lodging: Comfort Suites, $87-$160, double occupancy, (601) 261-5555. Hampton Inn, $58-$63, (601) 264-8080. Rooms at the historic 1907 Tally House are $60-$85, including full breakfast, (601) 582-3467.

Information: Area Development Partnership, P.O. Box 751, Hattiesburg, MS 39403-0751, (800) 238-4288 or www.hattiesburg-adp.org.

lecting and famous authors.

Hattiesburg was settled just south of the confluence of the Bouie and Leaf rivers, and the gently undulating terrain is marked by lakes, great oaks and towering pines. An exploration of recreational resources reveals an exceptional array of golf courses, public tennis courts, miles of landscaped walking and jogging trails, and water parks for swimming, fishing, boating, camping and hiking. South of town off U.S. Highway 49, Paul B. Johnson State Park has a 300-acre lake, cabins, nature trail, canoe and boat rentals, and fishing and picnic areas.

Hattiesburg's convenient hub location at the intersection of several highways means easy access to Jackson, New Orleans and popular Gulf Coast beaches, all within a two-hour drive.

Hattiesburg serves as southeast Mississippi's regional medical center and has won notice for the quality of its health care. Forrest General Hospital and Methodist Hospital have a total of 738 beds and 300 medical professionals. Hattiesburg Clinic has 80 physicians, making it the largest multispecialty group practice in the state. Both hospitals have programs that provide seniors with 100 percent of Medicare-approved hospital costs, plus health education, paperwork assistance and various cafeteria and gift-shop discounts.

A stellar array of museums, art galleries, parks and gardens promote interest in the visual arts, and performing-arts forums present plays and musical performances to enthusiastic audiences. The 1,000-seat Saenger Theatre hosts a variety of events; the restored art deco movie palace is a local landmark on the National Register of Historic Places. At noon on Thursdays during May and October, the Hattiesburg Arts Council sponsors brown-bag concerts in Fountain Park.

As expected in a college town, the university is a source of diverse cultural happenings. The music school features concerts by bands, choirs, a symphony orchestra and vocal artists, while the theater and dance departments perform each spring and fall. The C.W. Woods Art Gallery hosts major traveling shows as well as solo and group exhibitions. For sports fans, USM has an NCAA Division I athletic program.

Affordability figures prominently in Hattiesburg's increasing popularity with retirees. Retirement income such as Social Security benefits, pensions and IRAs are exempt from state income tax, and a generous $60,000 homestead exemption for homeowners age 65 and older helps ease property tax burdens.

When Tom Moseley compared taxes and household expenses such as insurance and utilities between his former home in Dunwoody, GA, and Hattiesburg, he found that living costs were reduced by more than $9,000 a year in Hattiesburg. Charles and Helen Short also noticed a substantial decrease in their cost of living. "Our property tax went from $5,000 to $1,000, and we went from 1,700 square feet in Rochester to 2,700 square feet here," says Helen.

Bob James, chairman of the Retirement Connection and a Coldwell Banker real-estate agent, says newcomers can find a variety of housing at very reasonable prices.

"Thirty- to 40-year-old, well-maintained subdivisions in town have condominiums and townhouses in the $60,000s and single-family homes in the $50,000s to $90,000s," he says. "There are several manufactured-home parks in the area with new homes selling for $50,000 to $75,000. Historic districts have a half-dozen homes on the market at any time, most priced from $120,000 to $250,000."

Lake Serene, a master-planned development outside the city, has homes on large wooded lots situated around several lakes for $150,000 to $300,000. Timberton, south of town with an 18-hole golf course and clubhouse, offers new homes for $140,000 to $300,000.

The Moseleys live in Canebrake, an upscale lakeside community of about 350 homes located six miles from town. Amenities here include security guards, walking trails, tennis courts and a golf course under construction. "About 20 retired couples live here," says Tom Moseley. "It's a nicer house, with tremendous amenities, in a nicer neighborhood than Dunwoody, and we paid one-third less for our house here.

"It also has 92 doctors living there," Tom continues. "I tell people (that) if I don't feel well, I stand out in my front yard and just yell out my symptoms and get advice from a dozen specialists."

The Litwillers also bought a house in Canebrake. Bill describes it as a two-story Arcadian-style home, similar to a Cape Cod with deep porches at the front and back. When they aren't playing golf, their favorite pastime, the Litwillers enjoy reading, computers, gardening and traveling.

Charles and Helen Short bought a 1-year-old house in Bent Creek, a subdivision eight miles from town that currently has 173 homes. "It's a young community. We are the old geezers, surrounded by young people. You can count the number of retirees on one hand," says Charles, who enjoys living among younger residents.

Hattiesburg was the recipient of 10 additional police officers via a federal grant under President Clinton's community-oriented policing initiative. Neighborhood enhancement teams patrol higher-crime areas by foot and bicycle, getting to know residents on a first-name basis and leading to a greater degree of cooperation and willingness to report criminal activity.

All three couples — the Moseleys, Litwillers and Shorts — were hard-pressed to come up with drawbacks to living in Hattiesburg. "If you get down to brass tacks," Charles Short says, "there's really not a thing we don't like."

For some, the heat may take some adjustments, though. "The first summer we were here it just about wiped us out," says Helen Short, "but now that we're accustomed to it we have no problem with it."

"We were attracted by a small city that literally has everything," says Nancy Litwiller. "The university is an integral part of the city. The Institute for Learning in Retirement is just wonderful. Medical facilities are outstanding. I think, bottom line, (it's) the people... so kind and so generous and so caring."

"Get connected!" advises Bill Litwiller. "Listen to what the connector has to say. He's a volunteer. He's not selling anything. He'll tell you what's here." ●

Hendersonville, North Carolina

TV's idyllic Mayberry comes to life in North Carolina mountain town

By Alan Silverman

The September morning was crisp and clear, once the sun had chased away the scraps of fog clinging to the Blue Ridge Mountains. It was a perfect day for the annual North Carolina Apple Festival in Hendersonville.

Hundreds of mountain craftsmen, folk musicians and food vendors set up booths along Main Street, where the crowd grew to 200,000 by afternoon.

Retired residents Ken and Ginny Brown browsed through the booths, munching on Greek gyros sandwiches and freshly picked apples. They stopped by Higgins Copy Shop on Main Street to say hello.

"They're so friendly. There's a box sitting by the copier. You make your copies and drop your money in the box. That's pretty much how most folks are around here," says Ginny, 66.

Later, the Browns set up lawn chairs outside the First Citizens Bank and listened to the Hendersonville community volunteer band cap off a perfect day.

Art and Anna Malowney staked out a spot on Main Street to watch the King Apple Parade and waved to friends they spotted in the crowd.

"This is what it's all about — friends coming together to celebrate everything that's good about this community," says Anna, 60.

If Hendersonville sounds a lot like the fictional town of Mayberry, from "The Andy Griffith Show" on television, it's no wonder. The two have a lot in common.

Friendly small-town atmosphere, a picturesque setting and a nice climate have combined to make Hendersonville a premier destination for retirees such as the Browns and the Malowneys.

The town, on a plateau between the Blue Ridge Mountains and the Great Smoky Mountains, is 15 miles north of the North Carolina-South Carolina border. The Blue Ridge Parkway, one of the country's most scenic drives, cuts across the northern end of the county about 10 miles from town.

The climate and the 2,200-foot elevation have helped make this the sixth-largest apple-producing region in the country. In the fall, acres and acres of apple orchards ripen along U.S. 64, and visitors can stop at any of 14 orchards to pick fruit.

Hendersonville has a rich history as a resort community that dates back more than 100 years. Doctors initially prescribed the clean mountain air as a remedy for respiratory illnesses such as tuberculosis. Today the area's natural attractions and mountain crafts make it a popular destination for sightseeing, shopping, hiking and rafting. It's close to the Great Smoky Mountains National Park, which draws the most visitors of all parks.

The population is only 9,624 within the town, though it jumps to 81,856 when adjacent unincorporated areas are included. Summer tourists push the population above 100,000 at times.

The historic downtown has changed little since the early tourist days. It still looks like something off a Norman Rockwell canvas, with brightly colored awnings shading craft galleries, antique shops and restaurants along Main Street.

The quaint, usually quiet atmosphere attracted Harry and Anne Myers, 68 and 65, who moved here from their native Huntington, WV.

"On our second visit here I was asking about 20 questions of a lady at the Visitors Center," recalls Harry, a former director of operations for Ashland Ethanol. "Suddenly, a man standing nearby said, 'I can answer some of those questions.' He was a complete stranger — he didn't even work at the Visitors Center — but he took time to answer all my questions. The friendliness of the people here really overwhelmed us at first."

The Myerses considered Blacksburg, Williamsburg and Winchester, VA, along with New Bern, Wilmington and Hendersonville, NC. Over the next two years, they made three trips to Hendersonville.

"The first time we came, it rained three out of the four days we were here," Harry says. Despite the rain, they fell in love with the area.

"We moved on the ninth of January," Harry recalls. "It was 55 degrees and so nice the movers wanted to know if they could stay with us." Last year when they were visiting in Huntington, they convinced Anne's sister to move to nearby Brevard.

The area's moderate climate came as a welcome relief to the Malowneys when they moved here from Bartlesville, OK. They settled in Flat Rock, a smaller community adjacent to Hendersonville.

During their 37 years of marriage, the couple moved 16 times with Art's job as a marketing representative with Phillips Petroleum. They endured the smog of Los Angeles, the humidity of Houston and, most recently, the constant winds of Oklahoma. So by the time Phillips Petroleum offered Art, 62, a "golden handshake," he and Anna knew the type of climate they were seeking.

"We wanted four seasons that weren't too cold in the winter or too hot in the summer," Anna says.

They also liked Hendersonville's friendly small-town atmosphere combined with its proximity to metropolitan areas. Atlanta is a three-hour drive to the southwest, and Winston-Salem is about the same distance to the northeast. Charlotte is less than two hours east. Asheville, the largest city in western North Carolina and another retirement hot spot, is 22 miles north. At one point the unincorporated areas of Hendersonville and Asheville are less than three miles apart.

The natural lay of the land and mild summers have made the Henderson-ville area a favorite among avid golfers like the Browns, who moved here from Berea, OH.

"We came here to golf each year for eight years. We always hated leaving the mountains. So when it came time, we decided we wanted to retire here," says Ken, 67, a former pilot for Republic Steel Corp.

For retirement, the Browns wanted to lower their cost of living, particularly on real estate taxes. Ken estimates his property taxes in Ohio were five times higher than what he now pays.

The low property taxes are a major attraction, "especially to folks from the Midwest and Northeast," says Roger Hill, president of the Hendersonville Board of Realtors.

The area's cultural attractions also are a drawing card. The heart of the area's performing arts is the Flat Rock Playhouse, four miles south of town in historic Flat Rock. The playhouse, designated the state theater of North Carolina, has hosted performers such as Burt Reynolds, Elizabeth Ashley, David Forsyth and Lee Marvin. From May through September, it offers live performances of Broadway, off-Broadway and original shows.

Hendersonville, NC

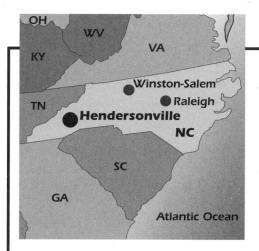

Population: 9,624 in town, 81,856 in the county.

Location: In western North Carolina between the Blue Ridge Mountains and the Great Smokies, 22 miles south of Asheville and 15 miles north of the North Carolina-South Carolina border.

Climate:

	High	Low
January	48	28
July	87	67

Average relative humidity: 60%

Rain: 55 inches.

Snow: 14-16 inches.

Moderate climate has four distinct seasons, though none is severe normally. Thunderstorms are common during spring and summer, but tornadoes are virtually non-existent. Heavy snowfalls are uncommon, though the blizzard of '93 left up to 18 inches at one time. Elevation is 2,200 feet.

Cost of living: Average (specific index not available).

Average housing cost: $130,950

Sales tax: 6%

Sales tax exemptions: Prescription drugs, eyeglasses, some medical supplies.

State income tax: Graduated in three steps from 6% to 7.75%, depending on income.

Income tax exemptions: Social Security benefits. Each taxpayer also can exempt up to $4,000 in local, state or federal government retirement benefits and up to $2,000 in private retirement benefits, but the total of these exemptions cannot exceed $4,000 per person.

Intangibles tax: None.

Estate tax: None, except the state's "pick-up" portion of the federal tax, applicable to taxable estates above $675,000.

Property tax: City tax rate is $11.35 per $1,000 in valuation, with homes assessed at 100% of market value. In Hendersonville, the yearly tax on a $131,000 home is $1,487.

Homestead exemption: $15,000 off assessed value for those age 65 and older with income below $11,000.

Security: 113.6 crimes per 1,000 residents, higher than the national average of 46.2 crimes per 1,000 residents.

Religion: The county has 212 houses of worship, representing many denominations and including a synagogue.

Education: Blue Ridge Community College maintains a Center for Lifelong Learning as part of its Continuing Education Program; center membership is a one-time $25 fee. Opportunity House offers ongoing classes in arts and crafts; its annual membership is $38 for a couple, $20 for a single.

Transportation: There is no public transportation. The Asheville-Hendersonville Regional Airport has daily flights.

Health: There are more than 100 physicians and two hospitals, Margaret Pardee Memorial Hospital with 262 beds and Park Ridge Hospital with 100 beds, both offering acute care. The Blue Ridge Health Center has four clinics, including one specializing in geriatrics.

Housing options: Besides single-family homes, condominiums and townhomes, the area has 16 retirement communities, 13 retirement homes and seven nursing homes. Homes start in the mid-$180,000s at **Cummings Cove**, (800) 958-2905, and **Carriage Park**, (800) 639-8721. Manufactured-home communities include **Riverwind**, (800) 452-3058, with homes on lots starting in the $80,000s, and **Dana Hill**, (828) 692-8477, with homes on lots starting in the mid-$50,000s.

Visitor lodging: The area is known for bed-and-breakfast inns, including the Claddagh, (828) 697-7778, $105-$149 double occupancy; the Waverly Inn, (828) 693-9193, $129-$159; Woodfield Inn, (828) 693-6016, $109-$189; and the Flat Rock Inn, (828) 696-3273, $125-$135. There are about 60 small hotels and motels in the area.

Information: Greater Hendersonville Chamber of Commerce, 330 N. King St., Hendersonville, NC 28792, (828) 692-1413 or www.hendersonvillechamber. org. Hendersonville Visitors Center, (828) 693-9708, or the Hendersonville Welcome Wagon, (828) 692-2377.

Flat Rock also supports three other acting companies, a symphony orchestra and a chorale group. Across the street from the Flat Rock Playhouse is Connemara, home of Carl Sandburg. It was here that Sandburg penned his only novel, "Remembrance Rock," and his "Complete Poems," which won a Pulitzer Prize in 1951.

Twenty-two miles southwest lies Brevard, home of the Brevard Music Center, which regularly attracts singers such as Tony Bennett and traveling symphonic and chorale groups. Because of Brevard's proximity, many Hendersonville retirees work as volunteers for the Brevard Music Association.

None of the three couples had friends or relatives living in the area when they arrived, but all say making friends was easy.

"Our neighbors were very friendly. We had just gotten the phone installed and one neighbor called and invited us to dinner," says Harry.

The Browns relied on their church for contacts.

"We became active within a month," says Ginny, adding that they also joined the Welcome Wagon and Club of Seniors.

Like the Browns, many newcomers to Hendersonville find social contacts through their religious affiliations. The town is situated in the buckle of America's Bible Belt with Southern Baptist being the predominant religious group among the 212 places of worship in the county.

Another major avenue to social contacts is the Hendersonville Welcome Wagon, one of the largest in the country. The Malowneys joined soon after they moved to town.

"They put us in this huge hall, jammed with people. We thought it was such fun. You get to meet so many new people," says Anna, who headed the membership committee with her husband. Once new members are acquainted, they split into smaller groups offering ongoing activities such as bridge, golfing and hiking.

Volunteerism is strong among the 39 percent of residents who are age 55 and older. Anna is on the local board of the American Cancer Society, and husband Art volunteers as an AARP tax adviser and as a member of the United Way Allocation Committee.

The Opportunity House, a cultural and social center, is completely volunteer-driven, and the majority of its 2,000 members are retirees. Among its programs are regular classes in art, dancing and crafts.

"We have a woodcarvers group that meets twice a week, a lapidary group, a woodworking shop open to members, bridge, pinochle, canasta and a sewing group that meets once a week that sews for the community," says Beverly French, vice-president for Opportunity House. The majority of instructors are retirees, and nearly all staff members are volunteers.

While Hendersonville's climate is praised as an ideal four seasons, it does have a drawback. The ample moisture — an average of 55 inches of rain annually — creates a breeding ground for pollens, molds and spores.

"You need to investigate the area before making a decision," Ken advises. "The allergens may not agree with some people."

The Malowneys say there were no downside surprises to their move.

"It has given us everything we were looking for when we moved here," says Art. He recommends Hendersonville to other retirees, joking, though, that "we don't want to see it grow too fast."●

Hilton Head, South Carolina

South Carolina island booms in nature-friendly environment

By Betsy and John Braden

Looking for fertile new sugar and indigo fields on behalf of Barbados planters, English sea captain William Hilton in 1663 stumbled upon the island off South Carolina that now bears his name. Sighting only white sand beaches, virgin forest and Yemassee and Ewascus Indians then, he would be amazed at the prospect that greets today's travelers.

"The island is getting pretty full but it isn't bulging at the seams yet," says Pat Cowan, 64. Four years ago he and his wife, Norma, 64, bid permanent adieu to Akron, OH, which had been their home on and off for 40 years. Pat retired from Uniroyal Goodrich, and Norma transferred her B.F. Goodrich telemarketing position to their new home.

"We looked hard at the Isle of Palms (near Charleston), but we felt more at home on Hilton Head," says Pat, who had been visiting the island yearly since 1961.

In the 1950s, young Charles Fraser masterminded Sea Pines Plantation, the island's first development. He broke ground in more ways than one by carefully integrating resort and residential features with the natural environment. In doing so, he set the tone and standard for all subsequent development on the island.

Along the still-pristine sands, among the canopied forests and around the picturesque coves that beguiled Capt. Hilton, the 42-square-mile island now enfolds 16 hotels, 11 condominium resorts, 21 golf courses, 300 tennis courts, 300 shops, 150 restaurants, nine marinas and nine movie screens.

From a relative handful of property owners, the island has grown to an estimated 30,000 permanent residents. The first sprinkling of homes has proliferated to more than 10,000 within 12 plantations — the gated, residential compounds that have replaced the cotton plantations of yore. The larger plantations contain a number of different housing styles, usually grouped together, as well as hotels, yacht clubs and other amenities.

Still, development keeps a-coming. About 500 homes a year take shape among the oaks, pines and palmettos.

"Something like 100 new houses are being built within our community of Hilton Head Plantation alone," Pat says. That brings the plantation's total to 2,700 homes; 20 years ago there were two.

Already-large grocery stores are expanding and department and home improvement stores are multiplying. The island's main thoroughfare has been expanded to four lanes and connects to the mainland via a milelong bridge spanning the Intracoastal Waterway.

Growth on the mainland has been equally explosive. Seventeen golf courses lie within easy motoring distance, and an exclusive golf community is taking shape near Rose Hill, six miles inland. Del Webb Corp., the leading developer of active adult communities, located its first project on the East Coast just 13 miles inland from Hilton Head. Its Sun City Hilton Head is expected to have 8,600 homes when completed.

Despite all the development on the island, several thousand homesites still are available. Observers predict, however, that "build-out" is only a few years ago.

Summer brings crowds of vacationers — and high humidity, mosquitoes and pesky gnats known as "no-see-ums." The influx, which swells the daily ranks to 150,000 from June through August, is a double-edged sword.

"We can't do things on the spur of the moment like we can in the winter," Pat says. "It's harder to get dinner reservations and tee times, and traffic to the southern end of the island is congested."

The Cowans' solution? Plan ahead and be prepared for traffic congestion. Also, when looking for a homesite, locate close to your activities of interest. For instance, the Cowans keep their sailboat near where they live on the northern end of the island.

Beach parking also can be vexing in the summer. Although the 12-mile, traffic-free strand is open to everyone, public access points are limited. The opening of a fourth access point, with more than 200 parking spaces, should alleviate past problems. Again, the Cowans have their own solution: They hop on their bicycles, pedal along one of the island's many bike paths to the closest access and ride as far down the beach as they wish.

Pat notes that while the number of tourists may be annoying, their presence makes possible many of the amenities that year-round residents enjoy. From Easter weekend through Labor Day, free concerts and performances take place nightly at Shelter Cove Harbour, with spectacular fireworks every Thursday. Bed-tax monies "support beach renourishment, charities, road maintenance and many island activities — so many, that my trouble is finding a day off to rest," he jokes.

Outdoor sports naturally predominate on this barrier island where wintertime temperatures seldom fall below 40 degrees Fahrenheit. In addition to the obvious lures of golf, tennis, fishing, boating and swimming, residents can enjoy shrimping, crabbing, kayaking, kite-flying, birding, biking and hiking. They can go horseback riding and rollerblading, or watch the championship tennis, golf and windsurfing competitions that come to Hilton Head annually.

Even the small Museum of Hilton Head Island has been called a "museum without walls" because of its popular docent-led walks among the island's dunes and beaches, Civil War forts and early Indian and plantation ruins. Tours also explore the Pinckney Island National Wildlife Refuge and the 600 acres that Fraser preserved within Sea Pines Plantation.

In these and other protected areas, chances are good of spotting deer, bobcat, otter, mink, alligator and possibly wild boar.

Less well-publicized are the diverse cultural options, many of which fill the slacker winter calendar. Eighteen arts organizations, including the mu-

seum, a playhouse, orchestra, dance theater, art league and gallery, jazz and choral societies, a low-country singing group and barbershop quartets operate under the umbrella Cultural Council. A new arts center built to showcase such talent opened in 1996. Arts patrons hope to open a

Hilton Head, SC

Population: 30,377 year-round, 150,000 in the summer.

Location: A 42-square-mile barrier island off South Carolina, about 90 miles southwest of Charleston and 35 miles northeast of Savannah, GA.

Climate: High Low
January 59 38
July 89 71

Average relative humidity: 53%
Rain: 49.4 inches.
Temperate climate with four seasons. Summers are hot and humid with afternoon thunderstorms common. Winters can bring freezing temperatures and a trace of snow. The area is vulnerable to tropical storms and hurricanes from June through November. The last hurricane to affect Hilton Head was Hugo in 1989; two others have blown through since 1979. Federal Flood Insurance, which covers water damage from a hurricane, can increase homeowners insurance costs by more than $400 per year.

Cost of living: 112.6, based on national average of 100.

Average housing cost: $200,000; new homes average $225,000.

Sales tax: 5%

Sales tax exemptions: Prescription drugs, some medical supplies, most services.

State income tax: Graduated in six

steps from 2.5% to 7%, depending on income.

Income tax exemptions: Social Security benefits. Retirees under age 65 who are drawing income from qualified retirement plans may deduct up to $3,000 of that income. At age 65, residents may deduct up to $15,000 in income.

Intangibles tax: None.

Estate tax: None, except the state's "pick-up" portion of the federal tax, applicable to taxable estates above $675,000.

Property tax: $21.21 to $25.24 per $100 of assessed value, with $23.02 being the most common rate. Homes assessed at 4% of market value. Yearly tax on a $200,000 home taxed at the $23.02 rate is $1,841. With the homestead exemption noted below, the tax is $1,657.

Homestead exemption: $20,000 off market value for residents age 65 or older; none for those under 65 unless disabled.

Security: 65 crimes per 1,000 residents in Beaufort County, higher than the national average of 46.2 crimes per 1,000 residents.

Religion: Worship sites serve all major religions except Islam.

Education: Technical College of the Low Country and the University of South Carolina-Hilton Head offer a range of courses through their Offices of Continuing Education.

Transportation: The island has no public bus transportation. USAir serves Hilton Head Airport with commuter flights from Charlotte, NC. Regularly scheduled limousine service goes to nearby Savannah International Airport, which is served by several major carriers.

Health: The 68-bed Hilton Head Medical Center, staffed by more than 60 physicians, offers a full range of med-

ical care. Air-ambulance service connects Hilton Head with three Savannah hospitals, and there are several major hospitals in Charleston including the Medical University of South Carolina. There is also a U.S. Navy Hospital at the nearby Parris Island Marine Training Center.

Housing options: Most homes and condominiums (called villas) are located in 11 residential developments referred to as plantations. Each is an independent development; there is no central property source. Resale prices range from $70,000 to more than $2 million; several thousand homesites still are available. Many homeowners are part-time residents who lease or rent their condos on daily, weekly or seasonal bases. Such rentals are good options for those who want to check out the area for retirement. **The Village of Victoria Square**, a new development of single-family homes, has two-bedroom, two-bath, 1,396-square-foot homes for $205,900-$235,900, and three-bedroom, three-and-a-half-bathroom, 1,621-to-2,099-square-foot homes for $215,900-$243,900, (843) 785-9055.

Visitor lodging: As a major resort, Hilton Head offers more than 9,000 rooms in 27 hotels, motels and villa (condominium) resorts, a wide variety of rental homes and an RV resort; a campground is nearby on the mainland. Through Seashore Vacations, (800) 845-0077, an oceanfront two-bedroom villa rents for $950-$1,525 a week, depending on the season; golfside villas are $525-$875 a week. From November through late March, rental costs drop.

Information: Hilton Head Island Chamber of Commerce, P.O. Box 5647, Hilton Head Island, SC 29938, (843) 785-3673 or www.hiltonhead chamber.com.

1,000-seat hall for the orchestra in the not-too-distant future.

Through the SHARE Senior Center and Kreation Station, divisions of the city and county recreation commissions, there is a variety of planned instruction and recreation for retirees. Options include travel lectures, crafts sessions, intramural softball, computer classes, square dancing, shag dancing (a South Carolina specialty since the 1960s), rollerblading, pottery, sculpture, calligraphy, sewing, floral arranging and financial planning.

Benefit soirees and black-tie galas also fill agendas, providing respite from the normal sockless, tieless regimen of the island.

"There are more than enough cultural activities to keep me happy, and if not, we can always zip over to Savannah or Charleston," says Mary Ellen McConnell, 61, formerly of Basking Ridge, NJ.

Except for an occasional day trip to the nearby antebellum town of Beaufort, she and her husband, Jack, 70, don't go off-island much because of Jack's work with a non-profit medical clinic he established four years ago. Jack, a physician, pioneered the development of Tylenol and magnetic resonance imaging (MRI) when he was corporate director of medical research at Johnson & Johnson. Drawing from a large group of retired medical personnel on the island who wanted to contribute their talents, Jack began the privately funded Volunteers in Medicine Clinic. As its board chairman, he oversees a paid staff of five, 110 volunteer doctors, dentists and nurses in 11 specialties and 170 lay volunteers.

"If you retire and wish to take from the retirement site, that may satisfy you for a year or so. But if you wish to give something back to the place where you're living, it can go on forever, and you're better for it. At the end of the day there is a deep soul-satisfying joy," Jack says.

Hilton Head has tremendous opportunities for volunteerism, with a volunteer center to coordinate the needs, Mary Ellen says, naming cultural organizations, a hospice and a literacy group in addition to the clinic.

Before relocating, Mary Ellen and Jack scoured potential retirement spots between the Eastern Shore of Maryland and the southwestern coast of Florida.

"Our criteria included a warm climate, a change of seasons and easy access to medical care, cultural events and shopping," says Mary Ellen. "But we weren't looking for the ideal resort life so much as a place with a real sense of community where we could get involved. Those who live on Hilton Head care deeply about it, even though most weren't born here."

Kay and Marvin Summers, who relocated from Potomac, MD, three years ago when both were 55, think the fact that so many Hilton Headers once were newcomers themselves makes them especially welcoming and outgoing. In their case, the couple who lived next door to them in Sea Pines Plantation gave a get-acquainted bash for them to meet their neighbors. Marvin, a former IBM manager, and Kay, a homemaker, have since made other fast friends through the plantation's fitness facility and sports groups.

Although many newcomers unite through church and organizational activities, most socializing tends to take place within plantation boundaries.

"Hilton Head Plantation has a very active women's association that coordinates bridge, gourmet groups, book clubs and other interests. If yours isn't there, you can organize it yourself," says Mary Ellen. "Plus, Jack and I found the intergenerational experience that we were looking for. We are among families of all ages, from preschool to retirees, and I feel like I'm living in a small town when the school bus drives by my house."

While Hilton Head is a retirement haven, it is not age-restricted. Thousands of young workers and professionals are employed on the island, contributing to the need for four schools serving youngsters of kindergarten age through high school.

At the same time, the advancing age of those who retired to Hilton Head 20 or 30 years ago means that health and other related services have increased dramatically. An 88-bed nursing home has been built near the Hilton Head Hospital, itself a fully accredited facility that is equipped to handle all medical conditions except heart surgery.

In the 1980s, The Seabrook of Hilton Head Island opened as the community's first comprehensive retirement complex, established as a nonprofit entity through the efforts of a local retiree. Seabrook was joined three years ago by The Cypress on a 180-acre campus that includes a nursing wing for Alzheimer's patients. A third, TidePointe, debuted in 1996 within Sea Pines Plantation. All three have skilled-nursing pavilions, recreational amenities, clubhouses, dining rooms, social programs and a choice of living arrangements that include studios, patio homes and one- and two-bedroom units, some with a den. Prices range from about $75,000 to $500,000.

These facilities have been crucial for today's fiftysomething and sixtysomething retirees whose parents relocated with them. "My mother lived with us for one and a half years after we moved, but at 89 she needed more care," says Pat Cowan. "Now she's looked after by professionals and is only five minutes away from us."

Despite the island's growth, none of the couples plans to move away. "I can't think of one reason why we should," says Jack McConnell. "Our children are scattered across the country and all of them love to come visit us here on vacation." ●

Hot Springs, Arkansas

In the Arkansas mountains, retirees find cosmopolitan living without the congestion

By Marcia Schnedler

Native American paths led from all directions to the sacred Valley of Peace, where 47 hot, healing springs bubbled from the rolling Ouachita (Wash-i-taw) Mountains. This was neutral ground, even in times of war, where strangers from faraway places met, made friends and traded ideas as well as useful and exotic items.

So from time immemorial, Hot Springs has been a place of relaxation, rejuvenation and hospitality. This storied Spa City has attracted everyone from American presidents to Al Capone and his gangster pals.

In 1832, Hot Springs became America's first national reserve. Today, its row of opulent early 20th-century bathhouses is part of Hot Springs National Park, which also encompasses forested mountain ridges and valleys surrounding the town.

But this Garland County seat, with a population of 37,000, is much more than a collection of thermal baths. The historic area and manicured parks around Bathhouse Row serve as the centerpiece of a growing district of fine arts, family attractions, shopping and dining spots. The town's calendar is packed with festivals and events, from the Arkansas Senior Olympics to Oktoberfest, documentary film and music festivals and an extravaganza of Christmas lights.

Hot Springs is surrounded by streams and five sparkling lakes — including Arkansas' largest man-made body of water — and is perched at the edge of a national forest that leads west into Oklahoma. Boaters, anglers, hunters, hikers, canoeists, bird-watchers, golfers and others who love the outdoors flock to the region.

Garland County has a lower-than-average cost of living, mild winters and a housing market varied enough in price, location and amenities to fit divergent wants, needs and budgets. It's no surprise, then, that Hot Springs attracts not only vacationers, but active retirees.

When Glenn and Dolores Quade retired from jobs in northern Illinois and Wisconsin, they bought a new car and headed west on an 8,500-mile journey. Looping back, they stopped at Dolores' father's winter home in Hot Springs.

"We pulled in here in mid-February and it was 72 degrees," says Glenn, 71. "We were impressed by the town and its quaint charm, and by the people themselves. If you were looking at a map, people would ask if they could help you find something. If a shop didn't have what you needed, they'd call their competitors to find where you could get it."

So they promptly bought a 3,000-square-foot home on the shore of Lake Hamilton on the south end of Hot Springs. They planned to use it during the winter.

"My mom and dad had always had two homes for the seasons, and I thought I was just going to do the same thing," says Dolores, 64. "But on the way home, Glenn asked why we wanted two homes, particularly since the weather is nice in Hot Springs all year around. I do like seasonal change, and springs and falls here are especially gorgeous, while winter is a soft season."

Another transplanted couple, Fred Sims, 68, and his wife, Betty, 64, had traveled the United States and the world thanks to his job as an oil refinery technologist. Betty had worked in the retail business whenever possible. When they retired in 1991, they lived in Baton Rouge, LA.

"I was 62 the first time I visited Hot Springs," Fred recalls. "I fell in love with the terrain — the hills, the mountains, the lakes. I really enjoy fishing, boating and small-game hunting. But the really great thing is just getting out in those woods."

In addition to milder weather and outdoor recreation, they found the cost of living lower in Hot Springs in everything from groceries and gasoline to utilities. And, as an added bonus, their daughter and her family live in Hot Springs, too.

The Simses decided on a Spanish-style home in a Hot Springs neighborhood. "We like being close to grocery stores, hospitals, organizations and our grandchildren, who often stop by on their way home from high school," Fred says. "And we fell in love with the First Baptist Church near us."

The average housing price in Hot Springs is $117,000. "In the older sections of the city, homes sell for $30,000 to $40,000. And you can find a nice, well-maintained, three-bedroom, two-bath home with a two-car garage in the $80,000 range," says Carol Caldwell, who operates Century 21 Caldwell Realty. "In new areas near Lake Hamilton, you'll pay around $140,000 for a 2,300-square-foot home, a very good value. You can find homes in the $175,00 to-$1 million range in one fast-growing area, but they don't appeal much to retirees," she adds.

"You'll also find some very nice mobile home parks with manufactured homes on permanent foundations, and clubhouses," she says. "You can buy a house and lot there for around $60,000. Although the average rental price is around $450, the type of place in which a retiree would like to live, with two bedrooms, is in the $600-to-$650 range."

Hot Springs' crime rate is above the national average, but "that is extremely misleading," Carol Caldwell says. "It occurs in a certain neighborhood among people who know each other. I am single and have lived alone here for many years with no problems or fears.

"In fact, more than once I've inadvertently left a good camera and binoculars out in plain sight on my boat that I keep at a neighbor's condo. And the water skis sit out in the open all summer."

The Hot Springs area offers hundreds of activities, and both the Quades and the Simses leave themselves little time to relax. Betty Sims works 16 hours a week to receive medical benefits, Fred says, while he works at the Oaklawn thoroughbred racetrack — the only one in Arkansas — during its January-through-April season.

"It's a lot of fun meeting people, and it lets us travel during late spring through fall," Fred says. He also enjoys hunting and fishing trips with his son-in-law.

The Simses have volunteered at a new medical clinic for low-income families run by a group of Hot Springs churches. And Fred is active in the Masons as a member of a Shrine clown unit.

"We do a lot for children, help in fund raising for diabetes research, and go all over Arkansas in parades and meeting kids," Fred says. Betty volunteers through her church and such other groups as the Women's Welcome Club. She plays cards four times a month, and enjoys working with handicrafts, such as making toy bears for one

Hot Springs, AR

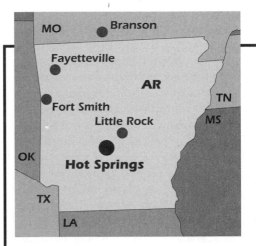

Population: 37,023 in Hot Springs, 12,946 in Hot Springs Village, 84,500 in Garland County.

Location: Hot Springs is in central Arkansas about 50 miles southwest of Little Rock. It lies in a valley of the rolling Ouachita Mountains and is surrounded by lakes and national forests. Hot Springs claims the only national park within a city thanks to the thermal waters that gave the town its name.

Climate:

	High	Low
January	43	31
July	82	67

Average relative humidity: 55%

Rain: Average annual rainfall is 54.3 inches, fairly evenly distributed but slightly higher January through May.

Snow: Averages about four inches annually and usually does not remain on the ground beyond 24 to 48 hours.

Cost of living: 93.8, based on national average of 100.

Average housing cost: $117,000 in Hot Springs. In Hot Springs Village, resale homes range from $60,000 to $800,000, and townhomes from $50,000 to $320,000.

Sales tax: 6.6% on most items, plus an additional 3% tourism tax is collected from hotels, motels and restaurants.

Sales tax exemptions: Prescription drugs and medical services.

State income tax: Graduated in six steps from 1% to 7%, depending on income

Income tax exemptions: Social Security benefits and $6,000 of employer-sponsored pensions exempt.

Intangibles tax: None.

Estate tax: None, except the state's "pick-up" portion of the federal tax, applicable to taxable estates above $675,000.

Inheritance tax: None.

Property tax: Property is assessed at 20% of the market value. The effective rate is determined by the school district in which the property is located. In Hot Springs school district No. 6, the rate is $41.87 per $1,000 of assessed value. In Lake Hamilton No. 5, it is $39.67. In Hot Springs Village, it is $34.60-$34.80, depending on location. The annual tax on a home in district No. 6 valued at $117,000 would be approximately $980.

Homestead exemption: Available to low-income residents 62 and older who own, occupy and pay taxes on their home and have a household income of no more than $25,000.

Security: 99 crimes per 1,000 residents, higher than the national average of 46.2 crimes per 1,000 residents.

Religion: Hot Springs has more than 90 churches representing 32 denominations. Hot Springs Village has more than 16 churches with new congregations under formation.

Education: Garland County Community College, with an enrollment of 2,300, offers continuing-education programs. Hot Springs also has two vocational-technical schools with adult education, plus continuing education at three senior and community centers. Henderson State University and Ouachita Baptist University are in Arkadelphia, 36 miles south, and the University of Arkansas is in Little Rock, 50 miles away.

Transportation: Hot Springs has an intracity transit system, one bus line, a municipal airport served by one commercial airline, and a shuttle service to Little Rock National Airport.

Health: Hot Springs and the Garland County area are served by three major hospitals with a total of 572 beds, 128 practicing physicians, 28 clinics and seven nursing homes. Among their specialties are acute care, arthritis and other rehabilitation programs, home health care, cardiology, cancer and radiation therapy centers. In Hot Springs Village are a medical and diagnostic clinic, cardiac rehabilitation unit, an urgent-care center, and a long-term care facility with independent-living apartments.

Housing options: Quite varied, from the gated **Hot Springs Village** with wooded, golf-front and lake-side lots with townhouses to custom-built homes, to in-town homes and apartments in Hot Springs, waterfront homes and condos on nearby lakes, and upscale mobile home parks. For information about Hot Springs Village, call Cooper Communities, (800) 266-7373. **Meyers Realty/ Better Homes and Gardens**, (501) 624-5622 or (800) 467-0622, frequently works with relocating retirees and offers a relocation packet. The company's Web site is www.meyersrealty.com.

Visitor lodging: Arlington Resort Hotel and Spa, $58-$112, (501) 623-7771. Lake Hamilton Resort, $79-$94, (501) 767-8576. Econo Lodge, $59, (501) 525-1660. In Hot Springs Village, Village Villas Vacation Rentals, $59-$210, (800) 411-8070.

Information: Ask for a free relocation packet from the Greater Hot Springs Chamber of Commerce, P.O. Box 6090, Hot Springs, AR 71902, (800) 467-INFO or www.hotsprings.dina.org. For a statewide retirement and relocation guide, call (800) NATURAL.

of the local hospitals.

Glenn Quade has helped organize the state Senior Olympics held at Hot Springs each year, and both he and Dolores volunteer at the Mid-America and Hot Springs museums. Glenn, who enjoys woodworking, even made some of the Hot Springs Museum's display cases. Dolores also volunteers at a local hospital.

The couple takes advantage of the adult-education program at Garland County Community College. "Glenn is a gourmet cook and has taken classes there," Dolores says. He's also just finished remodeling their kitchen to incorporate commercial-quality appliances and counter tops. Dolores is a master gardener and has taken classes in flower arranging.

As jazz fans, they belong to the local society and look forward to Hot Springs' annual jazz and blues festival. They own two boats and go fishing occasionally, and Dolores is an avid swimmer — even plunging in on her Oct. 11 birthday.

Hot Springs Village, a gated Cooper Community about 12 miles north of Hot Springs itself, offers an equally active lifestyle that suited Larry and Beverly Severson. When they retired, they were living in northern Illinois. They and their children had been downhill skiers, owning a condominium in Steamboat Springs, CO. But that didn't appeal to the Seversons as a year-round retirement location, and they gave the condo to their sons. Marco Island, FL, which they had visited with friends, didn't attract them, either.

"People were too old there," Larry says. Then they looked over Hot Springs Village on the way north from a visit to Dallas. They immediately were enchanted by the beautiful terrain — and the golf. Beverly, 71, is an avid golfer, and they built a 2,200-square-foot home on a lot overlooking a course.

"Being from Door County, WI, I missed the water," Larry says. So they sold their first home and built a 3,300-square-foot place, including a boat dock for their party barge, on the shore of Lake Balboa, the largest of the community's six spring-fed lakes.

Beverly golfs three or four times a week on one of Hot Springs Village's seven 18-hole courses, where green fees are $5. Several of the courses have restaurants and driving ranges. There also is a country club, which the Seversons

joined as social members.

The Seversons are active church members, and Beverly has served as president of several local organizations.

Hot Springs Village, with a population of about 12,946, boasts 13 lighted, pro-surfaced tennis courts, a fitness center with an indoor pool, whirlpool, sauna and massage, and a family-oriented games area with outdoor pools, basketball courts, miniature golf course and fenced-in playground. Its $2.5 million performing arts center offers concerts, plays and other cultural activities, while the community center is the site of meetings of more than 100 social and civic clubs. All of these amenities are owned by the property owners association and are funded by a monthly assessment fee of $26.

While 83 percent of Hot Springs Village residents are retired, more than 50 percent are under age 65. Some 450 school-age children also live there.

The price of home sites at Hot Springs Village varies. The average lot size is 90 by 160 feet, about a third of an acre. An interior lot runs $6,000 to $10,000, while one close to golf or a lake will cost $8,000 to $25,000. A golf-front lot averages $30,000, and a lake-front lot $120,000. Resale homes range from approximately $60,000 to $800,000, with townhomes running from about $50,000 to $320,000.

Hot Springs Village has medical offices, banks, restaurants, grocery stores, service stations, a florist, video store, beauty salons, clothing stores, stockbrokers, attorneys, hardware store, travel agency, bakery and even a watch repair shop.

Hot Springs itself offers an even greater variety of shopping opportunities, including such department stores as Dillard's, J.C. Penney and Sears, as well as furniture and antiques shops and clothing and accessories boutiques.

And there are the bathhouses. "Betty loves the baths and the pedicures and manicures and massages," Fred Sims says.

"Glenn gives me the whole works on my birthday," Dolores Quade says.

They and other retirees, as well as younger residents and visitors, especially love the old downtown that has made a remarkable comeback in recent years.

Its crown jewel is the Fordyce Bath-

house, the most opulent of the eight remaining spas along Bathhouse Row. Outfitted in fine wood, marble, stained glass, period furnishings and old-time exercise and therapeutic equipment, it serves as the national park's visitor center and museum. The Buckstaff is the only 1920s bathhouse still in operation, but newer ones can be found at the venerable Arlington and Majestic hotels as well as the more modern Hilton.

Up and down Central Avenue, across from Bathhouse Row, are more than 20 fine arts, crafts and antiques galleries that sponsor a monthly Friday-night Gallery Walk. Just down the street is Hot Springs' newest museum, Window to the World, opened in a restored department store and brothel that had been empty since 1958. Sue Koenig, who retired after 31 years of teaching in Denver and Saudi Arabia, had collected thousands of exquisite handmade handicrafts, costumes and other items from dozens of trips around the world. She visited friends in Hot Springs Village, liked the area, then found and remodeled the old building to display some 23,000 pounds of art.

In the same tradition as Sue Koenig's museum, Hot Springs offers a variety of ethnic as well as American restaurants. "There are restaurants galore, from German, Chinese and Japanese to Thai, Italian and Greek," Glenn says.

Fred enjoys two excellent steakhouses, Hamilton House and Coy's, and as a former Louisianan approves of the cooking at Cajun Boilers. Or they can dig into the down-home barbecue at McClard's, one of Bill Clinton's favorite hangouts when he was growing up in Hot Springs.

Most of all, these relocated retirees enjoy the friendly, active environment. "We have a lot of friends who visit us here, and the first thing they have to do is the baths," Fred says. "Some friends like art, and there is some very, very good local talent here. We enjoy walking down, getting a sandwich, hearing a concert. And Sunday afternoon, after church, it's the Arlington Hotel brunch with big-band music."

Like many newcomers to Hot Springs, the Simses quickly felt at home in their new town.

"I found a lot in common with the people here," says Fred Sims. "It doesn't take you long to fit in."●

Jackson Hole, Wyoming

A chic, Old West town anchors this alpine valley in northwest Wyoming

By Mary Lu Abbott

In the summer, Joe and Gainor Bennett walk outside their home and cast for cutthroat trout in the Snake River, and in the winter they slip on skis to explore white meadows, all beneath one of nature's most spectacular canvases, the majestic Teton Range in Wyoming.

"I go cross-country skiing along the river with our dogs," says Gainor. "We always see deer. Sometimes we see moose — they're big critters. They bring you to attention."

Close encounters with moose aren't uncommon in any season in the beautiful alpine valley known as Jackson Hole. Rather ungainly looking with flattened antlers, moose munch their way along the banks of streams and rivers, enjoying willow and cottonwood trees in particular. Buffalo, elk, eagle, osprey, great blue heron, trumpeter swan, otter, beaver and bear also call this region home. So do many retirees such as the Bennetts, both 65, who moved here in 1990 from Salt Lake City, UT, where he was in the mining business.

"We like the outdoors — we ski, bicycle, fish — and we wanted a country setting. We're not golfers and didn't want a Southern golfing community," Gainor says, adding that they were familiar with Jackson Hole from vacationing and visiting relatives in the area.

Many visitors succumb to the magnetism of this mountain-ringed valley, which stretches about 60 miles from the town of Jackson on the south to the entrance of Yellowstone National Park on the north. Presiding over the broad sage-covered flats bisected by the Snake River are the high glacier-carved peaks of Grand Teton National Park, perhaps the most dramatic alpine scenery in the country.

From the valley floor of about 6,500 feet elevation, the Tetons jut abruptly upward more than a mile, with seven peaks topping 12,000 feet and the Grand Teton crowning the range at 13,770 feet. With glaciers and canyons in clear view, the peaks run most of the length of the valley,

possessing an in-your-face closeness that is unusual to find without hiking to higher elevations. Against a deep blue sky and reflected in lakes beneath them, the towering Tetons at times seem like a painted backdrop.

Jack and Carole Nunn, who both attended the University of Wyoming at Laramie, had honeymooned and vacationed in the area before moving here from Boulder, CO, in 1995.

"We loved it and said if the opportunity ever presented itself to live there, let's move," says Jack, 52, who was a bank president in Boulder and is a native of Casper, WY. When their kids were grown, Jack and Carole, 50, decided they wanted something new, so they traded the Colorado Rockies for the Tetons. "We like the mountains, the open space and the fewer people here."

A pathologist from El Paso, TX, Dr. Richard Juel, 56, first saw Jackson Hole about 10 years ago when he spoke at a professional conference. "I came in September and the aspens turned (colors) over the four days I was here," he says. "I went home and told Susan (his wife), 'This is it.' I fell in love with Jackson."

Richard sold his clinical lab in 1991, and he and Susan took a road trip through Colorado to the Tetons to look at possible places to retire. There was no question where they wanted to settle when Susan saw Jackson Hole for the first time. The next year they bought a home southwest of Jackson, outside the community of Wilson, and split time between here and El Paso, where Susan, 48, still had a computer consulting business. In 1994, they decided to forsake the desert permanently for Jackson Hole, where their home sits on 14 acres with two streams and views of both the Tetons and the Gros Ventre Range to the east.

The Bennetts, the Nunns and the Juels are part of a boom that has hit Jackson Hole in the last decade, pumping the population of the county from about 11,000 in 1990 to an estimated 15,000

today. Long a popular gateway to the Grand Tetons and Yellowstone in the summer and a highly regarded ski resort, Jackson Hole has caught the fancy of many urbanites seeking a return to nature and a quieter lifestyle. Some newcomers exited the fast lanes suffering from burnout in high-pressure jobs, while others have taken early retirement, sometimes still dabbling in their businesses. A few movie stars, including Harrison Ford, hang their hats here.

Where the Marlboro Man meets Ralph Lauren and Martha Stewart, Jackson Hole succeeds in being both the real and the trendy Old West. Working cattle spreads sit beside guest ranches, and real wranglers down beers with city slickers at saloons. Everyone dresses casual, wood stoves still provide heat in some places, and old log cabins have become cozy restaurants.

Despite the area growth, Jackson remains a small town of about 5,500 residents. Elk antlers form arches around the town square, and wooden sidewalks pass chic Western storefronts such as Eddie Bauer, the Nature Company and, yes, a Ralph Lauren outlet.

"I haven't had a tie on that I recall since moving here," says Jack.

Don't mistake this jeans-and-boots, outdoorsy environment for a back-woods place, though. It's sophisticated, chic country with good restaurants and cultural opportunities to satisfy the many former urban dwellers who have moved here. The top card is the Grand Teton Music Festival, entering its 37th year of classical concerts that have gained international attention.

Each summer, a resident company of 200 musicians gathered from major symphonies around the country performs orchestra and chamber music in a concert hall at the foot of the ski resort at Teton Village, 11 miles northwest of Jackson. The July-August series enjoys enthusiastic support among Jackson Hole residents. In the winter, individual artists and ensembles are brought in for performances at the National Museum of Wildlife Art Cook Auditorium on the north edge of Jackson.

Given Jackson Hole's isolation and small population, Jack says many people are surprised at the high quality of the festival and other cultural attractions here. A major arts center, Jackson Hole has an estimated 40 galleries and museums, a summer dance festival, a live theater, arts and crafts festivals and special events. It has just opened a new library. The National Museum of Wildlife Art houses 2,000 paintings, sculptures and photographs in a low-profile stone building overlooking the National Elk Refuge. Besides its exhibits, the museum sponsors

discussions on art, the environment and music. Gainor says many residents also take advantage of educational programs at the Snake River Institute and the Teton Science School.

Mountain men in the early 1800s christened the area, using the word "hole" for a high valley amid mountains and naming it for fur trapper Davey Jackson. French-Canadian trappers called the highest peaks Les Trois Tetons, or "the three breasts," now known as the Grand, the Middle and the South Teton. With the creation of Yellowstone to the north as the nation's first national park in 1872, fur trapping gave way to big-game hunters, tourists and settlers who established cattle ranch-

ing as the major business in the valley.

In 1929, the Teton Range became a national park. The late John D. Rockefeller Jr. fell in love with the area and began buying valley land fronting the mountains to keep it from being overdeveloped. In 1950, he donated 33,000 acres to expand the park, which now includes most of the valley starting on the north edge of Jackson and extending to the tip of Jackson Lake about six miles from the south entrance to Yellowstone. Between the town and the park lies the elk refuge, a long flat meadow where up to 10,000 elk migrate to spend the winter.

The preservation of the land as parks, forests and wilderness has contributed to

Jackson Hole, WY

Population: About 5,500 in Jackson, the county seat, and 15,000 in Teton County.

Location: In northwest Wyoming, with the "hole," as fur trappers called a high alpine valley, running about 60 miles from the town of Jackson on the south to the entrance of Yellowstone National Park on the north and encompassing Grand Teton National Park. The valley is about 20 miles wide, rising in elevation from 6,200 feet in Jackson to 6,800 toward the north end; mountains ringing the valley top 13,000 feet.

Climate:

	High	Low
January	28	2
July	79	41

Average relative humidity: 50%

Rain: 15.27 inches.

Snow: 87 inches.

Cost of living: Above average (specific index not available).

Median housing cost: $290,000 for single-family homes, $150,000 for condominiums.

Sales tax: 6%

Sales tax exemptions: Professional services, prescription drugs.

State income tax: None.

Intangibles tax: None.

Estate tax: None, except the state's "pick-up" portion of the federal tax, applicable to taxable estates above $675,000.

Property tax: In Jackson, $59.53 per $1,000 in assessed value. In the county, $60.29 per $1,000, with homes assessed at 9.5% of market value. Annual property tax on a $290,000 home in Jackson is about $1,640; in the county, it is about $1,661. In some areas, separate water and sewer fees may apply.

Homestead exemption: None.

Security: 37.8 crimes per 1,000 residents in Teton County, and 61.7 crimes per 1,000 residents in Jackson, compared to a national average of 46.2 crimes per 1,000 residents.

Religion: About two dozen places of worship are located in the area, including the beautiful, small Chapel of Transfiguration in Grand Teton National Park.

Education: Continuing-education classes are offered in Jackson through the University of Wyoming at Laramie and Central Wyoming Community College in Riverton.

Transportation: There's local bus service within town, to the airport and to Teton Village at the Jackson Hole Mountain Resort. The airport has daily jet service.

Health: St. John's Hospital, a full-service facility with 40 beds, 50 doctors on staff and a nursing home with 60 beds, pro-

vides most types of health care, though residents go elsewhere for more critical problems, such as heart bypasses. Salt Lake City, UT, 265 miles away, is a regional medical center.

Housing options: With national parks and forests covering 97 percent of county land, there's limited space for development of homes. While Jackson has old and new homes and condos, many newcomers prefer to buy or build outside town to get views of the Tetons, but be prepared for prices as high as the mountains. **Bar B Bar Meadows**, north of town, has lots from $400,000. To the west of town, **Teton Pines** and **Spring Creek Resort** are popular, but you'll pay $600,000 or more for a condo and from $700,000 for lots. South of town, **Rafter J** has homes in the $350,000 range, though not all have Teton views. **Jackson Hole Realty**, (888) 733-9009, can provide information on subdivisions and developments throughout the area.

Visitor lodging: Jackson Lake Lodge, in Grand Teton National Park, open from mid-May through mid-October, from $115, (800) 628-9988. Renaissance Resort and Spa at Jackson Hole, open all year, from $215 with AARP discount, (800) 445-4655. Lodging in town, at Teton Village and in the park includes numerous small motels, guest ranches and cabins.

Information: Jackson Hole Chamber of Commerce, P.O. Box 550, Jackson, WY 83001, (307) 733-3316 or www.jackson holechamber.com.

Jackson Hole being part of the largest undeveloped natural ecosystem in the temperate zones today. And, it has left only 3 percent of Teton County privately owned and available for development, thus making land—and homes—extremely prized, particularly if there's a mountain view.

With the boom of interest in the area in the last decade, housing costs have skyrocketed. While the median housing value is about $290,000 for a single-family home, newcomers will encounter price tags of $500,000 and higher in some popular areas.

"I've seen a doubling of property value in our area in the last five years," says Richard.

While property values are up, Jack thinks housing costs aren't as unrealistically high now as they were a few years ago. The Nunns recently bought a new home that they had considered when they first arrived in 1995. They had been put off by its high price tag and instead chose an older home and remodeled it. When the new home didn't sell, the Nunns looked at it again, got a better deal and moved into it in 1997.

"Houses are still expensive here," Jack cautions. "There are very few single-family homes under $200,000."

"Be prepared to pay more than you think to get what you want (in a house)," says Gainor, who adds that many who are thinking of building a log home are shocked to learn such construction may run $200 a square foot.

While housing is costly to buy, homeowners get a break with comparatively low property taxes, in part because homes are assessed at 9.5 percent of market value. The annual tax on a $290,000 home is a little over $1,600. Overall, Jackson Hole is tax-friendly; there's no state income tax, though there is a sales tax of 6 percent.

Gainor says food prices also help boost the cost of living above average. "We can get anything — even fresh fish every day — but prices are dear because of transportation. We seem to be at the end of the food chain," she says. It's 265 miles to Salt Lake City, the nearest metropolitan area.

Though Jackson has numerous stores, the scope of shopping is somewhat limited. Most of the apparel stores stock casual, outdoors-oriented wear. "We have the high end and the low end — for instance, Scandia Downs and Kmart," says Gainor. "We support the local shops, but I keep my catalogs for some middle-of-the-road and traditional things like suits."

The couples say crime in the area is minimal. Jack adds, "We were used to locking our car all the time. The joke up here is that if (residents) took the keys out of the ignition, they wouldn't be able to find them."

"By and large, it's a trusting, open community. If you're going to be gone only a short while, many people normally don't lock their houses. The UPS and FedEx men just open the door and throw things in," says Gainor.

St. John's Hospital in Jackson serves the valley, providing all types of care except such procedures as heart surgery. "We have the best equipment and best care for a community this size that I've ever seen," says Richard, the pathologist.

Newcomers seem to have little trouble making friends. "We've met wonderful people. It's been easy to establish the type of friendships you had where you had been 25 years. The people here are active and talented," says Jack.

The music festival and social events connected with it foster friendships. All three couples are active supporters of the festival. Gainor is chairwoman of the festival auxiliary, and Carole is among its members. Gainor's husband, Joe, is a vice president of the board, and Susan serves as a trustee. Joe and Jack also are involved in other community organizations.

While Jackson Hole has many amenities, it is small. "Sometimes you get 'valley fever'— you want to get out. Sometimes you need a city fix," Gainor says.

All of the couples do sound a warning about the weather: The winters are long, cold and hard. The average high temperatures for December (26 degrees) and January (28 degrees) are below freezing, and for November, February and March are only in the high 30s. Nighttime temperatures below zero are common in midwinter.

"We have snow six months of the year. November starts getting seriously cold, and by early December we have a foot of snow," says Gainor. "If you don't really enjoy a good long winter, it's not the place to move to."

Jack says, "You have to enjoy outdoor sports in the winter to live here on a full-time basis. If you get out and enjoy the winter, it's livable." While Jackson Hole has low humidity and sunny days that ameliorate the cold, Jack thinks the area has more overcast days than winters in Colorado.

Winter brings cross-country skiing, and downhill skiing at Jackson Hole Mountain Resort, Snow King Ski Area in Jackson and Grand Targhee Ski Resort on the back side of the Tetons, plus snowshoeing, dog-sledding, snowmobiling, ice skating and other activities.

Many residents escape during the transition months as fall turns to winter and as winter gives way to spring. "In November, you can't hike, bike or ski and the fishing season is over. Late April and May are the mud season (when snow is melting). These are great times at other places in the country, though, so many people go away then," Gainor says.

Gainor cautions gardeners about the area's short growing period, with only about 45 days that are considered frost-free. She says some things such as tomatoes and squash can't be grown because the nights are too cold. For nine months, the low temperature averages 32 degrees or colder; June and August have an average low temperature of 37 degrees and July climbs to 41 degrees, all still quite nippy.

While winter may take some adjustment, late spring, summer and fall are glorious. Snow usually has melted in the valley by May, though the mountains still are cloaked in white, glistening against deep blue skies. Over the summer, snow melts off the lower part of the Tetons but remains at high elevations. Starting in June, wildflowers begin to carpet the valley, each having its own season to paint the flats, meadows and canyons blue, lavender, yellow, red, orange, white and pink.

Newborn elk, buffalo, moose and deer play in the protective sight of their mothers. While most of the elk and buffalo migrate northward, many moose stay in the valley, often wandering onto the highway to create traffic jams of tourists who can't quite believe they're seeing the real thing. Bear sometimes are spotted in the mountains and valley.

Come September, snow falls on the peaks, frost coats the area and aspens turn Jackson Hole a brilliant gold. The valley is filled with the sound of male elks bugling as they gather their harems and move southward to the refuge. Residents put up their fly-fishing rods and kayaks and bring out the skis and snowshoes. It's all in the nature of living here.●

Jupiter, Florida

Retirees give high marks to this Florida Gold Coast town

By Molly Arost Staub

In some respects, Jupiter is typical of Florida's lure for retirees — it enjoys warm weather and sunshine, it boasts lower costs of living than many other areas of the country, and it has the opportunities and facilities for year-round golfing, tennis and boating. But Jupiter has its own special charm that makes it one of the last outposts of rural ambiance and unhurried lifestyles before you hit the hustle and bustle of South Florida's larger cities.

Ideally situated for aficionados of water sports, Jupiter basks on the Intracoastal Waterway south of the federally designated "wild and scenic" Loxahatchee River. Parks provide ramps for waterway access, and boats and skis can be rented at a variety of marinas. And for some retirees, Jupiter's superior health-care facilities provide icing for the cake.

Typical are Bob and Annamarie Broeder, who were lured by the winter climate and good weather for golf. Before moving here in 1993, they began visiting Annamarie's brother in Jupiter in 1985, then rented a condo before buying their current unit in Indian Creek, a development boasting an 18-hole golf course and clubhouse.

Previously they had lived in Grass Valley, CA, for 17 years. "We visited Phoenix but found it too hot," says Bob, 72, machine shop supervisor at Stanford University before he retired. Besides playing golf, he walks two miles daily and has become active in the Elks Club. He also helps provide transportation for seniors who need rides to their medical appointments.

Annamarie, 67, likes the social scene in Jupiter. "It's really easy making friends here in a condominium development," she says. "We meet people at the pool and in golf club events."

Avid travelers, they like to cruise from Miami — easily accessible to South Floridians — aboard Carnival, Royal Caribbean and Holland America vessels. They also travel on Jupiter Parks and Recreation Department-sponsored trips to Walt Disney World, Cypress Gardens, Universal Studios and Branson, MO. "There are nice activities and trips for seniors," Annamarie says.

She and Bob love the winter climate, and they return to California in the summer when South Florida gets hot and muggy. Bob suggests that anyone considering retiring to Florida's Atlantic coast "rent for three months during the summer to see if you can handle the heat." As for expenses, he says, "utilities and taxes are less here, and real estate is much less expensive."

Both are impressed with the area's medical facilities, which Bob says are "better equipped to handle seniors" than most hospitals. "We live a 10-minute trip to the hospital. What I miss least about where we formerly lived was the one-hour drive to the hospital," he says.

Besides the lack of snow skiing, which was nearby when they lived in California, about the only thing the Broeders miss is not having a garage and garden in their condo lifestyle. "We like to putter in the lawn and can't do that here," says Annamarie.

Another activity Bob loves is fishing, and opportunities are plentiful along the Gold Coast and its Atlantic beaches. Although fishing licenses are required for fresh- and saltwater fishing, he appreciates that they are free to residents over 65. Year-round boating lures many here, and numerous marinas cater to their needs.

Fishermen, nature lovers and beach aficionados enjoy the nearby John D. MacArthur Beach State Park, a sea turtle nesting area from May through August, where ocean swimming and diving are available, and Jonathan Dickinson State Park featuring campgrounds, canoe rentals and boat ramps.

The fishing and good weather are products of the Gulf Stream, which runs close to shore in this area. A long maritime association is illustrated by the signature red-brick Jupiter Lighthouse, built in 1860, which boasts a museum of lighthouse memorabilia and local artifacts.

Another couple pleased with the myriad activities here is Tom and Mary Kirby. "You almost never find us home because we're always so busy," says Tom, 75.

When he and Mary, 73, aren't doing volunteer work at the parks and recreation department in Jupiter — such as working in the art gallery or helping organize five-kilometer runs and an annual beach cleanup — they're liable to be at the new Roger Dean Stadium watching spring training games of the Montreal Expos and St. Louis Cardinals or farm teams in the summer. They've made many friends through their volunteer work, "and my wife is an excellent cook," Tom says of Mary, who also enjoys painting.

Those interested in the arts find many opportunities in nearby West Palm Beach at the Norton Gallery of Art and Palm Beach's galleries — not to mention the legendary shopping along tony Worth Avenue. Broadway shows and concerts are held regularly at the Kravis Center for the Performing Arts, and more theater is available at Palm Beach's Royal Poinciana Playhouse.

The couple's choice of Jupiter also was influenced by family concerns. After living 25 years in Farmingdale, NY, they moved to Jupiter in 1985, primarily because their daughter lived here. Tom had worked as a bookbinder at McGraw-Hill for 19 years, then in construction and at the Cedar Creek Water Treatment Plant on Long Island. Mary was an assistant manager at Chemical Bank.

"I would never move back," Mary says. "And we have two grandchildren here."

Nearby attractions to lure the grandchildren (whether they're residents or visitors) beyond the ocean and pool include the expanding Dreher Park Zoo and Lion Country Safari. The Burt Reynolds Ranch and Film Studios includes a museum exhibiting movie memorabilia from the native son's films, plus a small petting farm for little ones.

Two county parks, Burt Reynolds East and Burt Reynolds West (reflecting the actor's many contributions to the area and the pride Jupiter has in him), offer boat ramps, picnic areas and the Florida History Center and Museum, spotlighting prehistoric, Seminole Indian and Spanish colonial influences.

The Kirbys previously considered Ocala, FL, and bought property there, but the section where it was located was never developed. They visited the Jupiter area many times over an eight-year period but unfortunately found themselves victims of crime soon after they moved. "Someone broke into our car before the plates were off the car," Tom says.

Jupiter, FL

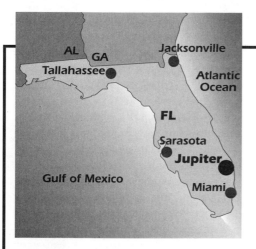

Population: 28,711
Location: On the east coast of Palm Beach County north of West Palm Beach.
Climate:

	High	Low
January	74	54
July	90	73

Average relative humidity: 76%
Rain: 58.5 inches.
Cost of living: About average (specific index not available).
Average housing cost: $160,000
Sales tax: State tax is 6%, and there's a 4% Palm Beach County bed tax on lodging and rental accommodations.
Sales tax exemptions: Food and medicine.
State income tax: None.
Intangibles tax: Assessed on stocks, bonds and other specified assets, with some investments exempt. Tax rate is $1 per $1,000 of value for assets under $100,000 for individuals or $200,000 for couples and $1.50 per $1,000 of value for greater amounts. The first $20,000 of assets ($40,000 for couples) is exempt.
Estate tax: None, except the state's "pickup" portion of the federal tax, applicable to taxable estates above $675,000.

Inheritance tax: None.
Property tax: $21.08 per $1,000 of assessed value, with property assessed at 100 percent of market value. The annual tax for a home assessed at $160,000 would be about $3,372.80, with the homestead exemption noted below.
Homestead exemption: $25,000 off the assessed value of a permanent, primary residence.
Security: 55.8 crimes per 1,000 residents, higher than the national average of 46.2 crimes per 1,000 residents.
Religion: There are 29 churches and one synagogue in Jupiter.
Education: Florida Atlantic University offers courses at its convenient Northern Palm Beach Campus in Palm Beach Gardens. Palm Beach Community College's Edward M. Eissey campus in Palm Beach Gardens offers academic courses and continuing education for retirees at its Etta Ress Institute of New Dimensions.
Transportation: Palm Beach International Airport is a major airport 20 minutes from Jupiter. North County Airport in West Palm Beach opened in 1994. Amtrak serves major U.S. destinations from West Palm Beach, and Tri-Rail is a commuter rail service running between West Palm Beach and Miami, with special trains added for major events. Palm Tran is a countywide bus system. Several cruise ships depart from the Port of Palm Beach.
Health: The 156-bed Jupiter Medical Center is totally comprised of private rooms. Its highly regarded departments include the Comprehensive Cancer Care Center, Women's Diagnostics, Diabetes Education, Health and Rehabilitation, Sleep Disorders Center and Pain Management Clinic.
Housing options: The following are mixed-dwelling communities, including condominiums, villas (semidetached homes) and single-family homes. **Indian Creek**, is a community about 14 years old with resales ranging from $110,000 to $150,000 for single-family homes, $80,000-$115,000 for condominiums. For information, contact a local real estate agency. **Jonathan's Landing**, (561) 745-9777, offers 1,200 homes ranging from $120,000 to $3 million. All are resales except a few remaining new homes at the top end of the price spectrum, and monthly maintenance fees average $325. **Admiral's Cove**, (561) 744-8800, is an upscale community with most homes located on the Intracoastal Waterway. They range from $250,000 to $4 million with an average monthly maintenance fee of $500.

Visitor lodging: The only oceanfront property, the Jupiter Beach Resort, has been heading toward full timeshare ownership but still functions as a luxury hotel with rates of $200-$450 in high season, (800) 228-8810. Numerous motels and campgrounds include the Best Western Intracoastal Inn, $129-$139, (561) 575-2936, and Wellesley Inn at Jupiter, $125-$155, including continental breakfast, (561) 575-7201.
Information: Jupiter-Tequesta-Juno Beach Chamber of Commerce, 800 N. U.S. Highway 1, Jupiter, FL 33477, (800) 616-7402 or www.jupiterfl.org.

"Then we built the house of our dreams in Jupiter Farms, but I got sick and panicked, so we bought a condominium in the Indian Creek development nine years ago," says Tom. "It has an 18-hole golf course, a clubhouse and tennis courts. We feel safe here."

Health care is another powerful draw for the Kirbys. "I rave about the medical facilities, which are great, especially for the elderly," says Tom. "I've been in the emergency room about 15 times at the hospital at the Jupiter Medical Center. And the Comprehensive Cancer Care Center is wonderful."

He admits he misses the change of seasons "and visiting places with nice trees and hills. But at my age, I wouldn't like the cold." The summer season also can be a drawback, "muggy and buggy," he says. The thing he misses least, though, is New York traffic. "People don't know what a traffic jam is until they've been in one in New York City," he says.

And he also doesn't miss the higher cost of living in New York. "There's no comparison between the cost of living here and up north, and housing costs 40 percent less here," says Tom, noting that heating expenses and real estate taxes also are lower.

Their condo has appreciated in value since they bought it, he says.

But another couple, Sophie and Charlie Dineen, found the cost of living in Jupiter higher than they experienced in their preretirement communities in Alabama and New York. Charlie, 70, a former regional president for Manufacturers Hanover Trust, lived in Olean, NY, about 80 miles south of Buffalo, and Sophie, 60, moved to Jupiter from Tuscaloosa, AL.

Charlie considers South Florida an expensive place to live, although he notes that lower real estate taxes and the lack of a state income tax reduce costs. But he says it costs more to dine at restaurants than in upstate New York, and "dry-cleaning costs are unbelievable here."

Still, they're happy they chose Jupiter. "I had a seasonal place at PGA (in Palm Beach Gardens) and had always planned to move to Florida," says Charlie, who retired and moved to Jupiter in 1987. "I didn't consider any other place. I didn't want any part of the winter weather any longer. I love to play golf, and there's only a 10- to 12-week window when you can golf in western New York. Now I play golf five days a week."

After his wife died, he met and married Sophie 10 years ago. But she owned a horse and wanted to live in an area where her equine companion could be boarded nearby. "Jupiter had places to board a horse — there's a big community of horses in Jupiter Farms," she says, explaining their decision to buy in the Ranch Colony development of The Links. "Jupiter was a small town 10 years ago," Sophie says, "and it's still kind of rural."

What Charlie misses most are his four children and seven grandchildren, who all live in New York. He also misses having a basement, and he has had difficulty finding reliable workmen for chores around the house. "I think we were taken the first few years," he says.

"Another mistake I made, based on the seasonal community I lived in, was that I envisioned that everything had to be in pastel colors," he adds. "I gave away some beautiful wood furniture and antiques to my kids. Now I'm sorry I didn't keep it."

But he rates Jupiter's hospitals and medical care very highly. "I'm very pleased with the excellent care by the doctors and nurses and the Jupiter Medical Center, where I've been three times," he says. It's a refrain echoed by many seniors in these parts.●

Kerrville, Texas

Texas Hill Country entices retirees to wide-open spaces

By Judy Wade

Kerrville, in the heart of the Texas Hill Country, has the signs of an affluent community. Expansive homes with scenic views are set on large acreages, and cultural events include performances by the visiting Bolshoi Ballet.

Yet in Texas tradition, Kerrville residents are among the friendliest, most down-home folks to be found anywhere. Like the surrounding terrain, the town's residents are open, easily extending welcomes to newcomers.

"They just seem to accept you," says Harvey Fritter, 76, noting that the warmheartedness of the residents is one reason he and his wife, Marsha, retired here from Hyattsville, MD.

"I grew up in a little Texas town called Roscoe and really wanted to come back (to Texas)," says Marsha, 71. Her requirements included a good library, hospital, social events and a healthy climate. The Fritters also wanted a place with less congestion, traffic and crime.

The Fritters custom-built their retirement home in Riverhill, a planned country club development on Kerrville's south edge. An 18-hole golf course is part of Riverhill's private, member-owned country club. Social events are held in an elegant old mansion-turned-clubhouse.

About 500 families, a mix of young career couples and retired professionals, have moved to Riverhill since it opened in 1974, and about 200 parcels still are available for building. Lots with a view or on the golf course are in prime demand, says Marsha.

For their retirement, Jack and Betsy Smith chose a manufactured home in Ingram, a riverfront community six miles north of Kerrville. Also former Texans, they were coaxed back to their home state by the open, friendly people. They came from the chilly climate of Aurora, CO.

Betsy, 64, says coming to Kerrville was like going to college. "Everyone is new and looking for new friends," she says. "The clubhouse is a great place to meet people."

Jack, 68, a retired personnel director, says there's not enough time to develop as many friendships as they would like.

"At one time we knew all 70 families living here, but with 160 here now, we just can't keep up," Betsy adds.

Ingram Oaks is a planned manufactured-housing retirement community adjacent to the Guadalupe River. Residents have access to a private dock for fishing and water sports. A pool, tennis courts, whirlpool and game room are part of the recreational complex. The $175 monthly lot lease includes all amenities, water and garbage pickup.

About 160 homes of a projected 220 are occupied. Many residents have added decks to their homes, providing outdoor living space to take advantage of the sunny climate. In front of one well-tended home, a pink snow shovel proclaims that the occupants are "retired from Indiana" and, presumably, from the need to ever again shovel snow.

Jack and Betsy purchased their double-wide manufactured home in Kerrville and had it moved to their lot in Ingram Oaks. Betsy has accented its traditional decor with her own oil paintings of the surrounding area and of her East Texas childhood home. Both the Fritters and the Smiths have homes that take advantage of the tranquil, pastoral views that are part of the Hill Country.

Elton H. "Al" and Mauryne Donaubauer, each 75, opted to buy a home across from the elementary school in town when they retired here from Fayetteville, AR. They also considered Alpine, in West Texas, and New Braunfels, where he had lived as a child. The friendly people and the climate made Kerrville their top choice.

"Next to San Diego, it's the best climate in the country," says Al.

About an hour northwest of San Antonio and less than two hours west of Austin, Kerrville has a dry, moderate climate. Summers are hot, but the humidity is lower than in the sultry Gulf Coast area, and with an elevation of about 1,600 feet, evenings tend to cool off. January lows can hit freezing, but snow and sleet are rare, normally occurring only once every three or four years.

A cost of living below the national average also lures retirees to Kerrville, which has a population of about 20,000.

"Our money goes further here," says Marsha Fritter. "We get a lot more for our money in terms of medical costs."

Jack Smith appreciates the proximity of a well-respected Veterans Affairs hospital.

Returning Texans as well as those new to the Lone Star State say the community feeling in Kerrville is tied to a strong sense of history. The town's roots date to 1869 when Capt. Charles A. Schreiner, a Texas Ranger, established a general merchandising business. By 1900 the Charles Schreiner Co. owned more than 600,000 acres of prime Texas land. The captain's efforts are remembered today at Schreiner College, a four-year liberal arts institution, and Schreiner's Department Store, a shopping mainstay.

Substituting for a traditional downtown is Olde Town, a three-block stretch of Water Street. Restored buildings from the late 1800s house art galleries, antique shops and boutiques that face onto a street paved with red brick and lined with lampposts.

An area of gas stations and service establishments is bisected by busy

State Route 16, locally called Sidney Baker Highway. Beyond, the town spreads out like a pattern on a quilt, with homes and ranches dotting the countryside. Low-level construction dominates; there are no high-rises. Many structures are built of limestone, which is native to the area.

Unobstructed views of the Guadalupe River, which runs through the heart of Kerrville, are part of the charm of many riverside homes. Parks with shade trees and picnic tables along its banks invite leisurely strolls and alfresco meals.

With more than a third of Kerrville residents retired, senior sensibilities run high. The Dietert Claim Senior Citizen Center offers physical fitness classes, quilting, bridge and guitar lessons as well as line, folk, square and round dancing. Clubs cater to the special interests of a dozen different groups, including retired teachers and stamp collectors. A 70-member mixed chorus meets regularly, and the Trailblazers walking club goes on area hikes.

The multipurpose activity center was dubbed a "claim" by its founders, civic leaders Mr. and Mrs. Harry W. Dietert, because it is for seniors "to stake a claim to pan out boredom, isolation and loneliness from their lives," says activities director Mabel Hurt.

Mabel, a Kerrville native who has worked at the center more than 20 years, says about 2,500 seniors use the center every month. Lunch is served five days a week for a suggested $2 donation. The center's in-home

Kerrville, TX

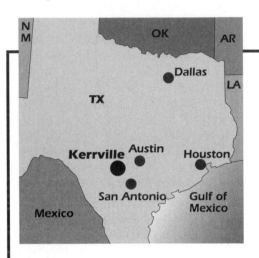

Population: 19,818 in town, 42,623 in Kerr County.

Location: Highest point in wooded, rolling Texas Hill Country on the Guadalupe River, an hour northwest of San Antonio.

Climate:

	High	Low
January	61	33
July	94	68

Average relative humidity: 55%

Rain: 32 inches.

Winters are usually pleasant, with occasional cold weather each year and light snow every few years; summer days can be hot. Thunderstorms, particularly in spring and summer, can be intense, cause flooding of the Guadalupe River and spawn tornadoes. Elevation is 1,645 feet.

Cost of living: Below average (specific index not available).

Average housing cost: $108,000

Sales tax: 8.25%

Sales tax exemptions: Groceries, medical supplies, prescription drugs, professional services.

State income tax: None.

Intangibles tax: None.

Estate tax: None, except the state's "pick-up" portion of the federal tax, applicable to taxable estates above $675,000.

Property tax: Rate is $23 per $1,000 of assessed value, with homes appraised at 100% of market value. Yearly tax on a $108,000 home is $2,484 before homestead exemption.

Homestead exemption: $5,000 exemption off the school district portion of the tax and $3,000 off the county portion ($10,000 additional for residents age 65 and older).

Security: 36.8 crimes per 1,000 residents, lower than the national average of 46.2 crimes per 1,000 residents.

Religion: More than 50 churches represent 16 denominations.

Education: Schreiner College, a postsecondary liberal arts college, offers baccalaureate and associate degrees and has night college courses. Tivy High School has continuing-education classes.

Transportation: There's no local bus service. San Antonio, 62 miles southeast, has the nearest commercial airline service.

Health: Sid Peterson Memorial Hospital has 148 beds, 75 physicians on staff and a connecting professional building. Kerrville boasts dialysis, cardiac rehabilitation and cancer radiation centers, and Kerrville State Hospital accepts psychiatric patients. A 221-bed medical/surgical Veterans Affairs hospital also has 154 nursing home beds. Assisted-living services and nursing care are available at Alpine Terrace, with retirement apartments adjacent at The Hills.

Housing options: There are various types of housing in town, along the river and in the hills; limestone and wood are commonly used in construction. At **Riverhill,** (830) 257-1400, a country club community, lots begin at about $30,000. Homes range in price from $100,000-$575,000. **Comanche Trace Ranch**, (877) 467-6282, a new master-planned golf community along the Guadalupe River, has garden homes from $185,000 to $250,000 and single-family homes from $250,000 to over $1 million. **Ingram Oaks,** (830) 367-2426, a manufactured-housing retirement community northwest of Kerrville across from the Guadalupe River, leases lots from $175 per month. That includes water, garbage pickup, septic system and use of a recreation center, pool and tennis courts. Many attractive apartments line the banks of the Guadalupe, some with short-term leases for winter visitors, ranging from $595 to $1,575 per month.

Visitor lodging: Inn of the Hills River Resort, $78-$91 double, (800) 292-5690; Kerrville Econolodge Inn, $69 double, (800) 225-1374; Y.O. Ranch Holiday Inn, $109 double, (830) 257-4440; rates may be lower in winter. At Riverhill, a country club community, rental cottages are $85 per night in summer, $65 in winter, (830) 896-1400.

Information: Kerrville Chamber of Commerce, 1700 Sidney Baker, Kerrville, TX 78028, (830) 896-1155 or www.kerrville tx.com.

care department helps assess needs of area seniors, then provides assistance to help them remain independent and in their homes.

The Senior Games, officially sanctioned by the U.S. National Senior Sports Organization, are held in Kerrville each spring for athletes who want to qualify to compete in the state and national Senior Olympic Games. As a national qualifying site, the town hosts athletes age 50 and older who excel in tennis, swimming, track and field events and other sports. This year more than 800 senior athletes participated.

"Most qualifying sites have their games underwritten by large companies and corporations," says Karen Tucker, executive director of the games. "We think it's a tribute to the generosity and flourishing volunteer spirit of our citizens that our senior games are supported entirely by private donations."

"I've never seen people so willing to contribute," says Al Donaubauer, who has served in several fund-raising positions, including financial committee chairman of the games. The local Senior Games has an annual price tag of about $70,000.

Feeding the mind as well as the body, the arts also play an important part in shaping Kerrville's personality. Betsy Smith sometimes volunteers at The Gazebo, the display and sales boutique for members of the Hill Country Arts Foundation. The Hill Country Museum, in the restored Victorian mansion built by Charles Schreiner in 1879, portrays the affluent life in the Hill Country's early days. The annual Texas State Arts and Crafts Fair, held two weekends each summer, showcases the jury-selected works of 200 resident artists and craftsmen and attracts more than 200,000 visitors.

Perhaps the best known and most unusual center of culture is the Cowboy Artists of America Museum. The airy, Southwest-style building with mesquite floors richly complements an ever-changing selection of Western paintings and sculpture. The nation's most distinguished living Western artists, including Joe Beeler, Bill Nebeker and Howard Terpning, follow the legacies of Frederic Remington and Charles M. Russell in celebrating the Old West. A shady courtyard is paved with bricks imprinted with each artist's signature and footprint.

Although big-city shopping forays to San Antonio and Austin are always options, life's necessities are readily available in the supermarkets and service shops of Kerrville.

Interesting boutiques scattered throughout town purvey Western wear, gifts, designer clothes and unique local art. You can purchase the work of local artist James Avery, a nationally acclaimed designer of gold and silver jewelry, in a retail shop just north of Kerrville.

Kerrville's environs could come from the pages of a Zane Grey novel. Views stretch for miles, across vast expanses of sky and rolling hills that rise to a plateau. Live oak, pin oak, mesquite, cedar and cypress trees add greenery, and clear, cool streams cut through rocky limestone ledges where caves often are found.

South of the city, Bandera was the staging area for the great cattle drives of yesteryear. When ranching fell on hard times in the 1930s, an enterprising rancher took in "dudes" to help him through the Depression, and an industry was born.

The area's reputation for preserving a Western tradition is emphasized by the success of these guest ranches. The Y.O. Ranch, founded by Charles Schreiner, invites visitors to see its large herd of longhorns, native wildlife and free-roaming exotic animals. (There is a nominal fee to tour the grounds.) Zebra, giraffe, ostrich, ibex, oryx, eland and 50 other species are bred to sell to zoos and exotic wildlife ranches, and some breeds can be hunted for fees that often are hefty.

White-tailed deer are so numerous in the area that motorists are cautioned to be on the alert for them, especially at night.

Guest cabins at the Y.O. Ranch include restorations of an 1852 schoolhouse and an 1880 stagecoach stop. These accommodations permit ranch guests to enjoy the history of Texas in modern comfort while making preservation of the cabins economically possible.

The area is popular for vacationing from spring through fall, and thousands of children come to summer camps here.

San Antonio is convenient for entertainment, offering numerous festivals, sports events and concerts. It's home to Sea World and Fiesta Texas, popular theme parks. For those in need of a beach fix, Sea World's Lost Lagoon comes complete with two- to three-foot surf and swaying palms. At Fiesta Texas, a theme park that bills itself as "the town built just for fun," Fiesta Bay Boardwalk simulates a seaside boardwalk of the '50s and '60s, with a ferris wheel, roller rink, miniature golf course and paddle boats. Limestone quarry walls around the park become giant screens for a spectacular after-dark laser show that traces the state's colorful history.

Kerrville's multifaceted appeal attracts a diversity of retirees. Marsha Fritter declares, "We thank God every day that we chose this area."

Betsy Smith says that their new retirement lifestyle makes her feel younger. The city's invitation to "lose your heart to the hills" is one that both couples say they have accepted with pleasure.●

Key West, Florida

Creative spirit and Caribbean flavor spice island lifestyle in Florida

By Jay Clarke

Bob Cornell never had been to Key West until just before he retired. He and his wife, Flo, both restoration buffs, decided to check out the Key West historic district while on a visit in Miami.

"We saw this restoration area and spied a little house that looked very inviting, about 125 years old," says Bob, 66.

They lived in Cambridge, OH, and had been looking for a place to relocate when they retired. They had visited Charleston, SC, several times to tour its restored homes, but Flo doesn't like cold weather.

"We saw Key West and knew it was what we wanted," says Bob. The Cornells fell in love with the tropical island and its historic architecture.

He had experience restoring homes, and Flo was in the antiques business. They bought the old house and spent three years refurbishing it, eventually earning a restoration award for their work.

"Every day we get up and see the sun is shining, we thank God we're here in Key West," he says.

Unlike the Cornells, Bob Elliott came to Key West knowing the area well. A Naval dentist, Bob had been stationed in Guantanamo Bay, Cuba, for two years in the 1970s.

"I loved it, loved the cuisine, loved the climate," says Bob, 73, of his stay in Cuba, only 90 miles from the tip of the Keys.

Key West was much like Guantanamo, so soon after his return to the States, he bought an apartment in Key West and moved to the island.

"It's the closest thing in the USA to Guantanamo," says Bob, who rose to become a rear admiral and chief of the Navy's dental corps. "It's changed some, but the climate's the same. I like the people, the flora, the casual way of life."

Indeed, the casual lifestyle always has been a keystone here, and if you want proof, just visit the daily sunset celebration. This is no staid toast to the end of the day, but a raucous and unpredictable beginning of the night.

At Mallory Dock, jugglers toss flaming brands into the air and balance bottles on their chins. Pantomimes wander through the crowd, while another entrepreneur gathers an audience to watch his trained cats jump through a burning hoop. The smell of Italian peppers and onion, of popcorn and souvlaki, wafts over the sunset-watchers from mobile food stands, while the Cookie Lady maneuvers her tricycle through the masses, hawking sugared goodies.

It's a completely unstructured ritual, yet in a town where traditions are few, this is one of them.

Strolling on Duval Street is another — at least for visitors. It's a tourist Broadway, a mishmash of commerce evidenced by T-shirt shops next to elegant boutiques, fine art galleries by souvenir emporiums, fast-food spots rivaling gourmet restaurants. And bars, lots of bars.

These are the haunts of tourists, but few retirees make their way there.

"Just driving downtown is difficult, so when I go, I go early or late," says Barbara Larcom, who moved with her husband, Paul, to Key West from Connecticut 21 years ago. She recalls that one time when she took her granddaughter to Duval Street, the sidewalks were so crowded with tourists that they had to walk in the street.

"After a block of this, my granddaughter said, 'I've had enough. Let's go home,'" Barbara, 73, recalls.

Still, Barbara has no desire to return to New Canaan, CT, where they lived before retirement: "I don't miss it. I miss my friends, but they find their way here. So does my family. We have four children, all married, and they love to come to Key West."

Bob Cornell agrees: "We don't go back home much. I send the kids money so they can come visit us at Christmas."

The Cornells knew no one when they moved to Key West, yet found themselves quickly accepted into the community, Flo says.

"Bob had a ruptured appendix during the night, before we even became full-time residents. He had to have emergency surgery, and the next day almost everybody on the block was in his hospital room to see him. They didn't know him well, but they just dropped by to wish him well. That really touched us. That wouldn't have happened if we had been in Cambridge (their previous home in Ohio). There is a very strong sense of family in Key West," Flo says.

Key West residents also rate high with Al McCarthy, who moved here from Troy, NY, with his partner 14 years ago. "People here are friendly and caring. This is the most caring community I've ever seen," says Al, 65.

Friendly and caring they may be, but cookie-cutter they are not. Key Westers run the gamut from normal 9-to-5 wage earners to reclusive iconoclasts, from old sea dogs to young entrepreneurs, from couples with young children to couples of the same sex.

The diverse character of Key West always has attracted creative people. Over the years, many writers and artists have succumbed to the lure of the Keys and its main town.

Hemingway moved to Key West in 1931 and in the upstairs study of his home wrote many short stories and novels, including "Death in the Afternoon," "The Green Hills of Africa" and "To Have and Have Not."

Visitors today can tour his home, now a museum, but they will see little that dates to his stay on the island. One legacy is the pack of six-toed cats roaming the grounds.

Hemingway moved away from Key

West before World War II, but he is remembered every July, when Hemingway fans stage a look-alike contest and costume party during a somewhat irreverent festival called Hemingway Days.

Tennessee Williams lived on Duncan Street and while here wrote "The Night of the Iguana" and "The Rose Tattoo." Other writers who lived and worked in Key West include the late John Hersey, Allison Lurie, Elizabeth Bishop, Thomas McGuane and Phillip Caputo.

With this kind of heritage, it's not surprising that theater and the arts are strong. Flo notes that Key West has five live theaters, opera and numerous art galleries.

"There's so much to do, you just can't do it all," Flo says.

Key West's intimate connection with the sea is also a major lure for both residents and visitors. During the 19th century, Key West was the base for "wreckers," scavengers who made a living salvaging goods from ships wrecked on the reefs offshore. Later, sponge divers and turtle trappers prospered here.

With turtles now an endangered species and the sponge beds depleted, Key West's turtle kraals (pens) and sponge boats are long gone. But a fleet of shrimp boats still operates here, along with dive boats, sunset cruisers and sailing catamarans that cater to tourists.

In an island community such as this, it's not surprising that boating is a major passion.

"We both love the water, and when we first moved here we had a sailboat," says Barbara, who lives on a canal. "We can't physically handle a

Key West, FL

Population: 27,255
Location: At the tip of the Florida Keys, 168 miles from Miami on the famed Overseas Highway. It is the southernmost point in the continental United States and is only 90 miles from Cuba.

Climate: High Low
January 72 66
July 89 80

Average relative humidity: 67%
Rain: 39.42 inches.

Subtropical climate, with wet season June through October; September is the wettest month and the most likely one for hurricanes. Ocean breezes temper the summer heat. Hurricane season is June through November; since 1960, nine hurricanes have come within about 65 miles of Key West. Elevation is 5 feet.

Cost of living: 112.43 in Monroe County, based on state average of 100.

Average housing cost: $342,000 (condos average $228,000).

Sales tax: 7%

Sales tax exemptions: Medical services, prescription drugs, most groceries.

State income tax: None.

Intangibles tax: Assessed on stocks, bonds and other specified assets. Tax rate is $1 per $1,000 of value for assets under $100,000 for individuals or $200,000 for couples, and $1.50 per $1,000 of value for greater amounts; first $20,000 for individuals and $40,000 for couples is exempt. Some investments are exempt.

Estate tax: None, except the state's "pick-up" portion of the federal tax, applicable to taxable estates above $675,000.

Property tax: $15.92 per $1,000 of assessed value, with homes assessed at 100%. Yearly tax on a $342,000 home is $5,046, with the homestead exemption noted below.

Homestead exemption: $25,000 off assessed value for primary, permanent residence.

Security: 105.4 crimes per 1,000 residents, higher than the national average of 46.2 crimes per 1,000 residents.

Religion: There are more than two dozen churches, representing different denominations, and two synagogues.

Education: Florida Keys Community College, a state junior college, offers a two-year degree and continuing-education classes.

Transportation: Five Florida cities have non-stop flights to Key West International Airport; air service to other cities is generally through Miami. Buses run regularly between Key West and Miami. Key West has a local bus system, and the county can provide local transportation for needy seniors.

Health: Florida Keys Health System, the only hospital in Key West, has 169 beds, a 24-hour emergency room and a separate 49-bed psychiatric unit. The nearest mainland hospital is in Homestead; Miami, three to four hours away by car, has many options in advanced medical services. Helicopter medical evacuation is available.

Housing options: New two-bedroom condos start at $145,500 at **SaltPond Condominiums**. At **Seaside**, a new development, two-bedroom townhouses are $159,900-$235,900; three bedrooms are $325,900-$459,000. **Flagler's Landing** has custom-built townhomes on the bay starting at $399,000 for 1,430 square feet. **Key West Golf Club** offers two-bedroom bungalows for $175,000-$250,000 and three bedrooms for $235,000-$330,000. For information, call Jeff Dunaway at **Key West Realty**, (800) 654-5131.

Visitor lodging: There's a wide range of hotels and motels, with prices varying by season. Comfort Inn, $99-$139, (305) 294-3773. Southernmost Motel, $105-$125 in summer, $155-$275 in winter, (305) 296-6577. Key West also has several dozen bed-and-breakfast guest houses, many at moderate rates. Visitors planning a stay of a week or more should consider renting a house; two-bedroom rentals start at about $1,000 a week in summer, twice that in winter.

Information: Key West Chamber of Commerce, 402 Wall St., Key West, FL 33040, (305) 294-2587 or www.fla-keys.com/keywest.

sailboat anymore, so we've gone to stinkpotting (motorized boats)."

Boating still occupies a big role in the Cornells' lives. They're active in the Power Squadron, a group whose activities include classes in boating safety. Bob has been the squadron commander. Besides boating in local waters, the Cornells make more ambitious journeys, going to the Bahamas and the Dry Tortugas, a cluster of islands about 70 miles off Key West and the site of historic Fort Jefferson.

Many retirees take an active role in the community. Barbara says she and Paul, 79, have done a lot of volunteer work, though they've tapered off their activities recently. She helped with house tours during Old Island Days, a popular festival, and was on the board of Old Island Restoration. Paul was active in church work.

Bob Elliott's list of activities sounds like a who's who: president of the American Red Cross advisory board, president of the Retired Officers Association, vice president of the Key West Historical Society, member of the church school board. He's also president of the Academy of Dentistry International, a position that has taken him to meetings as far away as Vietnam. His wife, Carol, 69, volunteers in the hospital and runs a thrift shop.

Al has served on the Key West Historical Society, the hospital board and the fine arts and architectural review board for the town.

However heartwarming, satisfying and salubrious living is in the Keys, it is not cheap. Though the cost of living was less some years back, Key West today is not a place for people on a low budget to retire.

"The cost of living is extremely high," says Al. "Housing is very high, and being a resort community, restaurants also are expensive."

However, there are trade-offs on costs, the Cornells note.

"A pair of shorts and a clean pair of sneakers for church and you're set — that's a little bit of an exaggeration, but you dress for comfort here and not for show," Bob says.

The Cornells say they have no heating costs and spend little on air-conditioning because their home was built to catch the breezes, which blow frequently and help cut the tropic heat.

Like most people who moved some years ago to this southernmost town in the lower 48 states, Al bought property when prices were lower. He has seen its value increase dramatically; he sold his first Key West home at a profit and is living in his second remodeled house.

Bob Cornell says their home in the historic district has increased almost four times in value in the six years they've owned it. The Cornells live in a wooden "conch" house; conch re-

fers to the early settlers, who were nicknamed after the large seashell common to the area.

Bob says the house started as a cottage. "You add on here and you add on there (over the years). That is a major part of the unique architecture of Key West," he says.

Key West has a mixture of housing, from small cottages to larger Victorian homes, many often set in lush gardens of tropical flora. White picket fences give an all-American feeling to some areas, while in others brightly colored houses are reminiscent of the Caribbean islands.

The thread that runs true with most retirees one talks to is that whatever the ills that plague Key West — high prices, tourist encroachment, tight housing — it's still a place they love and would find difficult to leave.

"I don't have the enthusiasm for Key West I had before," says Barbara, "but I love my friends, love where we live and love the climate."

While colorful — in scenery and characters — it's not glitzy, says Flo, who adds: "I love the weather, the friendliness of the people, the creativity that exists here. I like being able to walk everywhere."

Flo would encourage other retirees to consider settling in Key West with one caveat: "Don't come down and try to change it into New York City or Cleveland. Leave it as Key West."●

Lake Conroe, Texas

Forested area near Houston is a haven for golf, tennis, sailing and fishing

By Diane Freeman

With nine lush golf courses nearby and country club resort communities lining the waterfront, the Lake Conroe region in southeast Texas is drawing more and more retirees to its quiet shores.

Perched at the edge of the Texas piney woods just 40 miles north of Houston, the Lake Conroe area first attracted Houstonians as a weekend retreat, then was discovered by retirees from elsewhere in Texas and from other states.

It's an ideal setting for those who want a recreational lifestyle — tennis, golf, sailing, fishing — close to extensive metropolitan amenities — cultural pursuits, diverse cuisine and outstanding health care. Lake Conroe residents are close enough to take advantage of Houston's attractions but far removed from the hassles of day-to-day city living.

The 22,000-acre lake, situated five miles west of the small town of Conroe, was completed in 1973, forming a reservoir. Fishermen brag of catching bass, walleye, striped bass, catfish, bream, hybrid perch and crappie. Pleasure boaters enjoy the south end of the lake where water-skiing and sailing are popular. The Conroe Yacht Club has boat slips and sponsors racing events. Boat rentals and lessons are available.

But the lake may take second place in popularity to golf in this part of Texas. Montgomery County has more golf holes per capita than any other county in the state. About 15 minutes south of Conroe in the master-planned community of The Woodlands lies the Tournament Players Course, home to the annual Shell Houston Open. Mild winters in this part of Texas allow golfers on the courses nearly year-round.

Natives of New York state, Bob and Joanne Quinn moved to April Sound, a waterfront resort community on Lake Conroe, after living in Fort Worth for 10 years. They had family living in Houston.

Both are artists and liked April Sound's clubhouse policy of displaying art works of residents without fees or commissions. The couple also liked the 24-hour security gate at the entrance to the subdivision.

"It's very affordable in relation to other country club dues and fees," he says.

Bob made friends easily on the golf course. Although all ages live in April Sound, which has both private homes and condominiums, the development's residents are principally retirees, he says.

Joanne, a portrait and still-life artist, gives art lessons through the Conroe Art League. Bob is a member of the Kiwanis Club and the Men's Golf Association.

"Everyone is very outgoing and friendly. The women's group makes you feel right at home," Joanne says.

Bob and Ginger Bell moved to the Walden subdivision on Lake Conroe. The couple had lived in Palm Desert, CA, six years where Bob managed a tennis club. But California was too expensive, and Walden has proved kinder to the budget.

"We wanted a place with a diverse population, near a good medical center," says Bob. The club was large enough for a variety of friends, and the lake community provided plenty of recreational opportunities.

Another couple, Chuck and Ethel Everett, considered living in California but also nixed that idea because of the state's high cost of living. After living in Baton Rouge, LA, 11 years, they moved to Walden, bought a waterfront lot and leased a townhouse until their new home was built.

"We liked the aesthetics created by the lake," Ethel says. "It's complemented by lakeside homes and the golf course. It's not crowded, and Conroe gives you a good flavor of small-town life. We go in and shop."

The Everetts had lived all over the world before they moved to Walden. Chuck's job as a complex manager for the U.S. Department of Energy had taken them to stints in Italy, New Zealand, Thailand, the Philippines and England.

"Ethel always wanted to live on the water," he says, in citing the primary reason they settled at Walden.

"The number two reason was we wanted a neighborhood with strong deed restrictions to protect the property owners from unwelcome intrusions. All of the streets are paved — (we have) storm sewers and no open drainage ditches. And there are great recreational opportunities here, especially for tennis and golf," he says.

The Everetts found new friends easily, through joining the local chapter of the American Association of Retired Persons and tennis and golf associations. Chuck also is a member of the Kiwanis Club.

Chuck said retirees occupy a large percentage of homes in the Walden development; about 30 percent are weekend homes for people who live and work in Houston.

Besides the attractions provided by the lake and golf courses, the Sam Houston National Forest, a piney woods wilderness that meanders through three counties, is located about 13 miles north of Conroe.

The 161,320-acre forest has campground sites and a 140-mile Lone Star Hiking Trail. Its wildlife includes the endangered bald eagle, deer, raccoon and wild boar. Deer hunting is allowed on a seasonal basis.

This wealth of forestry gave Conroe its start in the lumber and timber business about a century ago. In 1881, Isaac Conroe, for whom the town was later named, moved his small sawmill from Halton to the rolling, forested plains area that is now Conroe.

In 1932 oil was discovered by George Strake. The Conroe oilfield, southeast of the city, changed the town's economy for the next 50 years. The field is the 10th largest ever to have been discovered in the continental United States.

Today Conroe has a population of 36,067 and is the seat of Montgomery County, which boasts a population of 286,000 and is considered in the Houston metropolitan area, though it's about a one-hour drive north of the main city.

While the Conroe cost of living is below average, it's still partly a bedroom community for Houston, and that location keeps prices relatively high. The local sales tax is 8.25 percent and property taxes in Montgomery County are assessed at a rate of $4.74 per $1,000, plus add-ons.

While Houston has a rich diversity of ethnic, regional and gourmet cuisine, Conroe's restaurants are primarily limited to the fast-food variety, from hamburgers to Chinese, Mexican, seafood and barbecue.

The Texas Medical Center in Houston offers world-renowned health care in all fields, often leading the way in research and innovative care. The Conroe area has three hospitals with 450 beds and a psychiatric hospital with 156 beds. One of the hospitals provides full health care service including a cardiac care unit and kidney dialysis.

Houston's George Bush Intercontinental Airport, with international service, is about 30 miles south of Conroe. Outside the Conroe city limits is the Montgomery County Airport, which has several private general aviation aircraft.

Educational opportunities abound in the area. Montgomery College, a branch of the North Harris Montgomery County College District, has a campus just south of Conroe. In Huntsville north of Conroe is a four-year liberal arts college, Sam Houston State University, and

Lake Conroe, TX

Population: 36,067 in Conroe, 286,000 in Montgomery County.
Location: 22,000-acre reservoir with several home developments outside Conroe, about 40 miles north of Houston. In rolling hills and piney woods section of southeast Texas and adjacent to the Sam Houston National Forest.

Climate:[1]

	High	Low
January	62	41
July	94	73

Average relative humidity: 59%
Rain: 51 inches.
Mild winters with short cold snaps; hot, muggy summers.
Cost of living: 91.5 in Conroe, based on national average of 100.
Average housing cost: $107,863
Sales tax: 8.25%
Sales tax exemptions: Groceries, prescription drugs, professional services, some medical supplies.
State income tax: None.

Intangibles tax: None.
Estate tax: None, except the state's "pick-up" portion of the federal tax, applicable to taxable estates above $675,000.
Property taxes: County rate is $4.74 per $1,000 but assessments are added by various water and school districts, depending on location of property. Homes are assessed at 100% of market value. Basic county property tax is about $512 for a $108,000 home.
Homestead exemption: $25,000 exemption on assessed value for persons 65 and older.
Security: 66.3 crimes per 1,000 residents in Conroe, higher than the national average of 46.2 crimes per 1,000 residents.
Religion: A large number of churches and several synagogues are in the area.
Education: Montgomery College has a campus just south of Conroe. Sam Houston State University is north of Conroe in Huntsville.
Transportation: No public transportation. Houston Intercontinental Airport is 30 miles away.
Health: Three hospitals with 450 beds in the area.
Housing options: Walden, (409) 582-1013, is a 1,400-acre lake-side golf resort with tennis center. Condos start in the low $30,000s and single-family homes in the low $100,000s. It also has

patio homes and townhouses in the $70,000s. It has a 24-hour security patrol, with a Montgomery County Sheriff's Department substation and unit on the property. Golf membership is $12,000 plus $155 a month; a full-service marina is available for additional charge. **Bentwater**, (713) 552-9525, is a 1,400-acre lake-side development with courtyard homes starting at $200,000 and single-family housing starting at $249,000. Building lots start in the mid-$20,000s to $500,000s. It has a 24-hour security gate, guard and patrol, plus a yacht club and marina, country club and 36 holes of golf. **April Sound**, (409) 447-2400, is a 1,000-acre lake-side golf resort (27 holes) with condos from $39,000-$140,000, waterfront townhomes from $120,000-$275,000, and single-family homes from $100,000-$600,000. It has a 24-hour security gate with guard and patrol. Country club membership is required (transferable to new owner with a one-time transfer fee and monthly maintenance fee).
Visitor lodging: Del Lago Resort, $129-$149 double, (409) 582-6100; April Plaza Marina and Motel, $55 double, (409) 588-1144.
Information: Conroe Chamber of Commerce, P.O. Box 2347, Conroe, TX 77305, (409) 756-6644 or www.conroe.org.

[1]Temperatures and relative humidity based on Houston readings.

within 40 miles are 11 state and private universities.

Retirees have a hard time thinking of negatives about the Lake Conroe region.

"We played golf right through July and August this year," says Bob Quinn.

But the Bells noted that the area's high humidity makes summers muggy.

Although winters are pleasant and mild with daytime temperatures in the mid-50s to 70s, summers bring long stretches of 90-degree heat.

Chuck Everett noted that taxes are high. "The municipal utility district taxes are determined by the size of the bonds issued to build the utilities, and apparently there was no attempt to hold down costs when they were built," he says.

None of these detractions was a surprise to the retirees. The Quinns visited Lake Conroe about a dozen times before deciding to move here. They rented an apartment in Houston and scouted the area with a real estate agent for two months. They bought their home in 1985 in a depressed market, and it has rebounded in value.

In April Sound a one-bedroom, one-bath condo starts at $39,000 while waterfront townhomes start at $120,000. Single-family homes run $100,000-$600,000.

The Everetts checked out several lake areas in Texas over the course of 18 months before deciding to move to Walden. "We were trying to pick up a foreclosure, but we couldn't find the right house so we bought a lot and built," Chuck says.

The Everetts knew their furnishings wouldn't fit the style of their new home, so they liquidated everything. "We put ads in the paper and had several garage sales," he says.

Cost of living was a major factor when the Everetts considered relocating. "We are basically living on a pension with some investment income so we had to take that into consideration," he says.

Traveling doesn't appeal to the Everetts as much now that they're settled near the lake.

"We don't like to leave our home – we enjoy it so much," Ethel says.●

Lake Havasu City, Arizona

Water, mountains and desert meld in popular Arizona oasis

By Judy Wade

In 1963 when chain-saw magnate Robert P. McCulloch began constructing Lake Havasu City, the place looked dismal.

The lake, formed when Parker Dam 21 miles to the south impounded the Colorado River, was surrounded by dirt terraces, bare of trees and vegetation. A single Spartan motel didn't do much to entice visitors.

McCulloch was a visionary, however. He promised a job with his company to anyone willing to relocate. Early guests were flown in to a rough, graded airstrip and then taken to see lakeview lots selling for $5,000.

Still, the place languished. Phoenix newspaper articles joked about the "big mudhole," smugly pointing out that summer temperatures there topped even Phoenix's legendary heat. For almost two decades Lake Havasu City's progress was unremarkable.

Then in the mid-'80s, the town began to boom, thanks in part to an anomaly in the Arizona desert, the London Bridge. Brought to Havasu by McCulloch and reconstructed in 1971, the bridge became a major tourist attraction, helping visitors discover the developing recreation area.

Today Lake Havasu City is a sparkling oasis with about 45,000 residents. The once-harsh landscape is green with golf courses and gardens. Imaginative resorts cluster at lakeside, and good restaurants offer eclectic dining. Beyond city borders, the Sonoran Desert melts into the foothills of the Mohave Mountains on one side and the Chemehuevi on the other.

The population is growing at a rate of 5 percent per year. Almost one-third of residents are seniors. Winter visitors continue to swell the numbers between Christmas and Easter, but the city is becoming much more of a year-round community. Fewer and fewer snowbirds migrate home, note local residents.

By 2010 the city is expected to max out at around 60,000 residents. Because it is surrounded by state land there is no space to expand unless the city is able to acquire publicly held property.

The appeal of water and weather lured John and Oweita Augsburger to Havasu.

"We lived on a lake in northern Indiana, and I was raised on the Gulf of Mexico, so we both like water," says Oweita, 51. "Here you have everything — mountains, water, sun and the convenience of Las Vegas, Phoenix and Los Angeles." The cities are within three to five or so hours by car, and there are commuter flights to Phoenix and Los Angeles.

The Augsburgers had vacationed at Lake Havasu City for 20 years but did look elsewhere in Arizona and in the Caribbean before deciding on the site for retirement. They built a mountainside adobe-style home with a lake view.

While climate is a big drawing card, it also may be the city's most apparent flaw. Beautiful warm winter days with temperatures in the mid-70s give way to July and August scorchers that can top 110 degrees. John, 59, suggests retreating to the 7,000-foot Hualapai Mountains, an hour away, where temperatures can be 30 degrees cooler. Some residents leave the city for several weeks during the late summer.

Retirees Jean and Bob Ramsdell aren't fond of the heat either, but say the trade-off is worth it.

"You might have two bad months, but I still like the other 10," says Bob, 76. "We have air-conditioned homes, cars and stores. If I have to run around, I do it early in the morning."

The Ramsdells moved to Havasu from Massachusetts, finding that their chronic sinus conditions were greatly alleviated in the dry desert climate.

Many Havasu residents rely on the 45-mile-long lake to help stay cool. Its waters are in the pleasant 80s from about mid-April into early fall, chilling to the mid-50s during winter months. On its shores, the natural sand beach of Rotary Community Park has shaded picnic tables and volleyball and softball areas.

Streets curve up and away from the lake, providing many homesites with views. Although architectural styles vary, Spanish-Mediterranean home designs prevail. There are no planned subdivisions or retirement communities because lots have been sold individually or in small groups. Young families, retirees and winter-only residents share neighborhoods.

Lot prices have skyrocketed — a lot that sold for $17,000 in 1976 is now on the market for $65,000. Golf-course lots can go for as much as $158,000. While $100,000 homes are the norm, custom homes can cost $600,000. Less pricey options are manufactured homes; three areas are zoned for them, two of which offer deeded lots for sale.

The London Bridge remains a focal point in the community. In the 1960s, when it was still British, the stone landmark was indeed, as the nursery rhyme declared, falling down, sinking into the Thames under the burden of increased traffic. Entrepreneurial Londoners put it on the market and McCulloch submitted the winning $2.46 million bid. The bridge was dismantled, its pieces numbered and transported to Lake Havasu. Today excursion boats and pleasure craft pass under its arches, passengers craning to see numbers still visible on many blocks.

The bridge seems appropriate in the Arizona desert in a Disneyesque sort of way, especially since Lake Havasu City was planned by C. V. Wood, who also designed Disneyland.

London Bridge is not just a quirky anachronism, though. It provides access to parks, a hotel and other businesses on a sliver of land called The Island. It also shelters the shops of English Village at its mainland end.

The city's two premier golf courses offer sweeping views of the bridge and lake. Hitting the links in 100-plus temperatures may sound like a bid for heatstroke, but courses open at daylight. Residents can get in 18 holes and be home by late morning, before temperatures peak. Late afternoon usually is the hottest time of the day. London Bridge Golf Club, where the Ramsdells belong, has two championship courses, where weekday greens fees are $50 and $35, including cart; lower rates apply after 1 p.m. Havasu Island and Queens Bay golf courses are other options.

Well-priced eateries, from the fun and funky to truly elegant, encourage dining out. At the unexpectedly European Cafe Mocha Tree, linen tablecloths and crystal chandeliers set the scene for French-style cuisine served by waiters in tuxedo shirts and cummerbunds. Bridgewater Cafe in the London Bridge Resort is famous for its opulent Sunday champagne brunch.

While water is the attraction for many, Havasu's arid side fascinates others. Especially in the spring the Sonoran Desert is alive with yellow creosote, red barrel cactus, brilliant orange-red ocotillo and the many-armed saguaros. Locals highly recommend an initial exploration with Outback Off-Road Adventures. Guests bounce along in a six-passenger Bronco 4x4 with a trained naturalist whose knowledge of plants and animals makes it possible to see life where none seems to exist.

A favorite excursion is a 20-minute ride across the lake on the Colorado River Express to the California side and Havasu Landing Resort and Casino. Because it is part of the Chemehuevi Indian Reservation, the resort can offer slot machines and electronic games of chance. Visitors often linger for lunch or supper at the casino lounge and restaurant.

A trip upriver to Topock Gorge and

Lake Havasu City, AZ

Population: 44,739 in Lake Havasu City, 209,865 in Mohave County.
Location: In the Sonoran desert on 45-mile-long Lake Havasu, created by damming the Colorado River. Founded in 1964, it sits on Arizona's boundary with California.

Climate:

	High	Low
January	67	43
July	110	83

Average relative humidity: 29%, but there are big seasonal differences. January averages 65%, June 15%.
Rain: 3.8 inches.
Extremely hot summers, moderate winters with an occasional freeze. Elevation 600 feet.
Cost of living: 98.3, based on national average of 100.
Average housing cost: $118,000 for a single-family home. Unfurnished three-bedroom, two-bath homes rent for an average $750 a month, or $800 with pool. Unfurnished one-bedroom apartments start at $400.
Sales tax: 7%
Sales tax exemptions: Prescription drugs, groceries.
State income tax: Graduated in five steps from 2.9% to 5.17%, depending on income.
Income tax exemptions: Social Security and up to $2,500 of federal, state and local government pensions are exempt.
Intangibles tax: None.
Estate tax: None, except the state's "pick-up" portion of the federal tax, applicable to taxable estates above $675,000.
Property tax: $94.70 per $1,000 of assessed valuation, with homes assessed at 10% of market value. Taxes on a $118,000 home are about $1,117 a year.
Homestead exemption: None.
Security: 32 crimes per 1,000 residents, lower than the national average of 46.2 crimes per 1,000 residents.
Religion: More than 30 churches represent 24 denominations.
Education: Mohave Community College, Lake Havasu Campus, offers degree programs and waives the $30 registration fee for students age 55 and older.
Transportation: There's no city bus service but an on-call van service delivers passengers door to door for $3 per destination. The airport has commuter flights to Phoenix and Los Angeles.
Health: Havasu Regional Medical Center has a 99-bed, full-service acute-care facility and a 19-bed transitional-care unit. It's staffed by 60 physicians and visiting specialists and is state-certified as an advanced life-support base.
Housing options: Many single-family homes, apartments and condos and three mobile-home parks. Three-bedroom, two-bath single-family homes run from $72,900-$189,900. **Queens Bay Condominiums**, in five locations, start at $40,000. There are no planned retirement communities. Lots are sold individually or in small groups for development. Independent retirement apartment living with 24-hour assistance is available at **1221 Claremont**, (520) 855-4843, a retirement residence that provides three meals a day.
Visitor lodging: Havasu Dunes resort condominiums, (800) 438-6493, one-bedroom units start at $95 a night; London Bridge Resort, (800) 624-7939, double rooms start at $119.
Information: Lake Havasu Area Chamber of Commerce, 314 London Bridge Road, Lake Havasu City, AZ 86403, (800) 242-8278, (520) 855-4115 or www.havasuchamber.com.

National Wildlife Refuge reveals another side of Havasu's aquatic nature. Via excursion boat or private craft, it's easy to spot many of the birds that are protected here. To those who are imaginative, the random shapes of surrounding cliffs, softened by centuries of river water, become an alligator, fish, dolphin, hippo and gorilla. Near the waterline, ancient Indian petroglyphs are clearly visible.

Havasu's arts calendar is filled with theater productions and art shows. The Lake Havasu Community Orchestra presents a number of yearly concerts featuring pops and the classics, and popular drama in a dinner theater setting is offered by the Drury Lane Repertory Players.

Recent Havasu Light Opera productions included "You're a Good Man, Charlie Brown." The 123-member Lake Havasu Art Guild sponsors a spring juried show, which attracts exhibitors from throughout the Southwest. Mohave Community College's Discovery Series presents talks, choral concerts, dance programs and other events. Residents go to Phoenix and Las Vegas for more cosmopolitan cultural venues.

The Lake Havasu Senior Center offers line-dancing classes, yoga, bingo and bridge and workout classes as well as noon lunches. Health-maintenance support includes blood pressure check and nutrition education. Writers, artists and entertainers frequently present programs and workshops.

Havasu Regional Medical Center provides 24-hour emergency care, surgical capabilities, a transitional-care unit and a home health-care agency. An extensive network of senior services may be accessed through the Interagency Council.

Many Havasu residents own houseboats, ideal for exploring the lake's placid waters and the coves and inlets along its irregular shoreline. These "floating condos" also are for rent. At 46 to 52 feet, or about the size of a large motor home, most houseboats have standard-size beds, completely equipped galleys, living rooms and barbecue areas on deck. Some can accommodate 10 to 12 guests. Houseboats also provide a base from which fishermen can pursue the wily trout, bass, bluegill, crappie and catfish.

The new Aquatic Recreation Center is a good respite when lake waters are chilly or when summer's sun proves too intense. Colorful windsurfers float from the ceiling. "Surf" in the wave pool washes up on a cement "beach" that's fringed with frankly fake palm trees. Plastic coconuts periodically dump water on anyone underneath. A four-story water slide keeps kids busy, and a gently sloping shoreline-style entry is used for the aquatic wheelchair, available to anyone who needs it. A single admission to the center is $6, or $5 for seniors; yearly memberships are available.

Havasu is a planned community, taking the time to get things right. As chairman of the finance committee, Bob Ramsdell wrote the city's first budget and has served as mayor. When the Ramsdells moved here in 1977 there were 8,000 people. Now there are about 45,000, but "we still love it," Bob says.

Adds Jean, 75, "Since it was so small to begin with, shopping was a bit of a problem. We didn't have the stores we were used to." Now there are four major supermarkets, a Wal-Mart and dozens of other retail stores.

The Ramsdells say their taxes are much lower in Lake Havasu City — about $800 vs. more than $3,000 paid in "Taxachusetts," as Bob puts it. "We have a high electrical bill here, but when I add in the fuel costs from the other house to the electric bill, it's cheaper here," he adds.

Jean misses the colorful display of fall leaves they had in Massachusetts, but Bob says he misses nothing. "I gave up my two proudest possessions — my lawn mower and my snow blower."

Both the Ramsdells and the Augsburgers say that despite Lake Havasu City's growth, it still has the feel of a small town. "There's lots of gossip. With such an influx of people from all over the United States, I didn't expect that," says Oweita.

Pre-retirees considering Havasu should spend a summer there before making a year-around commitment, cautions John.

Bob advises retirees to reach out when they move to Lake Havasu City. "Go to the Senior Center, to your church, to town meetings, raise your right hand and they'll keep you so busy you'll never know that you're retired. And that way you develop friends, too," he says.●

Las Vegas, Nevada

From affordable living to plentiful recreation, retirees find that this desert city has it all

By Adele Malott

Las Vegas Valley at night is a soup bowl of stars, an oasis of lights hugged up close by the Spring Mountains. For several decades this view has welcomed millions of vacationers arriving from throughout the world.

But for newcomers moving to the Las Vegas area each month, it now says "welcome home" to people like Ken and Marlene Rengert, who came to Las Vegas six years ago after Ken retired from the Air Force in Rantoul, IL. The Rengerts are great travelers — gone as much as 75 percent of the time some years — so the view of their new hometown from an airplane window when they return is one they know well.

Marlene Rengert says that when the plane crests the mountains, she likes to see the lights laid out beneath her. And when she's home, she tells her friends, "It's like having Christmas lights in the back yard all year long." The Rengerts chose a three-bedroom ranch home on Sunrise Mountain with views of the city lights for their retirement oasis.

Las Vegas did begin as an oasis for the Spanish and Mexicans who used the Old Spanish Trail to travel between Santa Fe and Southern California. These travelers named the area "Las Vegas," meaning "the meadows" — an image difficult to imagine when looking at the towers of neon and construction gantries that now dominate the skyline.

Las Vegas started to take shape in 1905 when the San Pedro, Los Angeles and Salt Lake Railroad (Union Pacific) auctioned off building sites for the spot it had chosen to change crews and get water for its trains. Another growth spurt pumped the city in the early 1930s when construction of Hoover Dam began, and again in the '40s when Bugsy Siegel built the Flamingo Hotel as a gaming spa for the mob, then in the 1960s when Howard Hughes came to town, and the '70s when the mammoth MGM Grand was built. Now, every third or fourth year a new wave of construction adds to the skyline.

All the superlatives to describe Las Vegas have been used up as a tightening time-line spiral of boom and boom and boom has thrust the city repeatedly to the top of many different kinds of "fastest-growing" lists. So it is no surprise that people from all backgrounds, occupations and parts of the United States in search of a retirement home find what they want in Las Vegas. Retirees comprise the fastest-growing segment of Las Vegas' population, and the National Association of Home Builders predicts the city will be the most popular seniors housing market in the coming decade.

Many, like Terry and Claudia Culp, who moved to Las Vegas in 1998 from Buffalo, NY, are quick to emphasize that the Las Vegas in which they live is not the Las Vegas they were accustomed to reading about. Terry explains that the typical Easterner's view of Las Vegas "is a misinterpretation that assumes that all there is to do is to lay out in the sun or gamble. As it turns out, Las Vegas is totally different than what I envisioned," he says as he describes his discoveries. "Valley of Fire is absolutely gorgeous. I had heard about Lake Mead, but it is much bigger than I thought. Another surprise is Lake Powell — it's not that far away. And Hoover Dam is a little touristy, but you have to do it once, right?"

Perhaps one reason the Las Vegas Strip works so hard for the attention of visitors is that its glitter and glitz must compete with vast natural spectacles like Valley of Fire and Red Rock Canyon, places that could serve as God's own statuary gardens filled with sandstone creations named Elephant Rock and the Seven Sisters. These two geological parks are the east and west bookends for Las Vegas, and both draw millions of visitors annually.

Lake Mead National Recreation Area is the massive playground that resulted from creating a needed flood- and drought-control project. With 822 miles of shoreline, Lake Mead offers a bonanza of water sports, as does Lake Mohave, created by the construction of Davis Dam nearly 50 years after Hoover Dam. Hoover was built to rein in the Colorado River's rampages and supply electrical power for much of the Southwest.

The enormous Hoover Dam construction project jump-started southern Nevada's economy in post-Depression years and today offers tourists a chance to take river rafting and excursion boat trips through Black Canyon at the base of the dam, which towers 726 feet overhead. River rafters are intrigued with often-told ghost stories that describe the moans and cries of construction workers trapped in the dam wall.

The Culps undertook methodical research to find their new home after they sold a family business in Buffalo and left 70-hour work weeks behind. They believed they would prefer the Southwest and began buying books and retirement publications to research their choices. Then they chose eight cities to look at critically during a 3,000-mile trek across the country: Lake Havasu City, Page, Phoenix and Tucson in Arizona, Santa Fe and Albuquerque in New Mexico, and Reno/Sparks and Las Vegas in Nevada. Each stop included visits with chamber of commerce officials and real estate agents. And once they decided on Las Vegas, they moved into an apartment to give themselves time to get a feel for the area until they found their 2,600-square-foot home in Henderson, southeast of downtown.

"There were a lot of pluses for each city we looked at, but when we boiled it all down, Las Vegas was the most attractive," says Terry Culp. "The small-town feel was a big advantage and, because Las Vegas is so easy and

Las Vegas, NV

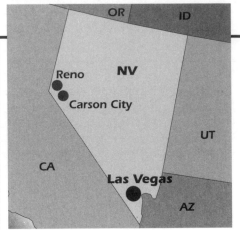

Population: 1.2 million

Location: In a broad desert valley in the southern tip of Nevada surrounded by mountains. The valley's elevation is about 1,200 feet, with surrounding mountains rising from 2,000 to 12,000 feet. Las Vegas is at the crossroads of I-15 (connecting southern California, Arizona and Utah), I-95 (from the northwest) and I-93/95 from the southeast.

Climate:

	High	Low
January	57	34
July	108	76

Average relative humidity: 31%

Rain: 3.8 inches

Cost of living: 106.4%, based on national average of 100.

Average housing costs: $148,575 for a new three-bedroom home of 1,800 square feet. Median sales price of an established home is $128,107. A 950-square-foot apartment rents for an average of $774 per month.

Sales tax: 7.25%

Sales tax exemptions: Food for consumption at home, prescription drugs, vegetable plants and seeds, propane and fuel for home heating.

State income tax: None.

Intangibles tax: None.

Estate tax: None, except the state's "pick-up" portion of the federal tax applicable to taxable estates of more than $675,000.

Property tax: $2.50-$4 per $100 in assessed value depending on the taxing district within Clark County, with homes assessed at 35% of taxable value. The annual tax for a home valued at $148,000 would be $1,295 to $2,072.

Homestead exemption: None.

Security: 59.4 crimes per 1,000 residents, higher than the national average of 46.2 crimes per 1,000 residents.

Religion: There are 584 churches serving the Las Vegas Valley.

Education: Two two-year colleges, Community College of Southern Nevada and Las Vegas College, and one four-year college, University of Nevada at Las Vegas. Those who are 62 or older can attend fall and spring semester credit classes at UNLV on a space-available basis without paying credit or tuition fees. Summer credit courses are offered at half-price. The Clark County School District offers a large number of adult education programs, as do area park and recreation departments.

Transportation: McCarran International Airport, 10 minutes south of the business district, is ranked as the nation's 10th-busiest airport with daily traffic of about 800 flights and 83,000 passengers. Public bus transportation is provided by CAT (Citizens Area Transit). Trolleys also run along the Strip and from downtown to a mall and the Stratosphere Hotel. A new project is the Senior Neighborhood Trolley Routes that stop at various senior centers and shops.

Health: 10 hospitals boast a combined staff of 7,000 physicians and specialized care centers such as a bone marrow transplant facility, diabetes treatment center, coronary heart disease reversal program and a burn-care center.

Housing options: There is a vast array of housing choices available from townhouses, condominiums and apartment complexes to single-family homes (many of them on new golf courses). Nearby cities such as Henderson and Boulder City also are claiming their share of new residents. There are a number of active-adult housing developments. **Sun City MacDonald Ranch**, (800) 764-9322, 10 miles south of downtown Las Vegas in Henderson, has homes starting at $117,400. The 55-and-older communi-ty features a fitness center, community center and golf course. Also in Henderson, **Anthem** incorporates three types of neighborhoods: a gated country club community, an active-adult community for residents 55 and older, and a traditional neighborhood geared to families; call (800) 4-DEL-WEBB for information. On the western rim of Las Vegas Valley, **Summerlin**, (800) 295-4554, is a 22,500-acre master-planned community currently comprised of 15 villages in various stages of development and covering a broad range of housing styles and prices, including the age-restricted **Sun City Summerlin**. Plans call for a total of 30 villages. One of the newest villages is **Siena**, (800) 856-7661, a guard-gated community with an 18-hole golf course, health and fitness center, and homes from the mid-$130,000s.

Visitor lodging: Las Vegas has a huge inventory of hotels and motels with more than 100,000 rooms, including 12 of the 13 largest hotels in the world. In addition, the city offers long-term stay and corporate apartment facilities for those needing more than casual or vacation accommodations. Space can be at a premium during high-traffic conventions. For more information, call the hotel reservations hot line of the Las Vegas Convention and Visitors Authority, (800) 332-5333.

Information: Las Vegas Chamber of Commerce, 3720 Howard Hughes Parkway, No. 100, Las Vegas, NV 89109, (702) 735-1616 or www.lvchamber. com. Ask for the biannual Las Vegas Relocation Guide. Las Vegas Convention and Visitors Authority, 3150 Paradise Road, Las Vegas, NV 89109, (702) 892-0711 or www.lasvegas24hours. com. Clark County Department of Comprehensive Planning, 500 S. Grand Central Parkway, No. 3012, Las Vegas, NV 89155-1741, (702) 455-4181. Aging Senior Division, Department of Human Resources, 340 N. 11th St., No. 203, Las Vegas, NV 89101, (702) 486-3545.

inexpensive to get in and out of, it was a good choice so our family and friends could visit." Terry laughs when he admits their decision was "sort of scientific" but also involved "our gut feelings."

Many of his views are seconded by Gail Imazaki, a nurse who retired to Las Vegas from Southern California in 1997. "You can live as quietly as you want, or you can get out and go to the clubs and shows," says Gail, who also researched a variety of locations, including Port Ludlow, WA, and Palm Desert and Roseville, CA.

Gail earned the crown of Ms. Senior Nevada in 1998 and was fourth runner-up in the national pageant, partly because of her dancing skills. A single senior, she now lives in a duplex on the eighth hole of Eagle Crest Golf Course in Sun City Summerlin, "with a spectacular view of the mountains that amazes me every morning when I wake up. I could never have afforded to live on the golf course in Los Angeles," she adds, noting that it is a location she enjoys even though she is not a player.

Gail ticks off the city's "pluses" in rapid order: "First, cheaper auto insurance; second, utilities much cheaper; third, no state (income) taxes." And then she laughs, "Another factor that swayed me were the inexpensive buffets. I rarely cook now, only microwave." But while Gail lists many good things about her choice, she admits Las Vegas is not perfect and worries that city amenities and services may not be able to keep up with rapid growth, especially in the area of health care.

The chance to spend more time dancing was one reason she decided to retire at age 60. As a registered nurse working on the open-heart surgery team at Good Samaritan Hospital in Los Angeles, Gail "was so busy I couldn't do my dancing." Now she practices in her dining room as well as attending recreation classes and serving as president of the Nevada chapter of the Cameo Club of Ms. Senior America, an alumni group.

Gail was persuaded to enter the Ms. Senior Nevada competition by Lori Sanchez, another Summerlin resident who claimed the Ms. Senior America title a few years earlier. The two met as performers putting on talent showcases at convalescent homes. Gail entered the Ms. Senior Nevada competition "with an attitude of meeting new ladies and for the experience — not to win," she says.

Representing Nevada also gave Gail a chance to "do some PR with senior citizens, to make sure they're well cared for. I can also help with referrals since a lot of seniors may not know about everything that's available to them in the way of services."

And there are many. Each Sunday's newspaper is filled with activities at dozens of senior facilities throughout the Las Vegas Valley, as well as news of health and financial assistance, discounts, volunteer opportunities, special continuing-education studies and seminars at the University of Nevada at Las Vegas. Terry Culp is enrolled in Spanish classes at the University of Nevada at Las Vegas and a computer class at the Community College of Southern Nevada.

Volunteering is part of what the Rengerts do, now that they are no longer in the military. Marlene Rengert helps at the hospital at Nellis Air Force Base, her church and as an AARP recruiter, while husband Ken is a tax aide volunteer for AARP.

When the Rengerts were moving from base to base during Ken's 30-year Air Force career, they learned about many areas in the United States. But Marlene Rengert says, "We fell in love with the desert and its warm, dry climate, which seems to make my rheumatoid arthritis less painful." While the weather was the top reason Las Vegas was right for the Rengerts, they also liked being close to a Veterans Administration hospital and connected to military roots at nearby Nellis Air Force Base.

Las Vegas is the kind of city that attracts more than the usual number of visitors, both friends and relatives of residents. But the Rengerts always look forward to visits from their four grandchildren (a fifth will soon be added to the family) and say Las Vegas' many parks and libraries help them entertain their young guests. Other favorite stops are attractions like the Wet 'n' Wild water park and the highly interactive Lied (pronounced "leed") Children's Museum. Here kids of all ages can try out gadgets, work at solving problems and enjoy the performances and workshops of artists-in-residence who showcase arts from photography to puppetry and creative writing to sculpture.

If the man-made attractions weren't enough, the Rengerts point out that the Grand Canyon is nearby, and residents can ski on Mount Charleston and explore historic mining towns. "We could have chosen anywhere. But we often say, 'Didn't we make a good decision?' and pat each other on the back," says Marlene. "We think we did a really good job choosing." ●

Lincoln City, Oregon

The jewel of the Central Oregon coast glitters with attraction for many

By Dana Tims

From signing the Emancipation Proclamation to delivering the Gettysburg Address to saving the Union, Abraham Lincoln is known to history for many acts of leadership. What the annals do not record about the 16th president, however, were his exploits in the Oregon Territory.

Why? Because he never had any. One can only ponder how Lincoln's life and the nation might have changed had he accepted an offer in 1849 to become governor of the newly formed Oregon Territory, a rough and wild section of country stretching from the West Coast to what is now Montana, Wyoming and Nevada.

A much different career path, one ultimately leading to Ford's Theater in Washington, DC, was chosen after his wife, Mary Todd Lincoln, told him that the untamed wilderness of the West was no place to raise children.

Lincoln City still is not for everyone, say members of the active senior community in the Oregon coastal town that bears the late president's name. But for those willing to put up with the boiling magnificence of a winter storm, summer breezes bending wildflowers low beneath stands of Sitka spruce and red alder on blustery Cascade Head, or a contemplative walk along more than seven miles of white-sand beaches, Lincoln City may be just the spot to call home.

Bounded on the east by scenic Devils Lake and to the west by the Pacific Ocean, Lincoln City long has been known as a haven for retirees. More than a third of the town's population of 6,785 residents, in fact, have pulled up stakes in other areas of the country and made the glittering Central Oregon coast their home.

George and Mary Jeffries had lived and worked in Chicago for six years before George retired in 1991 as director of workers compensation for CNA Insurance Co. Devotees of op-

era and theater, they loved the cultural accouterments available in a big city.

But when it came time to choose a retirement location, George and Mary gladly said goodbye to metropolis. The harsh winter weather, along with daunting daily traffic jams, had become too much. Having owned a small vacation cabin at Gleneden Beach, just south of Lincoln City, for years, they were well-acquainted with the area. Neither entertained thoughts of moving anywhere else. And they have not regretted their decision for a moment.

"We can't imagine having a better life," Mary says. "Everything we could ever want is right here in Lincoln City."

They immersed themselves in the area's abundant cultural and volunteer activities almost immediately. George, 65, fired up his long-dormant amateur acting career by building sets for Lincoln City's Theatre West. His love of literature landed him on the Friends of the Library board of directors, where he organizes weekly book sales that net enough money to buy such extras as a neon sign for the teen reading area and lighting to illuminate a stunning seascape painted and donated by another volunteer.

He also is an assistant gardener for the Connie Hansen Garden, a one-acre flowerfest of primroses, irises and perennials open to the public and named for the horticulturist who developed the parcel. In what little spare time he saves for himself, George painstakingly builds scale models of multimasted sailing ships.

"I wore suits for more than 40 years, and I just decided it was time to get rid of them," says George, who grew up in a small, informal town and still cherishes the ability to stump around Lincoln City's numerous art galleries and antique stores in casual clothes.

"When I was younger, going to the prom meant you had to wash your jeans. That's kind of how it is around here, too."

Mary, 64, writes a seniors column for the town's weekly newspaper, the *Lincoln City News Guard*. Her topics include everything from tax-cutting ballot measures to the impact on local traffic and congestion from Lincoln City's newest attraction, the Chinook Winds Casino and Convention Center. "I'm not a gambler, but it's been a big shot in the arm for the city," she says of the casino, which is owned and operated by the Confederated Tribes of Siletz.

An avid reader who always has at least three books going, Mary also is secretary of the Friends of the Library board of directors. She augments her love of literature by working 10 hours a week in a cozy downtown bookstore.

When the couple moved to Lincoln City, they paid $115,000 for a comfortable two-bedroom house with an ocean view. They currently are looking for a residence with a garage to accommodate George's woodworking needs. Now asking $135,000 for their home, they hope to find something closer to the ocean, although they know it will be a little more expensive.

Patti Smith, an agent with Lincoln City's Pete Anderson Realty, says land and home prices never have declined in the decade she has been in the business. But with prices now tending to be more stable than in the past, she says there's a buyer's market featuring plenty of options and choices.

"We've got everything here that seniors could want, including shopping, great health-care facilities and a fantastic beach," she says. "Lincoln City is a retired person's paradise."

Lincoln City's housing market is dominated by two-story residences, which are preferred by homeowners seeking a coveted view of the Pacific Ocean. While a number of planned developments aimed specifically at seniors are springing up around the area, many seniors still prefer to buy single-family residences, which average $130,000 to $165,000 for a two-bedroom, two-bath house.

"Our seniors are the ones who keep this town alive and hopping," Patti Smith says. "Without them, I don't know where we'd be."

Bill and Mary Kacy, both 68, have seen some significant changes in Lincoln City since they moved here in 1982 from their longtime home in Austin, TX. Foremost has been the increase in traffic along U.S. Highway 101, the coastal highway that effectively cleaves the town down the middle.

Lincoln City, OR

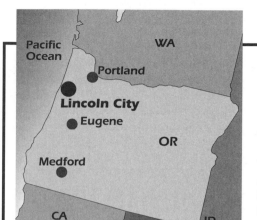

Population: 6,785 in the city, 42,500 in the county.

Location: Situated on the Central Oregon coast and bordered by the Salmon River to the north, Siletz Bay to the south and Devils Lake to the east. Lincoln City is 88 miles southwest of Oregon's largest city, Portland. Elevation is 11 feet.

Climate:

	High	Low
January	54	37
July	68	53

Average relative humidity: 62%
Rainfall: 71.8 inches.
Lincoln City has generally mild weather, with a winter storm season extending from mid-October to early March. Air quality is constantly refreshed with northwest winds in the summer and southwest winds in the winter.

Cost of living: 105.7 in Lincoln County, based on national average of 100.

Median housing cost: $160,000 for a single-family dwelling. Average rental $700.

Sales tax: None.

State income tax: Graduated in three steps from 5% to 9%, depending on income.

Income tax exemptions: Social Security benefits are exempt. You may be able to subtract some or all of your federal pension income, based on the number of months of federal service before and after Oct. 1, 1991.

Intangibles tax: None.

Estate tax: None, except the state's "pick-up" portion of the federal tax, applicable to taxable estates above $675,000.

Property taxes: $17.05 per $1,000 of assessed value. Homes are assessed at 100 percent of market value. The yearly tax on a $160,000 home is about $2,728.

Homestead exemption: None.

Security: 119 crimes per 1,000 residents, higher than the national average of 46.2 crimes per 1,000 residents.

Religion: Twenty-six local churches and temples represent all major religious denominations.

Education: Oregon Coast Community College, with satellite branches in Lincoln City and nearby Newport and Waldport, offers more than 100 credit courses along with a variety of noncredit adult education courses. Seniors receive a 50 percent discount on community education tuition. Evening and weekend seminars are provided to accommodate the needs of business persons and busy retirees.

Transportation: Central Coast Connections is the county-sponsored bus transport that runs daily from Otis Junction, just east of Lincoln City, south along the coast to Yachats and east to Toledo and Siletz.

Health: North Lincoln Hospital in Lincoln City provides a full staff of physicians and nurses, along with 49 beds and units specializing in dialysis, strokes and neurological rehabilitation. In 1996, the hospital built a home health care building. The hospital maintains a 24-hour emergency room and a diversity of professional courses for staff and community members via satellite. In addition, the area is served by five medical complexes and two care facilities, which provide the latest in rehabilitation services, respite care and hospice care.

Housing options: Many retirees buy single-family homes in existing neighborhoods in the city. Prices range from $50,000 to $500,000-plus along the coast. Only 30-35 new homes are built annually, almost all under buyer contract. Several retirement communities also are available. The **Dorchester House**, (541) 994-7175, is a restored historic hotel that now features 68 apartments for active seniors. Units rent for $1,000 and up for a 515-square-foot, one-bedroom apartment to $1,300 and up for a 672-square-foot, two-bedroom apartment. Services include weekly housekeeping and all meals. **Lincolnshire Retirement and Assisted Living**, (541) 994-7400, is a combination assisted- and independent-living facility overlooking quiet Devils Lake. It features 12 cottages and 52 studios and one-bedroom apartments. Monthly rents range from $1,500 for a studio to $1,800 for a one-bedroom unit, single occupancy (additional $425 for second occupant). Meals are provided and bus service is available to area medical and recreational facilities. **Hillside House**, (541) 994-8028, is an adult assisted-living facility with 33 units ranging from studios to one-bedroom apartments. Rents start at $1,500 per month for single occupants and go up, depending on the level of care. Additional occupants pay $500 per month.

Visitor lodging: Lincoln City has a wide variety of overnight accommodations and features more than 2,000 rooms, the largest number of coastal motel and hotel rooms between San Francisco and Seattle. Among the options: Inn at Spanish Head, $149-$215, (541) 996-2161; Best Western Lincoln Sands Inn, $189, (541) 994-4227; and Coho Inn, $107-$124, (541) 994-3684.

Information: Lincoln City Visitors and Convention Bureau, 801 S.W. Highway 101, Suite 1, Lincoln City, OR 97367, (800) 452-2151 or www.oregoncoast. org. Lincoln City Chamber of Commerce, P.O. Box 787, Lincoln City, OR 97367, (541) 994-3070 or www.lcchamber.com.

Area merchants, who for years opposed a proposed bypass around the town, now are supportive of the idea, especially since the town's 158,000-square-foot casino ensures that Lincoln City will never be without a steady influx of visitors. That shift of support, the Kacys say, could restore some of the charm lost to increased traffic.

However, both say that area seniors can manage very well, especially once they learn the side streets and shortcuts to such destinations as the county's quaint, turn-of-the-century covered wooden bridges, the North Lincoln County Historical Museum, the town's new senior community center, and North Lincoln Hospital with its state-of-the-art medical equipment.

The hospital serves the community with 49 beds, a full staff of physicians and nurses and units specializing in dialysis, strokes and neurological rehabilitation. Lincoln City also features five medical complexes and two care facilities providing services ranging from adult day care to hospice care.

Bill enjoys frequent rounds of golf at either Lakeside Golf Club's 18-hole course in Lincoln City or at the breathtaking ocean-view course at Salishan Lodge Golf Links just south in Gleneden Beach. "We have five courses within easy driving distance, and I can play all year around in a sweater," says Bill, who retired as regional director of public affairs for Union Carbide. "Our last year in Texas, it was over 100 degrees every day for two months. We could never go back to that."

He also has honed his computer programmer's skills by taking technology courses offered through Oregon Coast Community College. In addition, he volunteers at the hospital, where he serves on the board of directors.

The couple was forced to move from Texas because of Mary's respiratory problems. So while Bill remained behind to finish some last-minute work, Mary grabbed her Lhasa apso puppy, hopped in the car and headed solo to scout the West Coast. "I started at the southern end of Oregon and just drove north," says Mary, who managed the 25-story Westgate Building in Austin

before retirement. "When I got to Lincoln City, I just knew I had found what I was looking for."

Mary, a freelance writer, has been published in a number of newspapers and magazines. She also helped city planners write Lincoln City's transportation master plan. For an artistic outlet, the rugs, colorful shawls and decorative place mats she weaves on a 36-inch loom are sold at area gift shops.

The couple still lives in the house Mary discovered on that first venture, a two-bedroom, two-bath residence tucked among the alder and spruce on Cascade Head, a stunning promontory that juts into the ocean and features both canopied and wind-swept hiking trails. Only 35 houses and 30 condominiums, some of them used only as vacation getaways, dot Cascade Head, which has earned federal designation as the Salmon River Estuary Scenic Research Area.

The home faces south, saving the Kacys a bundle on utility costs. Splashes of afternoon sun in the winter prompt Mary to throw wide the doors to avoid overheating, while gentle sea breezes ensure that there is no need for air-conditioning in the summer.

During afternoon walks with their dog, Rowdy, the Kacys often stumble across a herd of 30 massive Roosevelt elk. They also have spotted bald eagles, cougars, black bears, deer and graceful, swooping peregrine falcons.

"Every morning when I get up and look out, I just thank God I'm here," Mary says. "It's just so natural and exhilarating. There's a very spiritual feel to it."

For recreation, the Kacys further the love of sailing they developed in Austin on forays at Devils Lake. A popular swimming, boating and picnicking spot, the 16,000-year-old expanse of cobalt-blue water drains into the ocean through the D River, which at only 200 yards in length is touted as the world's shortest river.

Lincoln City's small-town size has not limited amenities such as shopping. One of the region's largest factory-outlet sites, with 65 brand-name stores, including the only L.L. Bean outlet on the West Coast, greets bargain hunters. Although the area's reputation as an artist colony has faded somewhat in

recent years, galleries and antique stores number in the scores.

"I'm afraid the word is finally getting out about us," says LoriAnn Sheridan, executive director of the Lincoln City Chamber of Commerce, noting that the town has been listed in two books profiling America's most desirable places to live. "But every word of it is true."

Joyce and Robert "Scotty" Scotton decided to retire to Lincoln City after spending the first of their retirement years in the Fiji Islands as Peace Corps volunteers. Both Joyce, a university-level home education administrator, and Scotty, a retired police officer, say they have found full and happy lives in Lincoln City.

Among the special attractions for them is the ever-present power of the Pacific Ocean. They regularly meet and make new friends during long walks along the beach. Joyce loves the beach so much that she has developed a standard reply any time a tourist traipses into the Lincoln City Visitors and Convention Bureau, where she volunteers, and asks what do to first in town. "I say, 'Have you got sand between your toes yet?' I direct them straight to the beach, and I've never had a complaint from anyone yet."

As for Abe Lincoln, well, the late president did make it to Lincoln City after all — sort of, anyway. A statue of Lincoln astride a horse graces the heart of town. One of only three works of its kind in the world, the statue by renowned sculptor Anne Hyatt Huntington captures the period of Lincoln's life just after he had turned down the governorship of the wild Oregon Territory.

Huntington, who broke the mold after she cast the three works, donated the statue to Lincoln City in 1965, but only after securing several key agreements from city and state leaders. Among these was a requirement that Lincoln would always face west.

So while in life the president may not have personally followed a path leading to Lincoln City's perch on the Pacific Ocean, increasing numbers of retirees are making some personal history of their own by doing just that. And ending up being glad they did.●

Longboat Key, Florida

Pristine Florida island has it all — beaches, sports and cultural events

By Carol Godwin

If your retirement plans call for a location about as close to paradise as you can get, consider Longboat Key. Then pinch yourself because you're not dreaming, it really exists.

Adrift in the Gulf of Mexico along Florida's west coast, Longboat Key is an offshore barrier island 10.8 miles long and one-half mile wide at its widest point. Fringed with tall Australian pines and swaying sea oats, powder white sands spread along Gulf beaches, and finger canals reach into bayside neighborhoods where fine yachts are moored.

Longboat Key is free of minimalls, towering billboards and glaring neon signs. Its dedication to limited development makes the island an appealing and safe sanctuary for a variety of shorebirds as well as humans searching for a slice of serenity apart from the everyday world.

Linked by bridges to the mainland cities of Sarasota — known as Florida's cultural center — and Bradenton, Longboat Key is one of the world's most idyllic resort communities and an increasingly popular upscale retirement destination. Outdoor activities are enjoyed 12 months of the year. Anglers can cast a line into the turquoise waters off Longboat, marinas offer rental and charter boats, and joggers, rollerbladers and bikers share a 10-mile trail winding along Gulf of Mexico Drive, the island's only north-south road. Emerald fairways carpet both gulf- and bayside golf course communities, and tennis courts are an active part of the landscape.

A favorite saying among area real estate agents goes: "If we owned Heaven and Longboat Key, we'd rent out Heaven and live on Longboat."

Len and Fran Miller agree. "If God made a better place He saved it for Himself," says Len, 66, a mechanical contractor who retired with his wife to the island in 1990 from Wallingford, PA, a suburb of Philadelphia.

"We found this lovely place by mistake," says Fran, 65, who managed Len's office before retirement. "In 1979, we flew down to meet friends in Tampa and our travel agent booked us into the Holiday Inn on Longboat Key by mistake. We fell in love with Longboat and didn't want to leave. Since then we came back and forth, first for two weeks, then a month, then spent the winter, and finally seven years ago we bought a house and thought we'd spend six months here and six months in Pennsylvania."

"It took us a couple of months to figure out this is wrong," laughs Len. "Now we're here permanently."

The Millers looked elsewhere in Florida, at New Port Richey, Naples and Marco Island on the west coast, and Vero Beach and Fort Lauderdale on the east coast. But none was what they wanted and they kept returning to Longboat Key.

"You can't beat Longboat, it's so clean and pristine," says Len, and Fran adds, "We love it."

Circus king John Ringling envisioned such a paradise in the early 1900s when he purchased thousands of acres of land in Sarasota and neighboring St. Armands Key, Lido Key and the south end of Longboat. The ringmaster in the area's early development, Ringling quartered his "Greatest Show on Earth" in Sarasota each winter and employed his elephants to help dredge canals on Lido Key. He decorated St. Armands Key with Italian statuary he brought back from Europe and spent $3 million to partially build his grand hotel, the Ritz-Carlton, on the southern tip of Longboat Key.

Real estate boomed as Northern "snowbirds" clamored for a place in the sun. On broad Sarasota Bay, Ringling built a mansion for his beloved wife, Mable, fashioning it after the Doge's Palace in Venice and calling it Ca'd' Zan (House of John). On adjacent property, he built the John and Mable Ringling Museum of Art and filled it with treasures amassed during their travels throughout Europe.

Then came the great stock market crash and everyone suffered, including Ringling. His fabled Ritz-Carlton was never completed, its ghostly silhouette looming over Longboat Key's New Pass until the late 1950s. Arvida Realty Co. acquired the land, plus a vast portion of John Ringling's development projects. Nevertheless, the circus king made his mark, leaving the area with a rich cultural legacy that remains a hallmark of Sarasota.

Aross Sarasota Bay from Longboat Key, the Ringling Museum Complex now encompasses the official state art museum, the John and Mable Ringling Museum of Art with its magnificent open-air Italianate-style courtyard; the Ringling Home; sprawling grounds where the annual Medieval Fair is held; Circus Galleries that provide a glimpse of life under the big top; and a 19th-century theater imported from Asolo, Italy. Next door, the Asolo Center for the Performing Arts houses a laboratory theater for the Florida State University/Asolo Conservatory of Professional Actor Training. The center's main stage is a turn-of-the-century facility seating up to 500, which was first built as an opera house in Dunfermlin, Scotland. In 1987 its decorative detail was brought to Sarasota and incorporated into the theater.

Long a favorite retreat for writers and artists, the area is home to the Florida West Coast Symphony, the Sarasota Ballet of Florida, the Sarasota Opera, the Jazz Club of Sarasota, the internationally acclaimed Ringling School of Art and Design, the Marie Selby Botanical Gardens, numerous art galleries and little theater companies, plus intriguing shops, restaurants and sumptuous homes. And just offshore a paradise of an island, Longboat Key.

Fran enjoys being close to Sarasota and its cultural scene. She's active with St. Mary Star of the Sea Catholic Church, community choral groups and little theater and is a volunteer at Sarasota Memorial Hospital and at the Sarasota Convention and Visitors Bureau.

She frequently assists visitors to the area, many of them seniors who are looking for a place to retire. "When they say they want to buy a condo, I always advise to rent a place for six months before deciding to buy. That way you know the area and exactly where you want to be," says Fran. She and Len vacationed in several different condos before buying a home.

The Millers decided to locate on a canal, in a 2,600-square-foot, single-family home of Spanish design overlooking Sarasota Bay. Since purchasing the home in 1988, they figure it has

Longboat Key, FL

Population: 8,000 in summer, nearly 22,000 in winter.

Location: Barrier island across the bay from Sarasota on Florida's southwest coast about 60 miles south of Tampa. The Key is in Sarasota and Manatee counties.

Climate:

	High	Low
January	72	51
July	90	75

Average relative humidity: 58%

Rain: 53.09 inches.

Mild winters and long, hot summers with high humidity, but usually cooled by Gulf of Mexico breezes and afternoon thunderstorms. Hurricanes are a threat; however, over the past 110 years only one hurricane, in 1944, has directly hit the Sarasota area. Elevation 3 to 18 feet.

Cost of living: 104.3 in Sarasota, based on national average of 100.

Average housing cost: $411,000 for a condominium, $597,000 for a single-family home. Annual rent ranges from $750 to $2,500 a month, seasonal (winter) monthly rent from $2,000 to $5,000 and up.

Sales tax: 7%

Sales tax exemptions: Groceries, medicines, some professional services.

State income tax: None.

Intangibles tax: Assessed on stocks, bonds and other specified assets, with some investments exempt. Tax rate is $1 per $1,000 of value for assets under $100,000 for individuals or $200,000 for couples, and $1.50 per $1,000 of value for greater amounts; first $20,000 for individuals and $40,000 is exempt.

Estate tax: None, except the state's "pick-up" portion of the federal tax, applicable to taxable estates above $675,000.

Inheritance tax: None.

Property tax: In the beachside portion of Longboat Key, $36.76 per $1,000 of assessed value and in the bayside portion, $28.46 per $1,000 of assessed value, with all homes assessed at 100% of market value. (In Sarasota County portion, tax rates vary depending on location of the home.) Taxes on a $441,000 condominium are about $14,000 beachside, $11,000 bayside, with the homestead exemption noted below.

Homestead exemption: $25,000 off assessed value of permanent, primary residences.

Security: 17.8 crimes per 1,000 residents, lower than the national average of 46.2 crimes per 1,000 residents.

Religion: Four places of worship; an interfaith chapel, a Roman Catholic church, Episcopal church, and a Jewish temple. More options are available in Sarasota.

Education: On the mainland in Sarasota County: Sarasota County Technical Institute offers continuing adult education, New College-University of South Florida is part of the state university system, and the Ringling School of Art and Design has classes in every medium. In Manatee County, both Manatee Technical Institute and Manatee Community College offer continuing education.

Transportation: Public bus service by SCAT (Sarasota County Area Transit) serves the island. The Sarasota/Bradenton International Airport is about 14 miles away.

Health: Bay Isles Medical Center offers walk-in health care on the island. In Sarasota, 952-bed Sarasota Memorial Hospital, about seven miles away, and 168-bed Doctors Hospital, about 14 miles away, are acute-care facilities. Bradenton's 512-bed Manatee Memorial Hospital, offering acute care, is about 20 miles away.

Housing options: Single-family homes, condominiums, apartments and manufactured homes are available. Arvida's **Grand Bay** is a condominium community overlooking Sarasota Bay, with homes priced from $359,000 to $1.2 million and higher. **Islander Club** is an established beachfront high-rise condominium with units priced around $400,000. Resales at Arvida's **Seaplace** are possible for $198,000-$399,000. Contact Peter Snyder, Century 21 Dockside, (877) 941-0210 for more detailed information.

Visitor lodging: The Colony Beach and Tennis Resort, (800) 4-COLONY, is an 18-acre gulfside all-suite resort known for its world-class tennis facility and award-winning dining; nightly rates are $395-$645 high season, $195-$365 low season. The Resort at Longboat Key Club, (800) 237-8821, is gulf-front with condominium suites, most with kitchens, private beach, 45 holes of championship golf, 38 tennis courts, and superior dining; rates are $250-$985 high season, $140-$505 low season. Holiday Inn Longboat Key, (800) HOLIDAY, is beachfront with outdoor pool, indoor recreation center and four tennis courts; rates are $194-$309 high season, $189-$219 low season.

Information: Longboat Key Chamber of Commerce, 6854 Gulf of Mexico Drive, Longboat Key, FL 34228, (941) 383-2466 or www.longboatkeychamber.com. Sarasota Convention and Visitors Bureau, 655 N. Tamiami Trail, Sarasota, FL 34236, (800) 522-9799. Bradenton Area Convention and Visitors Bureau, P.O. Box 1000, Bradenton, FL 34206, (800) 4-MANATEE or www.sarasotafl.org.

almost doubled in value. Len jokes that some of the extra value is in his carpeted garage (where he builds his own golf clubs) complete with a few putting holes for those occasional rainy days he can't tee off for 18 with the men's league at Longboat Key Club.

Milt and Audrey Lucow came to Longboat Key in 1974, looked around and bought a condominium the same year. When it came time to retire, they never considered another site.

"It's like a vacation every day, and we stay so busy sometimes we don't know what day it is," says Audrey, 70, a professed housewife who doesn't cook but can make dinner reservations.

The Lucows live eight months a year in their 1,500-square-foot, gulf-front condominium at The Islander Club and four months in a condo in West Bloomfield, MI, outside Detroit, where Milt, 71, practiced law for 48 years.

"We fell in love with Longboat during the time we were snowbirds coming down for one week, two weeks, a month and then two and three months at a time. We made so many new friends and really enjoy the culture," says Audrey.

From their ninth-floor Islander Club condominium, the Lucows survey Harbourside Golf Course, Sarasota Bay and the city beyond. "We knew we'd retire here and bought a large apartment to begin with," says Milt. "At nights we see the city and marina lights, and it's beautiful."

Both avid golfers, Milt also is a regular on the tennis courts. He serves as vice president of the Islander Club Condo Association, and Audrey is chairman of the interior design committee. Actively involved in the Sarasota/Manatee Jewish Welfare Association, they are members of Longboat Key's Temple Beth Israel.

When Tom and Genevieve ("Gen") White, both 80, moved from the Washington, DC, area to Longboat Key in 1970, she cried all the way. "Now I love it!" she confesses. Gen represented the national building industry as "America's Foremost Homemaker" when she and Tom lived in New York City, then she opened an interior design business when they moved to the capital.

"I had a stroke, and my doctor knew about Longboat Key and suggested we take a look. We had looked up and down the east coast but never Florida's west coast. While I was designing a home for a retired admiral on Bird Key (a residential community in Sarasota Bay), we visited Longboat Key. Before we left we bought a house. That was 18 years ago, and we don't plan to go anywhere else. Longboat Key is the most beautiful, and Sarasota has all the arts."

A former North American representative for a machinery manufacturer and a real estate agent, Tom continues to stay active in real estate on the Key.

"Twenty years ago this (Longboat) wasn't the town it is today. The average price for a condo now is over $400,000 and the very expensive homes are moving for $4 (million) and $5 million. Some condos are going for $2.5 million," Tom says. The Whites paid nothing close to that for their three-bedroom condominium villa at Sutton Place, which has a private beach and two pools. Of about 80 families in the complex, 20 percent are retired.

Definitely not retiring in their approach to life, Tom and Gen have a boat and stay on the go. Even after four strokes, Gen says, "I believe everyone should have some goal at retirement. Those who don't are bored and grow old too fast." She is a voracious reader, Tom loves all sports especially golf, and they both are active in the Longboat Key Chamber of Commerce and All Angels by the Sea Episcopal Church.

What they like best about Longboat Key is "the way it's being run," Tom says. "We have a mayor and commission that do a beautiful job — we elected the best. They keep the Key pristine, with no fast-food places. Our paramedics, police and fire rescue can be at your side anywhere on the island within three and one-half minutes, sometimes sooner, with all the latest equipment. All ambulances are radio-equipped for en-route contact with doctors at the hospitals, and if the bridges (to the mainland) are out, a helicopter can fly you to the hospital."

The Millers praise the arts and entertainment in the area. In addition to all the options the mainland offers, the Longboat Key Art Center provides studios for instruction and art exhibits in varied media. The center has grown to be one of the best and largest art facilities on Florida's west coast, with more than 1,000 members and a faculty of 26. The area's art appreciation is also reflected in unique shopping meccas such as Longboat's Avenue of the Flowers and neighboring St. Armands Key's renowned St. Armands Circle, replete with Italian statuary set amid tropical foliage and sidewalk cafes.

"Prospective buyers get so enchanted with all the possibilities here they need a little time to sit back and consider the multitude of options and price ranges Longboat Key offers," said JoAnn Thorpe, a sales associate with Michael Saunders & Co.'s St. Armands Circle office. "There is a lifestyle for everyone — Gulf, bay, canal, golf, lake — all kinds of residences. The golfer or boater may know exactly where they want to be, but others may need a bit more time to think about where they wish to settle in this little paradise."

Thirty-seven years after acquiring much of Ringling's former real estate holdings, Arvida Realty Sales Ltd. continues to be the driving force in the benchmark development of Longboat Key. Its properties define the island from Gulf to bay.

Arvida's newest and final Longboat condominium community, Grand Bay, consists of 272 units in several multi-story buildings surrounded by the eighth and ninth holes of the Harbourside Golf Course and adjacent to the Harbourside Moorings Marina. Offering both Gulf and bay views, private elevators, tile entryways and open, bright floor plans, the condos range from $359,000 to more than $1.2 million.

The Lucows say the cost of living on Longboat Key is similar to where they lived before, but the Millers and the Whites have found it less expensive. All feel area health care is better.

The seasonal swell of traffic and winter's onslaught of snowbirds (as these retirees themselves used to be) are the only downsides to Longboat Key, they say. Winter visitors to the area boost the normal 8,000 population to nearly 22,000.

Len Miller wishes he and Fran had moved to Longboat Key 20 years ago. Tom White's advice to anyone considering the area for retirement is "COME. You're a long time dead so get down here!"●

Marble Falls, Texas

Lake-side tranquillity attracts residents to Texas Hill Country

By Judy Wade

There is no marble (it's granite) and there are no visible falls (they're now underwater), but despite the vagaries of its romantic name, Marble Falls does not disappoint.

The small Texas Hill Country town, dating back more than 100 years, sits by long, skinny Lake Marble Falls, the middle lake in a scenic chain that has become one of the state's most popular freshwater playgrounds.

Known as the Highland Lakes, the chain stretches northwest from Austin, the state capital, and includes lakes Buchanan, Inks, Lyndon B. Johnson, Travis and Austin.

In the 1930s the taming of the unpredictable Colorado River began with the construction of dams to harness the river's energy and control its wild swings from drought to flood. The lakes were a fortuitous side effect, and residents and visitors quickly realized their recreational potential.

Grassy parks, children's camps, campgrounds and marina facilities line the shores of Lake Marble Falls. All six lakes are computer-monitored so that the water remains at constant levels, providing excellent bass fishing, boating, sailing and other water sports.

With an amiable, sunny climate, the area fosters outdoor activities year-round. In spring, Texas bluebonnets, Indian paintbrush and black-eyed Susans carpet the banks of the lakes and surrounding hills with brilliant blues, reds and yellows. Summer is hot, but fall brings near-perfect weather — warm days and cool evenings — that often lingers through Thanksgiving. Winter usually is mild, though a dusting of snow is possible.

With a population of only 5,064, Marble Falls is the largest town in Burnet County. Outlying communities of homes have grown around Lake Marble Falls and adjacent Lake LBJ.

Although slightly less than 50 miles northwest of Austin and 85 miles north of San Antonio, the area feels far removed from the urban scene. Friendly locals are fond of saying that their idea of a traffic jam is three whitetails at a deer crossing or four painted buntings at the bird feeder.

Don't mistake small for backwards, though. In 1917 Marble Falls was the nation's first town to have a woman mayor elected by an all-male vote. Mrs. Ophelia (Birdie) Crosby Harwood did her sex proud by guiding the fledgling community through rough developmental times.

"We love this area," says Jaynet Baye, an artist. "People here are well-traveled because so many are military. They're not just set in their little world."

Jaynet, 62, and her husband, Firmin, 63, returned to Texas for retirement after traveling worldwide during his military career. San Antonio has several military bases, and many who serve there retire in the area.

Another couple, Paul and Enid Totten, came south to escape the chilly climate and big-city headaches of Euclid, OH, in the Cleveland area. They settled in Meadowlakes, adjacent to Marble Falls.

"We had always thought we would retire to Florida. My parents had retired there and one of our children went to college there, but when it came right down to it, when we went to Florida, it was too crowded," says Enid, 72.

They had property on Padre Island in south Texas but took suggestions to check out the Hill Country and Marble Falls before making a decision.

When the Tottens saw Meadowlakes, they didn't look any further. "We contracted to buy a house on our first visit here. We were the eighteenth family to move in," says Enid.

Paul, 73, says they enjoy swimming, golfing and riding their bikes down to the lake, which is only four blocks from their home.

Meadowlakes is an incorporated community with its own mayor and is protected with a 24-hour guard gate and perimeter fence. Although it is not age-restricted, about 75 percent of residents are retired. The community has a country club, 18-hole golf course, six lighted tennis courts, pool and restaurant. Most homes range from $100,000 to $250,000, with waterfront homes up to $450,000. Architectural restrictions guide the building of homes. Many of the residents are from Texas, California, Arizona and New Mexico.

Former New Jerseyites John and Barbara Racz chose to live in another popular community, Horseshoe Bay, about 15 minutes west of Marble Falls on Lake LBJ. It has homes along three championship golf courses and the lake, where residents have private docks and boat garages. Prices start at about $200,000. There are no age restrictions, but many retirees have settled here.

The Raczes bought their Horseshoe Bay lot while visiting friends there. Six years later they built a 4,000-square-foot retirement home. "We need all that space for our seven grandchildren," laughs Barbara, 61, whose colorful needlework decorates walls and pillows.

John, 61, notes that their home is built of limestone from nearby quarries. A fifth-generation German stonemason created a wall-size limestone fireplace, which complements white oak paneling with birch and maple accents.

Another popular "homesite" is the River View RV Park, which attracts a number of retirees who call their RV home and enjoy roaming the country. Directly on the south bank of Lake Marble Falls, the park draws all sorts of recreational vehicles, from tiny trailers to large fifth wheels (rigs pulled by a pickup truck), which make the park a temporary home the year-round.

Managers John and Mona Wefler (he's 68, she's 65) now consider the park their permanent digs. After eight years on the road as full-time RVers, they anchored their unit in Marble Falls because, they say, it's the friendliest place of any they've visited. The park has 38 sites, four directly on the waterfront, with barbecue pits and picnic tables.

Even though Marble Falls is small, it has two rental complexes that pro- vide seniors with assisted living as needed, 800 Claremont and Gateway Villa.

A commitment to history helps cement a sense of community in the town. The stone and log Adam R. Johnson House, built in 1860 by the city's founder, stands today on its original site. The Marble Falls Depot, now the chamber of commerce office, has been moved but has endured since its 1893 construction.

You can stop for a soda at 100-year-old Michel's Drug Store, the state's longest-serving pharmacy, which still dispenses frothy, old-fashioned fountain sodas. The 1880 double-galleried hotel known as the Roper House has become a professional building, and other historic structures along Main Street now house antique shops, galleries and crafts boutiques.

Area residents tend to take their safety for granted.

"I never lock my house or my car doors," says Gayle Dalton, 53. "I have friends in Houston who are concerned about the crime there and are planning to move to Marble Falls. I sent them a clipping from our local paper a few months back with a headline that said 'First Murder In Burnet County In Ten Years.' I told them they'd better hurry and move because our crime rate is soaring," she laughs.

While there are no official figures, the cost of living is considered about average, although the median housing price is a low $84,000.

Health care needs in Marble Falls

Marble Falls, TX

Population: 5,064 in Marble Falls, 10,702 in seven-mile radius.

Location: In Texas Hill Country on the Colorado River, 47 miles northwest of Austin, 85 miles north of San Antonio. In the middle of the Highland Lakes area, the largest chain of lakes in Texas.

Climate:

	High	Low
January	77	18
July	99	68

Average relative humidity: 40%
Rain: 30 inches.
Mild, fairly dry climate with hot summers. Area is subject to tornadoes, severe thunderstorms and occasional flooding. Winter brings occasional snowfalls.

Cost of living: Average (specific index not available).

Median housing cost: $84,000 (higher for lake communities).

Sales tax: 8.25%
Sales tax exemptions: Groceries, prescription drugs, professional services, medical supplies.
State income tax: None.
Intangibles tax: None.
Estate tax: None, except the state's "pick-up" portion of the federal tax, applicable to taxable estates above $675,000.
Property tax: Rate is $23.17 per $1,000 of assessed valuation, with homes assessed at 100% of market value. Yearly tax on an $84,000 home is $1,946 without any applicable exemptions.
Homestead exemption: $5,000, or $18,000 if age 65 or older, off assessed value for school portion of taxes; $3,000 off assessed value for county special road-tax portion.
Security: 38.7 crimes per 1,000 residents, lower than the national average of 46.2 crimes per 1,000 residents.
Religion: Nineteen churches represent a dozen denominations.
Education: Nearest colleges offering adult education courses are in Austin: The University of Texas at Austin, Austin Community College and St. Edwards University.
Transportation: No local transportation, but the Burnet County Commu-

nity Transit has buses that link towns within the county. Austin has the nearest commercial airport, 50 miles away.
Health: Highland Lakes Medical Center in Burnet, 12 miles north of Marble Falls, is an acute-care facility with 42 beds. StarFlight helicopter ambulance in Austin and Air Life in San Antonio serve the area. The town has five general practitioners and 10 specialized physicians.
Housing options: Horseshoe Bay, (800) 292-1545, on Lake LBJ has luxury homes on the waterfront and three golf courses; prices start at about $200,000. Homes in the gated community of **Meadowlakes**, on Lake Marble Falls, begin at about $100,000; property is available through real estate agents. **Gateway Villa**, (830) 693-1800, has assisted-living units starting at $1,535 a month, and **800 Claremont**, (830) 693-6446, has assisted-living apartments from about $1,500 a month.
Visitor lodging: Horseshoe Bay Resort & Conference Club, on Lake LBJ, from $181 for a double, (800) 252-9363. Best Western, $89, (830) 693-5122.
Information: Marble Falls/Lake LBJ Chamber of Commerce, 801 Highway 281, Marble Falls, TX 78654, (800) 759-8178 or www.marblefalls.org.

are met by 12 general practitioners and 25-30 specialized physicians. A number of specialists make weekly visits from larger towns. The closest hospital is Highland Lakes Medical Center in Burnet, 12 miles away. It's a 42-bed acute-care facility with a fully staffed emergency room and other services.

Paul Totten is among the Marble Falls volunteer Emergency Medical Service (EMS) corps that responds to area calls for urgent care. He's trained and certified in emergency medical procedures. Two air evacuation helicopter services transport serious medical cases to Austin or San Antonio.

The Senior Activity Center, open for a portion of every weekday, has potluck meals Monday and Friday noon followed by afternoon games. Exercise classes and crafts are offered on other days. Twice-a-month dances with live music keep members hopping, says president Judy Frasier, 71.

Judy says the area is great for finding a good husband.

"We've had a lot of marriages here within the club. I've been married just four years," Judy says. A $10 initiation fee and $5 per month dues allow access to all club activities.

Artists and crafts enthusiasts find a variety of activities through the Highland Arts Guild artists' co-op on Main Street. As part of the Highland Lakes Arts Council, the co-op promotes arts and crafts by offering exhibits, classes, workshops and demonstrations by members and visiting artists. Jaynet Baye's oils and pastels are among the works on display.

While Marble Falls High School sometimes offers evening college credit courses and continuing-education classes, opportunities for higher education are best sought in nearby Austin, which has both community college campuses and the University of Texas. Marble Falls does have a library, which has videotapes and compact discs as well as books and periodicals.

Dining-out choices tend toward inexpensive home-cooking cafes and barbecue, although the Captain's Quarters in Horseshoe Bay offers a fine dining experience.

Besides water sports on the lake, there are seven area golf courses, playable year-round. Scenic horseback trails, good deer hunting, and fishing for striped, white and largemouth bass as well as catfish and crappie are within minutes.

The closest Marble Falls gets to heavy metal is the Hill Country Flyer, five vintage passenger coaches pulled by 70-year-old Steam Engine 736 that huffs into nearby Burnet on weekends. A half-day excursion over sparkling rivers and through green valleys is $24 for adults, $10 for children.

There's little to fault about the area, the couples interviewed say. The Raczes like the small-town atmosphere but wish that Marble Falls had a hospital and better shopping. "We have to go to Austin for serious shopping," Barbara says.

Paul Totten says their first two winters were colder than expected, but others haven't been as cold since then.

So what about the missing falls and the elusive marble that gave the town its name?

The 20-foot cascade that once thundered into the Colorado River has long disappeared under waters that rose with the completion of the Max Starke Dam in 1951.

The huge pink monolith called Granite Mountain on the town's western edge secured Marbles Falls' place in Texas history. It was here that the Texas pink granite of the State Capitol building was quarried, a donation from far-sighted citizens in exchange for a rail connection with Austin.

No one in Marble Falls seems to care that it isn't marble.●

Maryville, Tennessee

Smoky Mountains town in eastern Tennessee attracts nature-loving retirees

By Richard L. Fox

Tucked in the foothills of eastern Tennessee's Smoky Mountains, Maryville's greatest asset is its enviable location.

Far from busy interstate highways and crowded urban centers, modern-day worries are forgotten — at least temporarily — when one is greeted daily by panoramic vistas of rolling, velvety slopes. A slower pace, small liberal arts college and abundance of outdoor recreation further add to the appeal of this quiet town of 24,000.

Maryville, the seat and geographical center of Blount County, cherishes its Smoky Mountains connection. Spring festivals celebrate regional heritage, wildlife and crafts, and in fall, residents and tourists alike take delight in a spectacular show of colorful foliage.

Many retirees, primarily attracted by the beauty of the mountains and lakes, live in rural planned developments outside Maryville and rely on the town for cultural, educational and social amenities.

"We love the isolation. We have bears, wild turkeys, deer and foxes roaming the area, and we live within walking distance of some wonderful hiking trails in the Great Smokies," says Bob Tiebout (pronounced Te-BOO). He and his wife, Lil, moved 22 times during his military career before settling in a gated community near Maryville in June 1994.

The Tiebouts began their search for a retirement town with a long list of requirements. "We wanted a planned community with plenty of space and facilities for outdoor recreation. We wanted a college town, quick access to air travel, and proximity to a military PX and medical facility. We got all of that — and a lot more," says Bob, 58.

The area's low cost of living and taxes that are among the lowest in the country were big incentives in their choice. "After spending our last two service years in Washington, DC, we were looking for economy," says Bob. "It's very economical here. Property taxes and utilities are very, very reasonable."

The Tiebouts found a home at Laurel Valley Country Club in Townsend. A scenic 16-mile drive south of Maryville, the 1,600-acre planned residential development backs up to Great Smoky Mountains National Park. Plans call for 450 homesites ranging in size from quarter-acre lots to 10-acre tracts. To date, about 170 homes have been constructed, with prices ranging from $150,000 to $850,000.

Laurel Valley offers a clubhouse, pool, sports bar and 18-hole golf course. Residents joke that the manned security gates are in place to keep out bears rather than criminals.

Opportunities for recreational activities abound throughout Blount County. Bicycling along lightly traveled roads is such a popular sport that the chamber of commerce offers a brochure with detailed descriptions of routes covering more than 100 miles.

For hiking, there are more than 125 miles of designated trails, including Greenbelt Park's two-mile lighted fitness trail and exercise course in the heart of Maryville.

Lakes Fort Loudoun, Tellico and Chilhowee and the Tennessee and Little Tennessee rivers form a semicircle to the west of Maryville. Sailboats, canoes, houseboats and cruisers ply these waters in search of fish, waterfowl and spectacular scenery.

To the south there is white-water rafting on the Nantahala and Ocoee rivers, and about 40 miles to the east is the Ober Gatlinburg Ski Resort.

Dr. Chuck and Jane Gariety vacationed in the Smoky Mountains for 15 years before moving permanently in 1992. "The mountains, climate and relaxed lifestyle that brought us here as vacationers keep us here as residents," says Jane, 64.

Formerly residents of Piqua, OH, the Garietys first bought property on Cherokee Lake northeast of Knoxville. After two years, the Garietys felt they had not formed strong attachments to that area. They also found that the glistening lake waters of summer nearly disappeared in winter when the Tennessee Valley Authority, which manages the lake, lowered the water level by 40 feet.

"If we had it to do over we would have moved here first," says Jane.

Like the Tiebouts, the Garietys moved to Laurel Oaks and appreciate its proximity to the national park. Chuck, 68, is a self-described do-it-yourselfer who enjoys woodworking and gardening. He took up golf after retirement and now lists it as his favorite recreational activity. Both Chuck and Jane love the mountainous landscape and the easy accessibility to area lakes.

As a bonus to Maryville's natural abundance, the urban trappings of several major cities are readily available. Travel from downtown Maryville to Knoxville is a quick 20 miles on the recently completed Pellissippi Parkway. Chattanooga is about 100 miles to the southwest, and Nashville is 194 miles west. McGhee Tyson Airport, the metropolitan Knoxville facility with more than 100 scheduled daily flights, is minutes away by car.

Maryville is off the major interstate highways, preventing heavy traffic from flowing through town. (From downtown Maryville, it is 17 miles to Interstate 40 and 22 miles to Interstate 75.) This has helped Maryville retain a peaceful and safe atmosphere, something retirees often cite as a factor in their decision to move here. According to FBI Uniform Crime Reports, Maryville reports 31.7 crimes per 1,000 persons, mostly thefts and burglaries. The national average is 46.2 per 1,000 residents.

"We wanted to be close to a large city, but far enough away not to be caught up in the traffic, crowds and crime," says Ed Crick.

Originally from Fort Washington, MD, Ed and his wife, Faye, ended a 10-year search for the right retirement town when they discovered Maryville. "We had looked all the way from Florida to Pennsylvania but couldn't find what we were looking for," explains Ed, 65, a retired federal auditor. "We visited Maryville for the first time in January 1993, left for two weeks, and came back and bought a lot. We've never second-guessed our decision."

Ed and Faye settled in Royal Oaks Country Club, a gatehouse-secure golf community within Maryville city limits. "It was a fairly new community with just 50 or 60 families at the time. We had an opportunity to get in on the ground floor and meet people as they came in. It now has around 160 households — mostly retired — and we know everyone who lives here," Ed says.

Faye, a former schoolteacher, serves on the official welcoming committee for Royal Oaks, and Ed is treasurer and on the board of directors for the

Maryville, TN

Population: 24,000 in Maryville, 100,000 in Blount County.

Location: In southeast Tennessee at an elevation of about 1,000 feet, within view of the Appalachian Mountains and Great Smoky Mountains National Park.

Climate:

	High	Low
January	47	30
July	87	68

Average relative humidity: 59%

Rain: 47 inches **Snow:** 12 inches

Cost of living: Below average (specific index not available).

Average housing cost: Approximately $100,000, according to the Blount County property assessor's office.

Sales tax: 8.25%

Sales tax exemptions: Prescription drugs, professional services, hearing aids, prosthetic devices.

State income tax: None on earned income, but there is a state tax of 6% on interest and dividend income from certain stocks, bonds, long-term notes and mortgages. Interest from CDs, savings accounts and federal, state or local government bonds is exempt.

Income tax exemptions: $1,250 exemption ($2,500 for married couples filing jointly). Individuals 65 or older with total annual income of $16,200 or less ($27,000 for joint filers) are exempt from the tax.

Intangibles tax: None.

Estate tax: None, except the state's "pick-up" portion of the federal tax, applicable to taxable estates above $675,000.

Inheritance tax: From 5.5% to 9.5%, based on amount of inheritance; spouse normally exempt.

Property tax: $44 per $1,000 of assessed value, with homes assessed at 25% of market value. Yearly tax on a $100,000 home is about $1,100.

Homestead exemption: An income-related exemption is available to homeowners age 65 and older.

Security: 31.7 crimes per 1,000 residents, lower than national average of 46.2 crimes per 1,000 residents.

Religion: There are 219 Protestant and two Catholic churches in Blount County.

Education: Maryville College is a liberal arts institution offering baccalaureate degrees in 33 majors. Pellissippi State Technical Community College has a campus in Blount County, and the University of Tennessee in Knoxville is about 30 minutes away.

Transportation: McGhee Tyson Airport (also called Metropolitan Knoxville Airport), only minutes from downtown Maryville, is served by five major carriers and six commuter airlines with 110 scheduled flights daily.

Health: Blount Memorial Hospital is a 334-bed, acute-care facility with a trauma center equipped for all medical emergencies except neurological and cardiac surgery. Eight hospitals and medical centers in Knoxville include the University of Tennessee Medical Center, a full-service facility with a trauma center and complete range of specialties.

Housing options: Recent listings include a new two-bedroom, two-bath home in **Laurel Valley Country Club**, (423) 448-2040, for $124,900; a two-bedroom, two-bath log cabin in a rural neighborhood for $76,900; and new three-bedroom, two-bath homes for $72,900-$89,900 in **Grand Vista**, a subdivision just outside city limits. **Royal Oaks Country Club**, (423) 448-2040, offers golf villas starting at $97,900 and custom single-family homes starting at $129,900. At **Rarity Bay**, (423) 884-3000, a 960-acre gated community southwest of Maryville on Lake Tellico, wooded homesites start at $37,000, golf course lots start at $44,000, and homesites on the waterfront are priced up to $235,000.

Visitor lodging: Rates at Airport Hilton-Alcoa start at $79 on weekends, (423) 970-4300. Rates at Hampton Inn-Townsend are $79-$84 with continental breakfast, (865) 448-9000. The Inn at Blackberry Farm, a 1,100-acre retreat, provides three meals daily and use of all amenities for $395-$845 per couple, per day, (800) 862-7610. Rustic cabins in secluded mountain settings are available in a wide range of prices; call the Smoky Mountains Visitors Bureau, (800) 525-6834.

Information: Blount County Chamber of Commerce, 201 S. Washington St., Maryville, TN 37804-5728, (865) 983-2241 or www.chamber.blount.tn.us.

property owners association. Ed also serves as a counselor for SCORE (Service Corps of Retired Executives), which advises small businesses. He does not plan to take on more activities any time soon: "I don't want to get so involved I don't have time for golf."

Ed and Faye both took up golf soon after moving to Royal Oaks and say it is their favorite hobby. The community boasts two of the county's seven 18-hole golf courses and eventually will have 750 single-family homes and 500 golf villas situated around the greens. Villas range from 1,676 to 2,586 square feet and are priced from approximately $97,900 to $179,900. Custom homes on a lake, in the woods or on the golf course run about $129,900 to $389,900.

There are housing options in Maryville for those not looking for gated, planned communities. New three-bedroom homes in town with 1,200-1,500 square feet are available for $72,900 to $89,900, while five-acre tracts in the suburbs can be purchased for $15,000 to $20,000.

A good hospital was high on the list of amenities Ed Crick sought in a retirement town. Health-care needs are met by 128 medical doctors and 464 registered nurses practicing in 334-bed Blount County Memorial Hospital. The hospital is equipped for all medical emergencies except neurological and cardiac surgery. In Knoxville there are more than 2,500 practitioners of every medical specialty and subspecialty.

Bob Tiebout, who used the facilities at famed Bethesda Naval Hospital while stationed in Washington, DC, is content with the local services. "We live within 20 minutes of Blount County Memorial and have access to Fort Sanders Regional Medical Cen-ter in Knoxville. We are more than satisfied with the health-care options in this area."

In the center of town stands the quiet, tree-lined campus of Maryville College. The liberal arts school with a Presbyterian Church connection was founded in 1819 and provided a way out of the mountains for many young people. Now it's one of the beacons attracting retirees to these mountains.

The 370-acre campus has 20 major buildings, including several listed on the National Register of Historic Places. With an enrollment of just 850, this small college contributes to the town's quality of life without dominating its pace and rhythms. The doors of its library are open to residents for study and browsing. Beautiful campus paths and serene wooded trails, easily accessible from downtown, are favorites among residents for walking, hiking and running.

The college's 1,200-seat Wilson Chapel and 400-seat Maryville College Playhouse theater offer orchestral and choral concerts and theatrical productions. Art gallery exhibits, the school's Appalachian Ballet Company and Division III NCAA athletic events add to the mix of activities available to the community through the college. There's also a series of non-credit courses designed for seniors.

The musically talented can toot their own horns by trying out for the Maryville-Alcoa College Community Orchestra. Made up of college musicians and residents of Maryville and nearby Alcoa, the orchestra performs six concerts a year.

Festivals are among the favorite rites of spring and fall in Maryville, and all conspire to foster an appreciation of the great outdoors. Coinciding with the blooming of the dog-woods in April is the Dogwood Arts Festival, sponsored by the chamber of commerce to raise funds for local charities. Events include an invitational softball tournament, arts and crafts show, a trout rodeo, Tour de Blount Bicycle Race, golf tournament and bluegrass jamboree.

Also in April, the Appalachian Wildflower Celebration features garden tours, bird-watching walks, wildflower hikes and wildlife programs. At the end of the month, the eight-day Townsend in the Smokies Spring Festival offers food, music and the natural beauty of the Great Smoky Mountains. The Autumn Leaves Arts and Crafts Fair in late September entertains the crowds who come to see the changing of colors that ushers in the fall season.

Civic organizations, many sponsored by the chamber of commerce, make an impact on the social, cultural and economic life of Maryville. Beautiful Blount, a group involved in beautification projects, recycling and litter education, and Blount County Partnership, a cooperative effort of four organizations, are among two dozen groups in town that work toward community improvement. Retirees work alongside civic leaders to recruit new industry, promote tourism, support education and develop cultural and philanthropic projects.

Maryville retirees find little to complain about. A few wish for better shopping and dining options, adding that Blount County is a "dry" county.

And though Bob Tiebout still misses the "camaraderie, and fervor of political drama" of military life in Washington, DC, he plans to stay in east Tennessee for the nature and the outdoor lifestyle he's come to enjoy.

"Every season has its own character, and all are beautiful," says Bob.●

Mountain Home, Arkansas

Arkansas Ozarks reel in residents who love the lakes and quiet life

By Brenda Blagg

Lakes loaded with lunker bass, rivers teeming with trout and a feeling of peace and security — these are the lures to Mountain Home, an Arkansas haven for retirees seeking life at a slower pace.

As one man put it, this is not the place for people who want the hustle and bustle of big-city life. Instead, retirees find "country quiet" and "breathtaking scenery" in the Ozark Mountains.

Many retirees are first hooked on the region when they come for family vacations, centered around fishing, boating and other water sports on scenic rivers and the area's twin lakes, Norfork and Bull Shoals.

Located in north-central Arkansas near the Missouri border, Mountain Home has a little over 10,000 residents and is the seat of Baxter County, which touts itself as "a good place to grow up and a good place to wind down." The county claims a population of more than 36,000 citizens now, with one of three citizens age 64 or older.

Floyd Cannedy, 69, and his wife, Iola, 65, both originally from the Midwest, moved to Mountain Home in 1994 from Hattiesburg, MS. For a couple of years, they had looked at possible retirement places, including some in Florida. Avid campers, they were in Branson, MO, when a camping buddy suggested they look at Mountain Home, less than 100 miles away.

"We just fell in love with the place," says Iola, explaining that their first stop was the local Presbyterian church. They knew "not a soul" in the town, but on that first Sunday were invited to join an impromptu group of 25 people for lunch.

"That's an every-Sunday occurrence," adds Floyd, noting that restaurants are accustomed to throwing tables together for unscheduled gatherings.

The friendliness and that first "open-arms welcome" convinced them that moving to Mountain Home was "the thing to do," says Floyd, who was in the insurance business.

The only thing they would do differently is "just move here quicker," says Iola, noting a popular bumper sticker that says: "We weren't raised in Mountain Home but we got here as fast as we could."

The Cannedys say the cost of living is a trade-off, with some things higher than in Mississippi and some lower; both states are known for low living costs compared to other areas. Overall, the Cannedys say it's costing them less to live in retirement especially since life is so casual in Mountain Home.

"Church is about the only place you see people dressed up," Floyd says.

With no relatives in town, the Cannedys and other retirees "buddy with each other," Floyd says. He describes Mountain Home as "a great domino-playing town" with a wide range of activities for seniors, including a "very lively" senior center.

The first time the Cannedys left town on one of their camping trips, they returned to find their lawn had been mowed. They extend the same courtesy to their neighbors now. "Everybody just kind of looks after each other...it's wonderful to know people care," says Floyd.

The Cannedys have few complaints or cautions for others who might move to Mountain Home. Some areas of town have drainage problems and utility service is interrupted in bad weather, they say. Summer brings tourists and increased traffic, but a recently completed bypass has alleviated traffic problems. Otherwise, says Iola, "It's a wonderful place to live."

Mountain Home looks like many small Southern towns. Once centered around a courthouse square, development has shifted to highways that slice through the town, stretching either to the twin lakes or to transportation corridors. While the commercial strips look like almost any other town, the historic courthouse and older homes and buildings lend some distinct character.

Vernon Wolfram, 70, and his wife, Vivian, 68, moved south from their Detroit-area home in 1990, fulfilling a promise made when they married in 1948. At the time they both lived in St. Louis, his hometown, but Vivian had spent part of her youth in Fort Smith, AR. She exacted a promise from Vernon that they would return to Arkansas when they retired.

"I told Vern it would be in Arkansas someplace — we just had to find where," she says.

When retirement time came, they narrowed the search to three towns — Bella Vista, Rogers and Mountain Home, all in northern Arkansas. The couple spent a week in each, touring and looking at prospective homes.

On the last of their weeklong outings, the only time they visited Mountain Home before their move, the Wolframs shot video of a three-bedroom house they liked. Back in Michigan, they looked at the video night after night, then called the real estate agent to cut a deal on their "perfect" retirement home.

Vivian says, "The books we read led us to Mountain Home — for economy, for the beauty of the land." And "for (low) taxes," Vern adds.

"When we came and found out how great the people were and we found this house in this area," Vivian says, "we knew it was right."

Vern, a former plant manager for Ford Motor Co., actually retired twice. After almost 30 years with Ford, he took an early retirement but soon went to work for a Ford supplier and worked another 10 years. The couple downsized their lives, moving three times in the Detroit area as their four children completed their education and left home.

"It took us 10 years to get here," says Vivian.

Their home, in a wooded subdivision near Lake Norfork, sits on a "lot and a half," which is large enough to accommodate a big vegetable garden, one of Vern's passions. The site is well away from what Vivian calls the "busy-ness" of town, yet Vern says the neighborhood has plenty of action. Anytime he's outside, he discovers he must wave to everyone who drives by – if he doesn't they'll stop to see if he's OK.

Vern speaks of a sense of community that stretches down the block and to the next street, not just to the next house or two as in his Michigan experience. When the Wolframs moved in, the neighbors welcomed them with food; now the Wolframs do the same for others moving into the fast-growing subdivision.

They had planned to learn to fish when they got to Mountain Home, but they haven't had time. Both are busy volunteers, active in their church and pursuing hobbies in writing and crafts. Vivian has published three compilations of recipes and a collection of her thoughts on life. They also are in a boating club, one of many area organizations that match resi-

dents with common interests from politics to pansies, square dancing to china painting.

Vern says the most pleasant surprise in their move was paying taxes the first time. Taxes on the house, two cars and a boat, he says, were just $600.

The Wolframs' one-level home, originally purchased for $75,000 six years ago, is valued at $115,000 now, but it is definitely not for sale. They don't miss the stairs or the snow and ice they had in Michigan.

Mountain Home does get snow, but it usually doesn't last long.

Four distinct seasons and the opportunity to play golf and fish year-round were among the draws for Mid-

Mountain Home, AR

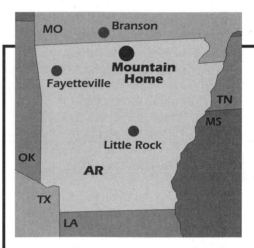

Population: 10,367 in town, 36,402 in Baxter County.

Location: In the Ozark Mountains of north-central Arkansas, 25 miles south of the Missouri border.

Climate:

	High	Low
January	46	24
July	91	67

Average relative humidity: 55%

Rain: 42 inches.

Snow: 8 inches.

Mild climate with four distinct seasons. Outdoor activities are possible most of the year. Snowfalls are usually light and melt quickly.

Cost of living: Below average (specific index not available).

Average housing cost: $90,614. Most homes under 10 years old in the area run $80,000-$120,000.

Sales tax: 6.625%

Sales tax exemptions: Medical/professional services and prescription drugs.

State income tax: Graduated in six steps from 1% to 7%, depending on income

Income tax exemptions: Social Security benefits and $6,000 of employer-sponsored pensions exempt.

Intangibles tax: None.

Estate tax: None, except the state's "pick-up" portion of the federal tax, applicable to taxable estates above $675,000.

Inheritance tax: None.

Property tax: In Mountain Home, $39.22 per $1,000 of assessed value, with homes assessed at 20 percent of market value. Yearly tax on a $90,614 home is $728. Also, specified personal property, including vehicles, livestock and farm equipment, is subject to taxes at the same rate as homes.

Homestead exemption: Local property taxes must be paid, but a rebate from the state is available to seniors with incomes below $15,000.

Security: 26.1 crimes per 1,000 residents, lower than the national average of 46.2 crimes per 1,000 residents.

Religion: About 50 churches represent a wide range of denominations.

Education: Arkansas State University-Mountain Home has two-year university classes and occupational, technical and vocational programs. Seniors may attend credit courses tuition-free

on a space-available basis.

Transportation: There is no local bus service. Baxter County Regional Airport has commuter service to St. Louis and Dallas, and there's long-distance bus service.

Health: Baxter County Regional Hospital in Mountain Home has 197 beds, more than 100 specialized physicians and 24-hour emergency room service. Other features include a Radiation Therapy Institute, cardiac-care unit and physical therapy unit.

Housing options: A variety of housing is available in town, in nearby communities and on the lakes and rivers. There are no planned retirement communities. Areas popular with retirees include Village Green and Indian Creek, older neighborhoods in town; and High Ridge, a development at nearby Lakeview, where new homes begin at $97,000. There also are independent-living facilities for seniors and five nursing homes.

Visitor lodging: Holiday Inn, (870) 425-5101, $62 for a double. Best Western Carriage Inn, (870) 425-6001, $65 for a double. Lakeside resorts are plentiful for around $500 a week, depending on amenities.

Information: Mountain Home Area Chamber of Commerce, P.O. Box 488, Mountain Home, AR 72653, (800) 822-3536 or www.mtnhomechamber.com.

westerners Joy and Merrill Eastman, both 69, who relocated from the Kansas City suburb of Overland Park, KS, in 1989. They settled in a community called Midway, on Route 5 midway between Mountain Home and Bull Shoals Lake.

They first planned to retire to Florida and had land there but "didn't want to fight the traffic in snowbird season," says Merrill, who had been general chairman for a railroad union.

A lower cost of living was a big factor in the Eastmans' choice of the area — including lower fees for golf, which Merrill enjoys, along with fishing. He keeps his boat in the water all year and considers a perfect day to be one in which he can fish half the day and golf the rest, or vice versa.

Joy misses the shopping opportunities they had in Kansas City and in Chicago, where they lived earlier. Mountain Home has no large malls so residents routinely make one-day outings to Springfield or Branson, MO, to shop and enjoy a wider range of entertainment.

Eugene Burroughs, 66, came home to Arkansas, bringing his wife Shirley, 45, and three youngest sons to Mountain Home after 14 years in California where he was a farm manager in the San Joaquin Valley.

"He wanted to fish. That was the main thing," says Shirley.

Eugene, who grew up in eastern Arkansas, had been thinking seriously about retiring for several years before settling on Mountain Home. Eugene always was provided a home by the farm management company, but he knew he wanted to buy his own place when he retired. "I started 20 years ago to plan for it," he says.

The Burroughs family moved in early 1995, and it's taking time for Shirley to adjust to being away from family in California, Nevada and Utah. She began volunteering at the local hospital and has made friends quickly.

Shirley and other retirees are proud of the town's medical services, the Baxter County Regional Hospital, a 197-bed facility with more than 100 active staff physicians.

Eugene considers Mountain Home a good choice for his retirement but warns those who need jobs that the wages are low. What he likes least about the place is that his sons "will have to leave here to go to work."

Elena and Victor Pollo moved from Chicago to Mountain Home more than 23 years ago. Both worked — he in watch and clock repair and she as executive secretary at Railway Express — but a heart problem soon forced Victor's early retirement. Now in their 80s, Elena and Victor are both retired but lead active lives.

Midwesterners make up a large portion of the retirees who have moved into the area. So many are from the Windy City itself that Mountain Home often is called "Little Chicago." The number of Illinois transplants in Baxter County is so high that the Mountain Home post office opens a special window to handle their business during the holidays.

Elena still misses the large department stores she rushed through to catch the commuter trains in Chicago, but she has no desire to go back to Chicago.

"You've got to understand this is different from a big city," says Elena. "It takes at least a year to make an adjustment."

Those who come here from urban areas will quickly note a lack of ethnic diversity in the community.

Like so many others, the Pollos connected with Mountain Home because of the fishing. Victor got his first glimpse of the region on a fishing trip years ago with friends. Later, when the couple visited, they happened onto what would become their retirement home.

In all their years in Mountain Home, the Pollos never considered a different house or a different town for retirement.●

Mount Dora, Florida

A century-old Florida town evokes New England charm

By Richard L. Fox

Scenic meandering pathways lead from downtown Mount Dora to the calm, blue waters of beautiful six-mile-long Lake Dora. For boat owners, the lake offers pleasant cruising waters as well as a popular shortcut to the city center from lakeside homes. It is connected by the Dora Canal to a chain of lakes leading to the St. Johns River and ultimately to the Atlantic Ocean, providing seagoing access that few inland towns can offer.

Bob and Mary Anderson had lived in rural Virginia 25 years when they discovered the small-town charm, convenience and historical legacy of Mount Dora. "We had built a room and porch on our house and planned to stay in Rockville," says Bob, 70. But then the couple planned a trip to Florida to help a neighbor who was moving in retirement, and Mary happened to see a newspaper article about Mount Dora.

"So we stopped by just for the fun of it, checked into Lakeside Inn, ordered a cocktail and watched the sunset over Lake Dora," says Bob, who retired from the office supplies industry. "The next day we drove home, sold our house and moved to Mount Dora."

Mount Dora — named for its 184-foot elevation in the generally flat Florida terrain — is an enchanting lakeside town of 9,500 residents, located 25 miles northwest of Orlando. It is characterized by its wide brick sidewalks, colorful outdoor cafes, and crafts and antique shops. Nine pretty tree-shaded parks dot the town's landscape, and they are especially attractive to seniors who enjoy tennis, shuffleboard and lawn bowling. The Mount Dora Lawn Bowling Club is the second-largest in the United States, with more than 300 members hosting local and regional competitions.

"We moved here because it was small, 'antiquish,' and we liked the preservation, old houses, the historical aspects," says Mary, 68. Mount Dora predates a rail line that opened in 1887, bringing passengers and freight to a town that had two general stores, three hotels, two churches, a drug store and a carriage factory.

"It has a nice, relaxed atmosphere and provides great access to the beaches, Disney World and Miami," adds Mary, who worked for Signet Bank in Richmond. Bob also likes the convenience of living in town, even a small one like Mount Dora. "We had never lived in a city and were tired of going 15 miles to buy groceries, attend church and enjoy city amenities," he says.

They wasted no time getting actively involved in the social and civic opportunities of their new home. "We joined everything in sight," Mary laughs. Bob joined the chamber of commerce and serves on the membership committee, and he was appointed to the city's historic preservation board. He also is on the board of trustees of the United Methodist Church. "You have to be active in civic affairs to enjoy retirement here," he says.

The relatively recent discovery by retirees and young working families of this quiet haven just minutes from Greater Orlando has had its impact on Mount Dora's population and real estate prices. The 1990 census recorded an 11 percent increase in population in the 1980s, from 6,483 to 7,196 residents. Today's count is approaching 10,000, roughly a 25 percent increase in the last 10 years. Like many retirees who were drawn to the town by its small-town atmosphere, newcomer Ed Jones says in resignation, "I hate to see it grow."

Ed and Betty Jones, from Wilmington, DE, had lived in Vero Beach and Clearwater during their working lives but sought something smaller for their retirement. "The towns had grown so much that they had lost the small-

town atmosphere we were looking for," says Betty, who was in sales prior to retirement. "We found it in Mount Dora, a place where we felt we could belong. It has lots of clubs and organizations, a nice library and very friendly people."

Waterfront housing is available along Lake Dora and on smaller lakes within a mile of the city. The quiet, tree-lined streets adjacent to downtown, resplendent with beautifully restored Victorian homes, churches and landmark commercial buildings, are popular with those who savor the history of this century-old town and the convenience of living within walking distance of the village center. Several master-planned developments offer affordable, active lifestyles just a few minutes from downtown.

In the early 1990s, Mount Dora's homes sold for $50,000 to $300,000, with a median price of $80,400, according to local appraisers. The current average price of homes sold is $133,119, says Chuck Cox, broker-owner of Baker Street Realty. However, two-bedroom homes in Silvan Shores, a charming, lakeside community, still are available for $75,000 to $100,000. Several attractive condominium and townhouse developments offered homes last year for $65,000 to $187,000. Homes within walking distance of downtown sell for $100,000 to $200,000, while most lakeshore homes are priced from $175,000 to $250,000. The Country Club of Mount Dora, a master-planned golf course development just minutes from downtown, has fairway homes and villas priced from the $100,000s to more than $500,000.

The Andersons chose a home built in 1955 on one of the smaller lakes in northwest Mount Dora, about a mile from downtown. Neighbors include residents in their 70s and 80s and young couples with children. Extensive renovations to the Andersons' home have paid off in substantial appreciation of their investment, but Bob doesn't like paying both city and county taxes — something he didn't have to do while living in rural Virginia. However, Mary claims that Virginia "had as many hidden taxes and 'gotchas' as Florida."

Though she wouldn't move "unless we win the lottery," Mary says she sometimes misses the peace and quiet of their home in rural Virginia. "Young people with loud car stereos can be a real nuisance," she says of life in Florida.

The Joneses also found a neighborhood they liked. "One reason we built in the Country Club of Mount Dora was its excellent tennis facilities," says Ed, 65, a retired engineering designer and one-time avid tennis player. Betty, also 65, enjoys the quiet, safe environment of her neighborhood, walks five days a week and spends her spare time volunteering at the chamber of commerce and the arts festival.

"There's always something going on downtown," adds Ed. Two dozen restaurants, mostly located within a six-block downtown area, range from casual sidewalk cafes and English-style tearooms to cozy, candlelit dining rooms with an international flair. These same streets harbor a dozen antiques and collectibles shops, and there's an annual Downtown Antique Fair. Renninger's Twin Markets, just outside town on U.S. Highway 441, sponsors the Antique Extravaganza in January, February and November, with more than 1,500 dealers participating.

In fact, Mount Dora leads the state as the home of major festivals. The 24th annual February Fine Arts Festival attracted almost 300,000 visitors, and the April Spring Festival, a celebration of music and literature, always packs the 300-seat Ice House Theatre, the 700-seat community building and every hotel in the area.

Mount Dora, FL

Population: 9,500
Location: In Central Florida, 25 miles northwest of Orlando.
Climate:

	High	Low
January	72	49
July	92	73

Average relative humidity: 85%
Rain: 54 inches.
Cost of living: 94 in Lake County, based on state average of 100.
Average housing cost: $133,119
Sales tax: 7%
Sales tax exemptions: Food and medicine.
State income tax: None.
Intangibles tax: Assessed on stocks, bonds and other specified assets, with some investments exempt. Tax rate is $1 per $1,000 of value for assets under $100,000 for individuals or $200,000 for couples; $1.50 per $1,000 of value for greater amounts. First $20,000 of assets ($40,000 for couples) is exempt.
Estate tax: None, except the state's "pick-up" portion of the federal tax, applicable to taxable estates above $675,000.
Property tax: The combined city-county tax rate is $21.95 per $1,000 of assessed value, with homes assessed at 100% of market value. The annual tax on a $133,000 home, with exemption noted below, is $2,371.
Homestead exemption: First $25,000 of assessed value on a primary, permanent residence.
Security: 82.9 crimes per 1,000 residents, higher than the national average of 46.2 crimes per 1,000 residents.
Religion: One Catholic and 27 Protestant churches.
Education: There are no college or university campuses in Mount Dora. Lake Sumter Community College in nearby Leesburg offers two-year associate of arts and sciences degrees, plus many continuing-education and noncredit courses. Lake County Vo-Tech in nearby Eustis offers vocational training and a school of cosmetology.
Transportation: Orlando International and Daytona Beach Regional airports are approximately 60 minutes from Mount Dora. Amtrak's East Coast auto-train stops in Sanford, 20 miles east of Mount Dora.
Health: Florida Hospital Waterman, five miles north in Eustis, is a full-service facility with 182 beds, 24-hour emergency room and 175 physicians on staff. Leesburg Regional Medical Center, 25 miles away, has 294 beds and serves a three-county area.
Housing options: Newcomers have a choice of lakeside and lake-view single-family homes, condominiums and townhouses, many within a short walking distance of downtown, priced from $65,000 to $300,000. In-town historic and contemporary homes sell for $100,000 to $200,000. At the **Country Club of Mount Dora**, (800) 213-6132, fairway homes and villas are priced from $120,000 to more than $500,000. **Waterman Village**, (352) 383-0051, a 50-acre rental retirement community, has 207 independent-living villas, 82 assisted-living units and a 120-bed nursing home. An additional 100 independent-living units are under construction. Prices range from $1,875-$2,500 a month for one person (add $400 for a second person), and include one meal a day, weekly housekeeping, security, scheduled transportation, emergency response system and events in the activities center.
Visitor lodging: Options include Lakeside Inn, $105-$205, (800) 556-5016 or (352) 383-4101, and Mount Dora Historic Inn, a restored 19th-century bed-and-breakfast inn located downtown, $85-$125, (800) 927-6344 or (352) 735-1212.
Information: Mount Dora Area Chamber of Commerce, P.O. Box 196, Mount Dora, FL 32757, (352) 383-2165 or www.mt-dora.com.

A bicycle festival is the largest and oldest cycling event in the country, bringing hundreds of cyclists from across the nation in early October. Later that month, an annual juried craft fair displays the talents of some 250 skilled artisans, drawing about 150,000 visitors.

John and Billie Keenon visited popular retirement towns in six states before settling on Mount Dora. Both in their mid-60s, they had lived in Little Rock, AR, for six years when they read about Mount Dora in Where to Retire magazine and decided to pay it a visit.

"Neither of us ever expected we would retire to Florida, but we fell in love with Mount Dora at first sight," Billie says. "And the people — real quality people — are so interested in the betterment of the community."

John, who spent his working years in the financial services industry, says he likes the wide assortment of activities and opportunities for participating in the community. He has served on the board of the Center for the Arts, the Mount Dora Chamber of Commerce and the Country Club of Mount Dora homeowners' association. "And I enjoy the concerts, Ice House Theatre performances and volunteering at the chamber of commerce," he says. His favorite recreational activities include golfing, boating and surfing the Internet.

"I play bridge, volunteer at the chamber, attend city council meetings and walk the dog," his wife, Billie, says. They describe their 2,200-square-foot contemporary home as light and airy with high ceilings. John feels it is appreciating in value. "They are still building and selling new homes, so it is likely prices are going up," he says.

Cost of living has not been a problem, all three couples say, agreeing that taxes in general are lower than in their previous home states. But there are plenty of opportunities to spend money, they say, citing the multitude of shopping, dining and entertainment outlets in the Greater Orlando area.

"In reality, the cost of living here is very reasonable," John Keenon says. "We still live the same lifestyle but eat out a lot more now." As for the Andersons, they credit financial planning with providing adequate income for their carefree retirement, along with one additional step taken some years ago. "We quit feeding our children money," Bob says with a laugh.

Although Mount Dora is sometimes called "New England of the South," thanks in part to some Victorian mansions near the downtown antiques district, the town is quintessential Florida when it comes to weather. Summers are hot and humid, with temperatures reaching into the 90s and humidity averaging 85 percent. Electrical storms are prevalent in late summer and early fall and winters are mild, with temperatures generally in the 50s to 70s.

Betty Jones misses the changing of seasons, but says, "Up North, there were a lot of gray, cloudy, rainy days. We don't get that much here." However, Billie Keenon doesn't like July and August in Mount Dora. "We try to go to Virginia to see our grandchildren in the summer," she says, "but sometimes it gets as hot there as here."

The Andersons are glad to put behind them the winter snowfalls back in Virginia. "Bob stood at the window and watched me shovel snow," Mary says of Virginia winters. "From November to April I hibernated," admits Bob.

Despite some misgivings about the hot summer temperatures, all three couples are glad they made the move and have no plans to relocate again. As John Keenon says, anyone considering Mount Dora as a retirement site "should put it on the top of their list." ●

Myrtle Beach, South Carolina

Those who vacation in this South Carolina resort find reasons to return permanently

By William Schemmel

Myrtle Beach didn't get its city charter until 1957. But fueled by sun-seeking retirees, the hub of the 60-mile Grand Strand resort and residential area on South Carolina's northern Atlantic coast has boomed into a metropolis of 180,000 residents and 12 million annual visitors.

The city takes the best of Nashville, Miami Beach and Disney World and blends them into a place where residents and visitors alike play year-round on 100 golf courses and enjoy 200 tennis courts, horseback riding, fishing, amusement parks, nature preserves and botanical gardens. They can unwind at trendy spots like Planet Hollywood, Hard Rock Cafe and NASCAR Cafe or showrooms featuring stars like Alabama, Kenny Rogers and the Gatlin Brothers. On another level, the entertainment calendar is crowded with touring Broadway musicals, plays and orchestra performances.

But for all these diversions, former New Jerseyites Charles and Betty Gary were won over by a tree.

"The huge live oak tree draping itself over our house was as big as anything in our decision to move to Myrtle Beach," recalls Charles, 78, a retired U.S. Army lieutenant colonel and former executive with New York Telephone Co. "I love that tree. I don't know what I'd do if anything happened to it."

The Garys bought their single-story, two-bedroom, two-bath house in Mount Gilead Place, a 99-home planned community in Garden City near the picturesque fishing village of Murrells Inlet. The community is a bonanza for fishermen because many homes sit along canals that lead into the inlet.

Population: 34,672 in Myrtle Beach, 180,000 in Horry (O-Ree) County.

Location: Extreme northeastern Atlantic coast of South Carolina, the hub of the 60-mile Grand Strand resort and residential area.

Climate:

	High	Low
January	60	40
July	90	70

Hot, humid summers tempered by ocean breezes. Mild winters with occasional below-freezing temperatures.

Average relative humidity: 57%

Rain: 50 inches

Cost of living: 103.8, based on national average of 100.

Average housing cost: $131,180 for a 1,800-square-foot home with three bedrooms, two baths and two-car garage. Average rent is $580 for a 950-square-foot, two-bedroom, two-bath apartment.

Sales tax: 5%

Sales tax exemptions: Prescriptions, dental prosthetics and hearing aids. Motor vehicles are charged a maximum $300 sales tax. Persons 85 and older are exempt from 1% of sales tax.

State income tax: Graduated in six steps from 2.5% to 7%, depending on income.

Income tax exemptions: Social Security benefits. Retirees under age 65 who are drawing income from qualified retirement plans may deduct up to $3,000 of that income. At age 65, residents may deduct up to $15,000 in income.

Intangibles tax: None.

Estate tax: None except the state's "pickup" portion of the federal tax, applicable to taxable estates above $675,000.

Property tax: $153.90 per $1,000 in unincorporated Horry County, $214.90 in Myrtle Beach. Residential property is assessed at 4% of actual appraised market value. The taxes on a $131,180 house in the county are $807.54, and in Myrtle Beach, $1,127.62.

Personal property tax: Same rates as above. Applies to cars, motor homes and boats, which are assessed at 10.5% of market value.

Homestead exemption: Homeowners age 65 and older who have established a one-year residency are eligible for a $20,000 homestead exemption.

Security: 207.4 crimes per 1,000 residents, higher than the national average of 46.2 crimes per 1,000 residents.

Religion: More than 100 churches and synagogues represent more than 20 denominations.

Education: Coastal Carolina University (4,500 students) offers a variety of full four-year programs and continuing-education courses. Full-time and part-time students enroll in evening classes at CCU's Wall School of Business. A high-tech two-way hookup with Winthrop University allows CCU students to earn nationally accredited MBA degrees.

Transportation: Coastal Rapid Public Transit Authority provides bus service in the Grand Strand area. Myrtle Beach International Airport is served by US Airways, Air Canada and Atlantic Southeast and COMAir (Delta Connections). Conway-Horry County Airport and Grand Strand Airport are available to private and corporate aircraft.

Health: Columbia Grand Strand Regional Medical Center in Myrtle Beach is a full-service acute-care medical center, providing comprehensive cardiac care, 24-hour emergency care and diagnostic services. Georgetown Memorial Hospital, in neighboring Georgetown County, has a high-tech nuclear medicine department, magnetic resonance imaging (MRI) and cardiac catheterization. Loris Community Hospital offers emergency and nonemergency family health care. Conway Hospital has a trauma center, a minor

"It's almost identical with our house in New Jersey," says Betty, 65, who retired as legal office manager for New York Telephone Co. "It has two great rooms, each opening into a sun room. We like to have our friends in, and it's large enough for a 50-person cocktail party."

Charles estimates that the house has appreciated in value about 15 percent since he and his wife purchased it in 1988. He says their property taxes are one-seventh what they paid on their former home in Lakehurst, NJ.

"We certainly feel safer here than we did in New Jersey," Charles adds. "We've never had any problems where we live in unincorporated southern Horry County. The city of Myrtle Beach, unfortunately, has a high crime rate, but most of it is concentrated in one part of town, and the city is taking steps to solve the problems in that area."

A downside, the Garys say, is traffic fueled by the Grand Strand's rapid development. But they add that traffic snarls, which are especially severe during the height of the summer tourist season, are mitigated by the opportunity to enjoy outdoor activities year-round.

"We used to do a lot of sailing, but we sold our sailboat when we moved here, so now we're walking, biking and golfing for exercise and recreation," says Charles.

"We miss the theater and music in New York City," he adds, "but cultural opportunities have improved tremendously since we moved here. And we certainly don't miss the cold weather in New York. The weather here is excellent. We get a taste of four seasons, and in the summer, the ocean breezes help cool things down."

They've also become active in local organizations, says Charles. "Along with Coastal Carolina University, we've hosted two Elderhostel programs at a local golf course. One of the first things we did after retirement was join the VISTA (Volunteers in Service to America) program. We're active in the chamber of commerce and Bike-the-Neck, a program to build a bike trail down to Georgetown. Betty is the board secretary for the Long Bay Symphony, and we're docents at Brookgreen Gardens."

America's oldest public sculpture garden, Brookgreen Gardens in neighboring Georgetown County south of Myrtle Beach was created in the 1930s. More than 450 19th- and early 20th-century sculptures grace formal gardens, alcoves, brick walkways, reflecting pools and fountains.

Also nearby are Huntington Beach and Myrtle Beach state parks, with protected beaches, fishing piers, campsites and other recreational amenities. North Carolina's hundreds of miles of Atlantic beaches begin at the state line a few minutes north of Myrtle Beach.

The Garys enjoy visits to historic

Myrtle Beach, SC

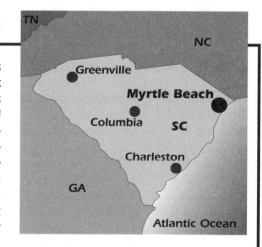

emergency treatment center, maternity and pediatric care, mammography, cardiac rehabilitation and emergency and nonemergency services.

Housing options: The Grand Strand has many resort-style residential communities with golf courses, tennis courts, swimming pools, clubhouses and other amenities. There also are many condominium communities on the ocean and fairways. **Tidewater Golf and Country Club,** (800) 843-3234, has homes overlooking fairways, marshes and the Intracoastal Waterway, with prices from the $130,000s. **The Park at Long Bay,** (888) 464-3700, eight miles from North Myrtle Beach, has manufactured homes in the range of $40,000-$79,900. Also offering manufactured homes are **Ocean Pines/Magnolia Grove,** at the southern end of the Grand Strand, and **Country Lakes,** near North Myrtle Beach. Homes are in the $60,000-$120,000 range. Residents, who must be age 55 or older, can take advantage of a clubhouse, swimming pool and organized activities. The communities are managed by Jensen's, (800) 458-6832. Centex Homes has four communities in the Myrtle Beach area: **SpringLake at Carolina Forest** offers homes for $120,000-$160,000; **The Tradition at Willbrook Plantation,** 18 miles south on Pawley's Island, has homes for $130,000-$250,000; **Mulberry Park at Indigo Creek,** eight miles south, has homes for $120,000-$170,000; **Muirfield at Blackmoor** has homes for $140,000-$200,000. Prices include homesite; for information call (800) 572-0708. **Seaside Village,** (800) 382-0388, two blocks from the beach, has two- and three-bedroom single-family homes from $133,900. At **Pawleys Plantation Golf and Country Club** on Pawleys Island, (800) 367-9959, home sites start at $29,000. Two- and three-bedroom villas, $100,000-$289,000, overlook the fairways of the Jack Nicklaus-designed golf course. **Heritage Plantation,** (800) 448-2010, has homesites from $40,000-$170,000 and homes from the $160,000s. **Ocean Creek,** (800) 747-6610, offers 57 wooded acres with 2.5 miles of protected beach. Condos and villas are $79,000-$275,000. Three-bedroom single-family homes at **Waterway Cove,** (843) 280-5370, start at $95,900. Three-bedroom homes with two-car garages at **The Oaks at Eastport,** (843) 249-3009, start at $133,500. **Legends,** (800) 552-2660, has two- and three-bedroom fairway villas from $120,000-$220,000 and single-family homesites from $30,000. Two- and three-bedroom condos at **The Moorings at Eastport,** (843) 249-3009, begin at $89,900.

Visitor lodgings: The Grand Strand has 55,000 hotel and motel rooms and rental condos. Prices are seasonal, and rooms facing the ocean and golf fairways usually are higher than those without views. At Bermuda Sands, oceanfront rates for two people currently are $280, (800) 448-8477. At Landmark Resort, ocean-front rate is $155, (800) 845-0658. At Beach Colony Resort, a suite with efficiency kitchen is $173, (800) 222-2141.

Information: Myrtle Beach Area Chamber of Commerce, P.O. Box 2115, Myrtle Beach, SC 29578, (843) 626-7444 or www.myrtlebeachlive.com.

Charleston 95 miles down the coast, where they can satisfy their cultural appetites at the annual Spoleto USA Music Festival in May and June.

Like the Garys, many retirees appreciate the Grand Strand's increasing cultural opportunities — including Larry and Mary Ellen Osius. The couple had what amounted to a 20-year preview of their retirement during frequent visits to Myrtle Beach before they moved permanently.

"We'd been coming here since the '70s to play golf," Larry says, "and we built a patio home in North Myrtle Beach in 1980. We came down a lot for long weekends and never considered any other retirement sites."

The couple moved from northern Virginia in 1990, where they had lived for 25 years. Larry, 67, former editor and publisher of Electrical Magazine, had achieved his career goals, and "life in northern Virginia was getting to be more and more of a hassle."

"I got tired of planning my day around every appointment because of the traffic problems," adds Mary Ellen, 67.

The Osiuses moved first into a patio home and then into their present home in the Little River community, near the North Carolina border, in 1992. "Our development backs up to the Cypress Bay Golf Course," Larry says. "We have a beautiful fairway in our back yard, and we play it as our home course, but we don't have to pay to maintain it. We're going to stay here as long as our health allows."

Larry also likes Broadway at the Beach, a 350-acre entertainment complex with 80 retail stores, an IMAX theater, 15 restaurants (including Hard Rock Cafe and Planet Hollywood), and the 2,700-seat Palace Theater, which hosts everything from Broadway musicals like "Cats" to such country singers as Kenny Rogers.

In addition, the Osiuses enjoy outings at Barefoot Landing, an oceanside shopping complex with 100 specialty shops, 14 restaurants, a paddle-wheel boat and a 2,000-seat theater. Other entertainment is available at the Dixie Stampede, a Western-style indoor horse show owned by Dolly Parton's Dollywood Productions, and the Gatlin Brothers' 2,000-seat home base.

Larry and Mary Ellen both had good experiences with surgeries at Grand Strand Hospital. On the downside, Larry dislikes "the tackiness of commercial signage on U.S. 17," traffic problems and video gaming, which is popular along the Grand Strand. And while he appreciates that property taxes are lower here than in Northern Virginia, he says auto insurance is "outrageous."

"But this has been a satisfactory retirement place for us," says Larry, a member of the Community Choral Society, which gives four annual concerts. Larry and Mary Ellen both volunteer with North Strand Helping Hand, a cooperative effort of nine churches, the city and United Way to provide food, shelter, transportation and clothing for the needy.

Mary Ellen says their move to Myrtle Beach "worked out well. We were so familiar with the area and were within walking distance of the beach, grocery stores, the library and other places we enjoy." But she advises other potential retirees not familiar with the area to "visit and not break their ties until they're sure this is where they want to be."

That's what Gary and Marlene Stahley did when they moved from Columbia, MD, their home for 25 years. Before making their move in January 1994, the Stahleys visited the area three times. Their one-story, traditional-style brick home is in South Creek, an inland planned community next to the Myrtle Beach National Golf Course. "This is the best-built house we've ever had," Marlene enthuses. "We're not in a retirement community, although most of the residents are retired. It's like living in a small town where you know everybody. Shortly after we moved in, I had back surgery and our neighbors brought us food. They really take care of you here."

Their move also was influenced by the Grand Strand's moderate year-round climate. "I wanted a change of seasons in a warmer climate — warm, but not too hot," says Marlene, 60, a former office manager for a periodontist. "And we had some good friends who had already moved here and liked the area."

Gary, 60, a former computer analyst for the U.S. Department of Defense, believes their house has appreciated in value, although he has no plans to sell it. "We aren't too concerned about it because we plan to be here for a long time," he says.

"The Myrtle Beach area has a lot of things that we enjoy," he adds. "When we lived in Columbia, we always went to the beaches in Maryland and Delaware, and it was natural for us to move to an area where we could still enjoy the beaches. We couldn't have stayed much longer in the Baltimore-Washington area. It was too expensive and getting worse all the time. People complain about the traffic in Myrtle Beach, but it's nothing compared to the Washington, DC, area."

Even so, Marlene hopes the city will work to control "increased traffic resulting from the new golf courses, the live entertainment complexes and all the new developments." Gary worries about air pollution caused by open burning and auto emissions.

Among the things they like best about their new home, Marlene says, is that "you can never complain that you have nothing to do. We appreciate the culture that is here. There's always a show, or something going on at Coastal Carolina University. The local talent is amazing."

She also had a positive firsthand experience with local health-care facilities. "When I had my back surgery, the care at Grand Strand Hospital was marvelous. Many new medical practices are opening, and health care is fine and getting better all the time. I also feel safer here."

Although the latest FBI Uniform Crime Reports show a higher-than-average crime rate in Myrtle Beach, local law enforcement officials point out that most violations are nonviolent thefts and frequently occur in heavily touristed areas. The FBI's methodology is tough on popular tourist towns since it looks at all crimes committed against residents and tourists alike and divides that figure by the number of residents only.

The Stahleys have become involved in many activities. Gary teaches a class in the Division of Extended Learning at Coastal Carolina University, giving them access to campus entertainment and other facilities. And there are courses of another kind. With all those tempting fairways designed by golf's biggest names, Gary has taken a serious interest in the game. Marlene also enjoys golf and is involved with her church and the South Creek community.

They recommend the area to other retirees. "I have no reservations about recommending the Grand Strand as a retirement place," Gary says. "But people have to understand that this is a tourist area and learn to live with it." ●

Naples, Florida

Pretty resort town on Florida's Gulf Coast blends culture, shopping and superb beaches

By Jay Clarke

It took Paul and Nancy Lappetito awhile to decide where they would spend their retirement years, but when they finally made up their minds, Naples was their choice. And they've never regretted their decision.

"I was a corporate nomad with National Cash Register for 33 years," explains Paul, 65, who lived in many cities as he climbed the corporate ladder. "So when I was going to retire in 1987, we checked out several places where we might like to live. We visited Hawaii, Southern California and Seattle, where we had a summer home.

"We were very interested in Palm Springs, but at a retirement party in Orlando, a friend suggested Naples," he says. "I liked it a lot. We bought a lot on our second visit here, then went back to Hawaii and Southern California to check them out again."

Naples still looked very good, so the Lappetitos went ahead and built a home on their golf course lot. "We liked the climate. There's no state income tax," says Paul. "Naples is safe and has good restaurants and cultural facilities. Then, too, we had a lot of friends in the East, and we wanted a place that our five children would be happy to visit.

"Most importantly," he adds, "we liked the people. They're mostly from the Midwest and they have Midwestern values. We knew nobody here at the time we bought our lot, but it was incredibly easy to make friends. People here are very friendly."

Lappetito, who was president of NCR Canada before he retired, is one of many high-ranking corporate executives who have made their retirement homes in this upscale Gulf Coast community. But Naples also is the town of choice for many retirees with more modest incomes.

Bob and Lois Geschrei had been coming to Bonita Springs and Marco Island, both near Naples, on vacations from their Cincinnati home since 1973. But when Bob, a financial consultant, retired at 56 in 1985, they tried several other locales — South Carolina and Tucson, AZ, among them.

"In 1992 we said, 'Let's go live on Marco.' We looked at Marco lots, but decided that unless we had a boat, we'd be bored. So we went to Naples," says Bob. "In four days, we chose a house. It was the first in the project, so we had the pick of the lots."

The Geschreis have a 1,600-square-foot home in a regular subdivision, not a retirement community, so their neighbors include families in all stages of life — a mix they both enjoy.

Taxes are lower in Naples than in Cincinnati, the Geschreis say, but water bills are higher ($80 a month), maybe in part because Bob is such an avid gardener. His love of gardening is one reason he picked a particularly spacious house lot. On it, he lovingly cares for an imposing array of flowering shrubs, ornamentals and a picture-perfect lawn.

And while they say Naples has fewer cultural facilities than Cincinnati, Bob points out that "for a small community, we have a lot of things that bigger cities don't — the philharmonic, art galleries, great shopping, a lot of restaurants."

Both Bob and Lois, who are 67 and 66 respectively, volunteer at the Naples Visitor Center three days a week, giving information to tourists — some of whom may wind up settling in Naples, as they did.

There's reason to think a lot more people may move to Naples. With a 77 percent increase in population, the town had the dubious honor of being the fastest-growing metropolitan area in the country during the 1980s.

Trying to cope with such increasing numbers is a trial, but so far Naples has been meeting the challenge. Despite its growth, Naples still has a small-town feel. Its subdivisions are tidy places. Shopping areas like Third Avenue South and the Waterside Mall are classy and well-maintained. A few high-rises have arisen, but they're all on the shore.

The public beach still is a place where friends meet, and a yen for night life can be satisfied in Miami or Fort Lauderdale, less than two hours away by car.

One of the most popular gathering spots is the fishing pier, whose silhouette appears on the city's official logo. Built more than 100 years ago as a dock for passenger and freight ships, it provided the only entry into the city until roads were built.

Anglers of all ages, from 8 to 80, come to the pier to try their luck. "It's like a jungle telegraph," says Bill Zinski, who with his wife, Pat, moved to Naples seven years ago. "When the fishing's good, everybody hears about it somehow and comes out to the pier. When it's not so good, they stay away."

People not only fish there, they gather on the pier and the adjacent beach to hold reunions and parties, celebrate birthdays, even recite nuptials. Destroyed several times during its 108 years of existence, the pier was reopened recently after reconstruction of its landward half.

Just as popular as the pier is the adjacent beach, which attracts sunseekers of all ages, from teenagers and twentysomethings to grandparents and eightysomethings. A beach at the north end of town also has achieved some renown. Delnor-Wiggins Pass State Recreation Area was once selected as one of the top 10 beaches in the United States by Dr. Stephen Leatherman of Florida International University. Leatherman is renowned for his annual list of best and worst beaches.

One reason the pier maintains its popularity is because it is situated at the foot of 12th Avenue South, just a couple of blocks from bustling Olde Naples, the restored downtown core of the city. Third Street South runs through the center of this four-square-block district, the site of trendy shops and boutiques.

Not far away is Fifth Avenue South, lined on both sides with restaurants, some with outdoor tables. And at the west end of the street, where it meets U.S. Highway 41 (the Tamiami Trail), are several hotels and a marina-turned-shopping-mall called Tin City.

A number of other hotels are situated on the beaches, including the top-rated Naples Ritz-Carlton and the Registry.

These assets contribute heavily to Naples' reputation as a highly desirable place to live. Strict zoning laws help, too.

"Naples doesn't have many, if any, tacky areas, even on U.S. 41 (the main highway through the city)," notes Paul Lappetito. Indeed, much of its growth is so recent that most of the city has a clean, almost antiseptic look.

Many subdivisions are enclosed by walls and laced with tree-lined, curving roads. Green lawns and lush land-scaping ring street after street of white and pastel homes. The average single-family home costs $179,917, but some homes in Naples go for more than $1 million. In fact, a five-bedroom estate on the Gulf recently sold for $7.9 million.

Baronial homes such as these are favored by captains of industry who have moved to Naples in retirement. And there are more than a few of them.

A recent article in the Naples Daily News followed the retirement activities of several chief executive officers and company presidents who have retired here. Bob Mulholland, 62, former president and chief executive

Naples, FL

Population: 20,629 in Naples, 220,000 in Collier County.

Location: On the Gulf of Mexico in southwest Florida at the intersection of U.S. Highway 41 (the Tamiami Trail) and Interstate 75.

Climate:

	High	Low
January	78	53
July	91	72

Average relative humidity: 67%

Rain: About 54 inches.

Rain falls mostly in the late summer months. Winters are mild.

Cost of living: Above average (specific index not available).

Average housing cost: $179,917 for single-family home, $107,145 for attached home, $173,337 for condominiums.

Sales tax: 6% levied by state. County also levies 3% tax on lodging and rental accommodations.

Sales tax exemptions: Groceries, medicines, professional services.

State income tax: None.

Intangibles tax: Assessed on stocks, bonds and other specified assets, with some investments exempt. Tax rate is $1 per $1,000 of value for assets under $100,000 for individuals or $200,000 for couples; $1.50 per $1,000 of value for greater amounts. First $20,000 of assets ($40,000 for couples) is exempt.

Estate tax: None, except the state's "pick-up" portion of the federal tax, applicable to taxable estates above $675,000.

Property tax: Millage rates vary within Collier County. Average rate in the county is about $15 per $1,000 of assessed value, with homes assessed at 100% of market value. Annual taxes on a $180,000 house are about $2,325, with the homestead exemption noted below.

Homestead exemption: $25,000 off assessed value of permanent, primary residence.

Security: 59.8 crimes per 1,000 residents, higher than the national average of 46.2 crimes per 1,000 residents.

Religion: There are many churches and synagogues in the city.

Education: International College and Edison Community College have branch facilities in Naples. Florida Gulfcoast University opened just north of Naples in 1997.

Transportation: Several major carriers operate from Southwest Florida International Airport in Fort Myers, 30 miles north of Naples. Naples Municipal Air-port caters to private aircraft and commuter lines, including Cape Air, American Eagle, US Airways and Comair (Delta).

Health: Naples Community Hospital has 400 beds and 24-hour emergency care. Its North Collier branch has 50 beds and 24-hour emergency care.

Housing options: Choices are broad. In the eastern suburb of **Golden Gate**, population about 5,000, a four-bedroom home with pool can start as low as $160,000. In Naples proper, prices are higher. Retirement and life-care communities, nursing homes and assisted-living establishments also are available. A number of developments, while not labeled retirement communities, nevertheless are mostly populated by retirees.

Visitor lodging: Naples has 5,000 hotel rooms, plus other rental accommodations. Prices are much higher in the winter high season than in summer. Some choices: Inn at Pelican Bay, $70-$80 summer, $145-$165 winter, (800) 597-8770; Naples Beach Hotel, $134-$185 summer, $255-$335 winter, (800) 237-7600; Ritz-Carlton, $200-$525 summer, $275-$625 winter, (800) 241-3333. For a list of lodgings, call the tourism bureau at (800) 605-7878 for a free directory.

Information: Naples Area Chamber of Commerce, 895 Fifth Ave. S., Naples, FL 34102-6605, (941) 262-6141 or www.naples-online.com.

officer of NBC, works with the Naples Institute, a group of current and retired professionals who discuss political issues that have an impact on the community. Ed Colodny, 69, former president and chief executive officer of USAir, still makes frequent trips to Washington, DC, where he serves on many councils and boards. Dick Henson, 86, former chief executive officer of Henson Aviation and Henson Airlines, still flies his personal jet to meetings around the country.

If there's anything they have in common, it is that they remain active in retirement. But keeping busy isn't limited to more affluent retirees.

Oscar Wooldridge, who just turned 80, was a chaplain, not a CEO, but he still plays tennis and goes biking, and that's one reason he retired here from Raleigh, NC. The climate in Naples lets him pursue those activities year-round.

Oscar got acquainted with Naples when he acquired a time share in a condo many years ago. Then he and his wife, Tew, 68, rented a condo for three months to see if they liked Naples enough to move here permanently. They did. So they bought their present condo four years ago.

"We like the climate, the recreational atmosphere and the people — they're pretty relaxed," says Oscar, who, despite his age and a recent knee operation, stays more active than most people 20 years younger.

Oscar, who retired 18 years ago, finds the cost of living higher in Naples than in Raleigh, but he says he hasn't had to make significant changes in his budget. However, he says he can't afford philharmonic concerts and other cultural opportunities that are more expensive in Naples than in Raleigh, where six colleges provided venues for low-priced entertainment.

The Wooldridges live in a condo community where 90 percent of the residents are retired. As is true of virtually all properties in Naples, the value of his condo has appreciated.

His advice to others who may be thinking of moving to Naples: "Come early, because it's filling up."

For Kay Wing, a Chicago widow, moving to Naples was a matter of keeping up with her friends.

"All my friends came here during the season. There was no one left back in Flossmoor," the Chicago suburb where she lived. "They were all in Florida," says Kay. "I went to one Christmas party here and ran into 40 friends from Flossmoor."

Living in a golf course development, she finds she can stay as busy as she wants. She enjoys golf and says she could be happy playing bridge with friends all day. Though it is not a retirement community, her development is populated mostly with retirees, so she has plenty of company.

In Chicago, she was vice president of a bank before she retired, and she was active in charitable organizations. In Naples, she serves on the finance committee of her church and is active in the Naples Philharmonic League.

Dining and shopping in Naples? It's on par with Chicago, she believes. So is entertainment, except for theater, which she feels is rather limited.

For three years before she moved permanently to Naples, Kay rented a house here for three months during the winter, something she recommends to anyone who is thinking of retiring here. She paid $3,000 a month in rent, an amount she admits was more than she cared to spend, but rentals are available at lower cost.

"There's nothing I miss in Chicago, other than being close to my children," says Kay. "I do miss seeing... my grandchildren."

However, her three children visit her in Naples. Most retirees find that their children are quite eager to visit Naples, particularly in the winter when snowstorms bedevil the North. Grandchildren love it, too, because Naples is only three hours from Disney World and the other theme parks of Orlando. For them, that's heaven.

It's pretty wonderful for parents and grandparents, too. As Bob Geschrei says, "When people ask me why I always have a smile on my face, I say, 'Why not? This is paradise.'" ●

Natchitoches, Louisiana

This historic town in north-central Louisiana works its charm on newcomers

By Honey Naylor

If you saw the 1988 movie "Steel Magnolias," you've already seen Natchitoches. Called Chinquapin in the film, Natchitoches was the boyhood home of Robert Harling, who wrote the smash-hit off-Broadway play on which the movie is based. The movie also was filmed here.

Natchitoches lazes on the banks of peaceful Cane River Lake, formed long ago when the Red River changed its course. (Since the waters don't flow, the 32-mile-long lake is not technically a river.) The green-grassy banks are shaded by ancient oak trees.

Front Street, in downtown Natchitoches overlooking the lake, is paved with brick laid around the turn of the century and is lined with small balconied structures decked in graceful wrought-iron trim. The town's 33-block historic district is on the National Register of Historic Places.

"We like the rolling hills around Natchitoches," says Ruth Malcolm, who with her husband, Leland, moved to the charming north-central Louisiana town in 1997.

Natchitoches (pronounced Nak-uh-tish) sits near the Kisatchie National Forest, a fit place for hiking and hunting, fishing and camping. Briarwood, nestled in the forest, was the home of Caroline Dormon, the first woman employed in forestry in the United States. She worked tirelessly with state and U.S. Forest Service leaders to establish the Kisatchie National Forest, now a nature preserve and the state's most complete botanical and wildlife sanctuary. In addition, the hill country around Natchitoches is virtually awash with lakes for boating, tubing and fishing — including Cane River Lake, Saline Lake, Black Lake, Clear Lake, Chaplin's Lake and Sibley Lake.

Ruth and Leland already were acquainted with the area and knew people here before moving. Both were born in south Louisiana — Ruth in

the small town of Welsh near Lake Charles and Leland in Fenton. Both have family nearby, and after considering other places for retirement — Salt Lake City, Austin and Atlanta — they chose Natchitoches largely because of the proximity to their birthplaces and to family.

Ruth confesses that readjustment to a small town has been difficult — and for reasons that are a bit out of the ordinary. The Malcolms not only had to adjust to small-town living, they had to repatriate. For 12 years they lived overseas in Bahrain, where Leland was a facilities manager. They miss friends who still live in the Middle East and worry about them. "We don't miss the bullets or the bombs," Leland says.

Indeed, it seems the greatest danger for the Malcolms, both 57, now is the possibility of being hit by a golf ball. "Our house is on a lane right beside the golf course," says Ruth of the home they own in a 10-house planned community. Their development requires a 2,000-square-foot minimum home size and prohibits fences because, as Ruth says, "golfers have to be able to get to their errant balls."

With this kind of proximity to a golf course, Ruth and Leland both have taken golf lessons, and they also obtained real estate licenses and work part-time. They already owned rental property in Natchitoches prior to moving and buying a house here.

Another newcomer, Ken Bates, also is a native Louisianian. Ken, a retired U.S. Army major, and his wife, Donna, both attended Northwestern State University in Natchitoches and were acquainted with this area prior to relocating here in 1993 from New Cumberland, PA. Proximity to family also was a consideration for them, as Ken's mother lives in a nearby town.

Ken and Donna were stationed in

Turkey when "Steel Magnolias" came out, but they've heard the many stories about the stars, the sets and the shoot since moving to Natchitoches.

That excitement has only slightly abated more than a decade later. Tour guides for Cane River City Belle Trolley and Cruises point out where the stars lived during the filming and where memorable scenes were shot. Almost everyone in town has a tale to tell about his or her part in making the film, no matter how small. Indeed, some had roles as extras.

The movie was a very big deal for this town of fewer than 18,000 people. During several months of filming, Natchitoches was home not only to Olympia Dukakis, Julia Roberts, Shirley MacLaine and Dylan McDermott, but to Dolly Parton, Sally Field, Daryl Hannah and Tom Skerritt, plus a sizable crew. The impact on the town was enormous, pumping millions of dollars into the local economy, and it was a shot in the arm for tourism. There now are 28 Natchitoches area bed-and-breakfast inns to help house tourists, many still drawn here by "Steel Magnolias."

They also come because of the area's rich history. That's another attraction for Donna Bates, who liked to explore Amish country when she lived in Pennsylvania.

Natchitoches is the oldest permanent European settlement in the Louisiana Purchase, a chunk of real estate that includes all of the territory between the Alleghenies and the Rockies. In 1682, the French explorer Robert Cavelier de La Salle followed the Mississippi River from Canada to the Gulf of Mexico and claimed for Louis XIV of France all of the land drained by the river.

In 1714, a young French Creole named Juchereau de St. Denis swashed and buckled his way to this site, which is named for the Natchitoches Indians. In 1803, President Thomas Jefferson bought the land from Napoleon Bonaparte, and the legendary Louisiana Purchase cost the young United States $15 million.

The Old Ducournau Building and the LaCoste Building are two 19th-century structures that form the core of downtown's Ducournau Square overlooking the lake. Their quaint carriageways lead from Front Street to courtyards in the rear, where small restored buildings once were stables or carriage houses. In the European style, the square's buildings have shops and restaurants at ground level and townhouses on upper floors.

Natchitoches sits on the cusp between south Louisiana, which was founded by the French, and north Louisiana, which was settled by English, Scots and Irish

Natchitoches, LA

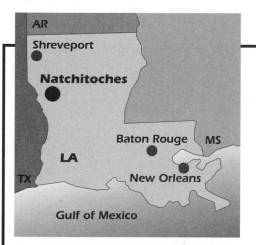

Population: 17,141 in the city of Natchitoches, seat of Natchitoches Parish, which has a population of 37,377.

Location: Natchitoches is in north-central Louisiana, about 60 miles northwest of Alexandria. Natchitoches Parish is bordered on the southeast by the Red River.

Climate:

	High	Low
January	56	36
July	93	73

Average relative humidity: 73%

Rain: 50.32 inches

Cost of living: Below average (specific index not available).

Average housing cost: A 1,500- to 1,600-square-foot, three-bedroom home is about $95,000. Homeowner insurance on such a home would run about $525 annually. For a 1,300-square-foot, two-bedroom condominium or townhouse, the cost is about $70,000-$80,000, with maintenance about $300 per month.

Sales tax: Combined city, parish and state sales tax is 8%. Groceries are taxed at 7%, and prescription drugs are taxed at 4%.

State income tax: For married couples filing jointly, graduated in three steps from 2% to 6%, depending on income.

Income tax exemptions: Social Security benefits and federal, state and local government pensions are ex-

empt.

Inheritance tax: Louisiana's inheritance tax will be phased out for deaths occuring after June 30, 2004. At this writing the following applies. Direct descendants, ascendants and surviving spouses are taxed at the following rate: Nothing is due on the first $25,000, 2% on the next $20,000, and 3% on the taxable amount in excess of $45,000. If the date of death occurred during the calendar year 1992 or thereafter, the total value to the surviving spouse is exempted from tax.

Estate tax: None, except the state's "pick-up" portion of the federal tax, applicable to taxable estates above $675,000.

Property tax: The tax rate in Natchitoches Parish is $107 per $1,000 of assessed value, with homes assessed at 10 percent of market value, and there's a $75,000 homestead exemption. Personal property is assessed at 15% of fair market value. In the city of Natchitoches, the tax rate is $17 per $1,000 of assessed value, with homes assessed at 10 percent of market value, and there's no homestead exemption. On a $100,000 home, you would pay parish taxes on $2,500 and city taxes on $10,000. Taxes due the parish would be $268, and taxes due the city would be $170, for a total bill of $438.

Homestead exemption: $75,000 on parish property taxes.

Security: 86 crimes per 1,000 residents, higher than the national average of 46.2 crimes per 1,000 residents.

Religion: Natchitoches has more than 90 houses of worship representing 30 denominations.

Education: Northwestern State University, with an enrollment of approx-

imately 9,000 students, offers community outreach programs, including continuing education, with courses and workshops on how to get out of debt, prelicensing real estate education, Cajun dancing, water aerobics and others.

Transportation: There is no public bus system, but the Council on Aging operates a van for seniors. Shreveport Regional Airport, 70 miles away, is served by 20 national airlines. Alexandria International Airport, 55 miles away, is served by four commuter airlines.

Health: The Natchitoches Parish Hospital, fully staffed with 27 physicians and specialists, has a 24-hour emergency room and services that include a long-term care unit, a senior care unit, a wellness program and Meals on Wheels.

Housing options: At **St. Clair Estates**, located between schools and the hospital, new homes are in the 1,500- to 2,500-square-foot range, priced from $125,000 to $175,000. At **Chinquapin** subdivision, new homes are 1,600 to 2,000 square feet. Patio homes, featuring two bedrooms and two baths and 1,300 square feet for about $85,000, also are popular with area retirees, local builders say.

Visitor lodging: Some 28 bed-and-breakfast inns range in rates from $65 to $125 per night. Ask for a bed-and-breakfast brochure from the chamber of commerce. Other options include Ryder Inn, $49-$90, (888) 252-8281, and Comfort Inn, $67-$140, (800) 228-5150.

Information: Natchitoches Area Chamber of Commerce, 550 Second St., P.O. Box 3, Natchitoches, LA 71458, (318) 352-6894, www.natchitocheschamber. org or www.natchitoches.net.

immigrants. The Bateses, both 50, appreciate the cultural diversity afforded by the area and by Northwestern State University.

The Bateses' home, which they have owned for four years, is a two-story French chateau-style house in an upscale neighborhood on the opposite side of the lake from the historic district. Ken notes that property taxes are much lower here than in Pennsylvania, and that Louisiana does not tax military retirement.

Indeed, much of Natchitoches' appeal is due to its affordability. The town offers a low cost of living and reasonably priced homes, and state and local taxes are below average.

Another recent newcomer, David Graham, says that the lower cost of living, along with the mild climate, was a factor in his move from Tennessee to Natchitoches. David, who says he's been thinking about possible retirement places "all my life," moved here with his wife, Carolyn, in 1997.

For 25 years the Grahams had lived in Germantown, TN, where David, 67, owned an insurance agency and Carolyn was an insurance claims administrator and a schoolteacher. They live in a one-story traditional house with gingerbread trim in a riverfront residential neighborhood. They enjoy participating in the cultural aspects of the area when not baby-sitting their 10 grandchildren.

The Grahams also had old friends here when they moved. But Carolyn echoes the Bateses, saying, "It's easy to make new friends if you join groups and become involved with the church."

The Grahams share a love of music: He sings in the church choir and she plays in a hand-bell choir and also plays piano and saxophone. In addition to music, Carolyn, 62, enjoys historic preservation and belongs to the Natchitoches Historical Society. David, a member of the Lions Club, plans to volunteer with the chamber of commerce.

"Natchitoches has so much more to offer," says David, referring to their choice of Natchitoches over Hot Springs, AR, another town they had considered. "There's so much to do, and there's a festival almost every week."

Indeed, there are festivals aplenty. Natchitoches is known in these parts for its Christmas Festival of Lights, when the downtown area is festooned with twinkling lights, and some 150,000 visitors come to see it. The festival kicks off the first Saturday in December with spectacular fireworks, parades both on and off the water, and a street fair with food, games, rides and music.

In October, historic homes are open to the public for a fall pilgrimage, and a jazz festival livens things up around St. Patrick's Day. An annual fiddlers championship is held at the nearby Rebel States Commemorative Area in Marthaville, and the annual folk festival is held on the campus of Northwestern State University in July.

A few miles south of town, Melrose Plantation, a national historic landmark, hosts the Melrose Plantation Arts and Crafts Festival each June. Some 25,000 people attend the festival, which features top-quality handcrafted baskets, pottery, dolls, sculptures, jewelry and other items. The plantation, open for tours throughout the year, was the home of the late Cammie Henry, a patron of the arts who welcomed writers to come to Melrose to live and work.

Lyle Saxon and Sherwood Anderson are among the writers who have stayed in this handsome mid-19th-century house, which also was the home of the late primitive artist Clementine Hunter. Among her works on display is a mural she painted on the interior walls of African House, one of the outbuildings included in the tour.

Melrose is one of several plantation homes open to the public south of Natchitoches. The Kate Chopin House bears the name of the 19th-century author of "The Awakening" who lived here with her husband. Chopin also wrote "Bayou Folk," a book about the people of this region, and a first-edition is displayed in a museum in the house.

Magnolia Plantation, whose stunning main mansion dates from the mid-18th century, is a national bicentennial farm. An antiques-filled bed-and-breakfast inn, as well as a still-working plantation, Magnolia will be a part of the Cane River National Heritage Area presently under development. Like Magnolia, nearby Beau Fort Plantation is a bed-and-breakfast inn with a wonderful collection of 18th- and 19th-century antiques.

In town, Northwestern State University offers symphony, ballet and theater, plus a raft of sports activities that ranges from football and baseball to rodeoing and rowing. In the spring, Cane River Lake attracts rowing teams from across the nation for practice and competition.

Donna Bates says she misses the change of seasons in Pennsylvania, and Ken misses the mountains — the highest point in all of Louisiana is just 520 feet above sea level. But they agree that it's hard to find friendlier people than the folks in Natchitoches. And Leland Malcolm has only one word of advice to retirees considering a move to charming Natchitoches: "Hurry."●

New Bern, North Carolina

Northern transplants find a warm welcome in this historic North Carolina port town

By Lan Sluder

Here's a formula for falling in love with a small town: Plan to arrive in the early evening. Come in over the high-rise bridge across the wide curve of water where two rivers meet the sound, where you can watch sailboats head back to the marina at day's end. Look as the setting sun frames the historic district on the waterfront and the twinkling lights of a bustling downtown. Catch a glimpse of expansive riverside homes with championship golf out the back door. Enjoy, even in deepest winter, a hint of warmth in the air and the soft gray of Spanish moss on oak trees, thanks to the moderating impact of the Gulf Stream not far away.

This is New Bern, NC, at its best. The first view of this picturesque port town in Craven County, 105 miles southeast of Raleigh, is capturing the hearts of more than a few retirees, and its agreeable combination of riverfront living, mild four-season climate, affordable housing, strong and diversified economy, interesting history, welcoming locals and wide-ranging recreational opportunities is winning them as full-time residents.

"My husband and I had made various trips, checking out towns, and when we drove into New Bern in 1997, we just looked at each other and said, 'We like this town — this is it,'" says Betty Ann Walker, who with her husband, Bill, decided to move to New Bern from Naples, FL.

Bill, 74, and Betty Ann, 53, spent just one day with a real estate agent, looked at only a half-dozen houses and quickly bought one, a 1970s-vintage brick rancher on a creek. Within a short time, the Walkers (they are nearly newly-weds, having been married less than three years) turned the house into a showplace, says Pam Michel of Coastal Homes Real Estate.

"We got twice the house here for the money than you could in Naples," says Betty Ann. Originally from Ontario, Canada, she had lived in Naples for 25 years.

Bill had lived in Illinois before moving to Naples, where he spent 11 years. "Half-backs" from Florida, those who moved to Florida from the Northeast or Midwest and then decided to move "half the way back," represent a growing group in towns like New Bern.

"In Naples we lived in a gated golfing community where everyone was over 65, and 80 percent of the residents left in the summer," says Betty Ann. In her neighborhood in New Bern, ages range from 4 to 94, and everybody lives here full time, she says.

The Walkers travel, garden, exercise and, like many retirees in the New Bern area, tool around the usually benign waters of the Neuse and Trent rivers and Pamlico Sound in their "yacht" — in this case, a 13-foot Boston Whaler.

"We were looking for a small town that didn't advertise itself on postcards," says Betty Ann. With the buzz New Bern is enjoying these days, the town may not need to do much advertising. The second-oldest town in North Carolina (Bath in Beaufort County claims to be the oldest incorporated town in the state) is suddenly one of the hottest retirement destinations in the region.

"Most of the retirees we get here, and we're getting a lot of them, are from the North — especially New York, New Jersey, Pennsylvania, the Washington area and from as far west as Ohio and Indiana," says Bob Bartram, co-owner of Century 21 Action Associates. "They're looking for a warm area, but not too warm," he says, noting that New Bern has four distinct seasons.

The average retiree pays around $200,000 for a home in New Bern, Bob says, though the range is wide, from around $75,000 to $700,000. Neighborhoods and communities around New Bern offer all types of housing options, from the country club environs of Trent Woods to houses from three centuries in the historic district and golf-oriented developments such as Taberna, developed by

Weyerhaeuser, where lot and home packages start around $160,000. There are waterfront projects such as Fairfield Harbour, which has two 18-hole golf courses, a 235-slip marina and housing options from condos to custom homes from $100,000 to $400,000, and there are time-shares, manufactured housing subdivisions and rural trailer parks.

Jeanne and Curt Collison are fairly typical of retirees from the North. Jeanne, 59 (her name is pronounced Jeanie), grew up on Martha's Vineyard, MA, and Curt, 60, in Rhode Island and New York. During the years when Curt worked for Ocean Spray, eventually becoming senior vice president, and Jeanne worked as a registered nurse, becoming charge nurse at a hospital emergency room, they lived in various towns in Massachusetts, Rhode Island, Connecticut and New Hampshire.

Following a stroke in 1992, Curt took early retirement, and the Collisons made a list of 16 things they felt were important in a retirement location. Among the most important were a warm climate with four seasons, proximity to a river or lake and within 25 miles of the ocean (but not directly on the ocean), a small town with history and fewer than 25,000 year-round residents, a location within a day's drive of the couple's three sons, and a place that's hospitable to Northern transplants.

Among the finalists were several small towns in eastern North Carolina, including Edenton, Bath and Beaufort. But after spending a week in New Bern, the town just "felt right for us," Curt says.

"We're antiques nuts and old house nuts," says Curt, so he and his wife were impressed with New Bern's vibrant 56-square-block downtown historic district. Founded by Swiss and German settlers in 1710 and named for Bern, Switzerland (Bern means bear in German, and a stylized bear is the town's omnipresent symbol), New Bern celebrates its past in a variety of historical attractions, most notably Tryon Palace. The Georgian-style palace, with 14 acres of gardens, is a reconstruction of the 18th-century residence of British colonial governor William Tryon. Most of the original structure, considered one of the grandest public buildings in the young country, was destroyed in a 1798 fire. New Bern also had the first printing press and the first newspaper in the state.

History lessons in New Bern needn't be stuffy, though. As proud as they are of the area's pre-Revolutionary history, residents appear equally proud that Pepsi-Cola was invented by pharmacist Caleb Bradham in New Bern in 1898. The "birthplace of Pepsi" at the corner of Middle and Pollack streets, now a gift shop with a soda fountain, is one of New Bern's most popular tourist attractions. New Bern's many B&Bs and motels stay busy year-round, and a new convention center complex on the riverfront doubtless will add to the attraction of the area for visitors.

In the heart of the historic district, the Collisons in late 1992 bought a three-story, 4,000-square-foot home, dating from 1817 with two later additions. In 1994 they began renovating it, a job that, while mostly completed, has continued to the present.

The Collisons say they love their historic home, described in New Bern promotional brochures as Federalist-Greek Revival with Victorian embellishments. "We especially love living in the historic district," says Curt. "It is a real tight community, including all ages, where you can sit on your front porch and know 90 percent of the people who walk by."

Active in the local preservation league, in antiques organizations and other groups, the Collisons say they have felt exceptionally welcome as lifelong Northerners in this Southern town. "We haven't even come close to seeing any anti-Yankee feeling — many of our closest friends were born and brought up here," he says.

Another couple who found their retirement paradise in New Bern are Dan and Vicki Larimer, who moved here in 1998 from the town of Jim Thorpe in Pennsylvania. Dan, 59, was an English professor at a community college, and Vicki, 58, ran the college's nursery school. The Larimers had become familiar with this part of North Carolina when they camped on the Outer Banks with their two daughters.

The Larimers bought in Taberna, a Weyerhaeuser development with golf course carved out of an area near the Croatan National Forest, a 155,000-acre national forest southeast of New Bern. Avid boaters, the Larimers own a 20-foot yawl that they sail on the Neuse and Trent rivers. They also are birders and have joined the local birding club. The Larimers say they enjoy the cultural activities available locally, including a Shakespeare festival, a concert series and an excellent library. They also enjoying biking or driving to visit the many quaint small towns around New Bern, including Swansboro, Oriental and Beaufort.

As with many retirees, weather and the water were the reasons Clair and Dorothy Smith chose New Bern. They began looking at the area in 1985, doing a lot of research, and eventually moved from Michigan to New Bern in 1993. They call it "a fabulous place to live." They chose a patio home at Greenbrier, a planned community with a golf course. Though boatless at present, the Smiths belong to a sailing club. Clair says he volunteers at the North Carolina Maritime Museum in nearby Beaufort, helping build and repair wooden boats.

New Bern, NC

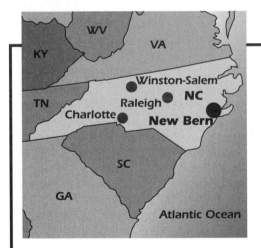

Population: 22,500 in New Bern, 91,000 in Craven County.

Location: New Bern, the county seat of Craven County, is at the confluence of the Neuse and Trent rivers in eastern North Carolina, about 105 miles (a little over two hours by car) southeast of Raleigh and about 35 miles (45 minutes by car) from coastal beaches.

Climate:

	High	Low
January	54	34
July	88	70

New Bern has a mild, four-season climate, with average mean daily temperature of 62, although summers are warm with highs in the upper 80s. Hurricane season is June-November.

Average relative humidity: 57%

Rain: 53 inches annually.

Cost of living: Average (specific index not available).

Average housing cost: The average residential sale in Craven County is $113,700. However, local real estate agents say retirees moving to the area are likely to spend $150,000 to $250,000 or more for a newer home in a desirable neighborhood. One- and two-bedroom apartments in desirable areas typically rent for $400 to $750 a month.

Sales tax: 6% (4% state and 2% local).

Sales tax exemptions: Prescription medicine, eyeglasses, some medical supplies and most services.

State income tax: Graduated in three steps from 6% to 7.75%, depending on income.

Income tax exemptions: Social Security benefits. Each taxpayer also can exempt up to $4,000 in local, state or federal government retirement benefits and up to $2,000 in private retirement benefits, but the total of these exemptions cannot exceed $4,000 per person.

Intangibles tax: None.

Estate tax: None, except the state's pickup portion of the federal tax, applicable to taxable estates above $675,000.

Property tax: $5.70 per $1,000 of assessed market value in Craven County. New Bern residents pay an additional $4.70 for a total of $10.40 per $1,000 of assessed value. Annual tax on a $150,000 home in New Bern would be about $1,560.

Homestead exemption: None.

Security: In Craven County, 48.4 crimes per 1,000 residents, slightly higher than the national average of 46.2 crimes per 1,000 residents.

Religion: The metropolitan area is home to about 225 churches and synagogues of more than 40 denominations.

Education: Retirees can take courses at a

Dorothy, who goes by the nickname Dottie, is a bridge player, member of a chorus and active in volunteer groups. She credits the local newcomers club, with some 400 members, as opening doors for her and other retirees. Although newcomers can stay in the club for only three years, they can graduate to an alumni group and stay in it indefinitely.

A different kind of club — "Uncle Sam's Club" — is the reason why another large group of retirees selects the New Bern area. About 18 miles away in Havelock is Cherry Point, the largest Marine Corps Air Station in the United States. At Jacksonville, about 36 miles from New Bern, is Camp Lejeune Marine Base, where new recruits go through the rigors of Marine boot camp. Career Marine and Navy personnel who have served at one of these bases often return here in retirement.

There's no scarcity of outdoor recreational activities in New Bern. Big-time fishing and boating abound on area rivers and sounds, with at least 13 marinas serving boaters. The Neuse River, a mile wide at New Bern and several miles wide downstream of the town, is more like a big bay or lake than a river. New Bern is home to eight area golf courses.

Good swimming beaches are a short distance from New Bern at Emerald Isle, Atlantic Beach, Hammocks Beach State Park and Topsail Beach. Only about 45 miles by car and a short ferry ride away is the Cape Lookout National Seashore. The island of Ocracoke, one of the jewels of the North Carolina Outer Banks, is 75 miles and a two-and-a-half-hour ferry trip away.

While New Bern isn't for the shop-'til-you-drop crowd, the suburbs have the usual array of Wal-Mart, Target, Kmart and other national stores. There's a small mall, Twin Rivers, anchored by J.C. Penney and Belk department stores. Downtown has an eclectic mix of antique and junque shops, boutiques and galleries. For serious shoppers, regional malls in Raleigh are about two hours away, and Wilmington is even closer.

If there's a serpent in this Eden, it's the possibility of hurricanes, say retirees here. Two hurricanes hit coastal North Carolina in 1996 and another in 1998. In 1999, record heavy rains resulting from Hurricane Floyd and other storms caused billions of dollars of damage in the state, although New Bern and the immediate area have been spared serious damage. Flooding is possible in New Bern, but severe storm surges — the killers in most hurricanes — are unlikely here because of New Bern's average elevation of 12 to 18 feet above sea level, the presence of barrier islands east of Pamlico Sound and the sheer distance of New Bern from the open ocean.

However, many retirees say the snows back home were twice as bad as the potential for hurricanes in eastern North Carolina. The infrequent snowfalls in New Bern rarely stay on the ground more than a day or so, although it did snow two to three inches on two occasions early this year, around the time a fluke storm dumped nearly two feet of snow on Raleigh, two hours away.

Some retirees say they also had to adjust to the heat and humidity of summers in New Bern. However, Bill Ball, 60, who with his wife, Judy, 58, relocated from Weirton, WV, in 1994, says the upside is that the warm climate helps his arthritis. "Spending three or four months walking around in 35 degrees and wet, I'd start having a personality change," says Bill. Now, while he's not cured of his arthritis, he no longer has black circles under his eyes from lack of sleep. "We like the basic mildness of the winter, and being hill people tired of hills, it's a pleasure to drive on flat land," he says.●

community college, Craven Community College, and at a campus of a four-year college, Mount Olive College. About 40 miles away in Greenville is East Carolina University, part of the University of North Carolina system and one of the largest universities in the state.

Transportation: Craven Regional Airport, a small but modern airport, is served by US Airways Express, offering flights to US Airways' hub in Charlotte, and Midway Airlines, with service to Raleigh-Durham. U.S. highways 70 and 17 are the major highway arteries. I-95 is the nearest interstate, 80 miles away.

Health: Craven Regional Medical Center in New Bern is a 314-bed, acute-care facility with more than 180 physicians on staff, supported by some 1,400 other staff. About two and a half hours away in Durham is Duke University Medical Center, one of the nation's leading hospitals.

Housing options: The New Bern area offers a wide choice of housing options, from 18th- and 19th-century homes in the downtown historic district ($100,000 to $500,000) to rural mobile home parks to riverfront and golf-course living in planned communities. Among the planned communities in the area are: **Taberna**, (800) 367-1278 or (252) 636-3700, with a private golf course and canoe dock on Brice's Creek and homesites from $29,000 to $200,000, or $140,000 to $450,000 for home and lot; **Evans Mill**, (800) 622-6297 or (252) 633-6100, country-style living on large lots, with lots from the high $20,000s, lots and homes from $155,000; **Greenbrier**, west of New Bern with a noted golf course, The Emerald, and homes from around $115,000 to $350,000; **Fairfield Harbour**, (800) 317-3303 or (252) 638-8011, about 10 miles from New Bern on the Neuse River, with two golf courses and a marina, condos and homes from $100,000 to $400,000. Among local real estate firms serving retirees moving to New Bern are **Coastal Homes Real Estate**, (888) 831-2620 or (252) 635-6500 and **Century 21 Action Associates**, (800) 521-2780 or (252) 633-0075. Retirement specialist Whit Morgan at **New Bern Real Estate** leads prospective residents on a free three-hour tour of New Bern and the surrounding area. For information call (800) 636-2992 or (252) 636-2200.

Visitor lodging: New Bern has a half-dozen bed-and-breakfast inns and a dozen motels. The 172-room Sheraton Grand, $105-$120, is New Bern's lodging leader, with a prime waterfront location near the new convention center, renovated rooms and many upscale amenities, (800) 326-3745 or (252) 638-3585. Comfort Suites, $76-$106, has a lovely Riverfront Park location, (800) 228-5150 or (252) 636-0022. The Airie, $89-$99, is a seven-room B&B in a converted Victorian home in the downtown historic district, complete with player piano in the parlor, (800) 849-5553 or (252) 636-5553.

Information: Chamber of Commerce of New Bern, P.O. Drawer C, 316 S. Front St., New Bern, NC 28563, (252) 637-3111 or www.newbernchamber.com. The chamber offers a relocation guide for $5.

North Fort Myers, Florida

Wide choice of lifestyles makes Florida Gulf Coast community popular

By Karen Feldman

It took Paul and Shirley Reitmeier 16 years to decide where to retire. When they did, they picked a place almost totally opposite their lifestyle in Alaska.

It was a decision that took them from a "northern exposure" to the sunny southwest Florida community of North Fort Myers. The Illinois couple, both 56 and retired from the telecommunications firm Unicom Inc., spent 16 years working in Alaska before buying a motor home and traveling across the country to their new life in Florida.

What made them pick North Fort Myers?

"There were a lot of places we could afford to live, but we wouldn't want to be there because of the environment or it was too remote from our family," Paul Reitmeier says.

They considered the St. Petersburg-Clearwater area but decided to head 125 miles south to North Fort Myers because it was less developed. Plus, they found a planned community that suited their tastes and budget.

They're among a growing number of retirees choosing this spot along Florida's Gulf Coast. The Fort Myers area has been among the nation's fastest-growing regions for more than 20 years. It is especially popular with Northerners who retire and head south for sunnier climes and a more affordable lifestyle.

North Fort Myers has seen its share of this rapid migration but has managed to avoid becoming overdeveloped. White-fenced horse ranches, pastures full of grazing cattle, unspoiled riverfront and a good measure of wetlands remain in this community wedged between Fort Myers and Cape Coral in Lee County.

There are waterfront and golf-course communities and a mixture of single-family homes, condominiums and mobile homes in a wide range of prices.

"You can move here for as little as $30,000 for a nice mobile home or you can buy a big estate if that's what you want," says Kerrey Zito, former executive director of the North Fort Myers Chamber of Commerce.

With nine golf courses, five marinas and at least two dozen planned communities to choose from, there is a development suited to most tastes and pocketbooks.

"North Fort Myers is Lee County's best-kept secret," says Thomas Cirignano, an agent with Century 21's AAIM Realty Group in North Fort Myers. "We still have plenty of country areas offering agricultural space for horse lovers and nurseries."

But, he notes, there is a variety of other housing choices and a growing number of amenities. That's what sold the Reitmeiers on their single-family home in the Sabal Springs development.

Sabal Springs has an 18-hole executive golf course, country club with restaurant, 24-hour security and tennis, among other features. There are a dozen home models, starting in the low $100,000s. Owners must be at least 40 years old and cannot have children younger than 18 living with them. Many residents are retirees, although Shirley says some still work.

Paul likes the fact that there is less traffic in North Fort Myers than in most parts of the county. "We're away from the major traffic patterns, yet we have good access," he says.

For George and Ruth Sherman, it was the proximity to water — and a relentless salesman — that prompted them to buy a condominium in North Fort Myers.

George, 69, a retired branch manager for Yorktown Cabinets, and Ruth, 68, a retired real estate manager, were attracted to the Riverbend development in North Fort Myers.

"What was really irresistible was the Caloosahatchee River and the ca-nals that run all the way around the property at Riverbend," Ruth says. "It is really a charming little area. We liked the golf course and condo, too."

Like many retirees, the Shermans are "snowbirds," spending the winter in Florida and the summer in cooler climes up North. In their case, up North is Annapolis, MD, where their summer house sits along the banks of the South River.

A plethora of affordable housing is one of the community's greatest draws, according to Edward Crimmins, a broker-agent with AAIM Realty Group.

"It's still possible to find very nice homes priced in the $80,000s with central air and heat, water and sewer," he says. "There are waterfront communities, golf communities, condo communities at almost any (price) level."

Cirignano says his waterfront home has appreciated in value about 25 percent over three years while homes in some other areas of the county have declined in value.

Tara Woods is a retirement community of manufactured homes that start in the mid-$60,000s. The development offers 24-hour security, shuffleboard, tennis courts, a courtesy van to Fort Myers shopping centers, swimming pool, exercise room and fishing.

At Foxmoor, condos start at $55,500, and residents have access to swimming, bike paths, tennis and fishing. There are also clustered patio homes and single-family houses in the development.

Heron's Glen Golf and Country Club offers championship golf, security and a host of amenities as well as custom-designed homes priced from $126,000, including lot and oversized two-car garage.

Admiralty Yacht Club, along the Caloosahatchee River, has condos starting at $90,000 with a lake view and climbing to $175,000 for a river view. There also are estate homes available beginning at $175,000.

Just east of Admiralty Yacht Club on the river is Daughtrey's Creek, where it's possible to buy a 2,200-square-foot home with pool on the water for about $250,000.

Says Crimmins, "The dollar will go about 25 percent further in North Fort Myers than elsewhere in Lee County for the same quality home."

While traffic during the winter tourist season can be annoying, the mild weather, social opportunities and cost of living more than offset the crowds for both the Reitmeiers and the Shermans.

"We have people here who are 80 years old and are still playing golf — very active," Ruth Sherman says.

Both couples say they were unprepared for Florida's burgeoning insect population, and Ruth Sherman discovered she was allergic to fire ants. But they say they have grown accustomed to the seasonal influx of mosquitoes and other bugs, including what are commonly called "no-see-ums," tiny gnats that bite and cause itching.

Housing costs and taxes are lower in Florida, the Shermans say, while recreation facilities, volunteer opportunities, crime and traffic congestion are about the same as in Annapolis.

The Reitmeiers miss the mountains and beauty of Alaska, but not enough to suffer through the long winters there. They say the climate, cost of living, health-care facilities and housing costs and availability are better in Florida than Alaska.

While there is no hospital in North Fort Myers, Cape Coral Hospital is just a couple of miles west of the town. Lee Memorial Hospital and Southwest Florida Regional Medical Center are both just a few miles south in Fort Myers.

Southwest Florida Regional performs organ transplants and in 1991 opened a Heart Institute and Emergency Center with a full range of cardiac services. Lee Memorial recently opened HealthPark, a massive and luxurious complex that combines doctors' offices, retail shops and a hospital that looks more like a resort than a medical complex. Many patients travel to Fort Myers from around the country for orthopedic and cataract surgery.

Besides numerous doctors' offices, North Fort Myers has Centra Care, an emergency clinic that operates until late in the evening and on weekends.

North Fort Myers, FL

Population: 46,478
Location: North of Fort Myers, on the Caloosahatchee River in southwest Florida.

Climate:

	High	Low
January	74	53
July	91	74

Average relative humidity: 56%
Rain: 54 inches.
Two-thirds of the annual rainfall arrives between June and September. Winters are mild and pleasant.
Cost of living: 95.2 in Fort Myers, based on national average of 100. Specific index not available for North Fort Myers.
Average housing cost: $115,000
Sales tax: 6.25%
Sales tax exemptions: Groceries, prescription drugs, medical services.
State income tax: None.

Intangibles tax: Assessed on stocks, bonds and other specified assets. Tax rate is $1 per $1,000 value for assets under $100,000 for individuals or $200,000 for couples, and $1.50 per $1,000 value for greater amounts; first $20,000 for individuals and $40,000 for couples is exempt. Some investments are exempt.
Estate tax: None, except the state's "pick-up" portion of the federal tax, applicable to taxable estates above $675,000.
Property tax: Rates are $20.57 per $1,000 of assessed value, with homes assessed at 100% of market value. Taxes on a $115,000 home are about $1,851 with exemption.
Homestead exemption: First $25,000 of assessed value on primary, permanent residence.
Security: 130.4 crimes per 1,000 residents in Fort Myers, higher than the national average of 46.2 crimes per 1,000 residents. Specific crime figures for the town of North Fort Myers are not available.
Religion: Has more than 25 Protestant churches, with synagogues and Catholic churches nearby.
Education: Edison Community College-University of South Florida campus is nearby in Fort Myers. Florida Gulf Coast University opened in Lee County in 1997.
Transportation: Lee County Transit Authority runs buses but routes and schedules are limited. Southwest Florida International Airport in Fort Myers is the nearest major airport.
Health: No hospitals in North Fort Myers, but extensive medical facilities with a full range of services including trauma care are within a few miles.
Housing options: One of the area's main attractions is its wide range of affordable communities for retirees, from manufactured-home subdivisions such as **Tara Woods**, where homes start in the mid-$60,000s, to **Admiralty Yacht Club**, where condos start at $90,000 and estate homes start at $175,000.
Visitor lodging: Best Western Robert E. Lee Motor Inn, (800) 274-5511 or (800) 528-1234, with river views, 108 spacious rooms and heated pool, $69-$89. Across the street is Hampton Inn, (800) HAMPTON, with 123 units, senior discounts, a pool, free local phone calls and continental breakfast, $53-$64 in the off-season, $99-$129 January through April.
Information: North Fort Myers Chamber of Commerce, 2787 N. Tamiami Trail, Suite 100, North Fort Myers, FL 33903, (941) 997-9111 or www.lee-county.com

With a median age of 55, the community offers its older residents some special amenities.

The North Fort Myers Senior Center gives residents age 55 and older a full slate of activities, including pool, card games, tennis, swimming, sing-alongs, puzzles and lots of opportunities to socialize.

For those new to retirement lifestyles, a variety of classes help them bone up on such pastimes as bridge, ceramics, languages, tennis, cribbage and shuffleboard. Dues are $36 a year.

A bingo hall across the street from the senior center operates from early morning to well into the night.

While a lack of cultural opportunities has long been a complaint of area residents, it's a gripe that's fading fast.

Harborside Convention Center, in downtown Fort Myers, provides a venue for top-name celebrities. The Barbara B. Mann Hall, at the Edison Community College-University of South Florida campus in Fort Myers, also offers shows and musical performances, and the Lee Civic Center hosts rock and country music performers, wrestling matches and other events.

A new state university, Florida Gulf Coast University, opened its doors in Lee County in 1997.

New residents can be assured that area attractions will entice friends and relatives to visit.

A trip to Southwest Florida isn't official unless you visit the Thomas Edison Winter Home and the Henry Ford estate next door. The homes of the two friends and industrial magnates lie just over the Caloosahatchee Bridge in Fort Myers, a short drive from North Fort Myers. Each Christmas, the homes are decorated for special holiday tours and musical performances.

For a journey into the heart of the area's marshes, head to Babcock Wilderness Adventures, just north of town in Charlotte County. Climb aboard a large swamp buggy and tour a portion of the Telegraph Cypress Swamp, where alligators, wild boar and bison roam. Tours are by reservation only. Call (941) 489-3911.

North Fort Myers itself boasts some noteworthy sites. Octagon Wildlife Sanctuary houses more than 200 exotic animals, including alligators, monkeys, lions and other animals that for one reason or another cannot live on their own in the wild.

ECHO — Educational Concern for Hunger Organization — is a demonstration farm on Durrance Road in the rural northeast portion of the community. The farm serves as a training base for missionaries, scientists and Peace Corps workers who pass along the techniques they learn to peoples of Third World countries. The group recently branched out into edible landscaping, offering a variety of plants for sale to the public. ECHO offers tours at 10 a.m. on Tuesdays, Fridays and Saturdays.

Every March, North Fort Myers hosts the Cracker Festival where mock Union and Confederacy forces re-enact the Battle of Fort Myers, the southernmost battle of the Civil War, which took place in 1864.

For a taste of what life must have been like in the area a century ago, when residents rode horses along dirt paths through the marshy woodlands, take a trail ride. DJ's Ranch offers trail rides daily, and some night rides that include a bonfire. At the Shell Factory, you can examine thousands of shells free of charge. The 70,000-square-foot facility has shells for sale, along with lots of souvenirs, T-shirts and crafts.●

Ocala, Florida

Retirees like rural setting, warm weather with seasons

By David Wilkening

Ocala's not your normal Florida scene — and that's one reason it's increasingly popular with retirees.

It's a small city in a rural setting, not a flashy coastal town. The terrain is hilly, perfect country for the many horse farms clustered in this north-central part of the state.

Palm trees are greatly outnumbered by sprawling old oak trees that shade homes and streets. Frame houses that conjure images of Northern residences add variety to the concrete-block structures so common in Florida. Although modern malls have brought in chain stores, Ocala still has a traditional downtown square that lends charm to the community.

With its somewhat sleepy atmosphere, plus a low cost of living and good climate, Ocala has attracted many retirees in recent years.

"We like the slow pace, and the people are friendly," says Julia Tierney, 57, who moved to Ocala from Washington, DC, with her husband, Francis, 67.

While many retirees have migrated here from the North, Ocala also is drawing retirees who've become disenchanted with other parts of Florida, particularly the southern area where congestion and crime are rising problems.

Marvin and Jean Van Merton, 71 and 60 respectively, retired from Oak Forest, IL, to Fort Myers first. She likes to joke that she prefers Ocala over the coast because "the cars don't rust like they do on the ocean." But there are more serious reasons for their move to Ocala.

"The coast was too crowded. There was too much traffic," says Jean. The Van Mertons like the more rural lifestyle Ocala offers. "We haven't found a better place to be," Jean says.

Ocala has become one of the fastest growing cities in the country. With a population of about 60,000, it is the largest city in Marion County, which has a population of 242,357.

Newcomers are quickly absorbed, in part because they are so common, according to the area's economic development council. Some 17 percent of the adults in Marion County have moved here within the past three years. Half of all residents have lived in the county less than 10 years, and a demographic profile of the county shows 29 percent of its residents are 65 or older.

Lester Crull, 72, and his wife, Marjorie, 60, moved here in 1990 from Waco, TX, but had lived much of their lives in Michigan. The Crulls like Ocala's country atmosphere and the variety of opportunities to do volunteer work, in hospitals and in programs to help shut-ins.

"We had gone past Ocala during other Florida trips," he says. "We knew it was more laid-back and a little cheaper than a lot of areas."

Indeed, the town is less costly than many other parts of Florida. Low cost of housing is a major reason that Ocala is more affordable. The average price of existing single-family homes is only $80,611, according to the economic development council. Apartments also are reasonable, with recent figures showing the average monthly rent at $450 for one bedroom and $565 for three bedrooms.

"There's a lot of varied housing. You can find just about anything you want," says Jean. The Van Mertons looked at several options before choosing a custom homebuilder.

Many retirees favor the more traditional-style homes familiar in the North, but here they come with pools, sun decks and other extras that reflect the active outdoor lifestyle.

Ocala's average property tax is in the middle range for the state, says Villie Smith, Marion County's assistant property appraiser.

While Ocala boasts the traditional sunny Florida weather, it has an added attraction: a sense of seasons.

Joseph C. Finzer, 77, came here 22 years ago from his job in research-engineering at Eastman Kodak in Rochester, NY. He wanted to escape the snow.

"Ocala is somewhat like the North in that there are four seasons," he says, adding that the changes are more subtle than up North but more distinct than in southern Florida. Ocala is drawing retirees from southern Florida, many of them transplants who fled Northern climates, then decided they missed seasonal changes. But they don't want severe winters.

In Ocala, winter is short and mild. In January the average low temperature is 43 degrees, and in summer, the average high is 91. The annual mean temperature is just about perfect, at 70.

Along with its attributes come some drawbacks.

Residents bemoan a lack of public transportation but note that the problem is common in smaller cities throughout the country.

The area is short on fine dining opportunities but does have many reasonably priced, family-style places where dinners start at $5.95. On the upper price end, dinner entrees start at $11.

Summers can be humid, even sticky hot. Some retirees have problems with allergies they didn't have elsewhere and complain about bugs that, like humans, thrive in the balmy climate.

Ocala, like other cities its size, can't offer the cultural smorgasbord possible in metropolitan areas. The Tierneys, for example, miss the cultural amenities of their native Washington, DC, but say Ocala is expanding its offerings.

"Just in the short time we've been here (two years) we've seen changes, such as the enlargement of the civic theater," says Julia.

Its Appleton Museum of Art has more than 6,000 pieces and has been praised by directors of the National Endowment for the Arts as being "a major museum that would be impressive in any community."

The Crulls think Ocala's cultural pursuits aren't as good as their previous residence, a college town, but they think it has other advantages.

Ocala, an Indian name, was Florida's southernmost tourist center for years until railroads began laying the tracks that would take visitors all the way down the coast.

In modern times, it's emerged as a cattle- and horse-breeding area. Today, 400 of the state's 600 horse-breeding farms are here, according to the state's Thoroughbred breeders association.

The area is also famous for its huge, 388,315-acre Ocala National Forest, a major recreation area for tourists and residents who enjoy fishing, hunting and camping.

Two other popular getaways are nearby. The Juniper Springs Recreation Area offers a tropical setting, with a huge rustic waterwheel churning 8 million gallons of cool spring water a day. At Silver Springs, glass-bottom boats take visitors over natural springs that have been bubbling for centuries. A 350-acre nature park at the attraction has been the setting for "Tarzan" and "James Bond" movies.

A drawing factor for Ocala is that it's centrally located, on major highways, but not in the midst of too much action. For instance, beaches are only 75 miles away on the Atlantic side and 40 miles on the Gulf side. And Orlando with its many family attractions is about 100 miles away.

In health care, Ocala has two full-service hospitals, as well as psychiatric and drug and alcohol centers. Shands Hospital in Gainesville, 35 miles north, offers outstanding specialized care.

Florida as a whole attracts many retirees because of its financial and physical climate. The state long has granted a $25,000 homestead exemption on taxes for property owners of all ages. The state has no personal income tax and no property tax on automobiles. It does have a sales tax of 6 percent, but groceries, medical and professional services and prescription drugs are exempt.

Whether they are seeking lower taxes or snowless winters, there are numerous reasons retirees are choosing to relocate here. Some reasons may be subtle, at least for Northerners who fled the cold but didn't want to totally escape their past.

"The good part about Ocala," says Finzer, "is that if you lived up North, it'll make you think a little about where you're from. But the good thing is that we don't get snow here."

Well, not usually, at least. It did snow briefly a few years ago. Finzer didn't mind — since it was only a flurry.●

Ocala, FL

Population: 60,000 in Ocala, 242,357 in Marion County.

Location: In north-central part of state, with hilly terrain that's become a center for Thoroughbred horse-breeding. Close to Ocala National Forest, with its hot springs parks.

Climate:

	High	Low
January	67	43
July	91	71

Average relative humidity: 55%
Rain: 53 inches.
Moderate climate. Mild winters; hot, humid summers.

Cost of living: 94.2 in Marion County, based on state average of 100.

Average housing cost: $80,611

Sales tax: 6%

Sales tax exemptions: Groceries, medical services, prescription drugs.

State income tax: None.

Intangibles tax: Assessed on stocks, bonds and other specified assets. Tax rate is $1 per $1,000 value for assets under $100,000 for individuals or $200,000 for couples, and $1.50 per $1,000 value for greater amounts; first $20,000 for individuals and $40,000 for couples is exempt. Some investments are exempt.

Estate tax: None, except the state's "pick-up" portion of the federal tax, applicable to taxable estates above $675,000.

Property tax: $23.68 per $1,000 of assessed value, with homes assessed at 100% of market value. Taxes on an $80,611 home would be $1,316 with homestead exemption.

Homestead exemption: First $25,000 of assessed value on primary, permanent residence.

Security: 119.7 crimes per 1,000 residents, higher than the national average of 46.2 crimes per 1,000 residents.

Religion: 135 Protestant churches, 5 Catholic churches and 3 synagogues in the Ocala area.

Education: Classes are available at Central Florida Community College in Ocala and the University of Florida in Gainesville.

Transportation: No public transportation is available, residents rely on cars. The nearest airport is Gainesville Regional Airport, 40 miles away.

Health: Ocala has two full-service hospitals, Ocala Regional Medical Center and Munroe Regional Medical Center. The county has three hospitals with a total of 703 beds and seven nursing homes with a total of 942 beds.

Housing options: A number of communities geared to retirees have been developed. **Oak Bend**, (800) 354-3636, offers manufactured homes from about $29,000-$50,000. **Oak Run Country Club**, (800) 874-0898, or (800) 342-9626 in Florida, has homes from the $70,000s to $150,000s. **Ocala Palms Golf & Country Club**, (800) 872-7256, has single-family homes from the $80,000s to $150,000s. The area also has several retirement centers.

Visitor lodging: Ocala Holiday Inn, doubles $82, (352) 629-0381.

Information: Ocala-Marion County Chamber of Commerce, P.O. Box 1210, Ocala, FL 34478, (352) 629-8051 or www.ocalacc.com.

Ormond Beach, Florida

Once a haven for the rich, this Florida community offers affordable housing

By David Wilkening

Nestled next to one of the world's most famous and busiest beaches is a quieter area that became known in the early part of the century as a winter home to many of America's richest families — including the Vanderbilts, the Astors and the Fords. Local lore has it that John D. Rockefeller settled here only after his staff spent five exhaustive years searching for the country's best retirement area.

Today you'll find that the small seaside town of Ormond Beach (population about 35,000) is home to many year-round residents. They may not be as famous or rich as those early settlers, but they like it here just the same.

Many of them shared with Rockefeller a desire to find the perfect retirement home. And many must have agreed with the oil tycoon's conclusion, because the area now has a large contingent of retirees from out-of-state.

"Ormond Beach was more residential and less touristy than other areas we looked at in Florida," explains Ruth Alvord, a 61-year-old widow who moved here from Buffalo, NY, in 1968 with her husband when he began receiving a disability pension.

"We liked the beauty of the location and the small-town flavor," she says. "I'm also near the river and the ocean. And I'm able to do things outdoors all year around."

Ormond Beach's fortunate geographical accident is to be on the Atlantic Ocean, about eight miles north of Daytona Beach and 90 miles south of Jacksonville. Orlando — the world's most popular tourist destination — is an hourlong ride by car. Historic St. Augustine is only a 30-minute drive.

Nearby Daytona Beach makes the news each year with its colorful auto racing and motorcycle madness, but Ormond Beach is better known for its tranquillity. It is a city in a parklike setting of tree-lined streets with residents often living in small houses only a few minutes by car, or even a few minutes on foot, from the ocean.

With sometimes-stiff ocean breezes helping keep the temperature at an annual average of 70 degrees, Ormond Beach offers a pleasant climate with many recreational opportunities near the water.

There are six golf courses — four public and two private — in Ormond Beach and many others within easy driving distance. Tennis enthusiasts have at their disposal two tennis complexes as well as 22 municipal courts popular with keenly competitive retirees. The city also operates baseball, soccer and football fields, picnic sites, horseshoe and shuffleboard courts and an extensive jogging trail.

All of this helped attract retirees like Joe and Patricia Lipscomb. Joe preferred what he saw in Ormond Beach to the many cities he visited throughout the world while traveling as a consulting engineer.

Joe, 68, had lived here in the 1950s before his job took him traveling. "Our children were born here. It was like coming home for us," says Joe, who was so eager to get here that he and his wife, Patricia, left their Pennsylvania home and headed for Florida on the very day that he retired.

They say they like the generally laid-back and slower-paced suburban lifestyle of Ormond Beach. They also like the variety of available housing. High-rise condos offering views of the Atlantic Ocean can cost upwards of $105,000 (the average area condo is $125,000), but Joe and others say that smaller homes only two or three blocks from the ocean still can be found for $60,000 to $70,000. Manufactured homes can be bought for even less.

Rental homes also are relatively inexpensive. The average two-bedroom rental is $450 to $500, and the median rent in the area is a reasonable $485, according to the local chamber of commerce.

The average single-family home sale last year was $100,000, according to local real estate agents. But homes priced under $79,000 represented almost a third of those sold.

Retirees like Joe Lipscomb who like to fish can choose between the Atlantic Ocean and the Halifax River, which are only about two blocks apart. "I do pretty well fishing, though I don't go out and slay them," he jokes. "At least I get to stand in the water and cool off."

Joe fishes in the Halifax for game fish, trout and mangrove snapper. He sometimes ventures a few blocks to fish the glistening blue waters of the Atlantic, where cavorting dolphins can sometimes be seen from the shoreline.

He readily admits that Ormond Beach does not have as much culture as would be found in a larger northern city. But he points out that for a smaller area, there's a surprising amount of high-toned activity. The London Symphony, for example, comes for an extended visit every two years. It's an event that the entire community embraces with unbridled enthusiasm.

The Ormond Beach Performing Arts Center sponsors children's theater, a school of dance, touring theatrical productions, community theater and a concert series. There are big-name concerts in Daytona Beach, and other regularly scheduled events such as summer's Jazz Matazz festival also offer a variety of entertainment.

The Seaside Music Theater in Daytona Beach brings in a variety of distinguished actors and directors and produces many popular plays. The Memorial Art Museum showcases rotating exhibits of Florida artists, and the nearby Museum of Arts and Science has a planetarium. A local landmark and restaurant can be found at the Ponce de Leon Lighthouse, built in 1887 and still offering a panoramic view of the entire area.

Another Northerner who liked what she saw when she first visited was Mary Panny, 71, who lives in a manufactured-home community with her husband, Ed, also 71. They like "the easy availability of everything," says Mary. "We're close to a lot of things, such as the beach and shopping."

They also are close to regional shopping malls and Walt Disney World in Orlando, about 60 miles away. So many visiting relatives have wanted to see the land of Mickey Mouse that the couple bought an annual pass to the theme park.

Still another couple, Vera and Charles Hood, moved from Birmingham, AL, soon after Charles, an executive with the telephone company, retired just over a decade ago. "We had visited my son, who lives here, and we thought this area was quieter and more residential than Birmingham," Charles explains.

In common with most residents, the Hoods like the proximity of the

Ormond Beach, FL

Population: 34,791

Location: Bordering the Atlantic Ocean and bisected by the Halifax River. About 90 miles south of Jacksonville, just north of Daytona Beach, and about 60 miles from Orlando.

Climate: High Low
January 68 47
July 90 73

Average relative humidity: 61%

Rain: 49 inches.

Cost of living: 95.6 in Volusia County, based on state average of 100.

Housing costs: Average home price is $100,000. Average rental rates are $450-$500 a month for a two-bedroom unit. Median rental cost is $485.

Sales tax: 6% levied by the state.

Sales tax exemptions: Groceries, medicines, some professional services.

State income tax: None.

Intangibles tax: Assessed on stocks, bonds and other specified assets, with some investments exempt. Tax rate is $1 per $1,000 of value for assets under $100,000 for individuals or $200,000 for couples, and $1.50 per $1,000 of value for greater amounts. First $20,000 for individuals ($40,000 for couples) is exempt.

Estate tax: None, except the state's "pick-up" portion of the federal tax, applicable to taxable estates above $675,000.

Property tax: $23.89 per $1,000 of assessed home value, with homes assessed at 80 percent of market value. Taxes on a $100,000 home are $1,433 with homestead exemption.

Homestead exemption: First $25,000 of assessed value on primary, permanent residence, plus $500 exemption for widows and widowers.

Security: 46.8 crimes per 1,000 residents, close to the national average of 46.2 crimes per 1,000 residents.

Religion: More than 250 houses of worship serve many faiths in Volusia County.

Education: Inexpensive adult-education courses ranging from fishing to watercolor painting to yoga are available at The Casements, former home of John D. Rockefeller. The Ormond Beach Senior Center has exercise and dance classes, computer instruction and foreign-language courses, among others. Daytona Beach Community College, a two-year school, also offers a variety of classes, including an especially popular adult-education course on how to write mystery novels. It's taught by local authors.

Transportation: Daytona Beach International Airport has 27 daily departures, with nonstop flights to Atlanta, Charlotte, Jacksonville, Miami, Newark, Orlando, Philadelphia and Raleigh-Durham. Scheduled airlines include Continental, Delta, Gulfstream and USAir. There are nearby municipal airports at Ormond Beach, DeLand and New Smyrna. Orlando International Airport, about 60 miles from Ormond Beach, has daily nonstop flights to more than 64 U.S. and 14 international cities.

Health: Hospitals include Memorial Hospital-Ormond Beach, with 205 beds, more than 300 physicians and Volusia County's only cardiovascular center performing open-heart surgery. Radiation therapy for cancer also is available. Other facilities in the area include Halifax Medical Center in Daytona Beach, which has 402 doctors and 748 nurses.

Housing options: The Falls at Ormond, (904) 673-2333, is the area's first manufactured-home community with such features as 24-hour security, clubhouse, pools, tennis courts and nine lakes. Homes start at $48,000. A newer manufactured-home community by the same builder is **Aberdeen at Ormond Beach**, (800) 898-5541, where homes start at $69,999. Another option is **Ormond in the Pines**, (904) 676-7463, but there's a waiting list of about two months for the 214 apartments that are owned and operated by the nationally known Holiday Retirement Corp. Rent starts at $995 a month, which includes three sit-down meals a day, housekeeping services and paid utilities. The facility has a social director and offers organized events.

Visitor lodging: Ormond Beach's newest hotel is the seven-story, 98-unit Coral Beach, (800) 553-4712. Ocean-view rooms generally are $50-$160 a night. Prices can go higher during special events.

Information: Ormond Beach Chamber of Commerce, 165 W. Granada Blvd., Ormond Beach, FL 32174, (904) 677-3454 or www.ormondchamber.com.

beach, as do John and Nancy Goss, 74 and 68 respectively. The Gosses, who were lifelong residents of New York City, considered Melbourne and Key West before retiring to Orlando. But then they were lured to Ormond by its beaches and climate.

"Ormond Beach is about three to four degrees cooler than Orlando because of its proximity to the ocean, which gives us a nice breeze," says John. Summers can be muggy, but residents say that ever-present air conditioning helps keep them cool.

If anyone gets a little hot under the collar in the dog days of summer, the near-perfect climate of winter months makes up for it. In January, for example, the average temperature is 63 degrees, compared to 82 degrees in July. The average annual rainfall is almost 49 inches, much of that coming between June and October, usually in the form of afternoon showers that cool the beaches before giving way to sunny skies.

Larry and Olive Gorman, both 70, moved to Ormond Beach for health reasons. He was in the computer business and she was a teacher in Albany, NY, before they retired first to a small town near Sarasota on Florida's Gulf Coast.

"It was very quiet and there was not much activity. At that time, there were hardly even any restaurants," Larry recalls. But the final straw came when he experienced heart problems and lost confidence in the local hospital.

"My wife didn't feel safe living there anymore. We happened to talk to a real estate agent who told us the hospital in Ormond Beach was world-famous for its heart specialists," says Larry. He later had successful heart surgery at Memorial Hospital-Ormond Beach, a 205-bed facility that is the county's only cardiovascular center performing open-heart surgery.

Larry also likes the wide selection of area restaurants. There are inexpensive hamburgers and milkshakes at the 1950s nostalgia-rich Doo-Wop-A-Doo. More sedate and upscale surroundings are found at such longtime favorites as Julian's Restaurant, known for its prime rib and live music.

The Gormans and others say Ormond Beach is retiree-friendly. There are early-bird dinner specials at affordable restaurants, and many merchants offer special senior discount days.

There are a few drawbacks, but local retirees don't seem to mind the noisy two-wheelers that sometimes venture into Ormond Beach from Daytona Beach, where motorcycle racing is becoming increasingly popular. "The motorcyclists are these people who like to sometimes run around in the woods and watch girls wrestle in coleslaw and stuff, but they go their way while we go ours. They don't really bother anybody, other than they make some noise," says Joe Lipscomb.

Like many Florida communities, Ormond Beach was little more than a settlement as recently as a century ago. It began to appear on the map when the East Coast Railway was extended in 1886. Two years later, the once-stately but now abandoned Ormond Hotel opened to cater to such society travelers as the Astors and the Rockefellers, who began migrating down from the North.

Situated in Volusia County, about 90 miles south of Jacksonville, Ormond acquired the no-longer-used nickname of "gateway to the tropics." In common with its more flashy big sister, Daytona Beach, Ormond also was popular with early auto enthusiasts.

Just after the turn of the century, Ransom Olds and Alexander Wilton, two early manufacturers of "horseless carriages," challenged each other to an auto race on the hard-packed sand of Ormond Beach. Each clocked an identical 57 miles per hour, yielding no victor but inaugurating a tradition of racing that continues today at world-famous Daytona International Speedway.

For some 60 years, owners and manufacturers of the world's best-known motor vehicles — Olds, Ford, Chevrolet and Kaiser — endeavored to set speed records on the wide beaches of Ormond and Daytona. A new motor sports attraction, Daytona USA on the grounds of Daytona International Speedway, chronicles this rich auto history.

Beach racing is a thing of the past, but motor vehicles (with some restrictions) still are allowed to drive along much of Volusia County's 43-mile stretch of hard-packed beaches. There are inevitable complaints, and it's likely that the vehicles eventually will be banned for safety and environmental reasons, though polls taken by the *Daytona Beach News Journal* generally have shown the local population to be evenly divided on the issue of driving on the beaches.

What would John D. Rockefeller have made of the evolution of Ormond Beach from a wealthy winter home of racing enthusiasts to a suburban-style community popular with retirees? It's hard to say, but one thing seems certain. The notoriously tight-fisted Rockefeller would almost certainly approve of Ormond Beach's tax rate, one of the lowest in Volusia County.

Yes, Rockefeller might still think this was the best place to retire.●

Oxford, Mississippi

A rich cultural and literary tradition enriches this unique Mississippi town

By Linda Herbst

If you ever tour the Deep South, make time to visit one of its jewels — Oxford, home of the University of Mississippi. Located on the picturesque route through the Mississippi Delta from Memphis to Natchez and New Orleans, Oxford has long been a favorite stopover for travelers meandering through the historic South.

Just an hour south of Memphis, the gracious curves of the area's rolling hills slope to level stretches of grassy valleys and pastureland. On the way into town, travelers often stop at the gates of one of the farmhouses that line the road. This particular one belongs to one of the nation's most popular writers, John Grisham, and is just one of Oxford's many literary landmarks. Beginning with Pulitzer and Nobel Prize winner William Faulkner, Oxford was the home and inspiration of nationally renowned novelists, poets, photographers, artists and musicians for the greater part of the 20th century.

It is its literary tradition, however, that sets Oxford apart from other arts meccas. Writers as diverse as Faulkner, Willie Morris, Larry Brown, Barry Hannah, Cynthia Shearer, John Grisham, Donna Tartt and Mary Hood have lived and worked in Oxford. Nearly every week world-renowned writers and poets visit Oxford and the university to read from their work and revel in what nearly all have called its "literary mystique." Residents and visitors alike have a hard time pinning down exactly what that mystique is all about, but one thing is for sure: The creative atmosphere here is intoxicating.

Once a year, usually in April, Oxford and the University of Mississippi host the Oxford Conference for the Book, a weeklong conference attended by the nation's foremost publishers, novelists, short story writers and journalists. The nonacademic conference is generally free and open to the Oxford community, and the whole town gets into the spirit of celebrating books. In August, the university hosts one of the most respected and longest-running literary conferences in the world, the Faulkner and Yoknapatawpha Conference.

Despite the Southern summer sun, the town seems to burst at its seams with distinguished Faulkner scholars from around the world, and once again the city revels in the excitement of being part of this important tradition. In many ways, Oxford is the manifestation of Faulkner's words: "The past is never dead. It's not even past." This is true of both the city of Oxford and the University of Mississippi, known as "Ole Miss," whose homes and public buildings house the sorrows and joys of the people who lived here during its frontier days, through the Civil War and the turbulent '60s. In its own way, Oxford's heritage is a story about the South from a perspective unparalleled in Southern history.

Aside from its literary traditions and historical value, Oxford's charms are so numerous that it is hard to choose the singular aspect that has placed it at the top of great places to settle for retirement. The overwhelming majority of retirees living in Oxford, however, are quick to point out that while Oxford is a great place to retire, it's not a retirement community.

"By that, I mean Oxford's a real place with a multigenerational population. It's not a controlled environment at all," says Bill Gurley, who with his wife, Clair, retired to Oxford several years ago from Greenwood, MS. Bill, a former bank president, maintains that the word "retirement" has great latitude. "For us, it doesn't necessarily mean strictly a time of leisure. Just because you don't have a job anymore doesn't mean you don't work," points out Bill, who has become a sales associate with a local real estate firm.

Bill and Clair's raised Louisiana cottage was completed in 1996. They were lucky to have found a lovely lot in an older, established neighborhood within easy walking distance of the town square. One of the most charming features of their three-bedroom home is its wraparound porch, which the Gurleys have decorated with ceiling fans and small groupings of easy chairs and cocktail tables. Bill and Clair can be seen nearly every nice afternoon enjoying the ease of this wonderful porch, and neighbors and friends are likely to join them.

Several years ago Clair Gurley was diagnosed with a heart problem, so quality of health care was a primary concern when it came time to decide on a retirement location. Baptist Memorial Hospital-North Mississippi, a 211-bed acute-care facility, has more than 70 medical and surgical physicians representing more than 30 specialty areas. It is one of the region's fastest-growing hospitals, serving a population of 200,000 in an eight-county area. Current expansion plans include an outpatient surgery center, cancer center and wellness and rehabilitation center.

The Gurleys also wanted to live in a college town. "The university and all that it offers — open-mindedness, continuing education, performing arts — were very important to us," says Clair. And with two daughters and two grandchildren living out of state, the Gurleys were pleased that Memphis International Airport was only 70 miles north of Oxford. The airport is located in the southernmost area of Memphis, so driving there doesn't require big-city traffic nerves.

Most of Oxford's retirees share Bill's energetic attitude toward retirement. Rev. Frank Poole and his wife, Mary, retired to Oxford in the summer of 1999 from Baton Rouge, LA. As part of the United Methodist tradition, Frank and Mary have made a lifelong commitment to ministry through music. They joined the Oxford-University Methodist Church and immediately became involved in its music traditions.

Frank and Mary love the atmosphere of small towns. In Oxford, they feel safe and independent from the constraints a larger place would put on them in terms of safety. Traffic can be hectic at times, but Mary says that because the weather is mostly nice, she and Frank feel safe enough to walk at any time of the day or night. Frank and Mary have moved into their newly constructed home but continue to add the finishing touches, and they also appreciate the level of trust they have with their contractor and the workmen who come and go at their home.

Mary's mother and father, Dr. and Mrs. A.B. Lewis, live directly behind them. The Lewises, both in their late 90s, have full-time sitters and house-

Oxford, MS

Population: The population of the city is 10,263, and enrollment at the University of Mississippi is about 10,800.

Location: Oxford is located in the hilly section of north Mississippi, 75 miles from Memphis, TN, and 165 miles from Jackson, MS, the state capital. Elevation is 380 feet.

Climate:

	High	Low
January	55	36
July	91	72

Average rainfall: 54 inches.

Average snowfall: 3 to 4 inches.

Cost of living: Below the national average at 91.4%.

Median housing cost: $120,000 for a single-family, three-bedroom home.

Sales tax: 7%

Sales tax exemptions: Residential water, gas and electricity, prescription drugs, payments made by Medicare and Medicaid, and health-care services.

State income tax: Graduated in three steps of 2%, 3% and 4% of taxable income.

Income tax exemptions: Qualified retirement income is exempt, including Social Security benefits, public and private pensions, IRAs and annuities. There is an additional $1,500 personal exemption for residents age 65 and older.

Intangibles tax: None.

Estate tax: None, except the state's "pickup" portion of the federal tax, applicable to taxable estates above $675,000.

Property tax: Property and automobiles are subject to ad valorem taxes. Automobiles are assessed at 30% of market value, and 6% of the assessed value is used as a tax credit. Residential property in Mississippi is assessed at 10% of its market value. A house valued at $125,000 would be assessed at $12,500. Based on the local tax rate of $86.15 per $1,000, the yearly tax would be $559.98, with the $6,000 exemption noted below.

Homestead exemption: There is a homestead exemption in the form of a tax credit of $240 for all homeowners. Residents age 65 and above can claim the first $6,000 of assessed value or $60,000 of market value as exempt from all ad valorem taxes.

Security: 31.6 crimes per 1,000 residents, lower than the national average of 46.2 crimes per 1,000 residents.

Religion: The Oxford area represents, supports and conducts services for a wide variety of beliefs including Protestant, Catholic and Jewish faiths.

Education: The University of Mississippi focuses on seven major schools of study: liberal arts, engineering, education, law, pharmacy, business and medicine. Masters and doctoral degrees are offered. Ole Miss is a participant in the Elderhostel program, and planning has begun on an institute for lifelong learning.

Transportation: Memphis International Airport is 70 miles north of Oxford and provides service to all major cities.

Health: Baptist Memorial Hospital is a 211-bed acute-care facility. It has more than 70 medical and surgical physicians representing more than 30 specialty areas. Leased by one of the largest not-for-profit health care systems in the country, Baptist Memorial Health Care Systems of Memphis, the hospital provides a full range of comprehensive medical care to all ages.

Housing options: Housing sites in the historic neighborhood are few, and houses generally cost more in that neighborhood. However, housing sites are available in newer housing developments that dot the county. At **St. Charles Place**, one mile south of Oxford Square, most homes have three bedrooms and two baths and range in price from $145,000 to $200,000. For more information, call Kessinger Real Estate, (662) 234-5555. **Grand Oaks** is set among rolling hills, with family homes that start at $350,000 on one side of the golf course development and three-bedroom golf villas ranging from $180,000 to $200,000 on the other side. For more information, contact Kessinger Real Estate, (662) 234-5555. At **Azalea Gardens**, an independent and assisted-living facility, services include transportation, activities, dining, housekeeping, beauty shop, massage therapist, exercise rooms, performances, arts and crafts, a full-time nurse and personal emergency response system. These services are available both to residents of the main facility as well as homeowners on the property. Popular new cottages for sale on the grounds have two bedrooms and range from $139,000 to $145,000. For a monthly fee, the management also takes care of 24-hour security, trash pickup and yard maintenance. For more information about Azalea Gardens, call (887) 234-9600.

Visitor lodging: There are eight hotels with more than 400 rooms, including three bed-and-breakfast inns. A sampling includes the Downtown Inn, $60-$70, (662) 234-3031; Oxford Days Inn, $49-$56, (662) 234-9500; Comfort Inn, $65, (662) 234-6000; and Oliver-Britt House, $49-$70, (662) 234-8043.

Information: Oxford-Lafayette County Chamber of Commerce, 299 W. Jackson Ave., P.O. Box 147, Oxford, MS 38655, (800) 880-6967, (601) 234-4651 or www.oxfordms.com. Oxford Tourism Council, P.O. Box 965, Oxford, MS 38655, (601) 234-4651. For information about Hometown Mississippi Retirement, call (800) 350-3323.

keepers, and Mary says it is a joy and a privilege to spend these last years with her parents. Dr. Lewis is the retired dean of liberal arts at the University of Mississippi. He and his wife have lived in Oxford for 40 years, so Oxford has been a second home to Frank and Mary in many ways.

One of the many aspects of Oxford and the university that the Pooles enjoy is the frequency and quality of concerts and theater performances on campus each season. From opera and Shakespeare to visiting symphonies and dance companies, the university's "artist series" is an affordable entertainment option.

"I was made for retirement," says Frank. "I have so much time now to concentrate on music."

"Some of the nicest evenings we've had here in Oxford have been those in which we've had a light supper, then walked to campus to a performance or concert," adds Mary. The Pooles live less than a quarter-mile from the university, which isn't necessarily a rarity in Oxford. Many retirees have chosen to live near the university and historic Oxford Square, and one can see the over-60 crowd walking side-by-side with coeds on any nice afternoon.

Aside from concerts and theater performances, the university offers an array of continuing-education classes, including wine tastings, music lessons, language classes, computer workshops, painting and sculpture lessons and cultural excursions to the Mississippi Delta and Memphis.

Usually, when asked, Oxford retirees either claim the wealth of cultural opportunities, the presence of the University of Mississippi, the literary heritage or the overwhelming sense of history as Oxford's biggest draws. "But don't forget the shopping and dining," says Clair Gurley.

Oxford's historic town square has a lively year-round festive atmosphere. The community boasts more than 50 restaurants, many of them unique to Oxford — gourmet coffeehouses, fine dining, Memphis-style barbecue and down-home cafes. In the spring and fall, students and residents dine on balconies overlooking the square, shop in the multitude of boutiques, gift and antique shops, or just pause for a neigh-

borly chat on one of the square's strategically placed park benches. Oxford's centrally located department store, Neilson's, is privately owned by an Oxford family and is considered the South's oldest store, established in 1848.

"Let's just say it fits every criteria for a retirement choice," says Shirley Perry, one of Oxford's newest retirees. "In doing my research, I found that Oxford was literally the only place that actually fit every criteria I had on my list — and the list was long, I can tell you."

Shirley retired to Oxford in September 1999, making the move from her longtime home in Boston, where she was a consultant to pharmaceutical and biotech industries in business development. "I had been thinking of where to retire for quite some time," says Shirley. "I literally subscribed to every magazine about the subject. I went to the library; I made calls and attended conferences. My criteria were very specific.

"It had to be a town versus a city, for one — someplace easy to negotiate, as well as one with a defined sense of community," she says. "It had to have regularly organized cultural events, since I've always loved community theater. It also had to have a sense of history and achievement. When I discovered that Oxford had all that and more — a university, a great healthcare community and a low cost of living — my decision was made."

Shirley's traditional brick house is in a lovely new neighborhood called South Oaks. Just three miles from the charm of the town square, South Oaks features spacious, wooded lots. Shirley's new four-bedroom home is built in what Shirley calls "Mississippi modern" style and sits on a half-acre corner lot. The one-story home has an imposing gabled roof, and the rooms are light and airy with high ceilings.

Writing and bicycling are two of Shirley's favorite hobbies. Despite the hills, Shirley finds cycling in Oxford a pleasure. The streets are safe and bicycle-friendly, she says, and there are many cyclists, young and old, on the streets. Plans are underway to create a bike path along the old railroad track that runs through town.

For most of her professional life, Shirley worked for the Central Intelligence Agency in Europe. She plans to begin

work on her memoirs as soon as her house is completed, and she finds the literary community and the many writers' groups and classes stimulating.

Small, safe, friendly, beautiful and cultural usually add up to expensive, but that's not necessarily true in Oxford. While the real estate market has boomed in the last few years, with values on some properties growing 100 percent or more, deals are still available. The average three-bedroom home is $120,000. Generally, properties at this price won't be located in the historic district, but Oxford has many welcoming neighborhoods, new and old. There are virtually no empty lots for sale in the historic part of town.

Occasionally there are houses for sale that can be remodeled or demolished and rebuilt. At press time there were five houses for sale in the historic district, ranging in price from $225,000 to $750,000.

New housing developments are abundant, however. These include St. Charles Place, designed in the mode of a small harbor town or New Orleans neighborhood; Grand Oaks, an upscale neighborhood on a lovely 18-hole golf course; and Azalea Gardens, an independent and assisted-living retirement community.

The average cost of living in Mississippi is 10 percent below the national average, and Mississippi residents benefit from the lowest per capita tax burden in the nation. In addition to low taxes in general, retirees living in Mississippi benefit from additional tax breaks. Social Security is not taxed, regardless of total income. Retirement income from IRAs, 401(k)s, Keoghs and qualified public and private pension plans are not taxable. The state welcomes, and even recruits, relocating retirees.

"I actually received an invitation to retire in Mississippi," says Shirley Perry, referring to the state's active retiree recruitment program, Hometown Mississippi Retirement. "I'd always heard about Southern hospitality, but now I'm experiencing it first-hand."

"We love the mixture of young and old, as well as the mixture of cultures here," says Frank Poole. "It's a small, but cosmopolitan town — all the benefits of a city without the negative side. We're having a great time enjoying our freedom together here."●

Palm Desert, California

Arts and culture mix with sports in Southern California oasis

By Judy Wade

For Bob and Jane Herrman, New Jerseyites transplanted to a suburb of Los Angeles, the decision on where to retire was based on economics.

"We wanted a view, which to us meant beachfront, and that was too expensive," says Bob. The couple then looked for other types of views, concentrating on areas near Los Angeles to stay close to their grandkids.

Eventually the Herrmans, both 64, traded waves for greens and decided on a three-bedroom condominium in Woodhaven Country Club in Palm Desert, CA. From their large covered patio they overlook a golf course lake and the fifth fairway.

Says Jane, "We love the weather here, we have good friends and we feel safe."

Although Palm Desert is an entity of its own, it's part of a multicity enclave of desert resort communities that includes Palm Springs, Indian Wells, Rancho Mirage, Cathedral City, La Quinta and Desert Hot Springs. They blend together with few distinguishing perimeters except for city signs, making it difficult to talk about one without including them all.

Collectively known as Palm Springs Desert Resorts, the area has a reputation of belonging to celebrities and the moneyed chic. It is true that the 45-mile Coachella Valley is one of the wealthiest areas in the nation. Yet clean, dry desert air and a cost of living lower than major metropolitan areas of California have attracted a population of 40,000 to Palm Desert, 30 percent of which is above age 60, according to statistics from the Riverside County Office on Aging.

Tidy rows of date palms (imported from Egypt) and the jagged San Jacinto and Santa Rosa mountains form a picture-postcard skyline. Low-rise construction and thoughtfully planned open spaces engender an uncrowded feeling even during winter months when visitors swell the valley's population by 100,000 or more. Streets named for Fred Waring, Bob Hope, Dinah Shore, Gene Autry, Gerald Ford and Frank Sinatra verify that the star-studded area pays tribute to the over-50s.

Palm Desert's personality emphasizes arts and culture while capitalizing on its oasislike appeal. The community is younger than adjacent Palm Springs and is carefully considering the direction it's taking as it grows. Traffic flows smoothly on wide, well-planned boulevards. Even when winter visitors are in residence, facilities do not seem overburdened. Some streets have golf cart lanes, and Town Center Mall has stations for recharging carts while owners shop.

Most of Palm Desert's retirees come from other parts of California. Figures kept by Del Webb's Sun City, an active adult retirement community a few miles from Palm Desert, identify 80 percent of purchasers as from the Los Angeles/Orange County/San Diego areas. For these retirees, accustomed to California prices, the state's above-average cost of living is not a surprise.

For out-of-staters like Dorothy and John Freeman from Winchester, TN, higher property taxes and automobile insurance were a bit of a shock. The couple moved to the area to abandon the cold and damp for a clime that helps alleviate the pneumonia that bothers John, 70.

The Freemans expected a buyer's market because they'd been told that California's real estate prices were severely depressed. But it was a challenge to find a home in their price range, says Dorothy, 68.

The Freemans purchased a condominium in a residential neighborhood. It was a good decision, says Dorothy, who loves the warmth and sunshine. "We're not golfers, but we've bought bicycles and we spend a lot of time riding around the neighborhood and in a nearby park," she says.

With a community mixture of retirees and winter visitors, young professionals and growing families, Palm Desert has a wide choice of residential options. Elegant country club communities with resort amenities proliferate along Country Club Drive. Single-family homes and condos in these posh developments begin at about $160,000.

According to real estate agent Leon Salant, a more reasonably priced option can be a manufactured home in a country club setting.

"In Palm Desert Greens, adjoining Palm Desert, resales range from $75,000 to more than $250,000, including the land," he says. A monthly fee covers maintenance of association-owned property, greens fees for the 18-hole course and 24-hour security. To own in Palm Desert Greens or Portola Country Club, another manufactured-home community nearby, one person must be age 55 or older.

Palm Desert's warm, dry, smog-free climate produces more than 300 sunny days a year. Golf courses are open all year. During summer months when the mercury can top out at 115, Bob Herrman says golfers simply adjust their schedules to play early in the day.

More than 87 area golf courses serve a seasonal population of 285,000-plus. About 30 courses are open to the general public, so anyone with a longing for the links may be able to play on courses that host the Bob Hope Chrysler Classic, the Nabisco Championship, the Skins Game and the Frank Sinatra Celebrity Invitational.

To make sure the greens are always grassier on these desert courses, an extensive groundwater basin beneath the sand is augmented with "imported" water from the Colorado River. Unlike drought-plagued Los Angeles, water here is plentiful. Water bills are quite low, but during summer months when air conditioning is a necessity, electric bills can soar well above $200 per month. Many residents opt for a level-pay plan on which monthly bills are a set amount year-round, thereby evening out the wide fluctuation between winter and summer.

Area medical care is excellent, but the cost runs higher than the national average. Desert Hospital in Palm Springs has the largest trauma and emergency care facility in the Coachella Valley. It also has rehabilitation and cancer centers and offers acute care. The paramedic system has an average response time of three to five minutes.

The Betty Ford Center, Dolores Hope Outpatient Center and Desert Orthopedic Center are part of the Eisenhower Medical Center in Rancho Mirage. This 239-bed nonprofit community hospital, with the capabilities of a major medical center, specializes in cardiology and cancer care.

For many, personal health concerns focus on wellness rather than illness, which is what enticed Charlie McDermid from Lake Tahoe, CA, to the desert.

"We wanted a healthy lifestyle," says McDermid, 61, a widower who plans to remarry. "We play golf or tennis every day." As a resident of Palm Valley Country Club, he finds all the activities he wants just outside his door.

Shoppers' needs also are close at hand. Besides the boutiques and designer shops expected in a resort community, large air-conditioned malls include Town Center with 150 stores

Palm Desert, CA

Population: 40,000 permanent residents (more in winter), 285,000 in the valley.

Location: In the Coachella Valley of Riverside County, 125 miles east of Los Angeles and 15 miles east of Palm Springs. Area also includes Cathedral City, Rancho Mirage, Indian Wells, Bermuda Dunes, La Quinta, Thousand Palms and Indio.

Climate:

	High	Low
January	70	38
July	107	77

Average relative humidity: 38%
Rain: 5 inches.
Lower humidity in summer helps keep soaring temperatures comfortable during mornings and evenings. Cool winter nights can dip to just above freezing.

Cost of living: Above average (specific index not available).

Median housing cost: $180,000 for a single-family home, but many lower-cost options are available, such as manufactured homes ($70,000) and gat-

ed condominium complexes with a median of $165,000.

Sales tax: 7.75%

Sales tax exemptions: Groceries, prescription drugs, professional services.

State income tax: Graduated from 1% to 9.3%, depending on income and filing status.

Income tax exemptions: Social Security benefits are exempt.

Intangibles tax: None.

Estate tax: None, except the state's "pick-up" portion of the federal tax, applicable to taxable estates above $675,000.

Property tax: Rate varies, but the average is about $12 per $1,000 of valuation, with homes assessed at 100 percent of market value. Tax on a $180,000 home is about $2,070 yearly, with the homestead exemption listed below.

Homestead exemption: $7,500 off assessed value for homeowner-occupant.

Security: 79.5 crimes per 1,000 residents, higher than the national average of 46.2 crimes per 1,000 residents.

Religion: More than 100 churches, synagogues and temples represent 40 denominations.

Education: College of the Desert is a two-year community college offering degree and certificate programs. California State University San Bernardino satellite campus offers four-year degrees and graduate studies.

Transportation: SunBus Transit Agency bus system links the valley's nine towns for a flat fare of 75 cents.

Health: Excellent care but expensive. In the area: Desert Hospital, Eisenhower Medical Center, John F. Kennedy Memorial Hospital, Canyon Springs Hospital and Counseling Center.

Housing options: Wide range of manufactured homes, condos, gated communities. **Del Webb's Sun City Palm Desert**, (800) 533-5932, in nearby Bermuda Dunes has homes from the low $100,000s. **Suncrest Country Club**, (760) 346-5866, leases manufactured-home lots around its nine-hole executive golf course. At **Palm Desert Greens**, (760) 346-8005, an established senior-oriented manufactured home community, some lots are available for resale through local realty agencies. **Hacienda de Monterey**, (800) 624-0236, has independent-living rental apartments and skilled nursing care; studio apartments with two meals a day begin at $1,250.

Visitor lodging: Palm Valley Country Club, one-bedroom golf course condos from $185 a night, (800) 869-1130; Holiday Inn Express, $79-$89, (800) 465-4329; Vacation Inn, $79, (800) 231-8675. Lodging rates typically are lower during summer months.

Information: Palm Desert Visitor Information Center, 72-990 Highway 111, Palm Desert, CA 92260, (800) 873-2428 or www.pdcc.org.

and Desert Fashion Plaza with Saks Fifth Avenue, Gucci, The Sharper Image, Victoria's Secret and 54 more trendy shops. At Desert Hills Factory Stores, 20 minutes west of Palm Springs, 52 factory outlets boast savings of 30 percent to 70 percent. Stores include Esprit, Eddie Bauer, Bass Shoes and Oneida Silver.

Nourishment for the mind as well as the body is found in Palm Desert's collection of retail art galleries. Along fashionable El Paseo and nearby Palm Canyon Drive, 30-some galleries offer contemporary paintings and sculpture, traditional arts and offbeat collectibles. Interesting restaurants and boutiques make El Paseo a favorite strolling street.

The entire community has become involved in the Art in Public Places program, referred to by residents as a museum without walls. Residents are directly involved in the selection and installation of art and sculpture in parks, public buildings and private businesses. So far more than a dozen sculptures have been placed around the city.

The McCallum Theater for the Performing Arts and the Annenberg Theater in the Palm Springs Desert Museum present classical, family and popular entertainment.

One of the area's most famous showplaces, the 1936 Plaza Theater in Palm Springs, is home to a razzle-dazzle, glitz-and-glamour revue called the Fabulous Palm Springs Follies. The entire cast is 50 to 86 years old. "Follies Ladies," former Rockettes, Copacabana and Las Vegas showgirls and dancers, perform production numbers a la the Ziegfeld Follies of the '30s and '40s.

Its producer, Riff Markowitz, 56, left Hollywood to retire. After two years of "memorizing the mountains," he accepted the producing challenge. "We chose 'seasoned citizens' as per-

formers because they actually were part of that magical age of American theatrical history," Markowitz says. Most live in the Palm Desert area.

College of the Desert has a highly regarded fine arts department, catering to older students with lower-division college, community and vocational programs. The palm-shaded campus also provides space for the San Bernardino satellite center where seniors can take classes for $7 a semester on a space-available basis. Chapman University offers certificate training, credentials and bachelor's and master's programs designed for the adult student.

Senior Lifestyle magazine, a monthly publication covering the Coachella Valley, includes a golf guide and restaurant section, which notes the popular money-saving early-bird specials. Publisher/editor Evan Israel says that because it caters to the high percentage of older residents, the magazine spotlights more than 300 activities for seniors in each issue.

Joslyn Senior Center serves more than 6,000 seniors a month, seven days a week. Computer classes are among the favorite programs, says Judy Graham, executive director. "People don't feel intimidated in classes with their peers. Computer classes now have waiting lists," she says.

The center's regulation croquet court, with a whites-only dress code, is popular for morning play.

The Coachella Valley Retired Senior Volunteer Program, known as RSVP, offers involvement for those age 55 and older. "We work with 90 non-profit public and private agencies that currently keep about 1,200 volunteers very busy," says director Lou Shultz. RSVP pairs a person's abilities and interests with various opportunities.

While some residents know every golf course and restaurant, others

choose the rich resources of nature for their entertainment. Half an hour away, Indian Canyons on the Agua Caliente Cahuilla Indian Reservation are open for hiking and picnicking. Within the canyons, oases verdant with fan palms create sharp contrasts to the stark desert.

A 14-minute trip on the Palm Springs Aerial Tramway puts the area in geographical perspective, providing a 180-degree overview of the Coachella Valley. From the desert floor, where temperatures can be higher than a hundred degrees, the 80-passenger enclosed cars rise to 8,516-foot slopes that often are covered with snow.

The ecology comes to life in the Living Desert, a 1,200-acre exotic botanical garden and wild animal park where native vegetation flourishes alongside plants from the deserts of the world. Marked paths and an exhibit building put guests close to bighorn sheep, golden eagles and other desert denizens, all in their natural habitat.

An hour away, Joshua Tree National Monument encompasses 568,000 acres of desert preserve. Coyotes and desert pack rats share terrain with dozens of cactus varieties and the many-armed Joshua trees, which early settlers thought looked like the Biblical Joshua praying to heaven. Visitors come for camping, hiking and rock climbing.

Despite its affluent image, desert life is informal. In keeping with a lively, active way of life, running shorts and golf togs are acceptable almost everywhere.

If you're not accustomed to a desert climate, John Freeman suggests you visit first: "Come and look. Stay for a while. Come during different times of the year. Then you'll get a true picture of what the desert is really like and how beautiful it can be."●

Paris, Tennessee

Friendly people and four-season climate give Tennessee community all-American charm

By William Schemmel

Nine years ago, when they began thinking seriously about retiring, Al and Mary Walker surveyed the country from Chesapeake Bay to the Arizona desert. Among their stacks of literature, they found a retirement guide that gave high praise to an unexpected place. It was their old hometown of Paris, TN.

The Walkers grew up in this western Tennessee town of less than 10,000 people. But for 33 years, Al's career as a nuclear energy engineer had moved the family to Philadelphia, Boston and Pittsburgh — and as far as Saudi Arabia and South America. The Walkers traveled around the world.

"The retirement guide made Paris sound so good, we decided we'd better come down and look it over," says Al. "We did a survey of the area. We talked to banks and people we still knew here. We liked what we saw, but we wondered whether we could fit in again after being away all these years. So, we decided to buy a house and give it a try for two years."

Now, the Walkers can't imagine living anywhere else. "The safety factor is one of the things retirees should look at closely," says Mary. "Paris and Henry County have a very low crime rate. We also have a wonderful four-season climate. And, unlike many small towns, our downtown courthouse square is very stable, with hardly any vacant storefronts."

Housing costs and property taxes are other retirement pluses, say the Walkers. Their 2,800-square-foot home on a wooded one-acre lot cost $70,000. They pay yearly property taxes of about $700.

And there are other advantages. Paris has plenty of ways to keep active retirees like the Walkers as busy as they want to be.

"This is a very active community," says Mary. "You can belong to civic clubs, garden clubs, political clubs and charitable organizations. You can get involved with chamber of commerce programs. The Arts Council produces a couple of plays a year, and they also bring in plays and performers from Nashville and Memphis."

"The people here are very open to newcomer participation," adds Al. "But you have to circulate and show an interest. If you sit back and wait to be called, you'll probably mold over."

Kentucky Lake, 16 miles east of downtown Paris, is easily the area's biggest attraction. The waterway was created by a Tennessee Valley Authority dam on the Tennessee River. Its 2,100-mile shoreline is a happy hunting ground for fishermen and a major playground for boaters, swimmers and water-skiers. It's separated from equally impressive Lake Barkley, on the Cumberland River, by Land Between the Lakes, a recreation-rich, 270-square-mile peninsula administered by the National Park Service.

All this fishing naturally calls for a celebration. Each April, more than 90,000 visitors come from all over the United States for what's billed as the world's biggest fish fry. During the weeklong festival, more than 13,000 pounds of Kentucky Lake catfish, bass and crappie are dispatched. Other highlights include parades, car shows, arts and crafts and a rodeo.

Unlike the Walkers, Lois and Pat Smith had never heard of Paris until they stopped here on their way home to Chicago. They ended up buying a house and have been Parisians for nine years.

"The years have just flown by," says Lois. "We love living here, and we can still drive back to Chicago in less than a day."

The Smiths' three-bedroom, ranch-style house is valued at about $120,000. The 2,000-square-foot home sits on a three-acre lot, with plenty of space for Pat's flourishing vegetable garden. It's in Country Club Estates, a neighborhood of well-spaced, meticulously kept homes developed about 20 years ago.

Avid golfers, the Smiths are a two-minute golf cart ride from Paris Country Club's nine-hole course. When they need a change of fairways, they drive 15 minutes to Paris Landing State Park. On Kentucky Lake, the 841-acre park's 18-hole course is the equal of many private courses. Seniors play free all day Monday. They can purchase a $300 annual pass for unlimited play on state park courses all over Tennessee. The resort-style park also has an inn with 100 motel-type rooms, a conference center, restaurant, swimming pools, tennis courts, marinas, fishing docks, picnic areas and other amenities.

Paris is about 40 miles north of Interstate 40 — the main east-west route between Nashville and Memphis — and about 60 miles west of Interstate 24, a busy route that links Nashville with freeways into St. Louis and Chicago. Residents say the area's location off the interstate highways is a mixed blessing. It keeps out "strip development" but sometimes discourages new business and industry.

Locally, small family-owned stores on the courthouse square are complemented by Wal-Mart and other chain stores. Most Parisians drive to Nashville (110 miles east) for heavy shopping, entertainment and air transportation. Airfares from Nashville, they say, are generally less expensive than from Memphis (133 miles west). Large regional shopping malls in Nashville's western suburbs are less than two hours by car.

Nashville's restaurants also are an attraction for Paris newcomers accustomed to fine dining. Prohibition of mixed drinks limits Paris restaurants mainly to small establishments specializing in steak and seafood. Package liquor, beer and wine are available.

Like Pat and Lois Smith, many Paris retirees are Midwesterners who originally came for vacations at Land Between the Lakes. Others come on business with industrial plants that the area has attracted in recent years.

"My wife and I came down on business in 1984," says former Detroiter Art Nellen. "We were staying out at Paris Landing State Park when my wife became ill. We were treated so well, we started thinking it would be a nice place to live."

Paris boasts a full-service hospital, the 142-bed Henry County Medical Center, with a 24-hour emergency room and facilities for nuclear medicine, cardiac/intensive care, outpatient surgery, physical therapy and other specialized treatment. A helicopter is available around the clock to fly patients to larger hospitals in Nashville and Memphis.

"The people here are wonderful and very accepting of outsiders," says Art. "I keep myself busy by going to the lake, working in my yard and doing projects for the chamber of commerce."

He helped organize a "Paris USA Convention" that attracted representatives of nine American cities named for the French capital, which also sent an official. (Chartered in 1823, Tennessee's Paris was named in tribute to the Marquis de Lafayette's aid to the American Revolution. Henry County was named for patriot Patrick Henry.) As a lasting landmark of the convention, the engineering school at Christian Brothers College in Memphis built a 65-foot scale model of the Eiffel Tower. It now sits in Paris' Memorial Park.

Other newcomers are military families assigned to nearby Fort Campbell, KY. About 1,200 Army officers retire from Fort Campbell every year, and many of them make their permanent homes in Paris and elsewhere in western Tennessee and Kentucky.

With its growing retirement community, Paris is experiencing a short-

Paris, TN

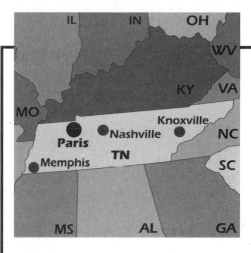

Population: 9,825 in Paris; 30,957 in Henry County.

Location: On Kentucky Lake in western Tennessee, 110 miles west of Nashville and 133 miles east of Memphis.

Climate:

	High	Low
January	45	26
July	90	70

Average relative humidity: 60%
Rain: 50 inches.
Snow: 11 inches.
Winters are moderately cold; summers are warm and humid. Most rainfall arrives in winter months.

Cost of living: Below average (specific index not available).

Average housing cost: $125,000 for a new three-bedroom in the lakes area. Homes in town average about $75,000.

Sales tax: 8.25%

Sales tax exemptions: Prescription drugs, professional services, hearing aids, prosthetic devices.

State income tax: None on earned income, but there is a state tax of 6% on interest and dividend income from certain stocks, bonds, long-term notes and mortgages. Interest from CDs, savings accounts and federal, state or local government bonds is exempt.

Income tax exemptions: $1,250 exemption ($2,500 for married couples filing jointly). Individuals 65 or older with total annual income of $16,200 or less ($27,000 for joint filers) are exempt from the tax.

Intangibles tax: None.

Estate tax: None, except the state's "pick-up" portion of the federal tax, applicable to taxable estates above $675,000.

Inheritance tax: From 5.5% to 9.5%, based on amount of inheritance; spouse normally exempt.

Property tax: City taxes are $33.90 per $1,000 of assessed value and county taxes are $22.30 per $1,000, with homes assessed at 25% of market value in both places. City tax on a $125,000 home is about $1,059, county tax about $700. Property values are re-evaluated every 10 years.

Homestead exemption: Homeowners age 65 and older with a household income of $10,000 or less are eligible for a state tax relief credit.

Security: Complete crime figures for Paris were not available at press time, but partial figures show 39.8 crimes per 1,000 residents, lower than the national average of 46.2 crimes per 1,000 residents.

Religion: About 100 Protestant churches and one Catholic church in Henry County.

Education: Four-year colleges at nearby Clarksville and Jackson, TN, and Murray, KY.

Transportation: No public transportation. 100 miles to Nashville International Airport.

Health: 142-bed Paris/Henry County Medical Center. Helicopter ambulance to hospitals in Nashville and Memphis.

Housing options: Affordable housing includes new and older homes in the city and in unincorporated areas of the county and a small selection of rental homes and apartments. Many retirees prefer living in one of many developments on Kentucky Lake and smaller lakes, where single-family homes and condominiums are available for $125,000 to $500,000 and higher.

Visitor lodging: Best Western Travelers Inn, $44 double, (800) 528-1234 or (901) 642-8881; Paris Landing State Park, from $56 double off-season (November-February) to $68-$72 in season, (901) 642-4311.

Information: Paris/Henry County Chamber of Commerce, P.O. Box 8, Paris, TN 38242-0008, (800) 345-1103, (901) 642-3431 or www.paris.tn.org.

age of available housing in some price ranges. Lois Smith says the shortage is especially acute in large $80,000-$90,000 houses that many retirees want. But she adds that there is a good supply of smaller houses in the $40,000-$50,000 range. Most of those are older homes inside the city. On the upper end, large homes on spacious lots in the new Country Woods area are $125,000 and up.

Many retirees want to live on Kentucky Lake. Originally from Wisconsin, Bill and Dot Jerstad were living in Jackson, TN, just 60 miles south of Paris, when a realty company invited them to look at lots on the lake.

"That was in 1959," Bill recalls. "The lots they showed us were on a ridge where you couldn't see the water. But we saw two other lots overlooking the water. We paid $1,400 for each of them, and in 1988, we built our home here."

Bill says they recently were offered $250,000 for their spacious one-level house, which is surrounded by gardens and lake-view patios.

To accommodate newcomers who want to live on Kentucky Lake, Buchanan Resort, a 50-year-old recreation area owned by a local family, has built a 70-unit lakeside condominium complex called Pleasant Place. The 1,800-square-foot, three-bedroom condos run from $150,000 and up, plus a monthly $150 maintenance fee. Each condo has a large outside deck overlooking the lake. Amenities include marinas, swimming pool, tennis courts and a restaurant.

The rolling, heavily wooded farmland around Paris is attractive to retirees like Grace and John Underwood. John, originally from Illinois, and Grace, a Henry County native, met while they were students at nearby Murray State University in Kentucky. They taught in western Tennessee public schools for 38 years.

"Family was one of the big reasons we decided to retire around Paris," says John, a former school principal. "At the time, one daughter and her husband lived just across the road and another daughter lived in Paris. Along with that, we've always enjoyed a rural atmosphere. Living conditions here are great. We have a definite change of seasons, and taxes and the cost of living are reasonable."

The Underwoods built a 1,600-square-foot "Tennessee tenant-style" house with most of the living space downstairs. An upstairs loft serves as Grace's workroom and a dormitory for visiting children and grandchildren.

"Before we started building, we studied our previous house to see what was really necessary," Grace says. "We wanted a house that was comfortable, functional, easy to clean and inexpensive to heat and cool."

To stay active and bring in added income, Grace specializes in restoring plaster picture frames, which were popular in the 1920s. John restores antique furniture in a workshop behind the house. They operate booths in downtown antiques stores. Their neighbors in the rural Palestine community, about 15 minutes from downtown, include 70 Mennonite families who relocated from Kentucky.

Unlike many small American towns, downtown Paris is alive and well. Small department stores, apparel, jewelry, sporting goods, drug and antique stores, banks and restaurants ring the tree-shaded Henry County Courthouse. Many of the buildings have been returned to their original 1890s look, with freshly painted facades and awnings. Parking is free on the street and in two city-owned lots.

Early in the morning, retirees gather around tables on the courthouse lawn for lively games of dominoes and pitch, a popular card game. When the weather is bad, they have a "reserved" room in the courthouse basement.

"We attribute the square's prosperity to two things," says Bryant Williams, editor emeritus of *The Post-Intelligencer*, Paris' daily newspaper. "First, the Downtown Merchants Association is very strong. They put pressure on the building owners to restore their turn-of-the-century look. They compete strongly with the shopping centers that have robbed so many small towns of their livelihood.

"Secondly, when the courthouse got into bad disrepair, we organized the Paris/Henry County Development Corp. as a non-profit organization so gifts would be tax-deductible. We raised about $75,000 to build brick sidewalks, new lawns and lighting fixtures. The county then got in the action and refurbished the courthouse inside and out. It's the second-oldest working courthouse in the state, and now it looks very much as it did when it was new in 1897."

To many residents, the downtown square symbolizes a way of life in Paris.

"We especially like the easy pace of life," says Art Nellen. "The climate's perfect, the cost of living is reasonable and you can be as active or inactive as you want to be."●

Pensacola, Florida

Colonial Spanish appeal adds to sparkling beaches of Florida's Panhandle

By Constance Snow

From Spanish galleons to the high-flying Blue Angels of Pensacola Naval Air Station, ancient and modern mariners have been attracted by the natural beauty of the coast of the Florida Panhandle. Clear turquoise waters lap at glistening sugar-white sand (99 percent pure quartz) on 40 miles of shoreline from Perdido Key to Navarre.

The first snowbirds to relocate in Florida hit Pensacola's beaches in 1559, establishing the state's earliest European settlement several years before St. Augustine, the oldest city in the United States. Pensacola was settled permanently in 1698.

Three centuries later, retirees are finding the same stunning natural attractions, now augmented by a town that's a Creole charmer. Old Pensacola's early Spanish cottages surrounding oak-shaded Seville Square have been converted into smart restaurants and shops. Nearby, New Orleans-style lacy iron-work decorates Spanish renaissance buildings of the Palafox Historic District. And, the North Hill Preservation District, with more than 500 houses in 50 blocks, is a living museum of Queen Anne, neoclassic, Tudor revival and Mediterranean architecture.

When Bill and Carol Ross wanted to retire from their jobs in Hong Kong with IBM, they found that Pensacola had the spark of cultural energy they had enjoyed in their years of living around the world. They also had worked in Atlanta and Washington, DC, and were eager to settle into a less hectic community for retirement.

"I moved 29 times with IBM, so I didn't really have roots anywhere," says Bill, 62, who was drawn to the "small-town amenities and friendly, honest people" of Pensacola. "It's sort of an easygoing lifestyle where the clerks in the stores really try to help you — not just sell you something."

Their search for a new home began with a map and a list of towns.

"When they (IBM) talked to Bill about the early retirement package," Carol says, "we sat down and started making a list of the things we wanted in a retirement community — a full university, close to water, a nice-sized town but not too big."

They decided to visit Pensacola first, then make day trips to Mobile, AL, and Panama City and Tallahassee, FL, before investigating other sites.

"We looked around for a week and we kept saying, 'We ought to drive over to Mobile one day' or 'We ought to drive over to Panama City one day,' but we never drove anywhere," says Carol, 48. "We liked it so much that we never went to the other places. We started looking for a house."

An ever-growing population of transplants from larger cities supports a booming arts colony that flourishes in the seaside village atmosphere. The historic Saenger Theatre, which hosts Broadway road shows from September through May, also is home to the Pensacola Symphony Orchestra, First City Dance, the Choral Society and the Pensacola Opera.

The downtown Civic Center seats 10,000 for concerts, sports, conventions and other major programs. Community productions are staged by the Pensacola Little Theatre, and the University of West Florida produces Artists in Residence Summer Theatre. Pensacola Junior College sponsors its own theatrical season as well as a lecture series.

A quirky setting in the former city jail (complete with iron-barred cells and looming stairwells) keeps the mood light at Pensacola Museum of Art, a regular stop for national touring exhibits. Local painters and crafts-people create the stock and man the sales desk at Quayside, the largest cooperative art gallery in the South. And each fall, the Greater Gulf Coast

Arts Festival attracts more than 100,000 visitors.

Meanwhile, the cultural calendar is peppered with a lively collection of other special events: the Fiesta of Five Flags, Fourth of July in Old Seville, Homecoming for the Blue Angels (the U.S. Navy's precision flight team), a chili cook-off, a jazz festival, a sea-food celebration and much more.

Like many area retirees, the Rosses are members of a thriving network of community volunteers.

Bill serves on the Advisory Council for the College of Business at the University of West Florida and sets up guided tours at the National Museum of Naval Aviation. Enthusiastic gardeners, Carol and Bill both pitch in with landscaping and carpentry for the local chapter of Habitat for Humanity, a nationwide "barn-raising" organization that helps elderly and low-income residents build their own houses.

The Pensacola area is rich with affordable housing. A typical 1,600-square-foot, single-level house (with two or three bedrooms, two baths and a garage) costs $96,000, with average property taxes of about $1,500.

Apartments average $550 per month, rental homes $700. Monthly rates for condominiums on Pensacola Beach range from $750 to $1,200 per month. And more than 25 retirement and life-care communities are located in the area, many with on-site medical facilities.

The Rosses worked with an architect for three years to create their own custom-designed house on a small, relatively undeveloped island where friendly porpoises swim right up to their front yard.

The intricate coastline of the Panhandle zigzags along bays, sounds and inlets, providing plenty of waterfront home sites. But efforts by local preservationists have established safeguards against the high-rise blight that plagues South Florida.

The Gulf Islands National Seashore is a 150-mile strip of barrier islands, natural harbors and submerged land, most of which is located in Pensacola. It was created in 1971 to protect and conserve the natural beauty of more than 100,000 acres of land and water for future generations and to defend the area against overdevelopment. On Santa Rosa Island and nearby mainland areas, 19th-century coastal defense forts and World War II batteries remain, and archaeological sites at Naval Live Oaks are a link to earlier settlements.

Jim and Janet Hess wrote "big water" on the first line of their wish list when they began planning his retirement from a bank in Muncie, the landlocked Indiana city where they had lived for 30 years.

An initial scouting trip to the Carolinas was rerouted because of bad weather. Then their southern detour to visit friends in Fort Walton Beach came to an abrupt halt about 40 miles up the Florida Gulf Coast.

"We took the three-mile bridge to Pensacola Beach and went no farther," says Janet. "We knew we had found home. The emerald-blue water and snow-white sand clinched it for us."

Self-described "water people," the Hesses spend many of their days swimming and exploring the shore-

Pensacola, FL

Population: 60,637 in Pensacola, 300,700 in Escambia County, 112,300 in Santa Rosa County.

Location: In the Panhandle on Florida's Gulf Coast. Pensacola and Pensacola Beach are in Escambia County, but the peninsula between them is in Santa Rosa County. Terrain is sandy beaches, salt marshes, Southern mixed forest. A series of natural harbors and waterways are protected by a necklace of tiny islands. Elevations vary from sea level to more than 300 feet inland.

Climate:

	High	Low
January	62	45
July	89	74

Average relative humidity: 73%
Rain: 60 inches.
Mild winters, hot and humid summers. Annual rainfall peaks with summer thunderstorm season. Snow is rare.
Cost of living: 96.9, based on national average of 100.
Average housing cost: $106,113.
Sales tax: 7%
Sales tax exemptions: Groceries, prescription drugs, medical services.
State income tax: None.
Intangibles tax: Assessed on stocks, bonds and other assets. Tax rate is $1 per $1,000 of value for assets under $100,000 for individuals or $200,000 for couples, and $1.50 per $1,000 value for greater amounts; first $20,000 for individuals and $40,000 for couples is exempt. Some investments are exempt.
Estate tax: None, except the state's "pick-up" portion of the federal tax, applicable to taxable estates above $675,000.
Property tax: $25.62 per $1,000 of assessed value downtown, $23.62 elsewhere in the city, $18.56 in unincorporated areas of the county. Assessment is based on 100% of market value. Yearly tax on an $106,000 house in the city is about $1,913 with the homestead exemption noted below.
Homestead exemption: $25,000 off assessed value on primary, permanent residence.
Security: 61.3 crimes per 1,000 residents, higher than the national average of 46.2 crimes per 1,000 residents.
Religion: More than 370 churches of various denominations and two synagogues.
Education: University of West Florida and Pensacola Christian College offer full four-year programs. Pensacola Junior College and George Stone Vocational College also serve the community.
Transportation: Escambia County Transit Authority's city buses offer routes and schedules with reduced rates for senior citizens. The Pensacola Regional Airport is served by several major airlines and commuter flights, and Amtrak stops en route between Los Angeles and Miami.
Health: Baptist Hospital (546 beds) has an emergency/trauma center and an electrophysiology laboratory for the diagnosis of heart disease. West Florida Regional Medical Center (547 beds) and Sacred Heart Hospital (431 beds) offer full-service acute care. Hospitals at Pensacola Naval Air Station and Eglin Air Force Base treat military retirees. Lifeflight Helicopter is a 24-hour air ambulance.
Housing options: Wide range of housing includes patio home subdivisions, townhouses and condos starting in the $40,000s. Waterfront property available on gulf, bay, sound, bayou and river. **Marcus Pointe**, (850) 484-9999, and **Champions Green**, (800) 445-2507 or (850) 932-9228, are two of many area golf course communities. **Sandy Key**, (800) 233-4469 or (850) 492-4469, and **Perdido Sun**, (800) 227-2390 or (850) 492-2390, are gulf-front condominium high-rises. **Azalea Trace**, (800) 828-8274 or (850) 478-5200, and **Homestead Village**, (800) 937-1735 or (850) 944-4366, are retirement communities.
Visitor lodging: On Pensacola Beach, Clarion, $143-$159 for one-bedroom suite with kitchenette, (800) 874-5303; Best Western, $134-$162 double with kitchenette, (800) 633-0266. There are more than 7,300 rooms available.
Information: There is a retirement/relocation specialist on staff at the Pensacola Area Chamber of Commerce, 117 W. Garden St., Pensacola, FL 32501, (850) 438-4081 or www.pensacolachamber.com.

line. They have moved three times in the Pensacola area, and now divide their time between Muncie, caring for Jim's 91-year-old mother, and their new condo on Pensacola Beach.

From the western tip of Perdido Key to the long barrier island of Santa Rosa (a skinny sandbar shared by the neighboring resorts of Navarre Beach and Pensacola Beach), Pensacola's clear waters are a boater's paradise.

Private and public marinas are plentiful. Snorkelers and scuba divers can paddle along natural reefs or venture into numerous wrecks, such as the USS Massachusetts, a 350-foot World War I battleship that sank in 1927 in just 30 feet of water.

Nearby, the spring-fed wilderness streams of the Coldwater, Blackwater and Sweetwater/Juniper creeks crisscross the "canoe capital" of Florida. Fishermen will find inexpensive charters as well as several public fishing piers. Hikers can tramp through Big Lagoon State Recreation Area or Bay Bluffs Park, where an elevated boardwalk descends Florida's only scenic bluffs, formed more than 20,000 years ago. More than 10 area golf courses are uncrowded and affordable.

The Hesses are actively recruiting their Northern friends — four other families have relocated to Pensacola because of their endorsement — but the couple has made many new friends as well. Janet is vice president of the women's group at St. Francis of Assisi Church, and Jim paints children's faces for the city's annual Cinco de Mayo Celebrations. Both help out with preparations for tongue-in-cheek extravaganzas staged by the flamboyant Krewe of Wrecks each Mardi Gras.

"One of the reasons we haven't been more involved is that Jim suffered a heart attack shortly after we moved here," says Janet, 59. "He had to have triple bypass surgery and has completely recuperated."

"I feel like a million dollars," agrees Jim, 60. "We have complete confidence in the Pensacola medical facilities and doctors, due to an excellent experience during this time."

Five hospitals with a total of 1,696 beds are serviced by Lifeflight Helicopter, a 24-hour air ambulance. The 546-bed Baptist Hospital boasts a state-of-the-art emergency and trauma center. One of 10 Florida facilities designated for the treatment of acute spinal cord injuries, it also operates the area's only electrophysiology laboratory for the diagnosis of heart disease.

Major hospital and commissary facilities are located at Pensacola Naval Air Station and Eglin Air Force Base. The Pensacola Naval Hospital was cited for superior care and treatment of retirees and dependents.

Area bases also offer clubs, boating, camping, golf, bowling, swimming and other amenities for military retirees, and several active associations welcome new members.

Those support services were a big part of the attraction for Ed Maddock, 71, a retired Navy commander, and wife Gloria, 70, a former library assistant. They had been stationed here in the early 1950s and returned in 1989, following a 23-year residence in Annandale, VA.

The Maddocks are history buffs who both volunteer at the National Museum of Naval Aviation. Gloria also works with the Corry Station Library. They left Virginia to escape cold weather and traffic congestion.

"After retirement," Ed says, "I got a job in downtown DC, only 10 miles from home, but it took an hour and a half to commute one-way." He enjoys Pensacola's easy driving, three seasons (spring, summer, fall), seafood and low cost of living: "I like sitting and watching my bank account grow."

Gloria says she likes this "small town with friendly people," although she's not too crazy about "the humidity in July and August. The temperatures are OK, but not the humidity."

The Rosses and Hesses also warn against Florida's muggy climate, as well as Pensacola's rather sketchy zoning laws. "I think there is a lack of community pride associated with taking advantage of the natural beauty," Bill Ross says. "You really run into some areas that look unattractive because of that, and then you run into some magnificently attractive areas."

"There will be a lovely house and then a dump beside it," Janet Hess agrees, noting a prevailing carefree attitude that is an attraction for many to the coastal resort. "The people are more laid back than I thought. If you have to get someone to do service work and the surf is up — forget it!"

Humidity and institutionalized laziness go with the territory in a beach town, but a citizens committee, appointed to promote Northwest Florida as a retirement location, has renewed emphasis on zoning and growth management. Their report calls for mandatory garbage pickup, additional funding for programs that improve community appearance and increased support for Pensacola's Clean and Green Program.

It seems a manageable goal for a town that already has been rated highly in several national surveys, including No. 2 in the nation for quality of life in a study of 130 U.S. cities by Joseph Gyourdo, a Wharton Business School finance professor at the University of Pennsylvania. Perdido Key is among America's top 20 beaches, according to a study by Stephen Leatherman of Florida International University that considered aesthetics, swimming conditions, weather, pollution and other factors.

And don't forget the city's stunning, albeit tastefully restrained, victory as the "sixth most-polite city in the nation," according to Marjabelle Young-Stewart, also known as the "empress of etiquette."

"That's up from No. 7 in my last survey," she says, "so it's getting better all the time."●

Petoskey, Michigan

Bay-front Michigan town satisfies retirees who like 'cool' living

By Dixie Franklin

The waters of Lake Michigan often settle to a glassy stillness as the evening hours approach, offering front-row seats to spectacular sunsets. The shore along Little Traverse Bay is backed by forests of pine, spruce, hemlock and mixed northern hardwood that blaze crimson and gold in autumn. Hills climb to Michigan's prime ski slopes when winter blankets the landscape.

In the bend of the bay is Petoskey, whose year-round population of 7,200 triples when summer residents return to their cottages and second homes. Petoskey could almost be a state of mind shared with the nearby communities of Bay View and Harbor Springs.

"The communities are in step with each other, and always have been," says Stafford Smith, who owns restaurants in all three.

Retirees have long found Petoskey attractive, drawn here by its natural beauty, support services and a growing number of peers. Retired executives, especially from Detroit, Chicago, Indianapolis and cities in Ohio, come first as vacationers, then build second homes and eventually retire here. The area draws more retirees from the region than from distant states.

"There's an easy flow of everyday living," says Dick Wise, who retired here twice. "You get to know almost everybody in town."

Wise and his wife, Betty, moved here in 1971, "looking for a better way of life" after he spent 20 years as an engineer for Ford Motor Co. in the Detroit area.

"Betty's heel marks are still on I-75 from when I dragged her up here in 1971, but now she wouldn't leave," Wise says.

He started a business, retired again eight years ago and now volunteers for the local Service Corps of Retired Executives (SCORE), sponsored by the Small Business Administration.

"A group of eight to 10 of us works with young entrepreneurs to help them get off to a good start," Wise says.

Petoskey is a mix of old and new, with lovely old churches and active service clubs. Street scenes in the Gaslight District along Lake, Howard and Bay streets include old-fashioned lampposts, flower boxes bursting with blooms and benches that encourage genteel loitering.

The Gaslight Shopping District has close to 60 shops and restaurants. Along its tree-lined streets are galleries, boutiques and gift shops. One of them, Symons General Store, is a nostalgic shop of charming clutter under high tin ceilings, with merchandise spilling out the door and onto the sidewalk.

One local gathering place is the Virginia McCune Community Arts Center, still known to many longtime residents as "the church" even though it has been years since Allen McCune bought the idle church building and donated it to the city in his wife's name. The art center hosts changing exhibits, with theater and arts and crafts. On Thursday evenings in June, July and August, women of the Epsilon Jazz Band liven up the stage of the First Presbyterian Church in performances reminiscent of old New Orleans. Most are seniors.

Down the hill past Symons General Store, a tunneled walkway runs under U.S. Highway 31 to a park on the harbor. Mauve banners line the park and marina, adding a splash of color to the boats along the docks. A stage built into the hillside hosts outdoor programs and evening performances.

Pink concrete sidewalks and curbs distinguish Bay View, formed in the 1800s as a Methodist Bible camp. Its personality has changed since its Bible camp days, but it still is primarily a summer community. Outstanding Victorian homes with decorative gingerbread trim, turrets and swirls are reminiscent of turn-of-the-century styles and helped put the town on the National Register of Historic Places.

Around the bay is Harbor Springs, primarily a second-home community for retirees whose main residence is farther south — although a few skiers and winter sports enthusiasts do stay to enjoy the snow. The year-round population is about 1,600.

Retirees seeking homes in the area naturally look first to the waterfront, but property facing the bay is very expensive, easily topping $400,000. Less-expensive alternatives, in the $175,000 range, can be found on the nearby inland lakes of Walloon, Burt and Crooked and the river systems that feed them, according to associate broker Gary Phillips of Re/Max Real Estate of Petoskey.

Many retirees choose homes in Petoskey neighborhoods, where good buys can be found for under $150,000. Single-family homes are more common than condominium units. Most construction is wood, and basements are common.

"Very rarely do I have a home listed with air-conditioning," Phillips says. "With the Northern air and the big lake to keep us cool, there may be one week of the year when we are a bit too warm."

Water recreation is a main attraction in the summer. Residents sail, boat and fish for lake trout and Coho salmon on Lake Michigan. Inland lakes and streams can produce nice catches of rainbow trout, walleye and bass.

Other popular activities include golf and tennis, bike riding and beachcombing along the waterline for Petoskey stones, which wash up on the shores of Lake Michigan. The hexagon-shaped green stone, a fossilized coral, has a distinctive flowerlike pattern that is easy to spot when it is wet or polished. Every pleasant evening finds couples out for a stroll, especially along the waterfront.

The Friendship Center offers 46 senior services, including transportation. Many retirees find time to work as volunteers through the Northern Michigan Hospital Auxiliary in Petoskey.

Retirees both take and give comfort at the hospital, which works closely with Burns Clinic, a nationally recognized regional referral facility. The 229-bed hospital has a medical staff of more than 125 physicians, including those affiliated with the clinic.

"Every major medical and surgical specialty is represented here, including a health information and physician referral program," says Diane Murray, public affairs manager at the hospital. She says patients often tease that their hospital rooms have better sunset views over the bay than local hotels do.

Herman and Mary Jo Tilly, originally from Indianapolis, volunteer at the hospital up to three times a week. He makes pharmacy runs, helps discharge patients and handles errands while Mary Jo works in the gift shop operated by the auxiliary.

"I was an engineer, and Mary Jo was a speech pathologist in the public schools. We have dealt with people all our lives and felt a need to continue," he says. "We get more out of it than we put in."

Other seniors volunteer their services at the Little Traverse Historical Society, housed in an 1892 railroad depot. While much of the museum contains typical regional historical collections, the display of Petoskey stones is outstanding. There also is a large collection of Ernest Hemingway memorabilia. Hemingway spent many summers at nearby Walloon Lake.

Some retirees stay year-round, but about 60 percent of them leave for at least part of the winter. Favorite getaway months are "the mud months of November and April," says Dave Williams, a retiree who is active as a volunteer in several organizations.

Winter snowfall is abundant with an annual average of 121 inches. But the winters that drive snowbirds south are eagerly anticipated by senior skiers. Downhill skiers head for the slopes at Boyne Mountain, Boyne Highlands and Nubs Nob ski resorts. There is an active over-70 ski club.

"Cross-country skiing is big with the older crowd," says Williams. "This is a very active group of seniors."

Not all retirees who stay for the winter are skiers; some simply enjoy the seasonal differences. In winter, without all the vacationers, the communities take on more of a hometown flavor. The landscape is beautiful in snow, and getting around isn't too difficult because roads are well-maintained.

"We're not great winter sports people, but we enjoy the holiday time of the year up North," Wise says. "The community goes all out for the holidays."●

Petoskey, MI

Population: 7,200 year-round, 25,000 during the summer.

Location: In the northern part of Lower Michigan on Little Traverse Bay of Lake Michigan. The terrain is gently rolling. The city, which was founded in 1895, was named for Chippewa Chief Pet-O-Sega.

Climate:

	High	Low
January	28	15
July	76	59

Average relative humidity: 60%

Rain: 32 inches.

Snow: 121 inches.

Idyllic summer days with lake breezes; cold winters with abundant snowfall.

Cost of living: Above average (specific index not available).

Average housing cost: Off the water, $120,000 for a two- to three-bedroom, two-bath house. On inland lakes and rivers, $170,000. On the bay, $350,000 and up. Condominiums average $125,000. New construction, $100-plus per square foot.

Sales tax: 6%

Sales tax exemptions: Groceries, prescription drugs, medical services.

State income tax: 4.4% of taxable income, based on federal adjusted gross income with modifications.

Income tax exemptions: Social Security benefits and federal, state and local government pensions are exempt, and there is a private pension deduction of $60,000 for a joint return.

Intangibles tax: None.

Estate tax: None, except the state's "pick-up" portion of the federal tax, applicable to taxable estates above $675,000.

Property tax: $39.74 per $1,000 of assessed value, with homes assessed at 50% of market value. On a $150,000 home, taxes would be $2,980 a year.

Homestead exemption: Up to $1,200 tax credit, depending on property tax paid in proportion to income.

Security: 28.4 crimes per 1,000 residents in Emmet County, lower than the national average of 46.2 crimes per 1,000 residents. Specific figures not available for Petoskey.

Religion: 36 churches, one synagogue.

Education: North Central Michigan College, a community college, waives tuition for students age 60 and older.

Transportation: No city bus service, though Friendship Center has transportation service for seniors. Pellston Regional Airport, about 20 miles away, provides commuter service.

Health: 229-bed Northern Michigan Hospital; 125 physicians.

Housing options: Most popular choice is a single-family home in Petoskey or one of the neighboring towns. There are no planned retirement communities. **Birchwood Farm Estate**, an upscale development north of Harbor Springs, attracts many retirees; the average price of a three-bedroom home with two-and-a-half baths is about $275,000. Homeowners who spend part of the year elsewhere can contract for year-round maintenance.

Visitor lodging: Apple Tree Inn, $64-$105, (231) 348-2900; Comfort Inn, $88-$118, (231) 347-3220.

Information: Petoskey Chamber of Commerce, 401 E. Mitchell St., Petoskey, MI 49770, (231) 347-4150 or www.petoskey.com.

Pinehurst, North Carolina

There's more than golf in the North Carolina Sandhills

By Tracey B. Holyfield

Golfers long have known the Pinehurst area is a great place to live. Now, retirees looking beyond the golf courses are finding other attractions that draw them to the Sandhills area of North Carolina.

From 1980 to 1990, the population of Pinehurst more than doubled, with a substantial number being retirees. According to data from the Moore County Economic Development Corporation, those 55 years and older currently make up more than 30 percent of the county population.

Retirees are drawn for many reasons: a central location, a mild four-season climate, a blend of town and country living in a setting among tall pine trees, and a friendly, safe atmosphere.

The Pinehurst area is halfway between New York and Florida. It's within a short drive of both the Blue Ridge Mountains and the Atlantic beaches of North Carolina.

The climate offers seasonal changes without the extreme cold of the North, and that's a major attraction for Northerners, such as Paul and Petie Graeter, ages 62 and 59. They moved to Pinehurst from Gates Mill, OH, near Cleveland.

"We lived next to Lake Erie and had about eight months of winter," Paul says.

In Pinehurst, where the average yearly temperature is 62 degrees, the Graeters enjoy a mild, dry climate that is pleasant year-round. Or almost year-round, according to Paul, who thinks the summer temperatures are hot. The average high in July is 91. Winters are mild, with an average low of only 33 December-February.

The quiet atmosphere in Pinehurst also was a drawing card for the Graeters. The village at Pinehurst is reminiscent of quaint, turn-of-the-century New England, with shops interspersed amid brick walks, wooden signposts and large shade trees.

"There are only two stoplights and no gridlock," says Paul.

Bob and Lee Stanley, 65 and 64 respectively, came from Rochester, MI. Bob characterizes Pinehurst as "a small town with a big-town feel."

Gordon and Dotte Tonnesen, ages 61 and 60, were drawn to Pinehurst for its country club atmosphere. They spent most of their lives in Great Kills, Staten Island, in the metropolitan New York City area.

"I have always wanted to retire in North Carolina, for its mild seasons, and live in a golfing community," Gordon says.

For golfers, Pinehurst is close to paradise, with seven golf courses and easy access to over 30 additional championship courses within a 15-mile radius. The Tonnesens like having access to a gun club, riding stables, tennis courts, 200-acre marina and optional membership at the Pinehurst Country Club.

"We just drove into the village of Pinehurst and said, 'This is it,' " Dotte recalls of their first — and only — visit.

In reality, she adds, their decision was based on more than the aesthetics of the area. Like the Graeters, the couple were looking for a mild climate and a central location. They also wanted to escape the congestion of the Northeast.

"The whole area is so open to retirement," says Dotte. "You can be as busy as you want. There are so many things here for retired people to do."

Dotte has volunteered for the chamber of commerce and also works with the Altar Guild of her church. Gordon is a member of the Men's Golf Association, the Shrine Club and a model railroad club. Both play golf two or three times weekly.

Pinehurst is one of several communities clustered in this area; not all have the same ambiance.

Norman and Marge Hawkins, ages 68 and 65, retirees from Miami Shores, FL, who have traveled extensively worldwide, chose Southern Pines.

"The other areas surround country clubs, and we didn't particularly want that," Marge says. "We spent a lot of years living in the right place and doing the right things at the right time. There's a little bit of magic here (in Southern Pines)."

The Hawkinses thought South Florida would be their retirement home "until it changed so much, became so violent." They were seeking a safe haven from increasing crime, which had begun to surround them in Florida and resulted in the loss of a loved one.

Rural areas and self-contained retirement communities, such as Knollwood Village where the Hawkinses live, are rarely troubled by serious crime.

Retirees Marty and Marge Cane, ages 63 and 59, former residents of New Milford, NJ, like the security in their private residential community of Seven Lakes, which has controlled access. Located 10 miles west of Pinehurst, Seven Lakes offers boating and fishing on 100-acre Lake Auman, two 18-hole top-rated golf courses, a fitness center, two private racquet clubs, an Olympic-size pool and stables.

The Canes found assimilation into the community was easy.

"Marty had been here six weeks and considered himself a true North Carolinian. His conversion was immediate and complete," she says.

Marge credits the friendliness of the people for their rapid adjustment.

"It was absolutely amazing. People on the golf course would find out that Marty was playing by himself and invite him for lunch or dinner," she says.

Jan Manning agrees about the hospitality of the Southerners and thinks it rubs off on retirees, too. She and her husband, Duane, both 66, retired to Southern Pines from San Diego.

Jan says they've met more retirees from out-of-state than native residents.

"Everyone feels they have to embrace Southern hospitality even though they may have been an obnoxious Northerner only months before," she says.

The Mannings studied different retirement sites for five years.

"The criteria we used were climate, cost of living, real estate (costs) and crime (low) — they all pointed to-ward Southern Pines," Duane says. They had visited the area because Jan's brother lives here in the winter.

During their research, the cost of living in some areas they liked became prohibitive, due to what Jan attributed to a growing number of retirees leaving metropolitan areas and buying homes in less-expensive, less-congested areas.

The Mannings considered settling in Eureka, in northern California. When they began pricing real estate, the home they felt they could afford "faced a house across the street with a goat tied in the front yard," she says.

The couple found prices more rea-sonable in Southern Pines. According to the Moore County Economic Development Corporation, the average housing cost is $154,000. In nearby Pinehurst, the average housing cost is $216,000. Overall in Moore County, the average housing cost is $135,000.

New, more expensive homes have driven the average upward; less expensive homes are available.

For the Stanleys, taxes were a major issue when selecting a place to retire. The couple's primary sources of income are his pension plan, an Individual Retirement Account and passbook savings. They looked close-

Pinehurst, NC

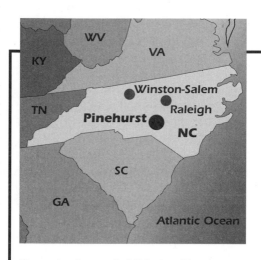

Population: 8,908 in Pinehurst, 10,412 in Southern Pines and 71,394 in Moore County.
Location: In the southern Piedmont region, between the Blue Ridge Mountains and the coast and about 70 miles south of Raleigh. Hilly, sandy soil, pine trees.

Climate:

	High	Low
January	55	33
July	91	67

Average relative humidity: 50%
Rain: 50 inches.
Mild climate with warm days, cool nights. Occasional, light snow.
Cost of living: Average (specific index not available).
Average housing cost: $216,000 in Pinehurst, $154,000 in Southern Pines.
Sales tax: 6%
Sales tax exemptions: Prescription drugs, eyeglasses, some medical supplies.
State income tax: Graduated in three steps from 6% to 7.75%, depending on income.

Income tax exemptions: Social Security benefits. Each taxpayer also can exempt up to $4,000 in local, state or federal government retirement benefits and up to $2,000 in private retirement benefits, but the total of these exemptions cannot exceed $4,000 per person.
Intangibles tax: None.
Estate tax: None, except the state's "pick-up" portion of the federal tax, applicable to taxable estates above $675,000.
Property tax: Pinehurst: $8.75 per $1,000 of valuation, with homes assessed at 100% of market value. Tax on a $216,000 home would be $1,890. Southern Pines: $12.03 per $1,000 of valuation with homes assessed at 100%. Tax on a $154,000 home would be $1,852.
Homestead exemption: Homeowners age 65 or older, or disabled, living in the home and earning $11,000 or less per year qualify for an exemption of $15,000.
Security: 19.6 crimes per 1,000 residents, lower than the national average of 46.2 crimes per 1,000 residents.
Religion: The area has 40 churches representing many denominations.
Education: Sandhills Community College offers degree programs and continuing-education courses.
Transportation: No public ground transportation. From the Moore County Airport, US Airways Express offers four commuter flights daily to Charlotte, NC. Raleigh-Durham International Airport is 80 miles away. There is Amtrak passenger service to New York and Miami.
Health: Moore Regional Hospital in Pinehurst, with 400 beds, has a heart center, 170 staff physicians and 34 medical specialties.
Housing options: Pinehurst has a number of country-club communities that cater to golfers. **The Carolina**, a gated golf community, has wooded homesites from the mid-$30,000s, golf-front homesites from the mid-$60,000s and homes from $250,000s and up. **Talamore Villas**, a golf club community, offers new villas from the mid-$100,000s to mid-$200,000s. **Midland Country Club** and **Knollwood Village** are golfing communities for seniors, offering attached single-family homes and condominiums from the $50,000s to $200,000s. Beautifully restored older homes are available in historic in-town neighborhoods and in nearby Southern Pines.
Visitor lodging: Pinehurst Resort and Country Club, doubles starting at $192 per person, double occupancy, including two meals, (800) 487-4653. Pine Crest Inn, $66 per person, double occupancy, including two meals, (910) 295-6121. Southern Pines Hampton Inn, $79 a room, (800) 333-9266. Numerous accommodations with golf packages available.
Information: Sandhills Area Chamber of Commerce, P.O. Box 458, Southern Pines, NC 28388, (910) 692-3926 or www.sandhills.net.

ly at North Carolina's sales, income and property taxes.

North Carolina has an income tax that is graduated in three steps from 6 percent to 7.75 percent. Social Security is exempt, and up to $2,000 in private pensions and $4,000 in government pensions is exempt. In Moore County, the sales tax is 6 percent; prescription drugs, eyeglasses and certain medical supplies are exempt.

In Pinehurst, the property tax on a $216,000 home would be about $1,890; in Southern Pines, the tax on a $154,000 home would be about $1,852.

The Stanleys think they would have fared better taxwise in Florida, but Bob considers there are trade-offs. "You give a little and take a little when it comes to choosing a place to retire," he says.

However, neither the Stanleys nor the Tonnesens were willing to give any regarding access to good medical facilities. Both men have suffered from heart conditions in the past.

The Moore Regional Hospital serves as a referral center for 14 counties and performs cardiac surgery regularly. Its respiratory care department is considered to be among the best in the Southeast.

The area also houses the St. Joseph of the Pines Health Center and Villas, a nursing hospital with 86 skilled nursing beds and four acute-care hospital beds plus retirement villas.

The area isn't without faults.

Jan cautions about the weather: "Sometimes it's sort of gray and dreary in comparison to San Diego, and that can really get you down."

The Tonnesens say there is no night life.

"I don't understand why," Gordon says. "They have some really nice restaurants here, but no dance bands except at the country club. And there it's like everyone is Cinderella. At midnight everyone is gone.

"If you go down the street after 10 o'clock, the only house with lights on is mine," he says.

Marge Hawkins says she misses the ethnic restaurants of South Florida but not the cockroaches of the tropical climate there.

Although the area has some fine shops and boutiques, it's short on variety in shopping. Residents drive to Raleigh, Charlotte or Greensboro to shop at large malls.

Moore County does have cultural opportunities but not as much as what most of these couples were accustomed to.

"We gave up the cultural aspects of San Diego for a totally suburban area," Duane says. "You can't have the best of all worlds."

For the Mannings it was important to have the peace and tranquility of a small town rather than the availability of culture. They figure that their travels will give them the cultural pursuits they want.

The trade-off is well worth it to Jan.

"I was working in my flowers the other day and heard something. I turned around and there was a gray fox. Coming home late one night, I had to stop my car because there were three deer in the road. Those things excite me, because I'm a farm girl. There's a perpetual floor show of beauty," she says.

For the Graeters, there's no better place. Says Petie, "We worked a lifetime to get to the point where we could retire and live a life of leisure, and we found the perfect place for that."●

Port Townsend, Washington

Moderate climate, waterfront charm pull retirees to historic town on Olympic Peninsula

By Loralee Wenger

Rene and Elaine Levy came to Port Townsend to buy a boat to enjoy during their retirement years and eventually bought a house instead. Don and Barbara Marseille were attracted by the moderate climate of Washington's Olympic Peninsula.

What both couples found was that Port Townsend is a hidden gem in an area of the Northwest already touted in many national surveys as one of the top-rated places to live.

Situated in the rain shadow of the Olympic Mountains, the historic seaport gets only 18 inches of rain a year and is blessed with more sunny days than Seattle, 50 miles south, enjoys. The town has attracted artists, writers and retirees charmed by its waterfront of old brick buildings and Victorian homes.

The Marseilles moved from the Chicago suburb of Hinsdale to Port Townsend for the weather. "I need to avoid the cold," says Barbara. "And Don doesn't do well in temperatures over 80 degrees."

Don, 62, charted the temperatures of various locations around the country. "We never really visited any other sites, because Don's chart indicated this was the best," says Barbara, 60. But she admits that the weather of Port Townsend is not for everyone. Skies often are overcast until noon.

The couple's move to Port Townsend came several years before they thought it would. While still living in Chicago, they saw an advertisement for a new Port Townsend home that resembled a turn-of-the-century farmhouse. It caught their attention. Barbara is an interior designer with a special interest in historic restoration and preservation.

"We came out to look at it and thought we would buy it and rent it out for 10 years," Barbara explained. But when they returned to Hinsdale, Don's company announced options for early retirement.

"Naturally, I jumped all over that," says the retired sales and marketing executive.

For people like Barbara who enjoy Victorian charm, Port Townsend is a living museum. In the late 1800s, the port was home to several sea captains who built mansions here for their families. Several homes, replete with widow's walks and gingerbread trim, still sit on the bluff overlooking downtown and the waterfront. Many of the dwellings have been preserved and converted to stylish accommodations that have made Port Townsend the Victorian bed-and-breakfast capital of the Northwest.

The location was discovered in 1792 by Capt. George Vancouver as he sailed through the Strait of Juan de Fuca. Over the next 100 years, the population of this seaport grew to 7,000 with hopes of reaching 20,000 as the center of Puget Sound shipping and commerce. Those hopes were dashed in the 1890s when the Union Pacific Railroad stopped in Tacoma, short of the Olympic Peninsula. Harbors at Seattle and Tacoma were developed about the same time.

During the next three decades, military establishments and a pulp and paper mill stabilized the population, but Port Townsend never grew to its earlier expectations. Fortunately, it has preserved its seafaring heritage and now is one of only four Victorian seaports on the National Register of Historic Places.

In 1976, the downtown area and residential section atop the bluff was designated a national historic district. Some 40 buildings in the downtown area are on the national register. Many century-old brick buildings along Water Street that housed mercantiles, hotels, businesses and brothels now are gift shops, antiques shops, art galleries, restaurants and hotels.

Several shops carry the wares of the town's artists and craftspeople — weavers, silversmiths, potters, sculptors and painters. Gallery Walks, featuring new exhibits in the local galleries, are held the first Saturday of each month from 5:30 to 8 p.m. March through December.

One of the newest restorations is the Rose Theater, for which Barbara Marseille volunteered to design the interior. This 1904 vaudeville theater, owned by Phil Johnson, a Port Townsend native, reopened in the summer of 1992. The theater includes the original stage front, wainscoting, historic hand-painted murals and a restored tin ceiling. The art nouveau interior features shades of maroon, raspberry and teal.

"The phenomenal people who live here are so involved in civic affairs and local politics," says Barbara. "I had a wonderful time working on the Rose. Because it was a volunteer job, I didn't have to keep time sheets. I channeled all my creativity into the project."

She is active on the Historic Preservation Commission and the Port Townsend Garden Club — a natural since the Marseilles' home sits on a third of an acre of gardens.

Don is a member of the board of the Centrum Foundation, a non-profit arts organization. It presents workshops and performances year-round, including a chamber music weekend in January, a jazz weekend in February and a festival of American fiddle tunes, a 10-day conference for writers and a jazz weekend in July.

Centrum's offices are at 446-acre Fort Worden State Park. The fort was built in the early 1900s as a harbor defense system for Puget Sound. Its balloon hangar was the site of a fight scene in "An Officer and a Gentleman," starring Debra Winger and Richard Gere. The park includes renovated officers' houses, the Port Wilson lighthouse, a boat launch, beach and the commanding officer's home, restored with period antiques and open for touring for a fee.

The Marseilles enjoy Port Townsend's musical performances, including the Port Townsend Symphony. Community events include a weeklong rhododendron festival in May, the Olympic Music Festival featuring the Philadelphia String Quartet on weekends June through August, a wooden boat festival in September, historic home tours twice a year, a square dance weekend in September and a Victorian Christmas tree-lighting ceremony early in December.

The Marseilles are very active, with Barbara practicing tai chi, controlled exercise movements developed in ancient China, four times a week and Don walking 27 miles weekly. For retirees with other interests, there are three 18-hole golf courses, 14 tennis courts and boat and kayak rentals in the community.

It was the need for this kind of active lifestyle that induced Rene and Elaine Levy to leave the isolation of their Texas ranch. The Levys are effervescent people who became accustomed to public contact through careers at American Airlines. Elaine, 53, is a retired flight attendant super-

Port Townsend, WA

Population: 8,200 in Port Townsend, 25,000 in Jefferson County.

Location: About two hours northwest of Seattle on the Olympic Peninsula.

Climate:

	High	Low
January	44	34
July	71	51

Average relative humidity: 70%
Rain: 18 inches.
Temperate climate. Freezes rare. Summers sunny with cool nights.

Cost of living: Average to slightly above average (specific index not available).

Average housing cost: $153,938.
Sales tax: 7.8%.
Sales tax exemptions: Prescription drugs, groceries, medical services.
State income tax: None.
Intangibles tax: None.
Estate tax: None, except the state's "pick-up" portion of the federal tax, applicable to taxable estates above $675,000.
Property tax: Rate is $14.45 per $1,000 of assessed value, with homes assessed at 100% of market value. Tax on a $153,938 home is $2,224.

Homestead exemption: Homeowners age 61 and older, with a gross household income of $28,000 or less, are eligible for certain property tax exemptions.

Security: 34.5 crimes per 1,000 residents, lower than the national average of 46.2 crimes per 1,000 residents.

Religion: 23 churches of numerous denominations and one synagogue.

Education: Peninsula College Continuing Education Center and Northwest School of Wooden Boats. Additional courses at Peninsula College in Port Angeles.

Transportation: Jefferson County Airport served by Ludlow Aviation charter flights. Seattle-Tacoma International Airport is 50 miles away via ferry. Washington State Ferries provide link with Keystone on Whidbey Island, just north of Seattle. County bus service connects with Greyhound and to other counties.

Health: Newly renovated, 55-bed Jefferson General Hospital, an outpatient clinic, a 94-bed nursing home, 25 physicians and 17 dentists. Outstanding specialty care available in Seattle.

Housing options: Most retirees live in single-family homes. Apartments for low to moderate incomes are available. There are no planned retirement communities. **Kala Point** is a 380-acre, 476-lot upscale planned community on the water with clubhouse, pool, health facilities, beach, tennis courts and boat ramp. About 75 percent of its residents are young, active retirees. Homes cost $125,000-$490,000, townhomes $100,000-$275,000. **Cape George,** a 665-lot planned community, is also home to deer, fox, raccoon and other wildlife. The community has a beach, marina and community center. Some Cape George areas allow mobile homes. Homes cost $80,000 to $300,000-plus. At nearby Port Ludlow, a resort community that once was a historic settlement and sawmill on Admiralty Inlet, is the **Resort at Port Ludlow**, a recipient of the National Association of Homebuilders' "Active Adult Community of the Year" award. The 750-acre, 1,000-lot resort has tennis courts, a beach, marina, hiking trails, championship golf course and extensive health-recreation center. Homes cost $127,634-$492,500, condominiums $122,950-$179,500.

Visitor lodging: Old Consulate Inn, $195-$210, (360) 385-6753; Ravenscroft Inn, $80-$190, (360) 385-2784; Manressa Castle, $70-$175, (360) 385-5750 or (800) 732-1281 in Washington.

Information: Port Townsend Chamber of Commerce, 2437 E. Sims Way, Port Townsend, WA 98368, (360) 385-2722 or www.ptchamber.org.

visor, and Rene, 65, is a retired pilot.

"The ranch became pretty lonely," says Elaine. "We missed our friends and colleagues."

They considered relocating to Cape Cod, where a son lives. Other options included the Chesapeake Bay area and the North Carolina coast. They visited Port Townsend to look at a boat they considered buying.

"We didn't like the boat, but we loved the town," says Rene. They didn't look any further.

"We love the sea here," explains Elaine. "It really is such a dominating factor that I never want to live anywhere away from the sea."

True to its historic seaport heritage, the town's marina draws boats and sailors from around the world. Adjacent to the marina is the Northwest School of Wooden Boats. More than 100 Port Townsend businesses are associated with boating, including sail-making and boat-building specialists.

Downtown along the waterfront is the Marine Science Center, housed in a historic building on the dock with large, open tables where marine animals can be viewed. There are at least five other marinas in the area.

"The primary thing is the feeling of the town," says Elaine. "It's such a wonderful mix of retired professionals and artisans and shipbuilders."

The Levys have made many friends in Port Townsend. In the past 30 years, the population ages 45 and older has increased from 32 percent to 43 percent. The population 60 and older has increased from just under 16 percent in 1960 to more than 27 percent in 1990.

Although the couple was sold on the town and its harbor, attractive housing and moderately priced goods and services were an added incentive to move here. Three-bedroom, two-bath homes cost an average of $125,000-$165,000. The comfortable home they bought eight years ago has nearly doubled in value. Its expansive view looks over the harbor and shipping lanes, nearby Whidbey Island, Indian Island and, in the distance, the lights of Seattle and Mount Rainier.

Their retirement lifestyle is funded by leasing pasture on their 500-acre ranch, an investment program and two pensions. Rene also works part-time as a self-employed investment counselor. Elaine teaches remedial reading in the local grade school.

The Levys were pleasantly surprised to find Fort Worden State Park and the Olympic National Park so close. Olympic National Park is a 900,000-acre wonderland with 60 miles of Pacific coastline, mountains, glaciers, lakes, rain forest, campgrounds and hiking trails. Some 40 miles west of Port Townsend is the Olympic Park Visitors Center at Port Angeles with exhibits of flora and fauna found in the park.

Hurricane Ridge is 45 miles southwest of Port Townsend. From the ridge, visitors can see across the Strait of Juan de Fuca to Victoria, BC, the Olympic Mountain range, and Mount Baker on the mainland.

Both couples are happy with their retirement choice of Port Townsend, but they caution that this hidden Victorian seaport is not for everyone.

"People who have had unlimited shopping and cultural activities (and who want to continue that lifestyle) should not come," warns Elaine.

"Come with the idea of contributing something to the town, not taking away, and you will be happy here," adds her husband.

Barbara Marseille echoes these sentiments. "Many people who live here are highly skilled, very bright people who have dropped out, but they have a strong sense of community," she says. "This is not a big city with a lot of government services or well-heeled industries.

"This town needs people who pull their weight." ●

Prescott, Arizona

Pine-scented air, Arizona history characterize mile-high town

By Judy Wade

Arizona summons images of roadrunners, sagebrush, cactus-studded desert and Spanish-style architecture. Not mile-high Prescott, though.

More than a million acres of national forest and the 1,400-acre Yavapai Indian Reservation surround the city, northwest of Phoenix. Natural wood homes with expansive windows and decking are niched among the craggy pine-covered slopes and gentle foothills of the Bradshaw Mountains.

At 5,347 feet above sea level, Prescott is a cool retreat from Arizona's low desert heat — and an increasingly popular place to retire.

Roy and Jacky Breitenbach, 62 and 52 respectively, took a methodical approach to discovering Prescott, appraising Carson City, NV, Vancouver, British Columbia, and three other Arizona towns before making a decision.

"We each made a list of the things we liked and disliked about towns we were considering. We both came up with Prescott as our first choice," says Jacky.

The Breitenbachs abandoned northern California in favor of central Arizona to custom-build their 3,000-square-foot mountainside home. In an area of two-thirds-acre homesites, its sweeping mountain view overlooks alligator juniper, ponderosa and piñon pines.

"Sites here are planned so you don't see your neighbors," says Jacky, adding that quails, blue jays, squirrels, doves, chipmunks and rabbits regularly visit their deck for handouts.

Twelve years ago former elementary school principal Joan Fleming of Casa Grande, south of Phoenix, bought a vacation home in Prescott with her husband, who has since passed away.

"From the day we bought, I tried to figure a way to take early retirement and move here permanently," says Joan, 67. She did just that, and has become such a part of the community that she has served as president of the Prescott Chamber of Commerce Board of Directors.

Community involvement is typical of Prescott retirees. The Breitenbachs are active in the Chamber of Commerce Ambassadors, who help welcome newcomers and study other towns to see how Prescott can learn from them.

Louis Franyi, 66, retired to Prescott from Indiana with his wife, Rosemary, 62. He successfully ran for a four-year term on the city council.

Additional involvement opportunities come through the Volunteer Center of Yavapai County, which is connected with more than 100 local agencies.

Prescott's clean air, mild four-season climate and near-ideal weather are attracting retirees at an ever-accelerating pace. Cloudless skies are a true blue, clear of the smoggy horizon smudge that blights Phoenix two hours to the south. On July days, the temperature lingers in the 70s, while it soars above 100 in southern Arizona. Winter brings some below-freezing nights and a smattering of snow, though it rarely stays on the ground more than a day.

Prescott's spirited past shows at Courthouse Plaza, the town's centerpiece. A statue of local hero Roughrider Bucky O'Neill greets visitors at one entrance, and at another a statue called "Cowboy at Rest" reminds guests of the area's Western heritage. A plaque tells of Prescott's founding in 1864 on Granite Creek, a source of placer gold.

Prescott is named for historian William Hickling Prescott. Believing the area's Indian ruins were of Aztec origin, the founding fathers named the city streets after figures such as Montezuma, Cortez and Alarcon, chronicled in Prescott's book on Mexico.

The original courthouse was erected in the plaza during Prescott's days as the state's Territorial Capital, created when President Abraham Lincoln saw the rich ore of the area as a possible source of funding for the Civil War. When the original building burned in the early 1900s, the present stately columned courthouse was built to serve as the seat of government for Yavapai County.

Today the square is the hub of town activities and special events, including Antiques in the Park, Faire on the Square, a Western art show and more. It takes on a carnival atmosphere during the annual June Territorial Prescott Days. It's also the place for strolling on shaded walks and for enjoying an impromptu lunch purchased from one of the shops bordering the square.

A few blocks away, on locust-shaded Mount Vernon Street, elegant, carefully restored Victorian homes tell of prosperous times when bright entrepreneurs came west to make money in farming, sheepherding and mining. At the turn of the century, Prescott was a rip-roaring Western town with 20 or more saloons operating 24 hours a day on Montezuma Street, known as "Whiskey Row." A few bars are still there.

The history of the area comes to life in the Sharlot Hall Museum, where docents relate tales of early Prescott as they point out artifacts from settler days. The museum includes several period buildings, including the Territorial Governor's Mansion built in 1864.

Rowdiness has given way to refinement in Prescott, where a population of about 36,000 enjoys outdoor activities and an active cultural arts scene.

The Prescott National Forest is the area's biggest recreational draw. Lakes, hiking trails, campsites and an equestrian facility are all within minutes of town.

"When I came here I was a city girl, and I've learned to fish for trout," says Jacky. "Any given morning I catch my limit of six. There are five lakes around here, and two are always stocked."

Nearby, Antelope Hills offers two well-kept 18-hole municipal golf courses. Prescott Country Club, 13 miles east of town, has an 18-hole course. Both are PGA-approved and open to the public.

Prescott Resort, on a bluff overlooking forests and granite mountains, is Arizona's only hotel casino. Slots and poker machines are permitted because the resort is on the Yavapai Indian Reservation. Paintings and sculptures by nationally recognized local artists give a gallery feel to the resort's public areas, and the 180-degree view from the Thumb Butte Room makes it a favorite local dining spot.

On the cultural side, an excellent 110,000-volume library includes large-print and talking books and public-use computers. A new performance hall at Yavapai Community College regularly attracts the Phoenix Symphony and recently hosted the Moscow Ballet.

The area's scenic beauty has in-spired many local artists whose works are shown in a number of private galleries.

"We've met wonderful people in our classes at Yavapai College," says Rosemary. "I take painting, and Lou is involved in advanced photographic studies."

Yavapai Community College, a public two-year school, offers discounts to students age 62 or older. Classes in creative writing, fine arts and current events are popular. Through the Elderhostel network, the college conducts weeklong trips to Sedona, the Verde Valley and the desert lowlands

Prescott, AZ

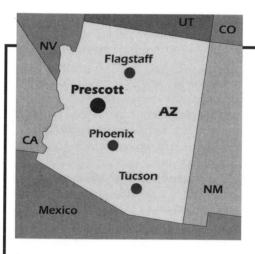

Population: 36,300 in Prescott, 152,500 in Yavapai County.
Location: In central Arizona in the Prescott National Forest, 89 miles north of Phoenix.
Climate:

	High	Low
January	50	20
July	89	56

Average relative humidity: 45%
Rain: 18.8 inches.
Snow: 20.6 inches.
Four-season climate with crisp, clean air is seen as beneficial to some respiratory ailments. At 5,347 feet elevation, Prescott is always much cooler than Phoenix.
Cost of living: 108.1, based on national average of 100.
Average housing cost: $173,675
Sales tax: 7.5%
Sales tax exemptions: Prescription drugs, medical services, prosthetics.
State income tax: Graduated in five steps from 2.9% to 5.17%, depending on income.
Income tax exemptions: Social Se-curity benefits and up to $2,500 of federal, state and local government pensions are exempt.
Intangibles tax: None.
Estate tax: None, except the state's "pick-up" portion of the federal tax, applicable to taxable estates above $675,000.
Property tax: Rate is $118 per $1,000 of assessed value, with homes assessed at 10% of the value determined by the state. Taxes on a $175,000 home are about $2,065.
Homestead exemption: None.
Security: 49.5 crimes per 1,000 residents, higher than the national average of 46.2 crimes per 1,000 residents.
Religion: Seventy churches and synagogues represent 48 denominations.
Education: Yavapai Community College has continuing-education classes at reduced rates for seniors. Prescott College and Embry-Riddle Aeronautical University offer four-year degree programs.
Transportation: Prescott Transit Authority provides hourly scheduled transportation within the city limits. Scheduled commuter service from Prescott connects with major airlines at Phoenix Sky Harbor International Airport, about 90 miles away.
Health: A total of 60 doctors, 40 dentists, 30 chiropractors and 30 other health-care specialists serve Prescott. Yavapai Regional Medical Center has 127 beds, offering emergency, surgi-cal, cardiac, home health, hospice and other care. The Department of Veterans Affairs Medical Center has 150 medical beds, a 60-bed nursing home and a 208-bed domiciliary.
Housing options: In town, small single-family resale homes begin at about $90,000. Most new homes are custom-built in developments. In **Yavapai Hills**, (800) 843-9568, lots are $30,000-$80,000. Paved roads with sidewalks, underground utilities, clubhouse, pool and tennis courts are in place, and contractors are building homes from the $120,000s to $300,000s. **Crystal Creek Homes and Realty**, (800) 553-0542, has a number of developments, including Timberridge, where lots are $44,900-$74,500. **Granite Gate Resort Retirement Community**, (800) 260-2596, offers independent apartments and assisted-living units in a luxury setting in the Granite Dells area; monthly rent for a studio apartment, with one meal daily and housekeeping weekly, is $1,295. Townhouses, condominiums and mobile homes are available in the area.
Visitor lodging: There are numerous hotels, motels, B&Bs, cabins, cottages and RV-mobile home parks. Best Western Prescottonian, $59-$72 double, (520) 445-3096; Prescott Resort, $139 double, (520) 776-1666.
Information: Prescott Chamber of Commerce, 117 W. Goodwin St., Prescott, AZ 86302, (800) 266-7534.

of western Arizona.

About the only convenience the city seems to lack is a large department store.

"But you can go up to Flagstaff and there's a nice mall, just an hour away," notes Joan.

All this sounds nearly idyllic, but residents acknowledge the town has problems, spawned by its recent growth spurt. Housing prices have skyrocketed, in part because of an influx of Californians who sell their homes for high prices and want to reinvest a large portion of their proceeds in a new home. As an example, Jacky says, newcomers are finding that a $350,000 home in California costs about $200,000 in Prescott.

Realtor Jeannie Furse says, "There is a shortage of affordable housing here. Rarely do you find a home in the $90,000s or even $110,000 range except for an older home with 700 or 800 square feet."

In Prescott Valley, eight miles to the east, three-bedroom, two-bath homes are available in the $90,000s and low $100,000s, says Jeannie. "But then you're not in the mountains and pines, which is why most people come to Prescott," she adds.

Some residents unhesitatingly label Prescott's growth as uncontrolled.

James Garner, who has edited the *Prescott Courier*, Yavapai County's daily newspaper, for the past 20 years,

sees the growth as overwhelming.

"We unfortunately didn't anticipate this pace and, therefore, didn't plan adequately for it," he says. He credits a 1970s article in the *Los Angeles Times* with starting the boom.

"The infrastructure is beginning to show the stress. The streets are crowded and deteriorating. We'll have to pass another sales tax issue. We have serious concerns about the water and sewer overload...same thing happened in Southern California," he says. "No one ever dreamed that a lot in Prescott would sell for $100,000."

Despite growth in other areas, Prescott's crime rate remains close to the national average. According to the latest statistics, there were three murders and only 20 robberies in one year. As the seat of Yavapai County, Prescott is home base for the Yavapai County Sheriff's Department with 75 officers, and the town has 50 officers.

The Breitenbachs don't worry about crime. Roy says, "Our sheriff claims that within 24 hours he'll catch anyone who commits a crime."

Several retirees mentioned a recently formed gang prevention program. "So far it hasn't been determined that there are any gangs here. They're mostly wannabes," says Joan, "but the city is watching, and they have a graffiti removal program so that graffiti is gone within hours."

While the town has doctors and a regional medical center, retirees report having to wait several months before doctors will accept new patients, and they say it's difficult to find local doctors who will take Medicare assignments.

Until five years ago most of Prescott's retirees were Arizona residents who migrated north. Although no official figures are kept, at least half of new residents seem to be from California, says a chamber of commerce representative.

While the brochure the chamber of commerce sends to prospective residents proclaims that Prescott is "Everybody's Hometown," a large contingent of the population hopes that "everybody" doesn't come at once. They would like to see the flood of newcomers stemmed for awhile so that the town can catch up with its recent growth.

Residents want time to plan a stable future that will maintain the area's quality of life, which has been a major attraction.

There's good-natured joshing about temporarily detouring people in other directions.

Editor James Garner jokes, "Retirees, we love 'em. They're building homes that no one ever dreamed of having in this town. But I still have time to run out and change all the road signs, don't I?"●

Punta Gorda, Florida

Florida city offers a sense of the past and an eye to the future

By Karen Feldman

When Spanish explorer Juan Ponce de Leon set sail in search of the fountain of youth, he made his way to Florida's shores, starting at the northeast in St. Augustine and wending his way down to Southwest Florida.

At Charlotte Harbor, he encountered the Calusa Indians and, judging from the fierce defense of their territory, became convinced that this was where the magical fountain must be. Why else would the Calusas fight so hard?

For Ponce de Leon, what is today Punta Gorda proved not to be the site of eternal youth, but of untimely death in 1513, when the Calusas killed him in battle.

Both the Calusas and the search for the fountain of youth are history. But many of the city's 12,768 residents find that simply living in this waterfront city, with its historic brick streets, miles of canals, manicured parks and golf courses, can be curative in itself. For those 50 and older, who comprise more than 60 percent of the city's population, it can come close to heaven.

Harriet Mielke, 62, moved to Punta Gorda from Detroit with her husband, Leonard, in 1992 and now volunteers at the chamber of commerce for Charlotte County, of which Punta Gorda is the county seat. "When I talk to prospects who visit the chamber, I tell them we have found Utopia," the former Detroit Public Schools employee says.

"It's a really diverse community," says Julie Mathis, executive director of the chamber. Recent publicity has focused attention on the area, drawing the curious who "come here and fall in love with it," she says.

It's a common occurrence. Bob and Jackie Meatty, both retired from the U.S. Department of State's Foreign Service, moved to Punta Gorda in 1995 from Alexandria, VA. They had seriously considered retiring in Charleston, SC, and checked out spots all along the Atlantic Coast from North Carolina on down.

After one visit to Punta Gorda, they decided it was where they wanted to be. They rented for five months, then purchased a single-family home with a large family room on a canal in Punta Gorda Isles, an upscale community where many homes are built on a multitude of canals that offer direct access to Charlotte Harbor and, beyond that, the Gulf of Mexico.

For Bob Meatty, 59, it was the "climate, lifestyle, ease of water access and a home on a canal" that convinced him. For 62-year-old Jackie, it was all those things as well as a lower cost of living. Jackie misses some of the cultural opportunities of the Washington, DC, area but happily lives without the metropolitan traffic.

As for Bob, "I don't miss anything." Low crime, moderately priced housing, lots of outdoor activities and a subtropical climate are the main attractions for them and for other Northerners looking for their place in the sun.

Although no one is sure of the exact spot at which Ponce de Leon landed, the city lays claim to the explorer and maintains Ponce de Leon Park on a choice piece of unspoiled land that looks out on Charlotte Harbor. His statue stands sentry over the park's entrance. Each March, the town celebrates his landing — with men dressing up as conquistadors and crossing Charlotte Harbor by boat to claim the city.

Other than the Calusas, most found the area inhospitable with its almost impassable crush of plants and ferocious mosquitoes. Eventually the English found their way to the region, settling a bit north of the harbor along the Peace River. In 1885, Col. Isaac Trabue from Kentucky bought the land from the British and named it Trabue. When the city incorporated in 1887, it returned to the more popular Spanish name, Punta Gorda. Trabue Cottage, the colonel's home, still stands.

Today, the city's downtown area has won recognition as a state historic district, and the city's Streetscape program is restoring its Old Florida look by adding to the historic red-brick streets, planting more trees and installing street lamps, benches and brick planters. Old wooden homes are being restored and have become highly sought real estate.

The city's residents are content to leave the busier pace and commercial development to Port Charlotte, its neighbor to the north across Charlotte Harbor. In Punta Gorda's downtown, cozy shops and restaurants share space with City Hall and the soon-to-be-replaced county courthouse.

In Punta Gorda Isles, just west of downtown, almost everyone has a car but also is likely to have one or more other forms of transportation: boats, bicycles and golf carts. It's not uncommon to see residents tooling along neighborhood streets in their golf carts, whether or not they are headed to the golf course.

For the Mielkes, it was their interest in boating through which they initially made friends. The Detroit couple didn't know a soul in Punta Gorda when they moved.

"The first year was very hard," Harriet Mielke says. "Once we joined the yacht club, though, we met a lot of people." After that, they made still more friends through tennis and golf. "This is a place where you can get up in the morning and find 10 people to play golf with," she says. "It's a great party town."

Punta Gorda, FL

Population: 12,768 in Punta Gorda, 136,773 in Charlotte County.

Location: On the southwest Gulf coast 100 miles south of Tampa.

Climate:

	High	Low
January	74	53
July	91	75

Average relative humidity: 56%

Rain: 52.55 inches.

Cost of living: Below average (specific index not available).

Median housing cost: $161,803 in the city. $51,954 for canal lots.

Sales tax: 7%

Sales tax exemptions: Most food items and medical and professional services.

State income tax: None.

Intangibles tax: Assessed on stocks, bonds and other specified assets, with some investments exempt. Tax rate is $1 per $1,000 of value for assets of less than $100,000 for individuals or $200,000 for couples, and $1.50 per $1,000 of value for greater amounts. First $20,000 per individual, or $40,000 for couples, is exempt.

Estate tax: None, except the state's "pick-up" portion of the federal tax, applicable to taxable estates of more than $675,000.

Property tax: $19.05 per $1,000 in Punta Gorda, with homes assessed at 100% of market value. Annual tax on a $161,803 home is about $2,606 with the homestead exemption noted below. The rate in unincorporated Charlotte County is $16.52 per $1,000, excluding special taxing districts in some areas.

Homestead exemption: $25,000 off assessed value of permanent, primary residence.

Security: 27.8 crimes per 1,000 residents, well below the national average of 46.2 crimes per 1,000 residents.

Religion: There are 20 churches and one synagogue in Punta Gorda and 40 churches and one synagogue in neighboring Port Charlotte.

Education: Edison Community College offers two-year associate degrees on the Punta Gorda campus. Florida Southern College Charlotte-DeSoto in Port Charlotte, a satellite of Florida Southern College in Lakeland, offers a bachelor of liberal arts degree, with some credit given for life experiences. The program is geared to students 40 and older. Florida Gulf Coast University is about 40 miles south in Fort Myers. It offers undergraduate and graduate degrees.

Transportation: Interstate 75 runs through the east side of the city, with access about a mile from downtown. Southwest Florida International Airport is about 35 miles south and easily reached via I-75. Charlotte County Airport, just east of the city, is a general aviation airport for smaller planes but no commercial lines.

Health: Charlotte Regional Medical Center is a 208-bed hospital offering 24-hour emergency care, a cardiac care unit, sports medicine and rehabilitation, two wellness centers, diabetes and sleep disorder centers, and treatment for psychiatric and chemical dependency disorders. In nearby Port Charlotte are Columbia Fawcett Memorial Hospital, a 254-bed full-service, acute-care hospital with 24-hour emergency treatment, and Bon Secours-St. Joseph Hospital, a 212-bed not-for-profit facility with 24-hour emergency services, a women's center and an affiliated nursing home, hospice care and assisted living.

Housing options: Single-family homes are the primary form of housing with prices ranging from $60,000 in modest neighborhoods to $1 million for more lavish dwellings that sit along the edge of Charlotte Harbor. There also are manufactured-home communities, where prices start in the $40,000s. **Punta Gorda Isles**, (800) 445-6560, just west of downtown, is a community that began in the early 1960s and continues to grow today. Most of the homes are on canals. Prices start at about $75,000 for an older two-bedroom home. New waterfront homes start at about $250,000 and go up to about $1 million. Downtown Punta Gorda, a state historic district, features mainly wooden structures, many of which have been refurbished in recent years. Convenient to downtown shops, waterfront parks and I-75, these in-demand properties range from $100,000 to about $400,000. **Burnt Store Marina**, south of the city, has a spectacular location on a wide stretch of Charlotte Harbor. This gated community offers waterfront condominiums from $89,900 and single-family homes from $119,950, (800) 237-4255 (Florida Design Communities). There's a large marina, tennis courts and a restaurant on property. **Burnt Store Meadows**, south of Burnt Store Marina, has more modest homes, with lots starting at about $4,000. **Blue Heron Pines**, a golf-course community for those age 55 and older, offers manufactured homes starting in the mid-$40,000s. Amenities include a clubhouse, exercise room and heated pool, (800) 635-4834. **Burnt Store Colony**, a manufactured-home community, also is geared to those 55 and older, with a clubhouse, pool, tennis courts and shuffleboard. Prices start in the low $40,000s, (800) 445-0943 or (941) 639-4009. On the east side of the city is **Ventura Lakes**, which offers manufactured homes starting at $49,900, a security gate, tennis courts, shuffleboard and clubhouse, (941) 575-6220 or (888) 575-6220.

Visitor lodging: Best Western in downtown Punta Gorda overlooks Charlotte Harbor, $79-$94 with discounts for AAA and AARP members, (800) 525-1022 or (941) 639-1165. Days Inn just off Interstate 75, $44-$150, (941) 637-7200. Other options include Punta Gorda RV Resort, $20 per day, $120 weekly, (941) 639-2010; Fisherman's Village Resort Club, $85-$100, (941) 639-8721; and Burnt Store Marina and Country Club Resort, $89-$99 summer, $150-$195 winter, (800) 859-7529.

Information: The Charlotte County Chamber of Commerce, 326 W. Marion, No. 112, Punta Gorda, 33950-4417, (941) 639-6330 or www.charlotte-florida.com/chamber.

Ed and Barbara Ring found much the same thing 12 years ago when they moved to Tropical Gulf Acres, a rural subdivision about seven miles south of the city limits. Their early friendships came through church and the Tropical Gulf Acres Civic Association, recalls Ed, 65.

But, even before that, Barbara, 63, says, "While we were building our home, our neighbors came by to chat."

The Rings had spent the better part of their married life traveling as Ed rose through the ranks in the U.S. Marines. They moved first to Port Charlotte but, after a couple of years, decided they "wanted a slower, quieter lifestyle," Ed says.

They were drawn to Tropical Gulf Acres because it was still relatively undeveloped and, as a result, most of their neighbors were birds and other wildlife. Their two-acre parcel sits on the banks of a pond.

Barbara says, "To me it's home — what we have been looking for after a nomadic military life. We have a bass in our pond that grew from a few inches to a foot long since we moved here and now follows us as we walk the bank of the pond. We feed him Cheerios."

The subdivision's 39 lakes attract osprey, ring-necked ducks "and a hawk that takes baths in the pond" behind the house, she says.

Nature's not far off even for those who live in more populated portions of the city. It's not uncommon to see fish leaping gracefully out of the water in backyard canals, or to see large turtles plodding along the roadside or sunning on a sea wall. Tiny lizards, called anoles, scamper about on sidewalks and climb screens around most homes.

Manatees, lumbering but docile sea mammals, make their way into the harbor and canals during cold weather, seeking warmer waters and the tons of sea grasses they need to eat to survive. Dolphins leaping about in the harbor, or playing in the wake of powerboats, are familiar sights. So are osprey, eagles, pelicans and all sorts of other birds.

Even the less-welcome alligator makes an occasional appearance, posing loglike in a canal, sunbathing in

grasses along the shore or, once in a while, getting disoriented and scurrying for cover under a car in the driveway. Feeding gators is illegal — the more accustomed they become to being fed by humans, the bolder they grow and the more likely they are to become aggressive. Those that venture too close to homes are picked up by wildlife officials.

Parks are numerous, too. Punta Gorda has six city parks, and there also are 34 county parks, four state facilities, and a federal wildlife refuge. There also are 15 public beach access sites, although none are in Punta Gorda itself. There's a small beach on Charlotte Harbor in Port Charlotte and, on the northwestern end of the county, access to the Gulf of Mexico in Englewood. South of Englewood is Boca Grande, an upscale island from which some of the world's best tarpon fishing takes place.

About 45 miles south, off the coast of Fort Myers, are the renowned beaches of Captiva and Sanibel islands. Sanibel is ranked one of the top three places in the world for shell collecting. There are several excellent public beaches and many places to dine and stay.

While residents describe Punta Gorda as on the sleepy side, there are quite a few things to see and do when not boating, fishing, playing golf or tennis.

There are lots of shops downtown and still more at the waterfront complex Fisherman's Village, which also has a marina and restaurants. For more extensive shopping, the Port Charlotte Town Center has department stores, 100 specialty shops and a food court.

The Florida Adventure Museum contains four exhibit galleries and offers traveling exhibits from around the country. The focus is on Florida-related themes. For artists and those who would like to be, the Visual Arts Center offers classes, programs, workshops and exhibits.

Babcock Wilderness Adventures consist of swamp buggy tours high above the waters of the 8,000-acre Telegraph Cypress Swamp and elsewhere on the 90,000-acre Crescent B Ranch, where visitors will see un-

spoiled Florida interpreted by well-trained guides.

The Charlotte Harbor Environmental Center offers environmental education and recreation, including guided tours of four miles of nature trails. And the Peace River Wildlife Center in Ponce de Leon Park protects and preserves native wildlife that has been orphaned, displaced or injured. Visitors are welcome.

Annual events include the aforementioned observance of Ponce de Leon's Landing in March. This also is the height of the tourist season and the month when the boys of summer head to the state for baseball spring training. The Texas Rangers train at the $6 million Charlotte County Stadium a few miles northwest of Port Charlotte. The Boston Red Sox train in Fort Myers, and the Minnesota Twins play just south of Fort Myers.

In April, the two-day Florida International Air Show swoops above and into Charlotte County Airport, featuring expert aerobatic and ground displays. The U.S. Navy Blue Angels and Army Golden Nights are frequent participants.

May brings warmer temperatures and fewer visitors, but the fun continues with the annual Charlotte Harbor Fishing Tournament and the annual Chili Challenge for Charity, which benefits the YMCA. At Christmas there's the Peace River Lighted Boat Parade and Holly Days, when Punta Gorda businesses hold open houses.

Volunteer opportunities abound at places such as the Charlotte County Chamber of Commerce, the Visual Arts Center, the Florida Adventure Museum, Port Charlotte Cultural Center and Charlotte Regional Medical Center. At the hospital, golf-cart driving volunteers give visitors lifts from their cars to the hospital entrance.

While Charlotte County is no longer the fastest-growing county in the nation, about 3,000 people a year continue to move in, far outstripping the numbers who leave.

The Meattys, the Mielkes and the Rings have no plans to relocate. "We like living where we are," Ed Ring says. "There's no place nicer."●

Reno, Nevada

Residents find Nevada city a winner in more ways than gaming

By Judy Wade

On the surface, most visitors see Reno as a city that glitters with bright neon signs, but that's only one side of its many personalities.

Not far from the glitzy casinos, nature paths invite quiet escapes for leisurely walks. Near downtown, historic homes are mixed with small office buildings, and on the city's outskirts, new residential developments blanket the hills.

Reno's all-encompassing persona is most emphatically shaped by rolling high-desert landscape ringed by mountains that glow beneath a usually cloudless blue sky.

Burgeoning growth has fused once-separate Reno and Sparks into a single metropolis of almost 300,000 residents, with city centers just three miles apart. They share a school and library system, jails and public transportation. Together they represent one of the state's fastest-growing areas, luring retirees in particular with senior-sensitive services and well-priced entertainment.

Mel and Edith Hamilton couldn't wait to leave the rainy climate of Portland, OR, for sunny Reno. In checking out places to retire, they ruled out California as too expensive, Phoenix because they found it too hot and Las Vegas because of heavy traffic.

They looked at planned retirement communities, but Edith, 67, says, "We need a mixed neighborhood because we like kids and dogs and young people."

The Hamiltons' new home — with their choice of colors, carpet and other amenities — is in a single-family residential subdivision with curving streets and pleasant parks near Peavine Mountain.

Ruth and Henry Wark, both 79, had retired in the early 1980s in Lancaster, CA, north of Los Angeles. Four years ago they pulled up stakes in favor of a retirement apartment in Reno's Classic Residence by Hyatt. The community in southwest Reno has views of Mount Rose and the Washoe Golf Course. Tidy frame buildings are connected to a central area with a dining room, library with fireplace, crafts room and lobby with concierge.

The Warks like Reno's setting, in particular its proximity to the mountains, pine trees and desert. Ruth adds, "There's an awful lot to see and do in the city if you never went out of it. There are a lot of good cultural things going on."

The Warks also enjoy Reno's variety of inexpensive restaurants and buffets. "If we want to play the nickel or quarter machines, we can eat right there, too," says Henry. Both couples report Reno's cost of living as similar to their former homes. According to ACCRA, an economic research firm that tracks costs of living, the latest index for the Reno-Sparks area is 113.7 vs. a national average of 100. Higher housing and health care costs in particular push Reno costs above average.

The Hamiltons note that groceries were less expensive in Portland and that Oregon has no sales tax but Nevada does; however, property taxes on their Reno home are about $2,100 less per year than on a similar home in Portland. Oregon had a state income tax but Nevada does not, thanks to the economic contributions of the state's gaming industries. However, the Hamiltons caution that Reno does assess a personal property tax on cars.

To retirees from California and other areas with high housing costs, the $158,000-plus price tag on an average single-family home in the Reno area doesn't look out of line. But to those coming from less costly areas, the prices can be prohibitive, and growth is slow in types of housing other than single-family units. Seniors do have an edge when securing apartments (average rent 1s $750 for two bedrooms), reports the monthly *Senior Spectrum* newspaper, because landlords like it that they "pay the rent on time and have no wild parties."

Cynthia Robinson, director at Classic Residence by Hyatt, says there is always a waiting list for apartments. "They're popular because they combine the privacy of a personal residence with the social aspects of a club," she says.

Henry Wark likes having most of their living costs covered at the apartment community. "Before, we had to write so many checks. Here we just write one for the rent and one for the phone," he says, noting that their rent also covers two meals a day.

One-bedroom apartments at Classic Residence begin at $1,915, with $375 for a second person. This includes daily breakfast and either lunch or dinner, weekly maid service and other amenities.

Residents say that Reno retains a cordial, small-town atmosphere despite its rapid growth in the last decade. Both the Hamiltons and Warks say it has been easy to make new friends.

It's also a convenient city. McCarran Boulevard circles the metropolitan area, providing a quick route from one point to another. The airport is less than 15 minutes from city center, and most casinos and restaurants are within about a 10-minute radius of the downtown area, which also has major cultural venues.

The Warks say that shopping opportunities are varied and easily accessible, with such companies as Macy's, Sears, J.C. Penney, K-Mart and Target in the area. Ruth favors 90-store enclosed Meadowood Mall.

While Reno is sunny year-round and adjacent to the desert, it sits at about 4,500 feet elevation and has a definite winter. From December through March, temperatures can dip well below freezing, and snowfall averages 27 inches a year. Below-zero temperatures can occur. Summers are pleasant, with highs rarely getting above the low 90s. Air conditioning is not a necessity and is offered only as an option by many new-home builders.

When going "over the hill" (to Tahoe in Reno-talk) during winter months, residents say that chains or snow tires and a shovel in the trunk are necessities. Unexpected storms can close roads, and places where snow has melted during the day quickly freeze to "black ice" at night.

Entertainment in the area runs the gamut from headliner shows and Broadway-type extravaganzas to the great outdoors. Casinos are low-key and unintimidating, most of them offering lessons to novices. It's possible to spend an hour or more with a dollar's worth of nickels playing slot poker. Aficionados say there's even a fairly good chance of coming out ahead.

Expansive buffets at most casinos cost as little as $4 or $5 for lunch, with $10 usually a top price for dinner. Fine dining options, more expensive but with gourmet food and elegant service, include Harrah's Reno Steak House and the Top of the Flamingo Hilton.

Although not nearly so visible as the casinos, Reno's cultural side sparkles as well. Across from the courthouse, the geodesic dome of the Pioneer Center for the Performing Arts dominates Virginia Street, the city's main thoroughfare. It is the home of the Reno Philharmonic and the Nevada Opera.

Nearby, along the silvery thread of the Truckee River that bisects Reno, the National Automobile Museum houses more than 200 antique, vintage and classic autos. A few blocks over, the enormous National Bowling Stadium looms like a giant bowling ball, attracting tournaments and sport bowlers from around the world.

Outside downtown, the Wilbur May Center houses treasures collected from travels around the world by May, son of the May Department Store founder. Its arboretum and botanical gardens are frequently used for local parties and weddings.

Fans of old movies will recognize the Washoe County Courthouse, a 1911 Classic Revival building incorporating the original 1873 courthouse. Once the nation's center for quick and legal severance of marital ties, the courthouse with its Corin-

Reno, NV

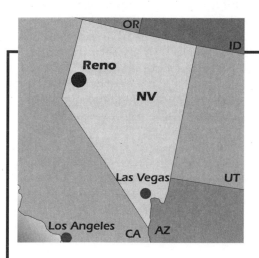

Population: 154,600 in Reno, 366,700 in Washoe County.

Location: At the base of the eastern slope of the Sierra Nevada mountains, 13 miles east of the Nevada-California state line.

Climate:

	High	Low
January	45	20
July	92	51

Average relative humidity: 30%
Rain: 7.53 inches.
Snow: 26.5 inches.
High desert with a sunny, dry, moderate four-season climate, but daily temperatures can vary as much as 45 degrees. Elevation is 4,498 feet.
Cost of living: 113.7
Average housing cost: $157,988 for a single-family home of about 2,000 square feet.
Sales tax: 7%
Sales tax exemptions: Prescription drugs, groceries.
State income tax: None.
Intangibles tax: None.
Estate tax: None, except the state's "pick-up" portion of the federal tax, applicable to taxable estates above $675,000.
Property tax: $33.50 per $1,000 of assessed valuation, with homes assessed at 35% of market value. Taxes on a $157,988 home are about $1,852 a year.
Personal property tax: A "privilege" tax applies to automobiles and varies according to year, make and model of car. The tax is paid yearly at the time license tag is renewed.
Homestead exemption: None.
Security: 60.7 crimes per 1,000 residents, higher than the national average of 46.2 per 1,000 residents.
Religion: 166 churches and synagogues represent numerous faiths.
Education: University of Nevada at Reno waives the $61 per credit fee to those age 62 and older.
Transportation: Citifare provides scheduled bus service in the metro-

politan area; Citi-Lift provides transportation for elderly and handicapped. Amtrak has daily service. Newly renovated Reno/Tahoe International Airport, less than 15 minutes from the center of the city, is served by major carriers. Van shuttles run frequently between Reno and Lake Tahoe.
Health: Eight medical facilities serving the region have a total of 1,594 beds and provide all types of health care.
Housing options: In northeast Reno, the city's fastest-growing area, **Canyon Creek** is being developed by Bailey & McGah, (702) 747-4600; homes are $126,950-$149,000. About six miles north of the city is **Stone Canyon**, developed by Lifestyle Homes, (702) 673-9000; prices run $93,500-$136,500.
Visitor lodging: Dozens of casino hotels are reasonably priced, though rates may vary depending on occupancy. Downtown, the Flamingo Hilton, (800) 648-4882, has doubles starting at $109. Atlantis, (800) 723-6500, also has doubles from $109.
Information: Greater Reno/Sparks Chamber of Commerce, 405 Marsh Ave., Reno, NV 89505, (775) 686-3030 or www.reno-sparkschamber.org.

thian portico became synonymous with divorce in countless flicks and news photos. Times have changed, though, and Reno now is known as a place to get married. Within blocks of the courthouse are numerous wedding chapels, offering packages complete with music, flowers and minister for those in a rush to tie the knot.

Reno's four-season climate creates outdoor recreation opportunities year-around. The Lake Tahoe area, less than an hour away, is a favorite getaway. In winter, it offers a wide variety of ski slopes and resorts, including Heavenly Valley, Alpine Meadows and Squaw Valley USA. When the weather warms, Reno residents hike the Tahoe Rim Trail and cruise the alpine lake's placid blue waters.

The Warks enjoy packing a picnic and driving through the Sierra Nevadas to Lake Tahoe or going to Pyramid Lake where serious anglers pursue cutthroat trout. Closer to home, they walk daily along paths and nature trails near their residence. Ruth even has tried hot-air ballooning, a popular sport in Reno's dry, still climate.

Golf enthusiasts have six course options in Reno and about 20 courses in the area, including nearby Lake Tahoe and Carson City. The beautiful Robert Trent Jones-designed course at the Resort at Squaw Creek near Lake Tahoe is surrounded by 10,000-foot Sierra Nevada peaks that are crisscrossed by ski trails most of the year. On Reno's public courses, greens fees with cart average about $36 for 18 holes. While many retirees from other areas find Reno's greens fees a bargain, the Hamiltons consider them high, compared to Portland's $6 public course greens fees — without cart.

Area medical care is good but costly, about 25 percent higher than the national average, according to AC-CRA figures. Among the major providers of health care are Washoe Medical Center, St. Mary's Regional Medical Center and the Northern Nevada Medical Center. The latter has the state's only geropsychiatric program, Senior Bridges, offering help for those with emotional health problems.

Health care and housing are high in part because the Reno area is relatively isolated geographically. The nearest major city, Sacramento, is 140 miles to the west. Goods and materials must be brought over the mountains by truck or train into the Great Basin. Commodities like building materials and goods that support a medical infrastructure reflect these transportation costs.

The Warks expressed some concern about crime. "When we got here four years ago there was no graffiti. Now there are gangs, graffiti and the crime element," says Henry.

The city's crime rate is higher than average — 60.7 crimes per 1,000 population at press time vs. a national average of 46.2 per 1,000 — but it dropped from 79.6 per 1,000 in 1993 and 71.8 per 1,000 in 1994. A representative for Reno's police department says that a high number of the crimes are casino-related larceny-theft.

Many of the casinos are on historic Virginia Street, spanned by a sparkling arch downtown. It's the latest in a series of welcome signs dating to 1899, when the original one greeted troops returning from the Spanish-American War. Today's art deco design has 800 linear feet of neon and 1,600 light bulbs that declare Reno the "Biggest Little City in the World" — a justifiable welcome, considering Reno's multiple personalities.●

Rockport, Texas

Texas Gulf Coast lures water and bird enthusiasts

By George L. Rosenblatt

For years, artists, anglers and whooping cranes have migrated to a friendly, nurturing environment along the middle Texas Gulf Coast. Now it's reeling in retirees too.

They're settling in or near Rockport, in a landscape quite different from the normal image of Texas — no big-city skyscrapers, vast stretches of arid land or oil well derricks.

Rockport lies on a flat coastal plain, which varies from swampy grasslands to shores marked by wind-bent trees and wide beaches backed in some places by undulating sand dunes.

"It was absolutely perfect for me," says retired U.S. Foreign Service officer Lynn Lee, 59, who settled on the coast in 1990 after three and a half years in Tegucigalpa, Honduras.

"I wanted to become an artist. Once I found Rockport, I looked no further," he adds.

In Rockport he found himself among like souls. The area is home to nearly 200 artists, who find inspiration in the water-dominated landscape, fishing boats and abundant birds and waterfowl.

Lynn met and married an artist, Joan Sumners Lee, 73, who had moved to the coastal town in the mid-1980s from her home in San Antonio.

"We live in paradise," says Joan, an opinion some might at least partially credit to her being a native Texan.

The Lees are not alone in their affection for Rockport. Bay and Gulf waters hook many a person lured by fishing, boating and beaches. Rockport's choicest homes are either at bayshore or linked to bay waters by canal.

"I found the home I loved with an artist studio in Key Allegro," says Lynn. "I wanted water and found I could get to the bay from my home via canal."

Don and Trish Butler also acknowledge aquatic allure as among influ-ences in their selecting Rockport. Their move followed more than 10 years in England and Australia, where Don served Ford-Mercury as vice president of international operations.

The Butlers had visited Rockport two weeks a year for the past 15 years until moving in "for the climate and the water," says Trish, 47. "We both golf and fish. Love boating."

They, too, settled in Key Allegro, a neighborhood of upscale homes.

Beyond climate and water, Rockport's draws for Gary and Nancy Cooper include interesting people from around the world plus the proximity of the outside world.

Gary, 64, and Nancy, 52, moved to Rockport from Santa Fe, NM, via a Peace Corps stint in Zaire. He had been vice president at S&M Drug Package Inc., while she was executive vice president and co-owner of Primacare Medical Centers.

The Coopers now live in the center of Rockport, in a 100-year-old home they restored and operate as the Blue Heron Inn.

"The geography offers so much," Gary says. "After Santa Fe, we decided we wanted warm and wet."

They came to the right place. Subtropical Aransas County soaks up an average of more than 37 inches of rainfall a year, and it basks in an annual mean temperature exceeding 70 degrees. The county's maximum altitude falls just short of 30 feet.

The town of 7,200 rests on a peninsula between Copano Bay on the inland side and Aransas Bay, separated from the Gulf of Mexico by a string of barrier islands. The town of Fulton lies only a hyphen north of Rockport, and the two communities often are linked in the same breath, mainly as popular summer beach resorts.

Within about a half-hour's drive south lie Corpus Christi and the Padre Island National Seashore, and about the same distance north is the Aransas National Wildlife Refuge.

The topography, the climate, the location and the vegetation all support a remarkable array of wildlife. Perhaps 500 species of birds spend all or part of at least one season in the Rockport area, which lies along the avian artery known as the Great North American Flyway.

Most prominent among those species are the endangered whooping cranes, which winter in Aransas National Wildlife Refuge. The whoopers can be seen, and their distinctive cry heard, from observation towers in the refuge or from special tour boats, which leave from Rockport.

One of the biggest feathers in Rockport's birding cap, however, flutters from the tiny hummingbird, thanks to the late Connie Hagar. An in-town wildlife sanctuary commemorates her 35 years of amateur bird-watching. Recognized as an expert in the field, she is credited with discovering the area as a major migratory milestone for hummingbirds.

The town draws tourists from early spring through late fall, though snowbirds from the Midwest and Canada also flock here in winter.

"This town is very open and welcoming," Nancy Cooper says.

"We have a broad scope of friends," adds her husband, Gary, citing local associations and volunteerism opportunities as starting points. "We developed friendships (here) faster than any place we lived before."

Long-timer Joan Sumners Lee adds that "you don't have to be here five minutes to make friends. Birding, fishing, arts are all easy ways to make friends."

Trish Butler credits the golf club with links to many local friendships and says retirement provided the opportunity to nurture those new associations.

"We've been members since it started but were never here long enough to get to know anyone until we retired," she says.

Spending more time with preferred pursuits does not equate with spending more money, however. All three couples agree that the general cost of living is lower here, especially in comparison to other locales they had considered.

"You can get a lot for your money here," says Don Butler, 61. Trish adds that "we spend less on clothes and food."

Lynn Lee says that the same three-bedroom, two-and-a-half-bath home he and Joan enjoy in Rockport would have cost "three times or more" in California or in Florida's Sanibel-Captiva area.

While the Coopers say they'd sell their bed-and-breakfast inn for the right price and move, both the Lees and the Butlers seem to have set their anchors firmly at the small seaside town.

All three couples actively participate in civic and arts organizations, as well as various other facets of local life. Water-based outdoor options lap at nearly every turn.

Rockport Beach Park features a 1-mile, white-sand beach, swimming areas with lifeguards, a natural saltwater pool, the Connie Hagar Wildlife Sanctuary, convenience and concession pavilions, an 800-foot fishing pier and a sector reserved for boating and water-skiing. The beach park is open year-round.

In the shadow of the Lyndon B. Johnson Causeway that today carries traffic across the narrows of Copano Bay, the original Copano Bay causeway is cast in a new role as possibly the world's longest (8,700 feet) fishing pier.

The town's premier landmark is the Fulton Mansion, built in the mid-

Rockport, TX

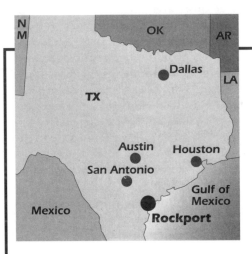

Population: 7,200 in Rockport, 1,400 in adjacent Fulton.

Location: On a small peninsula between two bays on the middle Texas Gulf Coast, called the Coastal Bend, about 35 miles northeast of Corpus Christi.

Climate:

	High	Low
January	64	50
July	90	79

Average relative humidity: 62%

Rain: 37.5 inches.

Subtropical climate with relatively mild winters, early short springs, late short autumns and long, hot summers. Hurricanes and tornadoes are possible; the last hurricane to hit the area directly was in 1970, though some other coastal storms have produced high water, heavy rains and stout winds. Elevation is 3.5 to 20 feet.

Cost of living: Below average (specific index not available).

Average housing cost: $96,000

Sales tax: 8.25%

Sales tax exemptions: Groceries, prescription drugs, medical supplies, professional services.

State income tax: None.

Intangibles tax: None.

Estate tax: None, except the state's "pick-up" portion of the federal tax, applicable to taxable estates above $675,000.

Property tax: Within Rockport, the tax rate is $23.50 per $1,000 in value, with property assessed at 100% of market value. Outside city limits, but within Aransas County and Aransas County Independent School District, the rate is $19.88 per $1,000. Yearly tax on a $96,000 home in Rockport is about $2,256 and in Aransas County about $1,908.

Homestead exemption: For persons age 65 and older, the different taxing entities (city, county, school district) grant exemptions varying from $7,500 to $15,000 off the assessed value. Veterans also qualify for exemptions.

Security: 86.4 crimes per 1,000 residents, higher than the national average of 46.2 crimes per 1,000 residents.

Religion: Houses of worship include 22 Protestant, two Roman Catholic and several other denominations.

Education: The Rockport Center for the Arts offers classes, workshops and lectures in fine arts and performing arts. At least a dozen universities, colleges, community colleges and other venues of advanced learning have campuses within 60 miles of Rockport.

Transportation: Buses run between Rockport, Fulton and other nearby communities; metered taxis serve the town. Corpus Christi International Airport is the nearest facility for major commercial carriers.

Health: The nearest full-service hospital emergency room is 11 miles away in Aransas Pass, and the nearest concentration of major hospital facilities is in Corpus Christi. The Aransas County Emergency Medical Services — one of the state's first ambulance/EMS operations providing advanced life-support systems — stations three state-of-the-art ambulances in Rockport.

Housing options: Key Allegro Island, a major residential development, has prices in varying ranges, from $60,000-$75,000 on the low end (homes off the water) to $150,000-$250,000 at the moderate level and $250,000-$650,000 at the top. Similarly priced homes can be found in the comparable developments known as **Rockport Country Club** and **Harbor Oaks**.

Visitor lodging: The Blue Heron Inn Bed and Breakfast, $100-$110, includes breakfast, (361) 729-7526. Laguna Reef Hotel/Suites, doubles starting at $75, discounted 10% for seniors, (800) 248-1057. For homes/condos to rent, sources include Security Real Estate Rentals, (800) 221-5028, and Key Allegro Rentals, (800) 348-1627. There also are RV parks.

Information: Rockport-Fulton Area Chamber of Commerce, Visitor Information Center, 404 Broadway, Rockport, TX 78382, (800) 242-0071 or www.rockport-fulton.org.

1870s by George W. Fulton, a Philadelphia-born pioneer in raising Texas cattle. His design included such unheard-of features as running water, flush toilets and refrigeration in functional, albeit primitive, forms.

The form of the cattle business that built Fulton's mansion was also primitive, in that it valued mainly hide and tallow. Beyond a relatively small proportion preserved and sold to the army, most of the meat was discarded.

After about two decades, changing times banished that bovine business, and Rockport's focus moved toward fishing and tourism as early as the 1880s.

Another revered area landmark is the Big Tree, an ancient live oak considered the largest in the state. It's 44 feet tall and its gnarled branches spread more than 90 feet. The tree is in Goose Island State Park north of town.

Varied aspects of area life appear in the art, artifacts and architecture of such local institutions as the Rockport Center for the Arts and the Texas Maritime Museum.

The Center for the Arts, in a restored, harborside Victorian home, encourages artistic endeavors through classes, gallery exhibitions and special events and programs.

Close by is the Texas Maritime Museum, which interprets the state's historic, economic and cultural links with the sea through artifacts, documents, interactive displays and rotating exhibits.

The area has a number of annual events, including the Hummer/Bird Celebration each September; the Rockport Seafair each Columbus Day weekend; the Fulton Oysterfest the first weekend in March; and the Rockport Art Festival the July Fourth weekend.

For all its offerings, Rockport, like anyplace else, does have drawbacks.

Among the aspects Trish Butler likes least is the "unsightly appearance" of some areas.

"Zoning ordinances are being implemented to improve the looks of some parts of the community," she notes. "They are getting better controls where there have been none before."

The Coopers would like to have a better, broader selection of dining options and better medical facilities closer — though Nancy says there's an excellent hospital 11 miles away, in Aransas Pass.

About the only real gripe the Lees have is the summer heat and humidity.

"But," concludes Lynn Lee, "when we get away for a couple of weeks, we start missing Rockport, and we can't wait to get home."●

Ruidoso, New Mexico

Housing is reasonably priced in this New Mexico mountain resort town

By Dave G. Houser

Named for the stream that bubbles briskly through it, Ruidoso (Spanish for "noisy") nestles in a high-mountain valley in south-central New Mexico, some 200 miles south of the big-city bustle of Albuquerque and the high-priced hustle of Santa Fe. And lately this out-of-the-way village of 10,000 has been making plenty of noise in the national media.

Long popular with the flatlanders of West Texas as a convenient alpine vacation getaway, noted for its horse racing and ski facilities, the area is gaining wider attention nowadays owing to a rash of articles, including one in *Woman's Day* that identified Ruidoso as one of the nation's best sports vacation values. *Vacations* magazine listed it among the top 10 small-town vacation sites in the nation; *Ski* magazine rated it one of the 10 best U.S. ski towns in which to live, and *U.S. News and World Report* included Ruidoso as one of the top seven places in the country for second-home ownership.

Not surprisingly, all the elements that have led to Ruidoso's increasing recognition as a vacation and second-home haven are attracting retirees in growing numbers as well.

"We wanted to be in the mountains," says Bob Macfarlane, a retired marketing manager who called El Paso, TX, home for 24 years before moving with wife Sue to Ruidoso in 1994. "We'd been coming here for years to ski and play golf, so the choice was a natural one for us," adds Macfarlane, 65, "and we really never considered anyplace else."

Escaping the traffic, crime and pollution of city life was another important consideration for the Macfarlanes, who found it necessary to install bars on the windows of their El Paso home for protection.

"Now we have clean air, no bars on the windows, no traffic jams and, in short, no problems," says Sue, 58, proudly showing the couple's elegant 2,200-square-foot, custom-built, mountaintop hideaway, purchased for $225,000 from the original owner, who built the home four years ago as a vacation residence.

According to local real estate broker Gary Lynch, more and more of the village's vacation properties — which constitute almost half of all homes — are being snapped up by new year-round residents, many of them retirees. The permanent population of Ruidoso has, in fact, doubled since 1990.

"We've seen the beginnings of a shift in recent years," says Lynch, "from second- to first-home purchases, and the same could be said for new construction. Still more folks are making the decision to retire to their second homes here."

While cool pines and mountain views are a definite draw, Ruidoso's greatest appeal to retirees may boil down to the affordability of its real estate.

In a survey by Century 21 Real Estate, Ruidoso ranked in the top 30 percent for market condition and affordability among 172 vacation-home markets nationwide.

"Even though prices have been on the rise since 1990," says Lynch, "in the context of a mountain resort community, Ruidoso remains among the most affordable markets you'll find anywhere."

Currently the median home price in Ruidoso is $130,000. Small cabins and condos, measuring 1,000 square feet or thereabouts, still can be found in the $45,000-to-$65,000 range, but the best values appear to be among higher-end properties, from $175,000 and up, which often include substantial acreage.

Pat and Lois Batchelor moved to Ruidoso four years ago when Pat retired from his appointment as Louisiana's commissioner of conservation. The Batchelors had built a retirement home in Lake Charles, LA, but after several visits to Ruidoso, they changed their minds, sold the property and moved west. They spent $280,000 on a 3,000-square-foot Santa Fe Territorial-style home in Ruidoso's White Mountain development.

"Friendly people, perfect weather, lots of golf courses and the prospect of slow-paced, small-town living were definite factors in our decision," says Pat, 69, "and great real-estate values cinched the move."

"Some friends of ours from New Orleans came for a visit last summer," says Lois, 61, "and they were so impressed with the place — and the prices — that they bought a lovely $100,000 condo after being here only four days. As a sequel to that," she adds, "they've just moved into a big new home near us and sold the condo — at a nice profit."

Glen and Carole Benham are among a growing number of Southern Californians who have taken up life among the pines of Lincoln County. Drawn by the region's recreational opportunities but concerned about how they'd take to the mountain winters, the Upland, CA, couple spent a year in a rented condo before deciding on the retirement move.

"That was all it took," says Glen, 69, a retired Los Angeles County sheriff's deputy. "We skied our brains out, played a lot of golf, fell in love with the people and got involved with the community. The next thing we knew, we were moving here to stay."

Like many newcomers, the Benhams purchased a condo initially and later parlayed that investment into the home of their choice — a 2,250-square-foot, two-story chalet with a glorious view of Sierra Blanca and the ski area.

Skiing is an obvious magnet to active retirees, and Ruidoso's Ski Apache certainly is popular with the senior set, thanks to its $140 season pass for skiers 62 and older.

Owned and operated by the Mescalero Apache tribe, whose mountainous 465,000-acre reservation borders Ruidoso to the southwest, Ski Apache is the nation's southernmost major ski area. With eight lifts (including the state's only gondola) servicing nearly 2,000 vertical feet of light powder, it boasts the largest lift capacity of any ski area in New Mexico. Ski season here normally runs from Thanksgiving to Easter.

Just as it does for the Macfarlanes, Batchelors and Benhams, golf figures prominently among the recreational pursuits of many of Ruidoso's retired residents. The area's four public and two private courses provide plenty of options. Most popular are The Links at Sierra Blanca, a challenging Scottish-style course that *Golf Digest* rates

Ruidoso, NM

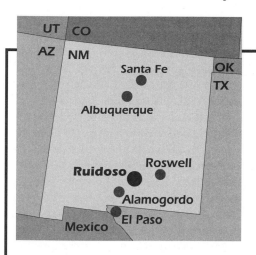

Population: 9,800 in Ruidoso and Ruidoso Downs, 15,974 in Lincoln County.
Location: Cradled on the heavily forested eastern slope of 12,003-foot Sierra Blanca Mountain in south-central New Mexico, 124 miles north of El Paso and 190 miles south of Albuquerque. Elevation is 6,800 feet.

Climate:

	High	Low
January	49	17
July	78	47

Average relative humidity: 30%
Rain: 23 inches **Snow:** 47 inches (180-300 inches at Ski Apache atop Sierra Blanca).
Ruidoso's climate offers more than 300 sunny days a year; winters can be cold.
Cost of living: Below average (specific index not available).
Average housing cost: $131,250
Sales tax: 6.9375% (called a gross receipts tax).
Sales tax exemptions: None.
State income tax: Graduated from 2.2% on incomes up to $8,000 to 8.2% on incomes above $65,000 for a single filer and $100,000 for married couples filing jointly.
Income tax exemptions: Social Security, plus varying exclusions for those age 65 and older with incomes of less than $22,000.
Estate tax: None, except the state's "pick-up" portion of the federal tax, applicable to taxable estates of more than $675,000.
Property tax: $30.72 per $1,000 of appraised value, with home assessment at 33.33% of market value. Yearly tax on a $131,000 home is about $1,341 without exemptions. In unincorporated areas of the county the rate averages $18.97 per $1,000 of appraised value.
Homestead exemption: There is a head-of-household exemption of $2,000 off the taxable value.
Security: 68.9 crimes per 1,000 residents, higher than the national average of 46.2 crimes per residents.
Religion: More than 50 churches representing 19 denominations.
Education: Continuing-education courses and some degree programs can be pursued at the Ruidoso branch of Eastern New Mexico University. Continuing-education (noncredit) courses are available at half-price to students 62 and older, and there's a special selection of courses catering to seniors. For those 65 and older, ENMU offers degree courses at $5 per credit hour, substantially less than regular fees that range from $22 to $107 per credit.
Transportation: There's no public transportation, but taxi service is available. Ruidoso is served by Lone Star Airlines, offering daily service to Roswell, NM, and Dallas.
Health: Recognized among the "100 Top U.S. Hospitals" in a national study, the 42-bed Lincoln County Medical Center is an affiliate of Presbyterian Healthcare Services. It is fully accredited by the Joint Commission for Accreditation for Health Care Organizations, and results of that organization's 1996 survey placed LCMC in the top 40 among more than 1,500 hospitals surveyed nationwide. It provides general and intensive care, 24-hour emergency service and full diagnostic and radiology services and is staffed by 12 physicians and 17 visiting specialists. Major regional health-care facilities are located nearby in Alamogordo (45 miles southwest) and Roswell (70 miles east). Ruidoso actively supports a talented roster of some two dozen alternative and holistic health-service providers. An 85-bed nursing facility, Ruidoso Care Center, features a 24-bed Alzheimer's Living Center and a 12-bed mental-care unit.
Housing options: Cabins and small condos still can be found in the $45,000-to-$65,000 range, but more realistic condo and single-family home prices range from $80,000 to $150,000. A good inventory of higher-end properties ($175,000 to $350,000) attracts affluent retirees, especially from Texas and California. Building lots (averaging $20,000) are readily available, and there's an abundance of developed acreage for homesites in the surrounding hills and valleys. At upscale **Ranches of Sonterra**, the area's newest development situated several miles north of the village, five- to 25-acre homesites are selling briskly at $25,000 to $100,000.
Visitor lodging: A popular year-round resort area, Ruidoso bristles with some 65 lodging options, ranging from rustic riverside cabins to a full-service resort. The latter is the 260-room Inn of the Mountain Gods, $110-$145, (505) 257-5141, a tribal enterprise of the Mescalero Apache. Other options include the Best Western Swiss Chalet Inn, $100, (505) 258-3333, and the new Holiday Inn Express, $109, (505) 257-3736.
Information: Ruidoso Valley Chamber of Commerce, 720 Sudderth Drive, P.O. Box 698, Ruidoso, NM 88355, (800) 253-2255, (505) 257-7395 or www.ruidoso.net.

one as of the 10 best public courses in New Mexico, and the verdant 6,834-yard, par-72 course at the Inn of the Mountain Gods. Both of these superb 18-hole courses are open to the public year-round.

Equine-related activities — racing, riding, roping and ranching — always have figured significantly in the life and times of Ruidoso. Ranching is the leading enterprise in Lincoln County, which sprawls over nearly 4,000 square miles (making it larger than Delaware and Rhode Island combined), and as the hub and largest community therein, Ruidoso is the natural setting for plenty of horse play.

Many folks maintain their own string of mounts, and there are a number of stables that provide steeds for riding the more than 300 miles of trails threading through nearby Lincoln National Forest and the White Mountain and Capitan Mountain wilderness areas. These same areas, encompassing nearly a million undeveloped acres, serve hikers, mountain bikers, hunters and fishermen as well.

Rodeos are popular summer events at neighboring Mescalero and Capitan, and the Lincoln County Cowboy Symposium each October offers some interesting insights into the traditions of the late American cowboy. Founded in the late 1850s as a lumber camp, Ruidoso can't lay claim to a colorful Wild West history, but nearby Lincoln has a legendary past as the setting for the violent Lincoln County War of 1878.

Scores of men died in this historic confrontation, some of them by the gun of outlaw William Bonney, alias Billy the Kid. Billy made Lincoln even more famous by killing Sheriff Matthew Brady, then gunning down two more deputies in a daring 1881 escape from Lincoln County Courthouse. Suspended in an 1880s time warp, the town remains pretty much intact today as a state historical monument.

Horse racing enthusiasts are likely aware of Ruidoso Downs, the nation's premier quarter horse racing venue and home to the annual All American Futurity. This Labor Day classic offers a $2 million purse and is by far the world's richest quarter horse race. During its 16-week summer season, the Downs also hosts the Southwest's finest thoroughbreds.

The striking new Museum of the Horse, fronting the track, is dedicated to the role of the horse in the evolution of the West and houses an impressive collection of more than 10,000 equine-related items. The museum has become a major attraction, and some experts have deemed it one of the finest small specialty museums in the country.

The unveiling in 1995 of internationally known sculptor Dave McGary's monumental bronze work, "Free Spirits at Noisy Water," which depicts seven breeds of American horses, at the entrance to the museum gained the attention of *USA Today* and other national media. This served to elevate both the museum's reputation and the area's artistic prominence.

Although lacking many of the cultural opportunities found in larger communities, Ruidoso is gaining attention for its flourishing art scene. Dave McGary's beautiful new midtown studio, Expressions in Bronze, anchors the growing Ruidoso art district, which numbers nearly two dozen galleries and studios.

The Hondo Valley, just east of Ruidoso, is home to a pair of famous names in the world of art. The late, great Southwestern artist Peter Hurd and equally talented wife Henriette Wyeth produced the bulk of their work on the family's Sentinel Ranch at San Patricio. Henriette and her artist son Michael Hurd maintain the Hurd-LaRinconada Gallery (and a classy bed-and-breakfast complex) at the ranch, exhibiting an extensive collection of Hurd-Wyeth works.

Theater and performing arts, heretofore limited largely to school plays and musicals and the productions of a local theater group, got a giant boost with the 1997 opening of the $17 million Spencer Theater of the Performing Arts. This ultra-modern, 500-seat facility brings to the community a variety of events, including Broadway shows, dance and classical, pop and jazz performances.

Another new facility that has added considerably to the quality of life and economic fortunes of the village is the Ruidoso Convention and Civic Events Center. Primarily intended to attract small conventions with its 33,000 square feet of exhibit and meeting space, the center also provides facilities for hosting special events, including the annual Christmas Jubilee, Oktoberfest, Ruidoso Arts Festival and the nationally known Golden Aspen Motorcycle Rally.

The village of Ruidoso itself tends to defy easy description. The terms "quaint" and "oddball" might relate to its colorful seven-mile-long main drag, Sudderth Drive, lined with an eclectic mix of souvenir and ski shops, art galleries, ice cream and espresso parlors and cowboy honky-tonks. Certainly the traditional concept of grid design was never applied here; there isn't much of a town proper beyond a block or two on either side of sinuous Sudderth Drive. Residential areas are scattered to the four winds, tucked away in canyons and straddling pine-covered hillsides.

The 3,200-member Mescalero tribe (direct descendants of the fabled Geronimo) plays a vital and productive role in the life and commerce of Ruidoso and Lincoln County. In addition to their popular Inn of the Mountain Gods and Ski Apache, the tribe operates successful cattle and timber industries and a Las Vegas-style casino at the resort.

But the enterprising Mescalero nation had fallen afoul of the community by making a deal — since abandoned — with a consortium of Eastern utility companies to permit a temporary low-level nuclear waste storage facility to be built on reservation land. Although the tribe is divided over the issue, leaders are reportedly continuing to pursue a similar deal. Beyond the reservation, opposition to the storage facility is strong, so the likelihood of such a dump site being built is questionable if not remote.

Although not without its shortcomings and controversies, Ruidoso is nearly ideal for active retirees who yearn for a friendly, small town and an outdoor-oriented lifestyle at an affordable price.●

St. Augustine, Florida

With 400-year history, this Florida town boasts colorful past

By Ruth Rejnis

With a history dating back more than 400 years, St. Augustine isn't your usual Florida boom town.

Its narrow streets, garden courtyards, a plaza and massive fort attest to a long Spanish colonial heritage. Add to that touches of British, Greek and Italian influence and a legacy as one of Florida's turn-of-the-century fashionable resorts.

The result is a congenial town of 12,481 that mixes the New World with the Old World.

St. Augustine is historically significant as the nation's oldest permanent European settlement. It was visited by Ponce de Leon in 1513, and in 1565 was claimed for Spain by adventuresome conquistador Pedro Menendez de Aviles.

A major tourist spot on the Atlantic side of north Florida, it attracts guests to its 144-block historic district, an area enshrined in the National Register of Historic Places. Although most of the original colonial Spanish buildings have succumbed to ravages of the ages, reconstructions help capture the spirit of old Spain that gives St. Augustine much of its appeal.

The city lies between the St. Johns River on the west and the Matanzas River and Bay (also the Intracoastal Waterway) to the east, two miles from the ocean. The quarter-mile Bridge of Lions links the downtown area to a string of small beach communities on Anastasia Island along coastal Highway A1A, the first of which is St. Augustine Beach.

Ron and Dot Firster, retired teachers from Butler, PA, were tourists for many years before taking up permanent residence.

"I spent most of 1945 here in the military," Ron, 67, recalls, "and I always planned to retire here. This was our favorite vacation spot, and we came here many times over the years."

Dot, also 67, says that they were attracted by the climate and the city's homey atmosphere.

While the area is popular as a retirement site, only a sixth of St. Johns County residents are age 65 and older. Retirees say it's easy to meet other seniors, though, through church, volunteer projects, bicycling, walking and other outdoor activities encouraged by the benign climate.

"One of the things I like about the town is its good civic spirit," says Norman Baker, a retired chamber of commerce executive from Columbus, OH, who moved here in 1984. "There's such a wide range of activities," he notes. "If you want to do it, it's here."

Norman, 76, and his wife, Jane, also 76 and a retired nurse, say they're kept as busy as they want to be with church and civic organizations. Both are tutors in Learn-to-Read of St. Johns County and have served on that association's board of directors.

Bob and Louise Ebbinghaus, who moved to St. Augustine from Port Chester, NY, also are active volunteer tutors. They put in several hours a week at local schools as part of the state-sponsored Retired Seniors Volunteer Program.

"We help teachers correct papers, help kids and do whatever else needs to be done," says Louise, 70, a former personnel assistant. She and her husband were recognized for their service with a state education award a few years ago.

The city's senior center has an active program schedule, and St. Augustine's historic attractions and programs staged with tourists in mind offer a busy year-round calendar. For example, Menendez Day each spring celebrates the conquistador's settling of the area, and summer brings Spanish Night Watch 1790, a torchlight procession through the Spanish Quarter by people in period dress. During

the holidays, visitors and residents look forward to 18th-century Christmas caroling.

Flagler College, a four-year liberal arts institution, adds to St. Augustine's cultural core. When oil magnate Henry Morrison Flagler developed a good deal of St. Augustine in the 1880s, he opened Ponce de Leon Hotel, now the college. The pink, vaguely Moorish complex is considered a Spanish Renaissance masterpiece.

Local real estate agents divide St. Augustine into three sections: houses in the historic district, those outside the district and homes at the beach.

"Houses in the historic district start at about $80,000 for a fixer-upper," says Janice Johnson of Johnson-Farrell Realty in St. Augustine. "They go up to $300,000. The average price is $150,000 for a moderate-quality historic home." Those houses are typically wood-frame. There are no condominiums in the historic district.

Elsewhere, homes range from around $50,000 for a condominium to more than $500,000 for an oceanfront single-family house.

All three couples interviewed live in St. Augustine Shores, a 2,500-unit planned community on the Matanzas River about eight miles south of downtown and two miles from the beach. The subdivision features single-family homes and condominiums, a golf course, clubhouse and pool.

Norman Baker estimates about 40 percent of the residents are retired. The lineup of social events at the clubhouse, he says, is a good one.

"You'd have to be a hermit not to make friends here," adds Bob Firster.

Cost of living in this part of Florida is lower than in the southern part of the state and is considerably below living costs in the Northeast or on the West Coast. It was the relatively inexpensive lifestyle that attracted the Ebbinghauses.

"We just couldn't afford to live in New York on a fixed income," says Bob, a 73-year-old former letter carrier. "It would have cost us $1,000 a month to rent a three-room house up there."

Louise adds, "We were happily surprised at the low taxes (in St. Augustine). The $25,000 (statewide) property tax exemption was a pleasant shock."

The climate enticed all three couples, they say. Hot summers are relieved by ocean breezes. By fall, temperatures cool down. Deciduous trees lose their leaves, although with the large number of palms, firs and other greenery, there is never the stark, bare look associated with areas that winter treats more harshly.

Shirt sleeves usually are adequate at midday during winter months, but morning and evening temperatures can drop to the 30s. That doesn't deter sunrise walkers and joggers, though, who simply bundle up in jackets, gloves and knit caps. Snowfall is rare.

Ocean swimming in winter is strictly for members of the Polar Bear Club, although lazing on the beach is certainly possible on sunny days.

"My daughter can come down here from New York in December and dash off to the beach when it's in the 60s, and I'm freezing," says Louise Ebbinghaus.

Hurricanes are a possibility, but the last big wind to hit St. Johns County

St. Augustine, FL

Population: 12,481 in St. Augustine, 4,115 in St. Augustine Beach, 109,894 in St. Johns County.

Location: About 90 miles south of the Florida-Georgia border and 50 miles north of Daytona Beach.

Climate:

	High	Low
January	70	47
July	89	71

Average relative humidity: 72%

Rain: 52 inches.

Cost of living: 99.2 for St. Johns County, based on state average of 100.

Average housing cost: $113,461 for a single-family home in St. Johns County.

Sales tax: 6%

Sales tax exemptions: Medical services, prescription drugs, groceries.

State income tax: None.

Intangibles tax: Assessed on stocks, bonds and other specified assets. Tax rate is $1 per $1,000 value for assets under $100,000 for individuals or $200,000 for couples, and $1.50 per $1,000 value for greater amounts; first $20,000 for individuals and $40,000 for couples is exempt. Some investments are exempt.

Estate tax: None, except the state's "pick-up" portion of the federal tax, applicable to taxable estates above $675,000.

Property tax: Rates are $25.12 per $1,000 of assessed value in St. Augustine and $19.62 in St. Augustine Beach, with assessments at 100% of market value. Yearly tax on a $113,461 home with the homestead exemption noted below is about $2,222 in the city, $1,735 at the beach. Both areas have a solid waste tax of $65 per household per year.

Homestead exemption: $25,000 off assessed value for primary, permanent residence.

Security: 90.1 crimes per 1,000 residents, higher than the national average of 46.2 crimes per 1,000 residents.

Religion: The town and beach areas have more than 80 churches and synagogues.

Education: Flagler College, a four-year liberal arts institution, is in the heart of St. Augustine. The town also has a branch of St. Johns River Community College, based in Palatka, about 30 miles southwest of St. Augustine. Various adult education courses are offered by the public schools.

Transportation: No public services. Jacksonville International Airport is about one hour away.

Health: Flagler Hospital is a 230-bed community hospital. It's augmented by more than a half-dozen hospitals and medical centers, including a branch of the Mayo Clinic, in Jacksonville, 25 miles north of St. Augustine.

Housing options: There's a wide range of houses and condominiums but few rental units in the area. **Coquina Crossing**, (800) 446-0699, has custom-manufactured homes from the $60,000s. **St. Augustine Shores**, a planned community on the Matanzas River eight miles south of the historic district, features single-family homes and condominiums for $75,000-$250,000. The subdivision, which still is adding new homes, offers a clubhouse, golf, pool and tennis courts: Sales and resales are available through local realty agencies. At St. Augustine Beach, **Commodores Club**, (904) 471-6968, is a lakeside patio-home community within walking distance of the beach and about six miles south of the downtown historic area. Homes are $125,000-$175,000. **Marsh Creek**, (904) 471-4343, at St. Augustine Beach, overlooking the marsh lands along the Matanzas River about six miles south of downtown, offers single-family and patio homes for $185,000-$750,000, with complete country club amenities. Luxury condominiums in **The Residences at World Golf Village**, (800) 279-1743, start in the low $300,000s.

Visitor lodging: Accommodations are available in all price ranges. Comfort Inn, (904) 824-5554, three blocks from the beach, is $79. Bed-and-breakfast inns in the historic district begin at about $80. Furnished time-share beach apartments are available for short-term rental. Call Resort Rentals of St. Augustine, (800) 727-4656, or Ocean Gallery Properties, (904) 471-6663. Rates are generally higher during the summer.

Information: St. Augustine & St. Johns County Chamber of Commerce, 1 Riberia St., St. Augustine, FL 32084, (904) 829-5681 or www.staugustinechamber.com.

was Hurricane Dora in 1964.

St. Johns County, which extends 43 miles along the east coast of Florida at its northeastern corner, is growing. Besides new housing developments, the new St. Johns Development, a 6,300-acre complex eight miles north of downtown, features homes, shops, the PGA Golf Hall of Fame and a golf academy. The airport, situated about five miles north of downtown, completed a $50 million expansion.

A number of large shopping malls serve St. Augustine, including an outlet center with 90-plus stores. Jacksonville, about 40 minutes by car, offers an even greater selection. In St. Augustine's downtown area, cobblestone St. George Street is lined with small shops and boutiques.

The area has a surprising number of good, well-priced restaurants, residents say. "We can afford to eat out a couple of times a week," says Louise Ebbinghaus. "Not at the best restaurants, but up there (in New York), we could eat out only about once a month."

St. Augustine offers engaging sightseeing to visitors from home. Grandchildren are delighted by the oddities at Ripley's Believe It or Not, the Castillo de San Marcos fortress, Potter's Wax Museum, the "authentic" old jail, the Fountain of Youth, and other attractions in the downtown area.

Marineland of Florida, the noted oceanarium, is just a few miles south of St. Augustine Beach. The St. Augustine Alligator Farm is at the beach. And for everyone, the St. Augustine Amphitheatre at the beach stages "The Cross & Sword," a colorful play depicting the settling of the city.

Retirees to St. Augustine say there's no shortage of company. Louise used to lead guests around, she says, "but now we sometimes just point them to downtown and give them the brochures about all they can see."

The city's geographical location is a plus for some. "I like the accessibility to major cities," says Bob Ebbinghaus. "You can get to New York (by car) with just one overnight stay." St. Augustine's historic district is about six miles east of Interstate 95, which runs from Florida to Maine. U.S. Route 1 runs through the town.

At the county's northern tip is Ponte Vedra Beach, an upscale community of about 25,000 where Sawgrass, the noted residential/recreational resort, is home to the national headquarters of the Professional Golf Association. The Players Championship, which features the top players in professional golf, is held there in March. The Association of Tennis Professionals international headquarters and facilities also are at Ponte Vedra Beach.

All three couples say that crime is no worse in St. Augustine than in their previous communities, and some say things are even a little better. Ron Firster expresses an awareness of areas prone to burglaries and muggings, but says those areas are easy to avoid.

What is an issue, though, is traffic, which even those most in love with the town concede can be dreadful at times. "When we came here, you could walk down the middle of the streets," says Bob. "It doesn't seem possible it has gotten so busy in 10 years."

Besides the influx of cars brought by winter visitors, the community also has horse-drawn carriages and open-air sightseeing trams offering guided tours of the historic district. Limited downtown parking and frequent congestion can cause frustrating delays. City leaders are grappling with the problem.

The city also is trying to determine the most efficient and best use for its historic area.

"I don't think enough is being done to capitalize on the natural beauty of St. Augustine," notes Norman Baker. "They could do a better job of putting a good face on the city."

The town's multifaceted past encompasses a melange of styles. Along with structures of both wood and shellstone from the Spanish colonial period, the era of Henry Flagler left its mark with grand public buildings. Flagler, the dominant figure in opening Florida to tourism at the turn of the century, built two major hotels in St. Augustine and headquartered his Florida East Coast Railroad here. Another major landmark besides Flagler College is Lightner Museum, the former Alcazar Hotel that opened in 1888.

Add to this mixture numerous shops selling T-shirts and souvenirs and the end result, according to some residents, doesn't blend as well as it could. Civic leaders are looking at the successful historic district in Charleston, SC, to learn how such a mix can work.

But the smattering of problems is not a worry to residents. Says Norman Baker, "I think it's a rare person who wants to move out of St. Augustine." ●

St. George, Utah

'Utah's Dixie' blends history, spectacular red rock setting

By Genevieve Rowles

More than a century ago, St. George's first "retiree" unwittingly set the stage for a retirement haven — some say heaven — that attracts today's new residents in increasing numbers.

The current popularity of St. George and surrounding Washington County was far in the future in the 1860s, when Brigham Young directed settlement of southwestern Utah's Virgin River Valley. Because of its relatively low 2,800-foot altitude, the scenic valley enjoys a much milder climate than most of Utah.

Young envisioned a future for the area, but it is doubtful that he foresaw today's thriving satellite communities, situated to take maximum advantage of the spectacular desert scenery. After sending several families here from Salt Lake City and directing them to plant cotton, the aging leader of the Mormon Church and governor of Utah Territory built himself a winter home in the settlement he called St. George.

Others called it "Utah's Dixie" because of the cotton venture. The cotton business failed, but the appellation stuck — along with St. George's reputation as a pleasant place in which to retire.

Today, a deeply etched contrast exists between historic St. George's tree-shaded pioneer-era homes, clustered around a white wedding-cake Mormon temple, and the sun-washed housing developments, condominiums and RV resorts that creep across the Virgin River Valley and climb the red sandstone bluffs above the city.

"We liked it and it fit," says Will Oborn of the expansive desert landscape, defined by towering ocher cliffs. The former NBC production manager and his wife, Nan, retired here from the Los Angeles area. A homemaker, Nan raised two children and enjoys visits from the couple's 10 grandchildren.

After investigating communities in Arizona, Oregon and California, the couple chose Kayenta, a carefully planned development of Southwestern-style custom homes tucked into a hilly landscape 10 miles northwest of St. George.

"Ours was Kayenta's 35th home," says Will of their 2,000-square-foot, adobe-style house, privately situated on an acre-and-a-half lot featuring natural desert plants. Now hundreds of custom homes are tucked among hills that rise above a southeast-facing mesa. In the winter "monsoon season," the ocher cliffs are faced with waterfalls, forming a dramatic backdrop.

"It's heaven for geologists and archaeologists," says Will, enthusiastically describing the avocation that he and Nan embraced soon after moving from the San Fernando Valley five years ago.

Kayenta's mix of professional people, artists and retirees from across the country produces a lively exchange of ideas that appeals to this energetic couple. It was this eclecticism that opened the door to the Oborns' new-found avocation.

Soon after the couple moved in, a neighbor invited Will to attend an archaeology meeting. He quickly was hooked. Both Will and Nan enrolled in archaeology and geology classes at Dixie College's Institute of Continued Learning. The St. George community college is a valued source of cultural activities for area residents.

Will put in 100 hours of classwork to earn his Utah avocational archaeologist certification. He helps with digs that uncover traces of the Anasazi Indians who populated the area 2,000 years ago. There is a sense of urgency to the digs, lest evidence of the area's rich aboriginal history become buried under housing developments. Bulldozers move in right behind the archaeologists.

Nan, who became an expert at reconstructing vessels from shards found in the digs, devotes countless hours to the meticulous work.

She also is a member of Kayenta's Architectural Control Committee, helping to ensure that the purity of the community's desert ambiance is maintained. Kayenta has no street lights, and yard lights are strictly controlled so that the stars winking in the black velvet desert sky may be fully enjoyed.

Year-round golf is a strong draw for the Oborns, as it is for most retirees in the St. George area. Eight courses accent the gorgeous scenery. Emerald greens and a cloudless azure sky seem to glow in counterpoint to red sandstone buttes.

While light snowfalls and overnight temperatures dipping below freezing are not uncommon, daytime winter temperatures in the mild 50s ensure great golfing. Springs and autumns bring crisp nights and days in the 70s. Summers are oven-hot with 100-degree-plus days. But the proximity of 7,000-foot-high Pine Valley, Snow Canyon, Gunlock Reservoir and other comparatively cool retreats helps to make the heat bearable.

Though seven area golf courses are open to the public, the Oborns joined the Bloomington Country Club, 14 miles distant, in order to take advantage of its fine dining. St. George runs more to fast-food outlets than quality restaurants. The Oborns think nothing of driving 18 miles to a favorite lunch spot or an hour to Zion National Park Lodge for dinner a couple of times a month.

The St. George area's widespread distances, and exploring the 10 state and national parks within a three-hour drive, have boosted the Oborns' gasoline budget since retirement. But they find entertainment expenses much lower than in Los Angeles.

"We could spend $60 a seat for an L.A. Music Center performance, but a season ticket to Dixie College's Community Concerts series costs only $55, and we get to hear the Utah Symphony and other fine performances," says Will.

Bernie and Thea Yeager's activities take a somewhat different direction, largely involving the city's active Senior Citizens Group. "We get good meals for $2 at the center, and have wonderful (center-organized) travel opportunities," says Thea.

The Yeagers find considerable scope for volunteering and hiking. While Bernie leads hikes to sites of historical interest, Thea fields prospective

St. George, UT

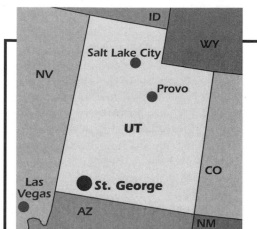

Population: 46,186 (about 82,000 in Washington County plus about 12,000 winter residents). About 17% are 65 or older.

Location: The city occupies a valley straddling Interstate 15 in the southwestern corner of the state, 106 miles east of Las Vegas and 395 miles south of Salt Lake City.

Climate:

	High	Low
January	54	30
July	102	69

Average relative humidity: Low (figures not available for St. George, but humidity averages 35% in nearby Milford).

Rain: 8 inches.

Cost of living: 102.2, based on national average of 100.

Average housing cost: $140,000. Small two-bedroom condos still can be found in the $70,000 to $80,000 range, but more realistic condo and single-family home prices begin at $90,000, topping out at $1,000,000.

Sales tax: 6%

Sales tax exemptions: Prescription drugs, professional services.

State income tax: Graduated in six steps from 2.3% to 7.2%, depending on income.

Income tax exemptions: Up to $7,500 of federal, state and private pension income is exempt for taxpayers age 65 and older. There is also a deduction of one-half of federal income tax paid.

Intangibles tax: None.

Estate tax: None, except the state's "pick-up" portion of the federal tax, applicable to taxable estates above $675,000.

Property tax: City rate is $14.77 per $1,000, based on 55% of market value. Yearly tax on a $140,000 home is about $1,173.

Homestead exemption: Homeowners age 65 and older may be eligible for an elderly exemption based on income.

Security: 33.3 crimes per 1,000 residents, lower than the national average of 46.2 crimes per 1,000 residents.

Religion: Most major Christian denominations are represented, and new churches are being built as congregations form. The Church of Jesus Christ of Latter-day Saints (Mormon) constitutes the largest single religion.

Education: Dixie College, a public four-year community college, serves over 5,000 students. Southern Utah University offers undergraduate and graduate courses through its local campus.

Transportation: Three bus and shuttle companies serve the area. St. George is served by Skywest Airlines, offering flights to Palm Springs, Phoenix and Salt Lake City. Las Vegas McCarran International Airport is 106 miles away.

Health: Dixie Regional Medical Center, an Inter-Mountain Health Care facility in St. George, is fully accredited by the Joint Commission for Accreditation for Health Care Organizations. The 137-bed regional referral center, staffed by 75 physicians, has 24-hour emergency service, a 12-bed long-term care center, and a full line of diagnostic, radiology and cancer treatment specialties, including cardiology treatment facilities. The St. George area's history of radioactive fallout received considerable publicity in the 1970s and '80s. In the early 1950s, nuclear testing in the Nevada desert wafted radioactive fallout over downwind St. George. Though cancer rates in persons living in St. George at the time of the testing accelerated in the years immediately following the incident, there is no evidence of lingering radiation hot spots that could affect new residents. Utah as a whole has one of the lowest incidences of cancer in the nation.

Housing options: The choice of home locations within a 10-mile radius of St. George includes Green Valley to the west, where home sales average $121,000, to less expensive Dixie Downs to the northwest and pricier Bloomington Hills to the south. Building lots are available in more distant Kayenta and Padre Canyon. **Sun River St. George**, (888) 688-6556, is an active-adult golf community with homes starting at $112,900. A few historic homes are available, but most housing options reflect the recent boom in development and custom-built homes. St. George area housing costs, as in other Western states, are escalating because of an influx of Californians accustomed to expensive housing.

Visitor lodging: Rates range from $20 to more than $200 at several dozen area motels, bed-and-breakfast inns and one guest ranch. Options include Motel 6, $45, (435) 628-7979, Four Points Sheraton, $74, (435) 628-0463, and Hampton Inn, $69-$74, (435) 652-1200.

Information: St. George Chamber of Commerce, 97 E. St. George Blvd., St. George, UT 84770, (435) 628-1658 or www.stgeorgechamber.com. Washington County Travel and Convention Bureau, 425 S. 700 East, St. George, UT 84770, (435) 634-5747.

newcomers' questions at the St. George Chamber of Commerce. Both play tennis and golf and are active in Mormon Temple work. The area's new residents represent a variety of religious persuasions, dropping the percentage of Mormons from 80 percent to about 50 percent.

"Our money goes a lot further here than in New Jersey," says Thea, a former home economics teacher and mother of seven. She and Bernie, a retired C.R. England truck terminal manager, purchased a home in Bloomington Hills, on St. George's southern edge, eight years ago when the city's runaway expansion was just building up steam.

But other than reduced auto insurance, entertainment and water costs (Kayenta has its own water system), the Oborns find living expenses comparable to those in the Los Angeles area. California sales taxes are higher, but Utah taxes more items. "I'm paying as much here as I did in California," says Will.

"Utah taxes everything, even food. But I would have paid twice as much tax in California for the same size house," says Will.

Many new residents chose the area partially because it is bisected by Interstate 15, considerably shortening driving distance to the bright lights of Las Vegas or to Cedar City, home of Southern Utah State University's summer Shakespearean Festival. Adequate services are a given. But while transplants wax euphoric over their new homes, others view the area's sudden growth with mixed feelings.

Many other communities in southwestern Utah share concerns in St. George over the desert ecology's ability to support continued growth. Today one of the fastest growing communities in the Southwest, St. George mushroomed from a sleepy town of 7,100 in 1970 to 11,350 in 1981 to today's 46,000-plus.

As a result, demands on water and other services are high. Washington County, growing at a comparable rate, also feels the pinch.

"We are keeping up with infrastructure needs," says community development director Bob Nicholson. "Right now our main problem is traffic." Nicholson says land (city limits go all the way to the Arizona border) and water (sources are adequate to supply needs for the next 20 years) are not issues, and the town's focus is quality growth in the 6 percent to 8 percent range over the long term.

Jay and Donna Curtis would like to see a slower rate of development and more sensitivity toward preserving the city's significant historic district. "We do need to have some growth, but it needs to be better controlled," says Donna.

She chuckles at a reference to the couple's relocation from the San Francisco Bay area 12 years ago as a retirement move. Traditional retirement seemed rash to Jay, a real estate broker, and to Donna, an escrow officer.

Reasoning that running a bed-and-breakfast inn would provide a sensible compromise, they purchased and restored the 1873 Woolley mansion, facing the Brigham Young House in the heart of St. George's historic district.

As St. George's historic preservation commissioner, Jay is protective of the city's colorful heritage. He and Donna, whose polygamous great-grandfather pioneered in St. George (their Seven Wives Inn is named in honor of his wives), strive to effect a balance between old and new. The inn's situation in one of St. George's most storied historic homes is incidental to the couple's concern that the current rush to develop may endanger St. George's old-fashioned small-town ambiance.

The experiences of the Oborns, Yeagers and Curtises are similar in that each couple knew what they wanted in a new location, and each found it in St. George. And in their own ways, each couple is taking full advantage of, and making valuable contributions to, southwestern Utah's unique marriage of nature and history.●

San Antonio, Texas

A colorful history and international flavor add spice to this Texas city

By Julie Cooper

It was March 6, 1836, when 189 valiant defenders of the Mission San Antonio de Valero fell at the hands of Mexican General Santa Anna and his troops, giving rise to the independence battle cry, "Remember the Alamo," as the fort is better known. More than 17 decades later, the Alamo and its poignant past are remembered fondly by thousands of visitors who annually pay homage to the most famous historical site in Texas.

For Ray and Barbara Clark, those fond feelings extended to the entire Alamo City, where they were stationed early in Ray's military career.

They couldn't forget the life they once had in San Antonio and finally fulfilled a dream to move back in retirement.

"We'd been trying to get back to San Antonio for 25 years," Barbara confesses. When Ray retired as an Air Force master sergeant in the mid-1970s, the couple was set to move to nearby Austin, where Ray had a job lined up with Texas Instruments. But family obligations took them back to Barbara's hometown of Evansville, IN.

The couple owned and operated a number of businesses in the Evansville area, including the 11th Frame Lounge and Cross-Eyed Cricket family restaurant. When retirement finally did dawn, the Clarks once again turned their eyes to the Lone Star State.

The eighth-largest city in the United States, San Antonio has one of the lowest costs of living among major cities. The seat of Bexar (pronounced Bear) County, San Antonio has a population of 1.19 million. The population of the metropolitan statistical area, which includes Bexar, Comal, Guadalupe and Wilson counties, is 1.57 million.

Whether they live in outlying Converse, Universal City or Garden Ridge, communities popular among newcomer retirees, most residents say they're from San Antonio. The city is about a three-hour drive from the Texas Gulf Coast and about four hours to the Mexico border. San Antonio is in south-central Texas and enjoys an average temperature of 68.7 degrees. Its proximity to the Texas Hill Country, with its rich history of 19th-century German settlements and wildflower-dotted pastures and roadsides in spring, is a big draw for Texas residents.

San Antonio ranks No. 1 with Texans as a vacation destination. Four interstate highways, five U.S. highways and five state highways make getting there a snap. The San Antonio International Airport serves the city and surrounding area and is just 13 miles from the downtown River Walk, an area along the San Antonio River that is packed with restaurants, clubs and shops. City attractions also include historic Market Square, museums, theme parks and scores of savory Mexican restaurants.

Before settling near San Antonio, the Clarks spent two years crisscrossing America in a 34-foot recreational vehicle. They found their 1,800-square-foot dream house in Carolina Crossing, a new gated community in Schertz, a booming community of 17,500 just north of San Antonio in Guadalupe County. The Clarks thought about a condo or garden home but wanted a small yard for their schnauzer, Shotzie. They bought a model home the same day it went on the market in February 1996

"We saved a good $1,200 to $1,300 a month by moving to San Antonio," says Barbara, 68. Ray, 67, estimates that the neighborhood includes about 30 percent active military and 30 percent retirees. Military retirees can use the exchange, commissary and pharmacy at Randolph Air Force Base in nearby Universal City.

The military presence in south-central Texas is a big plus with retirees. Lackland, Kelly (which is being phased out) and Brooks Air Force bases lie on the south side of town, while Randolph Air Force Base sits on the northern edge. Fort Sam Houston, northeast of downtown, has been an Army base since 1845.

If they so choose, the Clarks could use the medical services at Brook Army Medical Center, but they prefer to use an HMO to supplement Medicare. "The medical facilities are tremendous," Ray says. Major hospital systems include Baptist, Methodist, Christus Santa Rosa, Southwest General and Nix Medical Center, among the 36 hospitals serving the area.

The Air Force is part of the reason that Schertz has seen its population jump from 10,500 in 1990 to 17,500, according to city manager Kerry Sweat. "The large number of persons retired from the military is really how Schertz began," says Sweat of the town once called Cutoff by the railroads. "We have a lot of the advantages of the big city. We're close enough to enjoy it and still be a small town," he says.

Part of what they enjoy about San Antonio is a history that is a colorful draw for vacationers and residents alike. In 1718, Father Antonio Olivares, a missionary in south Texas, helped establish Mission San Antonio de Valero (the Alamo) and Villa de Bexar, the military outpost. The missions continued to grow as the Franciscans moved to convert the local Native Americans to Christianity. These missions still stand today along the historic Mission Trail and are active Catholic parish churches.

The flavor of Mexico is very much in evidence in multicultural San Antonio. In April, San Antonio holds its biggest party of the year when it celebrates Fiesta, a nine-day festival commemorating the area's rich history and cultures. Parades, parties, special exhibits, concerts and coronations are just some of the activities.

Fans of Western movies — whether it is John Wayne's "The Alamo" or Errol Flynn's "San Antonio" — won't be disappointed in the cowboy history that the area retains. Each February the city immerses itself in all things Western with the San Antonio Rodeo and Stock Show.

Trail riders and chuck wagons make a journey from all parts of South and Central Texas to meet up for the start of the

16-day rodeo, fair and livestock show.

Lascelles Wisdom, 55, doesn't have to wait for February to enjoy saddles

San Antonio, TX

Population: 1.19 million in San Antonio, 1.4 in Bexar County.

Location: In south-central Texas at the edge of the Gulf coastal plains, about 140 miles north of the Gulf of Mexico, 78 miles south of Austin, 270 miles south of Dallas and 197 miles west of Houston. Elevation is 701 feet.

Climate:

	High	Low
January	63	39
July	94	69

Average relative humidity: 50%

Rain: 28 inches.

Cost of living: 90.6, based on national average of 100.

Average housing cost: $117,041 for a new home.

Sales tax: 7.75%

Sales tax exemptions: Food and produce, pharmaceuticals and some agricultural services.

State income tax: None.

Intangibles tax: None.

Estate tax: None, except the state's "pick-up" portion of the federal tax, applicable to taxable estates above $675,000.

Property tax: Paid to the city, county, local school districts and a host of other special taxing districts. Taxes are assessed at 100% of the current market valuation. Rates are .3394580 per $100 valuation in Bexar County, .579790 in San Antonio, .3544 in Schertz and .5200 in Converse. There are 13 school districts in Bexar County with tax rates from 1.5 (Southwest ISD) to 1.76 (Somerset) per $100 valuation.

Homestead exemption: Each taxing entity caps exemptions for homeowners 65 and older at a different amount, the highest being the city of San Anto-

nio at $60,000. Bexar County exempts the first $50,000, and the Alamo Community College District exempts $30,000. Guadalupe County exempts $10,000 of the appraised value of a residential homestead. For homeowners under age 65, there is a $3,000 flood exemption and a $15,000 school district exemption; other exemptions may be available, depending on the neighborhood in which you live.

Security: 70.3 crimes per 1,000 residents, higher than the national average of 46.2 crimes per 1,000 residents.

Religion: More than 1,200 churches represent every denomination. There are nine synagogues.

Education: There are four campuses in the Alamo Community College District: Northwest Vista College, Palo Alto College, St. Phillip's College and San Antonio College. The University of Texas at San Antonio was established in 1973 as part of the UT system. Trinity University is a top-rated liberal arts school established in 1869. The University of Incarnate Word is a Catholic university with a current enrollment of 3,312. St. Mary's University is the oldest and largest Catholic University in Texas with three undergraduate schools, one graduate level and the only law school in San Antonio. The UT Health Science Center at San Antonio includes medicine, nursing, dental, allied health sciences and graduate-level bio-medical science. Our Lady of the Lake University offers undergraduate degrees in more than 40 areas, master's degrees in nine programs and a doctorate in psychology. The National University of Mexico also has a downtown campus offering classes in Spanish, English as a second language, Mexican arts, history, literature and computers.

Transportation: Via Metropolitan Transit serves the metropolitan area. Funded through a .5 percent sales tax, VIA operates a fleet of 529 buses. Bus fare is 75 cents and there are discounts for senior citizens and people with disabilities. The Park & Ride system serves special events such as Fiesta, Spurs games and events at the Alamodome.

Health: The San Antonio area has

more than 35 hospitals, including three military hospitals, mental health centers and rehabilitation centers. The Cancer Therapy and Research Center, a joint venture with UT Health Science Center, is dedicated to the cure and prevention of cancer and offers outpatient treatment and clinical research. The 700-acre South Texas Medical Center is the largest in Texas and represents a combined annual budget of $2.6 billion. The Center has more than 25,000 full-time employees.

Housing options: There are more than 145,000 rental housing units, including apartments, townhouses and duplexes in all sections of the metropolitan area. San Antonio's hottest area is in the northwest, with more than a quarter of the new homes sold in Bexar County during 1998. New developments include **The Ridge at Carolina Crossing**, from $110,000, (210) 658-6013; **The Springs at Stone Oak**, from $160,000, (210) 495-8815; and **Mainland Square**, from $87,900, (210) 543-2239. There also are build-to-suit sites of one-half to five acres starting in the mid-$40,000s. There are more than 47 retirement and life-care communities, which include assisted living, residential care and Alzheimer's care.

Visitor lodging: There are 25,000 rooms in hotels, motels, resorts and bed-and-breakfast lodgings. The Westin La Cantera opened in 1999; rates are $199-$215. A sister hotel, the 474-room Westin Riverwalk, opened in November; rates start at $119, (800) WESTIN-1. Historic hotels on or near the San Antonio River Walk include the Menger Hotel, La Mansion del Rio, Fairmount and St. Anthony Wyndham Grand Heritage.

Information: San Antonio Convention and Visitors Bureau, 201 E. Market St., San Antonio, TX 78205, (800) 447-3372 or www.sacvb. com. The San Antonio Chamber of Commerce, P.O. Box 1628, San Antonio, TX 78296, (210) 229-2100 or www.sachamber. com. The chamber has a Guide to San Antonio retirement package for $15, plus $4 postage and handling, (888) 242-3068.

and spurs. The recent retiree from Long Island, NY, has indulged his love of horses by purchasing eight thoroughbred racehorses. He stables them at Retama Park Racetrack, a new facility 15 minutes northeast of downtown San Antonio that offers thoroughbred racing July through October.

Lascelles and his wife, Netilda, 64, moved to San Antonio just last October. The Wisdoms had checked out Florida and South Carolina, where many of their friends had moved, as likely retirement spots. They chose Texas in part to be close to their daughter, Lorraine Smith, and her family.

Retirement came early for Lascelles when he accepted a buyout from Long Island Lighting Co. after 26 years as a welding engineer. He says he and his wife never considered staying in New York. "It is very expensive to retire and live in New York," Lascelles says. "My house was paid for, but the taxes were $8,200 a year."

The Wisdoms traded a five-bedroom "high ranch" for a newly built four-bedroom home in Converse in the northeast part of Bexar County. Netilda, who retired as an assistant rehabilitation aide in a nursing home, has tentative plans to do volunteer work. Currently, though, she's busy furnishing her new home. The Wisdoms left much of their furniture in New York rather than move it.

The average selling price for new homes in San Antonio is $117,041. The average monthly rental rate on a two-bedroom, two-bath unit is $560.

"I used to visit Lorraine and fell in love with San Antonio," Netilda says. "The people here are, let me say, different. The people here are friendly," she says with added emphasis.

There is an international flavor that permeates San Antonio. According to 1990 census figures, 55 percent of the population is Hispanic, 35 percent is Anglo and 7 percent is African-American. The low number of African-Americans among the populace does not bother the Wisdoms, both natives of Port Antonio, Jamaica.

"Where I lived in Jamaica, we were one people," Netilda says. "When we moved to Long Island, about 2 percent of the population was black," Lascelles adds.

Other recent retirees also have found San Antonio to be a friendly place to live.

"It's amazing how friendly the people are," says Nan Birmingham, 75. A former contributing editor for *Town & Country* magazine, Nan was ready to say goodbye to the New York winters and find a slower pace of life. She moved to San Antonio in 1998, partly to be closer to her only grandchild, Caitlin. Caitlin and her parents live 25 minutes away.

"I've finally stopped looking over my shoulder," Nan says, chuckling about the "innate suspicion" that many New Yorkers have for passers-by when it comes to crime. "I'm getting over it now," she says.

Nan sold her townhouse in the Bronx and opted to rent a spacious one-bedroom apartment in the Meridian, a gated complex near San Antonio's Quarry Market. Her ground-floor apartment borders the green space that backs into the complex. Nan estimates that a similar apartment in New York City would go for $3,500 a month — a far cry from the $1,270 a month she pays, and that includes use of a pool, health club, security and party room.

"I figure I've cut my overhead probably in half," says Nan, who likes to breakfast on her plant-filled terrace. She has turned half of her expansive kitchen into an office with computer and couch.

A native of California, Nan says she briefly considered San Francisco for retirement, and she watched a number of her friends retire to Florida and New Mexico. Besides traveling, which she does two to three months of the year, Nan enjoys the San Antonio Museum of Art, where she holds museum membership. One of the top art museums in Texas, SAMA is home to the Nelson A. Rockefeller Center for Latin American Art.

Other art draws include the McNay Art Museum, where admission is free but the art is priceless. The museum is housed in a Mediterranean-style mansion built in 1927. It holds Cezanne, Mondrian and bronzes by Rodin. And the Southwest School of Art and Craft is the place for learning the arts. Classes include photography, painting, ceramics, weaving and carving. The school is housed in the Old Ursuline Academy, begun in the late 1840s.

Both Nan Birmingham and the Clarks pitch Central Market as a fun spot to go near downtown. "It's my favorite place,"

Nan says. "When everyone said, 'Oh, you have to try the Central Market,' I envisioned Texas pickup trucks and fresh vegetables in an outdoor setting." She was surprised to find valet parking at a store once dubbed "Gucci B" by San Antonians. Central Market is part of the HEB Grocery Co., which has its corporate headquarters in San Antonio. A cooking school that offers weekly classes is another reason that Nan, a former cooking instructor, likes Central Market. And, "the price is right," she says.

The Clarks, who have authored a cookbook, frequently make the 20-mile drive from their home to Alamo Heights for a special shopping foray at Central Market. The longer growing season and proximity to Mexico mean more fresh fruits and vegetables at good prices almost year-round in San Antonio stores.

But if eating out is on the menu, there is more to the city than tacos and tamales. Former restaurateurs, the Clarks admit to a love affair with TexMex food and appreciate the spicy stuff. "We eat out about three times a week," says Barbara, noting that she and Ray usually stop for lunch when they are running errands. The early influences on the city's restaurants were Mexican and German, but the wide variety today boasts American, Continental, Chinese, Italian, Vietnamese, Indian and steakhouses too numerous to count.

On the negative side, what do retirees find to complain about? "The standing joke is we're running a B&B," Barbara says. The Clarks find their home popular among vacationing friends and relatives, but Barbara and Ray like to travel as well. They made five or six trips to Mexico in 1999 — "especially when friends come to visit," Barbara says.

Three months into their retirement, the Wisdoms were still adjusting to the way Texans drive. "I've got to get used to the driving in the center lane — those arrows are turning left and right and I don't know where to go," Lascelles says.

The Clarks are busy counting their blessings. "There's hardly a day that goes by that one of us doesn't say, 'I love Texas' or 'I love my house,' " Barbara says with a laugh. "I love Texas," Ray quips in agreement. "I love the attitude of the people here, and the patriotism," he adds.●

San Juan Capistrano, California

A deep sense of history permeates this Southern California town

By Mary-Ann Bendel

San Juan Capistrano, established in 1776, is the oldest community in a state that prides itself on being first with the latest trends. "This is a very special city," says Mayor Collene Campbell. "I think our city motto, 'Preserving the Past to Enhance the Future,' says it all."

The city welcomes retirees and has no trouble attracting them with its near-perfect climate. With the Pacific Ocean only a mile away, air conditioning is not needed and the winters are full of sunshine.

Much of the city centers around Mission San Juan Capistrano, considered the most romantic and the jewel in the chain of 21 Franciscan missions that are situated from San Diego to Sonoma. If you arrive in the early morning after a rare night of rain, the gardens will smell like they must have to followers of Father Junipero Serra, who founded the mission in 1776. It's also likely that you will find retiree Al Ravera and other volunteers working in the gardens to keep them beautiful. The 30 volunteers call themselves the Gardening Angels.

"We have to save this mission. It's a big part of California's history," says Al, who moved with his wife, Gloria, to San Juan Capistrano from Orange, CA, where he was director of city services. Like many seniors here, they are involved in volunteer work at the mission. "This is a very friendly community with a strong preservation mode," says Al, noting that people come from all over the world to see the mission's famous arches, hear the tolling of its bells and walk its time-worn paths.

When the Spanish missionaries arrived, local Native Americans helped build the mission and work the farms, make candles and soap and do the weaving and tanning. Adobe homes were built for families with ties to the mission. With the Mexican independence of 1821, mission lands were divested, and land grants put large "ranchos" in the hands of a few powerful families. With its location halfway between San Diego and Los Angeles, San Juan Capistrano became an overnight stage stop on the way to newly discovered gold fields in Northern California. But the Capistrano Valley developed as an agricultural center with a tight-knit group of farm families and merchants. They were relatively untouched by the explosion of development to the north and south.

All this history can be viewed at the San Juan Capistrano Historical Society in the O'Neill Museum, located in a Victorian-era home across from the railroad depot. The society has 4,000 photos dating to 1870, and a docent program helps visitors interpret the photo display on weekends. Don and Mary Tyron retired to the city 10 years ago, from San Pedro, CA, and they both volunteer a day each week at the society. "Most of us who work here are seniors," says Mary. "We talk to fourth graders and dress them up in old costumes. It's fun."

But San Juan Capistrano probably is best known for the return of the swallows to the mission every spring. The swallows migrate between San Juan Capistrano and Goya, Argentina, traditionally arriving in San Juan Capistrano on March 19, St. Joseph's Day. A festival has evolved around the swallow migration.

The Swallows Festival, or Fiesta de las Golondrinas, is a two-month-long celebration beginning in late February with a Taste of San Juan reception. In mid-March, Swallows Week kicks off with a ball followed by a full calendar of events. The annual Swallows Day Parade is famous as the largest nonmotorized parade in the United States. Horses and riders in old California costumes and marching bands make for a gala event.

"My father was a good friend of Gene Autry, who wrote a song about the swallows returning to San Juan Capistrano," says Gil Jones, a retiree who was born in Texas and raised in Oklahoma. That song inspired him to visit San Juan Capistrano, and he and his wife, Millie, moved here from Lake Forest, CA, in 1980. Although Gil and Millie say they are retired, Gil operates a minifarm complete with pony rides, a petting pen and an outdoor picnic area, and Millie teaches china painting classes in her home. "I've made many friends here through that endeavor," she says.

The busy couple believes San Juan Capistrano has attractions particularly amenable to seniors. "The city council here has always held seniors in high regard," says Gil, a former mayor. "There's a bond between the community and older residents not always found in other communities. There's a great deal of pride in the community, and it's a very small community, but you can go anyplace in the world and people have heard of it," he says. "It's very easy to become involved and be heard. Other towns are a little envious of how we operate and of our success at controlling growth and maintaining a large percentage of open space."

With a current population of 30,000, the plan is to expand to 40,000, and that will be the end of residential development. San Juan Capistrano's city government is committed to this plan to prevent the overbuilding that has impacted much of Southern California. It is a conscious decision by city government to preserve open land and protect beautiful ridge lines from development. "We are pretty close to build-out now," says city engineer Tony Foster, who believes San Juan Capistrano "is one of the more mellow places to live in Orange County."

Another retired couple enjoying life here is Les and Marie Blair, who had lived in the same house in Downey, CA, for 40 years before they decided to move. They always had wanted to live near the ocean, so six years ago they researched favorite coastal cities, chose San Juan Capistrano and never looked back. They bought a three-bedroom stucco home in an 8-year-old, 96-home planned community that encompasses all ages. One mile from downtown, their hilltop home overlooks the mission and downtown San Juan Capistrano. Married 58 years, Les will be 79 this summer and feels 50. Both he and

Marie jog and swim every day.

Les says San Juan Capistrano reminds him of Broken Arrow, OK, where he grew up. Marie adds, "I love this town, the mission and the history here."

They have had no trouble making friends. Because of their jogging, they meet a lot of people — and dogs. "We know some of the dogs better than their owners," Marie says with a laugh.

They also have found volunteering basic to their new life here. Les was assigned aboard the USS Pennsylvania in Pearl Harbor when it was attacked at the outset of World War II. He survived 17 naval battles in the Pacific and now visits local schools to share his experiences with young people. He also works with Alzheimer's patients, makes deliv-

eries for Meals on Wheels and has served as president of the Seniors Club. One of his proudest possessions is the Olympic torch he got to keep when he ran in the Olympic torch relay on the Pacific Coast Highway in 1996. Both he and Marie work with the Special Olympics and answer children's letters to Santa Claus. They dance West Coast swing, line dance and participate in dance contests, often winning.

Les believes their home has appreciated in value about $100,000 since they bought it six years ago, but Gil Jones says housing still is available at all income levels. "You can still get a two-bedroom condo for $80,000 — or a million-dollar mansion," he says.

As visitors drive around residential

San Juan Capistrano, CA

Population: 32,099

Location: The city is in southern Orange County in a picturesque coastal valley approximately 1.5 miles inland from the Pacific Ocean midway between Los Angeles and San Diego. San Juan Capistrano is 62 miles south of Los Angeles and 65 miles north of San Diego. Altitude is 104 feet above sea level.

Climate:

	High	Low
January	65	50
July	89	73

Average relative humidity: 65%

Rain: 10 inches.

San Juan Capistrano enjoys pleasant summers and moderate winters with offshore breezes prevailing.

Cost of living: Above average (specific index not available).

Median housing cost: $289,000

Sales tax: 7.75%

Sales tax exemptions: Food products, prescription medicines and services.

State income tax: Graduated from 1% to 9.3%, depending on income and filing status.

Income tax exemptions: Social Security payments are exempt.

Estate tax: None, except the state's "pick-up" portion of the federal tax, applicable to taxable estates above $675,000.

Property tax: The most common rate is 1.07663% of appraised value(the range is 1.07170% to 1.24134%). The annual tax on a home valued at $289,000 would be about $3,111, using the most common rate.

Homestead exemption: None.

Security: 23.4 crimes per 1,000 residents, lower than the national average of 46.2 crimes per 1,000 residents.

Religion: Most denominations are represented locally or in nearby communities.

Education: Options include Saddleback Community College in Mission Viejo, Irvine Valley College in Irvine, Orange Coast College in Costa Mesa, University of California at Irvine and California State University in Fullerton.

Transportation: Orange County Rapid Transit, Dial-a-Ride and Senior Van offer local transportation, and taxi service also is available. Amtrak and Metrolink make daily rail stops. John Wayne Airport is 20 miles north, Los Angeles International Airport is 65 miles north, and Lindberg

Field in San Diego is 65 miles south.

Health: San Clemente Medical Center, Mission Hospital in Mission Viejo (the regional trauma center), South Coast Medical Center in Laguna Beach (an acute-care hospital) and Saddleback Memorial Medical Center in Laguna Hills are within 10 miles of San Juan Capistrano. All are highly rated medical facilities.

Housing options: Mobile home options include **Capistrano Valley Mobile Estates**, (949) 493-4411, and **El Nido Mobile Home Estates**, (949) 493-2666. **The Seasons at San Juan**, (949) 487-0210, is an income-restricted apartment complex for seniors, with one-bedroom apartments renting for $600 a month. **Marriott Brighton Gardens**, (949) 248-8855, offers assisted living. **The Fountains at Sea Bluff** at Dana Point, (800) 846-4440, is a full-service condominium retirement development with prices from $114,000 to $498,000.

Visitor lodging: Best Western Capistrano Inn, $79-89, (949) 493-5661. Mission Inn Motel, $85 and up, (949) 234-0249. Ritz Carlton in Dana Point, $295-$595, (949) 240-2000. Blue Lantern Inn in Dana Point, $150-$500, (800) 950-1236.

Information: San Juan Capistrano Chamber of Commerce, P.O. Box 1878, San Juan Capistrano, CA 92693-1878, (949) 493-4700 or www.sanjuan chamber.com.

areas, they can't help but notice the preserved open spaces and ridges that are left natural. But there is a wide range of housing options, including rent-controlled apartments, luxury townhouses, affordable condominiums and planned developments. "People who retire here are happy campers," says Tom Hriber, a broker with Re/Max Real Estate Services. "San Juan Capistrano gives seniors a wide variance of home prices."

The city is attractive to seniors because it cares about their quality of life, says Tom Tomlinson, San Juan Capistrano's planning director. "In the late 1970s, the city established a cap on rent increases," he says. That offers assurance to seniors that they won't be forced out of their housing because of rate increases.

The Seasons at San Juan is an income-restricted apartment complex for active seniors 62 and older. To live here, residents cannot have an income of more than $30,000. Rent is based on ability to pay, with the average one-bedroom apartment renting for $600 a month. With 112 units, the seven-building garden apartment complex is attractive and affordable. "Seniors here call it paradise," says Jesse Talmo, property manager at the Seasons at San Juan.

For seniors who need physical assistance, options include the Marriott Brighton Gardens assisted-living development. It includes nursing and rehabilitative services as well as a special care center for people with Alzheimer's disease and related memory disorders. There also are full-service condominium buildings like the Fountains at Sea Bluff at Dana Point, which overlooks the Pacific Ocean. Fees of $2,000 a month include meals and transportation. One-bedroom units are priced from $114,000 to $246,000, and two-bedroom units are $178,000 to $498,000. "We spoil our residents in a resortlike atmosphere," says Meg Righton, marketing director at the Fountains at Sea Bluff.

There are several mobile home parks, including El Nido Mobile Home Park, which has about 150 homes that range from $50,000 to $70,000. Single-family homes run the gamut from historic adobes to elegant hillside estates. A number of single-family options usually can be found for $225,000 to $275,000.

Virgene and Jack Heath live in a mobile home in Capistrano Valley Mobile Estates, and they are more than satisfied with their 1,700-square-foot home. With a garden in back, life is good here, they say. Jack moved to San Juan Capistrano in 1973 while he still worked at an advertising job in Fullerton, CA, and decided to stay after he retired. "I fell in love with the coast," he says. He and Virgene take art classes together and walk at the nearby Dana Point Marina. They travel on cruises to places like the Panama Canal, Alaska and the Mississippi River.

Now 80 years old, Jack started an association for residents of his mobile home community and works with other retirees to keep large chain stores out of the city. San Juan Capistrano is determined to stave off the influx of development that has impacted much of Southern California. Intense development pressures in the early 1970s prompted citizens to create a general plan for the city that preserved historic resources and open space, limited development density and provided for ridge-line preservation. These measures, adopted in 1974, put San Juan Capistrano years ahead of many other California communities in terms of planning and should ensure the unique heritage of San Juan Capistrano for many years to come. Most retirees want to keep the quiet, rural atmosphere they now enjoy.

That rural atmosphere also helps make San Juan Capistrano popular among equestrians of all ages, and the horse population is one of the things Les Blair says he likes best about the area. San Juan Capistrano boasts eight stables and about 2,000 horses, a unique feature of this small city. There are 30 miles of trails on 1,400 acres of public lands that also are open to hikers and mountain bikers.

Besides riding, there is an opportunity for seniors to volunteer at the Fran Joswick Therapeutic Riding Center. The center provides therapeutic horseback riding in an effort to help disabled children and adults improve their cognitive, physical and psychological abilities. More than 200 volunteers help with lessons, office work, fund raising and maintenance of the stables.

"We have clients ranging in age from 2 to 82 with a wide range of ability level. Seniors are always welcome to help us," says Dana Butler, executive director of the Fran Joswick Center.

Another perquisite of this city is a recently built community center for all ages, from kids to seniors. The gym has volleyball courts, badminton courts and a basketball court that can go from college basketball dimensions to a court for 6-year-olds. The senior center there is a hub of activity, with bright activity rooms for a variety of interests. The center works with the Ruby Gerontology Center at Cal State-Fullerton in programs to improve neuromuscular strength and flexibility, thus cutting down on the risk for falls. The center also offers Saddleback College Emeritus Institute classes in sketching, nutrition, yoga and cooking for one or two. There are classes in film, history, law for the layman, literature and music at various locations in the community. "It warms your heart to see the joy here," says Elaine Tracy, senior citizen program coordinator for the city.

Even though the city is small, there is a lot to do. There are restaurants like El Adobe, President Nixon's favorite when he lived in San Clemente. The Depot at the train station is charming and a local favorite. The Dana Point Marina is a bike ride away. Besides many shops and restaurants, it has the new Orange County Marine Institute, another volunteer possibility.

In addition, the La Sala Library was designed by architect Michael Graves in 1983, and has received worldwide acclaim as the first structure of a new design genre, neoclassicism. The Los Rios Historic District comprises the oldest neighborhood in California, including three adobe homes built in 1794. It's a good area to stroll, shop and have a meal, and guided walking tours are available.

Lee Howard, a 73-year-old former professional ballplayer with the Pittsburgh Pirates, moved to San Juan Capistrano 14 years ago. "It's the only place in the world to live," he claims. Agrees Marie Blair, "I haven't had a bad day since moving here. The air is so clean. There's always a beautiful breeze."

Adds her husband, Les, "Come on down!"●

San Juan Islands, Washington

Coastal jewels of Washington boast gentle climate and picture-perfect scenery

By Stanton H. Patty

Dick Fales is only half-joking when he suggests that maybe it's time to "pull up the drawbridge" to Washington state's San Juan Islands.

"This is a very special place — and we want it to stay that way," says the former newspaper-syndicate manager.

Fales, 68, and his wife, Mary, 67, retired to Friday Harbor, the gathering place of the San Juans archipelago, after 17 years in New Canaan, CT.

The Faleses are not alone in longing for preservation of the islands' laid-back lifestyle as new settlers and visitors swarm the San Juans.

"Please tell people that it rains a lot and that the power goes out frequently," says Eugene Richey, 78, a retired engineering professor who lives on neighboring Lopez Island with his wife, Betty, 74.

Neither of the above is true — though power outages can occur. But Richey's puckish refrain gives a clue as to how a kind of possessiveness takes hold of contented residents.

Not long ago, these getaway islands, scattered like jade beads between northwestern Washington and British Columbia, attracted mostly summer-cottage owners and pleasure boaters from the Seattle area.

No longer.

Despite being cut off from the mainland — except for ferries and air taxis — population in the San Juans has grown from 8,000 to almost 14,000 in the past decade. Those are not big numbers by big-city standards, but they are whoppers for Washington's smallest county.

In addition, summertime ferry crowds are so heavy with cyclers, hikers, whale-watchers and other visitors that many residents plan their off-island trips for shopping and medical appointments in other seasons — or face aggravating delays boarding at the ferry piers.

Retirees figure significantly in the growth pattern. The Senior Services Division of the San Juan County government says the islands' over-60 population is almost 2.5 times the national average. And the fastest-growing segment is the 75-plus crowd.

The San Juans comprise about 600 islands and islets (the tally varies with high and low tides), with 172 having names. Only four are served by the Washington State Ferries fleet.

San Juan Island is the most populated and second largest of the chain. Friday Harbor, the county seat and the islands' largest community (pop. 1,790), is situated midway along the eastern shore. The town is about two hours by ferry from Anacortes, gateway city for the San Juans ferry route. The island is historic, as well as scenic. Back in 1859, the United States and England almost went to war over the killing of an English pig on San Juan Island. Truly.

Lopez Island is a favorite with cyclists because of its relatively flat terrain, uncrowded beaches and cozy bed-and-breakfast inns. It's the first stop on the ferry route from Anacortes.

Orcas Island is the largest (57 square miles) and most mountainous of the group. Moran State Park, with more than 20 miles of hiking trails, is a major visitor magnet. Eastsound, the main village, is an arts-and-crafts center. Shaw Island, only 8 square miles in size, is mainly private property. It has no overnight accommodations and attracts few travelers. A religious order operates the ferry slip.

Anacortes ("Anna-COURT-ess"), where most San Juans-bound ferry passengers board, is 78 highway miles north of Seattle. It's on Fidalgo Island but connected to the mainland by highway bridges. Washington ferries also cruise through the San Juans to Sidney, near the British Columbia capital of Victoria, on nearby Vancouver Island.

Both Anacortes and the mainland city of Bellingham — 89 miles north of Seattle on Interstate 5 — are off-island shopping centers for island residents. Bellingham is the southern terminus of the State of Alaska's ferry network, the Alaska Marine Highway System.

Besides state ferries, other island transportation options are excursion vessels, floatplanes and wheel planes.

All four of the main islands have clinics with resident physicians and nurses. There also are emergency medical technicians on each island. But for urgent care, San Juan residents count on medevac helicopters to reach hospitals in Bellingham and Anacortes. Island families may opt to pay $100 a year for the helicopter-lift insurance.

What is it about these bucolic islands that attracts retirees?

Maybe Capt. George Vancouver, the English navigator, had it right when he charted San Juan waters in 1792.

"The serenity of the climate, the innumerable pleasing landscapes... the most lovely country that can be imagined," was one of the lyrics the skipper wrote in his logbook.

Art and Mary Lumkes, who left the Chicago area for Friday Harbor, put it this way: "This is where God takes His vacation."

Art, 67, a retired interior designer, adds: "It seldom gets above 80 or below 40 degrees. Flowers bloom all year!"

For sure, the mild climate of the San Juans is a factor.

Jack Giard has been a volunteer weather observer on Lopez Island for 45 years. He says the San Juans get about 40 percent more sunshine and about 40 percent less rainfall than Seattle.

The reason: The islands lie in the "rain shadow" of the Olympic Mountains, only about 25 miles to the southwest.

While Dick and Mary Fales praise

the climate and say it was a factor in their moving to the islands, they also sound an alert that winter brings short days and rainy weather that can be depressing.

Scenery is another magnet. Morning mists rise over salt marshes and fields bright with wildflowers. Shores are notched with scores of sheltered coves where sailboats anchor in postcard settings.

Rich currents of the North Pacific Ocean rush in to nourish whales, salmon and other marine life. Bald eagles and blue herons call the forests and beaches home. Atop 2,409-foot Mount Constitution, on Orcas Island, visitors catch a view that sweeps from Washington to British Columbia, from the Olympics to faraway peaks of the Cascade Mountains.

On San Juan Island, not far from Friday Harbor, travelers pause at Lime Kiln Point State Park to watch for orcas (killer whales). And back in town there is a Whale Museum, where visitors listen to recordings of whale songs and learn about

San Juan Islands, WA

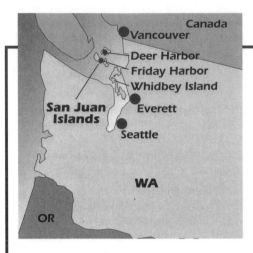

Population: 13,831 total on all islands; 7,000 on San Juan Island, including 1,790 in Friday Harbor, the largest community; 4,500 on Orcas Island.

Location: In northwestern Washington state, about 80 air miles north of Seattle. Of 172 named islands, only four — San Juan, Lopez, Orcas and Shaw — are served by Washington State Ferries.

Climate:[1]

	High	Low
January	43	35
July	70	50

Average relative humidity: 40%

Rain: 28.98 inches.

Snow: Up to 6 inches, depending on location.

Mild climate with warm, sometimes breezy summers and cool, often damp winters. The sun shines an average of 247 days a year. Severe windstorms are rare.

Cost of living: Above average (specific index not available).

Median housing cost: $232,000 on San Juan Island for a three-bedroom, two-bath home with a view.

Sales tax: 7.5%

Sales tax exemptions: Prescription drugs, groceries, medical services.

State income tax: None.

Intangibles tax: None.

Estate tax: None, except the state's "pickup" portion of the federal tax, applicable to taxable estates above $675,000.

Property tax: $10 per $1,000 of valuation, with property assessed at 100% of market value. Yearly tax on a $232,000 home would be $2,320.

Homestead exemption: Homeowners age 61 and older, with a gross household income of $28,000 or less, are eligible for certain property tax exemptions.

Security: 20.3 crimes per 1,000 residents in San Juan County, lower than the national average of 46.2 per 1,000 residents.

Religion: Eight places of worship, representing Protestant and Catholic denominations, on the four main islands.

Education: Skagit Valley College of Mount Vernon, WA, offers a broad range of adult-education courses at its outreach center in Friday Harbor. Fee is $12 per credit for people age 60 or older.

Transportation: Access from the mainland is by sea or air only. Ferries usually carry both cars and passengers, but some may take passengers only. Washington State Ferries provide year-round service between the port of Anacortes and four of the San Juan Islands — San Juan, Lopez, Orcas and Shaw. Air taxi service runs daily to Seattle-Tacoma International Airport and other points on the mainland. There is no public transit system in the islands. However, the San Juan County Health and Community Services Department sponsors senior centers on San Juan, Lopez and Orcas islands, and all three centers operate seniors' vans for both on-island and off-island trips. Vans take seniors to Anacortes, Bellingham and Seattle for medical appointments and shopping for a $10 fee per person, including ferry fare.

Health: There are emergency/primary care clinics on San Juan, Lopez and Orcas islands. The Friday Harbor clinic has four family physicians and two nurse practitioners; Lopez and Orcas clinics each have one family physician. Paramedics are on all three islands. Serious cases are routed to hospitals in Anacortes or Bellingham. Island families may opt to pay $100 a year for a plan that provides emergency lift by helicopter to Bellingham or Anacortes hospitals.

Housing options: There are no housing subdivisions or developments per se; most people buy individual properties that usually include some acreage. Some condominiums are available; **Cannery Landing**, a Friday Harbor waterfront development near the ferry pier, has about 40 units priced from $160,000 to $350,000. For housing information, contact Lynne Rogers, Windermere Real Estate, (800) 262-3596.

Visitor lodging: Inns at Friday Harbor, $79-$249, (800) 752-5752. Hillside House Bed and Breakfast in Friday Harbor, $115-$155, (800) 232-4730. On Lopez Island, Inn at Swifts Bay, $95-$185, (360) 468-3636. On Orcas Island, Orcas Hotel, $49-$189, (360) 376-4300.

Information: San Juan Islands Visitor Information Service, P.O. Box 65, Lopez Island, WA 98261, (360) 468-3663 or www.guidetosanjuans.com. San Juan Island Chamber of Commerce, P.O. Box 98, Friday Harbor, WA 98250, (360) 378-5240 or www.sanjuan island.org. Lopez Island Chamber of Commerce, P.O. Box 102, Lopez Island, WA 98261, (360) 468-4664 or www.lopezisland. com. Orcas Island Chamber of Commerce, P.O. Box 252, Eastsound, Orcas Island, WA 98245, (360) 376-2273 or www.orcasisland. org.

[1]Temperatures vary from island to island. These figures are for the only official weather station in the San Juans, at Olga on Orcas Island. Rainfall also varies, even on each island.

the islands' resident pods of orcas. Other visitors board charter boats in Friday Harbor for close-up views of the playful whales.

Friday Harbor is the main intersection of the San Juans. Its snug anchorage is hull-to-hull with pleasure craft and commercial fishing vessels. Ferries come and go with whistle toots. There are shops to browse and restaurants to sample. Winding country roads await vacationers with bicycles and rented mopeds.

Busy retirees say there is no shortage of things to do... boating, hiking, fishing, beachcombing, diving, cycling, camping, birding, gardening, volunteer work, etc.

Mary Fales, a retired speech therapist, volunteers with the Friday Harbor school system and helps raise money for scholarships sponsored by the American Association of University Women. She also belongs to a walking group. Her husband, Dick, helps with Lions Club fund-raisers for high-school scholarships. He also golfs and gardens.

Staying busy is easy, say Art and Mary Lumkes.

Both are active in the chamber of commerce. Mary, 60, formerly a manager for a Chicago mercantile company, also operates her own needlepoint shop in Friday Harbor. Art plays tennis and has taken cooking classes.

Over on Lopez Island, Eugene and Betty Richey, who moved to the San Juans from Seattle, quip that someday they may get around to completing their home. They designed the house (832 square feet on each of two floors) on a half-acre "across the street" from the sea.

"We've been doing about 90 percent of the work ourselves," says Betty. "Basically, it's about finished, but then..."

Her husband, she says, has become a first-rate cabinetmaker since moving to the San Juans.

"One has to learn to be fairly good at a lot of things to live on an island," says Eugene, a former University of Washington civil engineering professor.

Both of the Richeys took classes in teaching English as a second language and now volunteer in that field at a community college in Seattle. Mary Lumkes also volunteers as a tutor at Lopez Elementary School on her home island, and her husband manages the water system for their neighborhood.

Peter Scott, 68, a bachelor who moved to Lopez Island by way of California, New Mexico and other points, is active in a new organization called Sustaining Lopez. It's a cooperative effort to help island residents augment their income.

Peter, for example, plans to grow shallots for sale on a half-acre of his five-acre property. Another member grows tulips and produces jams and syrups for commercial markets. The County Extension Service provides expert advice for the island entrepreneurs.

Most retirees spend some time in the San Juans before settling here. The Faleses visited three times over two years before making a final decision. They also considered sites in Virginia and elsewhere in Washington. Once here they rented a series of houses while their home was being built on two acres of saltwater-view property.

The Lumkeses also made three prepurchase visits — in three seasons, winter, spring and fall — while also considering retirement areas in Vermont and New York. They bought a condo in Friday Harbor and lived in it for two and one-half years before purchasing their 10-year-old home.

The Richeys came to Lopez Island for a weekend visit. "We walked the beach one beautiful day, and a week later we started looking at property," Eugene recalls.

Peter visited a college chum on Lopez Island and "fell in love" with the pastoral island.

"There is no such place as paradise, but this is close," he says.

Peter left Santa Fe, NM ("too crowded, too commercial," he says), and once on Lopez hired a contractor to build a 1,700-square-foot cottage-style home that he designed. The house sits alone on five acres with a wide-angle view across a meadow, toward neighboring San Juan Island.

Life in the San Juans may be idyllic. Even so, as Eugene Richey says, one can become "a bit rockbound." Getting away is essential from time to time.

Getting away also saves money on groceries and other purchases. Living costs — especially for electricity, gasoline and food — are somewhat higher on the islands. Residents estimate an overall factor of about 10 percent over Seattle prices.

The Faleses maintain two shopping lists — one for supplies to be bought in Friday Harbor, the other for trips to Bellingham every two or three weeks. There are discount stores in Bellingham, near the Canadian border, and gasoline is cheaper in Anacortes, near the ferry landing. Fuel for the San Juans arrives on barges, which adds to the price.

The Lumkeses stay home during the summer season, when tourists pack the ferries, then go "off island" on monthly shopping trips the rest of the year.

The Richeys, who resided in Seattle for 28 years, still spend several weeks a year in the city, where they maintain an apartment. There are strong reasons: children, grandchildren, family physicians and dentists — and season tickets to University of Washington football games and the Seattle Repertory Theater.

In the islands, real-estate agents report a median housing cost of $232,000 for a three-bedroom, two-bath home with some acreage and a desirable view. Recent home sales were reported in the range of $175,000 to $280,000.

If there is a downside to life in the San Juans, it is the islanders' dependence on the oft-crowded ferries.

"Carry a good book and a bottle of wine if you have to wait in line for awhile," suggests Mary Lumkes.

There is no priority loading of ferries for island residents, but the islanders do have a system: They park their cars in the boarding line immediately after a ferry departs and leave for awhile. When they stroll back to the pier their vehicles are at the front of the line for the next ferry.

The retirees' advice to others who may be considering settling in the San Juan Islands:

"Be certain this is what you want before making the commitment," Dick urges.

Art adds: "Be prepared to get involved, because if you don't, you can become a lonely person. I know people here who are very lonely."

Mary Lumkes says: "If you come here to be entertained, forget it. You have to be able to provide your own entertainment."

Barring a medical catastrophe, none of the couples is planning to cast off from the San Juans for good.

"Bite your tongue!" Mary Lumkes says when her husband wonders about the possibility of future addresses.

Better yet, says Eugene, "let's pull up that drawbridge." ●

Santa Fe, New Mexico

The creative spirit thrives in New Mexico's multicultural capital

By John Villani

Nestled along the southern flanks of the Rocky Mountains, the arts mecca of Santa Fe presents a unique experience for retirees. Some refer to it as small-town life with all the trimmings, while others venture into philosophical discourses about the region's tricultural heritage and high-desert environment. But everyone agrees on the alluring charm of this city of 66,522 residents.

In recent years, Santa Fe has matured into a community of individualists, a place where people from across the globe have decided to put down roots and share in whatever magic it was that inspired Georgia O'Keeffe's masterful paintings. While there are several golf courses and two country clubs, Santa Fe's attractiveness as a place for retirement seems to transcend qualities that define other locales. It's for good reason this place is known as "the City Different."

Even though its charms have gotten national publicity, many visitors assume Santa Fe's climate is comparable to places like Scottsdale or San Antonio, which is not the case. While residents revel in plenty of year-round sunshine, Santa Fe's 7,000-foot elevation translates into four distinct seasons. Winter's first snowflakes fall in late October and reappear without fail through late April. That's why fireplaces are a common, and practical, feature in adobe homes and snow shovels are kept in garages.

Santa Fe recently celebrated the 400th anniversary of its founding by Spanish conquistadors, which means that before an English-speaking colony of Europeans ever set foot on Plymouth Rock, a Spanish-speaking colony of Europeans was flourishing in New Mexico. Today, Santa Fe and the rest of northern New Mexico remain predominantly Hispanic, and Spanish is commonly spoken on the streets and in supermarkets, government offices and local schools. In Santa Fe, Spanish culture and traditions are celebrated as the most important pieces of the American pie.

Native American traditions also are given the same deference as Hispanic culture. Eight Native American pueblos (known elsewhere as reservations) are located in northern New Mexico, some close enough to Santa Fe to allow pueblo residents to commute to jobs in the city. In this part of the country, people of European origin who are not Spanish are referred to as Anglos, an all-purpose term that conveniently lumps together Catholics, Moslems and Jews as well as Russians, Irish and Australians.

While Santa Fe's first artists were the Spanish santeros who created religious paintings and sculpture for the Catholic Church, it wasn't until the Santa Fe Railway's publicity campaigns in the years following World War I that this area began developing a reputation as an arts colony. Sent here to paint the landscape and Native Americans, some of those early 20th-century artists scratched out a living selling paintings to local businessmen and tourists or trading their work to settle up restaurant and bar bills.

After developing its reputation as an arts colony, Santa Fe began attracting a technicolor populace of eccentrics, renegades and visionaries that solidified its reputation as a place where alternative lifestyles were accepted. Today, as is the case in places such as Key West, FL, and Carmel, CA, Santa Fe is home to a large and economically powerful gay and lesbian community of all ages whose influence and input is woven into the town's fabric of daily life.

For those considering retirement to Santa Fe, becoming comfortable with the city's weather, culture and eclectic population is an absolute must. This is an exceedingly informal place where great restaurants combine with a diverse cultural life in a high-desert environment, creating an ideal climate for forming new friendships and expanding one's horizons. It's a heady mix that appeals to an urbane and culturally attuned retiree populace ready to wrap their lives around a part of the world that is culturally distinct.

"I find the adobe architecture to be very peaceful, and I really enjoy the way residential and commercial buildings fit in with the landscape," says Ted Meredith, a 55-year-old retired publishing executive who moved here with his wife, Nancy, in 1993. Nancy, 55, who had been in real estate as well as publishing, initially visited Santa Fe with Ted on the advice of their son, Douglas.

"At first we missed our friends back in Indianapolis and Connecticut, but after we moved to Santa Fe they all started visiting us... and have come back more than once," she says.

Ted, who lists among his recent achievements visits to the Los Angeles Dodgers fantasy camp, a car-racing course in Laguna Seca, CA, with the Skip Barber Racing School, and a motorcycle trip around the South Island of New Zealand with son Douglas, says that making new friends since moving to Santa Fe has been easy.

"We took out a membership at Las Campanas golf club, and that turned out to be a terrific meeting ground," he says. "There's so much to do here that I've even gotten used to not having the season tickets for professional hockey, football and basketball that we had when we lived near large cities."

For Nancy, an art lover who once volunteered her time at the Eiteljorg Museum, a renowned museum devoted to Native American art in Indianapolis, relocating to a community loaded with more than 200 art galleries and nearly a dozen art museums has been a rewarding experience.

"Santa Fe just brought us a wonderful opportunity to focus our interests in art," she says. "I've pursued my interest in Australian aboriginal art by taking a trip Down Under, and I have made friends with artists from Taos to Tasmania. I especially enjoy taking Australian artists around northern New Mexico when they're visiting here for an exhibition at Dreamtime Gallery."

David R. Anderson, a retired attorney, moved to Santa Fe from Washington, DC, in 1992 with wife Phoebe Girard. Politically involved and an avid collector of art, he wants to "be a good neighbor and friend with people who are from a different cultural tradition." He and Phoebe, who works for United Way, describe resulting friendships they've made as very rewarding.

A nine-year board member of Arena Stage Theatre in Washington, DC, David, 64, admits to having an abid-

ing love for the arts. These days he divides his creative energies between writing short stories and serving as a board member of Shakespeare in Santa Fe, a professional summer theater company. "Santa Fe is a small town where there's lots to do and where people are grateful for the efforts of volunteers like myself who have a natural bent toward community participation," he says.

"It's a distinctive and interesting place to live, and every morning when I go

Santa Fe, NM

Population: 66,522 in Santa Fe, 128,985 in Santa Fe County.
Location: Northern New Mexico at 7,000 feet in the Sangre de Cristo Mountains.

Climate:

	High	Low
January	40	19
July	82	57

Average relative humidity: 30%
Rain: 14 inches
Snow: 32 inches
Cost of living: 113.6, based on national average of 100.
Median housing cost: $183,500
Sales tax: Called a gross receipts tax locally, the rate is 6.3125% in the city and 5.875% in the county.
Sales tax exemptions: Prescription drugs.
State income tax: Graduated from 2.2% on incomes up to $8,000 to 8.2% on incomes above $65,000 for a single filer and $100,000 for married couples filing jointly.
State income tax exemptions: For married couples filing jointly, there is a low-income tax rebate on incomes falling under $22,000.
Income tax exemptions: Social Securi-

ty, plus varying exclusions for those age 65 and older with incomes of less than $22,000.
Intangibles tax: None.
Estate tax: None, except for the state's "pick-up portion" of the federal tax applicable to taxable estates above $675,000.
Property tax: $17.70 per $1,000 of assessed value, with homes assessed at one-third of appraised value. The annual tax on a $183,500 home, with exemption noted below, is about $1,070.
Homestead exemption: There is a head-of-household exemption of $2,000 off the assessed value of a primary residence.
Security: Specific figures for Santa Fe were not available. In Santa Fe County, 21.5 crimes per 1,000 residents, lower than the national average of 46.2 crimes per 1,000 residents.
Religion: Predominantly Catholic with every major religion represented along with Buddhist, Baha'i, Latter Day Saints, Quaker, Greek Orthodox and nondenominational congregations.
Education: Santa Fe Community College offers degree courses as well as noncredit adult-education courses both for day and night students. St. John's College and the College of Santa Fe are four-year institutions offering undergraduate and graduate degree programs.
Transportation: Santa Fe Trails, the city's transit system, uses buses powered by compressed natural gas in covering its 10 routes. Fare is 50 cents and most routes are operated seven days a week.

Santa Fe Airport is primarily used by private aircraft, but Mesa Airlines has several daily flights on twin-engine planes to and from Denver. Albuquerque International Airport is served by major airlines and is one hour south by car or shuttle.
Health: St. Vincent's Hospital, a full-service facility, is licensed for 268 beds and has 220 physicians on staff. The hospital also has a cardiac care unit and cancer treatment center.
Housing options: Las Campanas, (505) 989-8877, a gated community featuring a golf course, stables and clubhouse, has homesites starting at $250,000 with homes from $400,000 and up. **Shadowridge Apartments**, (505) 988-1919, offers a range of apartment sizes from $615 to $740. **El Castillo**, (505) 988-2577, a continuing-care retirement community, offers housing with entrance fees from $44,000 to $110,000.
Visitor lodging: El Rey Inn offers spacious motel rooms for $82-$135, (505) 982-1931. Adobe Abode has bed-and-breakfast accommodations in a historic downtown Santa Fe residence for $115-$155, (505) 983-3133. La Fonda, another historic downtown hotel, offers rooms for $189-$500, (800) 523-5002 or (505) 982-5511.
Information: Santa Fe County Chamber of Commerce, P.O. Box 1928, Santa Fe, NM 87504, (505) 983-7317 or www.santafechamber.com. Santa Fe Convention and Visitors Bureau, 201 W. Marcy St., Santa Fe, NM 87504-0909, (800) 777-2489 or www.santa fe.org.

outside to get my newspaper, I look up at the sky and immediately feel like I'm living in a resort. If there are any drawbacks to living here, it's the extremely dry climate and the constant sunshine, which take a toll on my skin."

Retired university professors Sarah Lanier Barber and Gloria Donadello moved to Santa Fe after spending their professional lives in New York City, sharing a classic loft apartment in the Soho neighborhood. "We fell in love with Santa Fe immediately, especially for its strong arts scene, its cosmopolitan, yet informal, friendliness, and its great restaurants," says Gloria. "We were looking for a multicultural place that was gay-friendly and someplace where we wouldn't have to turn on the air conditioning in February."

Since arriving here in 1991, Gloria and Sarah have been active in Santa Fe's community affairs, serving as co-founders of Hope House, a residence for people with AIDS. Sarah, 62, also is a founder and co-chairperson of the Lesbian and Gay Community Funding Partnership, while Gloria, 72, serves as co-chairperson of Santa Fe Festival Ballet. Like many other New York professionals who retire to Santa Fe, this couple has discovered that even in retirement their appointment books stay filled with music lessons, aerobics classes, social gatherings, art openings and evenings at the Santa Fe Opera.

Their comfortable adobe home has a spectacular view of the Sangre de Cristo Mountains and is filled with art collected primarily from local galleries. Sarah, who has spent the past five years mastering the cello, says that the cultural composition of northern New Mexico took time to understand. "I taught students from all over the world during my career, and I had lots of exposure to Puerto Ricans, Dominicans, Ecuadorians and other Latino people," she says. "But until I moved here, I had never had any contact with New Mexico's Hispanic culture, and I sure didn't know much about Native Americans."

"Santa Fe is an easy place to make friends, but it's also an expensive place to live and a place where the cultures tend to be more segregated than what we were used to in the city," says Gloria. "But on the other hand, it's culturally rich, you get great movies, and the people you meet are willing to extend themselves out to you in a deep and meaningful way. Without our being able to participate in the life of this community, our retirement experience wouldn't have been as rich as it is."

Bob and Bridget Nurock, who moved to Santa Fe from Philadelphia in 1993, surprised themselves when they "immediately bought a home in Santa Fe after spending a week's vacation here in April 1993. We couldn't believe it ourselves, but our feeling for the town was instantaneous," says Bridget, 52, a clinical social worker specializing in care of the elderly.

Bob, 60, a semiretired investment consultant specializing in stock market strategies for institutional investors, says that since moving to Santa Fe, he's reduced his workload "to about a seven on a scale of 10, and I'm fast headed in the direction of a low five. The main interest in my working life right now is painting, and I'm taking courses and working on my technique every day," he says.

Bob and Bridget both are avid skiers who enjoy living within a half-hour of Santa Fe Ski Area's 12,000-foot heights. They also are serious collectors of works by such artists as Santa Fe landscape painter Phyllis Kapp and serve on the boards of local organizations such as the Native American Preparatory School.

"Santa Fe is the kind of place that has so many activities going on that you never have any problems meeting people," says Bob. "Our shared interest in art has resulted in lots of friendships with artists and gallery owners, and we both enjoy the tricultural composition of this community. We're not necessarily country club-type people, so what matters for us is living close in to town, getting involved with the community, and sharing the love we have for the outdoors and for art. The best advice I have for anyone thinking of retiring here is to make up your mind that you're going to get involved in the life of this community."

"We dove into this place and don't have any regrets," says Bridget. "But if you're thinking of having a home built for you in Santa Fe, I promise you're going to learn about a whole new way of being patient."

That's a sentiment echoed by Jim Van Sant, a retired businessman from St. Louis who moved to Santa Fe in 1987 and now is the opera critic for Santa Fe's daily newspaper. "This place is hellishly expensive for just about all goods and services, and you're continually at the mercy of craftsmen of all kinds. Most folks I know need a couple of months away from here in midwinter, especially to places like San Miguel de Allende (in Mexico), which is much cheaper, yet still has a great cultural life," he says.

"I probably should add that one of the more curious things about retiring to Santa Fe is that you always have to protect yourself from having too many house guests. On the other hand, when you travel away from here, you come to realize that you have a certain status simply by virtue of having decided to live in Santa Fe. People listen to you a bit more, and I find it fun to live in such a high-profile small town."●

Sarasota, Florida

Vibrant city on Florida's Gulf Coast has an impressive cultural scene

By Karen Feldman

The lure of almost any Florida community includes a mild climate and countless opportunities for outdoor fun, but Sarasota boasts that plus something more: culture. Lots and lots of culture. Opera, ballet, theater, film festivals and the visual arts flourish in this small, sophisticated city on the state's southwest coast.

Much of the credit for this bounty goes to circus magnate John Ringling, who in 1927 decided to base his famed circus in Sarasota. Today his legacy lives on in many ways. John and Mable Ringling's estate, which includes the Ringling Museum of the Circus, the Ringling Museum of Art and his 30-room mansion, Ca'd'Zan (Venetian dialect for "House of John"), are resplendent treasures situated along Sarasota Bay in the heart of the city.

Although best-known for his circus success, Ringling made a fortune through shrewd investments in oil, railroads and real estate. Many of his business associates and acquaintances found their way to Sarasota, bringing their money, influence and desires for the finer things of life along with them. Today the Ringling estate remains a cultural hub of the city, and its influence radiates out in many directions.

Add to that 35 miles of pristine beaches along the Gulf of Mexico, five dozen golf courses, year-round fishing and a location convenient to Tampa and Orlando, and Sarasota weighs in as a serious contender even against much larger Florida cities.

"It's one of those rare special places that has big-city amenities without the hassle of being in a big city," says David May, president of the Greater Sarasota Chamber of Commerce.

It was just that combination that attracted Sam and Susan Kalush here in 1993, when they decided to move south from Michigan. The retired cardiac surgeon and his wife, an interior designer, considered the central Piedmont and Research Triangle regions of North Carolina and many other Florida towns. After several visits to Sarasota, they were sold.

Why? "The warm climate, and it was large enough to offer the amenities of culture, entertainment and good restaurants," says Sam, 58, who also cites its proximity to Tampa and the ocean. "You are not overwhelmed by a big urban environment with urban center problems," he says.

"It has the feel of a small town," agrees Susan, 56.

The city's population stands at about 55,000, with another 250,000 in the rest of the county. Development, which has thrived for more than a decade, continues at a brisk pace. With the growing population comes "a wide range of retail establishments and restaurants that make it an interesting place to live and to entertain," says David May.

For Joe and Lolly Hascal, the move from Louisville, KY, to Sarasota was a foregone conclusion. Joe, 75, had owned a condo on Siesta Key, a barrier island along Sarasota's western flank, and visited regularly for 17 years. After retiring from the men's retail clothing business, he and Lolly, 71, a mental health counselor and educator, bought a duplex in the 125-unit Crestwood Villas. They moved in November 1994, quickly and easily making friends at the community's pool and clubhouse.

When it comes to housing, the options are many, including cozy, rambling old neighborhoods and sleek, well-manicured new ones. There are waterfront and country club communities and options downtown among the art galleries and cafes or away from it all on large tracts with a country feel.

"There's housing here to meet all tastes, from apartments to a whole variety of single-family housing, villas and condos. There's a very good housing stock," says David May. "People used to paying housing costs in the Northeast or large communities like the Chicago metropolitan area will find it to be a very affordable market."

Renee Eppard, a broker with Re-Max Properties in Sarasota, agrees. "We have so many choices here it's unbelievable," she says. "Prices range from $60,000 for a 1,000-square-foot older condo to $3 million homes on the bay. And there's everything in between."

In order to take time to consider their options, the Kalushes first rented a home for about four months. They ended up buying a house in the development where they'd rented — Bent Tree, a subdivision of 575 homes with an 18-hole golf course. Their home is 3,200 square feet, an open, split plan with guest rooms on one end and the master suite on the other. It has a lakeside lot and a lanai, swimming pool and large open family room. "We spend a lot of time and eat a lot of meals outside on the lanai and around the pool," Susan says.

In general, Renee Eppard says, a new three-bedroom, two-bath home with a pool and a two-car garage runs $200,000 to $250,000 but can climb as high as $3 million for a beachfront location.

Many retirees prefer something smaller or want to skip the lawn and pool maintenance, so they choose a condominium development. Here again, prices range widely. From the basic older model that starts in the low $60,000s, prices rise to the $125,000-to-$300,000 range for a 2,500-square-foot luxury villa. Condos on Siesta and Lido keys start at about $250,000, while those on Longboat Key start at $500,000. Enjoying

America's 100 Best Places to Retire 257

a resurgence in popularity is the Sarasota Bayfront downtown, where luxury condos start at $800,000 and go up to $1.5 million.

Another plus for retirees, David May says, is "a whole range of assisted-living options. New projects have come on line to cater to the middle-income-and-up retiree who has the means and desire to live a good lifestyle."

That already has occurred to the Hascals. "When we get too feeble, they have gorgeous retirement places here," Lolly says.

Wherever they live, Sarasota residents have lots of reasons to leave their homes in pursuit of any number of interests. "For those who want to be active, there is an almost unlimited number of organizations that need talented volunteers," David May says. The Sarasota Volunteer Center refers several thousand volunteers to hundreds of local nonprofit organizations, providing an annual equivalent of $4.25 million in services.

Both the Kalushes and the Hascals

Sarasota, FL

Population: 55,000 in the city, 310,000 in Sarasota County.

Location: On the west coast of Florida, 60 miles south of the Tampa-St. Petersburg area. Easily accessible via Interstate 75 as well as the Sarasota-Bradenton International Airport and Tampa International Airport.

Climate:

	High	Low
January	72	50
July	91	72

Average relative humidity: 52%

Rain: About 60 inches annually.

Cost of living: 104.3, based on national average of 100.

Median housing cost: $150,000

Sales tax: 7%

Sales tax exemptions: Food and medicine.

State income tax: None.

Intangibles tax: Assessed on stocks, bonds and other specified assets, with some investments exempt. Tax rate is $1 per $1,000 of value for assets of less than $100,000 for individuals or $200,000 for couples, $1.50 per $1,000 of value for larger amounts. First $20,000 of assets ($40,000 per couple) is exempt.

Estate tax: None, except the state's "pick-up" portion of the federal tax, applicable to taxable estates of more than $675,000.

Property tax: $18.04 per $1,000 in Sarasota, with homes assessed at 100% of market value. The annual tax on a $150,000 home, with exemption noted below, is $2,225. Additional taxes vary depending on location and may include water management, lighting and other special assessments.

Homestead exemption: $25,000 off the assessed value of a permanent, primary residence.

Security: 88 crimes per 1,000 residents, above the national average of 46.2 crimes per 1,000 residents.

Religion: All major religions and many smaller ones are represented in the 150-plus churches and synagogues in Sarasota County.

Education: There are several colleges, including the University of South Florida, New College, Eckerd College, the Ringling School of Art and Design and the University of Sarasota. These colleges offer a variety of degrees ranging from associates to doctorates. Noncredit courses for adults also are available.

Transportation: Sarasota-Bradenton International Airport provides service to many U.S. cities with a combination of major air carriers and commuter carriers. Sarasota County Area Transit provides local bus service.

Health: There are two primary healthcare hospitals: Doctors Hospital offers a full range of services, including emergency treatment, radiology, pain management, chest pain care, hyperbaric medicine, a women's unit and a mature adult community center, and Sarasota Memorial Hospital offers urgent and emergency care, rehabilitation, chest pain treatment, cardiac care (including open-heart surgery), joint replacement, gerontology, outpatient surgery, a nursing facility and more,

including a 24-hour line for health questions and physician referral. In addition, there are several licensed nursing and congregate-care facilities.

Housing options: Apartments, condominiums, patio homes and single-family residences abound in the city and its metropolitan area. There are waterfront, downtown and country club communities to choose from, as well. Prices range from the low $60,000s to $3 million. Many communities have both independent and assisted-living options. Among those are **Bay Village**, (941) 966-5611; **The Fountains at Lake Pointe Woods**, (941) 923-4944; and **Kabernick House**, (941) 377-0781.

Visitor lodging: This popular tourist destination offers a wealth of hotels, motor inns and resorts. In or near downtown Sarasota are Hampton Inn Sarasota-Bradenton, $74-$114, (941) 351-7734; Holiday Inn Downtown by the Bay, $74-$89, (941) 365-1900; and Hyatt Sarasota, $99-$240, (941) 953-1234. On Siesta Key: The Palm Bay Club, $125-$500, (941) 349-1911, and The Turtle Beach Resort, $140-$325, (941) 349-4554. On Longboat Key: The Colony Beach and Tennis Resort, $195-$385, (941) 383-6464, and the Longboat Key Hilton Beach Resort, $129-$239, (941) 383-2451. Rates are per night, double occupancy, and are lowest from mid-April through mid-December, rising 20% to 60% from Christmas through Easter.

Information: The Sarasota Visitor Information Center, 655 N. Tamiami Trail, Sarasota, FL 34236, (941) 957-1877, (800) 522-9799 or www.sarasotafl.org. The Greater Sarasota Chamber of Commerce, 1819 Main St., Suite 240, Sarasota, FL 34236, (941) 955-8187 or www.sarasotachamber.org.

belong to that volunteer force. Sam volunteers his cardiology expertise at Senior Friendship Center, which offers low- or no-cost medical care and other health services to seniors by utilizing the retired medical community. He also instructs Red Cross courses on cardiopulmonary resuscitation and first aid. Susan volunteers at Doctors Hospital and serves as a tour guide at the Sarasota Florida House, an environmentally friendly house that serves as a model for the public. She's also the chairwoman of a social group at the country club. Joe volunteers at Senior Friendship Center as well, delivering meals, picking up groceries, running errands and visiting shut-ins. Lolly uses her training as a mental health counselor to lead a weekly support group and lectures once a month.

When not volunteering, Lolly also likes to folk dance and work on her computer while Joe shops and takes walks on the beach. Both enjoy swimming. For the Kalushes, golfing, fishing, boating, walking and bicycling are favorite pastimes.

David May says it's natural that most people think of the beaches and golf courses when they picture Sarasota, but he suggests exploring farther inland as well. "We have the largest state park (Myakka River State Park), beautiful inland waterways and wetlands that really make this area special for people who enjoy being outside," he says.

About nine miles east of Interstate 75, the park is easy to reach. Among its inhabitants are 200 species of birds, alligators, deer, feral pigs and bobcats. There are nature trails, observation decks, airboat and guided tram tours available. For yet another perspective, the state plans to add a rope walkway at treetop level, much like those found in rain forests.

Many current residents were once tourists looking for a warm-weather getaway. They found Sarasota and liked it so much that they eventually relocated. The many qualities that attract tourists are among those that appeal to residents, too.

The area has lots of Gulf access along the barrier islands of Lido Key, Longboat Key and Siesta Key. There's also lots of activity along the shoreline of sparkling Sarasota Bay.

The Ringling Estate, which overlooks the bay, sprawls over 66 acres, much of which is open for visitors to enjoy the trees, gardens and statuary. Within the Ringling Museum of Art, built in Italian Renaissance style, is a garden courtyard filled with reproductions of famous statues, including Michelangelo's "David." The estate is at its most startling each year during a Renaissance festival held in early March that fills the grounds with knights, wizards, ladies fair and other medieval characters.

Not far south along the water are the Marie Selby Botanical Gardens, nine lush acres filled with huge banyan trees, massive stands of bamboo, water lilies, cypress trees, orchids and Amazonian bromeliads. An elevated boardwalk winds through a mangrove swamp.

Tucked on a spit of land between Longboat and St. Armands keys, the Mote Marine Aquarium lets the public in to see the shark tank, sea turtles, a large touch tank and other marine exhibits. It also is headquarters for a group of marine researchers studying matters such as why sharks are immune to cancer and how that might aid humans in battling the disease.

St. Armands Key houses a collection of shops, galleries, restaurants and night spots arranged in a large circle ideal for browsing and dining. In downtown Sarasota, a number of art galleries, theaters and restaurants now draw crowds, too.

Greyhound racing takes place from late December to mid-April at the Sarasota Kennel Club. The Cincinnati Reds spend March and early April in spring training camp at Ed Smith Sports Complex. The Royal Lipizzan Stallions offer free shows from January through March at Col. Hermann's Ranch in neighboring Manatee County. There are also all the requisite water activities: fishing, canoeing, water-skiing, kayaking, dolphin watching, wildlife tours and swimming.

The city also is home to the Asolo Theatre Co., The Players, Sarasota Opera, the Sarasota Ballet of Florida, the Florida West Coast Symphony and a number of vocal and chamber ensembles. Big names in entertainment often appear at the Florida State University Center for the Performing Arts and the purple-hued Van Wezel Hall.

About an hour away are St. Petersburg and Tampa, home to the Salvador Dali Museum, Florida International Museum, The Florida Aquarium, the Museum of Fine Arts, the Tampa Bay Performing Arts Center and Busch Gardens. Orlando is about two hours east.

After living in the city for several years, neither the Kalushes nor the Hascals have plans to move. Their advice to others who are thinking about relocating and considering Sarasota: "It's an excellent choice," Sam says.

"I hate to encourage others," Susan adds. "It has gotten busier and busier in the last five years. When we first got here, we were very pleased because it wasn't so crowded. But I think it's still one of the prime places on the Gulf Coast."

Lolly Hascal expresses a similar sentiment: "You will love it." But, she jokes, "Wait 'til we leave." ●

Scottsdale, Arizona

A Phoenix suburb blends Southwestern and Mediterranean architecture with beautiful desert scenery

By Ron Butler

Forty years ago, Scottsdale was little more than a dirt road and a couple of saloons — Lulu Belle's and the Pink Pony. Then word got out and Scottsdale was swept up in the phenomenal Arizona population explosion that today makes the Phoenix-Scottsdale area one of the fast-growing urban centers in the country.

Just being in Scottsdale is an event — imagine living there. Situated seamlessly between Phoenix, Paradise Valley, Carefree and Tempe, Scottsdale's population is now near 200,000. Known for its outstanding architectural and landscape design, the impressive city also has impressive numbers — 125 art galleries (the biggest art center this side of Santa Fe), three libraries, 32 indoor theaters, one outdoor theater, 28 parks, four bowling alleys. There are three municipal swimming pools, 30 golf courses, 20 tennis parks, five museums, a civic center, baseball stadium, a Center for the Arts and the Scottsdale Community College.

Its downtown Civic Center Senior Center is groundbreaking in concept. "As part of the city of Scottsdale, we give our community a place to have fun, a place to be safe, and help to enhance the quality of life, especially for our senior population," says Human Services spokeswoman Cathie McDaniel. The center looks like a bank or office building outside, but inside there's a wide variety of social and recreational programs, health screenings, special events, organized outings, discussion groups and classes in everything from computer techniques to Spanish language. Only the special classes and concert and theater outings require fees. Everything else is free.

Throw in gorgeous desert scenery with proud mountain landscapes and a near-perfect climate, and it makes

you wonder why Nancy and Ned Benedict, 52 and 59 respectively, took so long to move there. They came from San Francisco three years ago. Ned spent 32 years as a career pilot for Federal Express. Nancy, his co-pilot if you will, is a homemaker.

The Benedicts live in a sprawling five-bedroom, three-and-a-half-bath ranch-style home in a gated, master-planned community north of town called Terravita, meaning harmony of life and land. Frequent visits to relatives in the area made them forsake San Francisco for the Arizona desert.

Golf is a big priority with the Benedicts. (Membership fee for the Terravita Club is $65,000. Greens fees for guests range from $35 to $100, depending on season.) The couple also enjoys excursions into the desert and trips to towns such as Tucson, Bisbee and Douglas in the southern part of the state to soak up all that Western ambiance. They enjoy eating out, with Roy's Pacific Rim Cuisine their current favorite, offering seared lemon grass-crusted salmon with watercress-ginger sauce, and grilled spiny lobster with bean thread noodles and macadamia nuts.

Eating out also is a favorite activity of Dr. Melvin Breeze, 85, and his wife Elizabeth, 84, who moved to Scottsdale from Portland, OR, five and a half years ago. They count 44 restaurants within walking distance of their Forum Pueblo Norte senior living community, and have tried them all.

Melvin is a retired pediatrician and gynecologist; Elizabeth was on the home economics staff at Oregon State University. Married in 1937, they have five children and five great-grandchildren.

It was a medical convention at the Wigwam resort in nearby Litchfield and subsequent conferences in the area that introduced Melvin to the

glories of desert living. He liked the people and loved the climate. He and Elizabeth have taken two apartments in the Forum, a Marriott retirement property, and combined them to make one large apartment with four bedrooms, a guest room and possibly the largest-screen TV set this side of the big sports bar on Scottsdale Road.

The Forum also has its own healthcare center and an assisted-living community. Services include one meal a day, downtown shuttle service, weekly housekeeping, free local calls, utilities, maintenance, heated swimming pool, shuffleboard and a putting green along with a wide range of organized social and cultural activities. The Breezes are members of the Scottsdale Arts Center and enjoy a full active life outside the Forum as well.

Norman and Cathy Arthur, 63 and 52 respectively, gave up the good life in Hawaii for the good life in Scottsdale six years ago and now reside in a gated community in the mountain foothills in the north part of town. He's a retired civil engineer; she's a computer consultant who still takes part-time assignments. They enjoy the desert scenery and often are part of it, taking long hikes and jogging 10 miles a day. They're often thrilled to spot a coyote or a bobcat or a pair of javelinas (wild pigs) along the way. They enjoy several challenging trails among the sheer red cliffs of Camelback Mountain, the area's best-known landmark, and they also play tennis but have an aversion to golf.

Their tastefully decorated home, with four bedrooms and three baths, is filled with Western artifacts and art — Hopi Kachina dolls, desert paintings, Indian blankets. Homes in the community are in the $300,000-to-$1.5 million range. The Arthurs also have a cabin in the summer recreation area of Pinetop, but it was primarily economic considerations that made Scottsdale a retirement choice. The cost of living in Scottsdale is about half of what it was in Hawaii, and there are all those pesky volcanoes.

They have a 17-year-old son living at home and another at school. The community has no age restrictions, so the Arthurs enjoy an eclectic group of neighbors, ranging from empty-nesters to retirees and even a couple of newlyweds on their second and third marriages. They like to read so it's not unusual to find them browsing the shelves at the fine downtown bookstores such as the Antiquarians Shop. Here serious collectors can pick up a signed, first edition of John Stein-

Scottsdale, AZ

Population: 195,490
Location: In south-central Arizona, bordered by Phoenix, Paradise Valley, Carefree and Tempe in the legendary Valley of the Sun.

Climate:

	High	Low
January	65	39
July	105	80

Humidity: 23%
Rain: 7.05 inches of rain per year.
Cost of living: 113, based on national average of 100.
Median housing costs: Home prices range from $60,000 to $6 million, averaging about $180,000. Apartments averaging 950 square feet with two bedrooms and one and a half to two baths rent for about $700 a month, excluding utilities.
Sales tax: 7.3%
Sales tax exemptions: Groceries and prescription drugs.
State income tax: Graduated in five steps from 2.9% to 5.17%, depending on income.
Income tax exemptions: Social Security and up to $2,500 of federal, state and local government pensions are exempt.
Estate tax: None, except the state's "pickup" portion of federal tax, applicable to taxable estates above $675,000.
Property tax: $9.24 per $100 assessed valuation, with homes assessed at 10% of market value. The annual

tax due on a $180,000 home would be about $1,663.
Homestead exemptions: None.
Security: 52.5 crimes per 1,000 residents, higher than the national average of 46.2 crimes per 1,000 residents.
Religion: Scottsdale has hundreds of churches and synagogues representing virtually every denomination.
Education: Scottsdale Community College offers an associate degree with credits transferable to university levels and technical degrees. A wide range of continuing-education classes and community service programs also are available. Arizona State University, the state's largest university with an enrollment of more than 40,000, is located in the neighboring community of Tempe.
Transportation: Nearly everyone in Arizona drives, but those who don't will find Scottsdale taxis among the most expensive anywhere. Figure about $1 a mile in this sprawling area. The Scottsdale Connection provides wheelchair-accessible bus service throughout Scottsdale with connecting service to major Phoenix and other regional transportation routes. Ollie the Trolley offers free transportation throughout downtown Scottsdale from mid-November to May. Dial-a-Ride is a low-cost transportation program operating in Scottsdale and Tempe for persons 65 and older. Proof of age (Medicare card or photo identification) is required. The Scottsdale Municipal Airport, one of the busiest single-runway facilities in the country, accommodates business and recreational flyers.
Health: Scottsdale is home to one of the three branches of the Mayo Clinic, a multispecialty outpatient clinic with more than 200 physicians and a medical support staff of more than 1,500. Scottsdale Healthcare is the largest single employer in Scottsdale with

more than 4,000 staff members and 1,350 active physicians.
Housing options: Medium-priced and luxury condominiums, townhouses, patio homes, ranch-style homes and two-story homes are all available in Scottsdale, making housing options one of its most attractive features. Of the more than 86,000 dwelling units currently occupied in Scottsdale, 67 percent are owned and 33 percent are rented. Scottsdale has several nationally recognized planned communities, such as McCormick Ranch, Gainy Ranch, Scottsdale Ranch, Desert Highlands, Grayhawk, Desert Mountain, Troon, Terravita, McDowell Mountain Ranch and Scottsdale Mountain. For information, call Neighborhood Resource Guide, (480) 312-7251.
Visitor lodging: Options range from glittering five-star resorts like the world-famous Phoenician, $195-$405, (480) 941-8200, and the Fairmont Scottsdale Princess, $149-$639, (480) 585-4848, to short-term rentals like the Adobe Apartment Hotel, (480) 945-3544. Days Inn Fashion Square, (480) 947-5411, is immediately adjacent to Scottsdale's most prestigious shopping mall and offers rates ranging from $39 for a standard room in low season to $130 for a suite in high season. For visitor information online, see the Scottsdale Convention and Visitors Bureau site at www.scottsdalecvb.com.
Information: Scottsdale Chamber of Commerce and Convention and Visitors Bureau, 7343 Scottsdale Mall, Scottsdale, AZ 85251, (800) 805-0471 or (480) 945-8481. Arizona Office of Senior Living, 3800 N. Central Ave., No. 1500, Phoenix, AZ 85012, (602) 280-1300, provides out-of-state retiree prospects with free relocation information. Web sites to check out include www.scottsdalechamber.com and www.scottsdale cvb.com.

beck's "In Dubious Battle" for $8,000, a first edition of Ernest Hemingway's "Death in the Afternoon" for $4,000 or Arthur Conan Doyle's "Hound of the Baskervilles" for $4,000.

Victor and Ann Phillips, 72 and 70 respectively, gave up Ohio's frigid winters to worship El Sol in Scottsdale 12 years ago. They lived in Oxford, a charming little town of cobbled streets and unique shops where both were affiliated with Miami University, he (following a 24-year military career) in business and she in library arts. They raised four children.

Today, home is a comfortable, art-filled, two-bedroom casita in the Classic Residence of Scottsdale, a senior living community by Hyatt and the Plaza companies that offers virtually all the amenities of a luxury resort. These include 24-hour concierge service, one meal a day (lunch or dinner), weekly housecleaning and linen service, shuttle service and a wide variety of health and fitness programs.

The scenery is all mountains and lofty saguaros. Ann, who keeps busy with volunteer church, library and bilingual school classes, complains that a persistent family of javelinas has been eating her flower garden, roots and all.

With their obvious love for art (their home is filled with Western oils, bronzes and tie-dye prints), the Phillipses couldn't have settled in a more compatible community. Scottsdale's art scene is world famous. Sculptor Bob Parks' magnificent downtown fountain with four life-sized Arabian stallions frolicking about — the most photographed landmark in Scottsdale — sets the tone.

For the past 20 years, Scottsdale galleries have treated visitors and locals to Thursday night Art Walks, the oldest such art event in the United States. Many of the best-known galleries are concentrated along Marshal Way and Main Street (the arts and antique district), with others clustered in the Fifth Avenue shopping area and Old Town. Buck Saunders Gallery on East Camelback Road was the first major gallery to feature the work of the late Ted DeGrazia, Arizona's best-known, most-loved artist, and was long his exclusive representative. Now many of the local galleries, most notably Anthony's, feature the works of this world-known painter.

For the downside of living in Scottsdale — ah, and you thought there wasn't any — progress seems to be the main culprit. Nearly everyone echoes the same complaint — too many people, too much traffic, limited bus service, too much building and banging. "There's so much work," says Ned Benedict, the former Federal Express pilot, "that many unqualified workers are filling the work force, taking forever to show up for a job when you call them, and then doing shoddy work."

Yet for all of its glitz and development, there's something about Scottsdale that calls to mind the small towns in Italy or Spain where old men spend their time sitting around the town square, sipping coffee or wine and discussing the cares of the day. You see the same men in downtown Scottsdale — but they're at trendy outdoor cappuccino bars, and they dress better.●

Seaside, Florida

An upscale new town sports an old-fashioned look in the Florida Panhandle

By Karen Feldman

Florida's Panhandle is an unlikely place to find a development that has set the standard for a new kind of community, one that blends the best features of old-fashioned villages with modern conveniences and environmental awareness. Yet the Panhandle, with its honky-tonk towns that sprawl along the edge of the Gulf of Mexico, is where the community of Seaside has flourished.

Most of the Panhandle's Gulf Coast developed helter-skelter as entrepreneurs crammed in as many motels, surf shops, eateries, and tattoo and piercing parlors as the market would bear. Apparently it will bear a lot, as the solid mass of commercial development along U.S. Highway 98, the main route along the Gulf, reveals.

But turn onto County Road 30A, and the development becomes less dense, the beach widens and palms line the roads of upscale condo communities. The scene sets the stage for Seaside, a testament to what can happen when one man with conviction turns his vision into reality.

That's what developer Robert Davis has proved with his creation of Seaside. While Seaside may not be a household name, anyone who has watched "The Truman Show," a movie starring Jim Carrey, has seen the idyllic 80-acre town with its pastel-hued cottages and white picket fences lining red-brick streets.

What Davis had in mind was a new type of community created by culling the best aspects of towns of the past. To find out what those were, Davis and his wife spent two years driving around Florida studying towns, their architecture and the qualities that gave them character. He and his team of architects then compiled the features that were to become the basis for this model town. Among these were white picket fences of varying designs around each home, screened porches with large overhangs, galvanized metal roofs, dirt footpaths and native landscaping.

What started as a couple of cottages built for about $65,000 each now encompasses 325 homes with prices that start at $255,000 and go upwards of $2 million. There are a dozen restaurants, an amphitheater for community events and a town center to which people walk for shopping and socializing. Across the highway is a large expanse of sugar-sand beach upon which the Gulf of Mexico laps gently.

Begun in 1982, Seaside is a teenager, both chronologically and in terms of maturity. Virtually all the empty lots have been sold and most have been built upon. Besides restaurants, there are shops, a gourmet supermarket, a bank, a post office, a fitness club and a small charter school. Yet to come are a chapel, a full complement of medical services and a significant number of full-time residents. Right now, about 10 percent of the homeowners occupy their cottages year-round, and another handful is in residence about half the year. Most homeowners spend a few weeks there annually and rent their homes to beach-loving vacationers the rest of the time.

Carroll and Felton Temple consider Seaside their primary residence, although they spend half the year in Charlotte, NC. Carroll, 67, is a retired medicinal chemist who worked for the Southern Research Institute in Birmingham, AL. Felton, 66, is a medical transcriptionist who still works when she chooses. The couple left Birmingham about a year ago and bought their Charlotte home.

During the 43 years in which they lived in Birmingham and raised a family, the Temples took many trips to Florida's Panhandle. It was during one of those trips in 1983 that they happened upon Seaside. Even then the fledgling community caught their eye. "There were three or four cottages here," Felton recalls. "I screamed for my husband to stop. I tried to get my husband interested in building a house, but he wouldn't do it."

Instead, they spent at least one vacation a year at Seaside, renting cottages owned by others. After eight years, Carroll came around. When they couldn't find an existing house to suit them, they built the four-bedroom cottage they dubbed Blue Heaven. The name comes from the University of North Carolina at Chapel Hill, where Carroll did his graduate work. The school's colors are blue and white and are referred to as Blue Heaven.

Blue also happens to be Felton's favorite color. Not surprisingly, the cottage is painted blue outside and "has a blue theme running more or less inside," Felton says. "One bedroom is blue with peach, another is blue with yellow, and so on."

While the couple's home is larger than many of the so-called cottages at Seaside, its whimsical name and decor are typical of the community's ambiance. Each cottage has a name neatly posted on the white picket fence or near the door, along with the homeowners' names, including those of their children and sometimes pets as well. The cottages have names such as Salad Days, Dreamweaver, Hakuna Matata, Freckles, Plum Lazy, Sunkissed and Ooh-La-La.

Felton says the couple didn't look anywhere else when they decided to build a second home. "We never considered any other place but Seaside. The Gulf is so beautiful. I liked the concept of little Victorian houses and cobblestone streets. You can't describe how pretty it is to anybody. They have to see it for themselves," says Felton, who notes that they put their cottage into the Seaside rental program during the summer, when it's too hot there for their tastes, and head north to Charlotte.

Charles and Sarah Modica discovered Seaside in much the same way as the Temples. In 1983, when they were vacationing at Panama City Beach, they drove out to see Seagrove Beach, just down the road from Seaside. From the road, they "saw a man sitting on the porch of a red house with his two dogs on his lap," Charles recalls. "That was Robert Davis and he was talking about what the city would look like."

At the time, Seaside consisted of two cottages on an unpaved street. "I said, 'Sarah, this man is crazy. Let's go,'" says Charles, who also thought the asking price of $65,000 for a house was on the high side back then. But his wife had other ideas, and the Modicas bought a lot and built the home they still occupy on Tupelo Street. Although it was to be a summer home, a respite from their grocery business in Alabama, Davis encour-

aged them to start an ice cream and sandwich shop on the beach. Sarah stayed and ran it while Charles continued to operate their grocery store in Alabama.

Seaside continued to grow and 10 years ago, Davis persuaded the Modicas to open a gourmet grocery store there. Charles, who was 61 at the time, objected that he was too old to start a new business, but Davis persisted. So the Modicas traveled around to see gourmet establishments in

New Orleans and elsewhere, then opened their store, Modica Market, which is stocked floor-to-ceiling with everything from basics like toilet paper and onions to high-end wines, gourmet breads, cheeses and fresh seafood. Their son, Charles Jr., is now part of the business as well.

Although Charles Sr., now 71, and his 67-year-old wife had visions of retiring at Seaside, he can't foresee that day coming. The business, open seven days a week, is

Seaside, FL

Population: During summer, the population averages 1,500. During winter, it ranges from 300 to 500.

Location: On Florida's northwest Gulf Coast between Panama City and Destin, 140 miles west of Tallahassee and 300 miles southwest of Atlanta.

Climate:

	High	Low
January	61	42
July	89	74

Average relative humidity: 49%

Rainfall: 60 inches annually.

Cost of living: Well above average (specific index not available).

Median housing cost: $850,000

Sales tax: 6%

Sales tax exemptions: Food and medicine.

State income tax: None.

Intangibles tax: Assessed on stocks, bonds and other specified assets, with some investments exempt. Tax rate is $1 per $1,000 of value for assets of less than $100,000 for individuals or $200,000 for couples, $1.50 per $1,000 of value for larger amounts. First $20,000 of assets ($40,000 per couple) is exempt.

Estate tax: None, except the state's "pick-up" portion of the federal tax, applicable to taxable estates of more

than $675,000.

Property tax: $15.84 per $1,000 in Seaside, with homes assessed at 85% of market value. The annual tax on an $850,000 home, with exemption noted below, is about $11,048.

Homestead exemption: $25,000 off the assessed value of a permanent, primary residence.

Security: 31.5 crimes per 1,000 residents, lower than the national average of 46.2 crimes per 1,000 residents.

Religion: A small nondenominational chapel is under construction at Seaside. In neighboring cities, houses of worship include Episcopal, Lutheran, Presbyterian, Roman Catholic, United Methodist, Unity, Jewish and interdenominational.

Education: The Seaside Institute is a nonprofit organization devoted to expanding the concept of town planning and living. It sponsors intellectual and cultural events throughout the year. The Seaside Neighborhood School is a charter school offering classes for about 90 students in grades 6 through 8.

Transportation: The self-contained community encourages foot and bicycle traffic only. The airport shuttle provides service to the Bay County Airport/Fanin Field in Panama City, 35 miles east of Seaside; Okaloosa County Airport in Fort Walton Beach, 45 miles west of Seaside; Pensacola Airport, 80 miles west of Seaside; and Tallahassee Airport, 140 miles east of Seaside. US Airways and Atlantic Southwest Airlines/Delta serve all four airports; Northwest Airlink serves Bay County, while Northwest flies into Oka-

loosa and Pensacola. American and Continental also serve Pensacola.

Health: There are plans to build a medical center that will house a resident physician as well as visiting specialists. Nearby are the Bay Medical Center and the Emerald Shores Medical Center. The closest hospital is in Panama City, about a 30-minute drive.

Housing options: Structures range from one-bedroom penthouses, which sell for $255,000 to $358,000, to six-bedroom cottages that cost upwards of $2 million.

Visitor lodging: The Seaside Cottage Rental Agency, (800) 277-8696 or www.seasidefl.com, serves as the agent for more than 270 privately owned rental cottages. Rental options range from one-bedroom cottages that sleep two or four to a six-bedroom house that sleeps 15. Rentals are least expensive in winter, rising in spring and fall and highest in summer. Many cottages must be rented for a minimum of three days. The three-night rate for a one-bedroom cottage is $448-$715 in winter, $553-$925 in the summer. Seaside Honeymoon Cottages offer couples a view of the Gulf starting at $357 per night. Beachside Cottages also have a Gulf view, accommodate small families and rent from $250 a night. The Seaside Motor Court offers old-fashioned motel accommodations with a nostalgic 1950s decor. Rooms rent for $145 a night. Josephine's French Country Inn, (800) 848-1840 or (850) 231-1939, offers bed-and-breakfast accommodations for $135-$215.

Information: Seaside Community Realty Inc., P.O. Box 4730, Seaside, FL 32459, (888) SEASIDE or www.seasidefl.com.

booming. He walks to work and enjoys his customers, including the children whose parents set up accounts at the store so the kids can go in and buy what they want on their own. "It's a close community," Charles says. "They take care of one another. It's like living in paradise."

While Seaside can't yet be considered a retirement town, it has the potential to become one. Most Seaside homebuyers now are well-heeled baby boomers with families who are looking for an investment or ensuring themselves a retirement place in the sun in a few years.

"If you look at fairly recent research on what people want out of a retirement community, what the plurality want is a small town with urban amenities," says developer Robert Davis. "College towns fit that bill rather well, and so does Seaside, with the added benefit of having a beach and warm weather, unlike Hanover (NH) and Amherst (MA)."

Davis, whose iconoclastic approach to development initially was ridiculed, only to later win high praise and many awards, is blunt about his dislike for the growing trend of adult-only housing developments spreading across Florida and other retirement states. "What people are looking for, I think, at least in this generation of preretirees, is a place very unlike the summer camps for the elderly," he says. "These concentrations of one age group, I think it's unhealthy for us as a culture and unhealthy for people who are so concentrated."

Davis, who is 55 and owns a home in Seaside, says, "I don't know many of my friends who picture themselves going off to live with our own age group. I would find it completely deadly. Yet I know a lot of people go to these places even if they don't want to segregate by age because the suburban environment where we have spent most of our lives is so completely unsupportive of people without driver's licenses.

"Seaside represents a place where people without driver's licenses can do just fine," he says. "They can walk to most of the things they need on a daily basis, and there's a van that will run errands for them, take them to the airport — basically, there's no reason that they need a driver's license to live comfortably."

Comfortable living without a car is what Seaside is all about. Even those who can drive are encouraged to park their cars at their cottages and leave them there for the duration of their stay. As a result, pedestrians, bicyclists and skaters have the streets to themselves.

The heart of the community is Central Square, where much of the commercial element is clustered. There's the MM Fitness Studio, an attorney's office, clothing stores, art galleries, a real estate broker, a wine bar and the Seaside Institute, a nonprofit organization that offers educational and cultural programs. Modica Market is nearby.

An outdoor amphitheater provides a communal gathering spot for a variety of activities, such as concerts, a summer film series and storytelling. There are wine festivals twice a year, architectural tours, a conference for writers and other cultural events.

Across the highway are more shops and eateries. PER-SPI-CAS-ITY, an open-air market like those found in Italy, features stalls with all sorts of clothing and accessories. There's also Piazza Nancy Drew, an open area with shops on which the fanciful paintings of well-known designer Nancy Drew create festive fronts. Bud & Alley's bistro and rooftop bar overlook the Gulf and feature rustic coastal cuisine such as crab cakes and seafood stew.

Among Seaside's most distinctive features are the nine beach pavilions that frame the entrances to the beach, providing access over the high dunes as well as bathroom facilities and yet another opportunity for architecture to shine. The pavilions, each designed by a different architect, also are popular gathering spots for watching the sun set. All lead to a smooth beach virtually devoid of shells. Big blue beach umbrellas shading lounge chairs line up like so many sandpipers facing the water. Besides the beach, amenities include three swimming pools, six tennis courts and a croquet lawn.

The town is divvied up into various smaller neighborhoods, such as Ruskin Place Artist Colony, where artists can create and sell their works on the ground floor, while townhomes with a New Orleans flavor occupy the upper floors. And although it was the town's beauty and location that prompted the Temples to build there, there's no disputing that it was a good investment. "Our house has more than doubled in value since we built

it — almost tripled," Felton says.

Jacky Barker, real estate broker for Seaside, says property values are climbing fast. "We've averaged 10 percent appreciation a year, but in the last couple of years it's run between 15 and 18 percent," she says.

When Robert Davis' grandfather, Birmingham department store owner J.S. Smolian, bought the remote 80-acre property in 1946, his family considered his $100-an-acre investment foolish. Davis inherited the land in 1978, and in the early 1980s, the most expensive lots ran about $20,000. "Those lots today would probably sell for $220,000 to $250,000," Barker says.

One-bedroom penthouses sell for $255,000 to $358,000, and townhouses run from $695,000 to $1.6 million. Cottages start at about $542,000 for a one-bedroom house with room to add on and rise to about $2 million for a four-bedroom dwelling that overlooks the water. Most cottages have three bedrooms and run $700,000 to $850,000, says Barker.

"People buy here because there is a sense of community," Barker says. "A lot of the folks have been renting here and their families just love it. They get to know other families. The children can roam the streets here without the parents having to worry about it."

When they do put their properties up for sale, there's very little flexibility in the price. "Some have more than one property," Barker says. "Their attitude is, 'If I'm going to sell it, this is what the price is going to be.'"

While they may be trailblazers, the Temples find Seaside almost ideal for retirement living. The only drawbacks, Felton says, are that "it's a little hot in the summer and they don't have very extensive medical facilities yet."

The Temples find plenty to keep themselves occupied, even in the winter when there are only about 300 people in residence. Felton likes to read and do needlepoint. Carroll likes to paint. They both like to take long walks around the town and along the beach.

"We also like to try out the different restaurants," Felton says. "The facilities for eating seafood around here are wonderful." To others considering retiring in Seaside, she only has one piece of advice: "Just do it."●

Sequim, Washington

Retirees find homes with views on Washington's Olympic Peninsula

By Richard L. Fox

The 8,000-foot peaks of the Olympic Mountains and the picturesque Strait of Juan de Fuca captivate many first-time visitors to Sequim. Unlike some better-known towns in this part of Washington's Olympic Peninsula, Sequim (pronounced "Skwim") is defined not so much by man-made structures as by its location, topography and congenial residents.

At the northern edge of the peninsula, the town of Sequim is clean and open, unpretentious and uncluttered. No tall buildings mar its skyline. It does not have a defined downtown; rather, shops, restaurants and motels are strung along a two-mile stretch of U.S. Highway 101 (called Washington Street in town), interspersed with art galleries, antique stores and gift shops. Among the shoppers and browsers are tourists who discover that Sequim's main street is the only available route to destinations farther out on the peninsula — a boon for shopkeepers but a matter of some concern for local drivers during peak season.

Byron and Barbara Nelson moved to Sequim in 1995 from Covina, CA, their home for 22 years. Going from the urban environment of Southern California to the peaceful surroundings of Sequim was a big change, according to Byron, a former police chief in Azusa, CA. "I don't hear sirens. I don't hear traffic noise. I don't see smog. I don't hear gunshots. Your home is safe. You can walk downtown any time of day or night without fear," he says.

Barbara, 56, was taken by the "fresh air, outstanding scenery, a slower pace, serenity and friendly people." For the Nelsons, the area's natural beauty is without parallel. "After retirement we took a six-week, 10,000-mile camping tour of the United States. New England (and) the East

Coast were beautiful in the fall, (but) when it was over, we agreed there was not a prettier place in the United States than where we were going to live," says Byron, 57.

The growing community boasts an active cadre of volunteers. The Retired Senior Volunteer Program advertises for grade-school tutors, aides for the courthouse information desk, senior center assistants and naturalists for the Dungeness Spit, the world's largest natural sand hook. Volunteers also staff the New Dungeness Lighthouse, a historic structure that has guided ships through the Strait of Juan de Fuca since 1857.

More than 160 organizations enlist the help of retirees such as Bryce and Gail Fish, both 56, who moved to Sequim from Madison, WI, in 1990.

Bryce and Gail knew the area before retirement, having lived near Seattle for three years during the 1960s. They visited several times, and after selling their lumber business, moved here permanently.

With longtime friends not far away in Bellevue, the Fishes settled quickly into their new community. Bryce serves on the boards of several clubs and service organizations, including the Citizens Advisory Committee for Schools and the Boys and Girls Club. Gail, a retired registered nurse, is a volunteer and well-loved fixture at the visitor center.

Most Sequim residents travel to Seattle for big-city shopping, dining and entertainment. Although the trip takes two to three hours, getting there can be infinitely more rewarding than an ordinary excursion to the mall. The quickest, most popular route starts with a slow-paced drive through small villages and thick virgin forests to Bainbridge Island, followed by a 30-minute ferry ride to Seattle.

The most scenic way to return home is to drive south to Olympia on Inter-

state 5, then north along Hwy. 101 between Olympic National Forest (keeping watch for deer and elk) and the Hood Canal (where you might spot a U.S. Trident submarine or aircraft carrier) and finally past Sequim Bay (where gray whales sometimes stray off-course during their Pacific coast migration).

Five airports offer daily flights out of the north Olympic Peninsula; those at Port Angeles and Port Townsend connect with Seattle-Tacoma International Airport (SeaTac) and several Canadian destinations, including Victoria and Vancouver in British Columbia.

"We enjoy going into Seattle," says Agnes Bell, 69, who moved with her husband, Bob, from Hamburg, NJ, in 1989. Before their move, "going into town" meant going into New York City. "We didn't want to do that anymore," says Bob, 70.

Bob and Agnes exchanged the hill country of western New Jersey for the hilly Sequim prairie and found that much of the environment looked comfortingly familiar. "One of our sons came out to visit us after we moved and said, 'I know why you're here. You're still living in Sussex County, NJ'," jokes Bob, a former postmaster.

"New Jersey is the home of my birth," adds Agnes, a retired executive secretary. "I lived there most of my life, but I must say I feel just as much at home here as I ever did there.

"I appreciate the weather here more because the highs and lows aren't as extreme," she continues. "I don't miss the ice and snow at all. I don't miss the mosquitoes, or the hot, hot summers with high humidity. We don't have that here."

Sequim's dry, sunny weather is an appreciated anomaly in the region. Thanks to the Olympic Mountains, which block rain clouds as they pass over the peninsula, Sequim tallies considerably more sunshine and less rain than towns just a few miles away. While Sequim averages 16 inches of rain a year, neighboring Port Angeles counts up to 25 inches, Seattle records around 30 inches, and the rain forests 60 miles west are deluged with more than 200 inches.

The low annual rainfall can be a two-edged sword — nice and dry for golfing, hiking and horseback-riding, but woefully short for meeting water supply and agricultural needs.

In 1895, the residents of Sequim and surrounding Dungeness Valley built flumes and irrigation ditches to bring water from the Dungeness River to the parched prairie surrounding it. Today more than 100 miles of irrigation ditches water the valley's farms and pastures, bringing agricultural prosperity (and a large herd of elk) to the area. The Sequim Irrigation Festival, which recently marked its 105th anniversary, is the town's biggest celebration and Washington's oldest continuing festival.

Housing options are plentiful, in locales from the shores of the Strait of Juan de Fuca to the southern hills. Choices include manufactured-home parks, established single-family neighborhoods, townhomes and condominiums, three-acre estates and five-acre minifarms.

Prices range from $39,500 for a double-wide manufactured home to $400,000 for a home on a large lot with a great view of the mountains or the strait. A two-bedroom condo may go for $66,500, a three-bedroom townhouse for $189,500, and a large custom home on a golf course for $225,000.

One-acre lots with views of the mountains or water start at more than $20,000. Water-view lots at Diamond Point by the bay are priced from $34,900 to $59,500, and lots on the strait start at $79,000.

At Bell Hill, just south of Sequim, lots start at $50,000. It's a popular place for retirees to settle, offering views of the strait with its parading tall ships, military and commercial vessels and occasionally the distant lights of Victoria twinkling across the water. Most of the time Bell Hill affords a bird's-eye view of downtown Sequim, surrounding res-

Sequim, WA

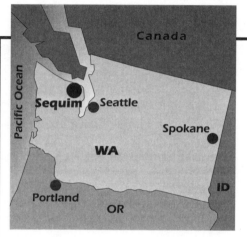

Population: 4,200 in Sequim, 26,000 in Dungeness Valley.

Location: In western Washington state, nestled between the Olympic Mountains and the Strait of Juan de Fuca on the north coast of the Olympic Peninsula. Elevation is 180 feet.

Climate:

	High	Low
January	46	32
July	71	52

Average relative humidity: 77%

Rain: 16 inches.

The area boasts 300 sunny days a year and moderate temperatures.

Cost of living: Above average (specific index not available).

Average housing cost: $139,500

Sales tax: 7.9%

Sales tax exemptions: Prescription drugs, groceries and medical services.

State income tax: None.

Intangibles tax: None.

Estate tax: None, except the state's "pick-up" portion of the federal tax, applicable to taxable estates above $675,000.

Property tax: In Sequim, $11.01 ($9.87-$10.86 in unincorporated Clallam County) per $1,000 of assessed value, with homes assessed at 100% of market value. Tax on a $139,500 home in Sequim is $1,536.

Homestead exemption: Homeowners age 61 or older, with a gross household income of $28,000 or less, are eligible for certain property tax exemptions.

Security: 60.8 crimes per 1,000 residents, higher than the national average of 46.2 crimes per 1,000 residents.

Religion: Twenty-one Protestant and two Catholic churches serve the Sequim-Dungeness Valley area.

Education: Peninsula College in Port Angeles is part of the state community college system. It offers associate degrees, Elderhostel, continuing education and public service programs. Senior citizens can choose from a variety of courses at reduced fees.

Transportation: Clallam County Transit Authority offers bus service between Olympic Peninsula towns. Ferry service provides access to Victoria, Whidbey Island, the San Juan Islands and Seattle. Fairchild Airport in Port Angeles (25 miles) and Jefferson County International Airport in Port Townsend (22 miles) provide daily connections with SeaTac International Airport south of Seattle.

Health: Olympic Medical Center, 17 miles west in Port Angeles, is a 126-bed, full-service facility with 24-hour emergency service. Seventy-seven physicians practice 20 medical specialties, with additional specialists from Seattle making regular local office visits.

Housing options: A wide variety of housing is available. Double-wide manufactured homes in adults-only parks are listed for $39,500-$84,000. One- and two-bedroom condos with clubhouse privileges are $66,500-$99,900. New three-bedroom townhomes with two-car garages on a golf course are priced at $189,500. Three-bedroom, two-bath custom homes in new developments start at $150,000. The 2,000-square-foot custom homes in Sunlands Country Club are priced from $225,000 and up. On Bell Hill, three-bedroom, two-bath homes on one or two acres go for $225,000-$400,000.

Visitor lodging: Best Western Sequim Bay Lodge, $79, (360) 683-0691. Ramada Limited Sequim, $79, (800) 683-1775.

Information: Sequim-Dungeness Valley Chamber of Commerce, P.O. Box 907, Sequim, WA 98382, (360) 683-6197 or www.cityofsequim.com.

idential neighborhoods, golf courses, parks, marinas and the waterfront Dungeness Recreation Area and Dungeness Spit.

Some residents warn that Bell Hill often is cloaked in clouds during winter months when dense fog settles in the higher elevations. As the day heats up, the clouds usually dissipate, but some newcomers have been known to move after one winter on Bell Hill.

Byron and Barbara Nelson built their home in Happy Valley, a rural area on the back side of Bell Hill that boasts views of the strait, valley, mountains and Vancouver Island. "At night you can see the lights of ships on the strait from our house," says Barbara. With a stable and pasture on five acres of land, the Nelsons have plenty of room to accommodate their horses and indulge their favorite recreational activity — riding.

Happy Valley provided the first proof that man hunted the mastodon in North America 12,000 to 14,000 years ago. Artifacts and fossils from the area are on display at the Museum and Arts Center, lending credence to theories that hunters chased the animals across land bridges over the Bering Strait.

Bob and Agnes Bell found a house in the early stages of construction in the Sunlands Country Club and Golf Course development and bought it before completion. "I love the view, the snow on top of the mountains. Every time I go out, I see a different view," says Agnes. "It's never the same."

Gail and Bryce Fish bought what Bryce calls a "country rambler in need of some TLC, with 20 acres of land." Located four miles west of Sequim between Highway 101 and the water, the home has an unobstructed view of the Olympic Mountains.

Bryce and Gail love hiking in the Olympic Mountains and sailing the waters of Sequim Bay and the strait, the latter a carry-over from their days in Wisconsin when they sailed the Great Lakes. There is snow skiing within a four-hour drive.

With some 300 sunny days and temperatures rarely above the low 80s, being outdoors is a way of life for most residents. Boating, bicycling, fishing and golfing are among the traditionally popular activities, but the uniqueness of Dungeness Spit makes it a popular site for hiking, bird-watching, beachcombing and crabbing. The bay formed by the spit is famous as the home of the Dungeness crab.

There are trails for horseback riding in parts of the Dungeness National Wildlife Refuge and Dungeness Spit. The spit is about five miles long and accessible only by foot; at low tide, hardy hikers like to make the 10-mile round-trip walk to New Dungeness Lighthouse at the end of the spit.

Agnes Bell is one of the inveterate walkers seen in the area on a regular basis. "It's only a mile from our house to the strait, and I walk it every day."

Agnes also is a member of MEOW (Machine Embroiderers of Oregon and Washington) and spends time with the group traveling and sewing. She also describes herself as a cyberspace granny. "I e-mail my grandchildren regularly," she says.

The nearest hospital is 126-bed Olympic Memorial, 17 miles west in Port Angeles. Sequim Medical Plaza has a medical staff practicing 22 specialties as well as facilities for surgery, radiology, laboratory technology, physical therapy and nutrition counseling.

Agnes credits the area's medical care as partly influencing their decision to move to Sequim. "We knew that as we got older we would need good medical attention," she says. "The very best doctors in Seattle come over to the medical center and see patients on a regular basis."

Bob goes to cardiac rehabilitation three times a week, and both he and Agnes use the facilities at the Sequim Aquatic Recreation Center to stay fit.

Bryce Fish has some advice for anyone considering a retirement move to Sequim. "You need to be financially secure since there aren't many jobs here to supplement income. You need to be able to entertain yourself. This is a natural environment that doesn't offer a lot of planned activities."

Says Gail Fish, "If you're planning on eating every meal out, don't come. There are some good restaurants, but not many." Shopping facilities also are modest by Madison standards, though Gail feels they're adequate.

"There are times when you need something that's not available, and you have to go to a larger city to find it," says Byron Nelson.

Bob Bell, mindful of the town's escalating growth rate, says with a mirthful smile, "Everyone should have as nice a retirement as we're having. But do it somewhere else!"●

Sierra Vista, Arizona

Arizona town has military ties and an affinity with nature

By Judy Wade

Sierra Vista defies the image of most Southern Arizona towns, owing its existence neither to mining nor cattle ranching. Rather, it grew up around the U.S. Army's Fort Huachuca, established in 1877 as a cavalry post to safeguard settlers.

Sierra Vista developed initially as a place to live for those supplying support services to the Army. Now there are about 11,700 military and civilian employees at the fort, with another 11,200 military family members living in town. Military retirees are attracted to Sierra Vista because of base privileges and medical facilities there.

The city's low cost of living and hometown personality have made Sierra Vista popular with other retirees as well. Its senior population increased by more than 200 percent during the last decade, and about a quarter of the city's residents consider themselves retired.

Chamber of commerce marketing efforts picture a happy couple with salt-and-pepper hair that have escaped to "the nicest little town under the sun." Yet big-city shopping and culture is readily accessible in Tucson, 70 miles to the northwest.

For Frank and Sally Solano, 65 and 68 respectively, moving to Sierra Vista was a homecoming of sorts. They retired to Sierra Vista from Cleveland, where Frank worked with the National Aeronautics and Space Administration and Sally was a homemaker. "Frank, who went to high school in nearby Douglas, AZ, worked as a student at Fort Huachuca in 1959," says Sally. "Sierra Vista wasn't even a town then. But he remembered the clean air, pristine atmosphere and lovely four-season climate. When we came back, we were shocked to see this little town here."

The Solanos live in an area of custom homes on large, open lots where deer, antelope, coyotes and quail roam freely. Sally says wild turkeys sometimes come in from the canyons south of town. "We can see mountain peaks in Mexico from here. In the Huachucas, we can see snow on Miller Peak, which is about 9,600 feet high, until Mother's Day," she says.

Situated on the eastern slope of the Huachuca Mountains overlooking the San Pedro River Valley, Sierra Vista's name means "mountain view" in Spanish. It is surrounded by the Mule, Dragoon and Whetstone mountains. Reliably good weather averages 75 degrees in summer and 50 degrees in winter.

The town itself, population 39,995, is low-key but with a sophistication created by relatively high income and educational levels among its residents.

The Sierra Vista Symphony performs regularly, and an annual concert series features nationally known artists. A Wednesday evening summer series at Veterans Memorial Park includes blues, jazz, pop and rock ensembles.

More than 75 restaurants create an eclectic dining-out scene. Residents have kiddingly dubbed Fry Boulevard, the town's main street, "French Fry Boulevard" because of the number of fast-food outlets strung along its length. But they are complemented by such restaurants as Ricardo's, which serves Mexican food, and the Mesquite Tree, with patio views of the Huachucas. Fine dining is offered at The Grille at Pueblo del Sol Country Club, where gourmet fare is presented in the evening and breakfast and lunch features inventive, well-priced menus.

Jan and Bob Cole, 56 and 68 respectively, moved from Phoenix where Bob owned a business-forms company. "We hardly feel retired because we volunteer with the Red Cross doing disaster relief all over the state and also with the chamber of commerce," says Jan. "It really keeps us busy."

Originally they bought property in Sedona, north of Phoenix, but discovered that the traffic and fast-paced lifestyle weren't what they wanted. "Everyone thinks about going north. They don't realize we're at more than 4,000 feet here, which creates a wonderful four-season climate," says Bob. Both say they like Sierra Vista's open spaces, mountain views and especially the supportive small-town ambiance.

Winterhaven is Sierra Vista's only master-planned, age-restricted (55 plus) community of single-family homes. Located within Country Club Estates, an existing golf-course community, Winterhaven has single-story homes bordering the mature, 25-year-old course and along winding streets. An RV park with hookups and storage will be completed at the edge of the property early this year.

Bob Strain, 64, a widower, lived in Sierra Vista for 10 years before he chose a Winterhaven home. "I trusted the alliance of the developers, Castle & Cooke, who are working with KE&G Homes, a local builder. And the opportunities for appreciation look good," he says. He chose an 1,831-square-foot floor plan with 10-foot ceilings, walk-in closets, two bedrooms and a den. Other plans with two to four bedrooms also are offered.

Even though he doesn't play golf, proximity to a course helped influence Strain. "It's kind of like being in the paratroops. You don't really like to jump out of airplanes but you like to hang out with people who do," he smiles. "And the golf community is a part of the ambiance that makes quality of life that much nicer."

Keith and Linda Howver, ages 63 and 50, lived in Mesa, AZ, before building their cul-de-sac home in Winterhaven. "We wanted to move someplace cooler, and we wanted more of a small town. At our age we like being in a retirement area, yet across the road there are all different ages," says Linda.

"Our lot has mountain views that will never be blocked," she says. The Howvers chose a floor plan and customized it, adding a fireplace to the master bedroom and bath, opting for ceramic tile rather than carpeting throughout.

The market for resale homes is booming, according to Jeanne Milczarek, a real-estate agent with Coldwell Banker. "Our average single-family-home listing is about $102,000," she says. "Condos run the gamut from $42,000 to well over $100,000, with manufactured homes and lots, depending on location, averaging $75,000 to $80,000."

Mack McCabe, a real-estate agent with Sierra Vista Realty, says that for the past 18 months the local multiple listing service reports a total of 1,236 sales of condominiums and single-family and manufactured homes with $90,150 the median sales price and $98,157 the average. "By far the greatest number are single-family homes. Our market is definitely in a good place right now, with prices sliding upward," he says.

But retiree Bobbie Snyder, 70, who moved to Sierra Vista with husband Joseph in 1983, is not so sure she likes the growth pattern that she sees. "In the 14 years we've lived here, our taxes have more than doubled. The new $25 million high school is not even paid for yet," she says, adding that their original property taxes were only about $400 per year.

The new Buena High School to which she refers was funded by a bond issue that passed by an overwhelming majority of voters. It accommodates 2,500 students and is the home of the Buena Performing Arts Center, the venue for community presentations that attract regional

Sierra Vista, AZ

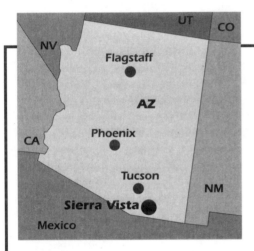

Population: 39,995 in Sierra Vista, 123,750 in Cochise County.

Location: In southeast Arizona, 70 miles southeast of Tucson among the Dragoon, Mule and Whetstone mountains at an elevation of 4,623 feet.

Climate:

	High	Low
January	58	34
July	89	66

Average relative humidity: 32%.
Rain: 14.6 inches
More than half of Sierra Vista's rain falls in July and August when monsoon conditions are right. Dustings of snow in December and January rarely last longer than half a day.

Cost of living: 99.3, based on national average of 100.

Housing cost: $90,150 median, $98,157 average.

Sales tax: 7%

Sales tax exemptions: Groceries, prescription medicines.

State income tax: Graduated in five steps from 2.9% to 5.17%, depending on income.

Income tax exemptions: Social Security and up to $2,500 of federal, state and local government pensions are exempt.

Intangibles tax: None.

Estate tax: None, except the state's "pick-up" portion of the federal tax, applicable to taxable estates above $675,000.

Property tax: $126.20 per $1,000 of assessed value, with homes assessed at 10% of market value. Annual taxes on a $100,000 home are about $1,262.

Homestead exemption: None.

Security: 41.6 crimes per 1,000 residents, lower than the national average of 46.2 crimes per 1,000 residents.

Religion: More than 30 churches and places of worship represent about 20 denominations.

Education: College-level courses are offered at the University of Arizona's Sierra Vista campus. Cochise Community College, Chapman College and Golden Gate University offer courses in a variety of fields.

Transportation: Sierra Vista Public Transit System has a 50-cent senior fare anywhere in the city. Scheduled bus service goes to Tucson, and America West Express, operated by Mesa Airlines, flies to Phoenix for connections to world destinations.

Health: Recently updated Sierra Vista Community Hospital has 24-hour emergency care and a complete range of facilities. Hacienda Rehabilitation and Care Center offers physical, occupational, speech and respiratory therapy as well as Alzheimer's care. Fort Huachuca also has a hospital.

Housing options: Winterhaven, (800) 837-6841, a Castle & Cooke development, is the city's only master-planned, age-restricted, active-adult community. Homes range from $103,990 to $172,990 including lot. Custom homes begin at $159,990 not including lot. Resale manufactured homes at **Sierra Vista Mobile Home Village,** (520) 459-1690, are $42,000-$75,000 with a $225 per month assessment that includes garbage pick-up, water, cable television and recreation center facilities. Apartment rentals at **The Oasis,** (520) 458-8321, begin at $370 per month for an unfurnished one-bedroom apartment, $599 for two bedrooms and two baths.

Visitor lodging: Best Western Mission Inn, $69, double occupancy, with senior discount and continental breakfast, (800) 528-1234. Ramsey Canyon Inn, $110-$132, (520) 378-3010. For prospective buyers, Winterhaven offers three days and two nights in an on-site home for $139, double occupancy, (800) 837-6841.

Information: Sierra Vista Chamber of Commerce, 21 E. Wilcox Drive, Sierra Vista, AZ 85635, (800) 288-3861, (520) 458-6940 or www.sierravistachamber.org.

audiences. Recent hot tickets have included the Count Basie Orchestra, the Kingston Trio, Ink Spots and the Lettermen. Other series feature classical performers. The center has wheelchair access for guests and facilities for the hearing-impaired.

"Education Row," of which the high school is a part, also includes a branch of the University of Arizona where seniors can take courses at no charge on a space-available basis. Cochise College offers two-year degree programs. Elderhostel opportunities include birding, hiking and bicycling trips.

The Oscar Yrun Community Center has an extensive senior program that includes noon lunch for a nominal fee. Monthly Dine-A-Nites allow older residents to try a variety of local restaurants. Recent bus outings have included Tucson's Gaslight Theater, an excursion on the San Pedro train through the National Riparian Conservation Area, a four-day trip to Mexico and a weeklong Branson, MO, sojourn. A new 31,000-square-foot public library opened next to City Hall in spring of 1999.

Sally Solano particularly likes Sierra Vista's proximity to Ramsey Canyon, a Nature Conservancy preserve at the hub of one of the country's finest birding areas. The 300-acre arroyo is a unique biological crossroads where more than a dozen species of hummingbirds gather from spring until early autumn.

The annual four-day Southwest Wings Birding Festival held in August attracts birders from all over the world and includes field trips, workshops, history and archaeology tours

and other programs. It is so popular that field trips fill up two months in advance and local hotels are completely booked.

The town's age diversity is a valued community asset, according to chamber of commerce representatives, who say that some retirees are practically "professional volunteers." The community relies heavily on the senior population to work with elementary-school children in reading and enrichment programs and with local youth clubs. A mediation and arbitration group sponsored by the county superior court includes close to 100 certified mediators and arbitrators, many of whom are retirees.

Former Iowa resident Roberta Dillig, 79, volunteers as the choreographer for the Rickety Rockettes, a dance group made up of women ages 58 to 86 who perform locally and in nearby cities. She recently competed in the Miss Senior Arizona Pageant where she exhibited her tap-dancing talent. "I was second runner-up. The two who beat me were only 62," she laughs.

The Sierra Vista Community Hospital recently has been renovated, adding new equipment and services that include a helicopter landing pad, a 51-bed medical/surgical department, intensive care and telemetry unit and 24-hour emergency department. Many seniors volunteer with the hospital auxiliary. A second hospital is located at Fort Huachuca.

City government, a manager/mayor system with six council members, keeps a close eye on situations affecting this high desert community, such

as the water supply, which is an ongoing issue. Sierra Vista sits on its own aquifer that is recharged twice a year, once by snow melt and once by a summer monsoon during which rainfall can total almost 14 inches. Some claim the aquifer has remained at approximately the same level over the last century, a contention vehemently denied by others.

"There is plenty of water for the city's growth," says Sierra Vista Herald managing editor John Moeur, "as long as it is a maintained and reasonable growth. What effect that will have on the San Pedro River, which is a key riparian habitat, is under debate, and no one has a lot of great answers."

The Herald, a daily newspaper, is an excellent source of information regarding annexations, city council proceedings, Fort Huachuca information and club meetings that include Rotary, Kiwanis, Veterans of Foreign Wars, Elks and bridge and chess clubs.

If there is a flaw in Sierra Vista, it may be that it does not yet have a major upscale department store. Target, Wal-Mart and J.C. Penney are there, but residents say they're waiting for a large mall with Dillard's or Robinson's/May. "And maybe a cafeteria," adds Roberta Dillig.

But a projected population of 50,000 may be as big as Sierra Vista ever gets, simply because it is bordered on two sides by Fort Huachuca, on another side by the San Pedro Riparian Area preserve, and on another by the Huachuca Mountains. There isn't a lot of space in which to expand.

And many residents like it that way.●

Siesta Key, Florida

It's a slow, casual lifestyle on Florida Gulf Coast island

By Karen Feldman

If ever there were a town whose name perfectly suited its nature, it's Siesta Key. Laid-back, casual and short on pretension, the barrier island community prides itself on its soothing pace.

Its beach extends the entire 8-mile length of the island, much of it a broad expanse of what's been voted the finest, whitest sand in the world. It, too, beckons visitors to settle in and chill out.

The island just southwest of the city of Sarasota is home to 12,000 residents year-round and twice that many in the winter. They are joined by some 350,000 tourists a year.

It's not uncommon for visitors to become residents.

"A lot of people stay for the winter season and buy a place before they leave," says Jean Kelly, a real estate associate with RE/MAX on the key and a Siesta Key resident for 43 years.

Diane Spencer, former executive director of the Siesta Key Chamber of Commerce, says that while some area communities tend toward formality, "Siesta Key is laid-back. The people are more free-spirited. We have a lot of independent thinkers, a lot of artists and musicians. These are people who have lived elsewhere, suffered the slings and arrows of life and ended up here."

For some, Siesta Key is their choice after considering a number of possibilities. For others, it's an annual vacation destination that eventually becomes a retirement home.

Bob and June Wood vacationed on Siesta Key for 23 years. Nine years ago, they left Lincoln, MA, and bought a gulf-front condo on the key.

"We had been coming for so long, it was like a second home," says June, 70. "We felt very comfortable here."

They had considered Honolulu and Southern California, but "kind of backed into the choice" of Siesta Key, says Bob,

70, who was with Polaroid. "We decided we couldn't afford to live in California and the distance from our family was too great in Honolulu."

Siesta Key was the only place that Jerry and Kathy Groom considered retiring. Jerry, 65, and Kathy, 60, had been fleeing to the island to escape the brutal Illinois winters for about five years before moving to their Siesta Key condo.

They enjoy the island lifestyle. "It's casual," says Jerry, who was with Levi Strauss. "It has a small-town atmosphere. We have the best of two worlds: Sarasota and Siesta Key."

Groom, recently inducted into the College Football Hall of Fame for his career as a Notre Dame center and linebacker, still works at keeping his 6-foot-4-inch frame in shape. He walks on the beach, swims and regularly exercises Murphy, the couple's 4-year-old Lhasa apso.

They scaled down from a four-bedroom home to a two-bedroom condo. Their sixth-floor unit has a broad view of the Gulf of Mexico and the public beach on the other side of Midnight Pass Road, one of the island's main thoroughfares.

"It's easy to travel out of a condo," says Jerry. "You just shut it up and go."

Don and Jan Metzler searched a 100-mile swath of the Florida Gulf Coast before relocating to Siesta Key from Utica, MI.

They liked Bonita Springs, a waterfront community south of Fort Myers, but opted for Siesta Key "because of the arts and culture," says Jan, 55, a professional artist. "Any day of the week, you can go to a show or art event."

The Metzlers bought a 3,000-square-foot home on a canal in a secluded neighborhood and spent a lot of time renovating it. Canals — some 50 miles of them — meander through the island community and lead to the Intracoastal Waterway, Sarasota Bay

and the Gulf of Mexico.

Waterways and their accompanying beaches may draw people to Siesta Key, but what clinches it for many visitors is the wealth of culture available in Sarasota, just east of Siesta Key.

Circus magnate John Ringling built his own bayfront estate at Sarasota in the mid-1920s and invested heavily in the area. His home, Ca'd'Zan (Venetian dialect for House of John), the Italian Renaissance Ringling Museum of Art, the 18th-century Asolo Theater and a circus gallery are run by the state and are among the city's top tourist attractions.

A bigger Asolo Center for the Performing Arts, a $10 million playhouse, houses an official state theatrical troupe and is also on the 38-acre Ringling estate. It presents a variety of plays throughout the year.

Nearby is the Van Wezel Performing Arts Hall, a lavender scallop-shaped landmark designed by Frank Lloyd Wright, which attracts nationally known artists and local productions with its high-quality acoustics.

The city also has its own ballet company, opera company and symphony. The downtown is chock-full of art galleries, restaurants and boutiques, which draw lots of shoppers during the winter season. So, too, does nearby St. Armands Key, which features a large circle of upscale shops and restaurants.

The Marie Selby Botanical Gardens, on the Sarasota bayfront just east of St. Armands Key, sprawls over 14 acres of lush property. It specializes in ecological preservation, has a world-class collection of orchids and other bromeliads, a museum of botany and arts, lots of plant sales, classes and special events.

Mote Marine Laboratory, just north of St. Armands, has tanks displaying plants and animals native to the bay and gulf, a 135,000-gallon outdoor shark tank and a 30-foot touch tank.

Among the region's best known annual events is the French Film Festival, which has drawn increasing national attention for the number of high-quality French films that make U.S. debuts there.

Siesta Key residents like knowing that culture is just a short drive away, but many also like not having to leave the island for much of anything else.

"You could really stay on the island if you wanted to," says Kathy Groom. "There are filling stations, banks, groceries, most of the places you need."

Most of these are clustered at the heart of the island in the shopping district, a busy center filled with restaurants, boutiques and T-shirt and tourist-ware emporiums.

There are tennis and volleyball courts and an exercise track at the public beach. People rollerblade and bicycle along the island's streets, and it's not unusual to see groups moving through graceful tai chi routines on the beach.

Diane Spencer likes to kayak in the gulf, renting equipment from a local shop. "The dolphins come up right beside me," she says. "I've been out several times and I'm a grandmother. It's wonderful."

Barrier islands always have been Florida's prime real estate. That's as true in Siesta Key as the rest of the

Siesta Key, FL

Population: 12,000 year-round, 24,000 in the winter.

Location: A barrier island on the Gulf of Mexico along the southwest Florida coast a few miles southwest of Sarasota.

Climate:

	High	Low
January	72	51
July	92	75

Average relative humidity: 70%
Rain: 47 inches.
Subtropical climate is hot and humid May through October, temperate and drier November through April with short-lived freezes possible. Hurricane season is June 1 to Nov. 30; most severe storms usually occur in September and October. Siesta Key is vulnerable to hurricanes, particularly in the Gulf of Mexico, but has not experienced damage recently.

Cost of living: 102.9 in Sarasota County, based on state average of 100.
Median housing cost: $400,000 for homes; condos about $350,000.
Sales tax: 7%
Sales tax exemptions: Medical services, prescription drugs, groceries.
State income tax: None.
Intangibles tax: Assessed on stocks, bonds and other specific assets. Tax rate is $1 per $1,000 value for assets under $100,000 for individuals or $200,000 for couples, and $1.50 per $1,000 value for greater amounts; first $20,000 for individuals and $40,000 for couples is exempt. Some investments are exempt.

Estate tax: None, except the state's "pick-up" portion of the federal tax, applicable to taxable estates above $675,000.

Property tax: Rate is $14.43 per $1,000 of assessed value, with homes assessed at 100% of market value. The yearly tax on a $300,000 home with $25,000 homestead exemption is about $3,968.

Homestead exemption: First $25,000 of assessed value of primary, permanent residence.

Security: 45.3 crimes per 1,000 residents in Sarasota County, lower than the national average of 46.2 crimes per 1,000 residents. Specific crime figures for Siesta Key are not available.

Religion: There are Episcopal, Catholic and Presbyterian churches on the island; all major religions and many smaller ones are represented in Sarasota.

Education: The University of South Florida offers those age 60 and older the opportunity to audit classes (no credit, no tests) without charge on a space-available basis.

Transportation: The Siesta Key Trolley runs the length of the island, making stops at many condos and restaurants; it also goes to downtown Sarasota. The Sarasota County Area Transit buses cover a similar route but with fewer stops. Sarasota-Bradenton International Airport is about 20 minutes away.

Health: There are no hospitals on Siesta Key, but next-door-neighbor Sarasota offers extensive medical services. Sarasota Memorial Hospital is a 952-bed, not-for-profit hospital with a full range of medical care. Its Senior-Care program has 16,000 members 50 years and older who receive health education, access to a senior care adviser, assistance completing health claims, discounts and physician referrals. Doctors Hospital, a private facility offering many services, moved into a new 168-bed complex including a medical office near the access route to Siesta Key. The hospital participates in the national Senior Friend program, offering discounts and special programs for a $15 annual fee.

Housing options: Condominiums and single-family homes are available, many of which have views of the gulf or bay. One-bedroom condos start at about $200,000 on the bay side and at about $400,000 on the gulf side. Houses start at $250,000 and top out at $5 million.

Visitor lodging: Best Western Siesta Beach Resort, (800) 223-5786, has rates starting at $141 from mid-December through mid-April and $78 the rest of the time. Many condo and apartment complexes rent units on a weekly or monthly basis. Contact the chamber of commerce or RE/MAX on the Key, (800) 486-4557, for information.

Information: The Siesta Key Chamber of Commerce, 5100 Ocean Blvd., Unit B, Siesta Key, FL 34242, (941) 349-3800 or www.siestakeychamber.com.

state. While properties cost more than in many mainland communities, many people find them affordable when compared to their previous residences, particularly in Northern states.

Jerry Groom is still kicking himself for not buying the condo next door when he could have snapped it up for $45,000 several years ago. Units in the small complex sell for about five times that now, and there's a waiting list of interested buyers.

The island's real estate market differs from much of the state because vacant land is scarce. In some cases, the land is worth more than the structure standing on it; as a result, some buyers are tearing down existing structures to build new homes.

Property values are on the rise all over the island. For instance, the Metzlers estimate that their canal-front home has doubled in value since they bought it seven years ago.

Houses on the Intracoastal Waterway start at about $400,000. In the Sandaling Club, a gated community of single-family homes, there's a $5 million house and maybe a few for as little as $400,000. Many run about $1 million or $2 million.

On the bay side of the island, one-bedroom condos start at about $200,000, with larger units running as much as $600,000. On the gulf, a one-bedroom condo is likely to run from $400,000 to $1 million.

But you can pay substantially less, as the Grooms did, by buying on the other side of the street from the waterfront. They've still got a prime view of the water, but at about half the price.

As a comparison, you can go just across the bridge to the mainland and get a one-bedroom condo for $75,000 at Casa del Mar, from which you can walk across the bridge to the beach.

Realtor Jean Kelly says the average age of a Siesta Key condo is about 17 years, but that virtually all of them are well-kept. She also says her agency has fewer condo listings now than it's ever had. "People are holding on to them because prices are going up," she says.

Many people buy condos and rent them out during the winter season. With only one motor inn on the island, there's a big market for condo rentals, with about 6,000 units available on the key. The going rate for a well-appointed, two-bedroom condo on the beach is about $1,500 a week.

Many retirees, particularly those coming from the North, find the cost of living here is less. Don Metzler, 57, who was a college professor, says, "What we paid in taxes alone there (in Michigan) would pay all taxes, utilities and insurance here."

The Grooms say their cost of living is lower than it was in Illinois mainly because of moving from a large home into a 1,300-square-foot condo. Both avid golfers, the Grooms found they could join two golf clubs in Sarasota for what it cost them to join one up north.

The retirees find little fault with the area.

"Even the rain isn't bad," Jerry says. "At least you don't have to shovel it."

Most residents do voice one complaint, though: During the winter season, traffic on the island's two main thoroughfares is painfully slow and congested.

But that, too, depends on your perspective.

"You do have to allow extra time to get most places in the winter," Kathy Groom says. "It's bad, but it's not as bad as Chicago."

And what's the rush? After all, this is Siesta Key.●

Thomasville, Georgia

An idyllic town draws retirees to the red hills of southern Georgia

By Mary Lu Abbott

Spring days are heady experiences around the Georgia town of Thomasville. A morning mist caresses rolling meadows and old moss-laden live oak and magnolia trees shading gracious plantations, most of which still are privately owned and enjoyed as leisure retreats. Fuchsia, scarlet and white azaleas and dogwood blossoms give way to roses perfuming the air in preparation for the town's annual rose show, celebrated since 1921.

Colorfully painted Victorian storefronts house several dozen shops and restaurants facing brick-paved streets downtown, where parking is free and only steps from the stores. A cool breeze snaps U.S. flags and bright banners along Broad Street that proclaim Thomasville a Great American Main Street award-winning town, one of five recognized last year for exceptional achievement in revitalization programs.

Ralph Fort recalls one spring when he and his wife came from Little Rock, AR, to visit their daughter in Thomasville. "We thought this had to be the prettiest town in the U.S.A. We thought it would be great to retire here," says Ralph. And, they did relocate here.

Norman and Ruth Smith were searching for an alternative retirement spot from their home in Leesburg, FL, when they visited Thomasville. "I walked down Main Street and thought to myself, 'Boy, this is beautiful,'" says Ruth. They decided to build a home here.

Hollywood couldn't dream up a more idyllic hometown than Thomasville. It is modern, yet exudes a lifestyle reminiscent of yesteryear. Residents go downtown to shop, eat and visit, greeting strangers as well as friends strolling along the sidewalk. While many downtown renovations have resulted in mainly tourist-oriented shops, Thomasville blends traditional and new businesses. Wander along Broad, Jackson, Madison and adjacent streets, and you will find children's, women's and men's clothing stores, shoe stores, jewelry shops, a lingerie boutique and a tailor, music and book shops, hardware, home furnishings and antique stores, a soda fountain and a drugstore, the latter in business since 1881. All are locally owned, not chains.

Adjacent to downtown are churches and neighborhoods with shaded sidewalks passing dozens of homes that date from antebellum through Victorian eras, most of them still occupied and lovingly preserved. Only a block off Broad Street, branches of a giant sprawling oak tree extend so far over the street that signs warn of low clearance. The oak is more than 300 years old.

"Thomasville has something special about it — its own personality. It's real Southern but yet very progressive — sometimes those two things don't go together," says Marjorie Fort, who was born in a nearby Florida town and retired to Thomasville from suburban Philadelphia.

Thomasville's size and location add to its appeal. It has about 20,000 residents, neither too small nor too large, and it's in a scenic pocket of pine forests known as the red hills, easily accessible yet removed from the fast-lane life. About 35 miles northeast of Tallahassee, FL, it is located on three not-too-busy U.S. highways, including a section of U.S. Highway 19 known as the Florida-Georgia Parkway. Still a farming center, it has one of the largest fresh produce markets in the state.

From its early days, Thomasville has been a prosperous community. Founded in 1826, it developed into an agricultural, commercial, social and political center, with cotton plantations fueling a major part of its growth. "There has always been money here," says Tom Hill, a Thomasville native and curator of the Thomas County Historical Society, which operates the Museum of History. He says the area attracted second sons of well-to-do families, the boys who would not inherit the home estate but were well-educated and had the backing to start businesses.

While the Civil War crippled the economy, Thomasville suffered far less than other Southern towns as it tapped a new industry: tourists. In the 1870s, wealthy Northerners were seeking resorts to escape for the winter and discovered Thomasville, a railroad terminus about 60 miles from the Gulf of Mexico. Its altitude of 273 feet kept it from being malaria-infested like much of Florida at the time, and the mild climate and pine-scented air had earned it a reputation as a health retreat.

Rather than turning their backs on the Northerners, local businessmen who had come through the war with some cash built large, blocklong hotels. Entire families arrived, often with servants, in late fall and stayed through spring. At the 400-foot-long Piney Woods Hotel, rooms were a princely sum of $4 a night with meals, but if you wanted a private bath, the rate jumped to $11. Among the names on the register: Mr. and Mrs. Cornelius Vanderbilt. Called "the best winter resort on three continents" by Harper's Bazaar in 1887, the town once boasted as many as 15 hotels and 25 boarding houses.

Many visitors liked the area so much that they built "winter cottages" in town or bought plantations or land at bargain prices where they established grand hunting estates. A staff of servants tended to the home, grounds, dogs and horses year-round, and the owners came seasonally, from November to March to hunt duck and quail, socialize and later play golf when a private course opened in 1896. Now part of the Glen Arven Country Club, it's one of the oldest continuously played private courses in the South.

With the taming of malaria, Florida began to siphon the tourist flow after the turn of the century, causing the demise of the Thomasville hotels, but many who had built homes here continued to come "for the season," and their descendants still do today. Within a 35-mile, three-county area stretching southward, there are 71 plantations covering about 300,000 acres, most of them originating in the antebellum period.

Hill says the plantations are unusual in several respects, including that so many still exist. Noting that most surviving plantations elsewhere have become tour homes and museums because residents could no longer afford their upkeep, Hill says owners still live in most of these plantations, coming to

enjoy "fox hunting, tea at four and dressing for dinner" during the winter.

Today's tourists can glimpse into the lifestyle of the rich and famous here at Pebble Hill Plantation, a 3,000-acre complex with everything from stables and kennels to a dog hospital, log-cabin school and main house with 43 rooms and 26 baths. It was donated by its

owners to be open to the public.

Established in the 1820s by an early settler, it was purchased in 1896 by the prominent Hanna family, industrialists in Cleveland, OH, and expanded into a renowned sporting retreat for hunting and polo. In the 1920s, the owners spent $1 million on a new dairy and stables complex,

Thomasville, GA

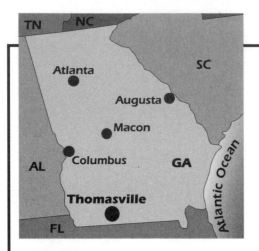

Population: 20,000. Thomasville is the largest community in Thomas County.

Location: In the southern red hills of Georgia, Thomasville is about 45 miles west of I-75 and Valdosta, GA, and about 35 miles northeast of Tallahassee, FL, and I-10. It's on U.S. highways 19, 319 and 84.

Climate:

	High	Low
January	63	39
July	92	71

Fall and winter are mild, spring brings a profusion of colorful blossoms, and summer is hot.

Average relative humidity: 50%

Rain: 52 inches.

Cost of living: Below average to average (specific index not available).

Average housing cost: $107,700 for a home, $400-$475 a month for a two-bedroom apartment.

Sales tax: 5%

Sales tax exemptions: Prescription drugs, medical services and some groceries.

State income tax: Graduated from 1% to 5% on first $7,000 (singles) or $10,000 (couples filing jointly), then 6% on greater amounts.

Income tax exemptions: Social Security benefits, and up to $13,000 in retirement income for those age 62 and older.

Intangibles tax: None

Estate tax: None, except the state's "pick-up" portion of the federal tax, applicable to taxable estates above $650,000.

Property tax: Thomasville residents pay a combined city-county rate of $28.07 per $1,000 valuation, with homes assessed at 40% of fair market value. Rates for county residents range from $16.10 to $19.70 per $1,000 in assessed value. Yearly taxes on a $107,700 home would be about $1,153 in town, $661-$809 in the county, including the $2,000 exemption noted below.

Homestead exemption: $2,000 off the 40% assessment value for permanent residents. Residents age 62 and older may qualify for further exemptions based on age and income.

Personal property tax: Same tax rates and assessment ratio apply to pleasure boats, but there's no $2,000 exemption.

Security: 96.8 crimes per 1,000 residents, higher than the national average of 46.2 crimes per 1,000 residents.

Religion: There are several dozen places of worship, including Jewish, Protestant and Catholic.

Education: Thomas College, with about 800 students, offers four-year degrees, continuing-education classes and special seniors programs.

Transportation: There's no public transportation system. The local airport serves private aircraft 24 hours a day. Commercial flights are available from Tallahassee, 35 miles southwest.

Health: The hub of a regional healthcare system of five hospitals and four nursing homes, the John D. Archbold Memorial Hospital in Thomasville has 264 beds and about 100 physicians in

35 specialties. Its extensive services include trauma, cancer, cardiac and rehabilitative care. The community has four nursing homes.

Housing options: Within the town and county are numerous choices in housing, from historic to modern homes at reasonable prices. Homes in convenient neighborhoods in town run from the $85,000s to $120,000s. Also in town, Lake Eagle is a new adult neighborhood with townhomes and free-standing houses starting at about $100,000. In the county, two popular developments are Tall Timbers with homes for the $90,000s to $130,000s and Tall Pines with prices in the low $100,000s to $175,000s. The Fairways, with condominiums from the $120,000s and higher-priced custom homes, is among developments near the Glen Arven Country Club, dating to the turn of the century. There's limited availability of rental housing in the area. For information on housing, contact a real estate agency; the largest is First Thomasville Realty, (912) 226-6515.

Visitor lodging: The area has about a dozen bed-and-breakfast inns, most of them in historic homes. Most notable is Melhana Plantation Resort, four miles outside town, which has luxury accommodations starting at $250 a night, (888) 920-3030 or (912) 226-2290. Other lodging in the area starts at about $75.

Information: Thomasville and Thomas County Chamber of Commerce, P.O. Box 560, Thomasville, GA 31799, (912) 226-9600, www.thomasville chamber.com. Thomasville Welcome Center, 135 N. Broad St., Thomasville, GA 31792, (800) 704-2350, www. thomasvillega.com.

and when most of the country was reeling from the Great Depression of the 1930s, the main house was rebuilt in the grand style seen today after a fire destroyed the older home. A staff of 36 was required to run the estate. President Dwight Eisenhower was among guests who came to hunt and play golf, and formal balls still are held at the home about five miles outside town.

At the neighboring Melhana Plantation, also once owned by the Hanna family, visitors can overnight in luxury and indulge in an updated estate lifestyle, strolling through gardens with peacocks, riding horses under a magnificent cathedral of oak and magnolia trees or lounging in a restored 1930s pool house. Turned into an elegant country-manor resort by local owners Charlie and Fran Lewis, Melhana has fine dining, spa services and 19 beautifully appointed rooms, with more accommodations planned as other historic buildings are renovated.

In town, the prized "winter cottage" is the 1885 Lapham-Patterson House, a whimsical golden-colored Queen Anne mansion unique in several architectural respects, most notably because it was built without any right angles or symmetry. Shoe merchant Charles Willard Lapham had suffered lung damage in the great Chicago fire of 1871, and at the time, the asymmetrical design was thought to be more like nature and thus healthier. Each of the 19 rooms has at least one door to the outside, and there are 53 windows. The Lapham-Patterson House is open for tours, and other homes can be seen on a self-guided walking and driving tour of the historic areas.

A century ago, Thomasville merchants and city leaders catered to their wealthy residents with upscale shops, good restaurants and an active cultural scene, and that tradition carries through today. "We're a high-end retail center," says Sharlene Celaya, executive director of Main Street development and tourism. "Downtown flourishes even though Thomasville has a mall. We used to go down to Tallahassee (to shop), but that trend has reversed. Now Tallahassee residents are tired of the traffic down there and come up here to shop. They

like the hospitality and service of our merchants."

Fran and Charlie Lewis echo the praises of downtown merchants, who get to know their customers, call when preferred merchandise arrives and gather a selection of clothes for a customer to take home, select from and pay for later.

The arts also are a priority. Local residents rescued a 1915 school with $3.3 million in private funds and turned it into the Thomasville Cultural Center, where a local theater group and dance troupe perform and two annual concert series bring in major artists. Thomas College, which has four-year degree programs, also serves as a cultural venue.

Over the years, wealthy winter visitors contributed greatly to the community, most notably in establishing the Archbold Medical Center, based in Thomasville and providing state-of-the-art health care to a 13-county area of Georgia and Florida through five hospitals, four nursing homes and other services. With about 1,400 staff and workers in Thomasville, it's the largest employer in the county.

While the last decade has brought numerous changes, they've been on the plus side, says Marjorie, who settled here after living 44 years in the Philadelphia area. When she and her husband, Harry Fisher, decided to retire, they wanted warmer weather, looked at sites in Florida where she has relatives, came to Thomasville and decided it was right for them. When he died a few years later, Marjorie remained in Thomasville, staying active in volunteer work with youngsters.

Ralph and Lois Fort also moved here in the 1980s, and Ralph, an engineer, became an avid tennis player. His wife died in 1991. Though the Forts and the Fishers had not known each other, a mutual friend tried to play matchmaker for Ralph and Marjorie, but plans for meetings always fell through, Ralph recalls. "I picked up the phone one night, called Marjorie, told her we were grown folks and why didn't we just go out and have dinner and meet each other ourselves. That started our romance," he says.

"I felt like the Lord brought us together. We felt so at home with each other right off," says Marjorie. They were married in 1993.

Norman and Ruth Smith decided to stay in Leesburg, FL, when his water-pollution control company was sold and he retired, but they grew discontented with their golf-course community. "The only thing people talked about was the club and how good or bad the food was. We didn't like that and started looking for a real community," says Ruth. They considered Tallahassee but found it too busy and moved to Thomasville in the late 1980s because it was "beautiful and a nice size," she says.

Chet and June Ledford had bought a farm in Ohio when he retired as an insurance agent, but after a number of years they decided it was more work than fun. They had come to the Thomasville area frequently to play golf. "We always liked the town and decided to move here," he says.

While all three couples say Thomasville residents are warm and friendly, some newcomers say that it can take time to become part of the social scene. "We found that people have lived here for generations, and it's not so easy to get acquainted as it is in Florida (where many residents are newcomers). It takes longer," says Ruth. But she calls Thomasville "a wonderful community" with a good art guild and numerous cultural events, and she and her husband have joined in community work.

Ralph and Marjorie made new friends through neighbors and their churches, and the Ledfords say the church and garden club served as their main entrees into local society.

The Ledfords often yearn for the rolling hills of Ohio. June says she was surprised that "the summers are too hot to grow iris and peonies" in Thomasville, and Chet dislikes "the pine straw dropping all the time — we use it for mulch and still have to carry it off." Ralph and Marjorie miss the colorful falls at their previous homes, and the Smiths sometimes wish for the easy lifestyle in Florida but are happy to be away from the heavy traffic.

Overall, the couples find the cost of living here about the same or easier on the pocketbook. They all would recommend that others consider Thomasville for retirement. "Come see it and talk to the people," says Marjorie. "I can't imagine anyone not liking Thomasville."●

Tucson, Arizona

A touch of the Old West mingles with urban sophistication in this Arizona oasis

By Ron Butler

"Geronimo Slept Here," proclaims a popular Tucson travel poster indicative of an allure that harkens to the Old West. With its 470,000-plus population, Tucson is one of the country's fasest-growing communities, a city that revels in the joy of its desert and its lively Western heritage.

This is the flavor that brought Roger and Edie Harvey, 65 and 63, respectively, to Tucson from their former home in Reno, NV, where Roger was an electrician and Edie was personnel director for a medical supply company. Tucson's Western ambiance — plus fabulous weather, easy prices and, considering that both Roger and Edie are avid golfers, its hole-in-one potential — is what lured the couple to Sun City Vistoso, a retirement community about 30 minutes from downtown Tucson.

A genuine feel of the Old West, with its galloping wide-open spaces and dusty bravado, still exists in Tucson and in neighboring places like Bisbee, Benson, Tombstone and Yuma, all within easy driving range. It exists in honky-tonks like the Maverick, where the two-step is the dance of choice. Cowboys and cowgirls, often wearing matching shirts, glide around the dance floor as though on roller skates, perhaps minus a wheel or two. Bean burritos and cold beer still comprise a breakfast standard, and the city's Sun Tran bus drivers all wear cowboy hats, although some modern-day local cowboys sport gold neck chains and boots that have never stepped in mud.

The Harveys, who have relatives in the area, visited Tucson regularly for six years before making the move, attracted in part by the lay of the land. The city's grid is surrounded by mountains: the Santa Ritas, the Catalinas and the Rincons, all subliminal landmarks for motorists. On rare rainy days when clouds hang low in the sky like a tarpaulin to obscure the details of the mountains, drivers often lose their sense of direction, driving south instead of north, east instead of west. But usually the weather is glorious, and sunglasses are sold by corner street vendors the way umbrellas are peddled in Seattle or New York City.

At night the city lights are kept at a dim twinkle, not to conserve energy but out of consideration for the scientists and astronomers at the Kitt Peak National Observatory, where the world's most powerful solar telescope peers into the galaxies. In the telescope's shadow, Yaqui, Pima and Tohono O'Oodham Indians still consult tribal medicine men for their aches and pains and harvest the desert for cactus fruit and building materials.

Golf is a year-round activity in Tucson, and Roger, with a 17 handicap, and Edie, who won't divulge hers, are on the course almost daily. The first thing visitors are likely to notice at their home is a golf cart loaded for bear. Membership at Sun City Golf Club is $3,300 for two; guests pay $65 for greens fees and cart.

Sun City Vistoso contains more than 2,500 homes, many with 12-foot ceilings and three-car garages, and most are in the $140,000-$300,000 range. Tucson has numerous housing options, including 10 retirement communities, 13 parks for recreational vehicles and mobile homes, and more than 25 active-adult retirement apartment complexes in addition to facilities for retirees needing assisted-living services.

In their retirement community, the Harveys have access to all kinds of social and community groups, travel clubs, a volunteer library and an easy, relaxed atmosphere that's conducive to making friends. But they also take advantage of Tucson's wealth of cultural activities. With two major learning institutions, the University of Arizona and fast-growing Pima College, there's something going on all the time — lectures, theater, dance, name entertainment and local talent.

Edie, an avid reader, is particularly impressed with the number of successful writers in Tucson. Authors such as Charles Bowden ("The Blue Desert," "Desierto") and Richard Shelton ("Going Back to Bisbee") follow a course set by the late naturalist Joseph Wood Krutch and writer Edward Abbey ("The Brave Cowboy," "Desert Solitaire") in defining, preserving and protecting the stark, awesome landscape. Top-selling writers such as Barbara Kingsolver ("The Poisonwood Bible," "The Bean Trees"), Tom Miller ("Trading With the Enemy," "The Panama Hat Trail") and Byrd Baylor ("Desert Voices") also call Tucson home. Larry McMurtry ("Lonesome Dove") spends almost enough time in Tucson to qualify as a local.

Also drawn to Tucson by its spectacular scenery, fabulous weather and laid-back Western ambiance are Warner and Liesel Zimmt, 77 and 60-something respectively. He's a Berlin-born chemist and archaeologist, and she's a retired office manager from Los Angeles. They were married just a year ago.

Zimmt, who has five degrees and all but speaks in equations, finds Tucson's academic atmosphere appealing. He volunteers several days a week at the University of Arizona in various research departments and as a research associate with the Arizona State Museum. He also works one day a week as a volunteer attendant at the Metropolitan Tucson Convention and Visitors Bureau information booth downtown.

The Zimmts live in a large two-story home in the Sabino Canyon area, not far from the eastern section of

Tucson's Saguaro National Park, formerly classified as a national monument before it became the country's 52nd national park. It contains thousands of acres of candelabra-shaped cactuses that annually attract more than 700,000 visitors. Many of the towering plants, some more than 60 feet high, have stood tall in the desert since before the time of Coronado.

Columnar, lofty and majestic, their limbs raised to the heavens as though in prayer, the saguaro is the very symbol of the Arizona desert. No Tucson travel advertisement is complete without one, nor is any Hollywood Western. They've even been transported to Spain and Italy to authenticate the scenery for "spaghetti Westerns."

Saguaro National Park actually consists of two sprawling sections of the Sonoran Desert east and west of town, about 30 miles apart. Designated driving loops offer a close-up look at the towering plants that grow in such profusion nowhere else in the world.

Within its dry sierras, canyons and mesas, Tucson and its southern Arizona boundaries contain 27 varieties of cactuses and a wide assortment of flora, wildlife and birds. Desert walks are popular, especially at sunrise.

The Southwest desert was long considered a scourge of man, arid and untamable, but now more and more people see in its raw, awesome beauty the last vestige of America's wilderness. For Warner and Liesel Zimmt, it represents the very essence of Tucson's lifestyle.

Also celebrating the desert is the Arizona-Sonora Desert Museum, an internationally known zoo in the 16,000-acre Tucson Mountain Park 12 miles west of town. Founded more than 36 years ago, its "cages" are sand dunes, water holes, dry washes, rock caves, shrubs and trees. Glass-panel viewing allows visitors to watch otters and beavers cavort underwater.

The museum maintains the precise

Tucson, AZ

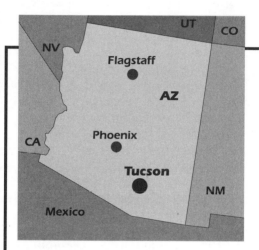

Population: More than 470,663 in Tucson, 830,375 in Pima County.
Location: Tucson is located in south-central Arizona 60 miles north of the Mexican border.
Climate:

	High	Low
January	64	38
July	99	74

Average relative humidity: 25%
Rain: 11 inches
Cost of living: 96.8, based on national average of 100.
Median housing cost: $109,900
Sales tax: 7%
Sales tax exemptions: Groceries and prescription drugs.
State income tax: Graduated in five steps from 2.9% to 5.17%, depending on income.
Income tax exemptions: Social Security and up to $2,500 of federal, state and local government pensions are exempt.
Estate tax: None, except the state's "pick-up" portion of federal tax, applicable to taxable estates above $675,000.
Property tax: Approximately $15-$17 per $100 of assessed value depending on the school district. Residential property is assessed at 10 percent of market value. The annual tax on a $109,900 home would be $1,648-$1,868.
Homestead exemption: None.
Security: 96.9 crimes per 1,000 residents, above the national average of 46.2 crimes per 1,000 residents.
Religion: More than 1,500 churches and synagogues represent virtually every denomination.
Education: Student enrollment at the University of Arizona is 31,000, and the university is the county's largest employer with a staff and faculty of more than 10,000. Pima Community College is the fifth-largest multicampus community college in the nation with more than 50,000 credit and noncredit students enrolled in more than 2,000 classes annually. The University of Phoenix, the largest private business school in the country, has a campus in Tucson. Prescott College has an adult degree program in Tucson, attracting older students who are continuing their educations or hoping to start over in a new career.
Transportation: Sun Tran offers bus service throughout Tucson. Fare is 85 cents (35 cents for passengers 65 and older).
Health: Tucson has 14 major hospitals, more than 2,000 doctors and more than 400 dentists. Tucson has the state's only medical school and is home of the Arizona Cancer Center and the University Medical Center. University Medical Center's transplant program is one of only nine in the nation.
Housing options: Apartments, condominiums and townhouses are available in all sections of the metropolitan area. Tucson has more than 25 adult retirement apartment complexes and 13 parks for recreational vehicles and mobile homes. In addition, there are several active-adult retirement communities, including **The Cascades,** (520) 886-3171; **Copper Crest,** (520) 883-6670; **Quail Ridge Estates,** (520) 825-9088; **SaddleBrooke,** (520) 825-3030; and **Villa Compana Retirement Residences,** (520) 886-3600.
Visitor lodging: There are 12,800 rooms in hotels, resorts, motels, bed-and-breakfast inns and guest ranches in the metropolitan area. About 2,150 rooms are in resort and luxury accommodations, including Sheraton El Conquistador, $129-$199, (800) 325-3535; Loews Ventana Canyon, $95-$345, (520) 299-2020; and Westward Look Resort, $99-$199, (520) 297-1151.
Information: Tucson Metropolitan Chamber of Commerce, P.O. Box 991, Tucson, AZ 85702-0991, (520) 792-1212 or www.tucsonchamber.org.

natural habitat of the animals, fish, birds and insects it houses and protects, from mountain lions to tarantulas and javelinas to rattlesnakes. The result is a zoo that seems not to be a zoo at all — always the best kind.

Along with the wildlife exhibits, underground limestone caves can be explored. They're part of the Earth Sciences Center, which also includes meteor and mineral displays. Visitors are encouraged to examine the stones and even study them under magnifying glasses. The Arizona-Sonora Desert Museum is one of the most popular tourist attractions in the state, second only to the Grand Canyon.

Tucson's informal entrepreneurial style — a throwback to frontier days — makes total retirement difficult. Many newcomers opt to open small businesses such as gift shops, bed-and-breakfast inns, restaurants and the like. Among them are Eve and Gerry Searle, 63 and 75, respectively. Eve was raised in Czechoslovakia and India, where her family moved to escape life under a communist dictatorship. In 1948 her family moved again, this time to Sydney, Australia, where Eve worked as a pilot and flying instructor.

While visiting Tucson, Eve thought a cattle roundup might be fun. That's where she met Gerry, a guy on a horse who looked to Eve like a movie star, and she wasn't far wrong. Gerry worked as a stuntman and rider on such Western hits as "High Chaparral," "Heaven With a Gun," "Dirty Dingus Magee" and "Monte Walsh" and was Lee Marvin's double in several films.

Eve and Gerry married and now own and operate the Grapevine Canyon Ranch at the base of Dragoon Mountain, some 85 miles southeast of Tucson. There's nothing else around for miles except mountains, canyons, mesquite, oak and manzanita. At an elevation of 5,000 feet, no lofty saguaros stab at the sky. There's only brush, small trees and crumbling adobe, the remains of early homesteads.

Eve is fascinated by the area's history. East is the Chiricahua Mountain Range, which includes Fort Bowie, the Chiricahua National Monument, Rucker Canyon in the Coronado National Forest, and Turkey Creek. The Chiricahua Mountain Range was the setting for Elliott Arnold's classic novel, "Blood Brother," about the friendship between Cochise and American scout Tom Jeffords. It was made into the film "Broken Arrow," with Jeff Chandler playing Cochise and Jimmy Stewart as the scout.

The Searles consider Grapevine Canyon Ranch as their nest egg and retirement home, which they share with numerous visitors. Many of them check out the stark, stunning landscape, spotting a lion or a bobcat off in the distance, or watch a hawk flying overhead in wide, watchful circles. It's the kind of vista that makes guests think that, heck, Tucson might not be a bad place to retire.

On the debit side, the outspoken Warner Zimmt finds Tucson bus service abominable for a city its size. Residents complain that service is too infrequent, the buses don't go far enough out of town, and hours are limited. Two lines, the Broadway and Speedway, whose buses run every 20 minutes or so, are praised, but the city's once-an-hour cross-town lines draw criticism.

Traffic in general also is a topic of concern to numerous Tucsonans. While city traffic hasn't reached the gridlock proportions of Phoenix, its sprawling sister city to the north, it continues to worsen. Tucson also has the highest automobile theft rate in the country. Cars parked at Tucson shopping centers seem especially attractive targets and sometimes are found across the border in Mexico. The border town of Nogales is only 60 miles to the south.

But when asked if there was anything about Tucson they didn't like, Roger and Edie Harvey had to think about it over tea and brownies in the living room of their spotless desert home filled with Indian and Mexican prints by a nationally known local artist, the late Ted DeGrazia. "I don't like snakes," says Edie, hard pressed for an answer.●

Venice, Florida

This Florida town's popularity with retirees dates to 1925

By Richard L. Fox

Take a casual stroll, drive or bicycle ride along Venice Avenue from downtown west to the Gulf of Mexico beaches, and you are struck by the charm, grace and beauty of Venice. Draped in tropical vegetation and shaded by huge oaks, Florida pines and palms, and built in the architectural styles of the canal city of northern Italy, this picturesque village exudes the trappings of a retirement paradise.

Blossoming orange trees, crape myrtles, azaleas and bougainvillea bring diverse fragrances and vivid colors to the wide median of this popular boulevard, which serves as a main conduit to many small parks and sporting venues for a growing colony of retirees. Legions of active, health-conscious seniors, numbering more than half the total population, frequent the tennis courts, lawn bowling greens and shuffleboard lanes within walking distance of their homes.

"There is a wonderful sense of community," says Gay McCarthy, who vacationed in Venice for several years from her home in Massachusetts before moving to Southwest Florida in retirement with her husband. "The people are extremely friendly."

The town's popularity with retirees has a long history. It was selected by the National Brotherhood of Locomotive Engineers as its retirement city in 1925 and has been building on that image ever since. A historic district and architectural review board were created to ensure that the city's original Northern Italian Renaissance architectural styles will be maintained, and plans for new construction or exterior renovation must meet this critical objective.

Its designation as a Florida Main Street City reinforces the preservation of its heritage. Downtown Venice is a safe, clean, visitor-friendly collection of gift shops, boutiques, art galleries, museums and restaurants, many housed in buildings listed on the National Register of Historic Places.

Casually dressed visitors and residents stroll palm-lined sidewalks, barely aware of passing traffic on its lightly traveled cobblestone streets. These same quiet avenues transition westward into elegant neighborhoods of small parks, manicured lawns and attractive, well-kept homes before arriving at water's edge.

When the Gulf Coast Intracoastal Waterway was constructed in 1963, downtown Venice was spared separation from the Gulf — an affliction of many coastal towns that requires extensive bridge networks. With the major north-south highways, Highway 41 (Tamiami Trail) and Highway 41 Bypass located east of downtown, an uninterrupted beach connection enhances local traffic flow, especially pedestrian traffic. Neighborhood growth patterns east of these arteries also have benefited, with less intrusion by nonlocal traffic into residential communities, and easy access to the interstate highway.

John and Betty Moody, natives of England, spent three years in the United States and abroad searching for a place to retire. Included in this odyssey was a winter in a 400-year-old cottage in England, three months on Longboat Key in Florida, and shorter stays in Oceanside and Carlsbad, CA, before settling in Nokomis, a tiny coastal enclave across Roberts Bay from Venice. John, 75, and Betty, 63, had lived a number of years in South Africa, Kenya and Zimbabwe and 12 years in Santa Barbara, CA, but they found what they were looking for on a secluded bay in Southwest Florida.

After service in the British Royal Navy in World War II, John settled in southern Africa in 1947. First engaged in real estate, he later manufactured travel trailers in Bulawayo, Zimbabwe, then trailers, pickup campers and motor homes in Durban, South Africa. Before marrying Betty in 1972 and moving to California in 1977, he manufactured mobile homes and developed retirement mobile-home parks in South Africa.

"We have four children in Georgia, New Hampshire and Maine, and they all love Florida," Betty says. "But the thing that brought us to Venice is its feeling of community. Sarasota (18 miles north) is a beautiful city, but I don't get the same feeling of community. Venice fits our interests and has the amenities we like. We love the climate and relaxed way of life."

They bought a "Florida home with all sliding glass doors opening into the pool area" in one of the "secret little neighborhoods" that make Venice so appealing, Betty says. Their home is on Hidden Bay, which flows into Shakett Creek, which becomes Dona Bay, eventually bisecting the Intracoastal Waterway before emptying into the Gulf of Mexico. By boat they navigate this three-mile passage in a matter of minutes. By automobile, they can cover the two miles from their home to Interstate 75 in five minutes.

Larry and Gay McCarthy owned a condominium in Venice for seven years and visited the area regularly from their home in Falmouth, MA, before moving here in 1994. Gay's late parents were longtime residents of Venice, and there was never any doubt about where she and Larry would live in retirement.

After 31 years in banking, the opportunity came shortly after the New World Bank of Cape Cod, where Larry, 56, was president, was acquired by another bank. A change of climate was a strong motivation for the move, Larry says, coupled with a lower cost of living and the fact that Florida has no state income tax.

They built a new home two years ago in Capri Isles, a master-planned subdivision three miles east of downtown. Gay describes it as "a typical Florida home" built on a former horse-riding farm.

Larry is a member of the Venice Rotary Club, sits on the Venice Foundation board and is a director of their homeowner's association. He also serves as chairman of the Senior Outreach Committee of the Venice Area Chamber of Commerce.

When he isn't busy volunteering, Larry enjoys landscaping and recent-ly took up golf — "I never had time to play before retirement" — at the urging of his sons, who enjoy golfing with him when they visit Florida.

Gay, 55, likes "the beauty of the town, its beaches and Gulf waters." When she isn't playing tennis, swimming, practicing aerobic exercises, walking, bicycling or gardening, Gay serves on the board of the Friends of Venice Art Center and as a member of Courtside Tennis Club and the YMCA.

Housing options are plentiful in the area. Many retirees choose older homes in tree-shaded neighborhoods within walking distance of downtown and the beaches. Some pick property on a canal or the bay in one of the quiet, unincorporated communities — Nokomis, Laurel, Osprey and South Venice — that encircle Venice. Still others prefer modern Florida ranch homes in upscale, gated, golf-course subdivisions like Waterford, Capri Isles, Calusa Lakes and Venice Golf and Country Club on the outskirts of the city.

Resident-owned condominiums vie with resort accommodations, yacht clubs and marinas for prized land on the Gulf. Cost-conscious retirees find that manufactured-home communities run the gamut from upscale, grandly designed Bay Indies to less-

Venice, FL

Population: 21,246 in Venice (the population doubles in winter) and 325,889 in Sarasota County.
Location: Florida Gulf Coast between Sarasota and Fort Myers.
Climate:

	High	Low
January	73	52
July	91	72

Average relative humidity: 62%
Rain: 47 inches.
Cost of living: 102.98 in Sarasota County based on state average of 100.
Housing costs: Average price of single-family home sales is $125,169. Average condominium sale is $90,532.
Sales tax: 7%
Sales tax exemptions: Groceries.
State income tax: None.
Intangibles tax: Assessed on stocks, bonds and other specified assets, with some investments exempt. First $20,000 of taxable assets ($40,000 for couples) is exempt. Tax rate is $1 per $1,000 of value for taxable assets under $100,000 for individuals or $200,000 for couples; $1.50 per $1,000 of value for greater amounts.
Estate tax: None, except the state's "pick-up" portion of the federal tax, applicable to taxable estates above $675,000.
Property tax: In the city, the rate is $17.52 per $1,000 of assessed value, with homes assessed at 100% of market value. In Sarasota County, the rate is $14.12 per $1,000. The yearly tax on a $125,000 home in Venice is $1,752 (with $25,000 exemption noted below).
Homestead exemption: First $25,000 of assessed value on primary, permanent residence.
Security: 26.5 crimes per 1,000 residents, lower than the national average of 46.2 crimes per 1,000 residents.
Religion: 88 Protestant churches and a Jewish synagogue.
Education: Manatee Community College, eight miles east of Venice, offers more than 90 fields of study. The University of South Florida, Nova University and the Ringling School of Art and Design offer a broad range of courses in Sarasota, 18 miles north.
Transportation: Sarasota County Area Transit (SCAT) provides bus service within the county. Sarasota-Bradenton International Airport is 25 miles north; Southwest Florida International Airport is 56 miles south.
Health: Bon Secours-Venice Hospital has 342 beds and is a full-service facility with 24-hour emergency service. There are 158 physicians on staff.
Housing options: Gulf-view condominiums are listed from $114,900 to $200,000. Gulf- and bay-front offerings run up to $750,000. **Bay Indies,** a manufactured-home community with excellent amenities, has resales from $20,000 to $60,000, (941) 485-5441. **Pelican Pointe Golf and Country Club,** a gated community, has homes from the $130,000s to the $300,000s, (941) 496-4663. **Calusa Lakes** has lake-front and golf course locations. Homesites are $49,900 to $89,000, maintenance-free homes are $156,500 to $225,000, and custom homes range from the $190,000s to the $300,000s, (941) 484-6004. **The Venice Golf and Country Club** has detached maintenance-free patio and custom single-family homes from the $180,000s, (941) 493-3100. **Village on the Isle** is a continuing-care retirement community, (941) 484-9753.
Visitor lodging: Veranda Inn, $52-$142 depending on season, (800) 345-9559. Best Western Sandbar Beach Resort, $109-$399, (800) 822-4853. The Quarterdeck Resort Condominiums, $610-$780 per week (depending on season) for a one-bedroom unit, (800) 845-0251.
Information: Venice Area Chamber of Commerce, 257 Tamiami Trail N., Venice, FL 34285-1908, (941) 488-2236 or www.venicechamber.com.

expensive sites.

For retirees who want health-care options, Village on the Isle, a non-profit continuing-care retirement community, has 228 residential apartments, 103 assisted-living units and a 60-bed skilled nursing facility. There is a one-time entrance fee and a monthly service fee. A priority program permits applicants to reserve the apartment of their choice for $1,000, which is applied to the entrance fee when residents move in. New residents must be at least 62 and in good health.

The McCarthys and Moodys rate health-care facilities equal to or better than those in their former hometowns. The 342-bed Bon Secours-Venice Hospital, a full-service facility with 24-hour emergency service, requires all of its medical staff to be board-certified in their specialties. But residents in the extreme north and south may have faster access to hospitals in one of the neighboring cities.

Sarasota Memorial, approximately 20 miles north of Venice, is a 952-bed regional center, the third-largest non-profit public hospital in Florida. It ranks among the top 25 in the country in the number of open-heart surgical procedures performed annually and is among the top 10 in joint replacements performed each year.

Englewood Community Hospital, about 20 miles south, has a 24-hour emergency care center, a cardiac care center, and helicopter port for quick transport of critically ill patients to better-equipped nearby hospitals.

The community offers many options for volunteers. Volunteer Center South, a nonprofit United Way agency, organizes and coordinates placement of volunteers in 70 organizations in the area and publishes a yearly "wishbook" listing the specific needs of these groups in terms of tax-deductible material donations, volunteering time and help with special projects. Last year, volunteerism alone involved 1,406 persons contributing 58,000 total hours of service.

Culturally, Venice may not receive the acclaim of its more famous sister city, Sarasota, but it boasts an impressive array of cultural arts organizations, including a community theater, dinner theater, opera and theater guilds, ballet company and symphony orchestra. The Venice Little Theater enjoys national renown with a full schedule of musicals, one-act plays and summer children's theater.

The Venice Art Center hosts year-round exhibits, sells original artworks, and offers classes for adults and children. Venice Community Center downtown seats more than 700 and is the main venue for cultural activities.

But Floridians like to spend most daylight hours outdoors, and Venetians are no exception. Fourteen miles of soft white-sand beaches from Osprey to Manasota Key draw sunbathers, swimmers, shell collectors and beach strollers. A sand replenishment project completed in 1996 widened a three-mile stretch along Venice Beach up to 300 feet deep, correcting an erosion problem and providing acres of additional space for beach-front activities. For those who prefer inland activities, 13 public and semiprivate golf courses in the greater Venice area are available to challenge the skills and endurance of the most inveterate golfers.

The highlight of the summer season is the Sharks Tooth and Seafood Festival, an annual event that takes place at the Venice Fishing Pier on the second weekend in August, attracting thousands of visitors from all over Florida. In addition to sharks-tooth hunts and culinary delights prepared by more than 25 area restaurants, this festive occasion features a juried display of original works by artists and craftsmen from around the state, and popular educational displays from the Mote Marine Laboratory of Sarasota and the Pelican Man's Bird Sanctuary, which rescues and rehabilitates injured pelicans and other wild birds.

In January, February and March, a series of senior street dances is sponsored by the Parks and Recreation Department, and the Sunset Serenade Concert Series January through April brings out large numbers of visitors and locals alike at the Gazebo in downtown Venice.

The Venice Area Chamber of Commerce sponsors a year-round program of wellness walks that feature free continental breakfasts, door-prize drawings and guest speakers in addition to the one-mile walk. Health-conscious retirees are well-represented at these events.

Continuing-education courses for retirees are available at the South County Adult and Community Education Center, and Manatee Community College eight miles east of Venice. The latter enrolls more than 1,500 full- and part-time students in more than 90 academic fields of study. Advanced courses are available at the University of South Florida and the Ringling School of Art and Design in Sarasota.

Betty Moody, who spent a number of years in executive positions with Max Factor, was surprised to find 18 members in the local chapter of the Daughters of the British Empire when she joined upon moving to Venice. Betty says she and her husband both enjoy walking, swimming, fishing and boating, but her favorite pastime is "assisting with line dancing in the Venice Senior Center."

Mustering all of the diplomacy for which the British are noted when asked what she likes least about Venice, Betty Moody grudgingly confides, "One would not be mean enough to say, 'the winters, when all the visitors come,' but I can think of nothing else." ●

Vero Beach, Florida

Strict rules protect land, water at Florida Atlantic Coast community

By Jay Clarke

Herman and Judith Niebuhr Jr., both professors at Temple University in Philadelphia, knew they wanted to retire in Florida. Their problem, as with many people approaching retirement age, was choosing just where in Florida to settle.

They checked out the Keys, West Palm Beach and Melbourne. Then they drove into Vero Beach.

"Once we saw it, it took us about 20 minutes to decide to move here," says Judith Niebuhr. "It's beautiful. It's like living in a park. And it turns out it's a great community as well."

People turn on quickly to Vero Beach. It's a tight little community with an upscale bent, an orderly place with strict rules to protect its land and waters and to keep development in line. It also offers a wealth of recreational opportunities, from boating, fishing and golf to Grapefruit League baseball, theater and active volunteerism.

That kind of ambiance has special appeal to retirees, especially when it is set in a caring community attuned to the needs of its older residents. In addition to its variety of housing options for retirees, Vero Beach has good supportive programs.

The not-for-profit Council on Aging, for example, maintains a senior center and offers a wide range of help and activities, from shuffleboard and art classes to transportation and meals for the elderly. The city has three accredited hospitals, a new library and excellent cultural facilities.

For many retirees, though, a large part of Vero's appeal lies in its opportunities for active lifestyles. The Niebuhrs are passionate about movements that help retirees put more activity and purpose in their lives.

"Research shows that if you keep an active, questing mind moving, you're apt to live longer," notes Herman "Reck" Niebuhr, 66. "Yet I see one guy pacing on his balcony of his condo all day long. And, you know, we've got retired CEOs living in John's Island who are worth a couple million bucks or so, and a third of them are going bananas.

"They live in a gilded cage, bored silly, looking for something to do — so they've gotten involved in what we're trying to do."

Reck is coordinating a Volunteer Action Center, a non-profit group sponsored by the Junior Service League. The center recruits and trains volunteers and fosters a sense of purpose that sometimes is lacking in the lives of retirees.

"And with so many single parents, or homes where both parents work, we have also developed a 'neighborhood grandparents' concept where we get involved with kids in the neighborhood," he says.

Keeping busy also is something Howard and Joyce Brand strive to achieve, but in a different way. Formerly of Wisconsin, the Brands, like the Niebuhrs, immediately were impressed with Vero Beach.

"It was such a clean little city. The ocean was right there with good access to inlets. We like to fish and boat. There were good golf courses close by. We have never been disappointed," says Howard.

They had wintered once in Lakeland and canvassed other locales in Florida before visiting Vero Beach one weekend. "That was it," says Howard. "We went back to Wisconsin, sold our home, loaded up the car and came back to Vero Beach."

The Brands, ardent boaters, keep busy setting up excursions for the Grady Bunch, a group of Grady White boat owners who travel together four or five times a year on trips around Florida. Both have been commodores of the Vero Beach Boat Club.

"It is hard to think about leaving your children and grandchildren, but we have been so busy we hardly have time to think about them. People here are awfully friendly. We really feel part of the community," says Joyce.

The Center for the Arts, Vero Beach's outstanding cultural facility, stages national and international exhibitions and has the largest museum art school in the state. Sports fans can watch major league baseball every spring when the Los Angeles Dodgers come to town. The Dodgers have taken spring practice in Vero Beach since 1948, when they were the pride of Brooklyn.

Dodgertown, their practice ground, is a sprawling complex that includes a convention center, a golf course (open to the public), a stadium, practice diamonds and rentable rooms and apartments, each with a street lamp whose globe is shaped like an outsized baseball. Roads in the complex are named after famous Dodger players, among them Jackie Robinson, Roy Campanella, Pee Wee Reese and Sandy Koufax.

Those are the most recognizable names one is likely to come across in Vero Beach, which likes to keep a low profile. More than just a way of life, it is a literal fact: By law, no building in the county can rise higher than three stories (five stories in town). Except for two grandfathered structures, Vero allows no high-rises, even on valuable beachfront property. Strict setbacks, square-footage requirements and high impact fees discourage rampant development.

That's quite a change from the Vero Beach of half a century ago, when one of its most prominent citizens was an eccentric who built three of the city's most unusual structures. Waldo Sexton, using no blueprints and simply shouting instructions to workers, incorporated driftwood, stone, odd lumber, mastodon bones and anything else that suited his fancy into his

Driftwood Inn, which the New York Times once described as "the damndest place you've ever seen."

He furnished it with eclectic items he acquired abroad or bought at estate auctions — among them Tiffany lamps and other items from Palm Beach mansions, and ship's bells from wherever he could get them. In one of the inn's rooms is Fanny Brice's couch; on the facade of another building is an original della Robbia.

Sexton died years ago, but his legacies live on. The weather-beaten Driftwood Inn still stands on the beach, and a block away is another of his unusual buildings, the Ocean Grill, one of the area's prime restaurants. The third structure, the Patio Restaurant, also survives in town; a mantle from the estate of car magnate Horace Dodge is among the decor.

In Sexton's day, the Driftwood and Ocean Grill were about the only developments on the beach. Today, the main beach road, Highway A1A, is lined with condominiums, resorts, tony housing developments and dozens of upscale businesses like stock brokerages and trendy boutiques.

The area's poshest developments lie on A1A. Places like John's Island, the Moorings, Sea Oaks, Sea Grove and Riomar are plush havens for retired nabobs of industry and commerce, and new ones are being developed. Windsor, a Galen Weston and Abercrombie & Kent project, attracts an international clientele. General Electric has put together Bermuda Bay, and Disney chose Vero Beach as the site for its first oceanside resort.

On the mainland side of the Indian River, the lagoon that extends for 156 miles on Florida's east coast, Vero has many less-pricey housing developments as well as continuing-care facilities and nursing homes for those

Vero Beach, FL

Population: 17,808 in Vero Beach, 111,000 in Indian River County.
Location: On the Atlantic Coast in mid-Florida, about halfway between West Palm Beach and Cape Canaveral.
Climate:

	High	Low
January	72	52
July	90	72

Average relative humidity: 60% Dry season runs from November to May, wet season June to October. A breeze from the ocean makes the summer heat more bearable.
Rain: 50 inches.
Cost of living: 100.9, based on national average of 100.
Median housing cost: Median cost of a three-bedroom, two-bath home is about $95,000. Average cost (higher because of the number of expensive homes) is $145,000.
Sales tax: 7%
Sales tax exemptions: Groceries, prescription drugs, medical services.
State income tax: None.
Intangibles tax: Assessed on stocks,

bonds and other specified assets. Tax rate is $1 per $1,000 value for assets under $100,000 for individuals or $200,000 for couples, and $1.50 per $1,000 value for greater amounts; first $20,000 for individuals and $40,000 for couples is exempt. Some investments are exempt.
Estate tax: None, except the state's "pick-up" portion of the federal tax, applicable to taxable estates above $675,000.
Property taxes: About $24 per $1,000 of assessed value. Homes are assessed at 100% of market value. Yearly tax on a $100,000 home is about $1,800, with the homestead exemption noted below.
Homestead exemption: $25,000 off assessed value on primary, permanent residence.
Security: 73.8 crimes per 1,000 residents, higher than the national average of 46.2 crimes per 1,000 residents.
Religion: The county has more than 100 churches of various denominations.
Education: Indian River Community College in Fort Pierce has a branch campus in Vero Beach. Florida Institute of Technology is situated in Melbourne, about 35 miles north.
Transportation: Community Coach bus system provides transportation through the Council on Aging. The nearest airport is Melbourne International Airport in Melbourne, 35 minutes away.

Health: Indian River County is served by two general hospitals and one rehabilitation hospital. The largest is Indian River Memorial Hospital, just north of Vero, with 347 beds. Sebastian River Medical Center has 133 beds. Both offer critical care. Treasure Coast Rehabilitation Hospital near Indian River Memorial has 70 beds.
Housing options: A wide range of housing styles are available, including **Isles of Vero Beach**, a retirement community of manufactured homes for sale or rent, (561) 778-7888; **Garden Grove**, a development of cluster-style homes, (561) 562-3700; and **Vista Properties**, which has several condominium developments in the area, (561) 569-3416. **Indian River Estates** is the area's largest continuing-care facility, (561) 770-0058; two smaller facilities include 24-bed **Elsie Miller Manor**, (561) 567-6769, and 22-bed **Hibiscus Manor**, (561) 562-6711.
Visitor lodging: Vero Beach attracts more than 500,000 visitors a year and has 1,700 rooms beachside and on the mainland. Moderate examples include the beachside Vero Beach Inn, $79, (561) 231-1600, and Comfort Inn in town, $68-$71, (561) 569-0900. Rates increase December through April.
Information: Vero Beach-Indian River County Chamber of Commerce, P.O. Box 2947, Vero Beach, FL 32961, (561) 567-3491 or www.vero-beach.fl.us/chamber.

in less robust health.

Single-family homes in Indian River County run "$30,000 to $3 million," according to real estate broker Chet Hogan. The median price for a three-bedroom, two-bath home in Indian River County is in the $80,000s, "but the average price is $114,000 because of all those expensive homes on the barrier island."

Also on the mainland is downtown Vero, which is sprucing up its look for tourists. The newly restored Heritage Center is of some historical interest; it is where William Jennings Bryan, "the Great Commoner," made his last public appearance in 1925.

Causeways cross the Indian River to connect the mainland with Memorial Island, site of the Center for the Arts and the Riverside Theater, an equity playhouse, and with the beach, which enjoys national renown.

But the Indian River itself, which is really not a river but an estuary lagoon, is one of Vero's prime attractions. Its brackish waters are home to some of America's best game fish — bluefish, cobia, grouper, king mackerel and tarpon among them — and the surrounding lands harbor almost 1,500 kinds of plants and 310 species of birds.

Running through the middle of it is the Intracoastal Waterway, the boat highway that runs from Florida to Maine. That waterway makes it easy to reach Sebastian Inlet State Park, the state's most popular state park 14 miles north of Vero, and nearby Pelican Island, America's first federal wildlife refuge.

Some towns that make a fine first impression sometimes lose their luster after a while. But Vero's sheen seems to last.

If the Brands had it to do over, would they do anything differently? "Yes," says Joyce. "We'd come down 10 years earlier."

The Niebuhrs also are happy with their move and have no plans to look elsewhere.

"We're done," says Reck Niebuhr. "It doesn't get any better than this."●

Vicksburg, Mississippi

Ole Man River sets the tone in this easygoing port city

By Bern Keating

In the spring, camellias, azaleas, banksia and peach trees grace the gardens of Greek Revival antebellum mansions in this slow-paced city of about 28,000 residents, a time capsule perched on the bluffs of the Mississippi River midway between Memphis and New Orleans.

Vicksburg's gracious Southern hospitality and Civil War landmarks are attractions to thousands of tourists each year, but an unsurpassed friendliness is what attracts newcomers like Jim and Sarah Pilgrim to relocate to Vicksburg in retirement. Jim, 62, moved to Vicksburg after retiring from his post in Little Rock, AR, as a regional official for an interstate electric power company.

"Of the 20 moves we made during my career from lineman to management, we enjoyed by far the widest circle of friends during our short stay in Vicksburg," says Jim, backed by Sarah's nods of agreement. "We remembered that when it came time to pick a spot for the rest of our lives."

Like seaports, river ports are traditionally more mixed ethnically, educationally and socially than inland cities, says Jim. Because of the constant comings and goings, residents tend to be less frightened of newcomers in port towns, he says.

And there are plenty of comings and goings in Vicksburg. Besides the port, the Vicksburg National Military Park attracts hordes of tourists from around the world. They come to walk the 1,800 acres of the magnificently preserved site of the 47-day siege that played a large part in the outcome of the Civil War.

"Also, the huge U.S. Army Corps of Engineers station here promotes a steady changeover of highly educated professionals who contribute their sophisticated leavening to the mixture," adds Jim.

Visitors to the small city are so numerous that they support 80 stylish restaurants and more modest cafes. There are 22 motels and hotels of major international and national franchises.

And there are 12 bed-and-breakfast inns lodged in stunning landmark buildings, like Anchuca, an 1820 Greek Revival mansion where Jefferson Davis, president of the defeated Confederacy, made a speech from the second-story balcony. A Union cannonball remains lodged in the parlor of Cedar Grove, built in 1840. Another bed-and-breakfast inn, Duff Green Mansion, served as a hospital for soldiers on both sides of the Civil War.

Other recent Vicksburg newcomers include James Bowman and his wife, Barbara, who both retired from the U.S. Army Medical Corps — James, 50, after 30 years of service and Barbara, 47, after 20 years. The Bowmans are African-American, and James admits he initially was dubious about moving to Mississippi. He worried they might not feel welcome, but his fears have been more than assuaged.

Two years before retirement from their post in Germany, James flew back to the states to investigate possible retirement locations. Still looking for a home, the South Carolina native accompanied his wife on a visit to her 11 siblings in Vicksburg — and found an astonishing friendliness that sold him on the city.

James located a lot on an upscale street east of town. After their retirement ceremony in Germany, the Bowmans moved into the impressive red brick house they built in a new development in Vicksburg.

"Soon after we moved in, I gave myself a 50th birthday party on our lawn," James remembers. "A crowd of 110 came to wish us well. All my neighbors were there."

Even Mississippi's scorching summer heat and humidity didn't discourage James. "After eight years of German snow and ice, this Vicksburg sun is just beginning to thaw me out," he chuckles.

Vicksburg's climate is, indeed, warm. July noontime temperatures average 92 with high humidity. But universal air conditioning has come to the rescue. Winters are almost semitropical, and years pass between snowfalls. Northerners are amused that schools and public offices close in panic when less than an inch of rapidly melting snow accumulates on the ground.

In the Edwards family, it was wife Edna, 63, who dragged Sam, 64, around the country in a recreational vehicle looking for a more solid home than a campsite on wheels. Though she hails from the highly touted retirement spot of Cape May, NJ, she didn't like the tourist hordes that she says have taken over the beaches there. And she thought Vicksburg was the friendliest spot they had found.

When Sam retired from his trucking job in Richmond, VA, Edna put the pressure on her husband to move to the Mississippi city. Sam had grown up in Yazoo City, MS, a small town near Vicksburg, and at first was not enthusiastic about moving back to his home state, fearing that Mississippi might not have kept pace with the times.

But Edna's arguments were persuasive. "Vicksburg has music, libraries, schools, art shows, theater. The town is spruced up and clean," says Edna. Shortly after moving into her suburban home, she was certain she had picked the right place when she spotted deer in her yard and a half-grown bobcat crossing the road in front of her house.

Medical facilities finally convinced Sam, a disabled veteran of the Korean War, that Vicksburg was a good move.

The Veterans Administration Hospital is only 42 miles east in Jackson, also the home of University Medical Center, which enjoys world renown for its surgical procedures. Vicksburg itself has two hospitals and about 100 doctors in all major specialties, and a new $100 million, 385-bed hospital is in the works. There also are five long-term care facilities, four home health agencies, one personal care home and three clinics.

Vicksburg is one of 20 certified retirement cities in the state's official retiree attraction program, Hometown Mississippi Retirement. Sam Edwards and Jim Pilgrim volunteer at the Retirement Development Center, where

Vicksburg, MS

Population: 27,496 in Vicksburg, 48,000 in Warren County.

Location: In western Mississippi on the bluffs of the Mississippi River, 220 miles south of Memphis, 220 miles north of New Orleans and 42 miles west of Jackson. Elevation is 200 feet.

Climate:

	High	Low
January	56	33
July	92	71

Average relative humidity: 58%

Rain: 55.37 inches.

Cost of living: 96.6, based on national average of 100.

Average housing cost: Cost of a new 2,000-square-foot brick home on a half-acre lot is about $120,000. Average cost of an established home is $78,000.

Sales tax: 7%

Sales tax exemptions: Prescription drugs.

State income tax: Graduated in three steps of 2%, 3% and 4% of taxable income.

Income tax exemptions: Qualified retirement income is exempt, including Social Security benefits, public and private pensions, IRAs and annuities. There is an additional $1,500 personal exemption for residents age 65 and older.

Intangibles tax: None.

Estate tax: None, except the state's "pick-up" portion of the federal tax, applicable to taxable estates above $675,000.

Property tax: $113.34 per $1,000 of the assessed value of a primary residence. Taxes are assessed on 10 percent of the home's value. Taxes on a $120,000 home would be $1,360.08, or $680.04 with the homestead exemption noted below.

Homestead exemption: There is a homestead exemption in the form of a $240 tax credit for all homeowners. Homeowners over age 65 are exempt from property taxes on the first $60,000 of the value of a primary residence. Persons with disabilities also can apply for homestead exemptions.

Security: 71.1 crimes per 1,000 residents, higher than the national average of 46.2 crimes per 1,000 residents.

Religion: There are more than 100 houses of worship serving 30 denominations and faiths in addition to a Jewish temple.

Education: The Vicksburg campus of Hinds Community College is the largest vocational-technical facility in the state and offers courses to retirees. At the U.S. Army Corps of Engineers Waterways Experiment Station, retirees can study for academic credit and graduate degrees granted by such cooperating universities as Louisiana State, Mississippi State and Texas A&M. Retirees willing to commute 42 miles east to Jackson can avail themselves of options at Belhaven College, Jackson State University, Millsaps College and the University of Mississippi Medical Center.

Transportation: Nearest commercial airport is Jackson International, 50 miles east. It is served by Delta, TWA, American Eagle, Southwest, Northwest Airlink and Continental Express. Delta Bus and Greyhound offer service through Vicksburg.

Health: Park View Regional Medical Center is a 240-bed general medical facility with about 85 physicians on staff. Vicksburg Medical Center is a 154-bed general medical and surgical hospital with 55 physicians on staff. A new $100 million, 385-bed hospital is in the works. Forty-two miles east in Jackson is the 155-acre University Medical Center campus, home of the prestigious University of Mississippi School of Medicine. It is especially known for its heart and kidney transplant units.

Housing options: Carlton Place is Vicksburg's first gated community. Another new community is **Turning Leaf**, which has four lakes, sports fields, walking trails and a 10-acre common area. Patio homes are available at **Mill Creek**, and housing in established neighborhoods is available in all price ranges, says Mike Davis, chairman of community relations on retiree relocation for the chamber of commerce and an agent with the 100-year-old **Century 21 P.L. Hennessey**, (601) 634-1921. Apartments are available, but house rentals are scarce.

Visitor lodging: Twenty-two hotels and motels and three campgrounds are available to visitors. Among the options are casino hotels and antebellum bed-and-breakfast mansions, including Cedar Grove Mansion Inn, $95-$185, (800) 862-1300; Anchuca, $85-$140, (888) 686-0111; and Duff Green Mansion, $95-$125, (800) 992-0037. At Harrah's Vicksburg Casino, rates start at $50 weeknights (Sunday-Thursday) and $65 weekends (Friday-Saturday), (800) 427-7247.

Information: Vicksburg-Warren County Chamber of Commerce, P.O. Box 709, Vicksburg, MS 39181, (888) VICKSBURG or visit www.vicksburg.org on the Internet. Ask for a free Mississippi Living guide from Hometown Mississippi Retirement, P.O. Box 849, Jackson, MS 39205-0849, (800) 350-3323 or visit www.mississippi.org on the Internet.

they provide information to relocating retirees. Jim also is readying himself for a new career as a student at the Hinds Community College branch campus in Vicksburg, where he is eyeing woodworking classes.

James Bowman has embarked on a second career with the school system. When he went to enroll his daughter at her new school, the principal quizzed James about his military career. The next thing James knew, he was the new instructor of the Reserve Officers Training Corps. James also is president of the nonprofit Magnificent Seven, a group of men who teach reading and writing to students, and has progressed from deacon to associate pastor at Mount Zion Baptist Church.

Other Vicksburg retirees work for the Red Cross and Salvation Army and in shelters for the abused and homeless. Some help with literacy and tutorial programs to help faltering students, and a prison ministry offers drug and alcohol counseling and assists families of prisoners with transportation and clothing. The Community Council provides daily hot meals at home for the frail elderly and transportation to group meals.

Between volunteer tasks, retirees find plenty to keep busy. The first job of a newcomer is to explore the sprawling beauty of the Vicksburg National Military Park, which nearly surrounds the city with its 1,300 state and regional statues and monuments to soldiers of both the Confederate and Union armies. After watching an 18-minute movie about the Siege of Vicksburg at the visitors center, the amateur historian can follow the course of the battle by walking in the very footsteps of the soldiers who stormed and defended the fortifications, now beautifully maintained.

Vicksburg offers several other museums, including the Old Court House, where the Confederate flag came down and the Stars and Stripes went up on July 4, 1863. At the Gray and Blue Naval Museum is the world's largest collection of Civil War-era gunboat models. Other museum stops include the Southern Cultural Heritage Center, where both Confederate and Union armies barracked during the Civil War; Jacqueline House, dedicated to the preservation of African-American culture; and Yesterday's Children Antique Doll and Toy Museum. The Biedenharn Museum of Coca-Cola Memorabilia celebrates the bottling of the first coke there in 1894, and you can get an ice-cream float at its old-fashioned soda fountain and candy store.

A hydrojet boat trip with Mississippi River Adventures takes visitors past Civil War fortifications as well as the four major 24-hour casinos — Harrah's, Isle of Capri, Ameristar and Rainbow — that profoundly affected the local economy and considerably enlivened nightlife after they opened in 1993-94.

Jim Pilgrim is among retirees who list hunting and fishing as hobbies. The forests around Vicksburg teem with deer and turkey, and annual dove and duck hunts keep outdoorsmen in the fields for long hours.

The Vicksburg Country Club has an 18-hole golf course as well as a driving range, putting green, tennis courts, swimming pool, pro shop and clubhouse. The Clear Creek Golf Course, with a clubhouse and golf shop, is open to the public. The city owns a swimming pool that it plans to cover for year-round use, and there are many tennis courts and soccer, softball and baseball facilities throughout the county.

A highlight of local festivals is the two-week Spring Pilgrimage in mid-March, when a dozen historic houses are open to the public. The city's nationally known melodrama, "Gold in the Hills," is performed during Spring Pilgrimage, and the audience is encouraged to cheer the hero and pelt the villain with peanuts. Run Through History, a road race, walk and fun run through Vicksburg National Military Park, is in March, and there's a spring arts and crafts show and three-day Riverfest street party in mid-April. A reenactment of the Vicksburg siege is in early July.

All are superbly equipped for making retirement fun. But Jim Pilgrim says it again: "Vicksburg is big enough to provide modern services and entertainment but small enough so the clerks in the stores call you by your first name. It is that friendliness that counts." ●

Waynesville, North Carolina

A mountain town in western North Carolina shows strong community spirit

By Richard L. Fox

Lodged on a plateau between western North Carolina's Great Smoky Mountains National Park and the Pisgah National Forest, Waynesville has many of the ingredients of a great vacation destination — except hordes of tourists. This slow-paced mountain hamlet is populated by working families and a growing cadre of relocated retirees lured by scenic vistas, outdoor recreation, a four-season climate and a safe environment.

Viewed from a nearby mountainside, Waynesville's eight-block downtown is marked by five church spires, lending an air of serenity to the otherwise busy central marketplace. The tree-lined sidewalks are alive with pedestrian activity as shoppers, diners and gallery-goers pass in and out of more than 100 establishments clustered along Main Street. Others are content to relax on benches in the shade, enjoying the measured hustle and bustle of the street against the calming vistas of the surrounding Balsam, Blue Ridge and Great Smoky mountains.

One always-busy downtown destination is the three-story, neoclassically styled Haywood County courthouse. Built in 1932, it stands as a symbol of stability and authority, fronted by an inviting entrance and surrounded by large trees. It is the fourth courthouse to occupy the site; the first was constructed four years after Haywood County was carved out of sprawling Buncombe County in 1808.

Originally called Mount Pleasant, Waynesville flirted with tourism early. For a brief time, the area gained some renown as a health resort after the construction of the White Sulphur Springs Hotel, the town's first lodging, in 1850. Despite advertising a healthy climate and an abundance of pure, cold spring water, the idea of down-to-earth Waynesville as a health resort never caught on.

Today, visitors who find their way to Waynesville are likely to have come from other parts of western North Carolina, like Maggie Valley, Cherokee or Highlands. The Folkmoot International Dance Festival, Church Street Art and Craft Show, Apple Festival and other annual events bring several thousand visitors to Waynesville for short stays or day trips.

A sign in Waynesville displays the often-used sentiment, "I was not born here, but I came as fast as I could." It's good advice for anyone considering a retirement move, says Bob Bottoms, 68, who with wife Virginia, 67, moved to Waynesville in 1994 after making six visits in five months.

Their first retirement move in 1983 took them from Pittsburgh, PA, to Hilton Head, SC. After 10 years, though, they felt that Hilton Head had become "too touristy, crowded and expensive," says Bob.

During the search for a new town, the Bottomses say they considered just about every southeastern state and even thought about retiring to New Zealand or Tahiti. But for now, Bob and Virginia have no plans to move again. "We have a 360-degree view of the mountains from our home, outstanding weather and the most beautiful mountain golf course I have ever seen," says Bob, retired general manager of international sales at U.S. Steel.

Waynesville's 2,658-foot elevation plays an important part in the town's popularity. In summer, pleasant warm days and invariably cool nights attract "lowlanders" seeking relief from humid, sweltering Augusts. Winters generally are mild, with infrequent snowfall rarely measuring more than one or two inches. In the surrounding higher mountain elevations, ski slopes are filled with skiers Novem-ber through March.

"The year-round climate is wonderful, with only February a time to get away to Florida," says Barbara Bennett, 52, who moved here with husband John, 74, from Princeton, NJ, in 1991.

"Princeton is a working man's community. We wanted a retirement community," says John. About two years after John retired as chief executive officer of a computer software company, the Bennetts moved to Waynesville.

They chose a site on a mountainside about 1,000 feet above Waynesville. Their custom-built home takes maximum advantage of the breathtaking vistas of the town and mountains beyond. Barbara, an interior designer, selected a floor plan and window placements for the best views.

In 1983 John and Erika Elshoff bought a home overlooking Waynesville that was 5,280 feet above sea level, and they came every summer from Treasure Island, FL, to enjoy the cool temperatures.

"I first laid eyes on Waynesville in the early 1960s and fell in love with it then," says John. When he retired as chief executive officer of a horticultural company in 1993, they moved to Waynesville full time, selling the vacation home and buying another place not quite so high up the mountain. "That (high elevation) is fine when you come here for the summer, but not for year-round living," says John, 64.

The Elshoffs' current home at 3,500 feet has six acres of land, a waterfall and trout pond. Erika says the beauty of the area and its climate strongly influenced her desire to relocate from the sunny Florida flat lands to mountainous, sometimes chilly, Waynesville. The "more tranquil pace of life, free of worry about crime" also was a big draw for her.

As more retirees settle in Waynesville, the town itself is changing to accommodate them. Residents anticipate some minor growing pains, but at the current population of about 9,400, it is the epitome of small-town living.

A sense of community is one of the elements that Virginia and Bob Bottoms sought when they chose Waynesville. "When we moved to our new home, it was very easy to make friends, mostly through the country club," says Virginia.

John Elshoff advises seeking out friends. "There are two ways to come to the mountains. If you are so inclined and don't want to make any effort, you can become a recluse. Or, you can reach out to people and not wait for them to come to you," he says.

"We found a lot of transplants looking for new friends, so it was easy," says Erika.

The relocating retiree population in Haywood County is far from reclusive, according to Kay Dossey, executive director of the Greater Haywood County Chamber of Commerce. "Retirees have had a tremendous impact on quality of life in this area. Barbara Bennett's fund raising has become legendary among the business community and major contributors in Haywood County," Dossey says.

Barbara credits others. "I like the fact that there are so many people willing to make the effort to come together and work for the improvement of the town. These efforts have made a big difference in just the few years we've been here."

The opportunity for involvement was Barbara's main incentive when the Bennetts selected Waynesville. "I wanted to be part of a growing town where I could make a contribution to the quality of life," she says.

Barbara volunteers her time and efforts to the Haywood County Arts Council. The council sponsors a diverse offering of cultural activities, such as free Sunday afternoon con-

Waynesville, NC

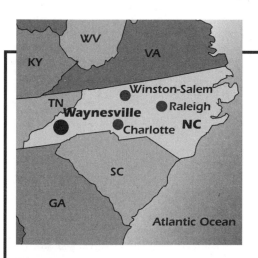

Population: 9,424 in town, 50,000 in Haywood County.

Location: In mountainous western North Carolina, bordered by Great Smoky Mountains National Park to the north and Pisgah National Forest to the south. The town's elevation is 2,658 feet.

Climate:

	High	Low
January	47	23
July	82	58

Average relative humidity: 58% in Asheville, about 30 miles away (figures for Waynesville not available).

Rain: 47 inches.

Cost of living: Below average (specific index not available).

Average housing cost: $108,000

Sales tax: 6%

Sales tax exemptions: Prescriptions, services and automobiles.

State income tax: Graduated in three steps from 6% to 7.75%, depending on income.

Income tax exemptions: Social Security benefits. Each taxpayer also can exempt up to $4,000 in local, state or federal government retirement benefits and up to $2,000 in private retirement benefits, but the total of these exemptions cannot exceed $4,000 per person.

Intangibles tax: None.

Estate tax: None, except the state's "pick-up" portion of the federal tax, applicable to taxable estates above $675,000.

Property tax: $10.10 in the city ($6.10 in the county) per $1,000 of assessed value, with homes assessed at 100% of appraised value. The annual tax on a $108,000 home in Waynesville is $1,090 without exemptions.

Homestead exemption: $20,000 off assessed value of permanent residence for those over age 65 with annual income of $15,000 or less.

Personal property tax: Same rate as real property, on the depreciated value of cars, boats, mobile homes and airplanes.

Security: 35.1 crimes per 1,000 residents, lower than the national average of 46.2 crimes per 1,000 residents.

Religion: One Catholic and 30 Protestant places of worship. Lake Junaluska Assembly, a worldwide religious group, is located here on a 250-acre lake.

Education: Haywood Community College, with an enrollment of more than 2,000, offers associate degrees in 30 disciplines and continuing-education courses; senior citizens pay no registration fees in the continuing-education program. The University of North Carolina at Asheville is 30 miles east, and Western Carolina University in Cullowhee is 25 miles southwest.

Transportation: No local bus service. Interstate 40 and four U.S. highways provide excellent highway access. Asheville Regional Airport, served by jets and commuter aircraft, is a 30-minute drive away.

Health: Haywood County Hospital is a 200-bed, full-service, regional facility with 24-hour emergency service and a staff practicing 24 medical specialties.

Housing options: A variety of choices from large estates to small farms, mountainside chalets to rustic and remote log cabins, contemporary, custom-built country club homes to condos and townhomes.

Visitor lodging: Best Western Smoky Mountain Inn, $79-$83, including continental breakfast, (828) 456-4402. Waynesville Country Club Inn, from $99, including breakfast and dinner, (828) 456-3551. Comfort Inn-Maggie Valley, $79, including continental breakfast, (828) 926-9106.

Information: Haywood County Chamber of Commerce, P.O. Drawer 600, Waynesville, NC 28786-0600, (828) 456-3021 or www.haywood-nc.com. Visitor information, (800) 334-9036.

certs in the public library and an annual two-week rehearsal residency by the Atlanta Ballet. The Folkmoot-USA program, part of International Festival Day, features dance troupes from around the world and brings thousands of spectators downtown. Stemming from the Folkmoot Festival, a new international school for ballet and dance opened four years ago.

The Haywood Arts Repertory Theatre, an amateur theater company offering four productions annually, celebrated the opening of a new $1 million, 250-seat theater recently. The Folk Art Center, youth theater, a museum and galleries showcase local talent.

As strong as the cultural movement is here, Waynesville is not an arts community in the tradition of Santa Fe, NM. Erika Elshoff cautions newcomers: "You can't come with a high-society attitude. It helps to love nature and outdoor activities."

National parks and forests comprise nearly 40 percent of Haywood County. More than 200 miles of hiking trails, including large sections of the Appalachian Trail, entice residents to the outdoors. Camping, canoeing, mountain biking, fishing, hunting, horseback riding, skiing and golf all are available.

North Carolina's oldest ski resort, Cataloochee Ski Area in Maggie Valley, can be reached in minutes, and white-water rafting outfitters are in nearby Nantahala, Asheville, Bryson City and Almond. The much-acclaimed, much-visited Blue Ridge Parkway eight miles southwest of town leads to many quaint villages, good for same-day exploration.

Laurel Ridge Country Club, a private course rated as one of the best in the country by *Golfweek* magazine in 1993 and 1994, and the 27-hole Waynesville Country Club course are among seven courses (six public and one private) in the county.

The influx of retirees has been cit-ed as the cause of rising home prices in Waynesville. "Waynesville has become such a popular living area that housing costs have really gone up in recent years," says Marty Prevost of MainStreet Realty. "There is a real shortage of nice homes in the $100,000-$150,000 price range — the price most downsizing retirees are looking for," she adds.

According to Prevost, the Waynesville Country Club area — one of the nicer, established neighborhoods — is built out, but resales sometimes are available in the $150,000-$295,000 range. She also notes that custom-built homes cost $80-$100 per square foot, depending on amenities, and a new 1,800- to 2,000-square-foot home on three-fourths to one acre of land likely will be priced at $200,000-$250,000.

Haywood County Tax Assessor Evelyn Cooper says the last reappraisal of residential real estate in 1996 revealed an average home valuation of $96,622 for the county, but she estimates that the next appraisal in 2007 will lift that figure to $108,000 or more. Bob Hill of the Haywood County Board of Realtors says homes are being sold at higher prices, though. "A comparison of listing prices of homes on the market today, with the tax re-evaluation, indicates most property-owners are pricing well above the appraised value. Real-estate prices are extremely volatile right now. Sellers don't want to get caught on the low side in a rising market," Hill says.

Retirees seeking luxury living may want to take a look at Smoky Mountain Sanctuary, an upscale gated community with underground utilities, clubhouse, helicopter landing pad and other perks. Two- to six-acre home sites are priced $60,000-$100,000, and a new five-bedroom, three-bath home has an asking price of $495,000. The Haywood County Hospital Foundation is responsible for creat-ing the new $900,000 Woman's Care Center and raised $5 million for the construction of a 50,000-square-foot health and fitness center.

Barbara Bennett is chairwoman of fund raising for the hospital foundation. With the foundation's help, Haywood Regional Medical Center, a 200-bed, full-service facility and the largest hospital west of Asheville, hired 27 new physicians during the last two years. The hospital also acquired new diagnostic equipment, including an MRI and CT scanner, and established a home health-care facility. In Asheville, Memorial Mission Medical Center (503 beds) and St. Joseph's Hospital (331) offer advanced medical technology and most specialties.

Among indications of the town's growing appreciation for its retirees are the special offerings for seniors at Haywood Community College. With an 83-acre main campus and 320-acre "teaching forest," it offers no-registration-fee continuing-education courses for senior citizens in clay, fiber, jewelry-making and woodwork. Higher-education courses are available at Western Carolina University in Cullowhee and the University of North Carolina at Asheville, each about 30 minutes away.

Downtown shops and area shopping centers provide for basic needs but are no substitute for the major malls and giant department stores in large urban areas. But Virginia Bottoms credits local merchants with serving the community well. "The shops on Main Street are nice, friendly places with quality merchandise," she says. And though John Elshoff cites the lack of upscale stores as a drawback, he adds upon reflection: "It's not a big deal."

When Erika Elshoff is asked if she'll ever move out of Waynesville, she says, "There are no hurricanes, no flooding, no fires, no earthquakes. Where else can you live and not have one or more of these conditions?"●

Whidbey Island, Washington

Retirees escape to life in the slow lane in Washington's Puget Sound

By Stanton H. Patty

There is a quiet place in Washington state's Puget Sound where bed-and-breakfast inns are sprouting like pretty flowers and retirees go fishing for fighting salmon.

It is Whidbey Island — only about an hour or so by freeway and ferry from Seattle traffic jams.

The 45-mile-long, seahorse-shaped island is a charmer: country towns with saltwater vistas and backdrops of lofty mountains, rolling pasture land and tall timber, uncrowded beaches and rugged bluffs, yachting marinas and golf courses. Plus there's an assortment of four state parks and an unusual national historical park.

All this scenery, a mild climate and the appeal of slow-tempo living have peopled the island with painters, potters, photographers, writers, actors and other creative types.

Five years ago Ray and Maureen Cooke decided to "quit the rat race" in Seattle and retire to Whidbey Island.

But retirement didn't quite stick. Now the Cookes are the owners of one of the island's most successful B&B establishments, Twickenham House.

"We've never had so much fun," says Maureen Cooke. "Sometimes we think we have just gone to heaven."

The move to Whidbey Island has brought a major change of pace — and lifestyle — for the couple. Ray, 65, had been a marketing and management consultant in, as he puts it, "Seattle's fast lane." Maureen's hobby was driving race cars around some of the Pacific Coast's fastest tracks.

Twickenham House (named for Ray's hometown in England) nestles into 10 acres of forest on the outskirts of a seaside village called Langley, near the south end of the island.

Wake-up calls may include the crow of a rooster. Permanent residents at Twickenham House include chickens, geese and goats. There are six rooms for guests. And the Cookes have added a British-style pub with dartboards and beer on draft.

"No stress here," says Maureen. That seems to be the theme across most of easygoing Whidbey Island.

It would be difficult even for a newcomer to get lost on Whidbey. One main road meanders the entire length of the island. And history and happenstance have scattered the island's three incorporated towns at convenient points for travelers.

The southern anchor is Langley (population 959), a snug harbor that is home to several noted artists. Coupeville (population 1,550), decked with Victorian homes of long-ago sea captains, is in the central section of the island and is the county seat. Oak Harbor (with a population of over 20,000) is Whidbey's largest community, its northern anchor. And next door to Oak Harbor is the Whidbey Island Naval Air Station, the island's largest employer.

There are four ways to reach Whidbey. Ferries cross from Mukilteo on the mainland, north of Seattle, to Clinton, a port on the south end of Whidbey Island, and from picturesque Port Townsend, on Washington's Olympic Peninsula, to Keystone Harbor in the central part of the island. There's a highway bridge across Deception Pass, at the north end of Whidbey, and Oak Harbor can be reached by air from Seattle-Tacoma International Airport. Harbor Airlines, a longtime commuter carrier, offers scheduled service daily for those in a hurry.

The Mukilteo-Clinton ferry crossing takes about 20 minutes. The Port Townsend-Keystone run is a 30-minute trip. Flight time between Seattle-Tacoma International Airport and Oak Harbor is about 25 minutes.

But there is no need to worry about highway directions. Whidbey Island has a free transit system (Monday through Saturday) that covers nearly the entire island, including the ferry landings. The

system — Island Transit — is financed with sales- and vehicle-excise tax receipts.

Retirees, who make up more than a third of the island's population of 55,000 or so contented folk, report no problems in staying busy. When they aren't biking or beachcombing or berry-picking and fishing, many seniors are involved in community projects.

Maureen Cooke, 51 — who still gets "off-island" occasionally to race her bright-red Lotus — is chairwoman of a campaign to raise funds for a performing-arts center in Langley.

Lois Fisher, 55, volunteers her time at a care clinic for bald eagles, hawks and other injured critters. Her husband, Gary, also 55, a retired Navy captain whose hobby is sheep-raising, is a volunteer adviser to island farmers through a Washington State University extension program.

Laurence Moses, 58, a retired Army colonel, lives in Oak Harbor and chairs a project to create a port district for the area. His wife, Lyn, also 58, is a volunteer with the Oak Harbor Police Department.

Why are retirees settling on Whidbey Island?

"It's many things," says Laurence. "Here we are, by the sea, looking at snowcapped mountains in two directions. That's pretty hard to do anyplace else."

The two mountain ranges within sight of Whidbey are the Olympic Mountains and the Cascades. The mountain walls help block much of the rain that falls with sometimes-dismal frequency elsewhere around Puget Sound.

The Moseses traveled the world during Laurence's 26-year Army career. They were in Heidelberg, Germany, when a Navy friend, who had been stationed at Whidbey, suggested the island as the ideal retirement spot.

"We came to take a look — and bought six acres of land," Laurence recalls. "It's just a great place."

Capt. George Vancouver, the English navigator, felt the same way when he explored Puget Sound back in 1792. This lyrical entry about Whidbey Island appeared in his log:

"The surrounding country presented a delightful prospect, consisting chiefly of spacious meadows, elegantly adorned with clumps of trees. In these beautiful pastures, bordering on an expansive sheet of water, the deer were seen playing in great numbers."

Vancouver decided to name the fair island for one of his trusted lieutenants, Joseph Whidbey. Puget Sound Indian tribes, of course, already knew all about Whidbey. They were waiting on shore to meet Vancouver with trade goods.

The Indians, however, did not encourage much more than early-day trade and tourism. The island's first settler, Thomas Glasgow, attempted to establish a land claim in 1848. But his reception was so chilly that he soon departed, leaving unharvested crops in his garden.

Whidbey Island, WA

Population: 55,000

Location: In Puget Sound, about one hour north of Seattle by highway and ferry (longer if traffic is heavy). Driving distance from Seattle to Oak Harbor, Whidbey Island's largest community, is 62 miles.

Climate:

	High	Low
January	44	38
July	71	51

Average relative humidity: 75%-80%

Rain: 20-35 inches, depending on area of island.

Cost of living: Average to slightly above average (specific index not available).

Average housing cost: Langley area, $269,000. Central Whidbey (Coupeville area), $215,000; more for waterfront property. Oak Harbor, $153,088.

Sales tax: 7.9%

Sales tax exemptions: Groceries, prescription drugs, medical services.

State income tax: None.

Intangibles tax: None.

Estate tax: None, except the state's "pickup" portion of the federal tax, applicable to taxable estates above $675,000.

Property tax: Homes are assessed at 100% of market value. For cities: Oak Harbor, $10.06; Coupeville, $9.84; Langley, $9.55. School levies account for the different rates. Tax on a $153,000 home in Oak Harbor is about $1,539 a year; on a $215,000 home in Coupeville, about $2,115; on a $269,000 home in Langley, about $2,569 a year.

Homestead exemption: Homeowners age 61 and older, with a gross household income of $28,000 or less, are eligible for certain property tax exemptions.

Security: Reported crimes per 1,000 residents is 22.1 in Coupeville, 54.8 in Langley and 29.3 in Oak Harbor, compared to the national average of 46.2 crimes per 1,000 residents. Reported crimes per 1,000 residents in Island County is 19.8.

Religion: 58 churches of numerous denominations.

Education: Skagit Valley College has a small campus in Oak Harbor and a branch in Langley, with about five courses offered for seniors each quarter. Western Washington University in Bellingham, north of Whidbey Island, offers a limited number of general courses to island residents.

Transportation: Whidbey Island is served by Washington State Ferries from Mukilteo, north of Seattle, and from Port Townsend on Washington's Olympic Peninsula. The Deception Pass Bridge, at the north end of the island, connects Whidbey to Washington's highway system. Island-based Oak Harbor Airlines has scheduled commuter service between Oak Harbor and Seattle-Tacoma International Airport. Island Transit operates free bus service (Monday through Saturday) that covers most of the island.

Health: The 51-bed Whidbey General Hospital in Coupeville has a 24-hour emergency room plus coronary and intensive care, cancer care and home health care. The 22-bed Oak Harbor Naval Hospital at Whidbey Island Naval Air Station offers health care to military personnel and dependents. Estimated 12 physicians on island. Nursing-home care available.

Housing options: Most retirees live in single-family homes. Apartments for low to moderate incomes are available. There are no planned retirement communities. One popular upscale development is **Useless Bay Colony**. There are 200 single-family homes; about half are occupied by retirees. Costs of new condo units are $230,000-$250,000, depending on size. Home prices average $200,000. Colony property owners are offered memberships at the nearby Useless Bay Country Club. The club has an 18-hole golf course; golf memberships are extra. Useless Bay Colony is near Clinton, on the southern end of the island.

Visitor lodging: Langley area — Harbour Inn, $75-$90, (360) 331-6900; Inverness Inn, $65-$85, (360) 321-5521. Central Whidbey (Coupeville area) — Inn at Penn Cove, $65-$125, (800) 688-2683; Coupeville Inn, $65-$95, (360) 678-6668; Captain Whidbey Inn (the island's best-known lodging place), $85-$225 with full breakfast, (800) 366-4097. Oak Harbor area — Acorn Motor Inn, $48-$78, (360) 675-6646; Auld Holland Inn, $45-$145, (360) 675-2288. In addition, the island has an estimated 40 bed-and-breakfast inns. The Whidbey Island B&B Association, (360) 679-2276, represents 12 of the B&Bs.

Information: Langley Chamber of Commerce, P.O. Box 403, Langley, WA 98260, (360) 221-6765. Central Whidbey Chamber of Commerce, P.O. Box 152, Coupeville, WA 98239, (360) 678-5434. Greater Oak Harbor Chamber of Commerce, P.O. Box 883, Oak Harbor, WA 98277, (360) 675-3535 or www.whidbey.net/oakchamber.

Then the Oregon Trail opened the Pacific Northwest to American settlers, and pioneer families began farming Whidbey's gentle acres. Later, enterprising New England sea captains, seeking lumber and other commodities for gold-rush California, began calling at Whidbey. Several returned with their families, giving the island a salty personality that continues to this time.

World War II brought construction of what became the Whidbey Island Naval Air Station. And now the island is one of Washington's fastest-growing areas.

There is some concern about growth, but residential property taxes still are relatively low and communities still are so small that things seem under comfortable control. The crime rate also is nominal, with 19.8 crimes reported per 1,000 residents in Island County. The national average is 46.2 crimes per 1,000 residents.

"We see two or three cars waiting at a stoplight in Oak Harbor and that's about as bad as things get," says Gary Fisher.

Maureen Cooke says island life is so muted that a shopping trip to nearby Seattle can be almost unsettling.

"We say that going to Seattle is 'going to America,' " says Maureen. "Our little piece of heaven here isn't the real world."

Gary Fisher remembers an evening not long ago when friends gathered at his home. Someone challenged the group to make a list of "What's wrong with Whidbey."

"We tried, we really did, but we couldn't think of anything we didn't like about the island," Gary reports. "It's all-around terrific . . . the climate, the surroundings, the proximity to things we like to do. It's a lifestyle."

One thing that potential residents should keep in mind, islanders say, is that while first-class medical care is available at Whidbey General Hospital in Coupeville, Whidbey is an island.

If an emergency should strike a resident in the southern end of the island, it is a drive of 30 miles or so to reach Whidbey General. If more urgent care is required, a ferry trip or a medical-evacuation flight would be involved. On the plus side, island fire departments have highly trained paramedics.

And while Whidbey has artistic abun-dance, ranging from theater groups to trendy galleries, newcomers should not expect all of the big-city cultural amenities.

"But it's not like we're stuck out here on a little island," says Laurence Moses. "We are within two hours of either the Seattle area or Vancouver, British Columbia."

Whidbey's trio of incorporated towns offers a medley of contrasts. Langley, South Whidbey's gathering place, counts 34 bed-and-breakfast inns with about 150 rooms.

The old-fashioned town dozes on a bluff overlooking spectacular seascapes. It looks like a motion-picture set built to portray an early-times steamboat port. And that's what Langley was.

Resolute citizens guard their vintage buildings and their bucolic lifestyle like precious jewels. There is a Design Review Board whose mandate it is to keep Langley as it was. You can be sure that the fresh crop of bed-and-breakfast establishments blends into old Langley. The townspeople wouldn't have it any other way.

A favorite stop in downtown Langley is a tiny park along First Street, where there is a lifelike bronze sculpture of a youth leaning on a railing. There is a bronze dog at his feet. "Boy and Dog" is the title. More often than not, the bronze lad is joined by visitors who want to be photographed with an arm around his shoulders.

Just down the street is an antique watering hole, the Dog House, a tavern dating to 1908. It has a place on the national historic register.

There is a watering hole for dogs, too. It's on a sidewalk in front of the local liquor store. Kindly employees keep water buckets topped for thirsty canines.

Tiny Coupeville, in the Central Whidbey area, one of Washington's oldest towns, is a jewel, a flashback to 19th-century seafaring times. A short downtown walking tour designed by the Island County Historical Society covers 26 buildings of historical value.

Oldest is the 1854-vintage home of Capt. Thomas Coupe, Coupeville's founder. The skipper also is remembered for maneuvering a fully rigged ship through the treacherous waters of nearby Deception Pass in 1852.

Nobody since has matched that bit of sailing skill.

Coupeville also happens to be part of that most unusual of national parks — Ebey's Landing National Historical Reserve. The reserve, first of its kind in the nation, was created by Congress in 1978 to preserve a historical record dating back more than a century.

More than 90 percent of the reserve's 17,000 acres is private property. Farms still are farmed, forests still are logged, and most of the historic buildings within the reserve still are used as residences and places of business. That includes the entire town of Coupeville.

A nine-member historical trust board, with local representation, sets the guidelines. Visitors are welcome to tour the reserve by car, bicycle or on foot. There are beaches for strolling, coves for picnicking and camping, old military forts to explore, lanes for biking and trails for hiking.

Visitors can check at the Island County Museum on Main Street for a self-guiding walking-tour map of old Coupeville.

Oak Harbor is Whidbey's version of an island metropolis. It is a Navy town on one hand, a thriving commercial hub on the other. The busy naval air station pumps millions of dollars into the island's economy.

Oak Harbor also comes with a rich history — shamrocks and tulips. Irish settlers came in the late 1850s to farm and fish. Dutch farmers, disillusioned with harsh conditions in the American Midwest, followed four decades later. In March, the Irish paint the town green for St. Patrick's Day; in April the Dutch parade through Oak Harbor in a celebration known as Holland Happenings.

Retirees say they'll never move from this pleasure island in the Pacific Northwest.

"The island would have to sink first," says Gary Fisher, the former Navy captain.

But beware: One visit and you may be shopping for property. Maureen Cooke of Twickenham House says four couples who registered as guests at the B&B since have become Whidbey residents.

The Cookes' advice to soon-to-retire active couples: "Don't wait — do it." ●

Wickenburg, Arizona

Cowboys and coyotes still roam this Old West town

By Judy Wade

It's hard not to like a town that erects a "No Fishing From Bridge" sign over a riverbed that's almost perpetually dry.

Wickenburg, in central Arizona, has had a sense of humor about itself since the late 1800s when it was a boom town celebrating glory holes and copper mines. Tales of its wealth were so exaggerated that any raconteur of overstated stories became known as a "Hassayamper" in honor of the Hassayampa River that now and then flows through Wickenburg.

More than a century after Henry Wickenburg discovered the nearby Vulture gold mine, this small Sonoran Desert town that bears his name doesn't have to work at maintaining its Old West ambiance. Surrounding ranches lend credibility to the cowboys in spurs and chaps at the local sandwich saloon. Three Western apparel and tack shops reinforce the charming image that helps sustain Wickenburg's most important economic staple — tourism.

So far, Wickenburg's small size has kept it free from the smog, traffic, pollution and crime problems that plague larger cities, although snowbirds seeking sunnier climes almost double the town's population to more than 12,000 during winter months.

Wickenburg grew by 27 percent (from 3,536 to 4,515) between 1980 and 1990, but growth poses no threat to its personality. The town is almost surrounded by property owned by the state and by the federal Bureau of Land Management, a situation that means large tracts simply aren't available for development. Even though city leaders actively court businesses in an effort to diversify the town's economic base, a height restriction of a story and a half keeps high-rise development on the farthest horizons of Wickenburg's future.

Retirees Jerry and Muriel Martin,

formerly of Montgomery, IL, bought a home in Wickenburg seven months after visiting the town. Traffic, taxes, weather and personal security were among reasons for the move, says 64-year-old Muriel. "We felt threatened when we went to the shopping mall (back home). Here we never even hear of a crime," she says.

Jerry, 65, concurs. "We investigated a lot of places through correspondence and ads. We first thought of Prescott, but when we found out it had 25 inches of snow we changed our minds. I've had bypass surgery, and I also have arthritis, so a warm climate was important."

The Martins' pleasant stucco home, with desert landscaping and a pool, is kept comfortable by a combination of air-conditioning and evaporative cooling.

"It's much cheaper to use the cooler than the air-conditioning," says Jerry of his 20-year-old home, "but you can't use the cooler when the humidity is high. We use air-conditioning only from around the first of July to late August, when it's very hot." After receiving a July bill of $300 for their all-electric home, the Martins opted for a level-pay plan of $180 per month year-round.

Dick and Hazel Conklin, both 64, left snowy Richland, IA, to spend two winters in Wickenburg before deciding on a permanent move. Says Dick, 64, "We came from a town of 600, and before settling here we considered Green Valley (near Tucson) and Sun City West (near Phoenix). But we prefer what we think of as outback country."

The Conklins' two-bedroom, two-bath home backs up to scenic open desert, and Hazel enjoys the active quail and coyote populations that parade just beyond their living-room window.

"We paid $18,000 for the 80-foot-

by-80-foot lot and the contractor charged $68,900" to build their 1,215-square-foot home, Dick says.

The Conklins experienced what Hazel calls "real estate shock. When we came out here and built something comparable (to our previous home), it was almost double the price we got for our house in Iowa."

The Martins, however, feel that costs have balanced out. "Housing is about the same. But our property tax in Illinois was $2,500, and in Wickenburg, it's about $700. Illinois didn't tax pensions, but Arizona does," says Jerry.

Housing costs are on a par with those in the Phoenix and Tucson areas. According to Wickenburg native Diana Garcia, a realty agent with Century 21, a new three-bedroom, two-bath, 1,800-square-foot home sells for $130,000-$160,000.

"A preowned home in a subdivision on a quarter-acre is approximately $93,000-$95,000, and that's a nice home," she says. Townhomes, condos and lower-priced homes are available.

One advantage of small-town living is a friendly, open attitude among its residents. James and Bennie Lotts moved from Kettering, OH, into an adult apartment complex in Wickenburg where "the residents were so friendly they just smothered us," says Bennie. "We were surprised at how everything fell into place so easily, and we were so readily accepted."

The Lottses, both 63, retired at age 47 and traveled for several years before settling in Wickenburg. They say they now spend less on shopping, eat at home more often and use their car less than they did during their working years.

"We have to watch our pennies, but it's fairly economical. We can walk to most places, and we manage the apartment complex where we live, which gives us a rent-free apartment and no electric bill," Bennie explains. The average age of residents in the complex is 70-plus.

Bennie dismisses the idea that you have to have a lot of money to relocate in retirement. "We've been retired all these years and haven't missed one meal. We don't have a lot, but we're happy. The average person (retiree) doesn't have a lot of money and still gets by," she says.

All three couples name community involvement as a key to feeling comfortable in their adopted town. Bennie Lotts is active in the hospital auxiliary and James volunteers to assist 24 elderly apartment residents with any need, day or night.

Muriel Martin spends free time as a board member of Las Senoras de Socorro, the fund-raising arm of the

Desert Caballeros Western Museum, and conducts children's tours. Jerry is active in the Elks and the chamber of commerce. Both are members of the Ambassadors Club, which welcomes new businesses to the area.

Cultural opportunities include Sunday afternoon concerts at the Community Center sponsored by Friends of Music, a civic group that exists on donations. Recent presentations have included the Phoenix Boys Choir and retired musicians from nearby Sun City.

Half a dozen art galleries purvey original Southwestern art, pottery and crafts by local artists. The Desert Caballeros Western Museum traces the town's history from prehistoric times, using miniature dioramas and a full-size reproduction of a turn-of-the-

century town. It also has an outstanding collection of Western art, including works by Charles Russell, Frederic Remington and others.

Wickenburg has two large food markets and two pharmacies, but residents report that shopping for clothes and furniture is best done in Phoenix, an hour's drive south. Many Wickenburg service and repair shops close at noon Saturday and don't open again until Monday. Says James Lotts, "If an appliance goes out on a weekend, you just have to live with it until Monday."

Considering that 31 percent of Wickenburg's population is 65 or older, it's not surprising to find an active senior center here. It serves lunches five days a week and organizes exercise classes, bingo and a band made

Wickenburg, AZ

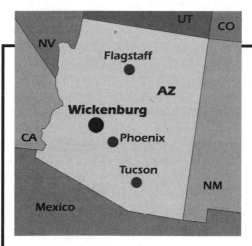

Population: 8,600 in summer, 12,000-plus in winter.
Location: About 50 miles northwest of Phoenix in central Arizona in foothills of Bradshaw Mountains; elevation 2,100 feet.
Climate:

	High	Low
January	63	30
July	104	70

Average relative humidity: 9% midsummer, 35% midwinter.
Rain: 11 inches.
Expect 345 sunny days a year in this semidesert terrain; summer temperatures average 10 degrees cooler than in Phoenix.
Cost of living: Average to slightly above (specific index not available).
Average housing cost: $155,000 for single-family home.
Sales tax: 6.5%.

Sales tax exemptions: Groceries, prescription drugs.
State income tax: Graduated in five steps from 2.9% to 5.17%, depending on income.
Income tax exemptions: Social Security benefits and up to $2,500 of federal, state and local government pensions are exempt.
Intangibles tax: None.
Estate tax: None, except the state's "pick-up" portion of the federal tax, applicable to taxable estates above $675,000.
Property tax: Rate is $109.90 per $1,000 of assessed value, with homes assessed at 10% of the value determined by the state. Tax on a $155,000 home is $1,703.
Homestead exemption: None.
Security: 35.9 crimes per 1,000 residents, lower than the national average of 46.2 crimes per 1,000 residents.
Religion: Churches include one Catholic and 16 Protestant.
Education: The Community Center offers inexpensive classes including computer training, water aerobics and crafts; many geared to seniors. Yavapai College and Rio Salado Community College also serve the area.
Transportation: No local bus service. There is commuter service to Sky Har-

bor International Airport in Phoenix, less than 50 miles away.
Health: One 80-bed acute-care hospital and an attached 40-bed nursing home are staffed by eight full-time physicians, including a general surgeon and an internist-cardiologist; 35 visiting specialists on the consulting staff. A municipally operated ambulance service is backed by helicopter ambulance service in Phoenix for transfer of patients needing more sophisticated care.
Housing options: Retirees have a wide choice of housing, with condos starting at about $46,000, older single-family homes starting at $80,000, manufactured homes on acreage starting at $69,000 and newer homes starting at about $100,000. Seven subdivisions have new homes priced from the mid-$100,000s to $300,000s.
Visitor lodging: Best Western Rancho Grande Motel, $62-$98 a night, (800) 528-1234. Americinn, $63, (520) 684-5461. Rancho de los Caballeros, $368-$616 per person, double occupancy, for three-night golf package with meals, (520) 684-5484.
Information: Wickenburg Chamber of Commerce, P.O. Drawer CC, Wickenburg, AZ 85390, (520) 684-5479 or www.wickenburgchamber.com.

up of retirees.

Explains 69-year-old Mary Ackley, center director, "Twice a week the Red Cross bus picks up seniors at their homes and takes them to Phoenix. It waits while they shop or go to medical appointments, then brings them home."

The expected chains like McDonald's and Taco Bell are part of Wickenburg's dining-out scene, as are two pizza parlors, a couple of steak houses and a deli. But the real gems are little places like Anita's, where a giant taco salad is $4 and a super-duper tostada (order it only if you're starving) is $4.75. It's not fancy, furniture is mismatched and tables are plastic-covered, but service is friendly and the food is great.

One of Wickenburg's biggest draws is its clean air and salubrious climate. Jerry Martin credits the climate with greatly diminishing his arthritis symptoms. Even during the hottest days of summer, late-afternoon breezes cool the desert, and residents say they open their windows at night and rarely sleep in air conditioning. Although Wickenburg occasionally gets some snow in winter, it rarely sticks for more than a few hours.

Golfers can become members of the Wickenburg Country Club, which, besides the 18-hole course, offers bridge, potluck dinners and other social events.

Another option for golfers, with a four-figure joining fee, is Los Caballeros Golf Club, acclaimed by *Golf Digest* as one of the top 10 courses in Arizona. Part of its claim to fame is that the parents of former Vice President Dan Quayle have a home along its fairways.

The Hassayampa River, which rarely makes an appearance in its sandy bed south of town, bubbles to the surface three miles to the southeast where it supports one of Arizona's finest Sonoran Desert streamside habitats. Its grassy banks, lined with cottonwoods and willows, form a ribbon of green that is a favorite spot for picnics. Visitors spot mule deer, mountain lions, bobcats, javelina and ring-tailed cats, all drawn to the river's edge. Local residents often volunteer at the Nature Conservancy, which protects the riparian area.

If there's any doubt about Wickenburg's small-town ambiance, it was dispelled when the town's first stoplight was installed 10 years ago at the corner of Tegner and Wickenburg Way. Local officials gave townspeople a 60-day no-ticket grace period so they could become accustomed to the new control.●

Williamsburg, Virginia

Colonial heritage and college-town appeal draw retirees to Virginia Peninsula

By Carol Godwin

Mention Williamsburg and images of early America cloaked in Colonial trappings come to mind — and rightly so. From 1699 to 1776, Williamsburg was the capital of England's oldest, largest, richest and most populous colony, a training ground for the men and women who led America to independence.

In its shops, taverns, government buildings, homes and streets, patriots like George Washington, Thomas Jefferson and Patrick Henry helped frame the structure of government for their state and their nation. Today Williamsburg is a composite of 20th-century lifestyles and rich Colonial heritage that remains steeped in a historic state of mind.

That's exactly what got John and Lisa Hewett thinking 30 years ago about eventually retiring in Williamsburg. "In the spring of 1964, we were passing through on vacation.... (We) stayed in a little house on Duke of Gloucester Street in Colonial Williamsburg and fell in love with the area," says Lisa.

"We were very intrigued with everything we saw and came back on a number of occasions before moving here in May 1994," says John, 64.

John and Lisa moved to Williamsburg from Pasadena, MD. John was headmaster at private schools for more than 25 years, and the Hewetts wanted to retire in a college town. They considered State College, PA, because their son lives nearby, "but it was too snowy," says Lisa, 63, a lifelong homemaker.

The Hewetts had lived in the Northeast — from Massachusetts to Maryland — and were seeking a warmer location in retirement. They also wanted a small community with an identity — and one with good art and music programs. In the fall of 1993, they purchased a home in First Colony, a residential community five miles west of Colonial Williamsburg.

"The house was 10 years old and extremely well cared for, and we've converted the attic into a studio," says Lisa.

"The community has tennis courts, swimming pool, recreation park, and marina and boat access," adds John. "We plan to live here as long as it makes sense to be here."

The Hewetts have found that their budget has not changed significantly since retiring to Williamsburg. "We are very conservative, with a New England background, and saved all of our lives," says John. "But I don't chintz when it comes to art supplies or books or educational opportunities," adds Lisa, who is enrolled in a portrait class.

Williamsburg is home of the second-oldest institution of higher education in the United States. The College of William and Mary was chartered in 1693. Seniors 60 and older can audit up to three courses per semester free.

The college also sponsors the Christopher Wren Association for Lifelong Learning, a self-supporting organization that invites area residents of retirement age to participate in a broad array of courses and lectures, field trips, tours, social occasions and fellowship — with no exams, no grades and no pressure. Courses are taught by current and retired volunteers from the college faculty, and instructors also are drawn from the association's own membership and from the community.

Williamsburg's college-town ambiance also attracted Sally Councill, 71, who has been enrolled in college classes for the sheer enjoyment of it since she moved to Williamsburg in 1993. She also participates in programs offered by Elderhostel Institute Network, which is associated with the Christopher Wren Association. Elderhostel offers unique adult educational experiences in the United States and abroad.

A widow since 1983, Sally says she loathes stories about children who "had to put mother in a retirement home."

"After my husband's death, I gave myself 10 years in the house and decided that at 70, while I was still independent, I would do my own 'putting,' " she says.

An avid traveler keenly interested in continuing to expand her horizons, she considered several communities in Pennsylvania and Virginia before moving from Bethesda, MD, to Williamsburg Landing, a continuing-care retirement community. Her colonial-style house overlooks College Creek, and her yard boasts a 10-foot spruce tree that's a magnet for birds.

"It's the cutest house you ever saw," says Sally. "I have a huge family room with plenty of space for my player piano, a living room, full dining room, kitchen, breakfast room, bedroom and two baths."

Sally doesn't own her home at Williamsburg Landing. She paid an entry fee based on specific options, and a monthly fee covers a range of amenities. One of them is Williamsburg Landing's state-of-the-art health-care facility. "I'm in perfect health now, but I'm here for the duration. My safety net is the total health care provided," she says.

Sally likes being close enough to Washington, DC, to drive back for special occasions, but she doesn't miss the city's traffic and congestion. She is quick to point out that Williamsburg is a sophisticated small town with an identity all its own.

Sally says it was easy to make friends at Williamsburg Landing. "It's like a college campus where all the students are 70 years old but don't know it," she says. "It's a caring, supportive community. We all stay busy, yet take care of each other without living in each other's pocket."

A major area attraction is Colonial Williamsburg, the nation's oldest outdoor living history museum. Populated with historic re-enactors clad in period dress, Colonial Williamsburg comprises 173 acres with 88 original 18th-century buildings and hundreds of structures that have been reconstructed on their original foundations. Educational tours and programs re-create daily life during the 1770s, when colonists were taking their first steps toward becoming Americans.

"One of the many perks of living in the

area is the Colonial Williamsburg Good Neighbor Card," says Arlene Geldreich, who with husband Dick moved to Will- iamsburg in August 1994. The Good Neighbor Card, a $33 value, is available free to residents of Williamsburg, James City County and the Bruton District of York County. It provides free admission to all Colonial Williamsburg exhibitions

Williamsburg, VA

Population: 12,400, plus about 7,500 university students.

Location: On the Virginia Peninsula midway between Richmond and the Virginia Beach seashore, about 155 miles south of Washington, DC. The city is bordered by the James and York rivers and lies in both York and James City counties.

Climate:

	High	Low
January	52	31
July	88	67

Average relative humidity: 70.25%
Rain: 56.63 inches.
Snow: 8.2 inches.

Winters usually are mild and summers, though warm and long, frequently are tempered by cool periods associated with northeasterly winds off the Atlantic. Temperatures of 100 degrees or higher occur infrequently, and extremely cold temperatures of zero or below are almost non-existent. Winters occasionally pass without a measurable amount of snowfall or with light snowfall that usually melts within 24 hours. Williamsburg lies north of the usual track of hurricanes and other tropical storms.

Cost of living: Below average (specific index not available).

Average housing cost: Average price for single-family homes, townhomes and condominiums in the Williamsburg area, including part of James City County and the Bruton District of York County, is approximately $170,000. Monthly rentals for single-family homes, townhomes and condominiums range from $550 to $1,600.

Sales tax: 4.5%

Sales tax exemptions: None.
State income tax: The tax is graduated from 2% on the first $3,000 of taxable income to 5.75% on the amount above $17,000.
State income tax: Graduated in four steps from 2% to 5.75%, depending on income.
Income tax exemptions: Social Security benefits. There is an $800 personal exemption for residents age 65 or older. There is a $6,000 deduction per person from adjusted gross income for residents age 62-64, and a $12,000 deduction per person for residents 65 or older.
Intangibles tax: None.
Estate tax: None, except the state's "pick-up" portion of the federal tax, applicable to taxable estates above $675,000.
Inheritance tax: None.
Property tax: In Williamsburg, 54 cents per $100 of assessed value, with homes assessed at 100% of market value. The rate is 86 cents in unincorporated areas of James City County and 84 cents in unincorporated areas of York County per $100 of assessed value. Tax on a $170,000 home in Williamsburg in James City County is about $2,380 a year.
Homestead exemption: There is a tax deferral for homeowners 65 and older, subject to income and net worth limits.
Security: 39.8 crimes per 1,000 residents, lower than the national average of 46.2 crimes per 1,000 residents.
Religion: More than 50 churches and synagogues represent 30 denominations.
Education: Seniors 60 and older can audit up to three courses free per semester at the College of William and Mary. The college's Christopher Wren Association for Lifelong Learning attracts a retiree student body. Thomas Nelson Community College in nearby Newport News offers 24 associate degrees and a full range of technical and vocational skills.
Transportation: James City Transit offers local bus service. Amtrak offers passenger service from Williamsburg. Area airports include the Newport News-Williamsburg International Airport, 20 minutes from downtown in Newport News; Norfolk International Airport and Richmond International Airport each are about 50 minutes away.
Health: The 139-bed Williamsburg Community Hospital provides full general medical, surgical and acute care. Eastern State Hospital provides psychiatric care. All facilities offer a range of inpatient and outpatient services. Also available are several quick-care facilities.
Housing options: On 2,500 forested acres, **Ford's Colony**, (800) 334-6033, has 54 holes of championship golf, tennis, swimming pool and nature trails; homesites begin at $70,000, homes at $275,000 and townhomes at $175,000. The new 90-acre **Patriots Colony,** (757) 220-9000, a continuing-care retirement community for retired military and senior government service employees, has apartments that range from $71,500 for a one-bedroom unit to $146,210 for a two-bedroom unit; villas range from $87,250 for a one-bedroom unit to $174,600 for a two-bedroom unit. On 133 wooded acres, **Williamsburg Landing,** (757) 253-0303, a continuing-care retirement community, has an entrance fee that entitles retirees to lifetime use of a residence ranging from $99,000 for a one-bedroom apartment to $292,000 for a 2,000-square-foot house. At the 2,900-acre residential resort community of **Kingsmill,** (757) 253-3393, lots range from $150,000 to $700,000, townhomes from $150,000 to $500,000, resort villas from $125,000 to $335,000, and single-family homes from $250,000 to $1 million.
Visitor lodging: More than 53 hotels and motels, 22 bed-and-breakfast inns and nine private guest homes are located in Williamsburg and Colonial Williamsburg. Many offer senior discounts. For a complete listing, contact the Williamsburg Hotel and Motel Association, (800) 899-9462.
Information: Williamsburg Area Convention and Visitors Bureau, P.O. Box 3585, Williamsburg, VA 23187-3585, (757) 253-0192 or www.visitwilliamsburg.com.

and museums, free use of the Colonial Williamsburg bus service, a 50 percent discount on tickets to evening programs, a 40 percent discount on up to 10 general-admission tickets annually, and more — perfect for when family and friends come to visit, Arlene adds. Nearby, historic Jamestown Settlement and the Yorktown Victory Center also provide free passes for area residents.

The Geldreichs first visited Williamsburg in 1963 while on vacation and thought then it would be a great place to retire. "We toured all over Florida (and) considered Naples and Captiva but felt they were too crowded for us," says Dick, 59, an accountant. They also visited Pinehurst, NC, but decided there was not enough variety beyond golf, says Dick.

He and Arlene, 57, a homemaker who recently graduated at the top of her college class in institutional management, lived at Packanack Lake in Wayne, NJ, for 21 years before retiring to Williamsburg.

The Geldreichs watched their new home go up at Ford's Colony, a gated community set on 2,500 acres rich with woodlands and wetlands. "Our house is a 4,300-square-foot cape colonial with a big kitchen, great room and two decks great for entertaining," says Arlene.

"We didn't want a retirement community, and I'd say the mix here is about 60 percent retired and 40 percent younger families with children of all ages," says Dick. "This is our seventh move, and we're in for the duration."

To complement 54 holes of championship golf, the dining room at Ford's Colony Country Club has received the American Automobile Association's Five Diamond rating. Laced with nature trails and natural environs that are home to wildlife, a portion of the community has been set aside never to be developed.

Williamsburg holds a special draw for retired military personnel. Several military installations and hospitals on the Virginia Peninsula and in nearby Washington, DC, are within proximity. The opening of the new Patriots Colony at Williamsburg, the first continuing-care retirement community in the area catering to retired military officers and senior government service employees, adds another dimension.

Retired Lt. Col. Lois White, a former U.S. Air Force nurse, and retired Senior Master Sgt. Donald White, a former U.S. Air Force medical technician, were among the first to arrive at Patriots Colony. They sold their home of 21 years in Manlius, NY, a suburb of Syracuse, and moved into an apartment in Williamsburg while waiting for construction to be completed on their Patriots Colony apartment.

"We started thinking about retirement in 1988, and most of the locations we were really interested in were retirement communities where the majority of those living there are former military," says Don, 63.

Previously stationed in Washington, DC, the Whites were somewhat familiar with the Williamsburg area and visited over a three-year period while considering their move. "We like the four seasons," says Lois, 65. The area's history and William and Mary's programs for senior citizens also were determining factors.

Pleased with their new 1,600-square-foot apartment, the Whites find it larger than those at many other continuing-care retirement communities. "Some other retirement communities don't have washers and dryers in each apartment; here they are standard in all units," says Lois. And with a nursing facility on the grounds, she knows that if she or Don ever needs nursing care, the other will be near at hand.

The Whites rent, rather than own, their Patriots Colony apartment. "We paid an upfront fee based on the square footage, and we pay a monthly fee that includes all taxes, housekeeping once a week, one meal per day, utilities, cable TV and the maintenance of all appliances," says Don.

Located about five miles from Williamsburg, Patriots Colony spreads over 90 wooded acres with a five-story highrise apartment building, villas, a community center with dining and recreational amenities, a fitness center, extended-care nursing facility and nature trails.

Another military couple, retired Col. Bob Mangum and wife Cary, both 60, chose a home near an area attraction — Busch Gardens Old Country, a major theme park. Their home is on a cul-de-sac in Kingsmill, a residential resort community developed by Anheuser-Busch Co.

When they bought their home in 1984, they were looking ahead to retirement. They had owned a home in Newport News for 17 years and moved in and out of it whenever Bob's career as a U.S. Army aviator brought the family back to the Virginia Peninsula.

Recently retired from the Army, Bob now is employed by McDonald Douglas Helicopter Co. and Cary is student personnel coordinator for a school of nursing in Newport News. They plan to fully retire in about a year.

"We like having the security, we're golfers, and the community met our needs for now and for retirement," says Cary. "We love the area but didn't want a strictly retirement community. Kingsmill is a good mixture of families with children and people of retirement age."

Located on the James River, Kingsmill has amenities that include tennis, health and golf clubs. "We joined the golf club," says Cary. "And Bob and I belong to a wine-and-dine club with 10 couples ranging in age from 45 to 75. We meet once a month at a different host home, enjoy wine and cheese, pick a restaurant and go out to dinner together. It's lots of fun."

The Mangums, Hewetts, Geldreichs, Whites and Sally Council all say the cost of living in Williamsburg is comparable to or lower than where they lived previously.

"My best advice to prospective retirees is to take advantage of the offers (that) residential, resort and retirement communities extend to come spend a few days and get to know a specific community and area," says Dick Geldreich. "Then compare, make lists and subscribe to the newspaper in the destinations you are seriously considering."

Don White's advice to those considering a continuing-care retirement community is to research the move thoroughly. Even with the many military moves Don and Lois White made in their careers, moving at 70 presents a different set of anxieties that can be lessened by thoughtful preparation, he says.

"You can't do too much research," he says. "Spend some time at different retirement locations and compare. Have something in common with the people who live there. Make the decision on your own. We have no children and did not want to be dependent on our siblings. Expect an adjustment period."

Sally Councill agrees that research is important. Through a subscription to the Williamsburg Landing newsletter, she knew a lot about the community before she moved in — right down to the name of the high scorer in bridge.●

Wilmington, North Carolina

Scenic coast and rich tradition make North Carolina port a star attraction

By Peggy Payne

When British actor Anthony Hopkins spent six winter weeks in Wilmington, NC, filming "The Road to Wellville," he lived at Graystone Inn, a neoclassic mansion in the riverfront historic district. On many evenings, he walked downtown to the Cafe Phoenix for supper.

Hopkins eventually moved on to other films in other locations, but he longed to stay in the city of Wilmington.

"He fell in love with the area," a Hollywood spokesman says. "He even considered looking for a home there, but the exigencies of his work and so on keep him from doing that."

Wilmington — the quiet, rich-in-tradition, Southern port where I grew up — in recent years has become startlingly hip. Movie stars filming here at Carolco Studios are captivated by the city. Dennis Hopper now has a residence in the area and Andy Griffith owns property here. Big-name stars aren't the only ones attracted to the area. Wilmington and its surrounding beaches are drawing increased numbers of retirees and people of all ages to relocate here.

George and Suzanne Taylor retired to Wilmington from Richmond, VA, where they had lived all their lives. George, 59, calls Wilmington "a good blend of small-town size, with the availability of cultural events of a much larger city."

It's one of the greatest places you could ever live," adds Suzanne, 57.

"This is certainly the hot spot of retirement right now," says Bill Bowman, who publishes the "North Carolina Relocation and Retirement Guide" and guidebooks to 11 other states.

The influx of both retirees and younger people began in the early '70s, says Bowman, who lives in Wilmington himself. The reasons for this burst of popularity are many, but "first and foremost," he cites the town's location.

The site — on a narrow peninsula between the Cape Fear River and the Atlantic Ocean — is the key to the town's history, its uncommon beauty and its distinct personality. The surrounding waters — the ocean, the deep river, the sounds and channels — have drawn people for centuries.

The first European explorer sailed into the Cape Fear region in 1524. Giovanni da Verrazano found the "sandie shoare," the fields and woods, to be "as pleasant and delectable to behold, as is possible to imagine."

Englishmen from Barbados settled on the riverbank in 1664, but the colony failed. In the early 18th century, pirates — among them Stede Bonnet and the fearsome Blackbeard — found excellent hiding places in this convoluted shoreline. As late as my childhood in the 1950s, people were still digging potholes in the sand of Money Island, looking for buried pirate treasure.

In 1725, a second town, Brunswick, was founded on the river, and plantations developed in the fertile, rice-growing land. Today the public can visit the Brunswick Town ruins, Poplar Grove Plantation and the gardens of Orton Plantation, with cypress ponds, immense live oaks, alligators and azaleas. If Orton looks familiar, you may have seen it and its more-Southern-than-Tara manor house in more than one recent movie.

Wilmington traces its roots to 1732, soon becoming an important port for shipbuilding and the transport of pine products. For a time in the mid-1800s, it was the home berth for blockade runners, the ships bringing supplies to the Confederacy during the Civil War.

Today, if you take a walk through the City Market downtown on Water Street, you can see past the rows of craft vendors to the sun on the river.

Fast-moving and deep enough for a battleship, the river has made Wilmington a place of trade and mingling cultures for a long time. This little market, for example, first opened for business in 1880. With its slight breeze off the water and view of river traffic, it still has the feel of a dock in the Caribbean.

Wilmington frequently is compared to the Southern ports of Charleston and Savannah. There are strong similarities: water-laced land, old homes, Southern history. There also are differences. Wilmington is smaller, and many people will tell you that it's a more open, easygoing town, an easier place to make friends. The openness of the community has impressed retired Navy Capt. Howard Loving and his wife, Elisabeth, who relocated to Wilmington from Hyattstown, MD, in 1994. They settled in a neighborhood that is about 50 years old, located eight minutes from downtown and 12 minutes from Wrightsville Beach.

The big surprise, according to Howard, 57, was "the ease with which you can meet people and get accepted. We have met neighbors on all the streets around us and gotten to be close enough that we share dinner together. You can't do that in too many places."

"You feel so welcomed," adds Elisabeth, 60, whose family lives in Le Havre, on the coast of France.

Local real estate agent Wendy Block works with many retirees interested in coming to the area and says most who visit wind up relocating here.

"Once they come here, we lose very few," Wendy says. "Wilmington people, by and large, have been receptive to people moving in. It's a warm, laid-back, easy community, a little more contemporary (than some other Southern ports)."

At the same time, a personal note: Wilmington is not SoHo. Though there is a lively arts activity and downtown nightlife, this is a town that also holds dear a sense of propriety and reserve.

A popular local guide and historian finds a historical basis for Wilmington's being open and somewhat reserved at the same time. Bobby Stanley Jenkins, a retired interior designer, has been active for more than 30 years in the successful preservation of the downtown historic district. Two hundred blocks of Wilmington are now listed on the National Register of Historic Places. To explore some of the older areas, Bobby began a Wilmington Adventure Walking Tour in his retirement.

He traces much of the personality of Wilmington to the fact that the town was settled by indentured servants and English second sons, often nobility who

Wilmington, NC

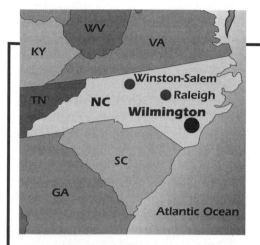

Population: 71,000 in Wilmington, 156,196 in New Hanover County.
Location: North Carolina's major port, on the state's southern coast near the mouth of Cape Fear River and 10 miles from Atlantic beaches.
Climate: High   Low
January   56 35
July   89 71
Average relative humidity: 56%
Rain: 53 inches.
Snow: 2 inches.
Four distinct seasons are tempered by maritime location; winters are mild, though coats may be needed, and summers are cooled by sea breezes. Area is subject to hurricanes; the last storm to cause significant damage was in 1984.
Cost of living: 102.6, based on national average of 100.
Average housing cost: $140,000.
Sales tax: 6%
Sales tax exemptions: Prescriptions, services and cars.
State income tax: Graduated in three steps from 6% to 7.75%, depending on income.
Income tax exemptions: Social Security benefits. Each taxpayer also can exempt up to $4,000 in local, state or federal government retirement benefits and up to $2,000 in private retirement benefits, but the total of these exemptions cannot exceed $4,000 per person.

Intangibles tax: None.
Estate tax: None, except the state's "pick-up" portion of the federal tax, applicable to taxable estates above $675,000.
Property tax: County rate is $5.65 per $1,000 of value and city rate is additional $4.70 for a total of $10.35 per $1,000 value in Wilmington, with property assessed at 100% of market value. Additional municipal rates for nearby beaches range from $2.35 to $4 per $1,000 of value. Outside a municipality, a $.25 per $1,000 fire district rate is added to the county tax. Yearly tax on a $140,000 home in Wilmington is $1,449.
Homestead exemption: People age 65 or over, or disabled, with an income of no more than $11,000 receive a $15,000 reduction in the property tax valuation of their permanent residence.
Security: 106.5 crimes per 1,000 residents, higher than the national average of 46.2 crimes per 1,000 residents.
Religion: More than 200 churches and synagogues are located in New Hanover County and represent most religious sects.
Education: The University of North Carolina at Wilmington offers baccalaureate, graduate and continuing-education courses. The university's Adult Scholars Leadership Program is designed to involve retirees with community projects. Shaw University has a four-year college degree program, and its Center for Alternative Program of Education (CAPE) offers a full schedule of evening classes. The region is also served by three community colleges: Cape Fear, Southeastern and Brunswick.
Transportation: There is local bus service. The New Hanover International Airport typically has 20 arrivals and departures a day by three carriers.

"International" service is limited to small private planes arriving from the Caribbean to clear customs procedures here.
Health: New Hanover Regional Medical Center has 628 beds in three hospitals: general acute care, psychiatric and rehabilitative. Also at the complex, the Center for Successful Aging offers care by specialists and educational and recreational activities. Columbia Cape Fear Memorial Hospital sponsors the Senior Wellness Clinic and Healthy Horizons, a 14,000-member health organization that offers services, classes, trips and discounts for people over 50.
Housing options: Wide selection available. Listings include: a Winds oceanfront beach condo at Carolina Beach, $79,000; a restored turn-of-the-century four-bedroom, four-fireplace home near downtown, $139,000; a ranch-style home on seven acres for $101,600; a pre-Revolutionary home with river views from terraces and decks, $650,000; or a big Victorian nearby for $259,900. On the Inland Waterway in the country club community of Landfall, homes start at $240,000. Or, you can choose a beach community, on nearby Figure 8 Island, Bald Head Island or at Wrightsville Beach.
Visitor lodging: Wilmington Hilton, (800) HILTONS, on the downtown riverfront, doubles for $85-$155 a night; Best Western Carolinian, (910) 763-4653, doubles from $44, including continental breakfast; an efficiency apartment at the Summer Sands at Wrightsville Beach, (910) 256-4175, from $125.
Information: Newcomer Information, Greater Wilmington Chamber of Commerce, 1 Estell Lee Place, Wilmington, NC 28401, (910) 762-2611 or www.wilmingtonchamber.org. There's a charge for publications; the Newcomer Package is $12, plus handling.

would not inherit family land or titles and, therefore, set off to seek their fortunes in the New World.

"In their native country, they would never have sat down together," Bobby says of the two types of settlers. But here, he says, they agreed among themselves that they would not perpetuate the class system that back in England had discriminated against both groups. That acceptance of differences and the international traffic of ships into the city have created a fabric of life that is at once "multicultural, multidimensional," yet based on the values of the early English.

Practically speaking, he says, "They will not judge you on the dollar value of your clothes but they'll judge the hell out of you…(over whether) it's the proper attire for the time and place."

The town does have a history of intolerance. In 1898, Wilmington erupted in race riots, which ushered in the era of Jim Crow segregation laws in the state. In 1971, racial tension again turned violent, resulting in the nationally controversial convictions of the "Wilmington 10." In recent years, however, racial politics took a different turn: The district attorney was removed from his job on the charge of using a racial slur to a black man in a bar. The incident underlines the fact that racial division still exists. On the whole, Wilmington is not a socially integrated town.

Yet in many respects, it is a cosmopolitan and sophisticated community. The basis for that again lies in geography and history.

"For years, we were isolated because of our geographic location, connected to the world by the Cape Fear River. We could not get inland to our state capital, but we always went to London," Bobby says. The port also provided ties with the Eastern Seaboard cities, where Wilmington's social and cultural scene attracted attention.

"You can stand on the corner of Third and Market streets and see more examples of famous American architects' works than in any other city in America," says Bobby. Architects who designed the Lincoln and Jefferson memorials in the nation's capital, Henry Bacon and John Russell Pope respectively, are among notables who did work in Wilmington.

Architecture in the historic district is largely Victorian with lots of gingerbread trim. Homes often have big porches and turrets. Similar to San Francisco's famed "painted ladies," these houses are in soft colors with a hint of a Caribbean influence.

The first play written and produced in America, "The Prince of Parthia," was presented here in 1767. In 1788, an amateur theatrical group, the Thalians, was formed. The Thalians continue today, one of the oldest theater groups in the country. Performances are now given 250 nights a year in the ornate 1855 Thalian Hall.

In recent years, the University of North Carolina at Wilmington has given the town a cultural and intellectual resource that the traffic of ships alone couldn't bring.

Bill McCann, who retired to Wilmington from Binghamton, NY, where he had worked for IBM, thinks the college helps distinguish the city.

"I think the university has a very, very positive influence on the community," he says.

McCann lives by a creek that runs into the Inland Waterway. He can walk across his back yard and step into his motorboat. Besides enjoying the water, he takes advantage of the cultural scene, attending plays and concerts.

One of the biggest events of the year is the North Carolina Azalea Festival, a spring celebration that locally rivals Christmas in pageantry. It's early in April and features a horse show and number of social events as well as garden tours.

A major attraction is the USS North Carolina, a large World War II battleship berthed across the river from downtown. It's open for touring year-round.

When it came time for the Taylors to retire, there was no question that Wilmington was the place. They had had a beach home here for 20 years. "We vacationed here every summer, came down about every month for a three-day weekend. George always said he was going to retire to Wilmington," Suzanne says.

"It had so much to offer — the city itself, the water, the college, cultural activities, Figure 8 Island (where the Taylor home is)," says George, former-

ly an engineer for Philip Morris.

"It has excellent restaurants and a wonderful downtown," says Elisabeth Loving.

In general, North Carolina residents are considered modest compared to their proud neighbors in Virginia and South Carolina. There's a common saying: "North Carolina is a vale of humility between two mountains of conceit." Wilmington, however, is an exception — its residents enjoy bragging about their city.

The arrival of the movie industry is simply one more ornament to justify that civic pride. Wilmington has appeared in a number of movies, including "Rambling Rose," "Teenage Mutant Ninja Turtles," and "Sleeping With the Enemy." Extras for movies are in demand. My mother, retired in Wilmington from the clothing business, was offered a small part as a nun but turned it down: Her first grandchild was due.

For the Lovings, the move to Wilmington has meant a savings in their cost of living. "I often paid $500 a month to heat that house in Maryland," Howard says of their former home. "Here I pay less than $750 for the season." While Wilmington's cost of living is slightly above the national average, the city is less costly than many cities in the Northeast, particularly the metropolitan areas.

Retirees have a difficult time finding any faults with the city. Suzanne Taylor, however, has noticed increased traffic and people congestion since they moved to the city in 1987. Her husband says airline service is limited and residents often have to go through Charlotte, NC, to get to their destinations.

Though none of the retirees interviewed mentioned crime as a problem, the city's crime rate is high, 106.5 crimes per 1,000 residents as compared to an overall national average of 46.2 crimes per 1,000 people, according to FBI Uniform Crime Reports.

Linda Rawley, community relations officer for the Wilmington Police Department, says much of the crime occurs in areas where drugs are a problem, adding that the high crime rate "is not citywide." She says the high number of arrests also reflects the city's aggressive enforcement of drug laws.●

Winter Haven, Florida

Florida town has feel of the country, but big-city amenities are easily accessible

By David Wilkening

Robert Price and his wife, Lillie, retired from suburban Chicago to rural Winter Haven, FL, population 28,972. Yet from their new home, they found metropolitan attractions just as easily accessible — and without a traffic hassle.

From this central Florida setting, inviting Atlantic or Gulf Coast beaches are about an hour's drive on normally uncrowded four-lane interstate highways, and cultural amenities are just as close.

The Prices — he's 65, she's 45 — say it's no more difficult to reach the art exhibits of Tampa, Orlando and Sarasota than it was to take in similar downtown Chicago attractions from their former home in Palos Park, IL.

Another couple, Dr. John Petre, 70, and his wife, Catherine, 68, from Erie, PA, live about a half-hour drive from the Prices in an even more rural area — yet they have season tickets to the Orlando Symphony Orchestra's pop concerts.

Why not, they ask? It's only an hour away on an interstate highway.

John and Barbara Riegler, both 61, from Beulah, a small town in northwestern Michigan, crisscrossed Florida for four years looking for the right retirement site. They shunned the state's well-known coastal cities for Winter Haven.

Its attraction? It's near everything and yet secluded, far removed from the "rat race you can get on either coast," as Robert Price puts it.

And it's less expensive, John Riegler adds.

For the Prices and Petres, the environment was a deciding factor in their choice of Winter Haven for retirement.

"We like the quality of life here, the restaurants, lakes, foliage, blue herons, egrets," says Robert Price. "We were surprised at the extent of the lakes and wildlife. Quite a few of the lakes have no population around them

and are probably like they were 10,000 years ago."

Price, who was a vice president of General Mills in Chicago before he retired, now serves as executive vice president of Central Florida Business Solutions in Winter Haven.

The Petres, who both were in the medical field (he as a urologist and she as a nurse), moved into a resort area called Grenelefe, a self-contained golf- and tennis-oriented community outside Winter Haven.

"The environment is similar to what we had in Pennsylvania — tall pine trees, high ridge country, beautiful lakes and oak trees," says John. "You are not allowed to cut a tree under any circumstance."

Winter Haven drew the Rieglers for several reasons. They liked the fact that it had little traffic but was close to such attractions as the beaches, Walt Disney World, Sea World and Universal Studios. And they found the cost of living — particularly recreation and housing — lower in Winter Haven.

"We're golfers, and the cost of golfing had a big impact as to why we went to central Florida as opposed to the coast," John says.

They bought a manufactured home in a community called Swiss Golf and Tennis Club on Lake Henry, where they play golf at least three times a week. The Rieglers spend half the year in Winter Haven and half at their second home on a lake near Traverse City, MI, where they operated supermarkets.

"When we go to Michigan, we get the boat out and get ready for our summer visitors. Down here, we get the golf clubs out and get ready for our winter visitors. It's a year-round vacation," John says.

Despite its quiet nature, Winter Haven sits in the heart of an area where 6.2 million people live within a two-

hour drive and 11.7 million within a four-hour drive. Modern airports at both Tampa and Orlando have won awards for their architecture and, more importantly, their convenience. Tampa — only an hour's drive away — offers its own share of tourist attractions, including Busch Gardens.

"One of the attractions of Winter Haven, I think, is that it's a little more laid-back atmosphere than, say, Orlando, which tends to appeal more to younger people," says Cliff Howell, a 57-year-old attorney who came to the town as a child in the early 1940s.

"The pace is a little less rapid, the costs are a little less, there's available land and the cost of a modest retirement home is less," Howell says.

At press time, the National Association of Homebuilders identified the Lakeland/Winter Haven area as the 16th most affordable place to live in the country. The association says 82.9 percent of the homes in the area can be purchased by households earning the area's median income. The average single-family home here costs $83,905, according to the local board of realtors.

In addition, an annual price index — released by the Florida governor's office and based on 117 items and services — shows the cost of living in Winter Haven and surrounding Polk County compares favorably with many other Florida counties.

The Prices, Petres and Rieglers — and many other retirees here — have migrated from regions that can be bitterly cold in winter.

"We had seven months of gray days," says Lillie Price of her eight years in the Chicago area. "I used to go to the tanning spa just for the bright light."

Winter Haven, by contrast, has mostly sunny days. It enjoys a balmy climate (average temperature is 73 degrees) with an advantage over coastal areas in that humidity generally is lower than in cities by the sea.

Retirees in Winter Haven find they don't have to go far to keep busy or to find recreation. Many activities revolve around the area's 177 parks and 50 lakes, which provide abundant opportunities for water sports and lakefront living. Citrus groves cover much of the gently rolling terrain. And, Winter Haven is home to Florida's famed Cypress Gardens.

Active retirees can choose among 37 golf courses and numerous tennis courts. For those not inclined toward outdoor activities, the Polk County area has 16 movie theaters, plus bowling alleys and various senior adult centers with organized activities.

Culturally, the Theatre of Winter Haven schedules eight productions a year in the city's 350-seat Chain O'Lakes Convention Center. It's known as one of the best community theaters in the Southeast. Other diversions include a variety of other theater and dance groups and such annual events as arts and crafts festivals and a well-known Bach Festival each March.

Despite its small size, Winter Haven boasts many amenities found in larger cities. There are more than a half-dozen banks and savings and loan offices in the city, for example, as well as a half-dozen stock brokerage firms.

Health care includes Winter Haven Hospital, a major not-for-profit facility with 579 beds. It has a 24-hour emergency room and all-inclusive medical facilities. Educationally, Polk Community College is popular with retirees. Its 130-acre campus offers a varied curriculum. Four-year colleges can be found in Tampa and Orlando.

Clubs and organizations here include dozens of social, fraternal and service groups. Local chapters of the

Winter Haven, FL

Population: 28,972 in Winter Haven, 479,699 in Polk County.

Location: At geographic center of state, 50 miles from Tampa on the Gulf Coast and Orlando, tourist capital and gateway to the Walt Disney World complex.

Climate:

	High	Low
January	72	49
July	96	74

Average relative humidity: 55%
Rain: 50 inches.
Climate balmy with mild, sunny winters and hot summers. Humidity high in the morning, lower in the afternoon and normally less than in coastal areas.

Cost of living: 95 for Polk County, based on state average of 100.

Average housing cost: $83,905 for a single-family home; $92,600 for a condo or patio home.

Sales tax: 7%

Sales tax exemptions: Most groceries, medical services, prescription drugs.

State income tax: None.

Intangibles tax: Assessed on stocks, bonds and other specified assets. Tax rate is $1 per $1,000 of value for assets under $100,000 for individuals or $200,000 for couples, and $1.50 per $1,000 value for greater amounts; first $20,000 for individuals and $40,000 for couples is exempt. Some investments are exempt.

Estate tax: None, except the state's "pick-up" portion of the federal tax, applicable to taxable estates above $675,000.

Property tax: $21.02 per $1,000 of assessed value with homes assessed at 100% of the appraised value. Yearly tax on an $83,905 home, with the homestead exemption noted below, is $1,238.

Homestead exemption: $25,000 off assessed value for primary, permanent residence.

Security: 99 crimes per 1,000 residents, higher than the national average of 46.2 crimes per 1,000 residents.

Religion: More than 80 churches of many denominations, plus one synagogue (reform).

Education: Varied classes at Polk Community College. Also within commuting distance: Florida Southern College, the University of South Florida, University of Central Florida, the University of Tampa, Warner Southern College and Webber College.

Transportation: Bus, taxi service available, but cars almost a necessity. Amtrak has daily service. Tampa International Airport and Orlando International Airport are both about one hour away.

Health: Seven general hospitals in the county. Winter Haven Hospital has 711 beds and 24-hour emergency service. There are also 10 medical clinics, two blood banks and about 300 physicians and dentists in area. Full medical services available.

Housing options: A mixture of single-family and condo apartments as well as up to a dozen manufactured-home communities and a half-dozen nursing homes. **Ruby Lake**, a gated lakefront community, has custom homes from the $130,000s, lakefront homes from the low $200,000s. **The Gates of Lake Region**, a new gated development, has lots priced from the $30,000s and homes from the $150,000s. **Cypresswood**, a master-planned golf community, has golf villas from the $70,000s, condos from the $80,000s and patio homes in the low $100,000s.

Visitor lodging: Howard Johnson, $54-$89 depending on season, located downtown, (863) 294-7321 or (800) 654-2000. Chain of Lakes Resort, $169 -$600 depending on season and room, or $550 and up per week (with kitchenettes), a mile from Cypress Gardens, (863) 324-6320.

Information: Winter Haven Chamber of Commerce, P.O. Box 1420, Winter Haven, FL 33882, (863) 293-2138 or www.winterhavenfl.com.

American Association of Retired Persons, Veterans of Foreign Wars Auxiliary and Rotary are active.

Early residents of Winter Haven made their living at a canning factory in the late 1800s. By 1911, the city of several hundred people decided it was big enough to build a city hall and pass speed ordinances for the 15 automobiles registered here. Today Winter Haven has a balanced economy based on tourism, commerce and industry, agriculture and phosphate mining.

Not everything is perfect in the Winter Haven area, of course. Summers are hot, though regular rain quenches some of the heat. Howell, who remembers Winter Haven in the early 1940s when it was a fifth of its present size, admits that traffic on main arteries gets congested sometimes — but nothing like Orlando or Tampa, he adds.

For anyone considering a move to Winter Haven, local retirees offer advice that can smooth the transition to a Florida lifestyle.

"I'd tell people to look at a map to find out where this is. I'd warn them it can be a secluded, rural environment," says John Petre, who adds that he has no desire to live anywhere other than the resort area of Grenelefe.

For retirees who prefer such resort communities away from town, shopping can involve a trip of several miles. But residents say the drive to find needed services is a fair trade for a less-crowded lifestyle.

Other advice comes from the Rieglers, who say their move to Florida for half of each year is a "dream fulfilled."

"You should rent for a season and make sure you like Florida and the community before buying. Do some intensive research," says John Riegler.

He says he has met people who moved to Florida and discovered they didn't like the casual lifestyle or the year-round warm climate or who simply missed their friends too much. "Some of them just went back home empty-handed," he says.●

Also Available From Vacation Publications

Retirement Relocation Magazine   **Print Cost Here**

❑ *Where to Retire*, one-year subscription, $10.95   _____

Retirement Relocation Books

❑ *Where to Retire in Florida* (Ratings for 99 Cities and Towns), Richard and Betty Fox, $16.95   _____

❑ *Choose the Southwest* (Retirement Discoveries for Every Budget), John Howells, $14.95   _____

❑ *Choose Mexico* (Live Well on $600 a Month), John Howells, $14.95   _____

❑ *Choose Costa Rica* (A Guide to Retirement and Investment), John Howells, $14.95   _____

❑ *Choose the Northwest* (Includes Washington, Oregon and British Columbia), John Howells, $14.95   _____

❑ *Where to Retire House Plans* (200 Beautiful and Efficient Designs for Retirement Lifestyles), $5.95   _____

Retirement Relocation Special Reports

❑   SR1   How to Plan and Execute a Successful Retirement Relocation, 48 pages, $3.95   _____

❑   SR2   America's Best Neighborhoods for Active Retirees, 64 pages, $3.95   _____

❑   SR4   Should You Retire to a Manufactured Home? 32 pages, $3.95   _____

❑   SR5   Retiring Outside the United States, 48 pages, $3.95   _____

❑   SR8   America's Most Affordable Retirement Towns, 48 pages, $3.95   _____

❑   MSS   How to Get the Most Out of Your Social Security, 32 pages, $3.95   _____

                                                                    Subtotal   _____

Texas residents only add 8.25% sales tax   Tax   _____
Add $2.50 postage and handling per book. Add $2.50 total postage and handling
  for any number of Special Reports. Postage included in magazine subscription price.   **Postage**   _____

                                                                    Total Due   _____

Name _____

Address _____

City, State, Zip _____

Check the appropriate boxes and fill in the price for each title ordered. Total at the bottom. Include your payment and return this order form or a copy to: Vacation Publications, 1502 Augusta Drive, Suite 415, Houston, TX 77057. **For faster service call (800) 338-4962 and order by credit card.**

Notes

Notes